Gardening for All

Edited by
Peter Hunt FLS

Contributors:
Harold Bagust
Kenneth Beckett DIP HORT (Wisley)
Alan Bloom VMH
Ann Bonar
P R Chapman
T K Colledge
H G Witham Fogg
Brian Furner FLS
John Garrity BA
Richard Gorer MA
Miles Hadfield
Ray Hanson
Denis Hardwicke
Cyril Harris
Gay Hellyer BSC
Will Ingwersen VMH
Rev E Morley Jones
Christine Kelway
F J Martin
Margaret Martin
F R McQuown MA FLS
A du Gard Pasley AILA
Ray Procter AHRHS
Tony Venison
Brian Walkden

This edition published 1978 by
Octopus Books Limited
59 Grosvenor Street, London W1
Seventh impression 1984
ISBN 0 7064 0685 0
© 1973 Octopus Books Limited
Produced by Mandarin Publishers Limited
22A Westlands Road
Quarry Bay, Hong Kong
Printed in Czechoslovakia
50315/6/br.

Gardening for All

octopus

Contents

Introduction

Gardening books of one sort and another have been published for centuries, during which time every conceivable aspect has been dealt with. Books range from step-by-step guides for the complete beginner to highly specialized monographs, to slim pamphlets describing particular methods of gardening. The price range of these publications is equally wide.

In GARDENING FOR ALL we bring you an encyclopedic work which covers in detail not only all the main gardening subjects but many other ancillary features such as the *Glossary*, which explains gardening and working terms, and *The Gardener's Year*, which covers the plants in season and the work to be done month by month throughout the year.

As its name suggests, this book caters for everyone. If you are a beginner you will find that each chapter presents its subject matter as clearly and completely as possible, though you may need to refer to the Glossary for definitions of certain terms and gardening methods. If you are more experienced and delight in growing particular plants such as chrysanthemums or dahlias to exhibition standard, then you will find much of value, provided by expert growers and exhibitors.

In fact all of the chapters have been written by gardeners who are well known for their ability to pass on their knowledge to others in easily understood terms, knowledge which has been handed down and added to over the centuries, all of which goes toward making this book an accumulation of gardening wisdom and experience.

A word more about this publication. Few people would think of building a house without preparing plans beforehand, yet far too many create gardens without adequate prior planning and, in the end, are dissatisfied with the results of their endeavours. For this reason GARDENING FOR ALL starts with a most important chapter on *Planning your Garden* in which it is shown that plans, simple or elaborate, can be drawn up for any size or shape of garden, provided the planning is done on the right lines. It is not necessary to have professional surveying instruments; most plans can be prepared by using such simple materials as pieces of string, a measuring tape, pegs, laths, a spirit level, a few large pieces of paper, plus some previous ideas of what you want your garden to look like and to provide for you in the way of flowers, fruit and vegetables, etc.

Plant categories are dealt with in separate chapters. You will find, for instance, chapters on Annuals; Hardy Perennials; Roses; Bulbs of all kinds; Trees and Shrubs (with particular emphasis on those that are suitable for the smaller garden); and Rock Gardens and Pools. Greenhouses are becoming increasingly popular and you will find much information on the various types and what you can grow in them. For those who like to grow plants in the house there is a chapter on Indoor Plants, which deals with the wide range of foliage and flowering plants, as well as cacti and other succulent plants, that are now so popular.

Many gardeners like to construct for themselves such garden features as archways, pergolas, etc. You will find detailed instructions on a wide range of these in the chapter called *The Handyman Gardener*.

There is also a complete chapter on Herbs and their uses and the making of Herb Gardens. If you need guidance on which jobs to do each month and which flowers, fruits and vegetables are in season, you will find it in *The Gardener's Year*.

Finally, you will find that GARDENING FOR ALL is crammed with colour pictures. Many of them illustrate the best varieties of garden plants, others are detailed drawings which will enable you to carry out essential tasks or construct various features.

Peter Hunt

Who Needs a Plan?

A new garden is at once a challenge and an opportunity. The very sight of some barren or weed grown plot brings out our latent desire to impose order and create our own particular version of paradise on the wilderness. Without very much thought the ground is cleared and dug, grass seed sown, odd beds prepared for plants gathered in a haphazard manner, a path, a clothes line, a shed appear as needed. Then, instead of fulfilment, there is a feeling of unease. Paradise was never like this? Perhaps a pergola, a rockery, a pool, a patio would improve things. Books, newspaper articles, magazines all suggest a new answer and more and more elements appear on the ground, unrelated to one another and to the needs of the owner. Small saplings, planted near the house, grow into large trees and darken the rooms, the various beds contain no colour and too many weeds, mud tracks are worn across the lawn because the paths do not lead in the right direction, there is no room for chairs on the terrace, the vegetables will not grow, and disillusion sets in. One can see all the stages of this kind of garden, in which one kind of chaos merely replaces another, on any train journey through a residential area. But what went wrong?

In almost every case these gardens were made without a plan, or at best with a few hazy ideas scribbled on an envelope. The makers did not really know what they wanted, had no clear idea of the finished product towards which they were working and inevitably the result was a muddle.

Years of growing time—and even in this period of instant gardening, time is still important—and endless labour have been wasted for very little result. And curiously enough it is the smallest gardens which need the most careful planning because every inch is vital and the slightest lack of decision can be seen immediately. So, faced with a barren plot full of brick ends, or a neglected wilderness, how does one set about preparing a plan which will satisfy all the needs of the family in a practical way, however long it may take to complete?

 **The Site**

First of all there is the site itself, and as this is the raw material with which you have to work, it merits very careful consideration. Although there are many aspects of it which will have to be considered and noted down, you will need a scale drawing which will form the basis of your work. There is very seldom any plan available, because the plans which form part of the title deeds of the normal house are on too small a scale to be very helpful, so you will have to provide one yourself. Unless your site is very large and very complicated you will not find the survey difficult.

You will need only very simple equipment. If it is possible to borrow two 100-ft. tape measures you will find them very useful but, if not, you will have to take some strong cord

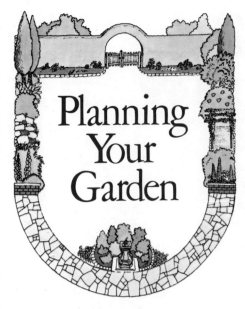

Planning Your Garden

which is not likely to stretch—a long clothes line for instance—and mark it off carefully into units of 5 ft. and 10 ft. As you will be using this cord to take long measurements, be sure that the divisions are accurately made and try to mark the 10 ft. divisions by means of differently coloured tags so that you can tell immediately where you have got to without counting along from the end every time. All the shorter measurements you can take with a steel tape. If the survey is large or you are working alone, an ordinary metal skewer fixed to the free end of your long tapes or cords will be useful, as you can fix it in the ground at key points and take several measurements from that position.

Make a rough sketch of the site—or just one part, if it is too large to do all at once—big enough to write in neatly all the measurements you are likely to need. This sketch does not have to be very accurate but it is as well to keep the general proportions—for instance the length of the house compared to the length of the garden—correct. But even that is not essential because the measurements will enable you to plot the work correctly afterwards.

Decide on a baseline from which to work. A straight, simple object like a boundary wall or fence, uncluttered by obstructions, is best although one sometimes has to invent a baseline formed by one of the tapes laid down and fixed in position. Measure this base, working away from the house, and mark with garden canes any significant distances, such as the 50 ft. mark, from which you may want to take subsequent measurements. Always try to take all your measurements in the same direction—say from the house outwards—because it makes it easier to plot the survey afterwards. Then measure an adjoining boundary or the other line more or less at right angles to your base line; 'more or less at right angles' because you should never assume that any apparent right angle is in fact true. The eye can accept quite wide variations in this. Having measured these two lines, complete a triangle by measuring the distance between the two free ends.

Starting again from the base line, fix the position of the other boundaries by forming another triangle or triangles if the plot is not a basic rectangle. At this stage it is best to treat the house as a simple block or even run a line straight across the back, picking up only the positions of the corners if the shape of the building is complex.

You have now the basic details of the plot shown as a series of triangles, each related to one another and all tied back to your essential base line. At this stage you could draw up the ground plan if you wished, but generally speaking it is as well to continue and fill in all the detailed information at the same time. The position of features which are close to boundary lines, or directly on the diagonal lines forming the sides of triangles, can be positioned as these main lines are measured. Even if the object is a foot or two away from the line, it is quite easy to judge a right angle over a short distance, and to measure outwards with the steel tape.

Objects inside the site—for instance existing trees or groups of shrubs—are measured separately by a series of small extra triangles and it is at this point that the intermediate measurements marked on the base line with canes can be useful, as they can form known points from which these smaller triangles can be measured. The small triangles may be linked together but they must always be tied back to the base line or other points whose position has already been measured.

This leaves the details of the house itself, and it is often more convenient to take these on a separate piece of paper, as a large number of separate measurements will need to be written down. Starting at one corner, work along the face of the house, noting the measurement to the outer edge of each window and doorway, width and number of steps, position of down pipes, manhole covers, etc. If there are projections or recesses, these will have to be measured separately and triangulated back to the corner of the house or some other measured point to make sure that they are really at right angles to the main structure.

If the site is large or of a complex shape it may be easier to divide it into sections, measuring each section separately. But you must ensure that the measurements of each section are complete in themselves and tied closely back to those of the adjoining section, or you may find that the total work is not accurate. One or two check measurements taken from the beginning of the base line, right through the sections to some fixed and measured point are often helpful in these cases.

Now to put this rough data into some definite and accurate form. The easiest base material to use is probably graph paper since it is already covered by a grid giving both a means of scale measurements and vertical/horizontal lines to work against. But it is not essential and large sheets of lined paper can also be used. If possible pin the paper to a large, smooth board of suitable size, as it will be very much easier to work on, and decide the scale at which you are going to work. In other words, at what size will each foot measured on the ground, appear on the paper? The scale should be some standard unit, easily measured with a ruler. For small gardens a $\frac{1}{4}$ in. to equal 1 ft. is a convenient measurement. For larger areas an $\frac{1}{8}$ in. to 1 ft. is easier because otherwise the size of the finished plan might become unmanageable.

Having seen from your notes roughly how the size of the garden will fill out the paper at the chosen scale, draw your base line, mark on it any intermediate measurements you took along it, and you are ready to begin. At this point you will need a large compass, possibly with an extending arm, so that you can measure the other two sides of your first triangle and strike them off as two arcs which will bisect at the point of the triangle. This will then give you the length and position of the second boundary. It is not necessary to draw in the diagonal lines forming the third side of each triangle because the bisecting arcs giving you the various fixed points, are all the reference you need. In the same way all the triangles can be plotted and the existing features drawn in. Finally the details of doors, windows and projections can be filled in on the block of the house. You will now have a representation, to a standard scale, of your plot, drawn on a flat sheet of paper.

But although your paper may be flat, your site is probably not, so it is time to think about levels. Surveyors use sophisticated levelling equipment but although this can sometimes be hired it is not easy for the amateur to use without instruction. Some levels can be found by direct measurement – the number and depth of steps from a door to outside ground level for instance, or the difference in the number of courses of brickwork exposed when ground level slopes past a brick wall. Others may be worked out by using two laths, a spirit level and your steel tape. Take a convenient fixed point, such as a manhole cover, to act as a datum point to which all your measurements will refer and rest the larger lath on edge across it. Hold the lath steady against a shorter lath held upright and adjust the level of the long lath by using the spirit level. Then measure the difference between the upper edge of the lath and the ground, using the steel tape. Drive a peg in level with the surface of the ground at the point you took the measurement, then repeat the process. The position of the pegs can afterwards be measured and plotted onto your survey and the various differences in level worked out. It is possible – though tedious – to take a whole grid of levels in this way, but usually only a few will be needed to give you the basic differences in level within the area of a normal garden.

Basic Information At this stage it might be useful to make one or two copies of the plan, as you will begin to collect basic information which might be applied more easily and clearly on separate sheets. If these extra copies were drawn on tracing paper, you could slip one or more of them over your basic plan sheet to give you the additional data you need when thinking of the final design.

Consider the question of sunlight and shadow, both in summer and winter. It is easy to plot their movement across your site on any given clear day, and to sketch in this pattern of movement on the plan. Ideally the movement at midsummer and midwinter should both be shown, as both will influence the final placing of trees and shrubs, and the choice of plant material for the different areas. If you cannot wait for six months to complete the two operations, you will have to plot one season and approximate the other, but this method is not so satisfactory unless you are very observant and have noticed the amazing effect of change in elevation of the sun at different seasons.

At the same time, make notes of areas which are particularly warm and sheltered, where heat is reflected from house walls and hard surfaces, those always shady and damp or permanently cold where frost and snow lie long after they have melted elsewhere.

Winds and draughts are another important element. Although we are mostly aware of the prevailing wind, this may not have the greatest effect on your particular garden. Often trees, hills or other buildings deflect the wind, bringing it in from some unexpected quarter while in urban areas downdraughts, wind tunnels between buildings and even minor whirlwinds in apparently sheltered courtyards can all cause havoc. These too can be noted on the plan as they are often very localized and may affect only part of quite a small garden.

Although most gardens will have the same amount of topsoil—or lack of it—over the whole area, this is not always so, and it is worth digging one or two trial holes to find out. Often builders fill in hollows with subsoil taken from foundations, or spread a layer of infertile subsoil over the ground near buildings. The most astonishing things are done to the soil and levels on new housing estates, and the unwary new owner is to be pitied if he should attempt to make a garden without investigating what lay beneath. If there is any significant variation the areas concerned should be noted on the plan and numbered soil samples sent off for analysis of pH value (to see whether it is acid or alkaline, which affects the types of plant you can grow) and mineral deficiencies.

Many new gardens are quite bare, but when an old garden has been split up into smaller plots, or some other site redeveloped, there are generally some existing trees and shrubs whose position, level in relation to surrounding ground and general size, shape and species (if known) should be carefully noted. Never destroy an existing plant, however poor or common it may seem, until you are quite sure that it cannot be incorporated in the new plan. Even if the final scheme does not require it, an existing shrub or tree, already established and probably capable of improvement by careful pruning and shaping, can give an

immediate air of maturity while the new planting grows up. After five or ten years, if it is no longer needed, it can be removed. Even an old, overgrown hedgerow in the wrong position will often yield a few saplings of interesting shape which will soon spread out and form nice trees when freed from the surrounding jungle. If you have inherited an existing garden, however neglected, do not do more than minimal tidying and lawn mowing for the first year, as all kinds of treasures may come to light which would otherwise be destroyed unseen. This year of limited activity will give you time to prepare a detailed survey, and get the feel of the place, so that the ensuing new garden will be far more interesting and practical than it could otherwise have been.

Then there are factors outside your own site which may nevertheless have an important bearing on your final design. If you are lucky you may have a view, either spectacular or merely pleasant, which can be seen from some parts of the garden and not from others. The best viewing positions should be noted, as these may affect the placing of seats or the shape of terraces. Often the good points are less obvious: a church spire glimpsed between two buildings, an old tree in a neighbouring garden, an interesting grouping of gables and chimneys seen against the sky are all features which could be used to draw the eye outside the garden and make it seem larger than it is. Again, the best views of these should be noted, together with the places where planting is needed to hide less desirable features and so draw attention to good ones. And there are the neighbours' windows which may dominate some parts of the garden while other areas are relatively private.

All open spaces are extrovert or introvert in character. In other words they can be outward looking, depending for all or part of their effect on views and objects beyond their boundaries, or they are inward looking with no views, or only bad ones, outside and needing to contain all their interest within themselves. It depends entirely on these outside factors what kind of garden you can have.

All this preparation may seem elaborate and complicated but if you consider the physical effort needed to make the garden, and the time it will take to grow, the planning stage falls into perspective as a small but vital part of the process.

The Zone of Influence

The first thing to do is to consider the site in relation to its surroundings. Every site has a zone of influence which may extend as far as the next street or even the next hill top if it happens to be in the country and can be seen as part of a larger landscape pattern in which hills, woods and fields form major elements. One must always remember that far more people will see a garden from outside looking inwards, either at short range or from a greater distance, than will ever see it in detail from within. It can be an interesting experi-

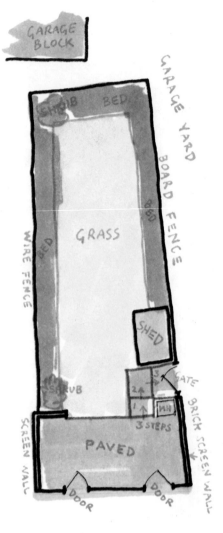

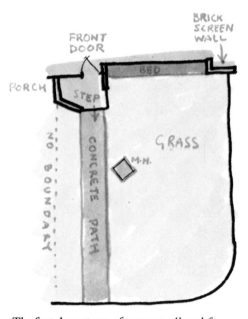

The first three stages of a survey. *Above left:* a sketch of a 'minimal' garden (front and back of house), drawn freehand and ready for survey measurements; the centre sketch has the detailed measurements. Some features which will be altered have not been measured. The right-hand

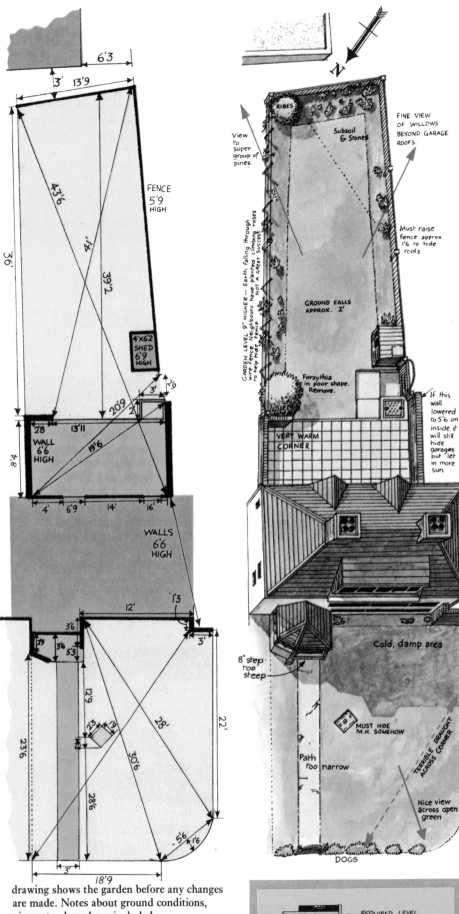

Labels within the survey drawing (left plan):

FENCE 5'9 HIGH

4'x62 SHED 6'9 HIGH

28 WALL 6'6 HIGH

WALLS 6'6 HIGH

Dimensions on left plan: 6'3 · 3' · 13'9 · 43'6 · 41' · 39'2 · 36' · 4'8 · 20'9 · 2' · 3' · 2'9 · 13'11 · 19'6 · 4' · 6'9 · 14' · 16' · 12' · 13 · 3'6 · 3' · 29 · 3'6 · 53 · 23 · 4'3 · 19 · 28' · 30'6 · 12'9 · 22' · 28'6 · 23'6 · 5'6 · 1'6 · 3' · 18'9

Labels within the survey drawing (right plan):

View to Super group of pines.

GARDEN LEVEL 9" HIGHER — Earth falling through wire fence. Neighbours have planted climbing roses to help hide fence. NOT A GREAT SUCCESS.

RIBES

Subsoil & Stones

FINE VIEW OF WILLOWS BEYOND GARAGE ROOFS.

Must raise fence approx. 1'6 to hide roofs

GROUND FALLS APPROX. 2'

Forsythia in poor shape. Remove.

If this wall lowered to 5'6 on inside, it will still hide garages but let in more sun.

VERY WARM CORNER

Cold, damp area

8" step too steep

MUST HIDE M.H. SOMEHOW

Path too narrow

TERRIBLE DRAUGHT ACROSS CORNER

Nice view across open green

DOGS

Bottom-left caption:

drawing shows the garden before any changes are made. Notes about ground conditions, views etc., have been included.
Right: a simple method of levelling. *Top:* a long lath is laid on edge across a fixed point, e.g. a manhole cover. Hold this lath steady against a shorter, upright lath, and use a spirit level to adjust the level of the longer lath.
Centre: measure the distance between the top of the lath and the ground and drive a peg in level with the fixed point.
Bottom: repeat the process as often as necessary and plot the differences in level on the survey.

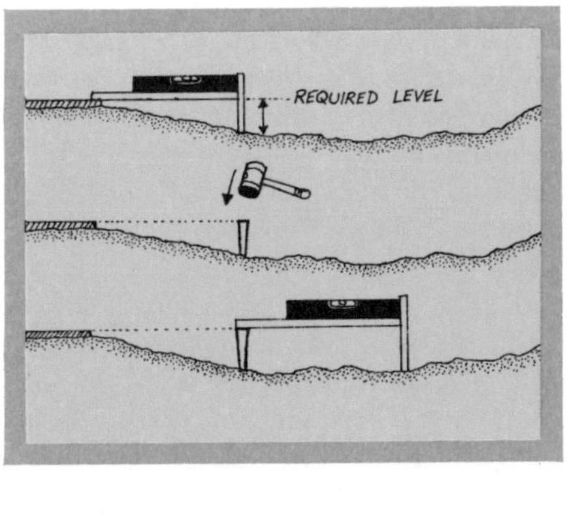

Levelling diagram label: REQUIRED LEVEL

ence looking at your potential garden from outside and realizing how much you can improve the general view for others. A carefully placed tree might hide drainpipes or a view of washing, or break up the long perspective of a dull street to make it seem more interesting. An urn or a patch of bright colour seen through a gateway might make all the difference at the end of a cul-de-sac, while in the wider view careful planting to conceal the hard lines of boundaries might help to blend a new garden into the countryside. Often visiting an unfamiliar area, it is the minor, unexpected touches which please most. A sudden cascade of roses over the top of a wall, the spray of a fountain in a patch of sunlight, an inviting garden path framed by trees. We forget that these effects were planned by someone and that we are often in a similar position to give pleasure to others.

Human Needs Once you have become familiar with the site and noted down all its physical characteristics both good and bad, it is time to consider very carefully the exact role the garden is to play in your life. Everyone has different priorities but it is very important at this stage to get these in the right order, because it is unlikely that any modern garden can fulfil all the needs and wishes of the various members of the family.

First there are the obvious needs: a place for children to play, room to sit in sun or shade, a washing line, a vegetable patch, space for cutting flowers, a working area for bonfires and compost heaps, a workshop or toolshed, are just a few elements.

Then there are the more elaborate requirements: a swimming pool, a tennis court, a croquet lawn, a sauna cabin, a greenhouse, a rose garden, rock garden, orchard, lily pool. Each of these is a major element round which a whole scheme might be evolved.

Less obvious, but still vitally important, are other basic human needs which are often forgotten today with fatal results in terms of human happiness. The need for privacy, not just from neighbours but from other members of the family. However harmonious our family life, there is often the need to be alone and the garden is an ideal setting for solitary thought.

With privacy go seclusion and the pleasures of the imagination. Children love to play in a world of make believe, hidden from grown up realities by a few shrubs or a spreading tree which will form the basis of any number of adventures. And it is not only children who need the pleasures of make believe. As the grown ups make their own world more and more intolerable, they too need a comforting touch of illusion to support them.

So what do you really want? Only you can make the decision. Prepare a list of elements and place them in order of priority, but unless you actually do this you are likely to find eventually that something important has been forgotten. So much depends on the way you live, the amount of time and money you are prepared to spend on maintaining the garden afterwards, the specific problems with which only you have to contend.

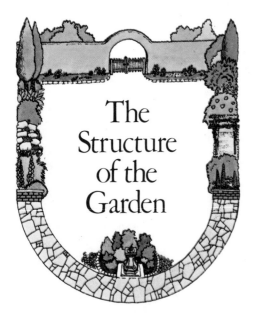

The Structure of the Garden

While deciding on the various elements which the garden must contain, it is as well to consider the structure which should form the basic outlines of any garden, large or small. So often the lack of this underlying structure results in the garden being a formless jumble rather than the satisfying composition which we subconsciously need.

Any garden, or landscape, consists of an arrangement of masses and voids. The masses may be formed by hills and woods or by buildings and banks of shrubs, while the voids are represented by lakes, rivers and fields or lawns, pools and beds of low-growing flowers. Basically a mass is formed by objects at or above eye level, while a void can be anything upon which one looks down. Voids are largely horizontal, masses are vertical and it is the balance between open void and closed mass, the contrast between horizontal and vertical which gives any garden its shape.

Masses do not have to be solid. A pergola, an avenue, a group of trees standing on a lawn, even a single tree with wide spreading branches, all give an effect of partial enclosure which still allows the eye to penetrate to open spaces beyond. It is this feeling of space flowing onward, flooding like water between the tree trunks, forming pools when held up by plant masses or buildings, which can give to the garden a sense of movement, interest and the illusion that the area is much larger than it is.

Illusion is important and the smaller the garden the greater the need to use all available arts to make it seem larger and more interesting than it really is. Bad proportions can be improved, ugly features hidden, small spaces enlarged and apparent privacy achieved by simple means. Once the basic principles are understood, they can be applied, varied and improved according to circumstance.

Space A small garden without defined boundaries, in a large open area will appear very small indeed, whereas if the boundaries are emphasized by strong vertical elements reaching above eye level, the space at once seems larger.

You have only to think of a house in the course of construction to see this fact emerge. When the foundations are first laid out on the ground, the whole house appears no larger than a reasonably sized room. When the walls are about waist height, the individual rooms emerge but appear very small. Once the walls have reached ceiling height the rooms are seen in their true proportion and may seem quite large. In the garden the same rule holds good, although there one has the ability to change the proportion by altering the heights of the walls and creating internal divisions which will contain a series of interlocking spaces of different kinds.

The partial division of a small area can make it seem larger and more interesting by emphasizing the half seen, allowing the eye to penetrate further in one direction than another and leaving the feeling all the time that there is something beyond.

Light and Shade Another means of altering proportion and apparent size is by the careful use of light and shade. In this country the contrast between the two is seldom as brilliant as it is abroad, but even so, shadow can conceal a great many bad points without using means which in themselves draw attention, to what is being hidden. Take the obvious case of dustbins in a courtyard garden. You can put them into a neat brick box with doors in front for easy access and flower boxes on top to brighten the effect. Certainly the bins are hidden and everyone will think 'How clever, that is where they hide the dustbins'. Alternatively you can have black bins, either bought that way or painted, and put them in the shadow of a large evergreen shrub or a slightly drooping bamboo. A dark painted trellis covered with ivy in front of which bright flowers are grouped in sunlight, completes the illusion. The eye is drawn to the sunlit flowers, everything beyond is vague and mysterious. The garden may extend for some distance but it is difficult to tell and the black bins stand unseen in the shadows.

Climbers Again, faced with a walled town garden many people start by painting the garden walls white. This is fine if you wish your garden to be a white box of sharply defined shape. Certain very formal types of garden rely on such emphasis for part of their effect, but if you feel confined and want an impression of greater space, this treatment is fatal. Better by far to overplant the walls with vines and creepers, not trained too neatly, which will swing forward in curtains of greenery, masking the boundaries in shadow and producing the feeling of a forest clearing.

The Uses of Water Water, even in the form of a tiny pool or fountain basin, can be a tremendous help to illusions of all kinds. Apart from the pleasure which the sound of moving and falling water always gives us, the greatest use of water in the garden is reflection. For this reason pools should always be painted black inside, for not only do they appear of limitless depth but they also produce the best reflections. Blue pools may be used to achieve special effects in that colour,

but all the other benefits of water are thereby lost.

Dark pools of this kind, in positions such as town courtyards where the lateral rays of the sun are cut off, can bring a brilliant patch of sky down to lighten what may otherwise be rather dark and dank surroundings. Larger pools can often be built to reflect objects in the garden or even outside it, giving double importance to some feature which you wish to emphasize. For instance, a long canal has been used in a town garden to mirror exactly a church spire which was the only redeeming feature of an otherwise very bleak outlook.

Because of its powers of reflection, the level of water in relation to the surrounding ground is very important. Try always to keep water level and ground level as close as possible. Water only 1 in. below ground level will appear to be 2 in. down because the depth of the edge is reflected–if it is 6 in. below it, therefore, appears to be 1 ft. down and the appearance already begins to be that of a well rather than a pool. For this reason you should always make pools slightly larger than you intend them to appear and the lower the intended water level the larger the actual water surface required to compensate.

Unless heavily masked by planting, water strongly emphasizes the exact form by which it is contained. This does not matter, indeed can be a positive asset, where a formal pool is concerned, provided that the shape is well proportioned, but it does lead to problems with the design of informal pools and water features. A brief study of pools and ponds in areas where these occur naturally will show that the more eccentric curves of garden ponds are largely the invention of their makers

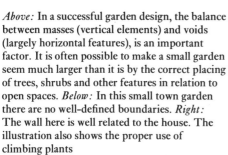

Above: In a successful garden design, the balance between masses (vertical elements) and voids (largely horizontal features), is an important factor. It is often possible to make a small garden seem much larger than it is by the correct placing of trees, shrubs and other features in relation to open spaces. *Below:* In this small town garden there are no well-defined boundaries. *Right:* The wall here is well related to the house. The illustration also shows the proper use of climbing plants

rather than an imitation of natural forms. In this, as in so many other aspects of garden design, when in doubt simplify. One large pool of simple shape is worth half a dozen contorted puddles joined by an unconvincing stream.

Ground Shaping Water, which looks happiest in a slight hollow, either natural or man made, leads to the consideration of ground shaping and levels. Few gardens are exactly flat and even in those which are, quite a minor excavation will produce enough soil to create interesting modulations of the ground surface. But do not undulate just for the sake of doing so. A slight valley formation will emphasize what lies at the end of it, whether a seat, a view, or an urn on a stand. A very gentle mound will give point to a group of trees standing on a lawn or alternatively a lawn slightly saucer shaped, surrounded by banks of shrubs, will appear intimate and secluded. A terrace raised only 6 in. above the rest of the garden will give the house much greater importance than if the two were on the same level. But if the terrace is too narrow for its length, the fault will be magnified if it is at a higher level.

Exterior proportions are not the same as those used indoors, simply because the scale of everything outside is larger. Many mean looking and unsatisfactory features have arisen because internal proportions have been used out of doors. When in doubt, make it larger, the steps wider and shallower, the terrace broader, the borders deeper. Our natural inclination is to design things which are too small, and are reduced to insignificance by the size of the outdoor world or the exuberance of the plant material which soon swamps our little beds and invades the narrow paths.

Structural Elements

Now, having considered some of the effects we can achieve, it is time to think about the various elements concerned in greater detail. Harmony of Materials and Shapes These fall into two classes, vertical structures including walls, fences, screens, gateways, pergolas and garden buildings, and horizontal structures of drives, paths, terraces and steps. Before examining any of these, one should look for a moment at the relationship of objects. Certain shapes and materials relate to one another, others do not and if we are to create satisfying gardens it is essential to achieve an underlying unity which will hold our designs together. To take some extreme examples, one would not choose to use precast concrete slabs as the terrace for an ancient brick farm house, or lay paths of rustic crazy paving to a steel and concrete building. Both would look incongruous and would irritate rather than give pleasure. But equally ridiculous things are done every day of the week.

Before deciding on any type of structure or material, study your house, the buildings which surround it, the materials and methods used in the locality, so that your own structures can become a part of their setting rather than something introduced and obviously alien. You may not particularly care for the materials and style of your house or the neighbourhood, but it is still wiser to employ these, even in some slightly different form, than to change the subject altogether. Of course there are gifted people who can mix the most dissimilar elements with success, but the remainder of us would be wiser to play safe. One does not need to make an exact copy of any particular feature, provided that the general feeling and intention of the new work blends in with what is existing.

Always try to make your new structures seem an inevitable outcome of the old by linking them firmly to the house or adjoining buildings, emphasizing the major features of these by carrying their lines and shapes out into the garden. For instance, where the upper half of a house is tile hung, the edge of the tile hanging will form a strong horizontal line which should be extended at the same level when a boundary wall joins or runs close to the building. This may mean a high wall, but the level can change at the next significant point such as the junction between house terrace and lawn. Never change the level unnecessarily or at some point which has no importance in the general design. Nothing is more irritating than a wall which descends in a series of pointless little jumps which do not relate in any way to the remainder of the garden.

If the façade of the building has a strong rhythm—for instance a series of columns of the same size between windows—these might be reflected in the paving pattern of the terrace and expressed as strips of stone crossing some other hard material such as brick or gravel. Arched glass doors opening onto a courtyard could be faced by brick arches of the same size, framing views of the garden or countryside.

Even on the most simple level, steps from lawn to terrace should lead obviously to a garden door or at least to some major architectural feature, rather than being directed straight at a blank piece of wall just because this happens to be in the middle of the terrace. If such a solution has to be arrived at, then at least let there be an important seat or urn placed to give apparent point to the arrangement.

Boundaries All too often boundaries and space divisions are made of materials whose only apparent virtue is cheapness, giving an air of meanness to the garden which no amount of subsequent care and planting can ever dispel. Nor are they cheap in the long term, as flimsy woven or wattle panels are impermanent and require frequent replacement, while trellis and rustic work last just long enough to become covered with climbing plants before collapsing in a tangle of broken woodwork and earwigs.

Much better, if these structures are to be expressed visually, or even used as supports for climbing plants, to construct them properly with appropriate materials at the outset, even if the cost means delaying completion of other parts of the garden for a year or two.

Walls are best made of brick or stone to match the house, although given really solid foundations and suitable design, either in staggered panels or with sufficient piers to give support, the brickwork need only be $4\frac{1}{2}$ in. instead of the normal 9-in. thickness, which will help to keep down the cost. Different types of wall have different characteristics. A run of wall with a flush face emphasizes length, walls of staggered shape or with frequent piers, especially if these are related to the ground plan, can make a narrow plot seem wider. Pierced walls, or those made of open concrete blocks, can suggest distance and depth, but such openwork elements are best used in short lengths or as panels framed in solid walling, as used alone in any quantity they can seem to dominate and have a rather irritating effect.

Painted walls in the garden, though sometimes necessary to relate to a painted house, create problems because they become quickly streaked with dirt and climbers make repainting difficult. It is better to give them a broad coping to throw off the rain, and to use them as a background to bold groups of foliage plants rather than plant directly against them.

Walls built solely as a background and support for climbers can be made of inexpensive concrete blocks, possibly with a brick coping to match the adjoining building. But remember that you will have to plant climbers on both sides of such walls if they are to be suitably concealed.

Where wooden fences, or panels of well-made hardwood trellis, are used near the house they can be given a much more architectural character by being set on a dwarf brick wall between brick piers so that they appear to have been designed as part of the general structure rather than added as an afterthought.

Gateways One of the most exciting things to come upon while exploring a strange town is a solid wooden door set in a high garden wall. The desire to turn the handle and look into the garden beyond is irresistible. Although we do not often have the chance to own such a door in a wall, it does teach us the importance of entrances of all kinds, each of which has a different character. Tall and narrow openings of this kind are exciting and mysterious. A broad opening in a high wall is expansive and hospitable, as though designed for a party, especially if emphasized at either side with finials of some suitable kind.

The character of the gates and doors themselves is important. Solid woodwork of good design is always useful, particularly on boundaries. Even the best wrought-iron work will only show to advantage against an absolutely plain background of grass, water, sky or simple paving. When a gate or door of open design is required to be seen against a complex background, then an arrangement of upright bars in wood or metal is generally best, as the repetition forms a grid of reference, giving point to the details beyond it.

Gates and walls which are below eye level are more difficult to deal with as they seem to imply an irritating obstacle to one's progress rather than a feature of consequence in themselves. Where they are necessary as a protection for (or against) dogs and children they are best made of simple vertical elements, not too closely spaced and painted black, to appear as unobtrusive as possible. The standard London cast-iron railing, which

gives protection while not impeding the view, is quite a good model to take, even though the scale and materials employed may not seem the same.

Anything of complicated design, whether castellated brick walls, wooden gates in the form of cartwheels or rising suns, or 'wrought-iron' fencing seemingly made from portions of tin cans painted black and stuck together, should all be avoided like the plague. And although ranch type fencing of painted horizontal boarding can look quite effective, it requires a great deal of maintenance to keep it in order.

Garden Buildings Garden buildings–sheds, summer houses, greenhouses and conservatories–create a number of problems which are not easily solved. Basically to have such structures designed and built specifically for any given position–as they should be–is very expensive whereas they can be obtained in prefabricated form quite cheaply. Naturally there are any number of designs and makers, and some of these may be more suitable than others for your given position. Unobtrusive siting and the use of matching materials–for instance the brick base of a greenhouse or conservatory should match the adjoining house or garden wall–can help considerably. So can matching major horizontals, such as fascia board or the line of the top of window frames, to similar elements on the façade of the house.

Pergolas At first sight the pergola, designed to create a shady walk protected from the sun in hot climates, is a strange introduction to the English garden. However, it is an excellent way of growing many types of climbing plants and can be visually very useful by extending the structure of the house into the garden and possibly linking it to some other building such as the garage or summer house which might otherwise appear as an isolated element. Here, too, proportions need to be generous, the width always being greater than the height, the structure sound and the materials related to the adjoining house, if the effect is to be satisfactory.

The isolated pergola, unrelated to other structures, is seldom successful, especially if it begins and ends at nothing in particular, which is too often the case. Pillars built in brick or stone, precast classical columns of simple shape, or slender metal uprights are all suitable in their place. Heavy beams set directly above the supports, or a more closely spaced pattern of lighter ones on continuous cross members, can form the roofing which should not be too solid or the finished effect when planted will tend to be dark. At all costs avoid structures made from flimsy rustic poles–if you can afford nothing better it would be wiser to forget about having a pergola and grow your climbers on pyramids made from three or four poles stoutly braced, which can look quite effective.

The Types of Hard Surface

Paths, drives, courtyards and terraces have all to be covered with hard wearing materials which will take vehicles, foot traffic, chairs and tables while remaining clean and easy to use at all times of year. Builders tend to put down a drive and path of plain concrete and leave it at that, but there are a great many more interesting materials which are equally suitable. Which you use, of course, depends on the style and material of your house, but the main possibilities are these:

Precast Paving   This, the most easily obtainable paving material on the market is simple to lay because sizes and depths of slab are fairly standard, whichever make is chosen. The disadvantages lie mainly in the hard mechanical finish and extraordinary colours produced. But many types have a pleasantly rough texture – which is also nonslip – and if quiet buffs, browns and cream colours are chosen the finished effect can be pleasant. Most colours weather down to softer tones and in appropriate settings some of the new slate-grey and purplish colours could be used successfully. At all costs avoid the crude raspberry reds and poison greens which look wrong everywhere, and do not use a large number of colours to achieve 'variety'. A fruit salad contains variety both of form and colour, but you do not necessarily want to look at it every day. A random mixture of the larger sizes is generally best, although in a small, formal area such as a courtyard, one of the stylized patterns suggested by the makers can look well. On the whole these rigid patterns tend to emphasize the machine-made form of the slabs, which is seldom a good thing.

Bricks   As the unit is small and regular, these are ideal for small scale work – narrow paths, parterres, designs involving curved lines, and panels which may be inset as part of a composition of stone or precast paving. It is best to use brick paviors, specifically made for the purpose and only 2 in. thick, but these are not so easy to obtain today. Engineering bricks are also suitable but they are expensive and have a very hard finish in strong red or blue/grey which will never fade or weather and, therefore, will not be suitable for every position. Over baked bricks, obtainable from some brickworks, are good although dark in colour, but are hard to lay as they are often warped and uneven in size and shape. Otherwise, really hard building bricks are suitable, but it is wise to get the suppliers to admit that they are suitable for outdoor paving before purchase. On no account use any kind of soft brick or common fletton, as these will crumble on exposure to frost.

Stone Paving   Various types of stone paving are obtainable in different parts of the country but the most commonly used and easily obtainable is York stone, either new or second-hand. This is an admirable material, with a pleasant texture and colour variation, obtainable in slabs large enough to provide a good sense of scale and fairly easily cut to pattern if required. It is best laid in a random pattern of rectangular slabs in different sizes, the joints between the stones pointed with cement tinted to match the stone colour and then raked back, so that it is scarcely visible and the forms of the individual stones stand out clearly. York stone has only two vices – apart from comparative expense which may be off-set by the thought that once properly laid it will remain almost for ever. The first is that second-hand paving is often of uneven thickness and, therefore, more difficult to lay, and the second is that it can become slippery in wet weather.

Granite Setts   At one time when all the roads, quay sides, tramways and other places laid with these square or oblong pieces of granite were being taken up, setts were easily obtainable. Nowadays they are hard to get and have always been hard to lay because the greater part of the sett is hidden below ground. They look effective as panels in a large stone terrace, or as a surface for an arrival or garage court largely used by wheeled rather than foot traffic.

Cobbles   This is another surface which is difficult to lay and uncomfortable to walk on, although this fact can be put to advantage to keep people away from certain areas, such as the edge of a retaining wall or a pond. They are best used as decorative panels in a setting of brick or stone. Only the end, or in some cases one edge, of the cobble stone is exposed; the remainder is buried to keep the stones in place. They need to be very closely set so that none of the supporting cement is visible, because nothing looks worse than a mass of concrete in which cobble stones are set singly, looking like currants in a plum duff. Swirling all over patterns can be made, using the variation in colour of the stones, and the different shapes of ends and edges, in a simplified version of those elaborate pebble pavings one sees sometimes in foreign gardens.

Gravel   The 'Prim gravel walks which ever winding go' of the Victorian garden have been out of favour for a long time. However, gravel properly laid and firmly held in place – preferably with brick or wood – is an excellent, hard-wearing and comparatively inexpensive surfacing material. With modern weed killers even keeping the gravel clean is no longer a problem. Unless a loose shingle effect is desired, proper binding gravel – or Breedon gravel which is really not gravel at all, but a form of crushed limestone – must be bought. The matt texture, quiet colouring and possibility of laying to any shape all give gravel the advantage over other materials.

Concrete   Concrete by itself is not an attractive material for the garden. However, it has certain advantages and much can be done to improve its cold colouring and unpleasantly smooth finish. By using different coloured sands, different aggregates and colouring agents which can be obtained for the purpose, the colour of the concrete can be changed from the usual hard grey/white to warm buff, tan and brownish shades more suitable to a garden setting. If an interesting aggregate is chosen it can be exposed before the concrete is absolutely dry, giving a pleasantly varied surface, or different textures can be applied while it is still damp by ribbing with a wooden lath, pressing coarse sacking on to the surface, or something similar. On no account draw paving patterns in the damp concrete with a pointed stick. They convince no one and merely look absurd. The fact that large areas of concrete cannot be laid without expansion joints to avoid cracking, can be turned to advantage by using patterns of wood strips, bricks on edge, panels of cobble stones, or similar materials to form an element in the design.

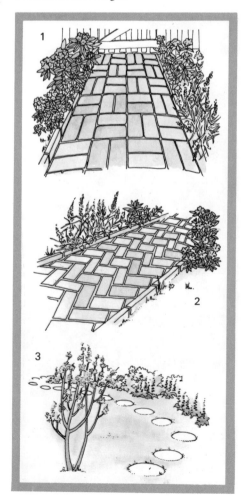

The Use of Hard Surfaces

Just as gardens are formed by the contrast of mass and void, open and closed spaces, so they need a proper balance between hard and soft elements. Either they can be largely soft with just enough hard surface to make them practical, like most country gardens, or the proportions may be reversed as they generally are in city sites. Where they are more nearly equal, the design is more difficult to handle and an exact 50:50 ratio seldom looks well. One should decide on the general intention before thinking of the detail, so that the completed work does not suffer the timidity and lack of purpose evident in many gardens.

Paths The first essential of any path is that it should be convenient to walk on and should take you where you want to go. If it fulfils these requirements comfortably it is of practical value and the exact form it takes will be dictated by the intended character of the garden of which it forms a part. Too many paths criss-crossing the ground can produce a restless and busy air, particularly as some of them are not needed. If dry ways are required in all directions it may be better to cease to think of them as paths, but to have a general pattern of interlocking hard and soft surfaces which together make a complete composition. Wherever practicable it should be possible for two people to walk comfortably abreast on a path and if the design demands that it should be curved, the curves must appear natural and inevitable, not forced and arbitrary.

Stepping Stones For casual use, where the line of a formal path would interrupt the flow of grass or planting, carefully placed stepping stones can provide an answer. They should be so spaced that a regular, easy pace will bring the foot well down on to each stone, rather than on to the edge with the risk of damaging the soft surface between them. Because grass or plants will tend to spread across the stone, the individual slabs should be large, so that there is not a constant edging problem, and where they cross lawns the stones must be set $\frac{1}{2}$ in. below the level of the turf to ensure that the mower blades can pass unharmed over the top. One should never use stepping stones where they will be used by wheelbarrows, because the wheel will wear a runnel of mud in the soft surface between them.

Mowing Stones Where grass abuts a vertical element such as a wall or step, it is essential to have a narrow strip of some hard material, once again sunk $\frac{1}{2}$ in. below the surface, to allow for easy mowing. The strip can be as narrow as a single brick, which will be almost invisible or it can be a broad band of stone or concrete forming part of an overall design. These wide bands are invaluable, also, between lawn and flower border, as they do away with the need for constant edging, which is always such a chore, and at the same time allow the plants to flop forward so that they can grow freely without the risk of being cut by the mower.

Terraces Most terraces are generally too wide for paths and too narrow for their proper purpose of forming a base to the house and a general area for sitting, entertaining and viewing the garden. No building looks its best rising straight from hard surface, so that a bed should always be left between house and terrace to give space for a foundation planting of low shrubs, foliage plants, bulbs and climbers if these are appropriate to the style of architecture. The material used for the terrace will naturally be influenced by the material of the building to which it is attached. Because the terrace is the first link on the horizontal plane between house and garden it must partake strongly of the character of both if it is to be effective. The architectural details of the house can often be reflected in the patterning and surface treatment of the terrace also, giving a further close link between the vertical and horizontal elements. Proportion is important and the classical width for a terrace is that it should equal the distance from ground to cornice (or in our case the eaves) as though, indeed, the face of the house were reflected again upon the ground. Although, where a bungalow is concerned the terrace would need to be wider to compensate for the low wall of the house behind. If you have not the space to allow for a terrace of this width, you should seriously consider whether a terrace is appropriate at all, or whether the whole of the garden should not in effect be the terrace in the form of an outdoor room directly related to the house. Not all this space needs to be paved, of course, because it can contain a certain amount of planting either in beds or carefully grouped

Bricks may be laid in various patterns to form pathways, such as the basket-weave pattern (1) and the herring-bone pattern (2). Stepping stones (3) make an interesting and unusual path across a lawn. *Below:* When using precast paving it is best to choose the quieter, muted colours and to use one colour only. *Right:* Bricks laid in running bond pattern to form a paved area

containers. The terrace needs a well defined edge, but unless there is a considerable drop it is better to avoid little hedges or irritating dwarf walls which cut up the view with little advantage. A single step, the full width of the terrace either up or down on to the lawn can be very effective, and even two or three long steps on which groups of easily changed pot plants can stand, will be very effective. The long horizontal lines of the steps will add greater importance to the house or give stability to the details of the garden beyond.

Steps Steps can be very much more than a means of proceeding from one level to another since they can provide interest, excitement, dignity and sculptural form. However, they must be comfortable to use. The formula for step design is that twice the rise plus the width of the tread should equal 26 in. and that, except very occasionally for some specific reason, the rise should never be more than 6 in. An easy proportion is a tread of 17 in. and a rise of $4\frac{1}{2}$ in., but a rise of less than this can be dangerous because it is difficult to see and easy to trip down. In general, the shallower the steps, the broader they should be, but final decisions on both these points will be influenced by the scale and proportions of their surroundings. The form of the step can either be that of a solid block, whether of hewn stone, shuttered concrete or brick, or formed from two distinct parts, the riser (which can be of brick or stone) and the tread formed from stone or precast concrete slabs. In this case the tread should overhang the riser by about $1\frac{1}{2}$ in., to give a deep line of shadow under the edge.

Retaining Walls Although these are strictly vertical features, they seem to belong with steps and terraces and so find their place here. Retaining walls should usually be made of (or at least faced with) the same material as the house to which they belong. If for some reason this is not possible they should be constructed from local stone or other material, or failing that be designed to be completely hidden by climbing and trailing plants. It is naturally essential that retaining walls should retain, and they must, therefore, be built on very solid foundations and can often be helped by a backing of rough concrete and reinforcing bars. Weep holes must always be left at the base of such walls to prevent water from being trapped behind and undermining the foundations. There was an unfortunate fashion in the earlier years of this century for making stone walls with earth joints in imitation of those retaining the steep-sided lanes in the stone counties. In the cracks were grown suitable plants and ferns but unless they were faultlessly made and maintained they either tended to collapse or become infested with deep-rooted weeds impossible to dislodge without demolishing the wall. Even worse was a fashion for leaving odd holes in the face of walls in order to grow tufts of trailing plants which merely resulted in the face of the wall having a spotty appearance.

Drives and Forecourts These features are the first introduction to house and garden and they should partake strongly of the character of the house to which they belong and should make an appropriate setting for it. The normal pattern of front garden, with a concrete garage run, a narrow bed, a path of some other material and then a patch of lawn and flower beds is very unsatisfactory. Often it could be better replaced by a forecourt, perhaps patterned in brick and paving, which would provide the hard standing needed for the car, dry access to the house, and space for planting, in one unified composition. This arrangement of strips of paving making a simple pattern with square or rectangular panels filled with some other hard surface where people and vehicles will pass, and with planting in the outer areas, is very satisfactory and capable of infinite variation. Naturally very solid foundations must be laid where cars will stand, but lighter ones can be employed for foot traffic. Long drives, of course, are best made with binding gravel, firmly edged, or with tarmacadam carefully tar sprayed and with grit or fine gravel well rolled in to conceal the black surface.

Decoration

Although the main decoration of the garden will naturally consist of living material, even the smallest garden can absorb one or two decorative objects, particularly if they are also useful. The temptation to have too many things, and to scatter them about as though a place had to be found for them somehow, must be sternly avoided if the garden is not to look like a cross between a scrap dealer's yard and a garden centre. The placing of any object whether seat, urn or fountain must

Left: A wide band of paving stones between the border and the lawn allows the plants to trail freely over the edge and the grass may be mown easily. *Below:* Informal steps made from stone slabs well cemented together for safety *Above right:* A well-placed seat in a quiet corner. Hostas provide colour and interest. *Right:* Plants in various containers. *Far right:* Colourful petunias in a half barrel

when viewed in silhouette against the light.

Fountains Much the same remarks apply to fountain figures as to other sculptures although seen in full sun with reflected light playing round them and themselves reflected in the waters of the pool, they need to be of higher visual quality than a statue half hidden in a shadowy grove. What is more we are always attracted to water, particularly when it is moving, and will examine its source carefully. If no suitable figure can be found, a simple shell or bowl, fixed to appear floating on the surface of the water, with a plain jet of water rising and falling in it, can be very effective and far better than a third-rate concrete Cupid. What is more the birds will bathe and drink in the shallow bowl, giving added life and pleasure. Where the pool is designed for reflection, a sedate bubble fountain scarcely disturbing the water surface, will be more appropriate.

Sundials, Birdbaths and Other Objects The sundial is a useful pivot and centre of attraction round which all kinds of garden patterns can evolve, but if one is honest and thinks of it in these terms only, because its original use no longer applies, then its true relevance in the garden is doubtful. Better, perhaps, a birdbath of good design, preferably with a small fresh water pipe laid on so that the water can be changed daily without resorting to buckets. This will bring far more life and interest to the garden than the silent dial. Apart from these obvious pieces there are other decorative possibilities, to be used with restraint and understanding. A sculptured plaque or the old carved keystone from a doorway set in a blank piece of wall, urns or finials on tops of gate piers or seen against the sky on the parapet of a house, an old bust giving point to the end of a free-standing wall, all have their place in certain types of design. For those who wish to relive their childhood there are great quantities of gnomes, concrete or porcelain animals with coloured eyes and other such things. But they belong to the world of the permanent funfair and have nothing whatever to do with gardens as such.

Seats and Furniture These items fall into two distinct classes, the permanent and the transient. Permanent seats and even tables can be both decorative and useful, either in natural wood or stone, or in painted wood or metal. The thing is to choose pieces which are not only pleasing in themselves but which reflect exactly the character of the place for which they are intended. One has only to experience the absolute absurdity of finding an elaborate white painted Victorian cast-iron seat beside a natural forest pool, to appreciate the importance of fitness for purpose. Where such permanent seats are to be used frequently they will need cushions kept easily to hand and covered in some plain dark coloured or at least neutral fabric. Since flower colour and the pattern of leaf or branch are what matters in the garden, obtrusive stripes, checks and vulgar florals should never be used. Where possible it is better to use cane, bamboo or woven willow furniture.

appear the inevitable outcome of the garden design, rather than an afterthought.

Urns Under this heading one can include all kinds of plant containers from the simple half-barrel stained or painted, to the most elaborate marble urn on a pedestal. The first consideration must be whether the principal attraction is to be the container or the planting. If the latter then simple shapes and generous provision for soil and good drainage are all-important. When possible choose containers which do not require maintenance in the form of painting, nor have to be taken into the house or under cover to preserve them from winter frost which is necessary with much earthenware and pottery imported from abroad. Pleasing groups can be built up using pots and bowls of contrasting form, some old such as bread crocks, household coppers or preserving pans and others new, in asbestos, concrete, stone or other appropriate materials (but hard shiny plastic is not appropriate in outdoor settings). Such groups might have a permanently planted backbone of small shrubs and foliage plants, leaving space for seasonal bedding which can be augmented with the addition of plants such as lilies in normal pots, set out while they are blooming and then removed to make way for something else. If the urn is to be considered as a decoration in itself it may require no planting or only some quiet trailing plants of a recessive nature. Again a simple design is best, chosen

to blend with the general character of the garden. Good reproductions of antique pieces cast in reconstructed stone are obtainable.

Statues It is unfortunate that there is so little good modern sculpture available for the garden although an approach to the local art school or technical college might produce interesting results. However, there are some good reproductions of antique pieces available in reasonable materials and visits to demolition sales and antique dealers can be rewarding. One does not have to stick to figures as such–a coat of arms on a stone panel, a large finial from a roof top or even a broken column tactfully draped in ivy would all be acceptable in the right setting. Primarily the intention is to draw the eye to a certain point, or to add an element of scale or punctuation to a part of the design. Both the placing and the object must appear inevitable in the given setting–if not, then the thing is irrelevant. Fine detail and materials are wasted in the garden, and provided that the balance, proportion and outline are good, one seldom looks more closely. Pale materials such as stone or marble are best against dark simple backgrounds, for example an alcove in a yew hedge, whereas bronze or lead figures are better in the open, seen against sky, water or mown grass. Elaborate carving or moulding needs to be placed in full sunlight against shadow, simple shapes or openwork modern 'constructions' in metal are most effective

Structural Planting

Structure does not only imply walls and terraces but it also includes trees and shrubs, hedges and grass which together form the natural masses and voids, vertical and horizontal elements. It is important at this point to realize that planting can be structural or decorative and that the two purposes should not be confused nor should they necessarily be combined. Failure to understand this basic principle has resulted in too many weak and shapeless gardens, lacking in character and purpose.

Trees These are the largest structural element in the garden, providing shade, wind shelter and a degree of privacy. Not many small gardens need or have room for large wind-breaks, but a group of trees can filter the wind or reduce the impact of draughts between buildings. In any type of structural planting it is the structure which comes first, so that even in a small garden a group or a curved line of trees providing shelter and privacy should consist of one variety of tree only. Choose the right tree where form, habit, colouring and cultural requirements fit that position and stick to it. The result will be visually and practically far more satisfactory than an ill-assorted collection of odd specimens, some of which will flourish better than others. Trees can also be used formally to provide architectural green elements on a large scale. Grown as espaliers or cordons they have long been familiar in the kitchen garden but standard trees planted 8–10 ft. apart, with their branches trained out espalier fashion above the top of the wall or fence, can soon provide privacy in small gardens. When the branches meet they are stopped and the ensuing twigs are trimmed to form what amounts to a hedge on legs. This training or pleaching of trees has been employed for hundreds of years, although it is more often encountered now in France than in England. The same basic method can be used to form open tunnels, arbours or complete pergolas of trees, trained out on wooden frameworks

while their branches are supple. But such constructions require quite a lot of maintenance. Feathered trees of suitable varieties, that is those with branches all the way down the trunk, before the nurseryman makes them into standards, can also be planted 3 ft. apart or so in lines and with careful trimming can be induced to form tall hedges. They will need careful support in the early stages, before they grow together.

Hedges The first thing to decide is the purpose for which the hedge is to be planted. If it is to be green architecture, a neatly trimmed expression of geometric shapes, then the hedging material should be chosen with that in mind, since certain plants clip more neatly than others. Again, if the hedge is to form a background to decorative planting it is essential that its tone should be dark and its texture matt. For such purposes yew would be ideal, while the loose growth, pale shiny foliage and coarse texture of laurel would be utterly unsuitable. If the hedge is to be largely free growing and is to be decorative in itself, then provided the growth of the chosen shrub is neat, well-furnished to the ground and suitable for growing in lines, the field is open for experiment both with evergreen and deciduous shrubs. However, if you wish to hide something it is pointless to try to do so with material which is in itself eye catching. If you think of those lines of Lombardy poplars which simply draw attention to the industrial developments which they are intended to hide, you will understand what is meant.

Shrubs A certain amount of structural shrub planting in the garden is often needed in addition to the backbone of trees and hedges, to give the required sense of form. But such shrubs must have the inherent quality of structure. Their solidity, form, habit of growth and tone value are of much greater consequence than the detail of flower or berry. Indeed, as a general rule all kinds of structure should be recessive in character, forming a background to the decorative objects and planting placed within it.

Grass This is almost the only structural planting on the horizontal plane and as such plays a very important part in British gardens. One of our problems is that it grows too easily–abroad, where good grass is hard to keep, much greater thought is given to the design and use of grass areas. Even in Britain, grass will not withstand a great deal of hard wear and continue to look attractive, so the first requirement is to design the grass shapes in such a way that they are not over used and that they are easy to maintain. To fulfil its function as a unifying, green matt textured carpet, holding together and flowing through all the other elements, the grass must be kept cut and, where appropriate, the edges trimmed. Simple forms and uncluttered shapes are, therefore, best. Do not try to achieve precise architectural forms with grass banks–the

idea is attractive but in the long run the neat angles and sharp planes are impossible to maintain unless they are hand cut with shears, an almost impossible task. Where you are dealing with large areas, good use can sometimes be made of the contrast between smoothly mown grass and grass cut less frequently which can provide a home for bulbs and wild flowers of all kinds. Beautiful interlocking abstract shapes in two tones of green can be achieved in this way, although a very careful programme will have to be evolved for cutting the longer grass, to ensure that the various bulbs and flowers it contains can all flower unharmed.

Plants as Decoration

'Isn't it pretty, I simply must have one of those' is a phrase which has rung the death knell of any number of gardens. Bought for some particular moment of flower or fruit, with no thought for the character or balance of the garden as a whole, any number of unrelated plants jostle in beds and borders, competing for our attention. The only effect they achieve is of discord and unease. If only those same people would first decide on a general theme, and then work within these limits, they could have satisfying, even spectacular results with no greater expenditure of time and effort.

Plant Form Colour photography has a great deal to answer for, since it is quite easy to take a pretty picture if the colours are harmonious, without thinking about composition, whereas with black and white work form, texture, light and shade are all important. All plants, if well grown, have a distinct outline which can be reduced to

abstract shapes so that you see them as pyramids or circles, verticals or horizontals, or some combination of these elements. Not only do they have form, they also have texture so that they can be seen as coarse or fine, light absorbent or light reflecting and so on. Before deciding on any individual plant it is much better to evolve a thoroughly satisfying planting scheme in purely abstract terms as an arrangement of sizes and shapes, forms and textures. Only when this composition is correct should you try to translate these elements into plants, but even then it is better to think of those plants as though they were black and white photographs, so that you can appreciate their formal structure, the shadow patterns which they cast, the way they hold their leaves or flowers, and whatever other qualities they may possess, without being confused by the separate problem of colour. And you must think of them at all times of year, the bare pattern of winter twigs as well as the heavy foliage of high summer, the hanging clusters of autumn fruit as well as the delicate wreaths of spring flowers, so that your picture is properly balanced. Once you have got this far you must choose from among plants of suitable shape and habit, those which will grow in your particular conditions.

The Fourth Dimension   In all garden work, time is a fourth dimension. No planting scheme is static and the effect next year, in five, ten, twenty-five, fifty years will all be different but must all be considered from the outset. Fortunately some plants mature quickly; others are very slow to reach maturity. So unless your outlook is very short term—and even then we should not think only of ourselves, but of those who

follow—the slow growing shrubs and trees must be put in first, spaced at the ·proper distances, while the large areas between will contain shrubs and plants of moderate growth. Between these can grow annuals, herbaceous plants, bulbs and shrubs such as brooms and tree lupins which mature quickly and are equally short lived. Before making a final choice, always try to see the plants you are proposing to use, growing in some park or garden at various seasons of the year. Some may have very off periods which may make them unsuitable for your purpose. Never choose a plant, however apparently attractive from the sole evidence of a cut spray exhibited at a flower show as this can be very deceptive.

Colour   The vexed question of colour, usually uppermost in people's minds, has been left deliberately until the last. To begin with, it is as well to remember that green is also a colour, and that one could make very satisfying compositions in that colour alone. Then there is the difference between the transient colour of flowers and the longer lasting colour of foliage, especially where conifers and evergreens are concerned, as they provide some of the brightest and most permanent colour effects. Do not neglect, either, the colour of tree trunks and young shoots which can do so much to cheer the winter landscape. The easiest way to handle colour, particularly in a small area, is to have a single theme and to stick to one colour at a time. For instance, a small garden, or part of a large one, planted in shades of yellow and gold only, in a general setting of grey foliage can be most exciting, and is comparatively simple to achieve. If this single colour device is found too constricting, then it is best to

keep firmly to one range of colour. Flower and foliage colours are generally based on blue or yellow. In the blue range, beside blue and purple are all the purplish reds, crimsons, bluish pinks and whites which have no hint of yellow in them. In the yellow range are scarlet, orange, flame, yellow pinks such as salmon and apricot, creams and whites inclined to yellow. If you work within one range of colour, setting it against a background of complementary foliage colours, the end result will still be very harmonious. Of course people with an eye for colour can achieve exciting contrasts between the two ranges but unless you are in that class it is wiser to play safe. With care, you can have quite different colour effects at different times of year, provided that the background planting is suitably neutral. The great thing to avoid is dotting little patches of unrelated colour about the place, each one taking away from the impact of its neighbours rather than building up into a total effect. Bedding plants or bulbs in boxes of mixed colours should never be used unless a particular patchwork effect is required against a very plain setting. A single variety or perhaps two or three shades of one colour are so much more useful. The colour of the atmosphere in this country is always blue, sometimes strongly so, and the blue quality of the light has an important influence on flower colour as it brings out and intensifies the colour of pale flowers giving them a life and character they could never have in a clearer less misty atmosphere. In the same way the blue light makes many of the bright colour contrasts which appear so stimulating in the strong yellow light of other parts of the world appear merely tawdry and vulgar.

Left: The various shades of red in these borders are subdued by the greens of the foliage
Above: Trees, shrubs and hardy perennials, with different rates of growth, show how time must be considered as the fourth dimension when planting a garden. *Right:* The various shades of green can be used effectively. Among other plants shown here are thyme, lavender, ballota, and *Iris pallida variegata*

Top: A town garden can be made more interesting if full use is made of the different shapes of plants

Above: A corner of a paved garden in which various plant forms and colours are used effectively

Bright colours should always be seen in sunlight, pale colours and white flowers gain added quality in the shade or against a shadowy background. If the garden is going to be used at night, the ability of some pale flowers to glow in the dark can be used to create a new pattern quite different to the familiar daytime scene.

Making the Design

Practical Considerations At this stage it is as well to take a piece of tracing paper, place it over your survey and put down the basic facts about the way in which you use your garden in diagrammatic form. For instance there is an obvious desire line between the gate and the front door, back door, garage entrance. There is probably one sheltered place in which you like to sit in the sun (your designing can create any shade you may need). There may be other inescapable factors, such as the need to park a boat or caravan in a particular position, other desire lines from back door to back gate and so forth. Although some of these may be shifted slightly, you cannot ignore them and they will have an important bearing on the final solution. Obviously the garden should not only be attractive but convenient. Kitchen gardens are best near the kitchens they are to serve, so are clothes' lines and small children's play areas. Areas for entertaining and general outdoor living must have good access from the house and should preferably not be approached by steps which make the carrying of chairs, cushions and loaded trays a hazardous undertaking. The service yard not only needs good access to all parts of the garden (and remember if you have steps, that barrows and mowers will need an alternative ramped approach) but also easy access to the road so that peat, manure and other garden materials can be delivered without being carried through the rest of the garden. The tennis court must be on a north/south axis to avoid problems from low lying evening sun, whereas the swimming pool needs to catch as much sun as possible but is better kept out of sight of the house because of its dreary aspect in the winter.

Putting Thoughts on Paper The practical needs and the site factors such as views, movement of sun and shadow etc., will form a framework almost as definite as the boundaries of the garden, and between these two sets of conditions you will have to prepare your design. Certain objects of fixed size, such as a tennis court, can be drawn to the same scale as the survey and cut out, so that they can be moved easily about the plan, but for the rest you must begin to sketch out your ideas on thin sheets of tracing paper stretched over the original survey. At this stage do not worry too much about keeping your lines precisely straight or every detail of the work neat; there is something inhibiting in working with exact precision when the most important thing is to get ideas to flow. Possibly you will already have a design in mind, and if this works out easily when put on paper all well and good. If it does not fit in properly, then do not try to force the issue. It is very easy to get obsessed with some particular idea and then make everything conform to it, but the result is seldom satisfactory and always looks forced and contrived (which indeed it is).

Do not be afraid of discarding partly finished sketches which do not seem to work, but do not throw them away altogether as some further development of your ideas may solve the problem which prevented one of them from satisfying you completely. If you are absolutely stuck it is better to leave the work altogether and return to it again. Sometimes it is even helpful to reverse all the decisions you have made – put the sitting area in the shade, the compost heap by the living room and so forth. Although naturally your finished plan will not really be like this, the total reversal of all preconceived ideas will often free your mind so that designing in exactly the opposite way to your first intentions can provide a key to some problem which will allow you to proceed as you wished.

All the time you are sketching things on paper, you must remember that the lines you are drawing represent real objects on the ground. It is important to visualize exactly how each element will look in that position. In your imagination you should be able to walk along the paths, mow the lawn, climb the steps, push a barrow round the corners and live at all times of day and all seasons of the year, in each projected design while you are drawing it.

If you can do this, you may well discover all kinds of faults and problems which are not immediately apparent. The path may not be wide enough to walk on with ease once the plants in the adjoining bed have grown to their full size, the curve of the lawn too tight for the turning circle of the mower, the corners too sharp for a fully loaded barrow, the steps steep and uncomfortable. This imaginative exercise is very important and can save making mistakes which would be difficult to remedy at a later stage.

Having satisfied yourself on paper that your scheme is a good one, you should draw it up neatly on tracing paper making sure that all the elements are exactly to scale, and that the shapes you are using are suitable for the materials you propose to use. For instance to design a $3\frac{1}{2}$ ft. wide path to be made with 2 ft. square slabs is obviously not practical. Any patterns you propose to make with different types of hard surface can also be worked out at this stage as can the positions of things such as water taps, outdoor electric points for use with lights or electrical equipment, heating systems for the greenhouse, the useful luxury of a telephone point in a summer house or changing pavilion far from the house, and similar items.

Never use your original plan out of doors. In most towns there is a drawing office, art shop or similar place where dyeline prints can be made quite cheaply from your

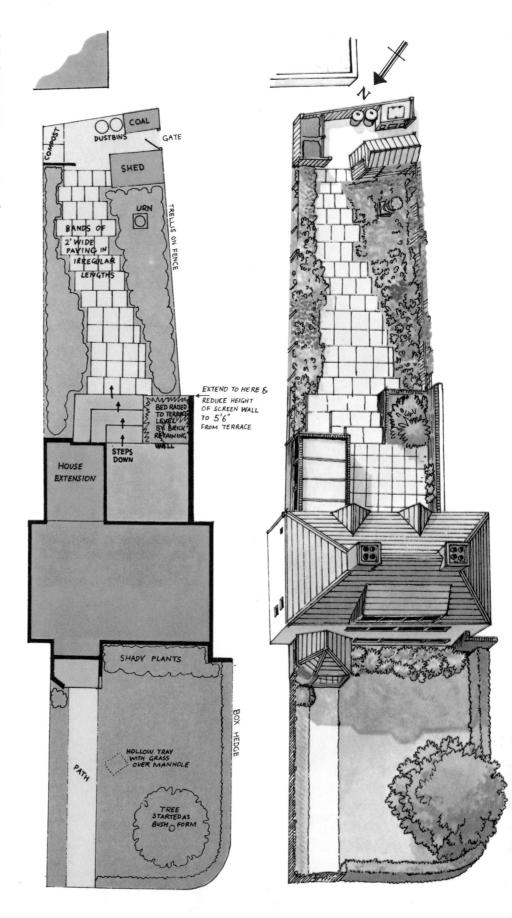

The original rough plan, as shown on page 13, has now been completed. The narrow path in the front garden has been widened and the manhole cover in the lawn has been hidden. A decorative tree in the bottom right hand corner provides protection. Plants which will thrive in shady places have been planted in the cold, damp area near the house. At the back, bands of paving stones provide access to the shed, dustbins, etc, the poorly shaped forsythia has been removed, and a brick retaining wall has been built to raise the bed to the level of the terrace

tracing paper plan. In this way you can have several copies made as you are bound to want to write in notes, mark distances and so forth on one, use another on the job where it will get wet and muddy, and keep clean copies for reference.

Before starting work you should always work out your whole design on the ground using pegs or garden canes and balls of cheap string. The most thorough way of doing this is to draw a grid on the plan, mark out the same grid full size on the ground, and then measure each point where the lines of the design intersect those of the grid on plan and transfer those measurements to the grid on the ground. In fact, it is seldom necessary to do this, as a certain number of measurements from known points such as the corners of the house, and measured positions on the boundaries, will generally suffice. At this point your paper scheme may need a little adjustment. However pleasing shapes may appear on plan, when translated to the ground and seen in perspective they do not look the same. Curves particularly look more extreme and may well need easing out to achieve the shape you intend. A garden hose can be very useful in drawing curves on the ground as it is heavy and solid enough to push into shape and will give the effect of the line more easily than a string which needs to be held in place with pegs.

Once the shapes are clearly marked out, do not rush to turn them into reality. A garden is a long term investment which may even go on to give pleasure to your children and grandchildren. Leave the pegs and strings

in place for a few days. Look at the layout from the bedrooms, the bathroom, the kitchen as well as the living room. See how it strikes you as you arrive home at night and leave in the morning, what it looks like in sun and shadow, by day and night. A solution which perhaps looked clever and original when first drawn may seem more contrived than restful when you have seen it on the ground for a few days.

When construction is in progress, you can be thinking about the planting, deciding on the heights and general shapes needed for shrub masses, the exact position and outline needed for trees. Tall garden canes can be stuck in to represent tree trunks and looked at from every angle to ensure that when planting time comes no mistakes are made – nothing is more irritating to find, having dug a magnificent hole and put in a shrub or tree with infinite care, that it is not quite in the right place.

One should never think of the garden completely in isolation, because there is always an interaction to a greater or lesser extent between interior and exterior views. Some buildings – for instance ancient cottages with tiny crooked windows set comparatively high – exclude their gardens, creating a cosy, womb-like effect within their low-beamed rooms. But most other houses acknowledge their gardens to a greater or lesser extent and in the modern house with its wide windows, the garden becomes almost a part of the interior. When it comes to colour, texture and shape, therefore, every effort should be made to integrate the furnishing

Below Left: It is not difficult to train laburnums over an archway to produce an effect like this, even in a small garden
Above: Roses and clematis on a pergola. Varieties can be chosen to flower at different times to ensure long continuity of colour

of the house and the planting of the garden to create a total picture.

Not only colour gives continuity, because different types of plant have very strong associations outside themselves. Laced pinks, auriculas, small moss roses, striped tulips and similar flowers with their air of Meissen bouquets belong to neat 18th century gardens with box edged beds and espalier fruit trees. Formal dark camellias, ferns, the roses 'Madame Pierre Oger' and 'La Reine Victoria', lilies-of-the-valley and certain other lilies are strongly Victorian in effect, while rhododendrons, hydrangeas, heavy headed paeonies and swags of rambler roses or climbing roses belong to different kinds of Edwardian gardens.

To sum up briefly then: decide exactly what kind of garden you need for your particular family and way of life, and consider how best this garden can be expressed in materials and shapes which will accord with your house and its surroundings. Make sure that everything down to the last plant and cushion has a definite part to play in the picture you are trying to create, and never think of any one element as an object in its own right. Remember the pleasure you can give to others who see your garden from the outside only, and do not be in too much of a hurry. Some of the things you build and plant will last a century or more.

Right: The garden at Great Dixter, Sussex

Bulbs, Corms & Tubers

Definitions

Bulbs, corms and tubers are the specially modified resting stages of certain plants which enable them to live, dormant (i.e. not actively growing), through some adverse climatic condition (usually drought). They all contain a store of concentrated food, and dormant buds, some of which in the bulbs and corms may have embryo flowers already formed inside them, so that when suitable growing conditions recur, the leaves and flowers are produced in a very short time. Because they are not actively growing they can be dug up, transported and sold in shops with little check to future growth.

Bulbs contain their food reserve in either special swollen scale-like leaves, loosely packed round the new bud, as in a lily bulb; or in tightly packed leaf bases encircling the bud, as in daffodil, tulip or onion (allium). In the second type the outside of the bulb is protected by dry, often skin-like, leaf bases. All parts spring from a very flattened stem area known as the 'plate', from the underside of which the roots grow.

Bulbous plants are members of either the lily family or the amaryllis family or of the genus *Iris*.

Corms differ from bulbs in that it is the stem, often flattened, which contains the food reserve. The main bud arises from the centre of the upper surface; other buds may often be seen at the sides. Protective scales are dry. Roots form around the edge of the scar of the previous year's corm.

Each bud is capable of making a new corm and so small cormels arise around the main corm and spread the plant. The plants producing the corms we are considering all belong to the Iris family.

The swollen area of a tuber may arise from a stem or from both root and shoot, but although a stem tuber will produce roots when it starts to grow it is rarely that a root tuber which has lost its shoot (bud) will grow another. Tubers may have scale leaves but more usually lack these. Tubers are not a method of propagation as small ones are not formed from them, as in bulbs and corms.

Tuberous begonias, dahlias and gladioli are dealt with in Favourite Garden Flowers.

When to Look for Bulbs, Corms and Tubers in the Shops The main outdoor planting season for bulbs, corms and tubers is in the autumn with bulbs on sale from mid-August to late November.

Lilies have a very long growing season and, if they have had to be transported over great distances, may not arrive in time for the autumn selling season. Buy them as soon as they arrive and plant immediately. If soil conditions are very bad pot them and plant out when conditions are good in the spring, do not store them.

Many corms, though dormant during the winter, are not completely hardy and are liable to be killed in the soil before growth can start in the spring. These are stored in frost-proof conditions and sold from late January to the end of April, for planting as soon as the soil (not the air) is frost-free. If potted up in a frost-free greenhouse they can be had in flower much earlier. Treated in this way they can be planted out as soon as air frosts are unlikely, but must be hardened off first.

There is a small group of plants which flower in autumn, often well before their leaves, the main growth of which is not till spring. They have a short summer dormant season and are sold in July-August.

Bulbs are sometimes marked 'prepared'. This means either that they have been heat treated so that they will flower before their normal season, or that they have been cool stored past their normal flowering season so that they flower later. These are available in August-September and should be planted immediately for growing indoors for Christmas flowering.

Greenhouse bulbs include those which are available in autumn but make their growth during the winter, e.g. ixias, *Gladiolus nana*. These can, of course, be planted outside in mild districts, and in any case can be put out by the spring. Holding them dry until the spring is not always a success. They also include those plants which while they can be grown quite successfully outside can be obtained much earlier by growing in a cool house. Varieties of narcissi and tulips which will stand this treatment are often marked as 'forcing' varieties.

Mixed crocus

True greenhouse plants are those which need a higher temperature than is likely to be experienced outdoors, especially during the period September to May. Their planting seasons vary enormously and depend not only on the season of flowering or growth but also on the amount of heat that can be supplied.

How to Select Bulbs, Corms and Tubers in a Shop Is the shop temperature suitable? If it freezes at night half-hardy bulbs may be damaged and go soft on the outside. If it is too hot (e.g. near the radiator or other source of heat), the bulbs will wither or start to grow shoots prematurely without root growth, and some fungal and bacterial diseases will attack bruised tissues. Tubers liable to wither, such as dahlias, should be prepacked in polythene. See that this is intact. Embryo buds are damaged by withdrawal of water during withering and also by high temperatures. Prepared bulbs lose the effect of the treatment in such conditions. Expensive bulbs should be in shavings, sawdust or peat moss.

Are the bulbs etc. clean? Dirty stock can carry soil-borne diseases and is likely to prevent you looking for bruising and other troubles. Is the stock well housed and properly labelled with variety name and grade as well as price? Narcissus bulbs can be single-nosed, double-nosed or mother bulbs. The more 'noses' the more main growths, each with a flower. Is a mother bulb, with three noses, going to give you a better display than three single-nosed bulbs – compare the prices. Single-nosed bulbs are best for using with a bulb planter, as they will not stick in the hole, but fall to the bottom. Bulbs for naturalizing should not contain a lot of very small bulbs which will not flower the same year.

Corms are sold by size, the cms denoting the circumference of the corm. Very big corms have fewer advantages than big bulbs, e.g. it is usually better to have one good spike per gladiolus than one and a small one. Exhibition growers choose medium size corms. Large cyclamen corms have fewer years ahead of them and often take longer to settle than small ones.

Hyacinths of medium size give one good spike against one and a small one of the very large bulb. It may pay you to pick off the small one when it starts to emerge to keep the good spike from growing lop-sidedly.

If you can handle the stock before purchasing do so carefully. If a sample of daffodils or irises has some bulbs which are

obviously underweight and are soft to the touch leave the lot as it will be impossible to make sure you are not introducing narcissus fly larvae (maggots) or other pest which has eaten out the interior. If when you carefully move a scale leaf or two you find a fungal disease and you are prepared to dip the bulbs in a fungicide before planting, hyacinths may still be all right to buy, but irises with ink disease (black patches) are to be avoided and so are tulips and gladioli with scabby patches (tulip fire and gladiolus scab). Why buy trouble? Show the shopkeeper and he can report to the grower who should not legally be selling diseased stock. Lily bulbs which have the scales falling off probably have basal rot. A similar disease may cause narcissi to have a faulty base plate without a complete ring of roots. Such bulbs spread their diseases to the soil and to other bulbs. They should be burnt.

The only other troubles likely to affect bulbs are not readily seen at this stage. They are best avoided by buying from a reputable source. Virus diseases may cause striped or yellowing foliage or broken colour in the flowers (desired in some tulips). There is no cure for virus diseases. Greenfly eggs may be on the bulb scales of small irises and aphids (i.e. greenflies, blackflies etc.) may attack any bulb in growth; especially susceptible are the fleshy leaves of lachenalias. An aphid spray or (indoors) aerosol should be used as soon as they are seen, as aphids may spread virus diseases.

In the shop it now remains to see that the assistant knows how to handle the stock and does not shovel up corms and tubers with a metal scoop that can remove the buds, and also be sure that each bag is properly labelled. It is maddening to have to wait until the bulbs flower in the wrong bowls to know that the hyacinth you thought was the blue one is in fact red.

Above: St Brigid anemones, available in brilliant colours, make fine cut flowers
Right: Sinningias, better known as gloxinias, are among the most decorative of greenhouse plants
Left: Tritonia crocata, the blazing star, is a close relative of the montbretia
Below: Bulb planting chart

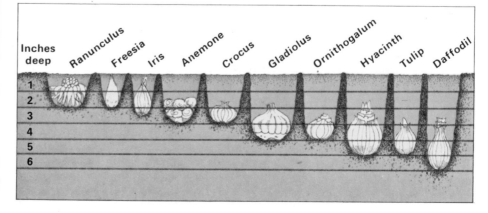

Bulb planting chart: Inches deep — Ranunculus, Freesia, Iris, Anemone, Crocus, Gladiolus, Ornithogalum, Hyacinth, Tulip, Daffodil

❧ General Cultivation ❧

Outdoors Although bulbs, corms and tubers carry their own food supply it is only good for one year at most and if you wish to have flowers year after year it is essential that they should be well fed. This is especially true of the highly-bred hyacinths, tulips and crocuses and some of the smaller irises. Always prepare the whole of the area to be planted in a bed, do not just dig out the holes, as these may act as drainage sumps in heavy ground, rotting the bulbs. Bonemeal and coarsely ground hoof and horn meal should be added to the soil, and also peat and sharp sand if the soil is very heavy. It is worth making up plenty of such a mixture for putting round the bulbs or corms wherever they are to go. When the ground has been prepared scatter the bulbs on the surface where they are to go and then dig out hole by hole with an ordinary trowel or a specially marked bulb trowel, planting and covering as you go. In this way you will not be digging where you have just planted. In formal planting mark out the distances along a trench.

If the bulbs are to go in turf this can be cut out with a special bulb planter after scattering the bulbs in drifts. If the bulbs are small and the turf close it is easier to lift the turf with a turfing iron or flat spade and place the little bulbs on the soil underneath, sprinkling the peat, sand and bonemeal mixture around them before replacing the turves carefully. Do not beat the turf down hard, but it can be watered to settle it.

Depth of planting Roughly speaking and if no special instructions are given the depth at which to plant a bulb is not more than twice its depth of soil above it and not less than its depth. Some bulbs make droppers (short stems) to take the new bulb to the optimum depth, others make contractile roots which pull the new bulb down. It may be possible to protect a half-hardy bulb outside from the effects of frost by planting it deeply, but some do not remain there but work their way to the surface.

Indoors, plants can be grown in pots filled with ordinary potting compost, in bowls or other undrained containers filled with a specially prepared bulb fibre, which is usually a fibrous or sphagnum peat with crushed shell and small pieces of charcoal, to prevent the fibre from becoming sour as a result of water collecting in the undrained bowl. The fibre has little feeding value, though the bulbs can be fed very carefully with a liquid feed. If grossly overwatered the roots in a bowl will drown for lack of air. If you think a bowl has been overwatered tilt it very carefully, holding the fibre in with one spreadeagled hand and drain off such water as appears.

Bulbs usually require sharp drainage and this can be assured by adding extra grit to a John Innes potting compost. These come in three grades of fertilizer. JIP 1 has one unit of base fertilizer, JIP 2 is richer, with double the amount and JIP 3 has three units and is for

Planting bulbs to flower indoors
1. A good layer of moist bulb fibre is placed in the container. 2. The bulbs are placed in position. 3. More moist fibre is pressed around the bulbs, leaving the tips exposed. 4. The container is placed in a polythene bag before being plunged under sand, ashes, etc.

very rich feeding, used only for very rapidly growing plants. Indoors, it is often more convenient to use a peat-based compost, which is cleaner and lighter.

Plants for the house should be started into growth in a cool dark place such as a cold cupboard or a plunge bed in the garden. This is merely a flat area on which the pots can be stood and covered completely with about 2 in. of moist peat, sand or washed ashes. These will fill in the spaces around the pots as well and keep the temperature very even. Boards or bricks can be placed round the outside or the bed can be made in a cold frame. Do not put bowls in a plunge bed out of doors or they may be flooded by rain. It may take as long as eight or ten weeks in a plunge bed before the pots are ready to bring into a warm place. By this time the bulbs or corms will have made a good root system which can take up enough water and food for the emerging shoot. If put into the warm straight away the shoot will often grow faster than the roots can feed it and the plant will collapse. Specially prepared hyacinths can generally be brought into the warmth after six weeks in the cool. The narcissi 'Paper White' and 'Soleil D'Or' do not seem to be any the worse for being brought straight into the warm if the bulbs have been properly ripened.

The planting depths for outside should not be followed inside. Large bulbs are usually planted with little or no compost over the last $\frac{1}{2}$–1 in. If the neck of the bulb is above the surface take care not to water into it. Plant the bulbs close, but not actually touching, and choose a bowl deep enough to contain all the roots which will otherwise come out at the surface, or through the drainage holes of too

small a pot. Pack the compost down round the bulbs which will shrink as the food is used up and may need top-dressing later on. Leave a space at the top to take the water.

A very fine display of daffodils can be obtained by planting a double layer in a large, deep pot. Plant the lower layer about half way up the pot and cover all but the tips of the noses with compost, then stagger the top layer above them so that all the noses have a straight run to the surface. Cover the top bulbs as usual.

Bulbs in the Greenhouse These are planted in pots of one of the JIP composts, often with sharp drainage below. Small bulbs should be covered with their own depth of soil and large ones may be only half submerged. Bulbs near the surface are more likely to need careful staking.

Bulbs being forced for cutting are often planted in deep boxes as appearance is not usually so important. Otherwise they are treated as bulbs in pots.

Bulbs for the alpine house or cold frame are usually small; they are often planted in pans but if a plant needs a deep root run a pot should be used. Very good drainage is necessary.

Tulip 'Engadin'

Lilium 'Cinnabar'.

Anemone blanda

Feeding Throughout the time that the plant is growing actively it should be fed. In pots there may be enough fertilizer in the compost to feed the plant for six weeks, but after that liquid feeds should be given once a fortnight. If a plant makes most of its growth during the winter it will need feeding during this season, even if you normally stop feeding in autumn and do not begin again until spring. Generally speaking the fertilizer used should be one with a rather high potash content to assist ripening which is very important in many bulbs from warm parts of the world. Never feed a plant in dry soil, always water it first.

Watering Many bulbs fail completely if they become dry at any time when they are growing, but only plants which are growing strongly need much water in winter as less is lost by evaporation than in summer, and such plants should be watered on the soil only as water on the leaves causes too sharp a drop in temperature and can lead to fungal infection becoming serious.

Ripening This is the name given to the complex chemical processes which occur inside the plants both before and after the leaves die down. Potash appears to be essential for these changes, as are the gradual withdrawal of water and, in many but not all, baking by sun heat. The plants most in need of this are those which experience drought during their resting period, e.g. nerines.

It is important with plants needing sun ripening to ensure that they do not get smothered with other plants, including weeds. Internal changes continue during the resting period and can be adversely affected by incorrect storage temperature.

Resting When the leaves of a bulb start to turn yellow watering must stop and the bulb be rested, unless experience shows otherwise. All the bulbs corms and tubers listed here have a definite resting period. Many can stand being dried right out; tulips like a thorough baking.

As far as many greenhouse pot plants are concerned the bulbs or corms are best left in the soil in the pot until it is time to start them into growth again. This prevents them withering as much as they would do in the open air and keeps them relatively safe.

Plants in the garden should be left to finish their growth before lifting, cleaning and sorting. If they are not to be lifted it may be wise to mark the site.

Grass with bulbs in it must not be mown until the foliage turns yellow, nor should the foliage be picked with the flowers. The leaves make the stored food.

Bulbs in bedding schemes may need to be moved before it is time to rest them. They can be lined up in trenches to finish their growth. Bulbs which were started in pots and plunged up to their rims in the formal beds are easier to cope with.

Bulbs which have been forced for use in the house or for cutting should not be used again for this purpose the following year.

Starting into Growth Bulbs still in pots can be put into fresh compost like new bulbs, or some of the old compost can be removed and replaced by fresh, or the whole pot ball can be transferred to a larger pot and top dressed. It is usually, but not always, necessary to water the soil to start growth. If a pot shows signs of growth it must be watered, but the amount given at first is usually modest.

Suitable sites There is some bulb, corm or tuber suitable for growing in almost any place you can name, though most prefer a sunny position. The following are some possibilities:

(1) Display beds devoted to nothing else: Hyacinths, greigii tulips, dahlias

(2) To grow through other bedding plants: Darwin tulips through wallflowers or forget-me-nots, Cannas through summer bedding plants or annuals

(3) To edge beds: Dutch crocuses, short alliums, muscari, zephyranthes, chionodoxa, scillas, puschkinia

(4) In clumps (groups) in mixed borders. Tall alliums, crocosmia, daffodils, summer snowflakes, crown imperial, camassia, some lilies, galtonia, dahlias, tall tulips

(5) In beds for cutting: gladioli, dahlias, narcissi, irises (Dutch, English and Spanish), St Brigid and De Caen anemones, some alliums

(6) Naturalized in long grass: Narcissi (daffodils)

(7) Naturalized in short turf: Tiny daffodils, fritillaries, muscari

(8) Naturalized under deciduous shrubs or trees: *Anemone blanda*, eranthis, cyclamen, snowdrops, colchicums

(9) Naturalized in thin woodland: Some alliums, bluebells, erythroniums, ornithogalum, *Galanthus nivalis*

(10) On rock gardens: Sprekelia, choice fritillaries, small irises, small narcissi, crocus species, some alliums

(11) Grown in alpine houses or cold frames: Winter-flowering crocuses, small irises, cyclamen, *Anemone blanda*, small fritillaries, autumn snowflakes, small South African corms

(12) Grown in hot borders under south-facing walls: Ixias, nerines, amaryllis, pancratium, babiana, sternbergia, sparaxia, crinum

(13) In warm but moist places: Tigridia, ranunculus, chincherinchee

(14) Grown in cool borders among evergreen shrubs: Most lilies, galtonia, colchicums

(15) Grown in pots or vases on a terrace: Hyacinths, daffodils, begonias

(16) Grown in pots or bowls indoors: Hyacinths, daffodils, early tulips, crocuses, muscari, scilla, dwarf irises, hippeastrum, vallota

(17) Grown in pots in a cool greenhouse: Begonias, gloxinias, lachenalias, veltheimias, nerines, hymenocallis, eucomis, some lilies, and begonias in hanging baskets

(18) Grown in pots or boxes in a cool greenhouse, but for cutting: *Gladiolus colvillei*. Dutch, Spanish and English irises, ixiolirion, freesias, tulips, narcissi, tritonia, chincherinchee, acidanthera

(19) In an intermediate greenhouse: Cyclamen, gloxinias, smithianthas, vallota. gloriosa as a climber, and achimenes in baskets

Bulbs, Corms & Tubers from A to Z

Achimenes (Gesneria family) (hot water plant) These greenhouse plants require a growing temperature of at least 60°F (16°C). Their fragile stems can be supported by twigs or allowed to fall out of a hanging basket. The small trumpet-shaped flowers, freely produced, are in shades of pink, violet blue and purple. The tubers are small scaly rhizomes, best started into growth in a box of peat and sand and then transferred to the hanging baskets when growing. In 5–6 in. pots space them 2–3 in. apart in peat-based compost and cover by ½ in. Start into growth from February to April for succession of bloom. Once in growth never allow them to dry out and keep the atmosphere humid by spraying or red spider mite may attack. Pinch out growing points to cause branching, especially when in hanging baskets. When in flower transfer to a cooler place will ensure a longer display, as will shading from direct sunshine. Dry slowly after flowering and store in their compost in a dry place at a temperature of 50 F (10 C).

Plants can be increased by soft cuttings in spring in a warm propagator, by seeds sown in March, in a temperature of 65–70°F (18–21°C), or by removing scales and sowing them like seeds. Forking tubers can be divided.

Acidanthera (Iris family) *A. bicolor murielae* is a half-hardy corm with 2½–3 ft. spikes of fragrant white flowers with maroon in the throat. The flowers are rarely open before October or November if planted outside in March–April, but this can be overcome by starting them in pots in a cool greenhouse or frame and planting out in late May–June. Alternatively they can be grown in beds in a cool greenhouse. Stake to prevent wind damage outside and lift before frost occurs.

Allium (Lily family) The ornamental onions are bulbs which produce heads of small flowers in soft colours on stems ranging from 3 in. to 4 ft. There are good plants for naturalizing in thin woodland, but most need a sunny site on the edge or in the body of a mixed border, on a rock garden or scree or even the protection of an alpine house. Many make good cut flowers. Some have a strong onion smell when bruised, therefore plant these where they will not be brushed against. The British wild ramsons, *Allium ursinum*, and also *Allium triquetrum* (both white) can be naturalized.

Amaryllis (Amaryllis family) (belladonna lily, Jersey lily) This is a slightly tender plant which can be grown outdoors in well-drained but well-fed warm borders, such as under a south or south-west wall where they can have the maximum amount of sunshine.

The large heads of fragrant, trumpet-shaped flowers are soft pink, but there is a good white called 'Hathor' and various deep pink forms. Flowers appear in September on 2–3 ft. stems before the leaves.

The bulbs are very large and work their necks out of the soil, but it is wise to start them just below the surface and to mulch well before frost occurs. Leave them to form dense clumps before lifting and replanting.

Anemone (Ranunculus family) *A. coronaria* hybrids, the poppy anemones, have large flowers, on 8–12 in. stems, in bright red, violet, lavender and purple, some shaded with white, single in De Caen varieties and semi-double in St Brigid. In mild districts flowers can be had in succession by planting the irregularly shaped tubers at any time; elsewhere they are usually put in in April, June and September. They require rich, moist, well-cultivated soil and are suitable for planting in the kitchen garden. Protect plants intended for winter flowering (from September–October planting) by cloches or frames.

A. blanda has little tubers. Soak the tubers before planting in autumn 1½ in. deep in a sunny position, or under deciduous shrubs pruned off the ground. White, pink, blue, violet and carmine forms occur.

Babiana (Iris family) (baboon plant) *B. stricta* makes an excellent cool greenhouse pot plant. It has 1 ft. high spikes of magenta, blue, purple or sulphur-yellow flowers and can be grown in sheltered borders.

Allium roseum flowers in June

Allium Species and Varieties

Name	Height in feet	Flower Colour	Type of head	Flowering	Site/Remarks
aflatunense	2½–4	rosy-purple	dense, globular	end May	border, cutting
albopilosum	2	lilac	large, globular starry flowers	June	sunny border, cutting
beesianum	¾–1	bright blue	hanging head	July	rock garden
caeruleum (syn. azureum)	1–2	blue	globular	June–July	sunny border
cernuum	1–1½	pink	hanging head	June	border, strong smelling
cyaneum	¾–1	turquoise	loose heads	July–August	rock garden
elatum	2½–3	rosy-purple	globular	end May	border
flavum	¾–1	yellow	loose heads bell flowers	July	border edge
giganteum	3–4	lilac–violet	large globular	July	border, cutting
karataviense	½–1¼	white–pale pink	large globular	July	border, cutting
moly	½–1	yellow	dense heads, starry flowers	June	naturalizing, border edge
narcissiflorum	¾	rose	hanging head, bell flowers	July	alpine house, scree in peaty compost
neapolitanum	1	white	loose heads	April–May	cool greenhouse, cutting
var. cowanii	1¼	white	loose heads	March–April	finer form
oreophilum (syn. ostrowskianum)	½–¾	rose	globular	May	rock garden, border edge
pulchellum	1¼–2	rose purple	loose heads, pointed in bud	July–August	border, cutting
rosenbachianum	2–2½	lilac	large, globular	May	border
roseum	¾–1	pink	loose heads	June–July	sunny edge, rock garden
schubertii	1–2	rose red	loose heads	April–May	border
siculum	2–3	dull red, striped blue-green	large, loose heads	May–June	border, cutting, flowers O.K. rest smells
sikkimense	¼–¾	dark blue	tiny heads	June–July	alpine house
sphaerocephalon	1–2	purple	globular	June–July	border
stipitatum	2½–3	rose purple	globular	July	border, strong smelling

Amaryllis belladonna needs a warm situation to produce its colourful flowers

The Indian Shot, *Canna indica*

Propagation methods

All kinds of bulbs and corms normally increase in number naturally. Thus a double-nosed daffodil will produce at least two bulbs which may in turn have more than one nose. Gladiolus corms frequently produce large numbers of cormels around the new corm. If left in the soil in a frost-free place these would quickly make flowering size corms. If the corm is lifted the cormels can be detached and grown on in a frame. Some bulbs make many small bulbs instead of one or two flowering size ones. Tulips need specially good feeding to prevent this happening too frequently.

Some lilies, e.g. *Lilium tigrinum*, make bulbils in the axils of the stem leaves. These can be collected and grown on when ready to drop to the earth. Sparaxis make small bulb-like cormels at the lower leaf nodes. These can be collected and grown on.

Most lilies can be increased by detaching the bulb scales and pushing them, bottom edge down into a pan of sand and peat; in a close propagating frame tiny bulbs will form on the lower edges.

Tubers are not so easy to increase as bulbs and corms and if the tuber is not of a shape that allows it to be cut into two or more pieces, each with a growth bud as well as some stored food it may not be possible to increase the plant other than by seed. Some are regularly grown from seed, e.g. cyclamen, others also from cuttings during the early stages of growth, e.g. dahlias, smithianas. When buying tubers it is sense to buy small ones which have only recently been grown from seed, as these will have a longer life.

Some bulbs can be grown to flowering size from seed in little over a year, but they are the exceptions. Most of the South African corms and many lilies flower in the third year, but tulips and daffodils may take as long as seven years to produce a flowering size bulb from seed.

In the greenhouse treat all these like freesias grown from corms but plant babianas deeper or they will make droppers to pull themselves down. Outdoors they flower in June, but in pots are earlier.

Camassia (Lily family) *C. quamash* varies in flower colour from purplish-blue to creamy-white. It likes good soil and produces fine clumps of flowers 2–3 ft. high. It flowers in June–July, but all the flowers on a spike come out at once, so giving it a rather short but striking flowering season. *C. leichtlinii*, with rather larger individual flowers on 3 ft. stems, has the same colour range and is very fine in its cream forms. All have large bulbs which need planting at least 4 in. deep.

Canna (Canna family) (Indian shot) Cannas have swollen rootstocks which will withstand drying right out during their resting period, October to March, though they do best if packed in just moist peat or left in the soil in their pots, only being knocked out to re-pot in fresh JIP 3. The varieties and hybrids of *C. indica* produce large, brilliantly coloured flowers, mainly yellow, orange or scarlet, often spotted with a darker red, on 2½–3½ ft. high stems, with broad green or dark red leaves.

Cannas are tender and need cool house temperatures even when at rest. Brought into leaf by moderate watering in March and kept growing steadily, in good rich soil, they will flower from June until the Autumn. If used outside, bring in before hard frosts occur. When necessary split up the clumps carefully before planting.

Chionodoxa (Lily family) (glory of the snow) *C. luciliae* produces its bright blue, white centred starry flowers in March or April, several on a 6-in. stem. It enjoys sunny places but does not object to some shade after the leaves have died down. It should be fed moderately. Plant in autumn 2 in. deep and leave the bulbs until they are overcrowded. It can also make a useful pan for indoors, planted in JIP 1 in autumn and treated like hyacinths in pots.

Colchicum (Lily family) (autumn crocus) The earliest to flower is the British wild *C. autumnale*, the rosy-lilac buds pushed up without any leaves being known as 'Naked Boys'. A whole group of 2-in. flowers is usually produced from each bulb and each flower flops over as soon as it has finished.

The best to grow are *C. byzantium* and *C. speciosum*, and their hybrids which have much bigger flowers rather like rose-pink or white tulips on stalks about 9 in. to 1 ft. high in September. Some like 'Water-lily', are double flowered. Others have chequered markings like fritillaries.

The big bulbs need planting during their short dormant season, in July for *C. autumnale*, and August for the later ones.

No leaves are produced until the following spring, when *C. byzantium* and *C. speciosum* produce big pleated leaves, which are much too dominant for the edge of most borders. They are best planted in front of shrubs or as a border to a vegetable plot where they enjoy the rich, limed soil.

Crinum (Amaryllis family) *C.* × *powellii* is a hybrid, hardier than either of its South African parents. It is a large bulb, up to 1 ft. high, which can be grown in tubs and wheeled out of a cool greenhouse during the summer, or planted permanently under a sunny wall in mild places. Its 2½–3 ft. stem has several buds on top which open successively, each flower being a large trumpet. It may be had in flower any time from July to September and varies from pure white to deep pink.

Spring planting is best; the necks gradually work out of the soil and need protection during cold weather.

Crocosmia (Iris family) The montbretias (*C.* × *crocosmiiflora*) are hybrids; the common form is hardy in most places. It has 2–3 ft. branching stems of small, trumpet-shaped, orange-red flowers, produced freely, even in poor soil, during August. They appreciate a sunny situation and moderate feeding. There are named hybrids with much bigger flowers which have the merit that they do not have long spreading stolons.

C. masonorum, 2½–3 ft., has arching growth. The deep orange-red flowers, produced in July, all face upwards.

Corms of choice varieties can be lifted in October and replanted in spring, but are best kept in slightly moist peat.

Crocus (Iris family) The large-flowered Dutch hybrids flower in March, and the little species crocus, by careful planning, will give flowers from September to March. The autumn and winter flowering ones are available from July to August and need to be put in immediately, as some will flower almost at once. The rest can be planted at any time during the autumn. The Dutch varieties are fine for edging beds and naturalizing in grass and the tiny ones are for alpine house or rock garden or, in many instances for planting under deciduous shrubs, or even for naturalizing in short grass (try *C. zonatus*, *C. speciosus*, *C. aureus* and *C. tomasinianus* for this). Plant the corms with not above 1 in. of soil over them. The flowers of the autumn flowering ones will come up before the leaves. Do not cut grass with crocus naturalized in it until the leaves have died down. The corms like to be well sun baked during the summer. All may be grown in pans, the Dutch ones in bulb fibre also, but must not be brought into a warm place until the flowers are nearly out.

Cyclamen (Primula family) The tubers of cyclamen get bigger each year but do not make other small tubers, which are only obtained from seedling plants, the sole method of increase. The large greenhouse cyclamen obtainable around Christmas have been raised from seed. Unlike most of the small 'hardy' cyclamen the best display is from the

new plant raised from seed after about 16 months in a warm greenhouse, and although the corm such a plant forms can be saved and grown for many more years it is not usual to do so.

Species cyclamen are sold either in leaf or as dry corms; the latter should be treated with great care as the loss of the dormant buds sets the plants back permanently. Corms should be lightly covered with sieved leaf mould or peat with some sharp sand and bonemeal, and should not have this pressed down. Similar compost should be used as a top-dressing every autumn before the flowers or leaves appear.

All cyclamen have the characteristic swept-back petals, many have a colour range from white through pink to carmine, often with throat markings of carmine on the pale flowers, and many have beautiful marbling on their leaves.

Endymion (Lily family) (bluebell) The English bluebell is *E. non-scripta* and the Spanish bluebell, *E. hispanicus*. The latter have stiffer, heavier-looking flower spikes and are usually sold mixed in colour, deep blue, sky-blue, lilac pink and white. Both flower in May and can be naturalized in thin woodland, but the bulbs of the Spanish bluebell are more frequently planted in groups in mixed borders or naturalized with daffodils in grass. These may now be found listed as *Scilla non-scripta* and *S. hispanica* (or *S. campanulata*).

Eranthis (Ranunculus family) (winter aconite) *E. hyemalis*, produces bright yellow flowers in February–March on 3–4 in. stems, each ruffed with green bracts. It forms excellent ground cover if planted 2 in. deep under deciduous shrubs or trees and will naturalize by seed. The tubers are obtainable in August and should be planted without delay. The plants divide successfully immediately after flowering.

Other kinds occasionally available are *E. cilicica*, with finely cut bronzy foliage, and *E.* × *tubergenii*, which lasts in flower longer but does not spread by self-sown seed.

Erythronium (Lily family) *E. dens-canis*, the dog's tooth violet has spotted leaves and nodding pink or white lily-like flowers on 6-in. stems in March–April. Plants do well on chalky soil and in light woodland, where they can be naturalized. They can also be grown in short turf or among shrubs, but must not become dried out in hot weather. Plant about 3 in. deep in autumn.

Other good erythroniums are *E. revolutum* 'White Beauty', to 2 ft. high, white marked with brown, April–May; *E. hendersonii*, pink with purplish markings stem, April; *E. tuolumnense*, light yellow with bright green unspotted leaves; its best hybrid is 'Pagoda', 1–1½ ft. All appreciate top-dressing with sieved leaf mould.

Eucomis (Lily family) (pineapple flower) Eucomis are cool greenhouse plants with thick stems which, in July and August, have small greenish-yellow flowers round the top foot or so of stem, which ends in a tuft of leaves – pineapple fashion. The best known is *E.*

Left: Crinum powellii is one of the most beautiful of summer-flowering bulbs. In milder gardens it may be grown outdoors, though it usually needs protection in winter. Otherwise, it is a fine plant for a cold greenhouse or conservatory, in a large pot or tub. Bottom left: The large-flowered Dutch crocus, available in a good colour range, are excellent for naturalizing in grass. The grass should not be cut until the crocus leaves have died down. Below: Colchicum speciosum, one of the autumn crocuses, produces its flowers in September. The large leaves do not appear then, but in the following spring. It is a plant for naturalizing towards the front of a shrub border. Plant the large bulbs in August. Bottom: Crocosmia masonorum, a relative of the montbretias, grows to 3 feet tall and has large, upward-facing, orange-red flowers.

Seed sown in flowering size pots in a propagating frame at 65–70°F (17–21°C) in February–March and grown on cool without any disturbance can be had in flower in November, by bringing them into the greenhouse (minimum 45°F (7°C)) in September.

Fritillaria (Lily family) *F. meleagris*, the snake's head fritillary will grow in most garden soils, especially in thin woodland, but must not dry out completely. It has hanging, wide, bell-like flowers, often white with green markings or purplish-pink, often chequered, on 1–1½ ft. stems in April.

F. imperialis, the crown imperial, may reach 3 ft. and has a ring of orange or yellow flowers high on the stem, which is topped with a tuft of leaves. The large bulbs are less liable to rot if started on their sides.

Galanthus (Amaryllis family) (snowdrops) The common snowdrop, *G. nivalis*, has many varieties which extend the flowering period from January–February to as early as October with *reginae-olgae* which flowers before its leaves, to the end of March with 'Straffan'. The most readily obtainable are *atkinsii*, about ten days earlier than the usual type and much taller (6–8 in.); 'Arnott's Seedling', another vigorous kind, and the double form. All grow well in thin woodland and should be planted 3 in. deep in autumn.

G. elwesii is best grown in full sun and should be given a chance to ripen without being overgrown by vegetation. The leaves are broad and the flower stems 6–8 in. long.

Galtonia (Lily family) (spire lily) *G. candicans* produces 3–4 ft. spikes of greenish-white, hyacinth-type flowers in summer. It makes fine groups in the middle or back of mixed borders. The large bulbs are best planted 5–6 in. deep in spring and once established can be mulched instead of being lifted in autumn. They do best in rich, moist soil.

Gloriosa (Lily family) One of the lily family's few climbing plants, this needs a warm greenhouse, 70°F (21°C) minimum from February to August. The large tubers should be planted 2 or 3 in 8-in. or larger pots of JIP 2 or planted in the greenhouse border. Cover with 2 in. of soil.

G. rothschildiana has long-stalked, bright red flowers like a Turk's cap lily, often with a yellow throat. The leaves have tendrils at the tips and these enable the plants to cling to whatever support is provided.

Other varieties of *G. rothschildiana* and also *G. superba*, the glory flower, are sometimes seen with yellow flowers. All need moist, but well-drained soil and a humid atmosphere in summer. *G. superba* can be grown in an intermediate house. From September to January, when completely dry, all can be housed at 55°F (13°C).

Top: The winter aconite (*Eranthis hyemalis*) flowers in early February, or even earlier in a mild winter. *Right: Fritillaria imperialis,* the crown imperial, flowers in April or May. *Far right: Erythronium revolutum,* a relative of the dog's tooth violet

comosa, (syn. *E. punctata*), occasionally grown in a sunny border. The large bulbs are best planted in 5-in. pots in February or March. Rest dry in the pots from November to February, in a frost-free place.

Freesia (Iris family) These are usually offered as coloured hybrids, the funnel-shaped flowers of which may be white, cream, yellow, orange, pinks, blues and mauves. The newer hybrids are usually scented whatever their colour. The wiry, arching stems may reach 2 ft. They are excellent for cutting from February to May.

Plant 7–9 in a 6-in. pot of JIP 1 in August, cover to a depth of 1 in., and put into a cool plunge bed under damp peat for a month until roots are well formed. The greenhouse must be well ventilated, with as dry an atmosphere as possible, with a minimum temperature of 45°F (7°C). The leaves must be supported. After flowering they can be kept growing in a north-facing frame till leaves die down when they should be stored in their pots, dry, until August. Specially prepared corms can be planted outdoors in April for flowering in late summer.

36

Right: Gloriosa rothschildiana

Leucojum vernum, popularly known as the spring snowflake, has white, green-tipped flowers which appear in February and March, on 6–8 in. stems, with bright green foliage. The bulbs should be planted in September, about 3 in. deep in sunny or partially shaded situations

Hippeastrum (Amaryllis family) *H. pratense* is the hardiest of these tender bulbs and can be grown in sunny south-walled borders or in a cool greenhouse. It makes a good pot plant, producing 1 ft. stems topped with 2 or 3 deep red trumpet-shaped flowers with yellow throats in spring or early summer.

The better known large greenhouse hybrids –sometimes incorrectly called amaryllis–can be had in flower practically any month of the year in the greenhouse or indoors depending on their treatment. Bulbs put on sale from August onwards have been prevented from spring flowering and should be planted as soon as available, when they can be had in flower from November onwards. (These may be described as 'prepared bulbs'.) They are followed by normally early-flowering varieties which carry the flowering season through to April. Later varieties carry the bloom round to July or even September if the bulbs are planted in succession.

The 3 ft. stems are usually topped with four enormous trumpet flowers which open in quick succession; there are frequently 2 or more stems per bulb. The bulbs are very large. Place them half into 4- or 5-in. pots of loam-based compost. The flower stems may come up before the strap-shaped leaves or with them. They must be fed liberally. Any small bulbs which have formed may be removed and should be grown on without any drying off. Dry out the big bulbs as the leaves yellow, store the pots on their sides in a temperature of 50°F (10°C), and leave them thus for about three months before starting the bulbs into growth.

Hyacinths (Lily family) The Roman hyacinths usually have several slender, loosely packed spikes per bulb; the more spectacular, stiff spiked 'Dutch' ones have the flowers closely packed. Both are very fragrant.

The Dutch hyacinths may be bought 'specially prepared' and these should be planted as soon as available to give flowers in the greenhouse or indoors by late December or early January. They force well.

For indoors they may be grown in water only, in special hyacinth glasses (discard the bulb after flowering); singly in 3½-in. pots, or close packed in larger pots or bowls, with their 'noses' just uncovered. Use bulb fibre for bowls and start these in a cold shed or shaded frame so that they are not drowned by rain; pots may be plunged in a cool place outdoors. Do not bring them into the warmth until the roots are well developed and the shoot is starting to grow (usually from 8–10 weeks). Then keep in full light.

Unprepared bulbs which flower about 3 weeks later may be planted in succession to flower from January to April.

Outdoors hyacinths should be planted in rich soil at least 5 in. deep in October–November. Use only unprepared bulbs. If used for formal bedding they should be replaced each season, but if fed well will make good clumps among shrubs.

The Roman hyacinths, which are white, pink or blue, are sometimes used on rock gardens, but are at their best indoors.

After flowering allow the leaves to die down naturally.

Ipheion (Amaryllis family) *I. uniflorum* (sometimes listed as *Brodiaea, Tritelia* or *Milla uniflora*), is a small South African, early-flowering bulb producing white or pale bluish-mauve funnel-shaped flowers 6 in. above the mass of grassy leaves. The best coloured is 'Wisley Blue'. It needs well-drained soil in a sunny place. Plant in autumn 1½ in. deep.

Ixia (Iris family) (African corn lily) These corms are not quite hardy outside in most gardens, but make interesting cool greenhouse plants flowering after the first spring rush. They are sold in mixed colours including deep carmine, white with red or yellow or purple centre, orange or yellow sometimes bronze outside, on 2 ft. tall arching stems. The flowers close in dull weather but when open fully make a wonderful display. Pot the rather small corms fairly close together in JIP 2, covered with at least 2 in. of soil. Ripen well after flowering.

I. viridiflora, an arresting plant, has blue-green flowers, darker at the centre, in May–June. It needs cool greenhouse treatment and proper ripening. It should be given bonemeal and protected from slugs and small snails.

Ixiolirion (Amaryllis family) *I. montanum* is a slightly tender bulb worth growing as a cut flower in a cool greenhouse. It produces its leaves in winter which prevents it being grown successfully outside. The flowers, on 15–18 in. stems, are in shades of blue, sometimes with violet banding, and bloom in May or June, *I. ledebourii* being earlier than the darker *I. palasii*. Plant in autumn in JIP 2.

Lachenalia (Lily family) (Cape cowslip) These cool greenhouse bulbs flower in early spring in airy conditions. Plant 5–7 close together in 5-in. pots in August–September, cover with ½–1 in. of JIP 2 and cover with moist peat in a plunge bed until growth starts. Then place the pots in a well-ventilated cool greenhouse.

L. aloides nelsonii has spikes of golden-yellow flowers tinged with green; other varieties have paler yellow flowers and may have red markings. *L. bulbifera* (syn *L. pendula*) has coral red or salmon tubular flowers marked with purple and green.

Lachenalias often have pleasantly mottled foliage. Their flower spikes are long lasting if kept at 45–50°F (7–10°C), but if brought indoors into 65°F (18°C) or more, the plants soon suffer. Ripen well after flowering by standing on a shelf under the ridge of the greenhouse, and reduce the water until the bulbs are dried out.

Leucojum (Amaryllis family) (snowflake) *L. aestivum*, the summer snowflake, flowers from April to May. It has heads of white, green-marked flowers on 1½–2 ft. stems and dark green strap-shaped leaves, and its large bulbs increase rapidly to make big clumps if planted in fairly damp soil. Plant 5 in. deep.

L. vernum has only one or two good sized flowers per 8 in. stem, but very fine bright green foliage and flowers that are out in February–March.

L. autumnale is less hardy but often does

Above: Lachenalia aloides nelsonii, a fine bulb for the cool greenhouse
Below: Ipheion uniflorum makes a good spreading clump, with grassy leaves, smelling of onions when crushed
Right: One of the many beautiful hippeastrums

well in a sunny, sheltered border. The flowers on 6–8-in. stems are very delicate looking, tinged with pink (not green) and usually come before the leaves. Plant 3 in. deep.

Lilium (Lily family) (lily) Lilies are often sold packed in peat or wood shavings to help retain their moisture and protect them. They should be planted as soon as available, from September to January, except for *L. candidum* and *L. testaceum* which are usually moved 'green', i.e. while still in leaf, after June–July flowering. Any lily can be moved successfully immediately after flowering if care is taken to keep the soil on the roots. As some flower in autumn and others have to come from Japan or N.W. America these may not be on sale until soil conditions outside are far from ideal. In this case pot them immediately and plant out later when conditions are correct.

HYACINTHS

Some recommended Dutch varieties: Those marked with an asterisk will force satisfactorily, even though some are late flowering.

White: Mont Blanc; *L'Innocence; Mme Sophie (double); Carnegie (late). **Yellow:** *Yellow Hammer; Gipsy Queen; *City of Haarlem (late). **Salmon:** *Oranje Boven (Salmonetta). **Pink–pale shades:** *Anne Marie (Ann Mary); *Princess Irene; *Lady Derby; Chestnut Flower (double). **Pink–deep shades:** *Pink Pearl; *Apollo. **Red:** *Jan (John) Bos (not for bedding); Eclipse (double); *La Victoire; *Hollyhock (double). **Pale Blue:** *Blue Haze (unusual eggshell blue); *Delft Blue; *Myosotis; Queen of the Blues. **Dark Blue:** *Ostara; *Concorde; King of the Blues. **Purple:** Purple King (mauve); General Kohler (double lavender).

Multiflora hyacinths are specially treated Dutch varieties which produce several small spikes in place of one large one.

Roman hyacinths are sold by colour, though 'Rosalie', a soft pink, is often available.

Species for rock garden: *Hyacinthus amethystinus*, 8 in.; *H. azureus* (often listed as *Scilla azureus*), 8 in. Both flowering March–April.

RECOMMENDED LILIES (Liliums)

Height in feet: 'C' indicates lime tolerance

Cup-shaped flowers (upward facing)
croceum (2½–4) June–July: deep orange; **dauricum** (2–3) July–Aug: yellow, orange, spotted maroon or black; **hollandicum (umbellatum)** (2–2½) June–July: yellow to orange-red; **Mid-Century Hybrids** (2–4) June–July: lemon yellow to crimson, some reflexed.

Bowl-shaped flowers (outward facing)
auratum (4–8) Aug–Sept: gold rays on white, crimson spots, fragrant. Good pot plant; **Crimson Beauty** (4–5) August: crimson rays and spots, otherwise similar. Good pot plant; **Imperial Silver** (5–6) August: all white with vermilion spots, petals reflexed at tips; **Imperial Gold** (5–6) August: yellow rays and maroon spots, petal tips reflexed.

Trumpet-shaped flowers (outward or partly downward facing)
Aurelian hybrids (4–5) July: yellow, apricot, pink or white, coloured centres; **Black Magic strain** (5–6) June–Aug: white, heavily shaded purple outside, fragrant; **brownii** (5) Sept: white, heavily shaded maroon, slightly fragrant; **canadense** (3) July: orange yellow, rather bell-shaped, long flower stalks. C; **candidum** (4–6) June–July: white, fragrant, the Madonna lily. C; **Golden Clarion strain** (3–5) July: yellow to gold, selected from the Aurelian hybrids. C; **Limelight** (4–6) July: Chartreuse yellow, shaded green, fragrant; **Olympic hybrids** (4–5) July: white, soft pink or pale green, shaded outside, fragrant. C; **Pink Perfection strain** (5–7) July: fuchsia pink, fragrant; **regale** (3–4) June–July: white, shaded yellow within and purple outside, fragrant. C; **rubellum** (1–1½) June: pink, 2–4 flowers only, fragrant, likes shade.

Reflexed Pendent Flowers (the most reflexed are known as Turk's cap lilies).
amabile (2–3) July: orange-red, black spots, pungent smelling, grow among shrubs. C; **Bellingham hybrids** (3–6) July: yellow, orange, red with maroon to black spots, some. C. Shade, Shuksan (3–4) orange spotted maroon is a named variety; **Bright Star** (3–4) July: almost flat, nearly outward facing flower in which the petal ends only are reflexed, white with orange star-shaped centre; **cernuum** (1–2) June–July: rose, spotted purple, fragrant. Flowers from seed in 3 years. Plant on rock garden or with low cover; **chalcedonicum** (2½–3½) July: scarlet. The red Turk's cap lily. C.; **Corsage** (3–4) June–July: outward-facing soft pink and cream with maroon spots. Anthers sterile, producing no pollen, so useful as a cut flower. Will force; **davidii** (4–5) July–Aug: orange-red, spotted brown, likes partial shade. C; **Fiesta hybrids** 3–5 July: yellow, orange to dark red with maroon or black spots; **hansonii** (4–5) July: light orange, spotted brown, some shade. C; **Harlequin hybrids** (4–5) June–July: pink, lilac, old rose, purple, white and cream, spotted maroon. C; **henryi** (5–6) August: yellow-orange with brown spots, dark purple stems, prefers lime. C; **martagon** (3–4) June–July: light purple to wine red, spotted purple, strong smelling. C; **martagon album** (3–4) June–July: the white form. Both naturalize in grass or light woodland; **monadelphum** (3–4) June: yellow, spotted maroon, fragrant. Good on marls. C; **Mrs R. O. Backhouse** (4–5) June–July: orange yellow, spotted maroon; **Paisley strain** (3–5) June: white, yellow, orange, tangerine, pink, mahogany red with maroon spots. C; **pardalinum** (4–6) July: orange shading to red, maroon spots. Prefers damp, but well-drained soil with some sun. The panther lily. Bulbs formed on rhizomes which spread out from the base of the plant. C; **pyrenaicum** (2–3) May–June: greenish yellow, spotted black, strong smelling. Naturalizes. C; **speciosum** (3–6) Aug–Sept: a very variable species with many named selections, good for forcing in cool greenhouse. Usually white suffused with more or less pink or crimson, often with deeper spots. There is a pure white form; **testaceum** (4–5) June–July: apricot-yellow, an old hybrid which likes lime. C; **tigrinum** (4–5) July–Sept: orange-red or lemon with black or maroon spots. Does not set seed, but produces bulbils on the stems. Tiger lily. C.

Cardiocrinum giganteum, formerly known as **Lilium giganteum,** is closely related to the lilies and forms spikes upwards of 6 feet, with fragrant white flowers, in July, and broad green leaves. It does well in light woodland.

'Golden Splendour' is the name given to a modern strain of hybrid lilies with trumpet-shaped flowers

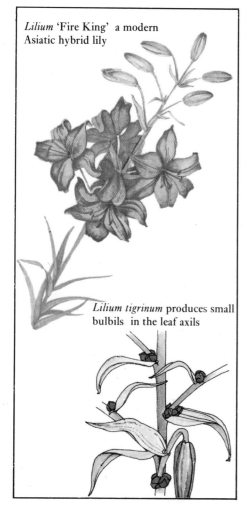

Lilium 'Fire King' a modern Asiatic hybrid lily

Lilium tigrinum produces small bulbils in the leaf axils

With the exception of *L. candidum* and other European lilies such as *L. martagon* which make roots from the base of the bulbs only, lilies should be planted with soil at least twice the depth of the bulb above it, thus a 2 in. deep bulb would need a hole 6–7 in. deep. This is because many lilies make roots from the stem in the first few inches of soil, in addition to those below the bulb. Sites for such lilies must be weed free, for hoeing near them is disastrous. Many lilies grow wild in the company of low-growing shrubs, the roots of which help to drain the soil, and others are found on steep slopes where moisture is flowing under the surface for much of the year, but all are on well-drained sites, and if necessary special beds must be made with extra peat and sharp sand to retain moisture but allow free drainage. Beds or even hummocks of such soil which will raise the roots and bulbs above the winter water table may make all the difference between success and failure. Some lilies will tolerate lime and others die if given it. Most lilies like to have their flowering stems in the sun, at least for part of the day, and grow well with a ground cover of low shrubs, or even annuals to protect their roots.

Lily bulbs should be examined to make sure there is no basal rot present, as this will cause the scales to fall away. Such bulbs should be burnt. The bulbs can be dusted with a fungicide to prevent the spread of the fungal disease which causes death of leaves and even of the whole shoot. Once the plants

are growing they can be protected from this disease by spraying with a systemic fungicide. Virus diseases are incurable, but their spread can be checked by spraying plants with a systemic insecticide which kills aphids which spread virus diseases. Some lilies are comparatively tolerant of virus diseases, but grow better without them, and others are killed by them. The easiest way to get virus-free stock is to raise the plants from seed and keep them sprayed. This works for most species but garden hybrids will not come true to form or colour. However, if 'strains' of lilies are bought rather than named varieties these will have been raised from seed, whereas the others will have been propagated from offsets, bulbils and by rooting scale leaves, and the risk of virus is greater with these.

Most lilies can be grown from seed, in fact *L. formosanum* and *L. philippinense*, white trumpet, cool greenhouse lilies, can be had in flower within a year of sowing the seed. However, many take three or four years and *L. martagon* takes six or seven to reach flowering size. *L. regale* flowers after two or three years.

In selecting lilies for gardens only species with similar cultural requirements to the garden hybrids have been chosen.

The garden hybrids are officially classified according to their breeding, but the shape and position of the flowers are more readily recognized in a garden and these are considered here.

Muscari (Lily family) (grape hyacinth) *M. armeniacum* is the kind most frequently of-

fered for sale. It makes little heads of honey-scented deep blue flowers on 6–8-in. stems, with lots of narrow, grassy leaves. Varieties are 'Heavenly Blue', deep blue; 'Cantab', paler blue; and a white form, though the white commonly sold is *M. botryoides alba*. *M. armeniacum* makes fine sheets of colour in April–May under deciduous shrubs and small trees and also looks well as an edging plant, but soon spreads. It will also naturalize in short turf. *M. botryoides* makes a good rock garden plant as it is not so invasive; its heads of little bells are smaller and a paler blue.

M. comosum is not so often seen as its variety *monstrosum*, the feather or tassel hyacinth. This has curious heads of dark violet-blue threads on 12–15-in. stems in May–June.

M. tubergenianum, the so-called 'Oxford and Cambridge' grape hyacinth, has pale and dark blue flowers on the same head. It is best grown on the rock garden where it will flower in March–April.

Plant *M. armeniacum*, *M. botryoides* and *M. tubergenianum* 3 in. deep and the others 4 in. deep in any good soil in a sunny position. They will all grow on limy soil. Split clumps as necessary after flowering.

Narcissus (Amaryllis family) (daffodil) In gardens the narcissi are best divided into the large hybrids–for use naturalized in long grass, in beds for cutting and display, and in pots outdoors and in–and the small species and their hybrids–for use in short turf, on rock gardens, in pans in the alpine house or indoors. The official classification is based on

Left: The magnificent flower spikes of *Lilium* 'Sutter's Gold', another modern hybrid strain
Above: A closely-planted 'river' of grape hyacinths (*Muscari armeniacum*)

flower colour and form, the relative length of the petal-like central ring or corona (which may be a trumpet, cup or eye) being of importance. The term daffodil is often restricted to the large trumpet forms, the others being called narcissi.

The bulbs of the small species are tiny; those of the garden hybrids are large and sold graded according to the number of 'noses' (growing points). Plant single-nosed bulbs with a bulb planter as there is no danger of them sticking half-way down the holes. The double and triple-nosed bulbs are fine for planting in borders or in pots where a close display of flowers is wanted in the first year.

Grass planted with daffodils must not be cut until the foliage has yellowed, nor should leaves be picked with flowers, for the foliage builds up the bulb with next year's flowers. If the grass is treated with normal lawn fertilizers there is no need to feed the bulbs (other than with bonemeal at planting), but bulbs in short turf must not receive lawn fertilizers as this will encourage the growth of coarse grasses with which the small bulbs will be unable to compete.

Daffodils should be planted as soon as available, before hyacinths and tulips. Large bulbs require holes 6 in. deep and small ones 3–4 in. Bulbs in pots can be placed shoulder to shoulder with the noses just under or just above the surface. If intended for forcing they must be plunged in a cool moist place (with the exception of the variety Paper White) until the roots have developed well.

NARCISSUS
Varieties specially recommended for forcing are marked *

In the following list of recommended varieties (separated into those above and below 12in. in height) the sequence of flowering is indicated by letters (VE very early, E early, M mid-season, L late, VL very late). Actual dates from year to year and place to place vary, but the sequence remains relatively constant even when a warm spell following cold weather telescopes the sections.

Yellow perianth, yellow trumpet: Dutch Master (17) VE; *Golden Harvest (18) VE; *King Alfred (19) E; Kingscourt (16) M; Unsurpassable (18) M; *Rembrandt (18) E; Unsurpassable (19) E.

White perianth, yellow trumpet: *Queen of Bicolors (18) M; *Trousseau (18) E.

White perianth, white trumpet: *Beersheba (14); *Cantatrice (16) M; Empress of Ireland (18) VE; *Mount Hood (18) M.

Yellow perianth, large cup, orange, yellow or red: *Carlton (17) E, yellow; Aranjuez (19) M; *Fortune (19) E, orange; Carbineer (18) M; *Red Devon (18) M; *Rustom Pasha (18) M, orange, edged red; *Scarlet Elegance (16) E, red.

White perianth, large coloured cup: Green Island (16) M, white, edged yellow; Queensland (18), M, pinkish; Polindra (20) M, yellow; Flower Record (16) M; Kilworth (20) M; Sempre Avanti (18) M, orange; Eddy Canzony (17) M, orange red; Mrs R. O. Backhouse (15) L; Louise de Coligny (17) M, pink.

White perianth, large white cup: *Ice Follies (16) M.

Reverse bicolor, large cup: Binkie (16) M; Spellbinder (20) M, deep lemon cup, pale lemon perianth.

Narcissus 'February Silver', a dwarf hybrid

Yellow perianth, small coloured cup: *Edward Buxton (19) E, orange, edged red; Birma (18) M, orange-scarlet.

White perianth, small coloured cup: Merlin (17) L, yellow/red; Barrett Browning (16) E, orange red; *Verger (16) M, red.

Double flowered, either one large or 2–4 small flowers per stem: Double White, *poeticus* (*albus plenus odoratus*) (14) latest of all narcissi (mid-May) white, fragrant; Golden Ducat (Double King Alfred) (18) M; Texas (20) M, yellow; White Lion (18); M, white and cream; Irene Copeland (14) E, white and apricot; Mary Copeland (14) L, white, lemon and orange; *Cheerfulness (19) L, cream, fragrant and *Yellow Cheerfulness (19) L; *N. pseudo-narcissus* Von Sion, double wild daffodil, (15) E, yellow and green.

Hybrids from Narcissus triandrus, which have several pendent flowers per stem; *Thalia (12) M; *Tresamble (14) L, white.

Hybrids from N. cyclamineus, with swept back perianth: *Charity May (12) M; *February Gold (15) VE; *Peeping Tom (14) VE, yellow.

Narcissus 'Actaea'

Hybrids from N. jonquilla, several small, fragrant flowers per stem: Cherie (14) L, white and apricot; *Trevithian (15) M, pale yellow.

Hybrids of N. tazetta, with many small flowers, usually fragrant and often producing foliage early in winter, which makes them tender but good for forcing: *Paper White (15) E; Geranium (16) M; *Soleil D'Or (18) E, yellow, orange, all tender: *Cragford (14) M, white, orange-red; Geranium (18) L, white, orange.

Hybrids resembling N. poeticus (the pheasant eye narcissus), white, red and green eye, scented: Actaea (20) M; and *N. poeticus recurvus,* the poet's narcissus or Old Pheasant's Eye variety (20) VL (May). Particularly useful for naturalizing.

Species or small hybrids like them: *N. asturiensis* (*minimus*) (2–3) VE, miniature yellow daffodil for pans, or turf; *bulbocodium,* hoop-petticoat daffodil (6) VE, yellow, wide trumpet, rushy foliage. Naturalize in turf. There are several forms; *canaliculatus* (*lacticolor*) (4) L, white, yellow, scented, small tazetta type, best on light soil; *N. odoratus* (12) otherwise similar; *cyclamineus* (14) VE (Jan–Feb) yellow, swept back perianth, likes damp position. Naturalize in turf or grow in pans. Small hybrids include Baby Doll (9) M, yellow; Beryl (8) E, primrose orange; February Silver (10) VE, white, lemon; Jack Snipe (5) M, white, primrose; Little Witch (9) E, yellow; *N. jonquilla* (12) L, deep yellow, fragrant; Baby Moon (12) VL, lemon, deep yellow; Bobbysoxer (8) L, yellow, deep yellow. *N. juncifolius* (3) M, yellow, flat cupped fragrant, rush-like leaves. *N. calcicola* (6) M. Flowers similar to *juncifolius,* but about 1 week earlier and with strap-shaped leaves; *N. nanus* (4) E, yellow trumpet. Good naturalizer in turf; *N. pseudo-narcissus* (Lent lily or wild daffodil) (6) E. Small bicolor for naturalizing, *W. P. Milner (10) M, better shaped flower, *pseudo-narcissus obvallaris* (Tenby daffodil) (10) VE, similar but earlier; *N. rupicola* (3) E, yellow, scented, rock garden or pans; *triandrus albus* (Angel's Tears) (4) L, creamy white, 2–5 flowers per stem; *N. triandrus concolor* (4) L, golden yellow; hybrid with *N. jonquilla* April Tears (7) L, yellow, *N. watieri* (3) similar to *N. rupicola,* but white and unscented, pans.

Narcissus cyclamineus, a dwarf species

Ornithogalum umbellatum, the Star of Bethlehem, does well in poor sandy soil, and is a good bulb to grow in a wild garden or in thin woodland. The greenish-white, star-shaped flowers are borne on 6–8 in. stems

Nerine (Amaryllis family)   These are South African bulbs although *N. sarniensis* is known as the Guernsey lily. The hardiest is *N. bow-denii*, which is grown successfully out of doors under south-facing walls even in the north of England and Scotland. The lovely clear pink flowers appear from September to November, and there is quite a variation in flower shade and time of flowering. The leaves die off in late summer, leaving a short period in July–August in which the large bulbs can be moved. Plant them at least 6 in. deep; they will gradually work their way upwards until the neck is above ground level, when they must be well mulched in frosty places or put down lower again. They look well planted out in a bed in a cool greenhouse. Keep them well fed with bonemeal when they are planted and with liquid fertilizer during growth.

N. sarniensis is not so tall, so vigorous or so hardy and needs cool greenhouse treatment. There are several hybrids in lovely shades of scarlet, salmon and wine shades as well as pinks and whites. Plant them singly in 4-in. pots with the neck of the bulb well out and never let the temperature fall below 45°F (7°C). Water the soil well only when growth Starts. After flowering continue feeding well until growth ceases. Dry them out and ripen them near the glass. Divide them only when it is essential, as they all flower best in crowded conditions.

Ornithogalum (Lily family)   The native *O. umbellatum*, the Star of Bethlehem, makes a fine wild garden or thin woodland bulb. It does well in poor, sandy soil, and has flattish heads of greenish-white, star-shaped flowers on 6–8-in. stems. *O. thyrsioides* is the chincherinchee, renowned for its longevity in water if picked in bud. It flowers in June–July, forming a long pointed head of white flowers. It is not quite hardy but can be treated like gladiolus (planted in March and lifted in October), or will grow permanently in warm but moist sheltered places, planted 6 in. deep, or in a cool greenhouse.

O. arabicum is also suitable for pots in a cool greenhouse. It has black-centred white flowers in heads like *O. umbellatum*. *O. nutans* produces 1-ft. stems of translucent greenish-white flowers in April and is a good shade plant.

Pancratium (Amaryllis family) (sea lily)   These are more or less tender plants with flowers borne on top of a long stem like amaryllis. They are usually white with green markings, with long spidery petals from a tube and are often beautifully fragrant. They are suitable for planting in JIP 2 in 5-in. pots in a cool greenhouse and can be stood outside during the summer in a sheltered place.

P. illyricum is sometimes grown outside in mild places, flowers in May or June and may have up to a dozen blooms which open in succession on 1½-ft. stems.

The bulbs should be rested during the winter when the leaves die down, and kept cool but frost free and dry, but not bone dry, until the spring.

Puschkinia (Lily family)   *P. scilloides* (syn. *P. libanotica*) produces 4–6-in. stems of pale blue flowers with a greenish stripe in March. There is also a white form. It makes a fine carpet planted 3 in. deep in autumn under deciduous shrubs or on a rock garden, especially in heavy soil. It also makes a good pan plant in JIP 1.

Ranunculus (Ranunculus family)   The tubers of *R. asiaticus* (sometimes sold as *R. grandiflora*) should be planted in holes 2–3 in. deep, claws downward, in pots or in clumps in a sunny border or in a special bed for flowers for cutting. Soak them for 24 hours before planting.

Plant carefully any time from October inside to April outside. They need well-drained, rich soil (JIP 3 and sharp grit) and produce large double flowers on stems 12–15 in. high, in shades of yellow, orange, pink and red. The normal season is May to June, but in a greenhouse they can be forced gently. They are normally sold mixed, but there are several strains differing in size, doubleness and height of flower and known as peony-flowered, French, Persian and Turban.

For cutting special beds are made with coarse rubble placed under about 1 ft. of compost containing coarse grit and also well-rotted manure, banked up like an asparagus bed. This ensures the necessary quick drainage and high level of feeding. They must not be allowed to dry out until the leaves die down after flowering. During August the tubers should be lifted and stored, preferably hung in paper (not polythene) bags in a frost-proof airy place until needed.

Scilla (Lily family) (squills)   The most readily obtainable are *S. bifolia*, *S. sibirica*, *S. tubergeniana* and *S. peruviana*. The first three are spring flowering and *S. bifolia* and *S. tubergeniana* are worth planting in pans of quick-draining compost in a cold frame or alpine house for flowering in March and April respectively. *S. sibirica* does well in sunny borders or in short turf, and makes a good show indoors planted in JIP 1 or bulb fibre. On 6–8-in. stems it bears deep bright blue flowers; there is also a white form. The flowers of *S. bifolia* are turquoise blue or pink or white. *S. tubergeniana* is almost white, but has a deep blue stripe down the centre. *S. peruviana* 8–10 in., has deep blue, lilac or white flowers massed in a 5–6 in. head, in May and June. It needs a warm border.

Sinningia (Gesneria family) (gloxinia)   These warm greenhouse plants have velvety leaves and brilliantly coloured purple, red, violet etc. flowers often with white throats to their trumpets, produced freely for many weeks. Tubers are planted, hollow side up,

singly in JIP 2 in 5-in. pots and covered with about 1 in. of soil, or they are pressed into boxes of moist peat and sand until they have produced both shoots and roots. This is useful for checking shoot damage in newly purchased tubers. These tubers will flower in summer and autumn the same year. The season can be extended by sowing seeds in June to flower early the following summer, or in January–February for later flowering the same year. Feed regularly. They need plenty of moisture throughout the year, but can be moved to slightly cooler conditions while actually in flower. Dry gradually and store at 50–55°F (10–13°C) in the pots.

Smithiana (Gesneria family) Once known as Gesneria or Naegelia, these require warm greenhouse treatment and are best grown from tubers planted singly in 5-in. pots in March in JIP 2 compost with extra grit or sand. The flowers are in lovely shades of yellow, orange, apricot and red, set off by deep green velvety leaves which damp off if heat and ventilation are inadequate. From March to August the temperature should be 60–70°F (16–21°C), and once the tubers have started growing well plentiful water must be applied to the soil, not the foliage. The plants reach $1\frac{1}{2}$–2 ft. and flower between July and November. During September and October the heat can be lowered slowly by about 10°F (6°C) and once flowering has finished they should be rested gradually and be stored in their pots, dry, at a temperature of 55°F (13°C) during the winter.

Particularly good plants are best increased by cuttings taken in early summer and rooted in a propagator.

Sparaxis (Iris family) (harlequin flower) These often have two or more colours per bloom in a wide range, including, white with yellow eye, bronze red with darker eye or with yellow eye, and purplish pink shades. They are best planted in March in a warm border

Left: Scilla sibirica, the Siberian squill, is a fine bulbous plant for a sunny place, or may be grown indoors in pots or bowls
Top: One of the most colourful bulbs for late summer and autumn is *Nerine bowdenii*, and can be grown outdoors even in Scotland
Above: The smithianas (once known as gesnerias or naegelias) are beautiful plants for the warm greenhouse

or grown in pots in a cool house, when they may be autumn planted. The flowers appear in April to late May according to treatment. Feed and ripen well, but when cleaning off the dead foliage do not pull it out in handfuls, but cut it short as the lower nodes will be found to contain small cormels which if left are the means of rapid increase. Many of the more brilliant colours are the result of crossing sparaxis species with the closely related *Streptanthera*.

Sprekelia (Amaryllis family) (Jacobean lily) *S. formosissima* is an interesting flower, very irregular in shape, looking like a 5-in. wide deep red orchid. The flowers are usually produced singly, occasionally in pairs. Plants are often grown in pots in cool greenhouses or in a frame, when they may flower as early as May, but in well-drained, sunny, warm sites outdoors flower in June. The large bulbs should be covered with their own depth of soil outside. Feed well and ripen thoroughly. Pot or plant when the foliage dies down.

Sternbergia (Amaryllis family) *S. lutea*, the lily of the field, produces bright golden-yellow crocus-like flowers about $2\frac{1}{2}$ in. high from late August. If the weather is bad at flowering time protect with a pane of glass, which will also assist ripening in a wet autumn. The bulbs are best planted in sunny place in July and should have 4 in. of soil above them. In short turf they should be

planted with a bulb planter, not by lifting the turves.

Tigridia (Iris family) (tiger flower) *T. pavonia*, a half-hardy Mexican bulb-shaped corm produces unusually brilliant flowers with the inner petals and bowl of the flower generally spotted red and making a tiger-face. The three petals which spread out flat are scarlet, cherry red, orange, buff or white; corms are usually sold as a mixture. The flowers last one day only but there are up to six on each 15–18-in. stem and they open in succession from June onwards. If treated like gladioli, planted 4–5 in. deep in late March or April and lifted before frosts, they usually flower in July. In warm sheltered places they can be left out if given a protective mulch. They need plenty of water and liquid feed during summer and then form good clumps.

Tritonia (Iris family) Tritonias are South African corms, and one only, *T. crocata* is freely available. The flowers are usually very brilliantly coloured, orange, a pale coppery shade, yellow or white. They flower in late spring or early summer in a warm, frost-free border or in pots in a cool greenhouse. They make good, long-lasting cut flowers. In pots treat them as freesias, planting them 7–9 in a 5-in. pot in JIP 3, and provide light support. After ripening keep them in the same size pot but replace some of the soil yearly in the autumn until the pot is full of corms.

Tulipa (Lily family) (tulip) Tulips have been favourite spring bedding and pot plants in Europe since the mid-16th century. The flowers are in all colours except true blues, usually solitary, but also 3-4 per stem, the garden hybrids ranging in height from 4-34 in. Good bulbs can be guaranteed to give a fine, even display the first season, but except in warm situations on sandy loam rarely produce so many or such large blooms in later years, though feeding with bonemeal and proper ripening do help, and by this treatment the smaller species may become established on sunny ledges of the rock garden. The bulbs should be planted from 4-6 in. deep according to their size, but should not be put in before October for the April flowering kinds and November for the May flowering ones.

If used for spring bedding, either alone or coming through a shorter ground cover of forget-me-nots, wallflowers or pansies, the bulbs will have to be lifted and allowed to finish their growth in trenches in a sunny position, unless discarded. Tulips in less conspicuous places should be allowed to die down before being lifted and placed in trays in a sunny place (cold greenhouse, frame or window) to complete their ripening. Only the large bulbs should be planted for display the following year, but the small ones can be grown on to flowering size in a sunny frame. They take up to seven years to flower from seed.

Some varieties can be forced, but it is very important to grow the bulbs in a plunge bed until growth is well up (4-6 in.) and then to bring them gradually into light and moderate warmth. They do not respond well to high temperatures and must be forced slowly.

Above: Tulipa tarda (dasystemon) is a low-growing species, about 3 in. high
Below: 'Rosy Wings', a Cottage tulip
Below right: 'Tol's Favourite', a Single Early tulip, flowering in April

Tulip species	Height in in.	Flowering time	Flower colour	Use
acuminata (cornuta) (Horned tulip)	20	May	yellow, streaked red, long twisted petals	as cut flower, pots
batalinii	7	April	primrose or yellow flushed pink	rock garden or pans
clusiana (Lady tulip)	15	late April	outer petals cherry, inner ones white, violet base	border or rock garden
eichleri	12	March	scarlet, pointed petals, black base	pots, border
fosteriana	10–18	mid-April	scarlet, crimson within, black base, broad petals, large flower	Princeps 10 in. borders Red Emperor 18 in. pots
greigii	9	April–May	scarlet or orange, base black ringed yellow. Leaves mottled with chocolate, flat	borders, pots, as edging to beds, as leaves are decorative
kaufmanniana (Water-lily tulip)	8	March–April	large; cream tinged pink outside, white or cream inside	fine garden tulip
linifolia	8	April–May	scarlet, violet base; leaves narrow, red-edged, wavy margins, flat on soil	high in rock garden to show red stems
orphanidea	10	March–April	orange shaded bronze and green yellow base, pointed petals	rock garden
praestans 'Fusilier'	10	early April	vermilion, 4–6 on a stem	pot plant, rock garden
pulchella violacea	4	Feb–March	reddish purple, cup shaped, base black or yellow	alpine house, rock garden
saxatilis	10	April	1–3 on a stem, pale lilac, yellow base. Flowers best if crowded.	confine in sunny bed by slates as spreads rapidly by stolons. Leafs early.
tarda (dasystemon)	6	April	3–6 on a stem, white, yellow inside	rock garden, in paving pockets, edging beds
turkestanica	9	Feb–March	5–9 on a stem, white, orange centres	rock garden, alpine house

The Scarborough lily, vallota

Vallota (Amaryllis family) (Scarborough lily) *V. speciosa* is a South African bulb for the cool or intermediate greenhouse. Bulbs can be planted singly in 3½-in. pots from May to July. Each year they should be moved into a larger pot without disturbing the clump. When they get grossly overcrowded and small bulbs are being squeezed up free from the mass it is time to divide and start afresh. Good soil should replace as much as possible of the old at each move and liquid feeding is essential to keep up the supply of flowering size bulbs.

The 3-in. trumpet-shaped flowers are rather like the smaller hippeastrums, but with more flowers in each head, on 1–1½-ft. stems, and are normally a brilliant vermilion, though both pink and cherry-red forms are available. They flower in late summer.

Vallotas can be grown successfully in a sunny window in JIP 2 with added coarse sand. Water carefully during the winter and remove from frost danger at night.

Veltheimia (Lily family) *V. capensis* (syn. *V. viridifolia*) flowers in early spring in a cool or intermediate house. The flowers form a red-hot poker type of spike but are straight sided, dull pink bells at the top of a speckled fleshy 15–18-in. stem. They are the sort of unusual flower colour for off-beat flower arrangements, and last well in water. The bulbs are large and can be lifted dry when dormant in the summer. They should be planted in September in JIP 2 and be kept growing throughout the winter, which means good light and an adequate temperature. The dried up ends of the leaf bases which form the bulb should be kept clear of the soil and care should be taken to water the soil and not into the neck of the bulb.

Zephyranthes (Amaryllis family) (flowers of the western wind) These are bulbs from warm regions in Central and South America, so only a few can be tried outdoors in the mildest parts, though they make good pot plants in a cool house.

Z. candida, with single white flowers like crocuses and rush-like foliage, is the hardiest and the most readily available. It flowers in September–October and makes a good edging plant. Also occasionally available are *Z. citrina*, a bright yellow with a greenish base, which is not quite so big; and *Z. grandiflora*, rosy pink and slightly larger in flower. Both are too tender for anything but a cool greenhouse.

TULIPS
The following varieties (arranged as far as possible by time of flowering) are recommended: forcing varieties are marked with an asterisk. Height, in inches in brackets.

Late March–April
Kaufmanniana varieties and hybrids: César Franck (8), red and yellow; Fritz Kreisler (8), flesh-pink, flushed rose, yellow base; Heart's Delight (8), carmine, edged rose and white, mottled foliage; Shakespeare (6), salmon, apricot and orange; Stresa (7), deep yellow and orange-red; The First (6), red outside, cream edged, cream inside.

Early April
Greigii varieties and hybrids: These all have leaves beautifully marked with chocolate, which they have passed on to some of the *Kaufmanniana* hybrids. Mixed *T. kaufmanniana* × *T. greigii* are sold as Peacock tulips. Cape Cod (8), yellow, striped red, black base; Margaret Herbst (20), scarlet; Oriental Splendour (18), carmine on outside of lemon yellow, black base; Plaisir (7), carmine, edged sulphur, vermilion inside; Red Riding Hood (8), scarlet.

April flowering
Early singles: *Bellona (15), yellow, fragrant; *Brilliant Star (12), scarlet; Cassini (14), deep crimson; *Diana (12), white; *General de Wet (13), orange-scarlet, fragrant; *Ibis (14), rose, pale margin; Keizerskroon (15), scarlet and yellow; Mon Trésor (13), yellow, fragrant; Pink Beauty (13), pink and white; *Van de Neer (12), plum-purple.
Mid-Season (mid-April to mid-May): *Triumph* (mid-April to mid-May); Crater (18), crimson; Elmus (18), cherry and white; First Lady (16), violet, purple; Garden Party (16), white, edged pink; Reforma (18), butter yellow.
Early doubles (about 7 days later): *Dante (10), blood red; David Teniers (12), violet-purple; *Electra (12), carmine, pink when forced; Maréchal Niel (12), yellow; *Murillo (10), pink and white; *Mr Van der Hoef (12), yellow; *Orange Nassau (12), orange-scarlet; *Peach Blossom (12), rose pink; Schonoord (12), white; Vuurbaak (12), scarlet.

Tulipa greigii 'Perlina'

Darwin Hybrids (end of April to mid-May): *Apeldoorn (26), orange-red, black base; Golden Springtime (26), yellow; *Gudoshnik (24), yellow, mahogany; Holland's Glory (20), scarlet; My Lady (24), vivid coral-flame, very large.
Lily-flowered (reflexed petals; end April–mid May): Aladdin (22), scarlet, cream edge, yellow base; Burgundy (18), a deep violet, good shape; *China Pink (22), pink, white base; Mariette (22), salmon-pink; Maytime (20), mauve-lilac, white edge; Maybole (24),

The Parrot tulip 'Estella Rijnveld'

rosy-red; Queen of Sheba (19), chestnut-red, orange edge; Red Shine (20), ruby-red, blue base; West Point (20), soft yellow; White Triumphator (26), white.
May flowering
Darwin Will not force before February: *Aristocrat (28), rosy magenta; Bleu Aimable (28), heliotrope; Charles Needham (26), scarlet, blue base; Clara Butt (24), rose, flushed salmon; Farncombe Sanders (30), red, white base; La Tulipe Noire (25), maroon-black; *Niphetos (28), lemon-yellow; Pride of Haarlem (26), deep carmine, blue base, fragrant; *Prunus (26), deep rose-pink; *Queen of Bartigons (26), salmon pink; Queen of Night (28), purple-black; Scarlett O'Hara (26), scarlet, blue base; Sunkist (28), golden-yellow; The Bishop (28), violet, blue base; Zwanenburg (29), white.
Breeder The old exhibition tulips of perfect globular shape, from which the Broken tulips known as Bizarre and Bybloemen arose: Dillenburg (26), orange; Louis XIV (30), purple, bronze edged.
Cottage or Single Late Advance (26), scarlet, blue base; *Carrara (22), white, (force from mid-Feb); Chappaqua (30), magenta; Inglescombe Yellow (21), yellow; Marshall Haig (26), scarlet; Mrs John T. Scheepers (24), soft yellow; Ossi Oswalda (26), cream, edged rose; Princess Margaret Rose (21), yellow, edged scarlet; Rosy Wings (22), pink, blue base; White City (Mount Erebus) (29), white.
Multiflowered with 3 or more flowers branching from one main stem: Claudette (22), ivory-white, edged rose; Emir (24), scarlet; Georgette (26), yellow, edged red.
Broken Coloured These are tulips which are infected with virus disease which has caused the break up of the colours, causing them to appear in streaks and patches. They should be kept away from other tulips as the infection is spread by aphids which infest the bulbs in store. Rembrandt tulips are broken Darwin tulips, others are broken breeder tulips: Mme de Pompadour (24), white, flamed violet-purple (Rembrandt); Absalon (22), yellow, flamed coffee-brown (Bizarre); Mayblossom (22), cream, flamed purple (Bybloemen).
Parrot These are tulips in which virus has caused distortion and splitting (lacination) of the petal edge. Similar, but shallower, division of the petal edge is known as 'fringed': Black Parrot (22), almost black; *Blue Parrot (24), violet and purple; Fantasy (22), soft rose, green markings; Orange Parrot (28), brownish orange, marked old gold, fragrant; Red Parrot (28), deep scarlet; Texas Gold (20), golden yellow, edged red, marked green; White Parrot (20), white; Fringed Beauty (12), red, yellow fringe; *viridiflora* (green tulips); *viridiflora praecox* (18), green, margined yellow; Artist (9), terracotta and green; Groenland (Greenland) (20), old rose, green and cream.
Double Late or Peony flowered: Eros (22), old rose; Nizza (16), sulphur-yellow, streaked red; Mount Tacoma (18), white; Uncle Tom (20), mahogany-red.

Annuals & Biennials

Seed is Nature's usual means of increasing plant life and it is also the simplest method for the gardener when it comes to raising annual, biennal and, in some instances, perennial flowering plants. Gardens of modern houses tend to get smaller and smaller, due to the high cost of land, therefore the thing to do is to grow only the best plants and to grow them well. Inferior seed takes just as much time to sow and grow, the results will never be first-rate and the saving of a few pence is false economy. Only the best is good enough for the experienced gardener, as he knows from years of trial and error.

Flower seeds, in common with vegetable and other crops, are bred with great care and the plant breeder maintains a stud-book in which he keeps the parentage of hybrid plants in the same manner as with race horses, pedigree dogs and the like. All this takes time and costs money, but the results are far superior to plants pollinated haphazardly by bees and other insects.

Vast numbers of plants are raised from seeds but as far as flowers are concerned they are known as hardy annual, half-hardy annual, biennial and perennial.

Hardy Annuals A hardy annual is a plant that is raised from seed, flowers, and dies a natural death within the four seasons. Given favourable weather a seed crop is harvested from such plants. However seed crops fail, or may be poor in some years, and it may take the seed grower a couple of years or longer to build up an adequate supply.

Half-hardy annuals These are usually raised from seed sown under glass and the seedlings planted out where they are to flower when the danger of frost is past. Or some half-hardy annuals may be sown in the open ground in late spring to provide a late display. Flowering will continue until the autumn frost cuts down the plants.

Biennials A biennial is sown one year, produces its flowers and dies the following year. Some biennials, the wallflower for instance, may prove to be short-lived perennials in some gardens, and the same applies to some half-hardy annuals, such as the antirrhinum, in a mild winter.

Perennials A perennial is a plant of any kind that lives for more than two years. It may be perennial in a greenhouse, others grown in the open are known as hardy perennials.

F_1 Hybrids Seed catalogues list many recent introductions as F_1 hybrids. This is the plant breeder's abbreviated way of recording that the seed is the result of a controlled cross of two known parent plants, or to the scientist, the first filial generation. Such seed produces plants of superior vigour and uniformity and often the flowers are of more intense colour and larger than ordinary hybrid seedlings. It is, however, a long and expensive process to obtain such seed, therefore it costs more per packet. Also the complicated breeding programme has to be repeated, as seed saved from F_1 hybrids grown in the garden, would prove far from reliable.

Cosmos bipinnatus

Cultivation

Hardy Annuals Seed of hardy annuals may be sown in the open ground where it is to flower; it is as easy as that. The main requirements are an open sunny position and a well-drained soil. Obviously the condition of the soil will be reflected in the quality of the flowers produced and to get the best results the ground should be forked over a few days before sowing and, where the soil is poor, work in bonemeal to a depth of 2 or 3 in. and at the rate of about 2 oz. to the square yard. This is a fairly slow-acting fertilizer that will provide nourishment as the roots get down to it. Fresh manure is not a good thing for annuals as it encourages much soft leaf growth and not flowers.

Before sowing rake the soil level, removing large stones and hard lumps of earth. Most flower seed is small and does need a reasonably fine surface soil in which to germinate. Sow the seed broadcast or in drills and in any case sow thinly for germination of annual flower seed is usually good. This will reduce the wasteful job of thinning. Pelleted seeds make small seeds much easier to handle and thin sowing is easily achieved. This means that the seedlings will have sufficient space to grow without the check caused by thinning or transplanting.

Do not attempt to sow seed when the soil is wet and sticky, be patient and wait until it dries out. Seed sowing is controlled by the weather not by the calendar. If cloches are available these should be placed over the ground where the seed is to be sown and will not only keep the soil from being saturated, but will help to warm the seed bed and thus assist germination when the sowing is done. After the seed has been sown cover it lightly with soil and water with a can fitted with a fine rose. Water it just sufficiently to make the surface soil moist and if cloches are being used these should be replaced to cover the seed bed. If the ends of the cloches are closed with sheets of glass or by some other means marauding birds will be deterred.

Cloches are certainly useful to assist germination and protect tiny seedlings from heavy rain, but they must be used with discretion. It is all too easy to leave them over a seed bed until the soil has baked hard and any seed that has germinated is cremated by the hot sun before the seedlings have had a chance to make an adequate root system.

This can happen even without cloches during a hot, dry spell and in such conditions small seedlings may be shaded by small branches of evergreens, or some other means.

Where thinning of seedlings is necessary this should be done when they are about 2–3 in. high and a final thinning should leave sufficient space for the plants to develop. After each thinning water the seedlings to settle the soil around the plants. The seedlings that have been removed may be planted elsewhere in the garden, but this is not successful with all annuals. As a rough guide to thinning the distance between each plant should be about three-quarters of the plant's ultimate height; e.g. plants which will grow 1 ft. tall should be thinned to 9 in. apart.

Half-hardy Annuals Many plants which we call half-hardy annuals are natives of much warmer lands where frost is unknown or a rare occurrence. Some are perennial in their native conditions. We must, therefore, encourage such seed to germinate with the aid of artificial heat in a greenhouse or frame as our conditions in February and March are too chilly in the open. Where the sowing is not done until April there should be sufficient heat from the sun to germinate the seed in an unheated greenhouse or frame. Some half-hardy annuals may be sown in the open in May or early June where they are to flower. These will, of course, not flower until late in the summer but are useful in prolonging the display after the plants raised under glass have finished flowering.

Seed of half-hardy annuals is sown in pots or boxes containing seed compost which is readily obtained these days in polythene bags at garden centres. It is moist and ready for use, which saves considerable time. Fill the container to within about $\frac{1}{2}$ in. of the top and press the compost down evenly and fairly firmly which is best done with a flat piece of board.

Sow the seed sparsely, then sprinkle a fine covering of compost over the seed and cover the container with a piece of glass, and a sheet of brown paper as shading. The compost should not require watering at this stage as it only needs to be moist. Remove the glass daily, wiping off the condensed moisture and reverse the glass when you replace it.

When the seed germinates remove the glass and paper and put the container in full light in the greenhouse or frame.

When the seedlings are large enough to handle, that is usually by the time they have developed two pairs of leaves, lift them carefully by levering up the soil with a dibber and prick them out into another box, spacing them about 2 in. apart. Plant them firmly and water them into the compost. Keep them growing steadily under glass until the beginning of May. Then, if the weather is reasonably mild, stand the boxes in the open for a week or so to harden the plants before they are planted out where they are to flower. If the boxes have been in a frame it is a simple matter

Above: Choose a sunny position for the colourful South African gazanias. *Left:* Petunia hybrids make a bright show in summer. *Centre:* Some of the eschscholzias or Californian poppies. *Below:* The best of the annual mallows, Lavatera 'Loveliness'

of just removing the frame light for this hardening-off process. Be sure that the boxes are standing level, and on a firm base, otherwise some plants may lack water. Give the boxes a good watering an hour or two before transplanting the seedlings so that they can be removed from the boxes with plenty of moist soil attached to their roots. Water them again when they are planted out.

Among the half-hardy annuals which may be sown direct in the open where they are to flower are aster, cosmos, African and French marigolds, mignonette and zinnia. The last two resent transplanting and germinate better when the soil is made firm after sowing. May or early June is the time to sow half-hardy annuals in the open in a sunny position and in well-drained soil.

Biennials Seed of biennial plants may be sown straight into a seed bed in the open ground in June, July or August. As the soil is warm germination is not delayed, provided the seed bed is kept moist. Another method is to sow in drills in a cold frame in March or April, or where only a small quantity of plants is required, to sow in pots or boxes in a cold frame or cold greenhouse. With the frame light in position there should be sufficient warmth to encourage germination. Artificial heat is unnecessary for seeds of hardy plants, in fact, it is not usually desirable.

Whichever method is used, sow thinly and do not make the common mistake of covering the seed with too much soil. As a general rule cover the seed with its own depth of soil. Nature just scatters it on the surface and lets the rain wash it in, but Nature is very wasteful, and sows with abandon.

Where the seed is sown in a cold frame leave some ventilation or the frame may get too hot. Some shading on the glass will also reduce the need for frequent watering and the same applies to seed sown in pots in a cold greenhouse which should be covered with brown paper or newspaper until the seed germinates. These are small points which make all the difference between failure and success. Biennials are sown one year and flower and produce seed the next, which completes their life cycle. Some will perpetuate themselves by self-sown seedlings, for instance, foxglove, forget-me-not, mullein, hollyhock, among many others.

Nasturtiums

The Uses of Annuals and Biennials

Beds and Borders Annuals are probably most widely used for filling gaps in borders, on the rock garden and elsewhere, for they provide splashes of welcome colour in a matter of months. A bed or border devoted entirely to hardy annuals can make a splendid carpet of colour during the summer months, but it does entail considerable work in weeding and maybe watering in the early stages.

For a small garden or one of moderate size, a mixed border of hardy herbaceous perennials and annuals will provide interest and colour from May to October without undue toil. With both types of plants it is possible, by making a careful choice, to include only such plants as require no staking and it is wise, in exposed gardens, to use low-growing plants that will not be battered by summer gales. (A list of such plants is given later.)

New Gardens One of the quickest ways of making a display in a new garden is by sowing hardy annuals, for seed sown in April where it is to flower will give a display from June onwards.

The choice of annuals is very wide and the range of colour all embracing which gives ample scope for those with bright ideas and those who like to try something different each year.

Containers For those whose gardening may be confined to window boxes, tubs or other containers on a roof garden or in a patio, half-hardy annuals are probably the best bet. These can be planted out as young plants in May and will soon start to flower. This is much more satisfactory, although it costs more than sowing seed of hardy annuals in window boxes which are usually too exposed for young seedlings to make good plants, even though the seed may germinate reasonably well in the first place. Suitable half-hardy annuals for growing in containers are antirrhinum, petunia, fragrant stocks, annual chrysanthemum, cherry pie (heliotrope), lobelia, *Phlox drummondii*, African and French marigolds and other showy plants.

Hanging baskets are also most decorative when filled with heliotrope, trailing lobelia, free-flowering nasturtium, petunia and other summer-flowering plants.

Edging and Paving Other uses of annuals are as dwarf edging plants for the front of a bed or border, or for sowing in crevices in paving. Among these is the low-growing *Limnanthes douglasii* with quite large white flowers with a yellow centre, which seeds itself without becoming a nuisance, mesembryanthemum with gay daisy-like flowers that thrives in well-drained soil and full sun, anagallis (pimpernel), and the creeping zinnia, *Sanvitalia procumbens*, with single yellow flowers with a black centre on 6 in. stems. This curious little plant is like a miniature sunflower and never fails to attract interest.

Above: Morning glory (Ipomoea)
Below: Nemesias are available in a very wide range of colours
Right: The most decorative variety of the annual corn cockle is *Agrostemma* 'Milas'

Cut Flowers Annuals provide a splendid selection of flowers for cutting and with a little planning flowers can be available over a long period. By sowing hardy annuals in the open in the autumn and making another sowing in the open in the spring a succession of welcome flowers will be assured. A list of annuals for cutting is given later.

Biennials are also most useful and effective in a border, particularly when planted in bold clumps. Wallflowers are probably among the most popular and there is a splendid range of colour. The fragrance on a warm day in May is glorious. For small gardens the 'Tom Thumb' varieties, about 9 in. high, are most valuable and decorative. These and other biennials are best planted in their flowering positions in the early autumn, but if necessary this can be deferred until March. If the winter happens to be severe, spring planting will prove to be the right choice, but autumn planting gives the wallflowers and other biennials more time to get established, in a reasonable winter.

Groups of sweet Williams in well-drained soil and a sunny position are delightful in early summer, and they are also useful for cutting. Other popular biennials include Canterbury bell, the blue cynoglossum with forget-me-not-like flowers borne on incurling sprays, polyanthus in many rich colours, honesty with its large flat seed pods which make decorative material when dried, Iceland poppy (*Papaver nudicaule*) and many different violas and pansies.

Annuals and Biennials for the Cool Greenhouse

Raising plants from seed is a most economical means of providing a long-lasting display for the cool greenhouse. Where a minimum temperature of about 45°F (7°C) can be maintained the choice of flowering and of decorative foliage plants is considerable. What is more many plants that we normally grow as annuals in the open may prove to be perennial when grown under glass, as they are in their native conditions.

For example, the fast-growing Mexican cup-and-saucer-vine, *Cobaea scandens*, also known as cathedral bells, has large purple and green cup-and-saucer flowers over a long period. This evergreen plant which clings by means of tendrils can make as much as 20 ft. of growth in a season, so it is too rampant for a small greenhouse but most decorative for a sunny wall in a large conservatory.

The popular morning glory (ipomoea or pharbitis) requires much less space, twining up supports to a height of about 10 ft. and bearing a succession of large sky-blue funnel-shaped flowers, as will the Chilean glory vine, *Eccremocarpus scaber*, which bears clusters of bright orange flowers for many months. Even in the open the last named will sometimes seed itself when grown in a sheltered sunny corner, so it is easy enough to raise from seed. All these flowering climbers can be grown in a sunny greenhouse border or will flower

happily when grown in pots or other containers.

Seeds of these plants, in common with many others, will germinate readily if sown under glass in March when the days are beginning to lengthen and to get warmer. An ideal temperature for germinating most seeds of this type is 65°F (18°C) and to maintain this as well as a moist atmosphere it will be found economical to have a propagating frame within the greenhouse. This need not be a costly affair, just four sides of a box and a sheet of glass will suffice. Such a frame heated by electrical soil-warming cable is convenient and economical in that the whole greenhouse does not have to be maintained at this temperature.

With an electrically heated frame the thermostat can be set at a slightly higher temperature to encourage germination and when this has taken place the temperature can gradually be lowered. Whatever means of heating a greenhouse or frame is used the aim should be to keep the temperature as constant as possible and to avoid wide fluctuations of day and night temperatures.

Most seeds germinate best in the dark and it is wise therefore to shade the frame, or the pots and boxes in which the seeds are sown, with brown paper. This will provide sufficient shade and at the same time reduce the amount of watering that may be necessary. The soil should be kept just moist in the early stages after sowing, but as germination takes place a little more watering will be required, and as

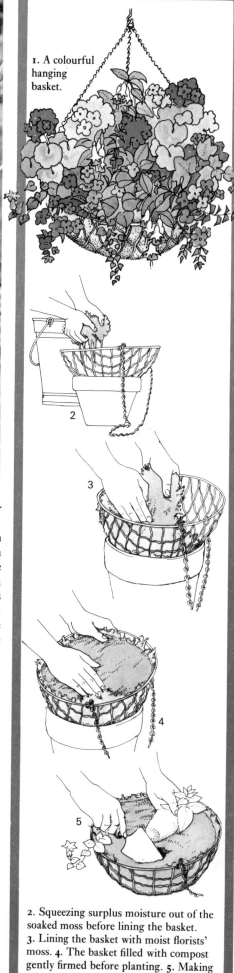

1. A colourful hanging basket.

2. Squeezing surplus moisture out of the soaked moss before lining the basket.
3. Lining the basket with moist florists' moss. 4. The basket filled with compost gently firmed before planting. 5. Making a hole with a trowel to receive a plant knocked out from a pot.

soon as the seed has germinated the shading should be removed. However, should germination coincide with a spell of really bright sunny weather it is as well to shade the tiny seedlings from the midday sun.

These days seed-sowing and potting composts, based on loam, or of the soilless, peat and sand type, are readily obtainable at garden shops in various sized polythene bags or cartons and are usually moist ready for use, which makes life easy in this respect.

While cyclamen are perennial tuberous-rooted plants they are often treated as biennials. They are easily raised from seed sown under glass in August and will flower within about 15 months, that is by Christmas the following year, when an individual plant will be quite an expensive item. Seed germinates readily in a temperature of 60°F (16°C), which means that the house or frame will need shading to keep the temperature down in August, and the atmosphere should be kept moist in hot weather by spraying water around the pathway in the greenhouse. When the seedlings have made two leaves prick them out in seed trays, or singly in small pots, and grow them on in gentle warmth. Put the little corms into larger pots when necessary, but do not bury the corm when potting, merely making it firm in the surface potting compost. There are various excellent large-flowering varieties in shades of salmon, crimson, mauve and white, also a new double flowered 'Kimono' strain of Japanese origin, in a pleasing range of mixed colours. After flowering, the corms can be discarded, or treated as perennials (see also the Part of this work dealing with The Greenhouse and Garden Frame). The dainty *Cyclamen persicum*, the parent of modern hybrids, has charming white or pink, sweetly fragrant flowers and is normally spring flowering.

Obviously one wants colour in the cool greenhouse during the winter and early spring and cyclamen will help to provide this for a long period. Other decorative plants that are easily raised from seed include *Primula malacoides* with candelabrum-like flowers on strong stems in shades of pink, lilac and mauve; the drum-head *Primula*

denticulata, which is in fact a hardy perennial but easily raised from seed, will flower from February onwards under glass. The long-lasting heads of flower are in shades of purple, mauve or white. And don't forget fragrant polyanthus and primroses in many colours. These flower for months in cool conditions.

Cinerarias sown in June should provide bold splashes of colour from February onwards. At this time the little *Limnanthes douglasii* should be a mass of yellow and white fragrant flowers and the sky-blue nemophila which also makes a charming pot plant for a partially shaded place in the cool house, should be in full flower. Schizanthus, butterfly flower, are available in an astonishing range of glorious colours—salmon, apricot, pink, yellow, mauve and purple. Many of the flowers have attractive markings. They thrive in cool house conditions as do calceolarias, but the latter do not usually start to flower until June, from seed sown the previous May.

The Chilean salpiglossis is remarkably beautiful, with a richness of colour and splendid veinings on the trumpet-shaped elegant flowers. The colour range includes rose, crimson, purple, cream and many blends. There are dwarf forms about 1 ft. in height and also large-flowered hybrids up to 3 ft. Seed sown under glass in August or September will make delightful flowering plants the following May.

There are numerous varieties of *Coleus blumei* which are grown for their decorative foliage. As they are natives of Java and Central Africa they like a warm, moist atmosphere which may make them a little difficult to accommodate in a cool greenhouse. Seed sown in warm conditions in February will provide large plants later in the year. While coleus are in fact perennial shrubby plants, given sufficient heat, they are more often treated as annuals. The nettle-like leaves are in various shades of red-bronze, yellow, green and maroon. The spikes of blue flowers are best pinched out to encourage bushy, leafy plants.

Seed of *Celosia plumosa* sown under glass

in March will provide summer-flowering annual pot plants of striking appearance with bright red, feathery tassels in summer. There is also a golden form. These fast-growing plants require a rich soil and plenty of light.

Some annuals which do not transplant easily may be sown thinly in pots in which they are to flower. After germination the seedlings should be thinned out to five or six plants to a pot, according to the size of the pot. It is as simple as that. Plants that can be treated in this way are the Californian poppy (eschscholzia), in shades of orange, copper, yellow, carmine and ivory; linaria, viscaria and the charming long-lasting mignonette (reseda), which is uniquely fragrant. Many other annuals can be sown in the normal way and will transplant quite readily when large enough to handle. A few pots of such plants will come in very useful to fill gaps in the sequence of flowering.

Other plants that will give a good display in a cool greenhouse are antirrhinum, brachycome, *Campanula isophylla*, of trailing habit and useful for growing over the edge of a shelf or in a hanging basket; *Campanula pyramidalis*, the chimney bellflower, with wide-open pale blue flowers borne on erect stems from 5–6 ft. in height, and clarkia sown in the autumn will flower freely the following spring. There are annual and biennial stocks (matthiola) which may be sown at different times of the year to provide colour and delicious fragrance for many weeks.

There is a wide range of hybrid petunias which are admirable as pot plants, in tubs or in hanging baskets. They are outstandingly colourful and long-lasting—large-flowered singles and doubles, compact bedding varieties, pendulous hybrids suitable for window boxes, some with fringed and ruffled flowers, bicolours and many self colours.

These are but a few of the flowering plants easily raised from seed which are so welcome in the cool greenhouse throughout the year.

Above: Colourful annuals form an edging to a border of hardy perennials
Left: The sweetly scented blooms of the flowering tobacco plant, *Nicotiana alata*

Right: Colour provided by annuals and bedding plants

Annuals for Special Purposes

Hardy annuals for Autumn Sowing in the open
Alyssum, Calendula (pot marigold), Centaurea (cornflower), Clarkia, *Delphinium ajacis* (larkspur), Eschscholzia (Californian poppy), Godetia, Iberis (candytuft), *Lathyrus odoratus* (sweet pea), *Limnanthes douglasii*, Nigella (love-in-a-mist), *Papaver nudicaule* (Shirley poppy), Saponaria, Scabiosa.

Hardy Annuals for Cut Flowers
Calendula (pot marigold), Centaurea (cornflower), *Delphinium ajacis* (larkspur), Gypsophila, *Lathyrus odoratus* (sweet pea), Nigella (love-in-a-mist), Saponaria, Scabiosa.

Annuals for Full Sun in Well-drained soil
(Hardy and Half-hardy)
Arctotis, Brachycome, Calandrinia, Clarkia, Dimorphotheca, Echium, Eschscholzia, Helipterum, Hibiscus, Linum (flax), Mesembryanthemum, Oenothera, Papaver (poppy), Portulaca, Salpiglossis, Sanvitalia, Sedum (stonecrop), Statice (limonium), Tagetes (African and French marigolds), Tropaeolum (nasturtium), Ursinia, Venidium, Zinnia.

Annual Climbers
Cobaea scandens, *Eccremocarpus scaber*, Gourds, Humulus (hop), Ipomoea (morning glory), *Lathyrus odoratus* (sweet pea), Maurandia, Quamoclit, Tropaeolum (nasturtium).

Annuals with Fragrant Flowers
Alyssum, Asperula, Centaurea (sweet sultan), Dianthus (pink), Exacum, Heliotrope (cherry pie), Hesperis (sweet rocket), *Lathyrus odoratus* (sweet pea), *Lupinus luteus* (yellow lupin), Matthiola (stocks), Nicotiana (tobacco plant), Oenothera (evening primrose), Reseda (mignonette), Tropaeolum (nasturtium) (Gleam hybrids).

Low-growing Annuals (from 9–18 in.)
Adonis, Anthemis, Centaurea (cornflower, dwarf forms), Collinsia, *Convolvulus tricolor*, *Coreopsis coronata*, *Coreopsis tinctoria*, Dimorphotheca, Eschscholzia, Gilia, Godetia (dwarf forms), Helipterum, Iberis (candytuft), Linaria, *Matthiola bicornis* (night-scented stock), Matthiola (ten-week stock), Omphalodes, Reseda (mignonette), Scabiosa (dwarf forms), *Tagetes patula* (dwarf French marigold), Ursinia.

Annuals for Moist Soil
Calendula (pot marigold), Helianthus (sunflower), *Limnanthes douglasii*, Linaria (toadflax), *Linum grandiflorum rubrum* (scarlet flax), Nemophila, Nigella (love-in-a-mist), Reseda (mignonette), *Saxifraga cymbalaria*.

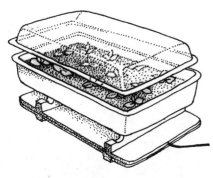

A simple propagating frame for raising annuals

Annuals & Biennials from A to Z

Adonis (pheasant's eye) H.A., 1–1½ ft. Easily grown from seed sown in the spring in a sunny position, *A. aestivalis* bears small crimson flowers in June and July. The deep green, finely-cut leaves are also attractive.

Ageratum (floss flower) H.H.A., 6–18 in. This is a popular bedding plant with masses of fluffy little powder-puff-like flowers from July until autumn frosts. The long-lasting flowers are mainly in shades of blue and retain their colour without fading. Sow under glass in February or March and plant out in a sunny bed, window-box or other container towards the end of May. Dwarf kinds also make neat plants when grown in pots to flower in a cool, greenhouse. Suitable varieties are 'Blue Mink', 6 in., powder blue; 'Blue Mist', 6 in., mid-blue, early flowering; 'Fairy Pink', 6 in., pale pink. There are also white varieties. *A. mexicanum* has soft lavender-blue flowers on 18-in. stems.

Agrostemma (corn cockle) H.A., 1½–2 ft. Magenta-red single flowers are borne on slender stems freely throughout the summer. A more decorative variety 'Milas' has large rosy-lilac flowers with conspicuous dark lines along each petal. The long, stiff stems make it useful as a cut flower as well as for the border. Seed may be sown in the open ground in the autumn or in the spring for later flowering.

Alonsoa (mask flower) H.H.A., 1–1½ ft. These South American plants thrive in a rich soil and in a sunny position. The most showy is *A. warscewiczii*, with bright scarlet flowers. There is also a dwarf form known as 'compacta', admirable as a pot plant for a cool greenhouse, where it is perennial. Sow in February or March under glass, in a temperature of 60°F (16°C) and plant out in May for a summer display.

Althaea (hollyhock) H.B., 4–5 ft. Easily raised from seed, the hollyhock may prove perennial, but is not long lived. Sow the seed in the open ground in May or June and transplant the seedlings to grow on, before putting them in their flowering sites in the autumn or early spring to flower in July and August. There are single and double varieties in shades of crimson, pink, yellow and white. There is also an annual form which should be sown under glass in February or March and planted out in May to flower from July onwards.

Alyssum (sweet alyssum) H.A., 4 in. A popular plant for edging, *A. maritimum* grows well in paving and window boxes. It flowers freely throughout the summer and early autumn and is easily raised from seed sown where it is to flower. Or seed may be sown under glass and the seedlings planted out about mid-May when the danger of frost should be past. The little heads of flower are sweetly fragrant. Recommended varieties include 'Lilac Queen', pale lilac; 'Little Dorrit' pure white; 'Rosie O' Day', deep rose-pink; 'Royal Carpet', violet-purple; 'Violet Queen', bright violet-purple.

Amaranthus (love-lies-bleeding) H.A., 3 ft. The long pendent tassels of crimson flowers are a curious sight from July to September. *A. caudatus* 'Viridis' has long greenish-yellow tassels. Sow in the open ground in April in well-drained soil and in a sunny position. It requires plenty of moisture during the growing season. In exposed districts it is best treated as a half-hardy plant. People either like it or it gives them the creeps.

Anagallis (pimpernel) H.H.A., 6–12 in. Seed of *A. linifolia* sown in the open in late May in well-drained soil on a rock garden or warm border will provide brilliantly coloured flowers from July to September. Mixed packets will provide shades of scarlet and blue, or separate colours are available.

Antirrhinum (snapdragon) H.H.A., 9 in.–3 ft. These long-flowering plants are usually treated as annuals although in mild districts they are short-lived perennials. For bedding purposes seed is sown in boxes or pots in a warm greenhouse in February or March.

Notes on Plant Descriptions

H.A. Indicates that the plant is best raised as a hardy annual by seed sown in the open ground in the spring, or in some instances in the autumn. This is stated where applicable. Such hardy annuals will withstand a normal winter in the open ground and will provide an earlier display than spring-sown seed.

H.H.A. denotes a half-hardy annual which is a plant that is liable to damage by spring frost or may be withered by perishing winds in the young stage. Such plants are raised from seed sown under glass in a temperature of about 60°F (15°C), either in a greenhouse or in an electrically heated propagating frame.

H.B. Indicates a hardy biennial that takes two years to flower from seed and then dies. The seed is usually sown in the open ground in the early summer, the seedlings later being transplanted in rows to grow on, before being moved to their flowering positions in the autumn or early spring.

H.H.P. This refers to a half-hardy perennial plant which may live for a number of years but requires the protection of a frost-free greenhouse during the winter. Such plants are often used for summer bedding displays; sometimes exceptionally good plants are increased by cuttings.

Above: The common marigold, *Calendula officinalis*, seeds itself freely. But there are much improved kinds, with flowers of various forms, in a fairly wide colour range. This one is 'Orange King'. *Below: Amaranthus caudatus* is popularly known as love-lies-bleeding. A half-hardy annual, seedlings should be planted out in late spring

Sturdy plants should be ready for planting out in a sunny bed by mid-May. Seed may be sown in the open ground in April for flowering in late summer, but these cannot be compared with plants raised under glass. The range of colour includes crimson, pink, orange-scarlet, yellow and white, and many subtle variations. The dwarf varieties are admirable for the front of a border or for window boxes and the taller varieties are useful for cut flowers. There is also a good selection of rust-resistant hybrids, which are advised where this disease is prevalent.

Arctotis H.H.A., 1–2 ft. These South African plants with daisy-like flowers require a well-drained soil and full sun. They are perennial in their native conditions but are easily raised from seed sown under glass in March in a temperature of 65°F (18°C). Harden off the seedlings before planting out in mid-May. The silvery-white flowers of *A. grandis*, 2 ft., have a mauve centre and a golden band. Young plants should be pinched back when about 6 in. high to encourage bushy growth.

Asperula (woodruff) H.A., 1 ft. A useful little plant for edging or for filling a gap at the front of a border. A native of Syria, *A. orientalis* is an easily grown plant producing fragrant, lavender-blue flowers from July onwards. It is of branching habit and is useful

for miniature floral arrangements. It enjoys a moist soil and partial shade and should be sown in April where it is to flower.

Bellis (double daisy) H.B., 6 in. *Bellis perennis* 'Monstrosa Flore Pleno' is a hardy perennial but is usually raised from seed sown in the open ground in early summer and transplanted to flowering positions in autumn. The button-like flowers are in shades of crimson to rose and white and are effective among other spring bedding plants and tulips.

Brachycome (Swan River daisy) H.H.A., 9–12 in. In sheltered gardens *B. iberidifolia* a little Australian plant may be treated as a hardy annual, but it is usually sown under glass in March and planted out in May. Easily grown in a dry, sunny position, it flowers throughout the summer until the autumn frosts. The star-like flowers are blue or white with a dark disk. As a pot plant it will flower for weeks in a cool greenhouse.

Calandrinia (rock purslane) H.H.A., 6 in. *C. umbellata* is a sun-loving plant from Peru which thrives on a rock garden ledge or on the top of a dry wall. The brilliant magenta-crimson flowers are borne in clusters from July to September, but do not open in dull weather. Sow the seed in April and May where it is to flower and thin the seedlings to 6 in. apart.

Calceolaria (slipperwort) H.H.A., 1–1½ ft. The dust-like seed of the pale yellow *C. scabiosaefolia* is sown under glass in early spring and after hardening off the young plants are put out when the danger of frost is over. In a sunny position or in dappled shade they flower from July to September.

Calendula (pot or garden marigold) H.A., 1½–2 ft. These showy plants derived from *C. officinalis* are among the hardiest and easiest to grow in almost any soil and in full sun. They flower continuously throughout the summer and autumn. Particularly in light soil they seed themselves happily but modern varieties tend to deteriorate quickly when grown in this way. Sow in spring or autumn where they are to flower. Young seedlings may be transplanted with success. There are numerous named varieties, many of American origin (F₁ hybrids), where they are known as the friendship flower. To get the best results purchase fresh seed each year. Good varieties include: 'Yellow Gitana', golden yellow, compact; 'Baby Gold', golden-yellow; 'Geisha Girl', large, incurved, warm orange blooms; 'Lemon Queen', lemon-yellow; 'Radio', bright orange, ball-shaped flowers with quilled petals.

Callistephus (China aster) H.H.A., 1–2½ ft. The diverse and colourful modern asters have been developed from *C. chinenis* but some seedsmen find they are better known as asters – not to be confused with the perennial Michaelmas daisies. Seed should be sown in a cool greenhouse in March or April, or in a sheltered garden in the open ground in early May. There are both double and single flowers and the colour range is all-embracing. Seedlings transplant quite readily when small. Grown *en masse* they make a splendid show in late summer and early autumn. The short-growing varieties make bushy, decorative plants in window boxes. 'Ostrich Plume', and 'Princess', both 2 ft., are admirable for cutting.

Campanula (Canterbury bell) H.B., 2½–3 ft. An old favourite among cottage gardeners, *C. medium* in shades of deep blue, lavender, deep pink and white is admirable in a mixed border in good soil and a sunny position. The cup and saucer varieties with large bell-like flowers and a saucer, or calyx, of the same colour are among the most popular. Sow the seed in the open in May or June, covering it very lightly with fine soil, and plant out in the flowering position in early autumn. They will flower the following June to August.

Celosia (cockscomb) H.H.A., 2 ft. The feathered forms of *C. plumosa*, of which 'Fairy Fountains' is perhaps one of the best, bear brilliant pyramidal plumes from July to September. The colours include shades of crimson, scarlet, orange and yellow and are seen to best effect with green foliage plants. Sow seed in a warm greenhouse in March, pot the seedlings individually and plant out in the open in mid-June in southern England. They thrive in a well-drained, light soil and in full sun. They also make decorative pot plants in a greenhouse for summer display.

Centaurea (cornflower, sweet sultan) H.A., 1–3 ft. The bright blue flowers of the cornflower, *C. cyanus*, are borne on tall stems and

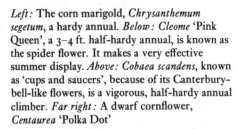

Left: The corn marigold, *Chrysanthemum segetum*, a hardy annual. *Below: Cleome* 'Pink Queen', a 3–4 ft. half-hardy annual, is known as the spider flower. It makes a very effective summer display. *Above: Cobaea scandens*, known as 'cups and saucers', because of its Canterbury-bell-like flowers, is a vigorous, half-hardy annual climber. *Far right:* A dwarf cornflower, *Centaurea* 'Polka Dot'

there are also pale blue, lilac, pink and white varieties, as well as dwarf varieties not exceeding 1 ft. in height. All are easily raised from seed sown from March to May, or in September in a sunny position and in reasonably well-drained soil. The taller varieties are excellent for cutting.

C. moschata (the sweet sultan) H.A. 1½ ft. is another popular annual with fragrant, fluffy heads of flower larger than those of cornflower, pale lilac in colour. There are giant varieties in shades of mauve, purple, rose, yellow and white. The flowers are most useful for cutting and will last many days in water if cut young. Sow as for cornflower. Both do well on chalky soil.

Cheiranthus (wallflower) H.B., 15 in. *C. × allionii*, is the Siberian wallflower with bright orange flowers from March to May. 'Golden Bedder' is a more mellow golden-yellow variety. The common wallflower, *C. cheiri*, 1½ ft. is perennial in some gardens but both these wallflowers are best treated as a biennial and sown in an open seed bed in May, or mid-June for the Siberian wallflower, and transplanted to flowering positions in October. The fragrance of wallflowers on a warm sunny day is glorious and they associate happily with tulips, forget-me-nots and polyanthus. The range of colour is splendid – blood red, scarlet, purple, pink, yellow, ivory white and there is a delightful strain of mixed colours known as 'Persian Carpet'. The 'Tom Thumb' varieties, 9 in. tall in various colours, are admirable for small beds, window boxes or for filling a gap at the front of a border.

Chrysanthemum H.A., 1–3 ft. *C. carinatum* (painted lady), 1½–2 ft. *C. coronarium* (crown daisy) 2–3 ft. *C. segetum* (corn marigold) 1–1½ ft. There are many gay varieties of annual chrysanthemums, single and double. All have daisy-like flowers on good stems and often have rings or zones of colour on white or cream petals. Among the best hardy annuals for summer flowering, they make excellent cut flowers. Seed should be sown in April in the open in a sunny position where they are to flower or in September for an early display the next year. They do not transplant readily, so it is a waste of time to plant out thinnings. They are not fussy about soil provided it is not excessively wet.

Clarkia H.A., 2 ft. Double-flowered *C. elegans* hybrids are deservedly popular; their slender spikes bear numerous flower heads in

shades of salmon-pink, carmine, rosy-purple and white. They are also most decorative as cut flowers. Sow in the open where they are to flower in March and April, or, in sheltered gardens in September to flower the following May and June. Clarkia does best in a light soil and will not tolerate heavy, wet soil. It is wise to support young plants with light twigs as they are liable to be broken off at ground level in a summer gale. For a spring display in a cold greenhouse sow the seed under glass in the autumn.

Cleome (spider plant) H.H.A., 3–4 ft. The large, airy flower trusses are an attractive pinky-mauve and borne erect on rigid, thorny stems from July to September. The plants are most effective when grown in bold clumps in the border. Sow the seed in March in a warm greenhouse and plant out in May in rich, well-drained soil. These fast-growing plants require ample moisture. 'Pink Queen' is an attractive apple-blossom pink; there is also a pure white variety.

Cobaea (cup and saucer plant) H.H.A., 10–20 ft. A vigorous Mexican twiner *C. scandens* bears large Canterbury bell-like flowers from July onwards on a warm wall. The flowers open green, becoming violet-purple. In a cool greenhouse it is perennial but requires ample space to spread. There is also a white variety. Soak the large seeds in water for a few hours before sowing and place them on their

sides in the soil, not flat. Sow under glass in March and pot on, planting out in early June.

Coleus H.H.P., 3 ft. These are ornamental foliage plants with attractive leaves in shades of green, copper, red and apricot, making them conspicuous for greenhouse or room decoration. Sow seed of *C. blumei* or named hybrids in February under glass in a temperature of 75°F (24°C) and grow on without a check to obtain strong, showy plants. Particularly striking varieties may be perpetuated by taking cuttings, 3 in. long, of non-flowering shoots in August or March.

Convolvulus H.A., 12–15 in. *C. tricolor* (syn. *C. minor*) is a bushy plant and is not to be confused with the climbing convolvulus. It has large, funnel-shaped deep blue, yellow and white flowers throughout the summer and is easily grown in poor soil and in full sun. Sow in March, April or September where it is to flower. Named varieties include 'Cambridge Blue', intense clear blue; 'Crimson Monarch', cherry crimson and 'Royal Marine', royal blue, of trailing habit.

Collinsia H.A., 1 ft. The Californian *C. bicolor* is an attractive plant with white upper lip and lilac lower lip, 'Salmon Beauty' is a free-flowering delicate salmon-rose. It is a useful plant for partial shade, or for a woodland garden. Sow in the open ground in March or April, or in a sheltered garden in September.

Coreopsis (tickseed) H.A., 1–2½ ft. Sometimes listed erroneously in catalogues as calliopsis, this is easily grown even in poor soil. Plants bear large, broad-petalled flowers on slender stems from July to September, in shades of yellow, brown and crimson with pleasing markings in contrasting colours. Coreopsis are readily raised from seed sown in the open in a sunny position in April, or under glass in March for earlier flowering.

Cosmos (cosmea) H.H.A., 2–3 ft. This is a most decorative plant with fern-like foliage and large, single or semi-double, daisy-form flowers on slender but wiry stems which make it useful for cutting from July to October. The colour range includes orange, yellow, deep rose to brilliant vermilion, red and white. Sow the seed under glass in February and March in a temperature of 60°F (16°C). Prick out the seedlings and plant out in May in light, well-drained soil and in full sun.

Cynoglossum (hound's tongue) H.H.A., 1½ ft. Although strictly biennial, *C. amabile* is usually grown as an annual, either sown under glass in March and planted out in May, or sown in the open in April for flowering in late summer. The fine seed should be sown thinly. The grey-green downy foliage and turquoise-blue drooping flowers, like large forget-me-nots, are charming. Plant in a moderately rich, well-drained soil and sun or dappled shade.

Annual dahlias

Dahlia H.H.A., $1\frac{1}{2}$–2 ft. Bedding varieties of dahlias are often treated as annuals as they are readily raised from seed. Sow the seed thinly in boxes towards the end of March. In a warm greenhouse it should germinate within ten days. When they are large enough prick out the seedlings or pot them individually. Plant out in mid-May in a sunny position and in a fertile soil. Dahlias require ample moisture during the growing season. Any outstanding plants should be lifted in the autumn after the first frost, and after the tubers have been washed and dried they should be stored in a frost-free place for the winter. They may be planted out the following spring and will start to flower in July. Or they can be put in a warm greenhouse in April to produce cuttings.

Delphinium (larkspur) H.A., $1\frac{1}{2}$–3 ft. Seed of annual delphiniums sown in March or April will produce flowering plants by about mid-July. Seedlings do not transplant well, therefore sow where the plants are to flower. For earlier flowering sow in the open in the autumn. The colour range includes shades of pink, lavender, mauve, rosy-scarlet and white and there are dwarf varieties ($1\frac{1}{2}$ ft.). The 3 ft. tall kinds with branching stock-flowered spikes are admirable for cutting.

Dianthus (pinks) H.H.A., 9–18 in. Seed of the annual varieties of carnations and pinks, such as Chabaud carnations (*D. caryophyllus*) and the Japanese pink (*D. chinensis* 'Heddewigii') and others should be sown thinly in pots and lightly covered with sifted soil. Do this in February or March and place the pots in a warm greenhouse where germination should be evident in a week or ten days. Prick out the seedlings into boxes when they are large enough to handle and harden off before planting out in May in well-drained soil and a sunny position. A great many varieties of dianthus will be found listed in seed catalogues, including *D. barbatus*, the sweet William, H.B., 6–18 in., obtainable in a glorious colour range. Sow these in April and plant out in July.

Digitalis (foxglove) H.B., 4–5 ft. The common foxglove (*D. purpurea*) makes a delightful picture in a woodland setting in partial shade, or it may be grown in a sunny position where the plants do not usually grow so tall. The colour range includes deep pink, purple, cream and white. There are several excellent strains; 'Excelsior Hybrids', with flowers carried horizontally all round the stem, revealing the beautiful markings within the florets and 'The Shirley', are of outstanding beauty. Sow seed in the open ground from May to July.

Dimorphotheca (star of the veldt) H.H.A., 1 ft. *D. aurantiaca*, a South African plant revels in a sunny position where it produces a succession of large, showy daisy-like flowers. In dull weather the flowers remain closed. It thrives in a light soil and when sown in the open in May in southern England it may be in flower within six weeks or so in favourable weather. In colder districts sow under glass in March and plant out in May. Colours include salmon, apricot, buff, orange with greenish-black centre and the large 'Glistening White' of spreading habit 6–9 in. high.

Eccremocarpus (Chilean glory flower) H.H.A., 8–10 ft. *E. scaber* is a fast-growing, deciduous, climbing plant. In mild districts it is perennial and will seed itself happily. Sow under glass in March and plant out against a warm, sunny wall or fence when all risk of frost is past. The clusters of orange-scarlet, yellow-tipped tubular flowers are freely produced throughout the summer and autumn.

Echium (viper's bugloss) H.A., 1–$1\frac{1}{2}$ ft. Compact little plants for the front of a border, echium hybrids bear many bell-like flowers in shades of blue, lavender, pink and white. They do well in poor, dry soil and in a sunny position. The cheerful heads of flowers withstand wind and rain remarkably well. 'Blue Bedder', bright blue, flowers from July to September and there are also good dwarf mixed hybrids.

Eschscholzia (Californian poppy) H.A., 1–$1\frac{1}{2}$ ft. These gay little poppies are easily raised from seed; in fact they seed themselves happily without being a nuisance. There are many varieties of *E. californica*, single, semi-double and double, in shades of yellow, orange, copper, carmine and ivory. For a hot, sunny bed there are few annuals of equal merit.

Felicia (kingfisher daisy) H.H.A., 4–6 in. Almost creeping in habit, *F. bergeriana*, is decorative on the rock garden or the front of a sunny border in light soil. Sow under glass in March and plant out in the open in early May. A profusion of small intense blue flowers is produced from June onwards. In dull weather the flowers open only partially to reveal the yellow centre.

Gaillardia (blanket flower) H.H.A., $1\frac{1}{2}$ ft. Perhaps not so well known as the perennial gaillardia, the annual *G. pulchella* has gay crimson-purple flowers tipped with yellow from July to October. The stiff, wiry stems make them useful for cutting. 'Indian Chief' is a striking copper-scarlet. Sow under glass in gentle heat in March, or in the open ground

Above: Helichrysum monstrosum, an Australian 'everlasting' provides much colour in the garden and may be cut and dried for winter decoration purposes
Below: Gazanias, otherwise known as treasure flowers, are among the most brilliant of all half-hardy annuals
Right: The 'Monarch' strain of godetias is low growing and consists of a variety of colours. The plants are suitable for bedding purposes
Below right: One of a number of colour forms of *Dimorphotheca* 'Buff Beauty', a half-hardy annual popularly known as star of the veldt

Below : Sweet William *(Dianthus barbatus)*

flowers are in a wide colour range. Sow in spring in light, well-drained soil and a sunny position where the plants are to flower.

Godetia H.A., 1–2½ ft. Gay plants with big, coloured cups, these are among the most popular of hardy annuals. There are dwarf and tall varieties, double and single, in shades of pink, mauve, salmon and white. The tall kinds make graceful cut flowers. Sow in March or April or in the autumn where they are to flower as seedlings do not transplant readily. They like a sunny position and a light soil.

Gypsophila (baby's breath) H.A., 1½ ft. The annual varieties are fast growing and when sown in the open in April will flower from June onwards. To ensure a continuity of flower sow at intervals of two or three weeks. Seed may also be sown in the autumn for spring flowering. *G. elegans* produces slender stems bearing dainty white flowers and 'Rosea' has pink flowers. They thrive in any good garden soil, preferably chalky. The flowers are admirable when used in arrangements with sweet peas, or to mask the stiffness of gladioli.

Helianthus (sunflower) H.A., 3–7 ft., or more. The giant sunflowers are useful for providing a quick screen and the seeds in the plate-like golden-yellow heads are a great attraction to birds in the autumn, but there are other sunflowers of greater garden merit and of more reasonable height. Seed should be sown in the open in April or in boxes under glass and seedlings planted out in mid-May. They like plenty of sun and are not fussy about soil. 'Autumn Beauty' (3 ft.), sulphur-yellow with copper zone; 'Sunburst' (4 ft.), a decorative multi-coloured strain are among the numerous varieties.

Helichrysum (everlasting flower) H.H.A., 1½–3 ft. The Australian helichrysums are the best known of the so-called everlastings. They are decorative in the garden in full sun and in a light soil and when cut and dried they are welcome for winter arrangements. The double form 'Monstrosum' of *H. bracteatum* has a popular range of colour – crimson, rose, silvery-pink, bronze and white. There are similar colours in dwarf, compact varieties which make bushy plants for the front of the border.

Helipterum H.A., 1–1½ ft. These Australian 'everlastings' are easily raised from seed sown in April where they are to flower. They do best in poor, well-drained soil and in full sun. The neat globular pink flowers are pleasing and there are also double pink and double white varieties.

Heliotropium (cherry pie, heliotrope) H.H.P., 15–24 in. These fragrant evergreen plants are really greenhouse perennials but hybrid varieties may be treated as half-hardy annuals. When sown in February in pots without a check, they can be planted out towards the end of May and will flower in the open from July onwards. The colours range from dark violet to lavender and white. 'Marine' is a splendid violet-purple; 'Marguerite' is dark blue with a white eye.

in April where plants are to flower. Choose a sunny position and well-drained soil.

Gazania (treasure flower) H.H.A., 6–9 in. These sun-loving, broad-petalled, daisies from South Africa are easily raised from seed sown under glass in a moderate temperature in March. Seedlings should be planted out in mid-May in full sun and a light soil. The modern hybrids are in shades of yellow, orange, brown, pink and ruby. The markings and zones of contrasting colours in the centre

of the flowers add considerably to their beauty.

Gilia (Queen Anne's thimble) H.A., 1½ ft. The blue, pincushion-like flowers and fern-like foliage of *G. capitata* are a delight from June to September. The dainty heads of *G. tricolor* (bird's eye) are in shades of lavender, pink and white with gold throat. *G. hybrida* (*Leptosiphon*) do not exceed 6 in. in height and are decorative on the rock garden or between flagstones in a path. The small, star-like

Iberis (candytuft) H.A., 6–15 in. *I. coronaria*, the rocket or giant-flowered candytuft, and *I. umbellata*, the common candytuft are most effective when sown in bold masses, but this does not mean sowing thickly. Sow in the open ground in September for early flowering the following summer, or in March or April for flowering the same summer. Candytufts do best in moist, rich soil, The dwarf varieties are useful for edging and are obtainable in shades of lilac, rose and white.

Impatiens (balsam) H.H.A., 1–2 ft. The original species (*I. balsamina*) from which the camellia-flowered and other hybrids have been raised comes from India, therefore do not attempt to plant out while there is still a danger of late frost. Sow the seed in March in a warm greenhouse. The dwarf and double varieties make attractive pot plants. The colour range includes pink, salmon, scarlet and white.

Ipomoea (morning glory) H.H.A., 8 ft. or more. This free-flowering twiner is usually catalogued as *I. rubrocaerulea*, although the correct botanical name is *I. tricolor*; to many people it is convolvulus. Call it what you will the large sky-blue trumpets, 4 in. across, are a magnificent sight from July to September. Germination can be erratic, but it helps if the hard seed cover is carefully chipped with a sharp knife. It is worth taking a little trouble with this spectacular plant. Sow the seeds singly in small pots in a warm greenhouse in March and plant out in a warm sheltered place and in well-drained soil in late May.

Kentranthus (often spelt centranthus) (valerian) H.A., 1–1½ ft. *K. macrosiphon* is easily raised from seed sown where it is to flower in a dry sunny position in spring. Blooms are produced from June to August. The grey-blue leaves and bright rose-pink, tubular flowers make this a showy plant.

Kochia (summer cypress, fire-bush) H.H.A., 3 ft. This neat, fast-growing foliage plant is burdened with the name *K. scoparia tricophila*. The finely-cut light green leaves turn coppery-red in the autumn, hence the name fire-bush. Sow the seeds singly in small pots, or three seeds in a 3½ in. pot under glass in April, later thinning to one plant. Plant out in the open in late May. The little seedlings should be watered carefully in the early stages as they are likely to damp off.

Lathyrus (sweet pea) H.A., 1–8 ft. These fast-growing plants, derived from *L. odoratus*, make deep roots and therefore require a deeply dug, fertile, sunny site. To obtain the best results sow the seed in pots or boxes in the autumn and over-winter them in a cold frame (beware of mice). Plant them out in the open in mid-March or early April. They should start to flower in June and, provided fading flowers are removed, will continue in flower for a couple of months or so. When planting out space the seedlings 1 ft. apart in the row and not less than 1 ft. between the rows. It is usual to have double rows growing up pea sticks, or they can be grown up tripods, or on netting firmly supported by strong metal posts, which may be used year after year. Seed catalogues list many fine modern hybrids in a diversity of colour and height, including 'Bijou' (1 ft.), 'Knee-hi' (3–4 ft.) and the early-flowering 'Galaxy' strain, tall, and often producing eight flowers to each long stem. See also Favourite Garden Flowers.

Lavatera (mallow) H.A., 3–4 ft. Easily grown, the annual mallow, *L. trimestris*, has hollyhock-like flowers throughout the summer. Sow the seed sparsely, in March and April, where it is to flower, in a sunny position. 'Loveliness' is the best bright carmine-rose and there is also a pure white variety. Allow these plants adequate space for under good cultivation they may reach a height of 4 ft. and make a bush 3 ft. wide.

Limnanthes (butter and eggs) H.A., 6 in. Sow the seed of *L. douglasii* in an open sunny position in September, where it is to flower the following spring, or in March to mid-May for later flowering. This cheerful little plant of spreading habit has shiny green leaves and bright yellow, fragrant, flowers, white at the tips, much loved by bees.

Linaria (toadflax) H.A., 9 in. Sow the seed of *L. maroccana* thinly in the open ground in March or April to obtain a display of snapdragon-like flowers from June to September. 'Fairy Bouquet' is of compact habit in shades of pink, yellow, lavender and salmon, with large flowers that last well when cut.

Linum (flax) H.A., 15 in. Sown in bold clumps in the open in a sunny position in spring, the scarlet flax, *L. grandiflorum* 'Rubrum', is a most effective summer-flowering annual. The common flax, *L. usitatissimum*, with pale blue flowers on slender stems is also delightful.

Lobelia H.H.A., 4–6 in. also trailing varieties. Seed of *L. erinus* and its varieties, is very small and it is easy to sow it too thickly, which means that it will damp off. Sow in pots containing a sandy compost, only lightly covering the seed with sifted soil. This should be done in February or early March in a warm greenhouse. Prick out the seedlings about a month later; these should become bushy plants ready to plant out towards the end of May. The trailing varieties are useful for window-boxes and hanging baskets but require ample and regular watering. Varieties are available in shades of blue; 'Rosamond' is deep carmine-red with a white eye, and there is a pure white variety.

Matthiola (night-scented stock) H.A., 1 ft. Sow seeds of *M. bicornis* in March or April where plants are to flower during the summer. The lilac-mauve flowers open in the evening and the fragrance on a warm summer night is delightful. Sown with candytuft there will be colour by day and scent by night.

M. incana (ten-week stocks) H.H.A., 1 ft. Sow seed thinly under glass in March and prick out the seedlings when large enough to handle. Give the plants plenty of light and air

and plant out 1 ft. apart where they are to flower when they have made bushy growth. The colour range is all embracing.

M. incana (East Lothian or intermediate stocks) H.H.A., 1½ ft. Sow under glass in February or early March, otherwise treat as for ten-week stocks. East Lothian stocks are vigorous, branching plants flowering in late summer and autumn. In sheltered gardens the East Lothians can be grown as biennials but are usually treated as half-hardy annuals. They are available in crimson, scarlet, rose, lavender, white, or in packets of mixed colours.

Mentzelia (blazing star) H.A., 2 ft. *M. lindleyi* may still be found in some seed catalogues listed as *Bartonia aurea*. Sown in the open ground in March or April, in a sunny position, this easily-grown plant will flower from June onwards. The large, single golden flowers have an attractive mass of golden stamens.

Mesembryanthemum (the Livingstone daisy) H.H.A., 6 in. Of South African origin, this annual, almost always sold under the name mesembryanthemum, but correctly known as *Dorotheanthus bellidiflorus*, requires the maximum sun and a rather dry soil. Of spreading habit it is most decorative trailing over a dry wall or growing in crazy paving. Sow under glass in March or April and plant out in May. The star-like flowers are in a wide range of brilliant colours.

Mimulus (monkey flower) H.H.A., 6 in.–2 ft.

Many mimulus are treated as half-hardy annuals although they may prove to be short-lived perennials. By sowing the seed under glass in March these quick-growing, moisture-loving plants will flower in the open in June and July. Seed sown in the open in partial shade in April will provide a later batch of colour. The seeds are very tiny and should only be lightly covered with sifted soil. The large trumpet-shaped flowers are in shades of red and yellow with attractive markings and blotches.

Moluccella (bells of Ireland) H.H.A., 2 ft. Germination of seed of *M. laevis* is unpredictable; sown under glass in March or April in a temperature of 65°F (18°C) germination may be satisfactory, and on other occasions it may germinate in the open in early May, provided the soil is light and warm. The little white flowers are insignificant; it is the large pale green, white-netted calyces that are so unusual and a delight to flower arrangers. The flowers may be dried for use in winter.

Myosotis (forget-me-not) H.B., 6–12 in. These are easily raised from seed sown in the open ground in June. Transplant the seedlings when they are large enough to handle and plant them out in the autumn where they are to flower. They are admirable when planted with tulips, wallflowers or polyanthus. They will grow in sun or partial shade and seed themselves happily. There are named varieties in several shades of blue and carmine-pink, and also white.

Far left: The Livingstone daisy, *Mesembryanthemum criniflorum* (botanically known as *Dorotheanthus bellidiflorus*), is a half-hardy annual available in many bright colours
Left: The candytuft *(Iberis umbellata)* is most effective when sown to form masses of colour
Above: In an annual bed, brilliant splashes of scarlet can be provided by sowing seeds of *Linum grandiflorum* 'Rubrum'

Mimulus cupreus, sometimes known as the monkey flower, is a moisture-loving plant which flowers in June and July from an early sowing under glass. It is a useful plant for a shady border or around the edge of a pool

Nemesia H.H.A., 8–12 in. Free-flowering little plants in a wide colour range, the varieties of *N. strumosa* are among the brightest of the bedding plants. Sow the seed in mid-March in a cool greenhouse and grow them steadily without a check. Prick out the seedlings into boxes and plant out in late May or early June. Be sure that the soil does not dry at any time. For winter flowering under glass as pot plants sow the seed in August.

Nemophila (baby blue eyes) H.A., 6–8 in. *N. insignis* (*N. menziesii*) is a useful spreading plant for moist conditions, in sun or partial shade. The feathery light green leaves and sky-blue flowers with a white eye make a cheerful picture for the front of a border or on a rock garden. Sow in the open in March or April, or, in sheltered gardens, in the autumn. There is also a white-flowered form.

Nicotiana (tobacco plant) H.H.A., 1½–2½ ft. Fragrance is one of the chief attractions when the flowers usually open in the evening, although if grown in partial shade they often remain open all day. 'Sensation' is a strain with flowers of mixed colours that do remain open in daylight. 'Lime Green' has unusual greenish-yellow flowers, popular for floral arrangements. Sow under glass in a moderate temperature in March. Plant out, when the risk of frost is past, in rich moist soil which has been deeply dug. They flower from July to September.

Nierembergia H.H.A., 9 in. Although strictly a perennial, *N. caerulea*, from the Argentine, is usually treated as an annual and sown under glass in February or early March and planted out towards the end of May. The large, cup-shaped, lavender-blue flowers with an attractive yellow throat are freely produced from July to September. 'Purple Robe' is a selected form with deep violet-purple flowers, with golden anthers.

Nigella (love-in-a-mist) H.A., 1½–2 ft. *N. damascena* is a favourite among hardy annuals and is easily grown. Sow in the open in September in a well-drained soil and a sunny position for flowering from May onwards. Seed sown in March or April will provide a long season of flower. Seedlings do not transplant readily, therefore sow where it is to flower. 'Miss Jekyll', sky-blue with dainty feathery foliage is a fine variety; 'Persian Jewels' is a pleasing mixture of pink, rosy-red, purple and mauve shades, also white.

Omphalodes (Venus's navelwort) H.A., 9–12 in. Resembling a forget-me-not, *O. linifolia*, bears masses of pure white flowers and grey-green leaves on slender stems from June to August. Sow in spring or early autumn in a light, well-drained soil where the plants are to flower. It is a decorative plant for the front of a border or on a rock garden.

Papaver (poppy) H.A., 1½–2½ ft. Easily raised from seed, the diverse annual poppies should be sown in March, April and May where they are to flower. Shirley poppies, derived from *P. rhoeas*, may also be sown in September to flower from May onwards. From the opium poppy, *P. somniferum*, have been raised many fine varieties, including double paeony-flowered and double carna-

Facing page: The brilliant colour range of salpiglossis, a half-hardy annual. Salpiglossis thrive in a rich soil and a warm, sheltered border
Left: Love-in-a-mist (*Nigella damascena*) is among the more popular annuals
Above: 'Pink Chiffon', one of the many varieties of *Papaver somniferum*, the opium poppy, has fully double flowers
Below: In *Nicotiana* 'Daylight', a flowering tobacco, the blooms remain open all day, instead of opening in the evening only

tion-flowered in many different colours. 'Pink Beauty' is a handsome double flower that shows up well against its grey foliage.

Penstemon (beard tongue) H.H.A., 1½ ft. Most penstemons are perennial but there is a hybrid race which is treated as an annual. In mild districts and in a well-drained soil they may survive the winter and start to flower earlier the following year. The elegant tubular flowers are borne on erect stems from July to September in mixed colours; pink, crimson, scarlet, mauve, white. Sow the seed under glass in March and plant out in a sunny place in May.

Petunia H.H.A., 9–15 in. Modern hybrid petunias are available in many different types; large-flowered singles and doubles, compact bedding varieties, pendulous forms suitable for hanging baskets or window boxes, bicolors, self-colours, some with fringed and ruffled flowers. They are sun-loving plants, although some of the new varieties are colourful even in a poor summer. The vigorous F_1 hybrids with large trumpet-shaped flowers of uniform colour are outstanding. Sow the seed under glass in March and grow the seedlings on steadily without a check. Prick out in boxes when large enough to handle and grow them on in the greenhouse. Put them in a cold frame to harden off before planting out in late May or early June in a fairly light soil and full sun.

Phacelia (California bluebell) H.A., 9 in.– 2 ft. P. campanularia, 9 in. has large bell-shaped brilliant blue flowers and greyish-green, red-tinted leaves, which make it a most desirable little plant of neat habit. Sow in the spring in a light well-drained soil and a sunny position, where it is to flower from June onwards. P. tanacetifolia, 2 ft. is a hairy plant with crowded spikes of lavender-blue flowers and is often cultivated by bee-keepers.

Phlox H.H.A., 6–12 in. P. drummondii is a popular, free-flowering bedding plant in shades of pink, salmon, crimson, violet and purple, many with a striking white eye; there are also pure white varieties. The compact varieties are about 6 in. high and the 'Grandiflora' hybrids up to 1 ft. Sow the seed in gentle heat in March and plant out from mid-May onwards in a sunny position, to flower from July until early October. Keep the young plants well watered.

Portulaca (Rose moss) H.H.A., 6 in. The dwarf, spreading P. grandiflora from Brazil requires a hot, sunny position in light well-drained soil. Sow the seed in May where plants are to flower as seedlings do not transplant readily. Cover the seed lightly with fine soil and keep moist until established. Plants make an effective carpet from July onwards. They are usually offered in mixed colours – double and single – scarlet, deep pink, yellow and white.

Quamoclit H.H.A., 10 ft. A fast-growing twining plant, Q. lobata is only suitable for very sheltered gardens or a greenhouse. The flowers are bright crimson, changing to orange-yellow and fading to cream. Sow the seed in small pots in a heated greenhouse in March or early April and move into larger pots when seedlings are well rooted. Plant out when the danger of frost is past in rich, moist soil.

Reseda (mignonette) H.A., 9–12 in. This is a plant of great charm and delicious fragrance. Sow the seed in light, well-drained soil, preferably containing lime, in April and May, where the plants are to flower. Germination is improved when the soil is made firm after sowing and the seed is only lightly covered with fine soil. By making two or more sowings a succession of flowers will be ensured. 'Crimson Fragrance' bears large, very fragrant, reddish spikes.

Ricinus (castor oil plant, castor bean) H.H.A., 4–6 ft. A decorative foliage plant, R. communis, has bronze-coloured leaves up to 2 ft. across. The flowers are insignificant but the seed pods, covered with soft spines, contain large bean-like seeds from which castor oil is obtained. Sow the seed singly in small pots in March in a greenhouse with a temperature of 60°F (16°C). Pot on the seedlings and plant out in June. Plants thrive in rich, moist soil but will probably need staking.

Rudbeckia (coneflower) H.H.A., 2 ft. The gay annual rudbeckias are easily raised from seed sown under glass in March and planted out in May in a sunny position. They are not fussy about soil. Listed in seed catalogues under *R. bicolor* 'Golden Flame' is a golden-yellow with a dark centre and 'Kelvedon Star' is deep yellow with a brown central disk and mahogany zone.

Salpiglossis (painted tongue) H.H.A., 2–3 ft. The elegant, trumpet-shaped flowers, many of which are beautifully veined, are in a brilliant range of colour. Sow the seed in a warm greenhouse in February or March. When large enough to handle prick out the seedlings singly into small pots and grow on

varieties should be supported with light twigs in good time or they may be damaged by summer gales. They are available in mixed colours and are admirable for cutting.

Sanvitalia (creeping zinnia) H.A., 6 in. Of prostrate habit *S. procumbens*. A Mexican plant, forms a carpet of small yellow flowers with a bold black centre. There is also a bright yellow double form. Sow in the open where it is to flower in a sunny position and in a well-drained soil in late April or May. Or it may be sown under glass in March and planted out in May. Sown in a bold mass it can be most effective.

Schizanthus (butterfly flower) H.H.A., $1\frac{1}{2}$–3 ft. Usually considered as highly decorative

plants for the cool greenhouse, schizanthus hybrids may be also grown in the garden in a sunny position, sheltered as much as possible from wind. For this purpose sow the seed under glass in a warm greenhouse in March and plant out towards the end of May. There are several good strains, some with beautiful markings on the petals, in shades of salmon, apricot, pink, yellow, mauve and purple.

Senecio (groundsel) H.H.A., 9–18 in. A refined version of the common groundsel, *S. elegans* can be quite effective when grown in a bold group. Sow in the open ground in April or May in a sunny position. Seedlings will transplant if necessary. It is usually obtainable in mixed colours – bright rose,

steadily until they are ready to plant out in early June. They like a rich soil and a warm, sheltered border. They are not plants for a cold, heavy soil and a windy garden, but are admirable as pot plants in a cool greenhouse.

Salvia (sage) H.H.A., 1–$1\frac{1}{2}$ ft. The vivid scarlet *S. splendens*, the scarlet sage, is a tender perennial usually treated as a half-hardy annual. Seed should be sown under glass in February or March in a temperature of about 68°F (20°C). When seedlings are large enough put them into pots singly and grow them on steadily, hardening them off before planting out in a sunny bed in late May or early June. *S. horminum*, H.A., $1\frac{1}{2}$ ft., should be sown in spring where it is to flower. 'Blue Beard' has attractive blue bracts.

Scabiosa (sweet scabious) H.A., $1\frac{1}{2}$–3 ft. Sown in the open in April or May the annual *S. atropurpurea*, or pincushion flower, will make a good show from August onwards. It can be brought into flower much earlier by sowing under glass in March and planting out in May in a sunny border. The taller

Opposite: The half-hardy annual nemesias are available in many bright colours
Above: The scarlet flowers of one of the half-hardy verbena hybrids, provide brilliant colour at the front of this border
Below: Petunias, in various colours, are among the most reliable of half-hardy annuals

Above: 'Picador', an African marigold
Right: Dahlia-like Zinnias, one of their many
flower forms

lavender, pink, white with yellow centre, in
both single and double.

Silene (catchfly) H.A., 9–18 in. From
southern Europe *S. armeria* has attractive
blue-green foliage and rose-pink clusters of
single flowers on erect stems in summer. More
widely grown is *S. pendula*, of compact habit,
with double flowers on 6–9 in. stems in
shades of salmon-pink, rosy-purple, ruby-
red and white. Sow in August or September
where the plants are to flower the next spring
or sow in the spring if the soil is heavy.

Tagetes (African and French marigolds)
H.H.A., 6 in.-3 ft. These are easily raised from
seed sown thinly in a cool greenhouse towards the end of March and planted out in a
sunny position at the end of May. *T. erecta* is
the bold African marigold which makes a
branching plant up to 3 ft. in height. There
are many modern F₁ hybrids in shades of
yellow, orange and lemon. These are an
improvement on the earlier rather harsh
colours. There are also dwarf American
hybrids (1 ft.). Very different are the petite
French marigolds which make compact plants
of symmetrical habit from 6–9 in. high. There
are single and double varieties in shades of
palest yellow, orange, gold and mahogany-
red some with dark foliage.

Tithonia (Mexican sunflower) H.H.A., 4 ft.
A vigorous, branching plant, *T. rotundifolia*
bears large, orange-red, broad-petalled
flowers in August and September. Sow the
seed in March under glass, pot the seedlings
and plant out in a light soil and full sun
towards the end of May.

Tropaeolum (nasturtium) H.A., 9 in., trailing and climbing. *T. majus* varieties are easily
grown provided simple rules are observed.
Do not sow too early as the seedlings may be
ruined by a late frost; poor soil is preferable
to rich which will only encourage leaf growth
to hide the flowers. Late April is time enough
to sow where they are to flower in southern
England. There are single, semi-double and
double flowered varieties in shades of glowing
scarlet, golden-yellow, cherry-rose, mahogany-red and mixed colours. *T. peregrinum*,
the canary creeper, is an attractive climbing
species to 10 ft. from Peru, bearing fringed

golden-yellow flowers from July onwards.
This likes a rich soil and should be sown in
sun or shade in late April or May.

Ursinia H.H.A., 9–15 in. Masses of daisy-
like flowers and graceful foliage make these
showy South African plants a welcome
addition to the summer display. Sow the
seed under glass in March and plant out in
mid-May in full sun and in a light, well-
drained soil. *U. anethoides*, 15 in., has large
brilliant orange flowers with chestnut-red
zone around the centre in July and August.
U. pulchra, 9 in., suitable for the rock garden
or front of the border, has rich orange flowers
with a dark central zone. Several named varieties are obtainable, including 'Aurora', with

a crimson-red centre to the rich orange
flowers, and 'Golden Bedder'.

Venidium (Namaqualand daisy) H.H.A., 2½
ft. Another sun-loving plant from South
Africa, *V. fastuosum*, bears large orange
flowers with a purple-black zone and shiny
black centre from July to September. Sow
under glass in March and plant out in mid-
May in a good loamy soil. Hybrids are
available in pleasing shades of yellow, straw,
orange and cream, their petals attractively
blotched at the base with darker colours.

Verbena (vervain) H.H.A., 6–15 in. The
hybrid verbenas are easily raised from seed
sown in a warm greenhouse in February or
March. Germination may be erratic and can
be delayed for several weeks. Prick out into
boxes and after hardening off, plant out in a
sunny position in May. The compact varieties
are admirable for window boxes or for the
front of a border. The 3 in. clusters of flowers
are freely borne from June to September.
The colour range includes scarlet, rose,
salmon, deep blue, lavender, some with a

white eye, and white.

Viola (pansy, viola) H.B., 6–9 in. Violas
usually have smaller flowers than pansies,
often self coloured, are of tufted habit and
are best treated as hardy biennials. Sow both
kinds in seed boxes in a cold frame in June or
July and keep the seedlings cool and moist.
When large enough to handle prick the seedlings out in rows and in September or
October plant out in flower beds. Do not let
them dry out at any time. They like a rich
moist soil, in sun or partial shade. Sowing
can also be done in March or April in the
open where they are to flower later the same
year. There are numerous special strains,
also winter-flowering varieties.

Viscaria H.A., 6–15 in. Annual viscarias,
mainly varieties of *V. oculata*, are easily grown
in ordinary garden soil. Seed should be sown
in March or April where plants are to flower.
They are free-flowering plants, effective *en
masse* at the front of a border, with showy
five-petal flowers in pink, scarlet, crimson,
blue and white, or as mixed colours. They are
also decorative as cool greenhouse pot plants.

Zinnia H.H.A., 9 in.–2½ ft. Sow the seed in a
warm greenhouse in April. There is nothing
to be gained by sowing earlier as seedlings
are liable to damp off during a cold spell.
Prick out into boxes when quite small, or
singly into small pots. Harden off carefully in
a cold frame before planting out in full sun
and in a rich, well-drained soil in early June.
There is a diverse selection from giant-
flowered and giant-dahlia-flowered varieties,
up to 2½ ft. high, to 'Lilliput' and 'Pompon',
9–12 in. and the American raised 'Thum-
belina' only 6 in. high. The range of colour
includes scarlet, pink, orange, lavender,
yellow and white.

According to the archaeologists, roses have existed for 30 million to 70 million years. Ever since civilization began they have given pleasure. They are referred to in Greek poetry and mythology, the Romans crowned their heroes with them and Shakespeare, Herrick, Keats and other poets sang their praises in their verses. However, roses as we know them now date from the end of the 18th century, when rosarians turned their hand to artificial hybridization. Since then the beautiful complex modern rose has been developed. Because of this complexity a completely new classification, based more on their qualities, remontancy and uses in the modern garden than their botany, is being adopted. In future, for example, hybrid tea roses will be called 'Large Flowered Bush Roses' and floribundas, 'Cluster Flowered Bush Roses'.

Changing living conditions that have made small gardens more popular have created a new approach to roses, which will be assisted by these new classifications. Repeat-flowering is becoming an important factor in selecting roses, because prolonged colour display is an essential in a restricted space. Whereas hitherto the choice has been largely confined to hybrid tea and floribunda roses, gardeners, particularly those with small gardens, should now look at the many other types that the vast rose family can offer and choose those that meet their needs. Gardeners should come to regard roses as flowering shrubs, which they are. Thus their use can be considered without inhibitions and their cultivation will be more easily appreciated.

Hybrid Tea and Floribunda Roses These two types are the most commonly found in gardens. At one time, they were two very distinctly different sorts, with their own characteristics – the hybrid teas producing their flowers singly, or at most in threes, on each stem, and the floribundas, which were more usually single or semi-double, in clusters. However, rose breeders have, by crossing hybrid teas and floribundas, and further intercrossing, developed floribunda roses that have large clusters of perfectly formed hybrid tea-shaped flowers. These are classified as 'Floribundas – hybrid tea type'. Also hybrid tea roses have been bred that produce their blooms in large clusters in much the same way as the floribundas. Excellent examples of these are 'Pink Favourite' and 'Fragrant Cloud'.

These developments are of considerable value to modern gardeners who particularly wish to enjoy hybrid tea roses where their space is restricted. When gardens were larger, hybrid tea and, to some extent, floribunda roses were nearly always grown in formal beds, usually in part of the garden entirely devoted to them. It was an accepted rule that they could be grown only in formal surroundings, although floribundas were permitted to co-exist with other flowering shrubs and plants. Growing hybrid teas in

Roses & Rose Growing

Using Roses in the Garden

formal beds is an excellent manner of displaying them if space allows. Nevertheless, there seems to be little justification for this restriction. In fact, if there is not sufficient space to do otherwise, and they are to be enjoyed, hybrid tea roses must be mixed with other plants in shrub borders, mixed beds and anywhere else where they can be fitted in. Moreover, if it is true that floribundas are suitable for informal positions, then our modern hybrid teas, with their similar clusters of blooms – 'New Generation Roses' as they have been styled – must be equally suitable.

There is another feature, particularly of present-day hybrid tea roses, which renders them less appropriate to formal bedding than those of former days. This is their great vigour, which most of them have inherited from that wonderful parent, 'Peace', that causes them to reach $4\frac{1}{2}$ ft. in height, making them too unwieldy for formal beds, though they can be satisfactorily inter-mixed with shrubs in small gardens. Some of the very tall ones, such as 'Uncle Walter', make excellent specimens in the lawn. Fortunately there are still some low-growing hybrid teas available for those who desire a formal rose garden.

Polyantha-Pompoms Where small areas are concerned, the almost forgotten, very hardy polyantha-pompoms, with their dainty clusters of colourful blooms, are valuable. They rarely grow more than 15 in. tall and can be usefully positioned in the foreground of mixed borders. Some varieties are subject to mildew, but 'Eblouissant', 'Ellen Poulsen', 'Jean Mermoz', and 'The Fairy' are far less susceptible.

Miniatures Even more diminutive are the miniature roses, ranging in height from the deep crimson 'Peon' at 5 in. to the clear yellow

'Irish Mist', a floribunda rose with blooms of hybrid tea shape

'Bit o' Sunshine', which can reach 18 in. All have recurrent-flowering, minute blossoms, that are exact replicas of either hybrid tea or floribunda roses. They are excellent for forward positions in borders, edging, and planting in rock gardens and sink gardens. They are also available as standards and climbers.

Species and Shrub Roses There are great opportunities for adorning modern gardens, with species and shrub roses. Many, such as *Rosa moyesii*, with its profusion of deep red blossoms, followed by large, bottle-shaped, red hips, and the *R. spinosissima* hybrid, 'Frühlingsgold', which is smothered with yellow flowers in May, are too large for most gardens, but there are other more modest growers, that can be planted as specimens in the lawn or among shrubs, as can the very beautiful *rugosa* shrubs, clear rose-pink 'Fraü Dagmar Hastrup', deep crimson 'Mrs Anthony Waterer', and the velvety, dark crimson, almost black, *gallica* shrub, 'Tuscany Superb'. There are also modern shrub roses that are repeat-flowering and not too large. These include the Kordes shrub roses, apricot-yellow 'Grandmaster', light crimson 'Elmshorn', and blood red 'Kassel', and the hybrid musk roses, 'Cornelia' and 'Felicia'. More recently developed are 'The David Austin New English Roses', which include among them the diminutive shrub type roses, crimson and purple 'The Knight' and warm pink, 'The Wife of Bath', both not more than 3 ft. in height.

Rose Hedges An excellent way of enjoying roses, particularly in a small garden, is to make a hedge of them. Suitable ones for this purpose are the white *rugosa*, 'Blanc Double de Coubert' (about 4 ft.), the hybrid musk, 'Penelope' (5 ft.), the floribunda – h.t. type, pink – 'Queen Elizabeth' (6–8 ft.) and the hybrid tea rose, 'Peace' ($4\frac{1}{2}$ ft.).

Climbing Roses The old-fashioned ramblers, such as 'Dorothy Perkins' and 'American Pillar', were once much cherished, but, because they flower once only in the summer, admittedly with a glorious display, and are so vigorous that it is essential that they are pruned and tied in immediately after they have flowered, present-day gardeners have little time for them. Fortunately, since 1930, when the pale flesh-pink, once-flowering 'Dr W. van Fleet', threw a sport, 'New Dawn', which was of the same colour, recurrent-flowering, but far less vigorous, there has been bred from it a range of modern climbing roses, which are very suitable for present-day conditions. In a small garden they can be most effectively used to clothe fences, walls, trellis, etc.

Among the roses that have stemmed from 'New Dawn' are 'Bantry Bay', 'Parade' and 'Schoolgirl'. The German hybridist Wilhelm Kordes, has been responsible for raising another very attractive group of climbers, known as the Kordes climbers or pillar roses.

The typical blooms of
(a) a hybrid tea rose and
(b) a floribunda variety
The difference is
becoming less distinct
as many modern
floribundas have hybrid
tea-sized blooms
Above left: Floribunda
rose 'Copper Pot'
Above right: Floribunda
rose 'Scented Air'
Below: 'Erfurt', a
modern shrub rose

They are all recurrent-flowering and modest growers. The best known are 'Dortmund', crimson with a white eye; crimson 'Hamburger Phoenix'; pale yellow 'Leverkusen', and red 'Parkdirektor Riggers'. Other modern, charming climbing roses are vermilion 'Danse du Feu', 'Golden Showers' and scarlet crimson 'Soldier Boy'. All these are characterized by their modest vigour, variety of colour and repeat flowering and have among them every form of flower that is found in all other types of roses. Mainly because of their long period of flowering, they have largely usurped the position of the climbing sports of hybrid teas and floribundas.

There are various ways in which climbing roses can be used. One trained up a post can form a very attractive specimen or make a colourful high point in a border. They are invaluable for clothing fences and walls, hiding sheds and covering dead tree stumps. They can be trained over archways, pergolas and draped ropes. An excellent use in a small garden is to form a hedge, by making them cover a post and wire fence, which is most space-saving, and with it little nutriment is sapped away from the surrounding soil. Some climbers when left untied, will sprawl over the ground and can be pegged down to cover ugly objects, such as manhole covers and boles of dead trees. 'Albertine', 'Excelsa', 'Max Graf', and 'Ritter von Barmstede' are excellent for this purpose.

They can also be trained to clamber into trees, which brightens them up at a time when they might be rather drab after their spring flowering has finished. This is an effective way in which to have one of the more vigorous climbers in a small garden. The selection of such roses can be made from the following: For trees up to 18 ft. high: 'Sander's White Rambler' and rosy-crimson 'Excelsa'; trees up to 30 ft. high: creamy yellow, tinged salmon, 'Lykkefund' and clear pink 'Climbing Cécile Brunner'.

Standard Roses These are usually hybrid tea or floribunda roses budded at the top of an upright stem about 4 ft. tall. Sometimes species or shrub roses are so treated, e.g. *R. xanthina spontanea* (Canary Bird). In addition, there are weeping standards, which are usually produced by budding ramblers, such as 'Excelsa'. These are particularly beautiful if planted as specimens in lawns. Standard roses are useful for giving height to a formal garden, but perhaps their greatest value is for planting in restricted areas, such as paved court-yards, patios and the like, where they can not only give the pleasure of having roses, but also allow other lovely plants to thrive at their feet.

Choosing and Buying Roses

The purpose for which roses are to be used is an important factor when making a choice. If possible, it is a good thing to make up one's mind regarding the requirements early in the summer. This gives plenty of time to see what best suits the need.

Left: Floribunda rose 'Southampton'

It is better to avoid making a final choice from a rose grower's catalogue, because, good though the illustrations often are, the colours are not always true; this also applies to roses exhibited at flower shows, such as Chelsea, which take place before the normal flowering season, because the roses are produced under glass. It should also be remembered that roses growing in a nurseryman's fields are maidens and, therefore, do not always manifest their ultimate characteristics.

Before making a decision, it is best to see roses growing under garden conditions in friends' gardens, public parks, rose grower's demonstration gardens or the display grounds of the Royal National Rose Society at St Albans. Always go to a reputable nurseryman, because he can be relied upon. Although bargains can sometimes be found, avoid cheap lines unless you are an expert. When buying you must see that the roses have several sturdy shoots emanating from at or near the union and at least three major roots and that they are free from pests, diseases and weeds. The British Standards Institution issue a specification (B.S. 3936 Nursery Stock: Part 2 – Roses, obtainable from British Standards Institution, 2 Park Street, London, W.1.) which is an excellent guide. Even if it is not declared, reputable rose growers supply roses meeting this standard.

Container-grown and pre-packed roses can be bought. They are a little more expensive than bare root roses. Although the choice of varieties is rather restricted, they are valuable for out-of-season planting. Container-grown roses are particularly useful for replacing dead roses in an old rose-bed.

Siting and Preparing Rose Beds

Conditions that Roses Like   Fortunately roses are quite easy to accommodate. They have, however, several dislikes. These are poorly drained soil, deep shade, particularly when the roots of trees deprive them of nutriment, and very alkaline (chalky) soil.

Choosing a Site   The site should ideally be in an open position, sunny for most of the day, preferably with some shade during part of the time. There should be no overhanging trees, although smaller shrubs often give the correct amount of shade and help to keep their roots cool.

Good Drainage   The soil must be well drained, because, firstly, roses strongly object to having their roots continuously in water and, secondly, in well-drained soil, air is sucked through by the water and it aerates the soil in the vicinity of the roots and thus stimulates the activity of the beneficial soil bacteria.

The drainage can be tested by digging a hole, 1 ft. deep and 1 ft. in diameter, and filling it with water. If it does not empty away within a day, it is necessary to improve the drainage. This can often be done effectively by raising the bed with soil well above the level of the surrounding ground or by digging a 2½ ft. deep trench across the bed and filling

it with stones up to 1 ft. from the top and then with top-soil.

Roots of Roses   Like other shrubs, the root system of a rose consists of two types of roots, viz., the tap-roots, which are long and strong so they penetrate well into the soil, giving good anchorage and a life line to more distant sources of water and nutriment, when they are needed; the surface roots, which emanate almost horizontally near the soil surface, collecting from the soil the rose's main supplies of moisture and plant foods.

The Ideal Soil for Roses   Firstly, the top-soil must be friable so that the surface roots can pass freely through it, have a high fertilizer content, which is not easily washed away by rain and it must be able to retain adequate water to assist the absorption of the necessary plant foods. Secondly, there should be beneath it a porous sub-soil, which allows good drainage and which is sufficiently broken up to allow the tap-roots to penetrate without hindrance.

The above soil specification is that of a medium loam, but many gardeners have not got this and it becomes necessary for them to make whatever earth they have in their gardens as near to this as possible. Apart from chalky soil, which will be referred to later, they normally have either clay soil of various degrees of heaviness or sandy soil. The practical difference between these is that sandy soil is very porous and allows rain to flow through it very quickly and is consequently poor, because the plant nutrients are rapidly washed away. On the other hand, clay soil retains the moisture, and, in extreme cases, is likely to become water-logged, but it remains fertile because the plant foods are not flushed out quickly. Thus to bring sandy soil nearer to the ideal, it is necessary to help it to retain water better; and, ideally to make clay more porous and so improve its drainage. Both objects can be achieved by adding humus-making materials, such as garden compost, rotted farmyard manure, peat, etc., although the addition of carbonate of lime or gypsum to clay soil also helps. These materials also serve to improve the sub-soil.

Digging   It is by the process of digging that any soil can be conditioned. There are two main methods that are used in preparing rose beds, viz. double digging and plain or simple digging. Which is employed depends upon the nature of the sub-soil. If it is hard and compacted, it needs to be broken up and then double digging is carried out, but if it is stony or consists of gravel, it is readily penetrable and simple digging can be adopted.

The procedure to be followed for double digging is as under:

(1) Dig a trench about 18 in. wide and 1 ft. deep, across the width of the site. Transfer the excavated top-soil to the further end of the plot.

(2) Break up the exposed sub-soil with a fork to a depth of 10 in.

(3) Incorporate some humus-making materials in the upper layer of the sub-soil and place about 2 in. on its surface.

Climbing and rambling roses are easily trained over archways. The construction of various different patterns of archways is described elsewhere, under 'Handyman Gardener'
Firmly constructed trellis-work provides admirable support for climbing and rambling roses
Below: 'Chaplin's Pink Climber' is a popular variety

(4) Dig a second similar trench, adjacent to the first, using the excavated top-soil to fill the first.

(5) Break up the sub-soil and add humus-making materials as in (2) and (3).

(6) Proceed similarly with further trenches until the last is reached. This should be filled with the top-soil transferred from the first.

The procedure for plain or simple digging is as follows:

(1) Excavate a trench of similar dimensions as given above and transfer the soil to the further end of the site.

(2) Fill this trench with soil produced by digging an adjacent trench, incorporating humus-making material in it as the work proceeds. Leave the sub-soil untouched.

(3) Continue this procedure until the last trench is reached. Then fill this one with the soil removed from the first.

Where the soil is very chalky, incorporate copious quantities of humus-making material in the course of digging.

Renovating Old Rose Beds Sometimes, when restoring an old, neglected garden, it is necessary to replace some very old, weakened or dead roses. The soil in which roses have grown for perhaps ten years or more, for some

reason which is not clearly understood, will not sustain new roses, despite the fact that established ones continue to flourish in it. This soil condition is known as 'rose sickness'. Replacement roses should not therefore be planted in it.

There are two ways to deal with this situation. The soil in the bed is removed to a depth of 18 in. and replaced by other soil in which roses have not been growing. As other plants are not affected, the old soil can be put anywhere where roses are not to be grown.

The second method, which takes about two years, is to green manure by sowing successive crops of mustard, trampling each down, moistening, covering with sulphate of ammonia and digging it in.

When making a garden provision should be made for making new beds close by the original ones in case replacements are necessary.

If it is only necessary to replace a few roses, this can be effectively done either by digging the soil from a hole, 12 in. across and 18 in. deep and replacing it with fresh soil, or placing in it centrally a container-grown rose with its top soil level with the surface of the bed and filling the annular space around it with *fresh* soil.

Top: The floribunda variety 'Tip Top' is of dwarf, bushy habit
Above: 'Bonn', a modern shrub rose, trained against a wire support

69

Feeding, Maintenance and Pruning

Once roses are planted they are destined to give great pleasure for many years to come. It is well worthwhile, therefore, to take a lot of trouble at this stage to carry out this operation with care. Allow newly dug ground to settle for at least six weeks before planting.

Pre-planting Preparations Usually when bare-root roses are delivered from a nursery they are ready to plant, but if they are not the following should be carried out:

(1) Cut away all damaged and broken roots and shorten unduly long ones.

(2) Remove all immature, dead and diseased shoots.

(3) Tear away at their point of origin any suckers.

(4) If the roses are dry, with shrivelling stems, they should be immersed in cold water for twenty-four hours, after which they will be plumped up.

(5) If the leaves are left on, remove them in order to minimize the loss of moisture while the roses are waiting to be planted.

(6) To reduce the risk of attack by fungus diseases all newly delivered roses should be dipped in a fungicide consisting of 8 oz. of Bordeaux mixture mixed with 2½ gals. of water, before planting.

A planting mixture should be made, consisting of a large bucketful of moist peat, two handfuls of sterilized bonemeal and one of hoof and horn meal.

Roses must not be planted during a severe frost. They should be stored in a frost-proof place until it is warmer. If they are in a polythene bag, they will be all right for two to three weeks, but after this they should be unwrapped and kept covered with damp sacking to keep them moist. Roses packed in paper should be unwrapped immediately and treated similarly.

Roses should not be planted out in soggy ground. If it is very wet they should be placed in a trench in a sheltered spot, their roots well covered with soil and trodden in and allowed to remain there until it dries up.

Time of Planting Bare-root roses can be planted at any time during the winter in open weather. Preferably it should be done, however, during October and November or from February onwards so as not to risk the possible deleterious effect of severe winter weather. Container and pre-packed roses can be planted at any time, but during a dry period, they should be copiously watered.

The distance apart roses are planted depends upon their vigour. Generally speaking, most bushes are satisfactory when placed 20 in. apart, but for more vigorous ones, including species and shrub roses, this distance might be safely increased to 30 in. upwards, according to their ultimate span.

Planting procedure When a bare-root rose has centrally-growing roots a hole is dug of such a diameter that the roots can be well spread out, and of such a depth that it is an inch or so greater than the distance between the enlarged portion on the stem (the union), where it was budded, and its crown, from where the roots radiate. Two good handfuls of the planting mixture are mixed with the soil at the bottom and heaped up to a 1 in. high central hump. The crown is positioned on this, the roots spread out and more planting mixture placed on top of them. After moving the plant gently up and down to eliminate air pockets the hole is filled about one-third with soil, then, holding the tip of the rose to prevent the union lowering, the soil is trodden in, working inwards to the central stem. The rest of the soil is added, left loose and levelled off. In heavy soil and wet weather treading must be done very lightly.

For bush roses with side-growing roots a wedge-shaped hole, which has about the same width as that for a rose with centrally growing roots, is dug. One side of it should have a slope of about the same angle as the roots are to the vertical stem. The planting mixture is mixed with the soil on this slope and the rose placed on it in such a position that the union is just about in the earth's surface. The roots are then spread out without any of them crossing. A further quantity of planting mixture and soil is put on top of them. Air pockets are eliminated by moving the plant up and down. The hole is then about one-third filled with soil and trodden in. This should begin above the tips of the roots and continue towards the stem. As before the top of the plant should be held to prevent it being lowered. The rest of the soil is then added, left loose and levelled.

To plant a container-grown rose, dig a hole deep enough for the surface of the soil in the container to be level with that of the bed, and wide enough to leave a 2 in. annular space all round it. Cut away the bottom of the container and remove the side by slitting it vertically. Gently pull out one or two short roots from the root ball. The rose should be put centrally in the hole, the annular space filled with soil and gently firmed.

Planting Climbing Roses Climbing roses are planted in the manner described for bush roses. If the position is at the base of a wall, the soil is usually dry there. It is better, therefore, to plant about 15 in. from it and train the shoots back to it. In addition a better choice for this purpose is a climber with side-growing roots, because they can be placed so that their ends are some distance from the wall, where more water will be available.

Planting Standard Roses The depth of planting a standard rose depends upon

whether its root-stock is briar, which has large thorns, or *R. rugosa*, which is recognised by its many spines. If the root stock is briar, the depth is as for bush roses, but where it is *rugosa*, it must be quite shallow, i.e. about 3 or 4 in. down. Otherwise the procedure is exactly as for a bush rose.

As standards are liable to sway in the wind, they must be staked. A stake, which should be 1 ft. longer than the distance between the crown of the rose and the union, is driven in between the spread-out roots, when planting, so that they are not damaged by being cut through, to such a depth that its top is just below the union. The stem is tied to the stake, using a special rose tie or tarred string with sacking or other fabric wrapped round the bark to protect it, at points just below the union, just above the soil and midway between these two.

Feeding Roses

Roses need to be kept regularly fed, but like human beings and animals they do not want to be overfed, and certainly not with the wrong foods. What they like most of all is a well-planned diet given to them at the appropriate times of the season.

In addition roses are thirsty plants and need copious quantities of water. It is important to water whenever there is a dry spell, no matter how early in the season it might be, and not just during a heat wave, when their leaves are drooping, because by then it might be too late. Without a good supply of water roses are unable to manufacture their food,

absorb the raw materials for this process from the soil and maintain the level of sap so that it can transport them to the places in the tissues, where they are converted.

Some gardeners think that organic or natural fertilizers are more beneficial to plants than inorganic or chemical ones. This is not completely true, because unlike animals, plants can only absorb plant food as simple chemical compounds. These are provided immediately by inorganic fertilizers, whereas the beneficial elements in organic fertilizers, which are complex substances cannot be taken up by the roots until they have been broken down into simple chemicals by the action of soil bacteria, which might take some weeks. Both types have their place in plant nutrition, because the organic fertilizers supply vital foods regularly over a long period and help to ensure their continuous presence in the soil, whereas the chemical fertilizers make supplies available to meet emergencies and special seasonal needs. Any nutritional advantages of organic fertilizers lie firstly in their soil-conditioning qualities as humus makers and the fact that they are sources of unspecified quantities of trace elements, required by plants in minute quantities. If inorganic fertilizers are used alone these have to be added.

Roses, like other plants, manufacture their own supplies of starches and sugar from carbon dioxide from the air and water from the earth through the agencies of the green colouring matter in the plants (chlorophyll) and sunlight. This is carried out in the vast majority of plants in the leaves. A good supply

Left : Many climbing and rambling roses may be grown as pillar roses, rather than trained against walls or fences. Some of the more vigorous shrub roses may be treated in the same way. This makes it possible to take advantage of the height of such roses where a wall or fence is not available.
Below : Where space is restricted, as it is in this garden, it is often preferable to grow roses in a formal bed. *Above right :* 'Paul's Scarlet Climber' on an old wall, forming a backing to a border of perennials. Space should be left between the border and the wall.

of moisture is necessary for this operation to be successful.

Apart from starch, however, roses need other vital substances if they are to flourish. Among these are proteins, chlorophyll, enzymes, nucleic acids and all sorts of other complicated compounds. These are all built up in the tissues from various elements that are obtained from the soil. This means that for good health, these must be continuously available in the earth. To be sure of this, it is necessary to feed.

Plant Foods These are divided into two groups, the major nutrient elements, and the minor nutrient elements or trace elements.

Nitrogen is a constituent of many of the most vital substances used by a rose. It is, therefore, essential for the maintenance of good health, but too much is bad, because nitrogen encourages leaf-growth and if given lavishly, produces lush growth, which is often weak and falls an easy prey to disease and frost. Nitrogen compounds should not, therefore, be put down late in the season. In addition, excess nitrogen encourages roses to grow abundant foliage at the expense of flowers. Plants deficient in nitrogen usually look feeble and have yellowish leaves.

Phosphorus (Phosphate) is also a vital constituent of rose foods. It is beneficial by encouraging earlier growth, the ripening of the wood, hardening plants to resist winter conditions and improving the root systems. Its shortage is manifested by stunted growth and leaves that are tinged red.

Potassium (Potash) plays a leading part in plant growth. Without it, stems are brittle and roses are very vulnerable to disease and frost. Also parts of the plant, where winter food supplies are stored, such as roots and seeds, are poorly developed. Roses deficient in this element usually have leaves that are yellow at their tips and round their edges.

Calcium not only helps to condition soil and keep it from becoming excessively acid, but is also important to roses because it is essential to the efficient working of the tissue cells. It is not very frequently deficient, but when it is, it is signified by malformation of the young leaves as they appear.

Magnesium is an important component of chlorophyll, which is essential to the food manufacturing process of roses. A severe shortage can be noted by the yellowing of first the older leaves and then the young ones.

Plant Foods Minor Nutrient or Trace Elements. Iron and Manganese are two of the most important trace elements because they are closely associated with the production of chlorophyll. Where they are deficient the younger leaves yellow, still leaving their veins green. (See Chlorosis.)

Other trace elements are copper, boron, molybdenum, and zinc.

1. Where large, perfectly formed blooms of hybrid tea varieties are needed for exhibition or for other purposes, it is often necessary to disbud. Remove surplus buds, indicated by the red lines, as soon as they are large enough to handle.

2. The red lines indicate where both hybrid tea and floribunda roses should be pruned in their first spring to ensure ample new growth and a good shape. **3.** This shows how hybrid tea roses are pruned in their second and subsequent springs. First cut out dead, diseased, weak and inward-growing shoots, then prune as indicated by the red lines.

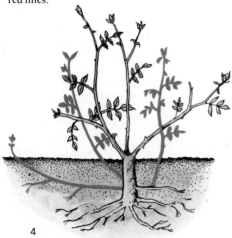

4

4. Suckers, shown in dark green, should be torn away, not cut, from their points of origin on the roots. **5.** This shows how to prune floribundas in their second year. After all unwanted wood has been removed, the spent flower clusters are cut from the previous year's growth (that emerging from the base) at the first or second outward-growing bud below them. The side shoots emerging just below them are pruned to three or four eyes from the main stem. All other stems are pruned to halfway. During the third and subsequent years, the dead clusters are removed similarly and all other growth, including that growing from just below the flower head, is pruned to half the length it attained last season. **6.** Incorrect pruning: the cut is too long and may not heal properly. **7.** Incorrect pruning: the cut has been made too close to the bud, which may in consequence be damaged. **8.** Incorrect pruning: the cut has been made too far from the bud and the shoot will die back. **9.** The right way to prune: the cut is sloping, level with the base of the bud opposite to it, finishing $\frac{1}{4}$ in. above it.
Far right: Rosa foetida bicolor, the 'Austrian Copper Brier', has bright orange-red single flowers from midsummer onwards.

A Feeding Programme A programme for feeding roses begins late in the winter after supplies of nutriments have become diminished. The first thing to do, preferably in February, provided the snows have gone, is to lay down a foundation for the future by distributing an organic fertilizer, which will break down over the ensuing months into simple chemical compounds and ensure that there is a basic supply that can be steadily absorbed by the plant. If it can be obtained, the substance to distribute is meat and bone-meal at the rate of two handfuls per square yard. Good substitutes are equivalent quantities of sterilized bonemeal, fish meal and John Innes Base Fertilizer.

Fertilizer is next applied in the spring, not earlier than April. This time it is a chemical fertilizer, which supplements the elements provided by the organic fertilizer, particularly when heavy rain has washed abnormally large quantities of a particular element away, or rapid growth, due to favourable weather conditions, has suddenly increased demand and so on. Generally, it is more satisfactory to put down a proprietary, ready-mixed rose fertilizer, of which there are several on the market. It is important to use one that is blended for roses and not a general fertilizer intended for vegetables, because sometimes the latter contains muriate of potash which is deadly to roses. Such rose fertilizer is distributed in accordance with the manufacturer's instructions. Usually these mixtures contain the trace elements that are needed by roses.

Although it is a lot more trouble, gardeners may mix their own fertilizer for roses. A recommended mixture is: Nitrate of potash 3 parts, Sulphate of ammonia $1\frac{1}{2}$ parts, Superphosphate of lime 8 parts, Sulphate of potash 4 parts, Sulphate of magnesium 1 part, Sulphate of iron $\frac{1}{4}$ part.

This is distributed at the rate of 2 oz. (about a handful) per sq. yd. once in April and again in May. Twenty pounds of this mixture is sufficient for 200 roses during the season.

It is important that no chemical fertilizer is applied after the end of July, otherwise lush growth might be produced, which will not withstand the winter.

Foliar Feeding This takes advantage of the fact that leaves absorb nutrients from liquids sprayed on them. It is not a substitute for the regular feeding programme, but something that can meet an emergency. There are several good foliar feeds on the market. They are best applied in the early morning or in the evening, but never in hot sun.

Rose Maintenance

Apart from pruning and fighting pests and diseases, which are discussed later, the maintenance of roses is not an onerous task.

Spring Ensure that any roses loosened by the ravages of winter weather are well trodden in.

Make sure that any broken stakes, posts, trellis, etc. are replaced or repaired. Particular attention should be paid to renewing worn out sacking that is protecting the bark and retying. This can often be done when the ground is too wet or too frosty to work.

Mulching helps to keep the soil moist, keeps its temperature steady, gives the roses a cool root-run. In addition, as the substances used for mulching provide humus they help to condition the soil and supply slowly-released plant foods. A mulch also keeps down weeds. It is also claimed that, because

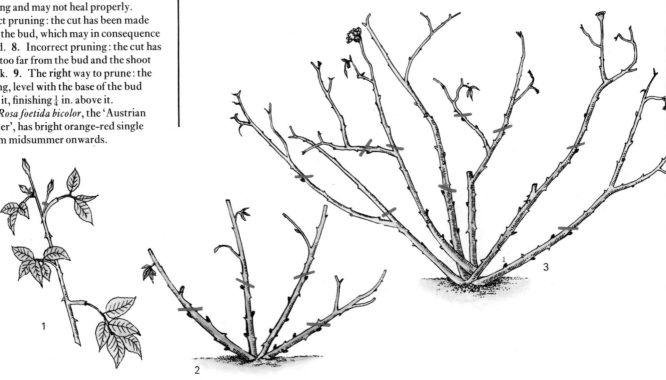

1

2

3

it prevents rain from splashing up from the ground on to the lower leaves of a rose bush, it reduces the spread of blackspot.

Rose beds should be mulched in May, when the soil has begun to warm up. A mulch is a layer, upwards of 2 in. thick, of an organic material. One of the best is well-rotted garden compost. Other suitable substances are moist peat, spent hops and rotted farmyard manure. Leave a small ring around the base of each rose, to avoid the risk of damage being done by the heating up of the mulch as it decomposes.

Summer Because weeds steal the moisture and plant foods intended for the roses, their suppression is important. The principal methods of doing this are: physical methods i.e. regular hoeing; mulching and chemical methods. The two main types of chemical weedkillers are:

(1) Contact: this type of weedicide is watered on to the leaves of the weeds in spring and summer. The chemicals are absorbed and the weeds soon die.

(2) Pre-emergent: this sort interferes with the growth of the seedling leaves and they do not emerge from the soil. It is applied in the winter.

Often during the spring, three shoots emerge from one bud centre. As soon as they are large enough to handle, the outside growths should be pinched off, and the centre one, which is usually the largest, should be allowed to develop.

Suckers are shoots that originate low down on the rose tree or beneath the ground. They grow from the root-stock and not the scion or budded variety. If they are allowed to remain, they sap nutriment from the main stems. The most satisfactory way of discern-ing a sucker is to note from which position it originated. If the shoot appears from below the union or from the root, it is a sucker and should be torn out, not cut away, at its point of origin, scraping away the soil, if it appears from below the ground. By tearing it out, the whole budding system is destroyed and there is little chance of it reappearing (see figure 4).

Some hybrid tea roses, instead of growing one terminal bud, develop three on a stem, while others grow their flowers in clusters. Disbudding consists in removing all the side-flowering shoots, when they are just large enough to handle, leaving one terminal flower-ing bud. Whether this is carried out is largely a matter of personal taste. Nothing should be done if a good, massed display of colour is desired, but if large perfect individual blooms, say for showing, are required, it should be carried out (see figure 1).

If there is to be good repeat-flowering, removing the spent blooms, as soon as they fade, is essential. The stems should be cut off at the first outward-growing leaf with five leaflets to avoid removing too many leaves, in which the plant produces its food.

When watering, the blooms and the leaves should not be wetted, because the former will become blemished and moisture on the latter will encourage fungus diseases. The use of a perforated hose, turned upside down and interwoven among the plants avoids these possibilities.

Autumn and Winter To prevent bush roses from being whipped by winds, cut back tall stems in November to halfway.

Roses should be sprayed, or watered, in December with 8 oz. of Bordeaux mixture mixed with $2\frac{1}{2}$ gals. of water, to minimize the effects of fungus diseases.

Modern Ways of Pruning Roses

In recent years there have been conflicts of opinion on various aspects of pruning. There is little need, however, for worry if it is borne in mind that roses are flowering shrubs. As far as pruning is concerned these are classified as either plants that bloom on the new wood produced during the current season or they flower on last year's shoots. The first types are pruned in late winter or early spring and the second as soon after flowering as possible. Nearly all roses except true ramblers fall into the first class, while the ramblers bloom on the previous season's wood and must, therefore, be pruned immediately after flower-ing. True ramblers are not so numerous in gardens as they once were.

Most shrubs go on growing until they are mature, but roses grow shoots, which, when they get to a certain size, wane and ultimately die and are replaced by new ones. This is a form of natural pruning, but as these dying shoots sap nutriment from the younger vigorous ones and are also potential centres for diseases it is the practice to encourage the growth of new shoots by cutting back the old, spent and diseased wood annually.

There are additional reasons for pruning. Among these are (a) to shape and restrict the shape of the plants to fit in the space allotted to them (b) to control the habit (c) to maintain youthfulness by encouraging the growth of new shoots from the base and (d) to restrict the number of flower shoots, when large exhibition blooms are required.

The Technique of Pruning The most common pruning tool is a pair of secateurs. It is essential that they are always kept very sharp; blunt secateurs may crush the stem,

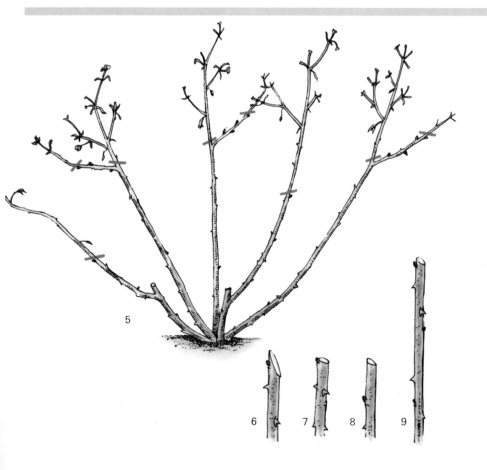

giving an opening for diseases to attack. The better tool is a pruning knife, which should be kept sharp by continuous whetting. It is not difficult to use and it is worthwhile learning how to do so.

Long-handled pruners are heavy-duty cutters, used for removing tough and old wood. Pruning saws are of value for cutting out stout stems; a pad (keyhole) saw is a useful pruning instrument because of its great flexibility.

Because of the risk of spreading diseases when pruning dip tools in an antiseptic solution when a badly affected tree is pruned. One recommended is a 10% solution of tri-sodium orthophosphate, which can be bought at a chemist's.

When to Prune
With the exception of true ramblers, roses are pruned during the winter or early spring. Exactly when depends upon the location and degree of exposure of the garden. The proper time to prune such roses is when the sap is just beginning to rise. In the south and milder places this is usually February, while in northern and exposed gardens it can be up to six weeks later. At this time, the cut will heal quickly, but in late spring or early autumn, the shoot will bleed and, if a frost comes, damage is likely to be caused.

Ramblers are pruned in the late summer, soon after their flowers fade. So that they do

not become unruly, the new shoots that remain should be tied in at the same time.

How to Prune
If a rose of any sort is examined, it will be found that each of its shoots has buds, which alternately point in opposite directions, i.e., in a bush rose they are outwards and inwards towards its centre. In pruning a bush rose, the cut is made just above an outward-pointing bud, as it is desirable to keep the centre open with no inward-growing shoots crossing it, or where a horizontally-trained shoot of a climber is being pruned, it would be an upward pointing bud, because it is in this direction that growth is required.

The proper way to prune is to make a sloping cut, which begins level with the base of the bud on the side opposite to it and ends at a point on the same side as the bud, which

is at a distance of ¼ in. from the base of the eye (see figure 9).

Unfortunately cutting is not always done properly and the following faults occur (see figures 6–8):
(1) The shoot is cut too far away from the bud. It then dies back and becomes exposed to fungus infection.
(2) The shoot is cut too close to the bud with consequential damage to the bud and malformation of the new shoot.
(3) The cut is too long, resulting in an excessive amount of pith being exposed, which prolongs the time of healing of the wound.

Bear in mind that if the cut is jagged the tissues will be damaged and may become a possible seat of infection.

Whenever a rose is pruned, always:
(1) Cut out all dead and diseased wood.
(2) Cut out all weak shoots, because while they remain they are using nourishment, that is required by the more robust ones.
(3) Remove all growth that is growing in the wrong direction.

Types of Pruning
Three different types of pruning are practised by rosarians:

HARD PRUNING This consists in cutting a shoot back to three or four buds from its base; e.g. in a bush rose to an outward growing bud and at a point which is usually 5–6 in. from the ground.

MODERATE PRUNING In this form of pruning, a shoot is cut back by about half its previous year's growth.

LIGHT PRUNING Here there is very little cutting away; usually the dead flowers or hips are removed by cutting at the first or second eye below the flower-bearing stalk.

Pruning Hybrid Tea and Floribunda Roses in the First Year
These should be hard pruned in the first spring after they have been planted, i.e. cut back to the third or fourth outward-growing bud from their base, to ensure that as many new shoots as possible spring from low down on the bush and that it

---

Left: Roses grown in formal beds. In such instances it is best to confine one variety to each bed. *Right:* A more natural effect is produced by growing roses informally

---

grows into a well-balanced, compact shape. If this is not done, the bush soon becomes leggy and unsightly (see figure 2).

SUBSEQUENT PRUNING OF HYBRID TEA ROSES The present-day roses, which are very vigorous, a quality that many have inherited from 'Peace', do not take kindly to hard pruning. In the main, they should be moderately pruned, otherwise they do not bloom so plentifully in the summer.

It is the modern practice to prune hybrid tea roses moderately, i.e. to cut their shoots back by half their previous year's growth. However, because of their great vigour, many soon become very tall and rather unwieldy for present-day small gardens. There are two ways in which this can be largely overcome.
(1) Moderate prune all shoots except two. These are hard pruned, i.e. cut back to two or

three buds from the base of the bush. This procedure can be repeated in successive years, selecting each time a different pair of shoots.
(2) Hard prune the bush every three years. This method seems to keep its size under control without any serious lowering of its flowering-power (see figure 3).

The second method is the better.

Pruning Floribunda Roses
Because the original floribundas stemmed from polyantha-pompom roses, they were first lightly pruned, i.e. only the clusters of dead flowers were removed. Because of their great vigour, this resulted in unwieldy bushes. When they were moderately pruned like modern hybrid teas, they lost their repeat-flowering, whereas with hard pruning they failed to grow and tended to die. The modern technique, aimed at keeping them in flower over a long period, is a combination of light pruning to produce early flowers and moderate pruning, which gives flowering shoots that produce colour later in the season. During the first year they are hard pruned, but, the procedure in the second year is slightly different from that of the third, which remains uniform for the rest of their lives. This modern technique is given below:

Pruning Floribunda Roses in their Second Year
(1) All the main shoots, which are the previous year's growth, and grown from the base

of the tree, are lightly pruned by cutting out the clusters of dead blooms at the first and second eye, whichever is growing outwards, below their base.
(2) Secondary shoots which have developed below the clusters should be cut back to three or four eyes from the main stem.
(3) All other shoots, which are emerging from the shoots that were hard pruned in their first year, should be cut back to half their length (see figure 5).

Pruning Floribunda Roses in their Third and Subsequent Years
(1) All one-year-old wood, that emanates low down on the bush, should be lightly pruned by cutting out the dead flower heads.
(2) All the remaining shoots are moderately pruned, i.e. they are cut back to about half their length.

Right: Rose 'Alec's Red'

Pruning Standard Roses Standard hybrid tea and floribunda roses are pruned in the same way as their dwarf counterparts. The object should be to preserve always an open centre to the head. With hybrid tea standards, moderate pruning is usually the best.

Pruning Weeping Standards The most effective of these are Group 1 Ramblers (see under 'Pruning Ramblers and Climbing Roses'), that have been budded at the top of tall stems of briar or *rugosa*. All the old wood, that has flowered is cut out near to their base as soon as the blooms are spent in the summer. The current year's growth is allowed to remain and flower the following season.

Pruning Polyantha-Pompom Roses After all dead, diseased, weak or inward-growing shoots have been removed, cut away clusters of dead flowers in late winter or early spring.

Pruning Shrub and Species Roses Apart from removing the dead blooms regularly, which enhances their power to repeat-flower, all that shrub and species roses require is to have cut away surplus growth to keep them in shape and their size under control. After some years, however, they tend to become bare at the base. This can be remedied by cutting one or two of the older shoots back to an outward-growing bud about 9 in. from the base. If this is done annually for two or three years, the roses will be completely rejuvenated.

Pruning Miniature Roses These roses, in the main, need to have diseased or dead wood and spent blooms only cut away, apart from any necessary thinning out and trimming to shape and size. Pruning is best done with a pair of nail scissors.

Pruning Ramblers and Climbing Roses There are four groups:

GROUP 1 RAMBLERS These climbing roses produce nearly all their new shoots from the base. The group includes 'Dorothy Perkins', 'Excelsa', 'François Juranville' and 'Sander's White Rambler'. All ramblers flower on the previous season's growth and it is necessary to prune them soon after they finish flowering in the summer. Pruning is done by cutting out all the old shoots at the base. At the same time it is equally as important to tie in all the new shoots, which will bloom in the following summer (see figure 10).

GROUP 2 RAMBLERS These mainly produce their new shoots at points on the old wood higher up the tree. Examples are the old ramblers 'Albéric Barbier', 'Albertine', 'American Pillar', 'Chaplin's Pink Climber', 'Easlea's Golden Rambler', 'Emily Gray' and 'New Dawn'.

The old wood is cut back to a point where a robust, young, green shoot emanates. This leading shoot is left and tied in ready for next year's flowering. All the shorter laterals are pruned back to a bud, 2 or 3 in. from where they originate. Old wood that has no new leading shoot should be removed to prevent overcrowding. This type of rambler tends to become bare at the base. This can be remedied by cutting one or two stems down to a bud 1 ft. from the ground (see figure 11).

GROUP 3 CLIMBERS This group contains the more vigorous climbing sports of the hybrid teas and floribundas, the stronger-growing large-flowered climbers, such as 'Casino' and 'Coral Dawn', and the climber 'Mermaid'.

The time to prune these is either late autumn or winter, and not in spring after the new growth has appeared. None of last year's new shoots should be pruned unless they are damaged or are occupying too great a space. All exhausted wood should be cut away and the laterals that flowered last year reduced to the third eye from their points of origin.

Most of these roses, especially the climbing sports should not be pruned in their first year, because the latter are liable to revert to their dwarf stature.

GROUP 4 CLIMBERS Included in this category are the climbing sports of 'Iceberg', 'Korona' and 'President Herbert Hoover', the large-flowered climbers, which are typified by 'Elegance', 'Golden Showers', 'Handel', 'Rosy Mantle', 'Schoolgirl' and 'White Cockade', the *Kordesii* climbers or pillar roses, 'Ritter von Barmstede' and 'Dortmund' and the Bourbon climber 'Zéphirine Drouhin'.

This group needs little attention other than a general clearing out of unwanted growth and pruning to control shape and size. During their first year remove only any dried out ends of stems, together with any dead wood and very twiggy shoots.

❧ Keeping Roses Healthy ☙

Roses are attacked by various pests and diseases. To fight them, it is important to be able to identify them and know what action to take.

Regular spraying with a chemical compound is important. As most, and foliar feeds as well, are mixable, labour can be saved by spraying simultaneously for various purposes. More recently it has been discovered that continuous spraying with the same preparation causes pests and diseases to become resistant. Thus frequent changes are desirable.

There are different types of sprayers, but the cheapest and most useful is the pressurized plastic kind. It need not be large—a 2 pt. size is adequate for 150 plants.

Pests These can be divided into two categories, viz., *sap-suckers*, which include greenflies and red spider mites and *leaf-and-bud-eaters*, such as caterpillars and sawflies.

Nowadays there are two types of insecticides: *systemic insecticides*, which enter the sap by absorption through the foliage and are used against the sap-sucking insects, and *contact insecticides*, which destroy leaf- and bud-eaters by direct contact with them. Systemics are of no value against the latter, because they do not imbibe sufficient sap to poison them.

The systemics are effective for about one month after spraying, whereas the contact types must be applied whenever the insects appear. A number of proprietary insecticides are mixtures of both.

Do not spray too soon, because the larvae of ladybirds, hover flies, lace-wing-flies and braconid wasps, which are the natural enemies of greenflies (aphids), appear at about the same time as the caterpillars. It is better to hand pick the latter and destroy them rather than spray them.

So that gardeners can detect hostile pests and diseases, their indications are given below.

Pests: Sap-Suckers GREENFLIES (APHIDS) These small green insects breed rapidly and soon engulf the rose trees; they are sometimes pink, red or brown in colour. By sucking the sap, they reduce the vigour of the plant, cripple the shoots and distort the leaves, which ultimately fall prematurely.

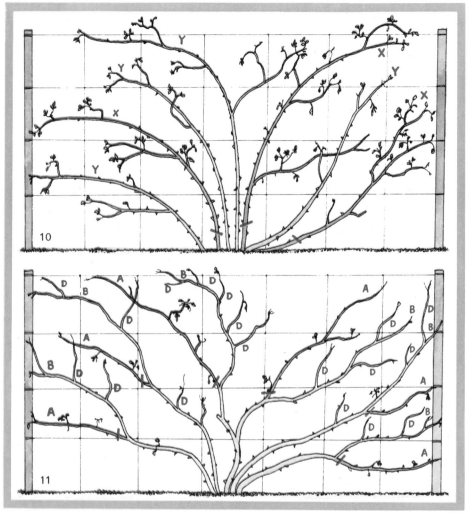

They must be dealt with expeditiously because not only do they damage the roses, they also exude a sweet, sticky fluid, honeydew, the natural food of the fungus, sooty mould, which by coating the leaves, interferes with their normal functioning. In addition, they are carriers of virus diseases.

THRIPS (also known as *Thunder-flies*). These small black or brown insects sometimes swarm all over roses, particularly in thundery weather. Their immature forms which are coloured pale pink to reddish, suck the sap. If they are present, leaves become mottled in appearance, young shoots are malformed and affected buds produce damaged blooms.

CAPSID BUGS The small, green wingless nymphs of these insects distort the leaves and flower buds. Often dark brown areas, which are sometimes mistaken for black spot, appear on the leaves.

RED SPIDER MITES These pests attack outdoor as well as greenhouse roses. They are very minute, red insects, that are so immobile that they may be mistaken for specks of dust. Their presence is shown by the development of a fine, silken web under the leaves, in which they live and breed. The leaves of infected roses become mottled and off-colour. If badly attacked, they turn yellow and fall. There is also loss of vigour.

Leaf and Bud-Eating Insects CATERPILLARS These, the larvae of moths and butterflies, manifest themselves in various ways, which include holes in the leaves, skeletonizing of the leaves, rolling of the leaves and injured buds. Sometimes they exude a sticky fluid.

LEAF-ROLLING SAWFLIES The adults of these insects are like queen ants. They deposit their eggs in the margins of the leaves, accompanied by a toxic fluid, which causes the leaves to roll and hang down.

ROSE SLUG SAWFLIES The larvae (grubs) of these insects usually devour the upperside of leaves and skeletonize them.

Diseases The principal diseases of roses are due to parasitic fungi, and do damage by stealing vital foods from their tissues.

BLACK SPOT This disease is well-known to all rose growers. Its attacks are at their worst in August and September, but it can strike at any time in the season.

It is recognized by the appearance of black or dark brown spots on the leaves, often initially the lower ones. They gradually increase in size and join together. The remaining part of the affected leaf becomes yellow and the leaves eventually fall off, leaving the plants bare.

No garden roses are immune from attack from this disease, but there are some that are less susceptible. A list of varieties that have been found to be more resistant to fungus diseases is given on the following page.

Hitherto fungicides used against black spot have been contact types, which form a protective coat, which must be renewed at intervals of a week or so, with more frequent

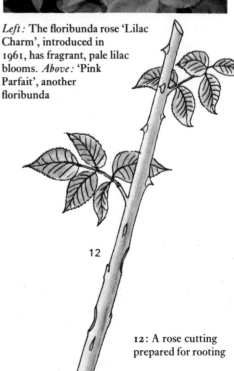

Left: The floribunda rose 'Lilac Charm', introduced in 1961, has fragrant, pale lilac blooms. *Above:* 'Pink Parfait', another floribunda

12: A rose cutting prepared for rooting

applications in wet weather. None of the compounds recommended provide a complete cure. Now there are systemic fungicides, however, that are effective against both black spot and mildew.

MILDEW This starts with white or greyish white spots on the young leaves and eventually spreads all over the plants, making them look as if they have been dusted with flour. The leaves become distorted. Dryness at the roots often makes plants susceptible to mildew. Thus by keeping roses well-watered, the incidence of the disease can be reduced.

Fortunately there appears to be a few garden roses that are very highly resistant to attack. These are listed on the right.

RUST This has three characteristics: it only seems to attack roses in certain areas in this country, it often remains for two years or so and then disappears, and its spores need to be frozen to germinate and attack the following year. The last two might be connected, because a mild winter might prevent freezing. The disease appears in April as rust-coloured swellings on the back of the leaves. In June, orange-coloured spores develop. These germinate and the infection is widely spread. Later in August, they turn black and in this form they live over the winter.

DIEBACK AND CANKER A stem on a rose will often turn brown and die. This can be the result of several different things, including frost damage, lack of water, careless pruning, causing jagged edges or being cut too high above a bud, the snapping of hardened shoots by high wind or rough handling, and by a fungus disease. The latter is *true dieback*; when the effect arises out of any of the other causes, it is commonly, but erroneously called 'dieback'.

Another fungus disease, stem canker, infects wounds, the cut end of stems after pruning, especially when blunt cutters are used, and dormant buds, which ultimately leads to browning and dying back. The first signs are yellow or reddish spotted or streaked, pimply or water-saturated portions of the stem. The brown area eventually extends some inches down the stem, usually terminating in a reddish-brown border where it abuts healthy tissues. Whatever may be the cause, the only remedy is to prune an affected stem back to a healthy bud, or cut it out altogether, if it has reached the union, otherwise the tree might die.

CHLOROSIS This is not a true disease, but an ailment, mainly caused by deficiency of iron and manganese. This can occur as far as the plant is concerned in soil in which there are ample quantities of these elements present, but where they are in a form in which they cannot be used by the rose, as often happens on alkaline (chalky) soil. The symptoms are yellowing of the leaves and stems in spring-time. They often eventually shrivel up and drop off. Also growth is stunted.

This condition cannot be remedied by distributing ordinary, simple compounds of iron or manganese. If it is serious, the soil must be watered in spring with a proprietary formulation which contains chelates of iron and manganese in a form that can be absorbed by roses, together with active magnesium, which is another vital plant food.

A Selection of Roses that are More Resistant to Fungus Diseases

HYBRID TEA ROSES
Alec's Red, Alexander, Blessings, Colour Wonder, Ernest H. Morse, John Waterer, Peace, Pink Favourite, Rose Gaujard, Silver Lining, Troika, Wendy Cussons.

FLORIBUNDA ROSES
Allgold, Apricot Nectar, Arthur Bell, Dickson's Flame, Elizabeth of Glamis, Golden Slippers, Lilac Charm, Pink Parfait, Queen Elizabeth, Scarlet Queen Elizabeth, Scented Air, Southampton.

Propagating Roses

Because of their complicated pedigrees, roses, except the species, do not reproduce faithfully from seed. Hence they are usually propagated by budding; nevertheless the more vigorous can be rooted from cuttings. Reds and pinks are normally successful, but not yellows. They are, however, not so vigorous as when budded.

Growing from Cuttings Hardwood cuttings, 1 ft. long and $\frac{1}{4}$ in. in diameter are taken in August or September, by cutting horizontally just below a lower bud and with a slanting slope above an upper eye. The lower leaves are removed, leaving two upper leaves, and also the eyes with a wedge-shaped cut (see Figure 12).

Place them 6 in. apart, in 2 in. of sand in a narrow wedge-shaped trench, which is filled with soil and gently trodden in, keeping them vertical. They should then be well watered. Rooting can be encouraged by wetting their lower ends and dipping them in hormone-rooting powder before planting.

In the autumn of the following year the rooted cuttings can be transplanted to their permanent quarters.

Budding Roses Budding is the process of uniting the rose cell tissue to that of a related plant, which has well-developed roots. The latter is called a rootstock. The most commonly used rootstocks are briar (*R. canina laxa*) and *R. multiflora* ('simplex') for bush roses and *R. rugosa* and briar for standards. Rootstocks are considered better when they are raised from seed.

The budding knife is a razor-sharp, pointed knife, with a handle with a thin, wedge-shaped end for lifting the bark.

The seedling rootstocks are planted about 8 in. apart, preferably in a straight line in a spare plot in February or March. The neck, i.e. the part between the first green shoot and the root fork, should be about 1 in. above the ground. For convenience when budding, they should be put in sloping towards the spot where the budder will ultimately work.

The shoot selected to provide buds should be one on which the blooms have just faded. As it should be fresh when the buds are taken, it should be left on the bush until the rootstock has been prepared.

In July or August on a day following rain or copious overnight watering, the soil is scraped away from the neck of the rootstock and it is washed clean with water. Next the budder to assist him in his work, should press the rootstock down with his knee to give him good access to the neck.

About 1 in. above the root fork, a cross-cut, about $\frac{1}{3}$ in. wide is made with the budding knife. Then from a point $\frac{3}{4}$ in. below it, a lengthwise cut is made to form a T-shaped incision with it. At the finish of making this cut, the bark is carefully lifted slightly with a twisting movement of the blade. The bark along the whole length of the slit is raised, using the wedge-shaped end of the handle (see figure 13).

To take a bud the selected shoot is cut, the thorns removed and the leaves trimmed back.

The budding knife is inserted into the stem about $\frac{1}{2}$ in. above a bud near its middle and the bark is cut thinly behind the bud until the blade is about that distance below it (see figure 14). The loosened bud is next gently torn away, taking a thin slip of bark with it (see figure 15).

Behind the bud there will be at this stage a thin layer of wood, which can be exposed by pulling away the strip of bark a little. This sliver of wood is removed, using the thumbnail, with a twisting movement (figure 16).

The bark containing the bud is next trimmed to form a wedge-shaped tongue on the side below it, so that the insertion into the incision on the rootstock is made easy (see figure 17).

Holding the small piece of leaf that has been left, the bud is next fitted into the T-cut on the rootstock, with the wedge-shaped end downwards. The lifted bark of the rootstock is replaced and the portion of bark above the bud is trimmed off in line with the horizontal cut (see figure 18).

The bud is made secure, either by tying with two turns below and three turns above of raffia or plastic budding tape. If the remaining piece of leaf-stalk dies in about three weeks, it is a sign that the bud has taken. The fastenings eventually rot away (see figures 19, 20 and 21).

In the following January or early February, when the weather is dry and frost-free, the rootstock is cut away at a point about 1 in. above the bud.

In the case of a *multiflora* ('simplex') rootstock, particularly, the young shoot might be torn away by high winds and it should, therefore be supported with a stake.

Budding Standards Except that their buds are joined to the rootstock at the top of a vertical stem, the budding procedure is the same as with a bush. In a briar rootstock, the buds are inserted in side shoots, whereas with *R. rugosa*, they are put into the main stem. As the ties do not rot, they must be cut after four weeks. The newly-budded roses are ready for planting out in their permanent quarters in the following October, or thereafter in suitable weather conditions.

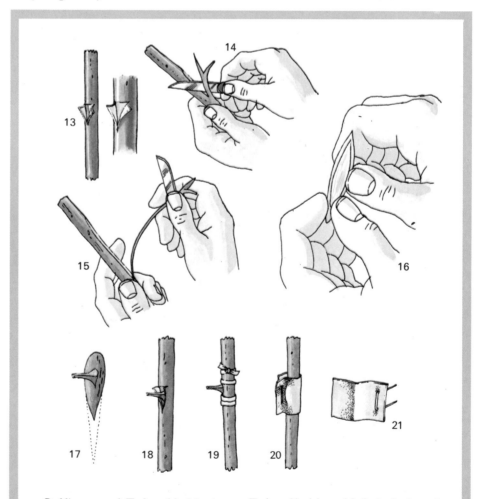

13: *Budding a rose:* A T-shaped incision is made in the bark and the bark is raised. 14: cutting out the bud. 15: The bud is gently torn away, taking a thin slip of bark with it. 16: The sliver of wood remaining is removed with a twisting action of the thumbnail. 17: The strip of bark is trimmed off so that the end below the bud is wedge-shaped. 18: The bud is inserted in the T-shaped incision, with the bark trimmed level with the horizontal cut. 19: The bud is tied in with raffia or plastic tape. 20: The bud fastened with the patented Fleischauer Tie, which consists of a patch of rubber fastened with a metal staple. The remaining leaf stalk is carefully cut away without disturbing the bud. 21: The patented Fleischauer Tie

One Hundred Roses Described

To enable gardeners to decide whether a particular rose is suitable for a purpose, their heights and vigour have been included, but it must be remembered that under very good weather and rich soil conditions, these are likely to be greater. The heights, unless specified, are graded as below: *short*: up to 2 ft. 3 in.; *medium*: 2 ft. 6 in.–3 ft. 6 in.; *tall*: 4 ft. upwards.

Hybrid Teas

Alec's Red This has large, full, perfectly formed, wonderfully perfumed cherry-red flowers, borne on strong stems. It is vigorous, a little under average height.

Anvil Sparks A unique rose with sweetly scented coral-red blooms, punctuated with golden yellow stripes and spots. It grows as a low compact bush. It can be used both in forward positions in borders and for bedding and its blooms are good for floral decoration.

Blessings It has full, fragrant, coral pink blooms with long pointed buds. Its growth is vigorous, bushy and branching. Medium height. Excellent bedding variety and very attractive for flower arranging. Resistant to disease.

Blue Moon The silvery-blue, full, shapely flowers are very fragrant. It is vigorous, of medium height. Good for floral decorations. The best of the 'blue' roses.

Bonsoir The large, full, well-shaped blooms are deep apple-blossom pink in the centre, paling to shell-pink on the edges, highly fragrant. It is vigorous, of medium height.

Chicago Peace With its rich pink, canary yellow and copper tones, this has been aptly described as a 'polychrome'. It has large, well-formed, slightly perfumed flowers. It is vigorous and tall-growing.

Double Delight An outstanding rose with unusual colouring. The centre petals are cream with crimson edges, the outer petals predominantly crimson. Medium height.

Duke of Windsor This rose is brilliant orange-vermilion. It has very fragrant, full blooms of moderate size. It is vigorous, but forms compact, bushy plants that are not more than 2 ft. tall. It is a little prone to mildew.

Ernest H. Morse The blooms are a striking rich, turkey-red, full and of good form, very strongly scented. It is vigorous, upright growing tall and disease resistant.

Grandpa Dickson Its lemon-yellow, very full, shapely, slightly scented flowers, fade to creamy yellow with a flushing of pink on their petal edges. Vigorous and tall, it is generally healthy. Long-lasting in water and excellent for showing and floral decorations.

John Waterer This has deep rose-red, large fragrant, full flowers, borne either singly or several together. It is vigorous, branching and tall, with strong flower stems, making it excellent for cutting.

Just Joey This has large, coppery-orange, full blooms, which pale towards the edges. Its buds are veined red. It is vigorous, upright and of medium height.

King's Ransom One of the best yellow hybrid teas—a bright shade and a good plant for cutting or bedding. Good disease resistance. Medium height.

Mischief This has beautifully formed, fragrant, salmon-pink flowers, highly resistant to wet. It grows to medium height. Its flowers grow in trusses.

Mullard Jubilee Its strongly perfumed flowers, moderately sized and very full, are a striking cerise pink, borne in clusters, as well as singly. It is robust, of medium height, resistant to diseases.

Peace This famous rose has large, well-formed, slightly fragrant, creamy yellow flowers, edged with pink. It is exceptionally vigorous and tall, and although over thirty years old, it is still a bestseller. Excellent for cutting, showing and borders.

Piccadilly A lovely rose with flowers scarlet, flushed gold, with gold reverses, moderately full and high-pointed, slightly scented. It is vigorous and upright, of moderate height. It is the best bicolour.

Pink Favourite Deep rose in colour, its flowers are large, full, perfectly formed and slightly perfumed, produced in large clusters, or, when disbudded, it produces excellent show blooms, and thus can be used for showing or grown informally. It is vigorous, of medium height, almost immune to diseases.

Red Devil This has very large, perfect, scented, very full blooms, crimson, with a slightly paler hue on the reverse. It is vigorous, healthy, tall, but objects to rain.

Royal Highness White with slight blush pink. It has large, perfectly shaped, sweetly scented blooms on strong stems. It is vigorous, growing just above medium height. An excellent exhibition rose.

Sunblest This rose has deep unfading yellow flowers which do not 'blow' prematurely in strong sunlight, borne on long straight stems. Vigorous, upright and tall.

Troika This has flowers that are bronze, shaded pink, and fragrant. It repeats flowering quickly. It is vigorous, upright-growing, of medium height and appears to be disease-resistant.

Wendy Cussons The beautiful large, well-formed, cerise pink flowers come fairly early. It has a strong old-fashioned rose scent. It is vigorous, upright and tall.

Whisky Mac With its medium-sized flowers, very shapely, strongly scented and golden orange in colour, this is an unusual rose of bushy growth, below medium height.

White Masterpiece Has very large white flowers with some green veining on the young buds. They stand up well to wet weather.

Floribundas

Allgold One of the best of the yellow floribundas, this has scented golden-yellow, well-formed flowers, semi-double and often 3 in. across. It is short and compact in growth.

Apricot Nectar This rose has freely produced, full, somewhat cupped, pleasantly scented, pale apricot flowers, with a golden base. Its flowering season is long. Vigorous, tall and spreading.

Arthur Bell This is another lovely yellow floribunda, with deep golden blooms, that change to creamy yellow with age. They are full, well-shaped, and very fragrant. It is vigorous, grows tall and upright and is usually very resistant to diseases.

Bonfire Night Orange-vermilion, slightly lighter on the reverse, the moderately full, well-formed flowers of this floribunda are produced in shapely clusters. It is a compact grower, of medium height. The blooms are much appreciated by flower arrangers.

Copper Pot This has neatly formed, moderately full, coppery orange blooms, a colour that is popular with flower arrangers. The fragrant flowers are often $3\frac{1}{2}$–4 in. across. It is moderately vigorous but forms a tall bush.

Elizabeth of Glamis This has light orange-salmon, full, finely shaped, fragrant blooms, which are carried in evenly spaced perfect trusses. It is vigorous, upright and little above average height.

Evelyn Fison This has large clusters of semi-double vivid scarlet flowers. It is vigorous, of medium height. Generally it is healthy, but a lookout should be kept for mildew. It faces bad weather well.

Golden Slippers Being short and compact but vigorous, this rose, with its orange-flame inside, gold outside, moderately full flowers, is valuable for small gardens.

Heaven Scent This is outstanding for its delicious fragrance. It is deep pink-rose in

colour and its full, double flowers are well-shaped. It is a strong grower, on the short side in height. It flowers early.

Iceberg The blooms, carried in small or medium trusses, are full, pure white, but the buds are sometimes tinged pink and the flowers are spotted pink in cool weather. It is vigorous and grows tall, sometimes reaching 10 ft. and making a good hedge.

Korresia One of the best yellow floribundas. The blooms, of hybrid tea shape, are nice for cutting but it also makes a good bedder. Medium vigour.

Meteor This rather older floribunda has withstood the test of time. It has brilliant vermilion, full flowers, 2½ in. across. Its growth is branching and short, and it is excellent for small gardens.

News This is a sensational shade of beetroot purple. Its moderately full fragrant blooms are brilliantly lit up by their bright golden stamens. Bushy and compact, it reaches medium height.

Orange Sensation The vermilion blooms are shaded orange at the base, moderately full and fragrant. It is vigorous and branching, a compact bush of medium height. It needs protection against mildew and black spot.

Picasso Its moderately full blooms rather prettily show their stamens in the centre of

It is also very healthy. Its moderately full flowers are apricot-orange in colour with a little flush of scarlet on the outside. It is vigorous, a little over medium height

Tip Top The large, full, salmon-pink blooms are borne in large trusses, produced freely and continuously. It is vigorous, but has a dwarf, bushy habit and is particularly attractive for use in small gardens.

Floribundas–H.T. Type

Courvoisier The strongly perfumed flowers are very full, ochre-yellow in colour and often 4-in. in diameter, borne either singly, or several together, on a stem. It is of medium height, upright.

Irish Mist The reddish salmon-pink flowers are large well-formed and hybrid tea in shape. It is vigorous in growth, of medium height.

Korbell Its abundance of long-lasting, moderately full, salmon-orange blooms with deeper edges makes this rose excellent for cutting and bedding.

Lively Lady The large double, well-formed, bright vermilion blooms have a pleasant scent. It is healthy, of vigorous habit, growing to medium height.

Marjorie Anderson This rose has full, high-centred, hybrid-tea form flowers

cerise-pink in colour. They are produced freely and continuously in clusters and are fairly strongly perfumed. It is vigorous and bushy growing 2½ ft. tall.

Moonraker The flowers which are 4½ in. in diameter are cream, which turns white in hot weather, and which is flushed with honey to amber in cool. The vigorous growth produces a tall, branching bush.

Queen Elizabeth Introduced in 1955, this lovely rose, with its large, pink, moderately full, hybrid tea-shaped blooms, finds a place in many gardens. Its blooms are borne on almost thornless, stout stems, sometimes singly, sometimes in large trusses. Very vigorous and upright, it reaches 6 ft. or more. It makes an excellent hedge.

Polyantha Pompoms

This group, historically important, because its members are the fore-runners of our glorious present-day floribundas, has become neglected in more recent years. With the increasing popularity of small gardens, they could easily come into their own again, particularly because they are dwarf, rarely exceeding 2 ft. in height, and recurrent blooming, bearing their colourful, small blooms in delicate clusters. They are excellent for edging, forward positions and bedding.

Left: 'Arthur Bell' is a floribunda rose with deep golden-yellow, very fragrant blooms
Above: 'Queen Elizabeth', a floribunda rose, has blooms of hybrid tea type. It makes a very vigorous, upright plant
Right: The very fragrant flowers of 'Duke of Windsor', a hybrid tea which grows about 2 ft. tall

the beautiful multicoloured petals. The whole ensemble might be likened to a pink, carmine and white pelargonium. It has a bushy, compact habit and a height of about 20 in. which make it suitable for small gardens. The blooms are excellent for floral decorations.

Satchmo The blooms are full, double and shapely, of the most outstanding, constant, vivid scarlet colour. It is vigorous, but grows a little below average height.

Southampton This has won many awards and is a fine choice for bedding or cutting.

Cécile Brunner This charming rose has tiny, pale pink, perfectly formed hybrid-tea type blooms, growing well-spaced in trusses. It is repeat-flowering. If it is lightly pruned, it makes a good specimen.

Eblouissant The large, scarlet crimson, semi-double blooms are 2 in. in diameter, borne in small clusters. It is very short.

Ellen Poulsen The small, deep pink flowers are very attractive. Growth is vigorous, spreading and height low.

Golden Salmon Supérieure This is an extremely bright, free-flowering rose, about 2 ft. high. Its blooms are a vivid golden-salmon.

Paul Crampel Free flowering, this has large clusters of small, orange-scarlet, semi-double flowers. It is moderately vigorous and makes a compact bush. It is excellent for more forward places in informal settings. Its colour is exactly that of the geranium, 'Paul Crampel', and it is an excellent permanent replacement for that bedding plant.

The Fairy This is very free-flowering with full, pale pink flowers. Growth is vigorous, spreading and low in height.

✿ Miniature Roses ✿

These bijou roses have blooms that are diminutive replicas of the hybrid tea and floribunda roses. The bushes are tiny and the flowers are in proportion to their size. There is a wide range of varieties available, in heights from 4–15 in. They are ideal for small gardens, and rock gardens, sink gardens and window boxes, but should be given a minimum depth of soil of 1 ft. In patios and terrace gardens, they can be most effectively used to create a miniature rose garden in a raised bed. Those marked below with an asterisk are obtainable as standards and it is also possible to buy the following as climbers: 'Yellow Jackie', bright red, 'Magic Wand', bright, rich pink, 'Pink Cameo', and 'Showoff', buff-yellow flowers with red and orange touches.

Angela Rippon The dainty double blooms are bright salmon. Height 12–15 in.

Baby Masquerade An exact replica of 'Masquerade', with its deep yellow buds opening to pink and changing to deep red, this grows 10–12 in. high.*

Easter Morning This exquisite rose has large double ivory flowers. It reaches a height of between 9 and 12 in.*

Little Flirt This has orange-red, reverse yellow, fragrant, full flowers. It is vigorous and reaches 12–14 in. high.*

Rosina (Josephine Wheatcroft) (Yellow Sweetheart) This has small semi-double, slightly scented, rich yellow blooms, in clusters. It grows 12–15 in. high.*

Scarlet Gem The flowers are very double and bright scarlet, on plants 9–12 in. high.*

✿ Climbing Roses ✿

Casino The hybrid tea-type, sweetly scented flowers are deep yellow in bud, soft yellow, when open. It is vigorous and grows to 10–12 ft. It is valuable for pillars and for covering fences. (Pruning Group 3.)

Copenhagen The recurrent blooms are large, full, scarlet and sweetly scented. Vigorous and compact to 8–10 ft., it is a good pillar rose. (Pruning Group 4.)

Coral Dawn This repeat-flowering climber has full, cupped, fragrant, pink flowers. Moderately vigorous, reaching 10 ft., it is a good pillar rose. (Pruning Group 3.)

Hamburger Phoenix This is repeat-flowering with large, rich crimson blooms. It is vigorous and grows to 9 ft. A good pillar rose, it is also valuable because it will flourish on a north wall. (Pruning Group 4.)

Handel This has moderately full, 3½ in. diameter, almost continuously flowering blooms, which are ivory with petal edges suffused a rich carmine. It is healthy, reaches 12–15 ft. and is useful for pillars and fences. (Pruning Group 4.)

Leverkusen A lovely rose, this has long sprays of golden, semi-double flowers, that are recurrent in summer and autumn. It reaches 9 ft. and is effective as a pillar rose, for walls and, because of its long stems, it can be used as a rambler. (Pruning Group 4.)

New Dawn The recurrent, shell-pink, delicately perfumed blooms are borne throughout the summer. It grows to 8 ft. and is useful for pillars, on a wall and as a hedge. (Pruning Group 2.)

Parkdirektor Riggers This splendid repeat-flowering climber, has 3 in. diameter semi-double, rich blood-red, velvety flowers with a golden centre of stamens. Vigorous, to 7–8 ft. tall, it grows well on pillars and north walls. (Pruning Group 3.)

Rosy Mantle The large, fragrant, hybrid tea-shaped, rosy-pink flowers are recurrent and last well when cut. Growth is vigorous, to 8–10 ft. It is a good pillar rose. (Pruning Group 4.)

Schoolgirl This is a recurrent climber in rich, soft copper-orange, with a spicy fragrance. It is vigorous, grows to 10 ft., a good pillar rose. (Pruning Group 4.)

Sympathie The hybrid tea-type flowers are bright red and very full. Vigorous, it grows to 9–12 ft., is useful for pillars and for a wall or fence. (Pruning Group 4.)

White Cockade The white, hybrid tea-shaped, pleasantly scented, recurrent flowers last well. It is vigorous and reaches 7 ft. It is a good pillar rose. (Pruning Group 4.)

Old-fashioned Shrub Roses

Blanc Double De Coubert (*Rugosa*) This has large, richly fragrant, snowy white, semi-double flowers with a buff and green centre. It is repeat flowering. It grows vigorously to 5–6 ft. It is excellent for hedging.

Frau Dagmar Hastrup (*Rugosa*) This has single, pink blooms with delicate veinings, which show their large, creamy centres. It is very free- and recurrent-flowering, and the flowers are followed in the autumn by large, rich red, tomato-shaped hips. It reaches 5 ft.

Mme Hardy (*Damask*) The exquisite, richly fragrant, large, white blooms are flat, perfectly cupped, with folded petals and a green button eye. Vigorous to 5–6 ft.

Mme Pierre Oger (*Bourbon*) This bears cup-shaped, very fragrant blooms, cream, flushed rosy pink, freely throughout the summer. Slender and erect, it reaches 6 ft. It makes an excellent specimen.

Tuscany (*Gallica*) A remarkable rose, with semi-double, intense dark purple-crimson, almost black, flowers, with brilliant golden stamens. It grows into a sturdy bush about 4 ft. tall. Popular with flower arrangers.

William Lobb ('Old Velvet Moss') (*Moss Rose*) The fully double, 3-in. diameter, richly-scented blooms are a medley of fuchsia purple and lilac with grey touches, giving them a shot-silk appearance. It grows vigorously to 7 ft. and is much appreciated by flower arrangers.

Above Left: Although basically ivory in colour, the petals of the climber 'Handel' are richly suffused with carmine, particularly along the edges
Left: The single crimson, yellow-centred flowers of 'Cocktail', a modern shrub rose which blooms well into the autumn
Top: The scarlet, sweetly-scented blooms of the recurrent-flowering climber 'Copenhagen'
Above: 'Canary Bird' (*Rosa xanthina spontanea*) is one of the earliest roses to flower

Modern Shrub Roses

Ballerina The masses of dainty, small, single, fragrant, apple-blossom pink flowers, with a white eye are borne in large clusters. It grows vigorously to about 5 ft.

Bonn The fragrant, moderately full, ver-milion blooms are 3 in. across. It is vigorous, upright and tall and easily reaches 5 ft.

Buff Beauty This rose has buff or apricot-yellow, large, fully double, very fragrant blooms in large clusters. It is repeat-flowering and its blossoms become very plentiful as the summer advances. It has a vigorous, spreading habit and reaches 5 ft.

Cocktail This has single crimson flowers with a pale yellow centre, borne in clusters. It is recurrent and free flowering. It grows up to 5 ft. high. Winter protection should be provided in very exposed gardens.

Cornelia The small, semi-double, very fragrant flowers are strawberry-pink, with a yellow base. It is repeat flowering. Growth is vigorous, to 5–6 ft. and it is excellent for hedging.

Elmshorn The small, fully double, light-crimson flowers, are produced almost continuously until December. Vigorous, upright and branching, it grows to 5–6 ft. and makes a good hedge.

Erfurt The large, semi-single, strongly perfumed citron-yellow flowers are edged brilliant pink. It is repeat-flowering. A very vigorous, bushy plant, it grows to 5 ft.

Fred Loads This is almost perpetual in flowering and produces masses of 4 in. wide, scented, single, vermilion flowers, in large heads. Very vigorous, upright and tall, it grows to at least 5 ft., makes a very good hedge and is excellent as a specimen.

Golden Chersonese A beautiful shrub rose, this has small, single yellow flowers, in May and June along the whole length of its shoots. It is very bushy.

Lavender Lassie A very charming, sweetly scented variety, this bears an abundance of huge trusses of lilac-pink, rosette-shaped flowers, up to 3 in. across. It is moderately vigorous in growth and reaches 4–6 ft. It is valuable for hedging and as a specimen.

Nevada The almost single blooms are creamy, sometimes tinged blush, with bright golden stamens. The flowers straddle the whole length of its arching, thornless branches, throughout the summer. Vigorous, to 8 ft.

Nymphenburg The pale salmon-pink blooms with gold tints are large, full and fragrant, produced periodically in clusters. Vigorous, it reaches 6 ft. and makes a colourful hedge.

Penelope Large, semi-double, very fragrant, creamy salmon-pink flowers are carried in large clusters. As the blooms age, they become off-white. It flowers freely and repeatedly throughout the summer. Moderately vigorous, it grows to 6 ft., and makes an attractive hedge.

The Knight This is another 'David Austin New English Rose'. It has the most beautiful, flat, full-centred carnation-like flowers not unlike those of the old *gallica* rose. The colour is rich crimson with touches of varying shades of purple. A tough grower, reaching 3 ft.

The Wife of Bath This charming little rose is one of the 'David Austin New English Roses', suitable for modern small gardens. It has small cupped, old-fashioned rose-type, warm pink, fragrant flowers. It is vigorous, but reaches 3 ft. in height only.

Wilhelm The flowers are semi-double, about 4 in. in diameter, velvety scarlet-crimson, borne almost continuously throughout the summer in great clusters. Vigorous, 6 ft. high, it makes a beautiful, strong hedge.

Species Roses for Modern Gardens

Rosa moyesii A splendid shrub, this has dusky red, single flowers with cream stamens. These are followed in the autumn by large, bright red, bottle-shaped hips. The dainty, fern-like foliage is dark green. It is very vigorous and will grow to 12 ft.

R. rubrifolia The attraction of this species lies in its lovely bluish-grey foliage, tinged with a deep rosy shade, and its red stems. Its purplish-red flowers are insignificant, but they are followed by attractive dark red hips. It grows vigorously to 6–8 ft., and for the sake of its foliage, it is sought after by flower arrangers.

R. sancta This is massed with 4 in. wide, apple-blossom pink single flowers, fading to white. They have huge golden centres and buds are rich pink. It grows to 3 ft.

R. xanthina spontanea ('Canary Bird') A very lovely species rose with rich yellow, single blooms 2½ in. in diameter. In May or sometimes in April the flowers straddle the long arching stems. It makes a very attractive shrub, 6 ft. high and 6 ft. across.

Colourful Hardy Perennials

No single word or term has yet been accepted to cover garden plants, as distinct from bulbs and shrubs, which flower year after year.

'Herbaceous plants', 'hardy perennials', 'border plants' are all inadequate or inaccurate in some respect. Strictly speaking, the word 'herbaceous' denotes the decay of each season's growth, with the plant itself remaining alive, but dormant. Delphiniums, phlox and many others have this habit but several, including iris and kniphofia do not, because they retain winter foliage.

The time is happily past when hardy perennials were relegated in so many gardens because the rewards they gave were disproportionate to the trouble entailed. One reason was because post-war demands for labour saving forced a swing to shrubs. The conventional herbaceous border was largely at fault because of its long narrow shape with a backing wall, hedge or fence. The plants suffered from overcrowding, weak growth and excessive competition for light and air. Quite often such borders were too narrow in relation to the height of the plants. All this accentuated the main disabilities to which perennials are prone if not given a fair chance – difficulty of access to the plants and the need for supports. Harmful competition between the ranker and the less vigorous kinds, and indiscriminate selection and planting almost invariably lead to trouble.

Adaptability This calls for a fair-minded approach when one considers that nature herself has set the limitations. The majority of garden plants have their origin somewhere in the wild. An original type may have been improved upon by breeding and hybridization, but the varieties or cultivars retain their main parental characteristics, including those of adaptability. A species which for millions of years has been accustomed to certain conditions of soil, moisture, sun or shade can scarcely be expected to flourish so well where its natural preferences are lacking.

Most perennials are adaptable to ordinary garden conditions, but it would be as much a mistake to plant something which naturally prefers shade or moist soil into a dry open situation as it would the other way round. It would also be a mistake to plant something rank or invasive near something that is by nature of slow or lowly growth.

Light and Air The problem of overcrowding is linked to this. Plants need light and air and overcrowding and overhanging by trees or other taller growth, which reduce these inevitably leads to stem weakness. Plants in close competition for light and air become excessively tall and spindly. It is a vicious circle and is the major cause of untidiness and the need for staking in congested borders, or those backed by tall trees, shrubs, hedges, fences or walls. Usually where staking is necessary, it is not the fault of the plants but of the conditions under which they are grown.

Island Beds Some years ago Mr Alan Bloom, the well-known nurseryman, who specializes in hardy perennials, experimented with 'island beds' and showed that not only were the plants shown to greater advantage, with all-round access, but very few needed staking, whereas the great majority had needed supports in the conventional one-sided borders. Although first-year growth was shorter, in succeeding years the growth was just as sturdy, and only such heavy spiked or headed plants as delphiniums and tall Michaelmas daisies needed support. Since then Mr Bloom has constantly advocated island beds as the best means of growing perennials. In the process, he has grown thousands of species and varieties.

Flanking Borders However, the small rectangular plot which most people have, with similar pots on either side, rules out the informality of island beds and such gardens admit of little choice but to go in for flanking borders. Even so in a small or otherwise inhospitable site, there are still ways and means of growing perennials successfully.

Selecting Plants The main thing is to select plants best suited to the place in which they are to grow. The range of available plants is sufficiently wide for this to be achieved, no matter how small the garden, or unkind the soil, so long as it is not completely hemmed in by tall buildings or overhung by large trees to exclude both light and air, and to compete for the available food and water. Even the conventional one-sided border with a high backing can be improved by growing kinds most suitable or adaptable to it. Such borders are usually far too narrow in relation to the height of the plants. Some plants are often invasive and attempts to grow shorter, choicer kinds as well have failed because of unfair competition. What is needed is a new approach, a new appreciation of garden worthiness and adaptability.

The range should include certain hardy bulbs or corms, such as crocosmia, which contribute greatly to the summer display, also certain dwarf perennials. If they are adaptable for growing in front of taller kinds, in ordinary soil conditions, then there are very good

An example of the type of
island bed recommended for
displaying hardy perennials
to their best advantage
Stepping stones behind a
backed bed allow for easy access
to the climbers on the wall
A standard type of back garden,
with two flanking beds
Above: A fine Oriental
poppy, *Papaver orientale*
'King George'

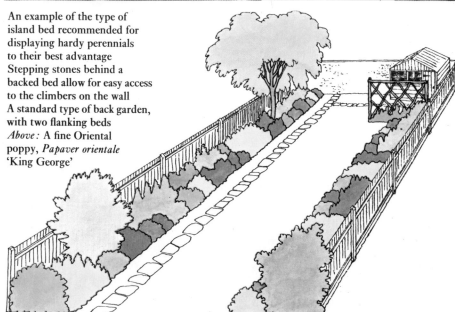

reasons for including them. Plants of, say,
6 to 12 in. tall are by no means out of place as
frontal groups and in small gardens where
beds have to be small, then dwarf plants are
both desirable and necessary.

Sites and Soils

Those moving into a newly-built house must
consider how to make the best use of the
available garden space. It may be completely
bare, a segment of farm or meadow land, and
such factors as slope, exposure, drainage, and
type of soil should be considered carefully.

Prepare the Site   Bearing in mind the need
to select plants best adapted to the site, the
preparation of a bed or border for hardy
plants should include drainage if the soil
appears excessively wet or sticky in winter or
hard baked in summer. Thorough digging
will usually suffice.

Summer and autumn are the best times for deep digging on heavy soil, as this will enable winter frosts to break down hard lumps and sods into a fine tilth for spring planting.

Eliminating Weeds There is a tendency nowadays to avoid manual labour, but there is nothing like hand digging. A spade is still the best tool for lighter soils, but for heavy or sticky soils a strong fork is best. Trenching, or double digging is necessary where there is a pan below the top spit. This will improve drainage and will enable surface-rooting weeds to be buried, but if the second spit is of subsoil then it should merely be broken up or turned over, not brought up to the surface. Perennial weeds, such as couch grass, must be eliminated, either by forking and raking during dry weather, or by weed killers. However, weed killers may be persistent, and they should never be used unless you know the long-term as well as the short-term effect they will have upon plant growth. Annual weeds are much easier to cope with. Contact sprays will kill them off quickly and leave the soil clear for plants within a few days. Normally such weeds as couch grass, mare's tail, creeping thistle and ground elder are so perniciously perennial that drastic measures are needed to kill them. If you are reluctant to use the lethal poisons which will ensure a complete kill, then it is best to fallow the ground rather than risk a permanent bed of hardy plants being ruined by perennial weeds.

Adding Humus On both light, poor soils and heavy clays, humus in the form of peat, compost or farmyard manure should be dug in. This will improve the texture, as well as the fertility of the soil, and give plants such a good start that nothing but occasional top dressings of fertilizer will be needed for years.

Grass-covered Sites This soil preparation applies to any site, new or old, but where the surface is grass covered, a rotary digger can be useful. If the turf is not wanted elsewhere or is of poor quality it will improve the soil fertility if it is buried, provided it is chopped up first. If an open trench is dug across the narrow end of a bed or border, the loose, chopped-up turf can be pushed in, using a spade or fork to cover it well as the plot is dug, trench by trench. Large lumps of turf dug in often result in lack of consolidation as they slowly shrink during the much slower process of rotting. Grassland usually harbours wireworms, but a dusting of a wireworm killer, dug in with the turf or lightly forked in before planting will deal with these pests.

Making Borders Conventional styles in gardening are hard to change, but those who wish to give hardy plants a fair chance will see that there are quite a few variations open to them. There is no doubt that island beds give the best reward, just as narrow, hemmed-in borders give the least return, in terms of value for money and effort in maintenance. An island bed can be sited anywhere provided all-round access is possible, even if it is only a narrow path on one side or end. A backed border can be converted into an island bed provided there is sufficient width. No matter what the backing is, rear access can be provided either by a narrow grass path or paving used as stepping stones. If the backing is a wall, it can be used for climbers and a strip allowed along the foot for bulbs or any of the wide variety of dwarf plants or climbers that like such a spot. The rear part of the bed itself should have as edging groups of dwarf early-flowering perennials such as bergenias, pulmonarias and epimediums, for even if the aspect is sunny, the taller perennials facing the adjoining groups will provide summer shading. This rear strip will prove a source of delight in spring and, even if colour has gone by summer, you still have easy access to the rest of the bed for maintenance work, and there will be far less staking required, because the weakening effect of the backing is greatly lessened.

Width is, however, an important factor. So many conventional one-sided borders are too narrow and should either be widened, or, if this is impracticable, then the tallest plants should be avoided. Some old borders have a gravelled path along the front—and perhaps a low box hedge as edging. In most instances the gravelled path is not necessary and could be dug up and incorporated as extra border width. The box hedging could be removed, as it has little ornamental value and harbours slugs and snails.

Sometimes a border is flanked by a grass path or lawn and this presents no physical problem, if you wish to increase the width of a conventional border, whether or not it is to be converted into a semi-island bed. A curved edge could enhance the layout if the general lines of the garden lend themselves to this treatment. But irregular curves, or a scalloped edge would be out of place if straight lines prevail elsewhere in the garden.

In island beds plants grow more sturdily, are less marred by supporting sticks, and can be viewed from all angles at a more convenient eye level. One-sided beds have become anachronisms; only those on a small

scale, where heights of plants are in keeping with the width of the border are worth considering. If the site is unsuitable for an island bed and you have to have a one-sided border, it will inevitably be more troublesome to maintain, unless you select the plants carefully.

Planning and Planting

Width of Border Whatever type of border you decide to plan and plant its success and potential interest will depend not only on a well-chosen site, well-prepared soil and the right selection of plants, but on its width. The narrower the bed, the lower the plants should be. Nothing looks more incongruous than plants flowering at 4 or 5 ft. in a bed only 4 or 5 ft. wide. They inevitably harm dwarfer, choicer plants growing beside them, regardless of aspect. A safe guide in selecting plants is to measure the plantable width of the border in feet, and halve it to arrive at the maximum height of plants it should contain. This restricts a 4 ft. wide border to plants of no

more than 2 ft. tall, but a little latitude can be allowed for the erect, spikey plants, such as kniphofias, to exceed the limit by a few inches. This is a rule that can be applied to any type of border–island or one-sided, bearing in mind that in island borders the tallest plants are placed in the centre, and in one-sided borders they are planted at the back.

Grouping should also be considered. Where space is very restricted and where variety is preferred, then there is a case for growing one plant only of each kind. But there is never any point in growing a single plant of the same kind in more than one position in the same bed or border. If the site is large enough, then plants should be grouped in threes, at least, in a bed of about 100 square feet in area, and in groups of up to 10 to 15 in the largest beds of a 1,000 sq. ft. or more.

Spacing Plants The space between plants in a group, should be less than that between the groups themselves. This is because the plants in a group will usually grow and mass together effectively when in flower. But they will probably differ in form and habit from neighbouring groups, and will need extra space to allow for this as well as to allow for vital light and air to give sturdy growth and for access for maintenance. The average spacing should be about five plants to the square yard. If, for example, groups are of five plants of a kind, this gives a planting distance of about 16 in. from plant to plant within a group. But the space around the group, up to the outer plants in adjoining groups should be 20 in. Spacing depends on the vigour of the plant; a single plant may occupy a square yard or nine plants of a dwarf, slow-growing plant may occupy the

same area.

Do not allow the more robust or rapid spreading kinds to overshadow or encroach on those that expand slowly. Those plants with a similar habit and vigour should be placed near to each other to avoid harmful competition. If you are prepared to plan you own bed or border, it is better not to use a stereotyped plan unless you are quite sure that the plants offered are suitable for the site. Making your own plan is not difficult. Planning on Paper First obtain a sheet of squared paper–each square inch subdivided into tenths. Using the most convenient scale that fits the paper, draw the outline of the bed or border. Within this outline, group spaces can be pencilled in faintly to begin with, once you have decided roughly on the area each group should occupy –depending on whether variety or a more massed display is preferred. A large variety of plants will call for smaller groups but a square yard at least will be needed if groups are to be large enough for massed colour, depending on the total space available.

It is better to space each group by means of numbers. If there are to be, say, 36 groups in a bed, get the numbers one to 36 down on paper, spaced over the area, and when you are satisfied draw in the outline of each group as indicated on the sample plan. Using the list of plants you have already chosen, the placing of each one becomes a stimulating task, as you take account of height, spread, colour and flowering season. At this stage it is useful to know something about the habits of the plants and this is where the descriptions of the plants which appear later will prove helpful.

Far left: The 3-ft. tall *Verbascum* 'Pink Domino', a modern hybrid suitable for an island bed
Left: Geranium psilostemon (*G. armenum*) is the most brilliantly coloured of the true geraniums or cranesbills
Above: The deep pink, trumpet-shaped flowers of *Incarvillea delavayi* open in May before the dark green leaves appear
Right: The large white flowers of the Christmas rose, *Helleborus niger*, are always welcome when they appear, usually in the New Year
Top: 'September Charm', a 3-ft. tall variety of *Anemone hupehensis*, flowers from August to October

Left: The bleeding heart, *Dicentra spectabilis*
Centre: Hostas or plantain lilies are among the best of foliage plants

Below: Oenothera fruticosa, a good herbaceous perennial

If in the process of making a new bed or border, an error in placing occurs it will show up during the first flowering season. Perhaps a dwarf kind should have been nearer the front or vice-versa, or two colours do not blend well. This matters little, for a switch can easily be made in autumn or spring, provided a note is made when the error is seen.

When to Plant Generally speaking, autumn planting is best–whether you are making adjustments or planting a complete new bed–provided the soil is in clean, friable condition. It may not be possible to obtain delivery of plants from a nursery in early October, the ideal time, but the whole of October is usually safe for planting except on heavy, sticky soils and in the coldest parts of the country. In warmer or drier districts and on well-drained soils, it is safe to plant in November too, except for a few kinds, notably *Aster amellus*, erigerons, pyrethrums, *Scabiosa caucasica*, nepetas and some of the grasses, which it is safer to plant in spring. In autumn the soil is still warm and new roots form quickly, so that in spring plants soon make up growth and do not lack for moisture. Watering in is seldom needed in autumn, but in spring it is often necessary.

Planting Planting a new bed poses few problems if you have a plan. When the consignment arrives, unpack and stand each plant or bundle upright, and sprinkle with water if dry. If the bed or border is all ready with its marker sticks or labels for each group in position, placing will be easy, but do not, if you can avoid it, lay out the plants too early lest sun or wind dry out the roots before they are safely covered with soil. If the soil is wet and sticky, move about the bed on one or two short planks, and do not tread in each plant too firmly. Lighter soils may be too dry, and if when you try to make a suitable hole with a trowel, you find that the soil tends to run back, then puddling is the answer. This is simply a matter of pouring water from the spout of a can, till the hole is almost full. The water will quickly soak away and then you can enlarge the hole sufficiently to take the plant and having inserted it with its roots well spread out, draw round some of the dry top soil and make a loose tilth round the plant.

Watering In spring, the soil is usually moist enough for planting until about mid-April, although even in March the soil can be so dry that puddling is necessary. If, after planting, plants show signs of distress, whether or not they were watered in initially, do not splash water over them. It is the roots that need moisture and a mere surface water-

ing can be harmfully deceptive as it may erode the soil, expose the roots or cake the surface without soaking in. What the plants need is a fine spray; this takes longer, but will penetrate more readily to the roots, with far less waste of water. The same method, preferably using a sprinkler with a fine nozzle, should be used during a summer drought on established plants which are showing signs of distress; it is best done in the evening, and after each overhead watering, especially on a newly planted bed, it is worth hoeing or raking over the surface, as it dries out again, so as to retain a fine tilth, a top layer of loose fine soil $\frac{1}{2}$ in. thick, which enables growth to keep fresh for much longer as water is drawn up from the soil below.

Mulching A new bed, with soil well-prepared will not need feeding for the first year or two if it is reasonably rich in humus. Sand, gravel, chalk or clay soils are often shallow and lack humus. Although leaf mould is hard to come by, peat is easy to obtain and apply, and is an excellent form of humus for such soils. It is useful by itself, either dug in or applied as a mulch that will retain moisture and keep down weeds. But if it is used in conjunction with an organic fertilizer it is most effective in promoting good growth. The best method where plants need both a feed and a mulch, is to apply the fertilizer in March, at about 2 oz. per square yard and immediately hoe it in to the top 2 in. of soil.

The spring-flowering leopard's bane, *Doronicum plantagineum*

This is worth while on any bed or border after the second season, but if a mulch, too, is needed, this should be applied during April or May, depending on weather, type of soil and locality. The soil at this time is warming up, and to mulch too early in late districts may retard growth a little, though it will catch up later. The warmer the district the earlier you can begin feeding, hoeing and mulching. Before peat is used as a mulch it should be thoroughly moistened (dry peat can absorb up to eight times its weight in water); in this condition it is easy to spread over bare patches of earth between the plants to a thickness of $\frac{1}{2}$ to 1 in. If you fork over a bed or border in autumn or winter, a peat mulch applied in spring will largely disappear, though it will continue to do good, as a soil improver.

Winter Digging This also improves the soil structure, although there is always a danger of damaging the roots of plants. This can be avoided by using a flat-tined potato-lifting fork, rather than a spade; the flat tines will keep each forkful more or less intact so that annual weeds can be turned in. At the same time any pieces of perennial weed which may appear can be picked out. Couch grass, ground elder, creeping cress, sorrel, thistle and the like are such nuisances that no effort should be spared to get rid of even the tiniest piece, even if it means taking up a border plant to do so.

Before winter digging begins remove last year's stalks. If you are not going to dig between the plants the dead stems may be cut back to ground level at any convenient time between November and February. This applies only to the truly herbaceous kinds, which lose each season's growth above ground and start growing again in spring. However, any foliage, for example that of kniphofias, that remains green over winter should be left until new spring growth is about to begin and then it is a matter merely of tidying up the decaying or sere outer leaves.

Other Methods of Growing For most people, a bed or border appeals as a well-defined feature in a garden. But hardy perennials may be grown in other ways. Many kinds can be grown in company with shrubs so that both are enhanced. Such erect and troublefree plants as hemerocallis flower from midsummer onwards to add more than a touch of colour to a background of shrubs. Apart from these, the wide range of ground-cover plants form a pleasing carpeting effect over what would otherwise be bare earth between shrubs, and most of these, too, will contribute colour.

Right: Aster amellus, one of the types of Michaelmas daisies

Acanthus (bear's breeches) Acanthus are best grown in isolated positions rather than in a mixed border. *A. longifolius*, *A. mollis* and *A. spinosus* will in time take up more than their allotted space as a group and then curbing becomes an annual task. *A. mollis* flowers less freely than the other two. All have long, jagged glossy green leaves and 3–4 ft. spikes of curiously hooded flowers, lavender-lilac tinged with white. They prefer a sunny place and well-drained soil, and a group by itself or in company with shrubs, can be very effective as they flower from early July onwards for many weeks.

Achillea (yarrow, milfoil) This genus includes a few good and showy plants, but also some of a weedy nature. All have flowers useful for cutting. *A. filipendulina* with plate-like heads of deep yellow on erect 4 ft. stems is deservedly popular. It is easily grown in any well-drained soil and needs the minimum of attention. It is usually offered under the name 'Gold Plate'. Stems cut at their best can be dried for winter decoration. *A.* 'Moonshine', 18 in. canary-yellow, with silvery leaves, is much dwarfer. It flowers from May to July. *A. millefolium* is the native milfoil. Deep pink, and almost red variants, such as 'Cerise Queen' make quite a brave show for a season or two, before they need curbing or replanting back into position. But heads on 3 ft. stems become top heavy and need support, as do the white achilleas, 'The Pearl' and 'Perry's White', both 3 ft. tall with double, button-type, white flowers in loose heads. All should be divided in early autumn or spring.

Aconitum (monkshood) Aconitums are related to delphiniums, but have a hood over the upper part of the flower–hence the common name. Several are good garden plants, and most of them will stand unaided. The hybrid *A. x arendsii* is a first-rate late flowering plant with strong 4 ft. spikes terminating in a bunch of amethyst-blue flowers in September and October. *A. bicolor* has more openly branches spikes on wiry stems about $3\frac{1}{2}$ ft. high and the blue-white flowers give a bright display for several weeks from mid-summer onwards. *A.* 'Bressingham Spire', $2\frac{1}{2}$–3 ft., grows rather like a well-foliaged tapering fir. The leaves are deep green and glossy and the terminal spike has violet-blue flowers, followed by secondary spikes, to cover the August to September period. The vigorous growing 'Newry Blue' flowers in June–July, but both this and the violet-blue 'Spark's Variety' have more open spikes, about $3\frac{1}{2}$ ft. tall. Aconitums should not be left unattended for too long, and if the plants are not mulched, they should be divided and replanted in enriched soil after about three years. This does not apply to the hybrid 'Ivorine', 3 ft., very neat and shapely in growth, with ivory-white flowers from late May to July–August; a splendid plant for sun or partial shade.

Alchemilla (lady's mantle) *A. mollis* will grow in any but the driest, starved situations and in sun or shade, forming a neat, ground-hugging clump of pretty maple-shaped grey-green hairy leaves. From this loose sprays of tiny yellowish-green flowers spread out and up to about 20 in. for many weeks. The plant divides easily and sets seed freely.

Anchusa (alkanet) Bright though they are these are not reliable plants. The popular varieties include 'Loddon Royalist', 'Morning Glory' and 'Opal'. The black, fleshy roots send up large coarse leaves and 4 ft. spikes of small but intensely blue flowers from late May to July. They usually need supporting. After July, there is a somewhat blank space, and all too often plants fail to survive the winter, especially in wetter or richer soils.

Anemone (windflower) *A. hupehensis* (long known as *A. japonica*) can contribute so much to the late summer display that no garden should be without these delightful plants. Though shades of pink and white are the only colours, it is the way their flowers are borne that makes them so charming. Individual flowers ranging from $1\frac{1}{2}$–3 in. across are like dog roses, with yellow-stamened centres. The wiry, branching stems are tipped by nodding flowers and close-set buds. Most varieties begin flowering in late July or early August and will continue until autumn. They need good drainage and a mainly sunny position and they are especially good on chalky soil.

Anthemis (golden marguerite) Most anthemis flower freely and for a long time, but they are short-lived plants, especially the varieties of *A. tinctoria*. The yellow, daisy flowers come on somewhat twiggy, not very erect plants, 2–$2\frac{1}{2}$ ft. high, from June to late August. If the woody rootstock fails to produce new basal growth in autumn plants will not survive. *A.* 'Grallagh Gold' is even trickier than the light yellow 'Wargrave' or 'Mrs Buxton', but the dwarfer species, *A. sancti-johannis*, 20 in., with deep yellow flowers, is more reliable.

Aquilegia (columbine) Very few aquilegias will come true from seed; for those who like a good range of colour and large, long-spurred flowers, such strains as 'McKana Hybrids', about 3 ft. high and 'Biedermeier', 20 in. high, are delightful for a year or two, until replacements are need. They are not fussy plants, and some will grow in shade.

Armeria (thrift) The common thrift is *A. maritima* which has produced some varieties and hybrids of real garden value. 'Vindictive' makes an effective edging; it will make a con-

tinuous evergreen row 1 ft. wide within a year or two. In May and June, it is ablaze with 8 in. drumstick heads of bright carmine-pink flowers. The white-flowered variety *alba* serves a similar purpose. The tallest, largest flowered and brightest armeria is *A. latifolia* 'Bee's Ruby' (the colour is, in fact, a deep carmine). The central root stem just below ground is so bare, that division is seldom possible. Cuttings are not easy to strike but basal cuttings taken in early autumn or spring and inserted in a cold frame sometimes root. Armerias need full sun and a very well-drained soil.

Aster (Michaelmas daisy) The garden would be dull in autumn if no Michaelmas daisies were to be seen. New varieties have been churned out over recent years, and although decided advances have been made, enhancing the range of height, colour and size of flower, it is a matter of personal preference when such a wide choice exists. One can only emphasize the need to choose varieties which do not need staking, and to replant every three years, using only the outer healthier shoots. Spring is the best time to divide asters.

Astilbe Astilbes grown in good moist soil are plants of incomparable beauty. They have attractive foliage and the plumed flower spikes are in every imaginable shade from white through pink, salmon and cerise to fiery red and deep red. Some are erect, others arch and droop, and heights vary from 6 in. to 6 ft. They do not need staking, are completely hardy and can be left alone for years, trouble-free and reliable, though they cannot stand hot, dry conditions. They appreciate a spring mulch to conserve moisture, and they can safely be divided when dormant. In general, the tallest astilbes are the strongest and least fussy about moisture, but these do not include the brightest colours. One of the best of the taller kinds is *A. taquetii superba*, about 4 ft., with straight imposing spikes of an intense lilac-purple shade, in July and

August. *A. davidii*, lilac-rose, and the varieties 'Tamarix', 'Salland', 'Venus', pale-pink, and 'Salmon Queen' are all tall and robust. Given the right conditions, the more colourful dwarfer hybrid astilbes, 1½–3 ft. tall, will flower for much longer, between late June and mid-August. 'Cologne', deep carmine-rose, 'Dusseldorf', salmon-pink, 'Rheinland', early, clear pink, 'Deutschland', a fine white, 'Fire' is intense red shade and 'Red Sentinel' almost brick-red, are about 2 ft. high. 'Glow' at 2½ ft. is stronger and 'Spinell' is another fiery shade. The 2½ ft. 'Federsee' is a rosy-red variety, and 'Bressingham Pink' has fine clear pink spikes. 'Fanal', deep red, is barely 2 ft. high, and 'Irrlicht' is white. *A. simplicifolia* 'Sprite', a sturdy miniature, has very dark foliage as background to the 12 in. ivory pink spikelets.

Bergenia (pig squeak) These are excellent space fillers for any but the hottest driest situations. The large shiny, almost evergreen leaves usually die off in late winter in readiness for the spring flowering period, when the stubby 9–12 in. spikes produce sprays of little bell-shaped flowers, usually pink – rather washy in older species, but deeper, bordering on red in such modern varieties as the dwarf 'Abendglut' (Evening Glow) and 'Ballawley', which is about the largest and finest of all. 'Silberlicht' is a free-flowering almost white shade. Where ground cover is more important than flowers any *B. cordifolia* form or *B. schmidtii* are cheaper. The value of bergenias is their bright foliage from May to March, and their ability to spread fairly quickly but unobtrusively in awkward places.

Brunnera *B. macrophylla* (formerly *Anchusa myosotidiflora*) differs from most anchusas by being a good reliable perennial, with less fleshy roots, forming clumps of rounded leaves which have weed smothering properties all summer. From April to July the sprays of tiny brilliant blue 'forget-me-not' flowers are borne on 2 ft. branching stems. In

Above: The herbaceous border in July. *Left:* The astilbes do best in moist soil. *Below:* Old clumps of Michaelmas daisies are often tough and are best divided by using two garden forks, back to back. Otherwise, as shown on the right, young portions may be removed from the outer edges of the clump and replanted, to save digging up and replanting the whole clump. *Right:* The golden marguerite (*anthemis*) variety 'Grallagh Gold', which flowers from June to late August

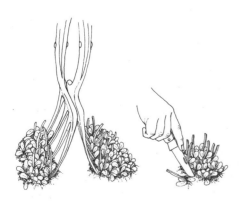

Top: The valerians (*Centranthus ruber* forms) are excellent plants for growing in the crevices of walls. *Left*: *Bergenia cordifolia* is one of the earliest herbaceous plants to flower in spring.

Above: One of the best of all bellflowers for the border is *Campanula lactiflora*, 4–5 ft. tall, available in various colour forms. *Below*: *Achillea filipendulina* 'Gold Plate'

good or moist soil, plants become fairly massive. A bright-leaved form *variegata*, is rather less robust; of its 6 in. wide leaves more than half is primrose yellow. It is best planted where hot sun does not scorch it.

Campanula (bellflower) This is an adaptable genus ranging from prostrate plants to those 5 or 6 ft. tall. With such diversity, recommendations will be easier to follow on the basis of height. The dwarfest, semi-prostrate hybrid 'Stella' can adorn not only a rock garden, a wall top, path edging or the front of a border, but makes a good pot plant for indoors or outdoors. It flowers from June to August, but if cut back, divided and re-vitalized it will flower again in autumn. Cultivation is easy in any reasonable soil, in sun or partial shade.

The varieties of *C. carpatica* are valuable for frontal groups. They are neat in habit, vary in height from 6–12 in. and have upward facing cup-shaped flowers, 1–2 in. across, from June to August. Colours vary from white to violet blue, and though easy to raise from seed, one must obtain named varieties to avoid mixed shades. *C. burghaltii* has long, near opaque smoky blue bells, dangling from 15–18 in. stems from June onwards. It is vigorous but not invasive. *C. vanhouttei* is similar in habit with equally large pale blue bells. *C. glomerata* has many forms; the best of this top-clustered group is *superba*, 3 ft., with upturned violet flowers in June and July. *C. lactiflora* is also variable; the deepest coloured named variety is 'Prichard's', growing erectly to 2½–3 ft., with open clusters of bell-shaped flowers. The pygmy variety of this long-flowering species is 'Pouffe', which makes a green cushion for the light blue flowers from June to September. The tallest, 'Loddon Anna', reaches 6 ft., with heads of near pink; '*alba*' is only a foot or so shorter. All these are reliable plants and will grow happily in shade as well as sun. *C. latifolia* (syn. *C. macrantha*) which flowers in June and July, and it is similarly adaptable, has strong 4 ft. spikes with large blue bells. There is a good white form – *alba*; 'Brantwood' is deep violet-blue, but the near opaque 'Gloaming' is an entrancing pale-sky-blue.

Catananche (Cupid's dart) *C. caerulea* has cornflower-like blooms on wiry stems from June to August. It reaches 2–2½ ft. in well-drained soil. Its faults are lack of longevity and a tendency to loll over so that flowers droop rather than stand up to face the sky, especially in damp weather. It is grown from seed sown in May, or root cuttings taken in March.

Centaurea (cornflower) This genus includes coarse as well as choicer species with heights varying from 2 in. to 6 ft. or more. The deep pink variety *steenbergii* is a great improvement on the species *C. dealbata*; 'John Coutts' is another improved variety with even larger flowers, of a lighter, clearer pink. Both reach 2½ ft. and flower freely in June and July. *C. macrocephala*, 5 ft. has yellow tufty flowers on more massive leafy plants. *C. hypoleuca* is charming with a pro-

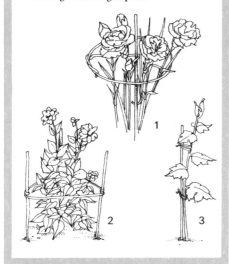

Below: Three different ways of staking and supporting perennials. (1) shows a plant ring, the leg of which is thrust into the ground beside the plant; (2) involves the use of three stakes and soft string or raffia. A single stake is used at (3). The aim should be to stake early so that the supports are hidden as the plants grow.
Right : Dictamnus albus purpureus, the burning bush or gas plant

fusion of clear pink flowers on compact grey-foliaged plants, with wiry, 1 ft. tall flowering stems from late May to July. *C. ruthenica* is distinctive for its shining foliage and gracefully slender 4 ft. stems carrying canary-yellow fluffy-headed flowers from June to August. All centaureas are best divided in early spring. They are easily-grown, vigorous plants, even in poor soil.

Centranthus (valerian) Many a garden would be the poorer without *Centranthus ruber* for it can colonize a neglected garden and can be seen naturalized on old walls as well as in old borders. Unwanted seedlings can be treated as weeds, leaving a group where it belongs to be self-replenishing. It grows 2-3 ft. tall and flowers freely. The usual deep, dull pink flowers are not specially attractive; the brighter red *coccinea* is better and there is also a white form, *alba*. If you consider it too common to grow among choicer plants, there is usually some odd dry corner where it can fill a need for colour.

Chrysanthemum Strictly, this genus includes pyrethrums and also marguerites or Shasta daisies. The white-flowered *C. maximum* 'Esther Read' is the best known, but other excellent varieties include 'Thomas Killin', 'Everest', large single white flowers; 'Wirral Supreme', double white, very large lacy-petalled single flowers; 'Cobham Gold', 'Moonlight', both flushed with yellow; 'Esther Read' and 'Jennifer Read', all doubles. But as a garden plant *C. corymbosum* is preferable. This has greyish foliage and grows stoutly to 3½ ft. and bears hundreds of 1 in. wide white daisies from June to August. Even after Michaelmas daisies are over *C. uliginosum*, 5–6 ft., comes into flower; it has single white, yellow-centred daisies 2 in.

across which add a last touch of summer to late autumn.

Cimicifuga (bugbane) These are effective and easy plants given reasonably good soil that does not dry out too much. All have slender tapering spikes of small fuzzy, pearl-white flowers in late summer and autumn. They need no attention for many years beyond an occasional mulch and feed. *C. cordifolia*, 3 ft. flowers in August and September; *C. racemosa* is best in the varieties 'White Pearl' or 'Elstead Variety', which are taller and later flowering, very effective when even Michaelmas daisies are fading.

Coreopsis *C. grandiflora* is easily raised from seed in such varieties as 'Sunburst' and 'Mayfield Giant', but they deteriorate after one season's profligate show of deep yellow flowers, rather laxly carried on thin 2 ft. stems. The midget 'Goldfink', 8 in., smothers itself in deep yellow, maroon-marked flowers from June to September, and usually survives the winter. If odd plants exhaust themselves, those remaining divide easily in the spring to make replacements. The most reliable and distinctive coreopsis is *C. verticillata*, which forms shapely 18 in. bushes decked with 1 in. yellow flowers from June to late August; and var. *grandiflora* is slightly deeper in colour.

Delphinium These majestic plants may be considered indispensable, but almost invariably they need staking in good time. They also need rich soil for best results and in some gardens slugs can be a menace. From seed sown under glass in spring it is possible for some plants to flower in late summer, otherwise sow outdoors to obtain stock to flower freely the following year after transplanting. Named varieties will not flower true from

seed, which mostly produce mixed shades of blue. A few strains come reasonably true such as the shorter-lived 'Pacific Hybrids'. Belladonna delphiniums, less tall with more open spikes, are in their way as attractive as the large-flowered varieties, though it is in the latter that double flowers occur.

Dicentra (bleeding heart) The true bleeding heart, *D. spectabilis*, has few faults as a hardy perennial, and it is worth a little extra attention to ensure that it gives of its best. The lush foliage and the arching sprays of dangling red and white lockets are a gladdening sight in May and June. The fanged, brittle roots should be planted carefully in well-drained good soil, where some sun but not the worst of the winds can reach the plant. Division is tricky, but young shoots, with a good base will root in a cold frame.

Dictamnus (fraxinella, burning bush) *D. albus* is a deeply rooting plant that likes full sun and perfect drainage where it will live for years to send up 3 ft. spikes of lilac-pink flowers from June to August. Division is difficult, propagation by root cuttings in autumn or spring is better; plants grown from seed are slow to reach maturity.

Doronicum (leopard's bane) These easily-grown plants make a bright display of yellow in spring. The earliest to thrust up their widely-rayed yellow daisies are the dwarfest. 'Goldzwerg' reaches only 6 in. and flowers from late March to May. It is followed quickly by the 18 in. 'Miss Mason'. This is the height of the outstanding fully double-flowered variety 'Spring Beauty'. 'Harpur Crewe' is tallest, with wide-rayed flowers on 3 ft. stems. Doronicums are easy to divide (preferably in early autumn) and respond to division and replanting every few years.

Above: Erigeron 'Felicity'

Echinacea (purple cone flower) *E. purpurea* (syn. *Rudbeckia purpurea*) has a special appeal, with its somewhat drooping petals accentuating the central cone on 3½ ft., stems. Named varieties as well as variable seedlings are offered. A better plant than the best-known variety 'The King' is the erect 'Robert Bloom' in a much warmer red shade. This is one of the 'Bressingham Hybrids' which show only slight colour variations. All flower from July to September. They like good deep soil, well drained but not too dry and can safely be divided in early spring.

Echinops (globe thistle) These deep-rooting plants are reliably hardy and perennial, but one or two are too massive for a small garden. All have greyish, jagged, slightly prickly leaves and branching stems which carry rounded flower heads of mainly light blue. *E. ritro*, 3 ft., is less troublesome than the taller kinds. Old plants are easier to divide than to dig up, and roots left in the ground will mostly sprout again.

Erigeron (fleabane) These useful members of the daisy family give a good display from May to August and some are useful for cutting. They are happy in open positions, in any well-drained soil and are best increased by division in spring. The most reliable include 'Darkest of All', 20 in., single-flowered, violet-blue, 'Foerster's Liebling', 20 in., near double, bright pink, 'Lilofee', 2½ ft., mauve blue, 'Prosperity', 20 in. light lavender-blue, almost double, 'Amity', 2 ft. lilac pink, 'Gaiety', 1½–2 ft., single pink, 'Sincerity', 2 ft. mauve-blue, single, long-flowering, and 'Dignity', 2 ft. violet-blue.

Eryngium (sea holly) By comparison with most flowers the eryngiums are freakish, as all have flowers without visible petals. In some the stems are as brightly coloured as the flower bracts and in others the flowers and leaves are green. Such species as *E. serra*, 6 ft., *E. bromeliifolium*, 4 ft. and *E. pandanifolium*, to 10 ft., grow from large green rosettes of vicious looking saw-edged leaves and send up stiffly branching spikes tipped with green spiny thimbles as flowers. *E. alpinum* is very handsome, with rounded green leaves and sturdy 2½ ft. stems crowned with large silver-blue flowers. *E. bourgatii* is reliable; it is very silvery with a tinge of blue in the 20 in. stems as well as in the terminal bract. *E. variifolium*, 2 ft., has marbled evergreen foliage. *E. giganteum*. 3 ft., is imposing, but only biennial. *E. planum* is easy, but the blue flowering tips are not as bright as in the widely-branching *E. tripartitum*, 3–3½ ft., which is the best of this group. Some eryngiums will grow well from seed, but the usual method of increase is from root cuttings in the spring.

Euphorbia (spurge) This vast genus includes a few good garden plants. All have bracts surrounding clustered flower heads. *E. charassias* and *E. veneta* (syn. *E. wulfenii*), are sub-shrubs, with year round blue-grey, somewhat succulent foliage, and build up into imposing plants 3 ft. high or more till they burst into almost a fountain of sulphur-yellow heads of flower in spring. They look well with shrubs or on a wall. One of the best of all spring-flowering herbaceous plants is *E. polychroma* (syn. *E. epithymoides*), 20 in., a sturdy, compact plant which produces heads of bright sulphur-yellow bracts in April and early May. *E. griffithii* 'Fireglow', 2½ ft., produces deep fiery heads in May and June. Of the more vigorous species, which have their uses as ground coverers, *E. cyparissias*, 10 in., spreads rapidly and has bluish-grey foliage and heads of sulphur-yellow. *E. amygdaloides* and *E. robbiae* are similar, with deep green foliage and a reasonable spread, but are more suitable among shrubs than in a perennial border.

Filipendula (meadowsweet) These are, with one or two exceptions, moisture-loving plants, which will grow well enough in full sun, provided the soil is moist. *F. hexapetala plena*, which will grow where the soil is quite dry, has reddish stems, 18–20 in. and snow-white heads in profusion during June–July. *F. hexapetala grandiflora*, 2½ ft., is single flowered· but has wide creamy-white heads. The remaining filipendulas are moisture loving. *F. digitata nana*, 9 in., has deep rosy-red flowers and *F. elegantissima*, 3 ft., hazy pink flower heads in June and July. Filipendulas can be divided in early autumn or spring and they benefit from an annual mulch.

Gaillardia (blanket flower) These are not very reliable perennials. They are easily grown from seed, though named varieties can

only be propagated by root cuttings – easier from roots left in the ground after plants have been chopped off, than from actual root cuttings. They prefer poor soil and dry conditions. Flowers are borne profusely from June to August, when cutting hard back is helpful. Good named varieties are – 'Croftway Yellow', 'Ipswich Beauty', yellow with maroon cone, 'Mandarin', fiery orange, 'Wirral Flame', browny-red, all 2½–3 ft. 'Goblin' is a 9-in. miniature.

Geranium (cranesbill) True geraniums are hardy garden plants, easily grown in sun or shade. *G. armenum*, (syn. *G. psilostemon*), 3½ ft., makes a dense bush given ample moisture; the flowers, over 1 in. across, borne from June to August, are fiercely magenta. 'Bressingham Flair' is less intense, with more pink in the flowers. *G. endressii*, about 20 in., forms dense mounds of light green and its sprays of light or bright pink flowers make a good show in June and July. *G. grandiflorum*, 15 in., clear blue, spreads too quickly for what it gives in flowers, but 'Johnson's Blue', 18 in., is very good indeed. *G. ibericum*, 2 ft., has dark leaves and rich deep blue flowers. *G. renardii* has light mauve-blue flowers, marked with delicate crimson veins. *G. sanguineum*, 1 ft., spreads slowly and has a long succession of magenta-rose flowers. 'Holden Variety' or '*splendens*', is a good clear pink and there is a white form, *album*. *G. sylvaticum* 'Mayflower', 18 in., has light blue flowers in May and June. The uncommon *G. wlassovianum* has deeper blue flowers from July to September, and is worth a place.

Geum (avens) For reliability *G. borisii*, 1 ft., rates highly with its intense orange single flowers in May and June. The shortest lived are the popular double red 'Mrs Bradshaw'

and double yellow 'Lady Stratheden'. These flower very freely, but after a couple of years they lose vigour and die. Other good hybrids which need replanting and dividing every two or three years are 'Fire Opal', orange-red and 'Rubin', deep red, all about 2 ft. 'Georgenberg', 1 ft., is single yellow, April to June.

Gypsophila (chalk plant) The tallest, but still popular baby's breath, *G. paniculata*, is not an ideal border plant, because of its floppy habit. The double-flowered 'Bristol Fairy' has little advantage over the single, longer-lived type. Both are charming in their way, with clouds of pure white flowers, but they need space, as well as free-drained soil, in which to make their expansive display from late June to September. But 'Bristol Fairy' can only be propagated by cuttings or grafting on to young seedlings of the single *G. paniculata*. There is a dwarfer, neater double-flowered variety, '*compacta plena*'. This grows 18 in. high and 2 ft. across and is to be preferred in a mixed bed or border. Two dwarfer double pink varieties are 'Pink Star', 18 in., with small pale pink flowers, and the more prostrate 'Rosy Veil'. All these will increase by cuttings in spring, and all are sun lovers and long flowering.

Helenium (sneezeweed) These are quite indispensable for providing a rich display of colour, but neglect can cause some disappointment. They need dividing and replanting every three years or so, in early autumn or spring, in enriched soil. Heleniums are very easy to grow in fully open positions. The tallest varieties should be avoided. 'Bruno', and 'Moerheim Gem', browny red and 'Butterpat', yellow, are in the 4 ft. range and flower from July to September. Earlier,

sturdy varieties are 'Bressingham Gold', 'Coppelia', 'Gold Fox' and 'Mahogany', all with orange and browny flame shades. 'Golden Youth', about 2½ ft., is a fine clear colour, and 'Wyndley', 2–2½ ft., is brown and orange.

Heliopsis (orange sunflower) These can be left alone for several years and relied upon to flower freely unsupported. All have basically yellow-green flowers as in 'Goldgreenheart', and the rich buttery-yellow 'Golden Plume', both semi-double. Good single varieties are 'Ballerina' and *H. patula*, both 3 ft., with 3 in. flowers from June to September. Divide in autumn or spring.

Helleborus (hellebore) The true Christmas rose (*H. niger*) has a never failing appeal even though it seldom opens in time for Christmas. But January and February flowering is exciting enough to make this a very desirable plant, though it is best placed in cool shade, not where it is over-hung or the soil is dry. Old plants do not move or divide easily; young seedling plants do best. Seed is slow to germinate and needs to be sown when fresh. *H. niger* is followed by the Lenten rose, *H. orientalis*, 12 to 18 in., and its hybrids, most rewarding plants, varying from white to deep pink and even plum purple. A few plants can fill permanently an odd corner even where it becomes quite dry in summer, so long as it is not sunbaked. Where it is moist enough, self-sown seedlings will appear, but mature plants can also be divided in autumn. *H. corsicus* has pale greenish-white flowers on 2 ft. stems in spring, and the 2 ft. tall *H. foetidus* with greenish flowers may become naturalized, even in dry shady places.

Hemerocallis (day lily) Many new varieties of this sterling garden plant have appeared in

Far left: The gaillardias are among the brightest of border plants, flowering from June to August
Left: Helenium 'Wyndley' grows 2–2½ ft. tall and flowers for many weeks from July onwards
Above: Echinacea 'Robert Bloom', a newer and beautiful variety of the purple cone flower
Right: Helleborus orientalis, is available in a range of colours, including the purplish-brown of this variety, *atropurpurea*

recent years. The rushy-leaved plants are robust without being invasive. They flower from June–August and are not pernickety about soil, shade or sun, but they respond to good treatment by giving a better, longer display of their richly-coloured trumpet flowers. A wide range of colour exists, including a reasonably good pink, 'Pink Damask', through every shade of yellow, orange and brown to the ruby-mahogany shade of 'Black Magic'. Where hemerocallis score is in the purer shades of yellow and orange. 'Hyperion' is a beauty, and so is the golden-yellow 'Doubloon'. 'Primrose Mascotte' is one of the best light yellows and 'Stafford', ruby orange; 'Golden Orchid', 'Golden Chimes', dwarf orange; 'Fandango', ruffled light orange; 'Larksong', lemon and 'Morocco Red' are all excellent. Most varieties grow into very large plants. Divide in autumn or spring.

Heuchera (coral flower) Heucheras have that rare combination of compact, well-foliaged evergreen growth and a show of brightly-coloured flowers carried daintily on

sprays or spikes for several weeks in early summer. On a well-grown plant hundreds of small, bell-shaped flowers are borne on wiry stems. Colours range from white to every shade of pink, and red including scarlet, coral, salmon and coppery-crimson. Heucheras must have good drainage, and are best in sun or only partial shade. They flower better in rich soil, yet they are draught resistant. Every three to four years mulch deeply with soil or compost, or dig them up and replant them deeply, using only the most vigorous shoots. 'Bressingham Hybrids' is a mixed strain in a wide colour range. They do not come true from seed and division is best after flowering ceases in July.

Heucherella 'Bridget Bloom', 15 in., is a splendid plant for fairly good light soil, in light shade, and may produce its sprays of light pink flowers almost as freely in autumn as at its normal period of May and June. This and H. tiarelloides are hybrids between a Heuchera and a Tiarella. H. tiarelloides makes modestly spreading ground cover with slightly

Left: Inula orientalis, one of the many daisy-flowered plants for the border, grows about 20 in. tall
Below: Many new day lilies (hemerocallis) have been bred in recent years and new colours have been introduced. This is 'Pink Damask'
Right: Hardy perennials in island beds at Bressingham Hall, Norfolk. This is an ideal way of growing these plants as they can be seen from all sides

golden-green leaves, producing in April and May 1 ft. spikes of pink flowers. It is easily grown in any but hot dry positions.

Hosta (plantain lily) These plants have come into their own of recent years, because of their hardiness, adaptability, reliable growth, good foliage and pleasing overall appearance. In any but parched or starved conditions they can be left for years to develop into solid clumps. They are happiest in cool shade. They vary in height from 8 in. to 4 ft. and can be used in a wide range of places from waterside to woodland conditions, for edging and for a mixed bed or border. *H. crispula*, 3 ft., has handsome leaves edged with creamy-buff and lavender-mauve flowers from June to August. *H. fortunei* and its varieties flower earlier. The species has large pointed blue-green leaves and 2 ft. stems of pale lavender flowers. *H. f. picta* comes through in spring with bright and very attractive variegations which last until flowering at midsummer, before turning green. 'Honeybells' is a green-leaved variety, with $2\frac{1}{2}$ ft. spikes of sweetly scented lavender trumpets. *H. lancifolia* has 20 in. lavender spikes in late summer. *H. rectifolia*, 4 ft., is a splendid free-flowering plant with lavender-mauve spikes. *H. undulata medio variegata* has brightly variegated leaves all summer and 12 to 18 in. spikes of deep mauve flowers. *H. ventricosa*, 3 ft., is easy and reliable. It bears its deep lavender trumpets freely in July and August and has bluish leaves; in its variety *variegata*, they are deep green and have streaks of yellow which make it one of the most attractive kinds. Hostas are best divided in early spring.

Incarvillea Once the deep fangy roots begin to sprout in early May, growth is rapid and

startling. In two or three weeks, the exotic looking deep reddish pink trumpet flowers begin to open. The deeply-cut dark green leaves follow. In *I. delavayi* the stems reach 2 ft. or more before the last flowers fade in early July. *I. grandiflora* begins flowering almost at ground level and seldom exceeds 1 ft. Old plants can be carefully divided, or plants may be raised from seed. They need well-drained soil and sun.

Inula This is another genus with yellow daisy flowers. *I. barbata* spreads fairly quickly, and bears $1\frac{1}{2}$ in. wide flowers many weeks from June onwards; *I. hookeri* is similar, but about twice as tall, at 2 to $2\frac{1}{2}$ ft., with large flowers. 'Golden Beauty', 2 ft., is a neat plant flowering from June to September. *I. ensifolia compacta*, a most useful little plant for frontal positions, is long-lived and trouble-free. Though *I. orientalis* grows only to 20 in. or so, the flowers are 3–4 in. across and finely rayed. All are easily increased by division.

Iris The most popular irises, the *germanicas*, June-flowering flag irises, are available in a wide range of colours. There are others that help to spread the flowering season. *I. pumila*, under 1 ft., is at its best in April and May, in shades of yellow, blue and white. *I. foetidissima*, the wild Gladwyn iris, will grow in quite deep shade. One seldom notices it flower, but cannot fail to notice the vermilion seeds revealed in autumn as the pods open. There is an excellent variegated form as there is of the old *I. pallida*–the 'poor man's orchid' of cottage gardens. *I. sibirica* is a moisture lover, and where suited will flower for four or five weeks. The growth is erect and rushy, with stems rising to $2\frac{1}{2}$ to $3\frac{1}{2}$ ft. in shades of blue and purple as well as white.

Kniphofia (red hot poker) All kniphofias like a sunny open position, and the range is now so wide that the five months from June to October can be covered, while heights range from $1\frac{1}{2}$–6 ft. when in flower. The early variety 'Atlanta' makes massive broad-leaved plants with heavy red and yellow 3 ft. spikes. 'Bee's Sunset', deep orange, 'Goldelse', 'Springtime', red and yellow, and *K. tubergenii*, light yellow, are all about 3 ft. and flower in June and August along with the salmon flushed ivory 'Jenny Bloom', and the white 'Maid of Orleans'; 'Bressingham Torch' and 'Bressingham Flame', also flower at this time. For late flowering–August to October, there are some of majestic stature, such as the brilliant flame 'Samuel's Sensation'. Division is best deferred until spring, although September is safe for early flowering varieties.

Liatris (gay feather) With erect or curving poker-like 3 ft. spikes of bright lilac purple flowers, these are showy, distinctive perennials. An unusual feature is that the fluffy flowers begin to open at the top of the stems, in contrast to nearly all spiky plants. The species *L. callilepis* is most often listed; *L. spicata* and *L. pycnostachya* are similar. Old plants are best dug up in the spring and rejuvenated by division and replanting in enriched soil.

Ligularia These thrive best in good deep soil and should not be planted in dry, windy positions. *L. clivorum* and its varieties have very large leaves and upright stems, 3–4 ft. high, carrying dozens of deep yellow, daisy-like flowers from early July to late August. 'Gregynog Gold' grows $3\frac{1}{2}$ ft. tall; 'Desdemona' has purplish leaves and deep yellow flowers 2–3 in. across. These are all good

waterside plants, spectacular when at their best, but they droop quickly on hot windy days. *L. przewalskii* is one of the easiest; its deeply jagged leaves do not spread widely and the 4–5 ft. spikes are slender but erect. The black stems contrast well with the somewhat ragged yellow flowers which open close to the upper half of the spike. 'The Rocket' is even more attractive with brighter flowers. All will divide in autumn or spring.

Limonium (*formerly Statice*) (sea lavender) The most reliable is *L. latifolia* which makes a large plant with a fair spread of shining green leaves and widely branching 2–3 ft. sprays of tiny blue flowers from July to September. For drying stems should be cut before the flowers begin to fade. The varieties 'Blue Cloud' and the deeper blue 'Violetta', have to be increased by root cuttings in spring. Plants do best in well-drained soil and open position.

Linum (flax) The blue *L. perenne*, $1\frac{1}{2}$ ft., seldom lives beyond two summers. *L. narbonense*, 20 in., is much longer lived in well-drained soil and where it is happy it is one of the finest of dwarf border plants. The flowers are richly blue, 1 in. across. *L. dolomiticum*, 18 in., a compact plant, has wide clusters of bright yellow rounded flowers $\frac{3}{4}$ in. across, from mid June to late August. *L. campanulatum* and *L. flavum* are similar.

Lupinus (lupin) With new varieties coming on to the market each year, the choice must rest with the purchaser, as far as named varieties are concerned. Many people prefer to have the cheaper seedling plants, even if they turn out to be a mixture of colours. Lupins grow better in neutral or acid soil rather than alkaline soil.

Lychnis (catchfly) *L. chalcedonica*, 2–3 ft., is a good perennial, with a head of small but intense red flowers from June to August. *L. coronaria* has silver-grey leaves and loose sprays of pink or carmine flowers for a long period. It grows best in a dry place. *L. viscaria*, 10 in., in the double form *plena*, has very bright pink flowers in June and July.

Lysimachia (loosestrife) These are mainly moisture-loving plants, robust enough to grow in drier soils. *L. clethroides* has white flowers and is very attractive with curved spikes in late summer. The yellow loosestrife, *L. punctata*, is very showy, with 3 ft. spikes of bright yellow flowers from June to August. Plants expand quickly and have to be curbed, but when small pieces are replanted, flowering is more prolonged.

Lythrum (purple loosestrife) These prefer moist soil. They flower freely from June to September. *L. salicaria* is taller and more robust than *L. virgatum*, and only named improvements of these wild types need be considered. 'Firecandle', 3 ft., has intense rosy red spikes, and 'Robert', $2\frac{1}{2}$ ft., is a compact plant with clear pink flowers. *L. virgatum* 'Rose Queen', 2 ft., is light pink, 'The Rocket', $2\frac{1}{2}$ ft., and has deeper, brighter flowers. All have a very tough woody root, but old plants will pull apart, and can be planted in autumn or spring.

Macleaya (plume poppy) These easily grown plants make strong spikes up to 6 ft., with powdered stems and pretty leaves, brownish beneath and bluish above, and large sprays of tiny flowers in late summer. In *M. cordata* the flowers are buff and it is an effective plant, by itself or against a dark background. *M. macrocarpa* has a wider branching flower spike, and the flowers are a brownish yellow; 'Coral Plume' is a slightly more colourful variation. The somewhat fleshy roots of macleayas tend to wander and shoot up among neighbouring plants. They will grow in quite dry soils and do not object to shade.

Meconopsis (Himalayan blue poppy) Few plants have achieved such an aura as *M. betonicifolia* (*M. baileyi*) with its 3 ft. spikes of 2 in. wide sky-blue flowers. It is easily grown from seed. *M. chelidonifolia*, $2\frac{1}{2}$ ft., is easy and fully perennial; it has 2 in. wide yellow flowers from June to August. All meconopsis prefer light leafy soil and some shade.

Monarda (bergamot) These are showy plants for the late June to September period. The flowers are of curious shape, having upward pointing petals, and come at the tips of the leafy stems which do not branch to any extent. These stems are however very profuse, and vary in height from $2\frac{1}{2}$–4 ft. according to soil and situation. They revel in deep moist soil, and form quite wide mats of surface growth where happy. Such spread may need curbing and it is often necessary to dig over the centre part of a group and fill back with vigorous pieces which have spread away, as an alternative to a complete replant in early spring. Bright colours are available in such named varieties as 'Cambridge Scarlet' and 'Adam', and the salmon red 'Prairie Glow'. 'Croftway Pink' and 'Melissa' are both good pinks and for purple there is 'Prairie Night'. The leaves have a distinctive and not unpleasant odour.

Nepeta (catmint) *N. faassenii* (syn. *N. mussinii*), gives a long succession of lavender-blue flowers on 1 ft. spikes, from grey-leaved plants, from June to September. Though adaptable to sun and partial shade, winter losses occur where drainage is poor. Division is best done in the spring. 'Six Hill's Giant' has sprays up to 2 ft. tall. 'Blue Beauty' has erect, 20 in. spikes of larger violet-blue flowers.

Oenothera There are several full perennial kinds that make a bright display with their big yellow cup-shaped flowers. *O. cinaeus* has bright leaves – buff, pink, purple-red in spring, fading to deep green as the loose sprays of rich yellow cups open. *O.* 'Fireworks', $1\frac{1}{2}$ ft., is a deep yellow, with purplish-green leaves, as

is 'Yellow River', 2 ft., with green foliage, and these and the 2 ft. tall 'Highlight', can easily be divided in early spring. The most distinctive is the virtually prostrate *O. missouriensis*, which from July to October bears 4 in. light canary yellow flowers. This needs sun and good drainage and can only be increased by seed.

Paeonia (peony) Among the longest lived of all perennials, paeonias should be planted with permanence in mind, space in which to expand in an open situation. They like a rich, deep soil and respond to mulching. Old plants can be divided, between August and October, carefully using a knife to separate the most vigorous chunks. Planting depth is important; the new buds should rest 1 in. below the surface. Varieties of the popular June-flowering Chinese peony (*P. lactiflora*) up to 3 ft. tall, have huge flowers in shades of pink, red and white, single, semi-double and double. Some are more fragrant than others. Consult a reliable catalogue for details of the numerous varieties. *P. officinalis* is the old cottage garden peony, 2 ft. tall, with very fragrant flowers, usually double, in red, crimson, pink and white.

Papaver For size of flower, *P. orientalis*, the Oriental poppy, can easily compete with paeonias. For brilliance of colour, they can excel them, but they are not so permanent. All flower from late May until late June. The most erect is the blood-red 'Goliath', $3–3\frac{1}{2}$ ft., though the orange scarlet 'Marcus Perry' is nearly as erect. Other varieties include brownish-red, various shades of pink, also white. All like a very well-drained soil, not too rich. Their fleshy roots are brittle and any pieces left when old plants are dug out will sprout again. Propagation is by 3 in. long root cuttings in spring.

Penstemon The showiest kinds are the least reliable as hardy perennials. Some are used as bedding plants by taking cuttings in late summer or autumn and keeping them under glass till planting out time in spring, when they quickly make bushy plants to flower from July to October. The trumpet-shaped flowers are borne on spikes up to $2\frac{1}{2}$ ft. tall. In milder localities the deep crimson 'Garnet' and the blood-red 'Firebird' (*P. schonholzeri*) will usually survive for several years, as will 'Pink Endurance'.

Phlox Among the brightest of border plants, phlox are happiest in light rather than heavy or alkaline soil. They should be divided every three years, or propagated by root cuttings to avoid attacks by phlox eelworm. The newest introductions do not necessarily supersede older varieties, and recommendations include older kinds which have stood the

Physalis franchetii (Chinese Lantern) is well known for its bright orange seed bags used in winter decorations, but the white flowers are insignificant. The roots have a tendency to ramp, and it is wise to grow these plants where they will not smother other perennials

test of time. The best dwarf white is still 'Mia Ruya'; 'White Admiral' at 3 ft. is taller. 'Mother of Pearl', 3 ft., is a vigorous, weatherproof pink suffused white; 'Mies Copijn' is soft pink and 'Dodo Hanbury Forbes' is somewhat deeper, with 'Windsor' a carmine-rose shade. 'Endurance', salmon-rose, 'Brigadier', orange-salmon; 'Spitfire' and the intensely bright 'Prince of Orange' should not be missed. The most reliable deep red is 'Starfire', with 'Tenor' an early flowering blood red; 'Aida', 'San Antonio' and 'Vintage Wine' are in the magenta range, with 'The King', 'Parma Violet' and 'Marlborough' for violet purples. Lavender-blue shades include 'Skylight' and 'Hampton Court', while 'Balmoral' has a tinge of lilac.

Physalis (Cape gooseberry, Chinese lantern) Though the showy orange seed bags of *P. franchetii* 2 ft., are excellent for floral decoration, as plants they are scarcely suitable among other perennials. The roots wander and the flowers are insignificant. Propagation by division is easy.

Physostegia (obedient plant) These are good reliable perennials for any soil, with tapering spikes, flowering from July to September. *P. speciosa*, 'Rose Bouquet', 2 ft., has a profusion of light rosy-lilac flowers; dwarfer 'Vivid', deep pink, flowers later, but the roots wander so widely that it pays to dig them up every spring and replant them where they belong. *P. virginica* 'Summer Snow' and the deeper rose-pink 'Summer Spire', are both about 3 ft. Physostegias have a vigorous rootstock of spreading, whitish crowns, which tend to fall apart when dug up, and in moist or rich soil need curbing after two or three years.

Platycodon (balloon flower) When the buds of *P. grandiflorum* expand, the petals are joined together to form a hollow globe of about walnut size, changing into a saucer-shaped, campanula-type flower. Platycodons have real merit; they are long lived, have fleshy roots, and need only well-drained soil. Heights vary from the 1 ft. tall variety *mariesii* in shades of light blue, to the 2 ft. of the tallest kinds of *P. grandiflorum* in white, blue and very pale pink. Seed-raised plants are variable in colour, but old plants will divide.

Polemonium (Jacob's ladder) Some of these are short lived and seed about to be-

Below: 'Gibson's Scarlet' is one of the best herbaceous potentillas

Right: Summer in the herbaceous border

come a nuisance. More reliable and seldom setting seed is *P. foliosissimum*, $2\frac{1}{2}$–3 ft., a good perennial with a much longer flowering period, from June till September, with heads of open petalled lavender-blue flowers. Polemoniums are not fussy plants, and when old can be divided to rejuvenate them, especially the dwarfer kinds, such as the light blue 'Sapphire', 15 in., flowering in May and June and 'Blue Pearl', 10 in., which also

flowers for several weeks in May and June.
Polygonatum (Solomon's seal) *P. multiflorum* and its forms, with arching sprays of green and white flowers, are best naturalized; they need cool soil for their tuberous roots to run and flower freely in June. They can be divided in autumn or spring.
Polygonum (knot-weed) Most polygonums have poker-shaped spikes of tiny closely-set flowers. In the robust *P. amplexicaule*, the 4–

5 ft. spikes top a rounded dense bush of pointed leaves, at least 3 ft. in diameter. The dull red variety *atrosanguineum* and the lighter, brighter red 'Firetail' can be recommended for reliability and for a three-month flowering season. The 3 ft. stems of *P. bistorta superbum* carry 4 in. long pokers of a clear light pink in May and June. *P. carneum* has smaller but deeper pink spikes in June and July and sometimes well into August.

Facing page: Pyrethrums add much colour to the border for some weeks from late May, and may flower again in autumn if they are cut back hard after they have first flowered
Above: The herbaceous paeonies flower in spring and are available in a wide colour range. This is the variety 'Lady Alexandra Duff'
Right: The numerous varieties of herbaceous phlox provide brilliant colour for many weeks in summer and early autumn
Far right: *Meconopsis betonicifolia*, the Himalayan blue poppy, is renowned for its sky-blue flowers

Potentilla (cinquefoil) For rich colourings, long flowering and reliability many of the potentillas rank highly. They are mostly dwarf plants, easily grown in ordinary soil and open positions, and all have green, grey or silvery strawberry-like foliage. *P. atrosanguinea* has silvery leaves, vigorous growth and sprays of bright red flowers, $\frac{3}{4}$ in. across. 'Flamenço', 2 ft., is similar, but with larger flowers and green leaves. Both flower from May to July, but from June to September the more prostrate but equally brilliant 'Gibson's Scarlet', 18 in., takes over. 'Firedance', orange salmon, 'Miss Willmott', pink and the good semi-double flowered 'Glory of Nancy', orange or red, 'William Rollison', flame orange and 'Yellow Queen', all grow about 18 in. Potentillas can be divided in autumn or spring.

Pulmonaria (lungwort) These adaptable spring-flowering plants can be used effectively in places one can more or less forget when summer comes. *P. angustifolia aurea*, 9 in., has brilliant blue bell-shaped flowers from March to May; 'Munstead Blue' is a little dwarfer and flowers later. *P. saccharata* is much coarser, and this and the red-flowered 'Bowles's Red', take up space with their large rough leaves. Of those with prettily white-spotted leaves, which are effective even when flowering is over 'Pink Dawn', 1 ft., is worth while, its flowers pink at first, fading to blue, to give at times a two-colour effect. All are easily propagated by division.

Pulsatilla (pasque flower) *P. vulgaris*, 9–10 in., is a deeply rooting plant, with grey-green ferny leaves, which in early spring sends up goblet-shaped flowers, surrounded by silvery gossamer calyces. Colours range from pale lavender to purple, and include white and ruby red, all with prominent golden stamens. The flowers are followed by prettily tufted seed heads. Seed, the only method of increase, must be sown when freshly gathered.

Pyrethrum The brightly coloured daisy-type flowers of pyrethrums are decorative from late May until July, but unless they have ample light and air space, they need supporting, even though they are mostly under 3 ft. high. Well-drained soil and sun are essential, and they prefer alkaline soils. It is best to plant in spring and, other than in March and early April, old plants can be lifted and divided immediately after flowering. Named varieties include single and double flowered white, various shades of pink, as well as rich salmon and crimson. Cut plants back hard after flowering.

Rudbeckia (cone flower) All the true perennial species are yellow, but their variations in form make all but the tallest of value. Tall kinds, varieties of *R. laciniata* include the well-known 5–6 ft. 'Autumn Sun'. 'Goldquelle', however, grows without support to a shapely 3–4 ft., bearing fully double chrome-yellow flowers 3 in. across from July to October. *R. deamii*, 2½ ft., makes a wonderful show from August to October with its black-eyed, deep-yellow, black-centred flowers.

The amazingly free 'Goldsturm', often begins in June or July and continues into autumn. No rudbeckias like to be in parched conditions and in good, reasonably moist soil will flower for much longer.

Salvia (sage) The best hardy salvias flower from June to August. *S.* × *superba* makes erect stems, 3½–4 ft. tall, topped with slender spikes of tiny lipped flowers which attract bees and butterflies. 'May Night', about 20 in., 'East Friesland', 1–1½ ft., both rather more compact and later, and 'Lubeca', 2½ ft., are all good varieties, long-lived, hardy and easy in any well-drained soil, easily increased by division or by basal cuttings in spring. *S. haematodes* is best grown from seed. In some gardens it will survive for years, while in others it may live for three or four years only. It is a showy plant, 3 ft. tall., with open branching spikes of light lavender blue in June and July.

Scabiosa (scabious) *S. caucasica* is a firm favourite, splendid for cutting. The flowers are in shades of blue and violet and there are also good white varieties, all about 2½ ft. tall, flowering from June to September. Scabious dislike wet, especially in winter and survive longest in well-drained alkaline soils. The open saucer-shaped flowers on wiry stems need to be cut or dead headed to encourage long flowering. They are best planted or divided in spring, but can also be raised from seed. *S. graminifolia*, 10 in. makes a compact mound of silvery, grassy leaves and gives a long succession of rounded pincushion heads of light lavender blue, from June to September; the variety 'Pincushion' has soft pink flower heads 1 in. across.

Sedum (butterfly or ice plant) The taller herbaceous sedums include such well-established favourites as *S. spectabilis*, 1–1½ ft. tall, with wide heads densely packed with glistening pink flowers in late summer. The varieties 'Brilliant', 'Carmen' and 'Meteor' do not differ greatly from one another. 'Autumn Joy', 2 ft., is a sturdy plant with heads up to 12–15 in. across, opening light pink in September, changing slowly to salmon-rose. *S. heterodontum*, 9–12 in., is another easy, somewhat fleshy-rooted, compact plant with fuzzy heads of a burnt orange colour and bluish foliage. The yellow-flowered *S. rhodiola*, the rose root sedum, is of a similar dwarf bushy habit. Plants are easily divided.

Sidalcea These graceful, spike-forming plants have mallow-like flowers in shades of pink to rosy-red between June and September. They are easy to grow in full sun with good drainage, and can be divided in spring. 'Mrs Alderson', 'Wm. Smith' and 'Rev. Page Roberts', to 4 ft., and 'Puck', 2½ ft., have light pink flowers. Deeper shades are 'Rose Queen', 'Wensleydale' and 'Croftway Red', all 3–4 ft. After flowering the spikes should be cut back to promote new basal growth.

Solidago (golden rod) Many solidagos are far too tall and invasive and any that grow over 4 ft. tall should be omitted. 'Mimosa' will reach 4 ft., but the compact plants do not seed about after the handsome yellow plumes have finished in September.

Those growing less than 4 ft. are worth having; the colour range varies from the deep yellow of 'Golden Mosa', 'Golden Shower' or 'Golden Falls' to the lighter shades of 'Lemore' and 'Leslie'. All grow to 2½–3 ft. and flower between July and September. 'Peter Pan', 3 ft., is earlier and has horizontal branches to the crested plume; 'Crown of Rays', 2 ft., is very bushy in habit, while 'Cloth of Gold', 18 in., has a vigorous outward spread. The neatest growing dwarfs are the miniatures, 'Queenie' and 'Golden Thumb', which form bright, almost golden-leaved bushes 9–12 in. high, flowering from August to October. These better solidagos are best planted or divided in spring.

Stachys *S. lanata* (donkey's ears), with its felted silvery leaves, is an easily grown mat-forming plant, bearing thin spikes of small pink flowers in June and July. It is a good ground cover plant in quite dry positions;

there is a non-flowering variety 'Silver Carpet'. *S. macrantha*, 2½ ft., is a charming plant with short spikes of rosy, purple-lipped flowers in June and July. *S. spicata rosea* has 1 ft. deep pink spikes, and in the variety *densiflorum* the flowers are closely packed on 15 in. stems. This is a showy plant, as is the sturdier 20 in. variety *robusta*. All these stachys are easily divided in spring or autumn.

Thalictrum (meadow rue) Without exception thalictrums do best in rich soils and dislike drought. They all have pretty, tiny leaves. *T. minus* (syn. *T. adiantifolium*) is the easiest, but its 2½ ft. sprays of buff-green flowers are by no means showy. *T. angustifolium* has the fuzzy yellow flower heads on strong 6 ft. stems from June to August, as does *T. glaucum*, 5 ft., with light yellow fluffy heads and blue-grey leaves. The earliest to flower is *T. aquilegifolium*, 3–4 ft., with bluish-grey foliage on strong branched stems which carry fluffy flower heads in shades of mauve and purple in early June; there is a desirable pure white variety. *T. dipterocarpum* makes a much smaller rootstock but makes a vast amount of top growth. This consists of small-leaved, much-branched 6 ft. stems which need support. It bears mauve-blue flowers from early July to September. 'Hewitt's Double' is less vigorous and not so tall and needs rich moist soil to give of its best.

Most species may be divided in spring.

Tradescantia (trinity flower, spiderwort) *T. virginiana* has rushy leaves and stems up to 2 ft. carrying clustered heads of 3-petalled flowers up to 1 in. across in bright colours from June to August. Named varieties are available in white, light blue, mid and deep-blue as well as purple and magenta, and smaller flowered doubles exist as well. By August they may be looking tatty, and are best cut back. They grow in an ordinary soil in sunny or partially shady situations.

Trollius (globe flower) Though not for hot dry positions, these can add much to the garden scene in early summer. The vital period when plants need moisture is after flowering and for the rest of the summer. Mulching with peat helps greatly and cuts down the need for watering. The 'globe' effect appears just before the buds open. *T. europaeus superbus*, 2 ft., is a reliable light yellow; 'Canary Bird' is paler and larger flowered. 'Goldquelle' has large mid-yellow flowers, while 'Orange Princess' and 'Fireglobe' are deeper yellow shades. The 3 ft. *T. ledebouri* is distinctive. The petals open to reveal an upstanding crest of stamens of egg yolk colour. It flowers in June and July.

Verbascum (mullein) Although some of the brightest of these are not fully perennial or long-lived, a collection of perennials needs such spike-forming plants to break up uniformity. The most reliable have the stoutest rootstocks, thick and fleshy or tap rooted. *V. chairii* (syn. *V. vernale*) is a good yellow. It has strong spikes 4–5 ft., which flower from June onwards. *V. thapsiforme* (syn. *V. densiflorum*), 4 ft., has similar yellow flowers. 'Gainsborough', 3 ft., is a lighter yellow with woolly-grey foliage, but dislikes winter wet. The bushy 2 ft. 'Golden Bush' is distinctive, reliable and long flowering. 'Pink Domino', 3 ft., has deep rose flowers. Verbascums do not need rich soil and do best in sandy or stony soil with perfect drainage to enable them to survive the winter. Increase named varieties from root cuttings in early spring.

Veronica (speedwell) This genus provides several good, easily grown plants. The varieties of *V. teucrium* are all blue and make a bright display in June and July. They include 'Shirley Blue', 1 ft., 'Crater Lake Blue', 15 in., 'Royal Blue', 18 in., 'Blue Fountain', 2 ft., all of mounded or bushy growth topped with short spikes. *V. gentianoides*, 2 ft., light blue, is at its best in May. Spikes come from mat-forming plants. *V. spicata*, 2 ft., bright blue, is also mat-forming, flowering in June and July. *V. spicata incana*, 15 in., has silver-grey leaves and violet-purple spikes. In the free-flowering 'Sarabande', the leaves are less silvery, as in the taller and less tidy 'Wendy'. Pretty pink-flowered 18 in. varieties are 'Barcarolle' and 'Minuet'. *V. exaltata*, 4 ft., light blue, is late flowering and sometimes needs support. This does not apply to the 4 ft. pale blue *V. virginica*, but both this and its pale pink variety *rosea* are soon over. By far the most attractive is the 5 ft. white-flowered *alba* which flowers in August and September.

Above: *Sedum spectabile*, the butterfly or rice plants. They grow 1–1½ feet tall, with wide heads densely packed with glistening pink flowers in late summer. Always attract butterflies

Right: The scabious, *Scabiosa caucasica*, available in various shades, mainly in the blue-violet range, provides excellent cut flowers. To encourage long flowering, the wiry-stemmed flowers need to be cut or dead headed. May be planted or sown in spring

Favourite Garden Flowers

 Chrysanthemums

Originating in the cooler northern regions of the Far East, the chrysanthemum responded quickly to the efforts of hybridists when the first plants were introduced to Europe in the 18th century. Their attraction lies in four main characteristics; flowers may be obtained in various forms and sizes, in virtually every colour other than blue; plants grow success-fully in almost every area, and are highly adaptable to soil, climate and treatment; by choosing suitable varieties, flowering can begin in the open garden in August and September, followed by the late-flowering types under glass from October to February. Perhaps the greatest attraction is the way the plant invites the grower's co-operation and intervention throughout the whole growing season.

Obtaining Plants The new grower should obtain his stock from a specialist nursery. In subsequent seasons it is possible to raise new stock from the stools of the previous year. A stool is what is left when the flowers have been cut and the main stem is shortened to about 12 in.

Propagation Though in many areas the chrysanthemum is hardy, it is better to take up the stools, wash them free of soil and then box them up in fresh compost. JIP1 will do very well. Keep the soil fairly dry throughout the winter and house the stools in a cold greenhouse or cold frame. In early spring the stool will send up young shoots and once growth has begun, give sufficient water to keep the soil moist. Growth can be hastened by applying gentle bottom heat but tempera-tures should not rise far above 50°F (10°C). Propagation may now proceed by either of two methods. If the shoots have roots already developed they may be taken off and boxed up to make new plants. For various reasons, better plants are obtained by taking cuttings.

Clean, healthy young shoots some 2-in. long should be cut or broken off and inserted 1 in. deep in a box or bed of JIP1. A thorough watering is then given and the container placed in a simple frame covered with butter muslin to shade the shoots from bright sun-light and to keep the air around them humid. This simple propagator may be placed either on the greenhouse bench or inside a cold frame. Since the optimum temperature for rooting is around 55°F (13°C) some slight warmth, particularly in the form of bottom heat, will help matters greatly. If rooting hormones are used, well-rooted plants should be produced in a month.

Most early-flowering varieties root easily in March and April but those which bloom later in the greenhouse require a start in January and February.

Growing On The young plants must be gradually prepared to face the outside con-ditions. Earlies are grown either in boxes or in a bed of soil on the floor of the cold frame. Whichever method is used, they should be given plenty of room to develop and nothing less than 4-in. spacing will do. Since late-flowering plants are usually flowered in pots it is as well to start them in 3-in. pots, either clay or plastic, in JIP1 or a soilless compost. As the pots fill with roots it will be necessary to move the plants to 5- or 6-in. pots. JIP2 will now be needed though again, the soilless type will serve. A final potting will be needed later on into 8- or 9-in. pots using JIP3 or 4. Make the compost little more than finger-firm so as to encourage rapid root extension. Late varieties can also be grown in the open garden and the plants lifted and replanted in the greenhouse in late September for flowering; the plants should be treated exactly as ad-vised for the early-flowering varieties.

While plants are in the frame, guard against over watering, frost and draughts. Gradually increase ventilation so that plants are hardened off by late April.

Soil Preparation Ideally the soil should be well drained yet retentive of moisture; fertile without being over-rich and open to all the light and air available. A liberal dressing of manure or other humus-forming material should be dug in during the winter and the surface left rough. About mid-April a dressing of 4 oz. per square yard of a balanced fertilizer should be forked in to a depth of a few inches only, leaving the main body of the soil undisturbed. Raking to produce a good tilth is best left until a day or two before

'Golden Seal', a late-flowering variety

planting in May, the actual date depending on the prevailing weather conditions.

Planting The canes should first be inserted and the plants placed close to them, each one secured by a loose tie and protected from slug damage by the application of bait.

Late-flowering plants in pots are moved out to their summer quarters at the same time. Insert a cane in each pot and set out the pots in lines, securing the canes to a wire stretched about 4 ft. above the ground. Leave at least 1 ft. between the pots and 2 ft. between rows to allow free access.

Bud development To obtain the best results it is helpful to understand the way in which a chrysanthemum plant develops. It begins with a single stem which extends until a flower bud appears in the growing point. This normally happens so early in the season that the bud fails to develop into a flower but forces the plant to break into lateral growth thus forming a bushy habit. This bud is known as the *break bud*. In their turn, the laterals extend and in due time form buds. According to the time of year, either a cluster of buds or one bud surrounded by leafy shoots will be produced. Such buds are known as *first crown buds*. Where leafy shoots are produced around this bud, they will grow on strongly and produce further buds known as *second crown buds* and if the grower does not intervene the result is a large first crown flower struggling into bloom at the base of a cluster of much smaller flowers.

It is best to ignore the break bud since it is usual to remove the growing point of the young plant before that bud appears and the resultant branching is just the same. Early-flowering types are usually flowered on first crowns so merely pinch out the growing point when the plant is well established in the garden (about June 1st). When lateral growths are a few inches long remove the strongest and weakest, aiming to leave four to six of equal strength. When the first crown buds appear remove the growths surrounding the central bud on each shoot and allow them to flower. Some late-flowering types give better blooms on second crowns and the procedure is as follows. Two dates are given in the catalogue of varieties, which indicate (a) when the plant is to be pinched first, and (b) when the laterals arising from that first pinch are to be stopped again by the removal of the growing points. The result will be a further crop of side-shoots which are allowed to produce their buds to be dealt with as before by the removal of all buds except the central one. Two pinches will give far more stems than one but resist the temptation to flower them all. To obtain flowers of good size and quality the limit should be set at six to eight.

Sprays and pompon types are exceptions. These branch naturally and all you need to do is to encourage the development of laterals by one pinch only, when the plants are 9–12 in. high. Since the beauty of these plants is in the large number of small starry blooms carried in sprays, no disbudding need be done. Nevertheless it may be wise to restrict the number of stems to ensure larger flowers.

Feeding By late May all plants will be growing away nicely in pots or the open garden and within some seven weeks the earlies will have to develop into mature bushes of up to eight stems each bearing its flower bud. Well-prepared, fertile ground will give fair results without further help but it is usually beneficial to give some added feed, firstly at the beginning of June to encourage quick establishment; secondly at the end of June to ensure that the plants are in vigorous health at the time the flower buds are being formed. Each time an application of a chrysanthemum fertilizer in powder or liquid form, is all that is required.

Because late-flowering plants are usually grown in pots, feeding is more important. Liquid feeds are by far the best. It doesn't really matter what the label says so long as the relationship between the nitrogen and potash content is correct for the particular purpose. During the rapid development of leaf and stem there should be roughly twice as much nitrogen as potash. As the buds appear and are being dealt with, give only clear water but start feeding again when the buds have begun to swell, but now the nitrogen and potash contents must be roughly the same. Do not give heavy doses every ten days or so but give about a quarter the recommended strength every time you water.

Watering Correct use of the watering can is crucial to good growing but it is something which has to be learned rather than taught. With pots the safest rule is to apply water just before the plant threatens to wilt. Both the leaves and the soil surface will give clear indication when that point has been reached and enough water should be applied to moisten thoroughly the whole soil ball.

After care Throughout the period of rapid growth it is necessary to control the plants. Remove surplus branches and shoots as soon as they are seen; tie flowering stems loosely to the cane every 9 in. or so. Never tie too tightly but, to avoid breakages, allow branches to sway a little in the breeze. Watch out for and deal with early pest infestations; the best insurance against pest damage is to keep the garden free of weeds.

Housing plants Late-flowering types are flowered under glass. In late September, when the buds are beginning to show the first signs of colour, it is time to house the plants. Remove all old leaves to about one third of the height from the pot, remove all surplus growths; tie up the plants securely and place extra canes if necessary. Spray with an insecticide and with a systemic fungicide to combat mildews.

The greenhouse must be thoroughly cleaned. Remove all debris and any growing plants before burning a sulphur candle. When the fumes have dispersed, wash the glass and every crevice with a jet of water from the hosepipe. Test the heating apparatus and seal every leak in the roof.

Ideally there should be plenty of space around the plants inside but in practice one tends to pack them in rather tightly. In fact, it is far better to leave a few poor prospects outside so as to give the better plants more light and air. For the first ten days or so, leave doors and ventilators fully open. Watering will rarely be required for several days but it is good practice to give a little water say every two days rather than to wait until a pot is bone dry. In this latter condition the water will run all over the floor and cause damp air—the worst enemy of flowers indoors. After this the ventilators should be used in conjunction with the heating apparatus to main a dry moving atmosphere at a steady temperature of around 50°F (10°C). Light shading may be helpful in bright weather.

Flowering Time This is not only the season of satisfaction and enjoyment, it also provides opportunity for planning future efforts. Look critically at the plants and their flowers with a view to choosing those which have exhibited both vigour and excellence. These should be clearly marked so that they can be retained for the propagation of new stock. In this way the collection can be kept at a high level of health. There is much to be gained by visiting the local shows so as to see what is new and to chat with fellow enthusiasts.

Cutting Blooms Chrysanthemum blooms will last longer if they are cut in the morning when the stems are full of sap. Place each stem in water immediately. Back at the house, bruise the lowest few inches of stem and remove all the leaves except the three or four beneath the bloom. Now set the stems in a deep container of water and place it in a dark, cool place such as a garage or outhouse, for about 24 hours. After this treatment the flowers will last for several weeks, particularly if any stems which are further shortened are again bruised at the base.

Outdoor plants need not be cut right down at flowering time; in a mild autumn, it is not unusual to have a second crop of delightful sprays. Blooms may be small but the enriched colour and profusion of the flowers will more than compensate for lack of size.

Neither early nor late-flowering types should be cut right down after flowering. It is better to allow the sap to run back for a few weeks before shortening the main stem to about 12–18 in. In this state the stools can be boxed as described earlier. A final shortening to a few inches can be carried out in the spring.

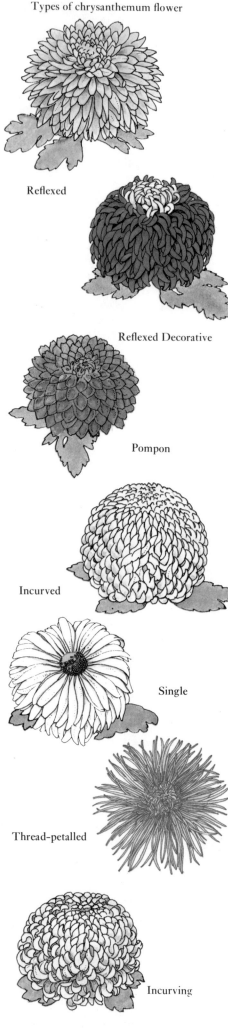

Types of chrysanthemum flower

Reflexed

Reflexed Decorative

Pompon

Incurved

Single

Thread-petalled

Incurving

Right: Well-grown, early-flowering chrysanthemums

Recommended Varieties

The selection of chrysanthemum varieties is extremely wide and numerous novelties are introduced each year. The following recommendations are made on the evidence available at the time of writing. There are many other lovely cultivars but those listed can be relied upon to give the least trouble and the greatest satisfaction.

1: Outdoor types which respond to disbudding to give blooms of fine quality for cutting, or may be allowed to carry large crops for border work.
Alice Jones: Light-bronze (3 ft.) September, Solid reflexed bloom
Bernard Zwager: Red (3½ ft.) Aug/Sept, **Cricket:** White (4 ft.) September, **Primrose Cricket** is also very good
Derek Bircumshaw: Large, tightly incurving golden yellow (3 ft.) Aug/Sept
Evelyn Bush: Large, incurving white. Full, solid blooms. There is also a more tightly incurved form – Incurving **Evelyn Bush** (4 ft.) Sept
Grace Riley: Bronze (4 ft.) September, Very large
Keystone: A purple of intermediate formation with a silver reverse. Outstanding for both exhibition and cutting. There are also sports in other colours, such as **Bronze Keystone** (red with gold reverse) and **Red Keystone** (4 ft.) Sept
Mexico: Red (4 ft.) September, Beautiful form
Oakfield Pearl: Salmon (3 ft.) Aug/Sept, Quite weatherproof
Rosedew: Pink (3 ft.) September, Waxy florets
Stardust: Yellow (3½ ft.) August, Rolled florets
Stephen Rowe: Yellow (3 ft.) August, Tightly incurved
Tracy Waller: Pink, reflexed. Large flowers (3½ ft.) Aug/Sept
Yvonne Arnaud: Purple (3½ ft.) Aug/Sept, Weatherproof

'Anna Marie'

2: Outdoor types requiring no disbudding. They produce a profusion of small flowers in sprays which are excellent for vases.
Anna Marie: White (3 ft.) August
Aurora Queen: Red (2 ft.) Aug/Sept, Very bright colour
Lucida: Yellow (3 ft.) Aug/Sept, Excellent
Gertrude: Pink (3 ft.) Aug/Sept, Heavy cropper
Madeleine Queen: Pink (3½ ft.) Aug/Sept, Strong stems
Nathalie: Purple (3½ ft.) September, Quite large flowers
Pamela: Bronze (3 ft.) August
Patricia: Red (3 ft.) August, Very sturdy grower
Pennine Crimson: A spectacular plant with deep red, double flowers (3½ ft.) Sept
Pennine Signal: Vivid red single flowers with gold centres (3½ ft.) Sept

'Fairie'

3: Spray types suitable for the front of a border but not giving stems long enough for cutting.
Cameo: Globular white flowers which open to show a yellowish centre. Still one of the best whites. Grows to about 2 ft.
Denise: A bright yellow semi-pompon. The flowers are carried on bushy plants. One of the best yellow varieties. Grows to about 1½ ft.
Fairie: This pink variety has several sports of different colours such as **Purple Fairie**. All are excellent, growing about 20 in. high and giving Pompon type blooms throughout August and later
Lemon Tench: a bushy plant not more than 18 in. high, with a profusion of yellow daisy-like flowers

4: Late-flowering varieties suitable for greenhouse decoration and cutting.
All have large double flowers and are best restricted to no more than eight blooms. Purely exhibition types have been omitted. The first mentioned in each colour group will flower in October and may bloom happily in a cold greenhouse. The others will need slight warmth in late October and November.
Snowcap: (4 ft.) October, Broad florets, free flowering
Ron Shoesmith: (4 ft.) Oct/Nov, Tightly incurved, long stems
Alan Rowe: (4½ ft.) Oct/Nov, Loosely incurving blooms
Yellow
Goldplate: (3½ ft.) October, Very large, rich gold flowers
Golden Gown: (4½ ft.) November, Most beautiful colour
John Rowe: (3½ ft.) November, Large incurved blooms

'Pamela'

Red
James Bond: (4 ft.) October, Broad florets
Pink
Amy Shoesmith: (4½ ft.) October, Incurving florets with lovely sheen
Fair Lady: (4 ft.) November, An incurved decorative of medium size
Joy Hughes: (5 ft.) November, Spiky florets. Grow in larger pots
Bronze
Heather James: (4 ft.) November, A bronze incurved decorative. Medium size
Lilian Shoesmith: (3½ ft.) November, Firm long-lasting flowers
Minstrel Boy: (4 ft.) November, Tightly incurved. Second crowns. Pinch May 30 and July 7
Purple
Daily Mirror: (5 ft.) November, An intermediate decorative. The large plum-purple flowers have a silvery reverse

'Goldplate'

5: Late-flowering varieties bearing single flowers like large daisies.
These should always be bisbudded to give one bloom per stem. Six to eight blooms per plant is the usual crop.
Cleone: This, together with its colour sports, is very reliable. It is white with just a pink blush when fresh and young. 5 ft.
Jinx: Pure white. Not as large as some but very beautiful. 4 ft.
Mason's Bronze: Orange-bronze bearing a profusion of slightly scented medium-size flowers; **Chesswood Beauty,** red, is a sport from this. 5 ft.
Peggy Stevens: A very large golden yellow 4 ft.
Woolman's Glory: A big flower of a dull bronze. The red sport is even better. 5 ft.
Note: All these singles do best on two pinches. The usual dates are April 15th and June 15th to give blooms in November.

6: Varieties suitable for producing cut flowers for the Christmas season.
All should be rooted in May if possible. A pinch towards the end of July should bring buds at the desired season. Three 'families' can be strongly recommended; each has a number of colour sports which can be recognized easily since each has the parent's name preceded by the colour of the sport.
Balcombe Perfection: The parent is bronze but the yellow, golden and red sports are equally good. Needs tying carefully. 4½ ft. Loosely incurving in formation.
Mayford Perfection: The parent is salmon-pink but all the sports can be strongly recommended. Incurving in form, the blooms are borne on very strong stems. Dwarfer than 'Balcombe Perfection'.
Shoesmith Salmon: The deep-rose parent has bronze, cerise, peach, ruby and yellow sports. The flowers are reflexing in formation. Stems are long and firm. 4½ ft.

Top: 'Patricia', an outdoor variety, which needs no disbudding. A very sturdy grower
Left: 'Lemon Tench', an outdoor spray kind, suitable for the front of a border
Above: 'Yvonne Arnaud' may be grown for cutting or garden decoration

107

Begonias, Fuchsias, Gladioli, Irises

ᔎ Begonias ᔍ

Large-flowered begonias are usually grown from tubers, but they can be grown from seed and they will flower about eight months after sowing if sufficient heat is available. There are many other kinds of begonias with fibrous roots, and some with rhizomes. Typical of this type are the *B. rex* cultivars with multi-coloured leaves. These will grow well along the edge of a greenhouse path, partly shaded by the staging. The most popular fibrous rooted begonias are those grouped under *B. semperflorens*, with green, bronze or variegated foliage, and white, pink or red flowers. Most have single flowers, but there are a few fully double varieties, chiefly grown as pot plants, while the single-flowered kinds are used for summer bedding. There are many others, some with silver spots on the foliage, many of which make good house plants.

Growing from Seed Sow seed of tuberous double varieties and *B. semperflorens* in January or early February, in soilless compost or J.I. seed compost. Sow in a clay half

pot or pan, and when using a soilless compost it should not be firmed down. Before sowing water the compost. Sprinkle the seed on the surface of the compost and do not cover it with additional compost, or with paper to exclude light. Place the pan in a heated propagator, and maintain a temperature of 60°–70°F (15°–21°C). The seed should germinate in 8–14 days, and the seedlings should be pricked out as soon as possible, into a similar compost, about 1 in. apart. Return them to the propagator if possible and, after a further 4–6 weeks, the seedlings should be touching each other, and they will then need spacing 2 in. apart. Return to the propagator again for a few weeks, but if this is not practicable, keep them as warm as possible and if it is dull or cool they will need very little water. By mid-May the seedlings should be hardened off in a frame prior to planting out in early June. They like some peat or similar material in the soil, and they can be planted in shade or full sun.

Greenhouse Cultivation Seedlings to be grown in pots in the greenhouse should be potted up into 3-in. pots in early May, in

1 part, by bulk, of JIP1 compost, mixed with 1 part of soilless compost. After a few weeks the plants will need potting on into 5-in. pots, and for these and all larger pots use 2 parts of JIP2, mixed with 1 part of soilless compost. The *B. semperflorens* varieties will flower in 5-in. pots but the tuberous doubles will need potting on into 6½–7½-in. pots. Clay pots are preferable as there is less danger of overwatering; if you use plastic pots add an extra part of coarse sand to the potting mix. In a greenhouse plants will need some shading from bright sunshine.

Begonias need cool conditions to produce sturdy plants with good blooms, and once all danger of frost is over the ventilators should be left open day and night to allow maximum circulation of air.

Disbudding Wherever you grow tuberous double begonias, it is best to remove the first flower buds. This allows the plants to become established before the strain of flowering and will result in larger and better formed flowers. Three blooms usually develop on each flowering stem, and with pot-grown plants the two outer blooms should be pinched off, leaving the larger double male bloom to open. The two outer blooms are usually females, and are always singles. The female blooms have a light green, three-winged seed capsule immediately behind the petals, but this is missing from all male blooms.

Feeding When in bloom tuberous double begonias will need a weekly feed with a weak tomato-type fertilizer, high in potash. Stop

feeding in early September. Plants will need less water as the cooler weather arrives, but it is vital that the compost should be kept moist and no attempt should be made to force the plants into dormancy by with-holding water. As top growth ceases moisture is needed at the roots to help build up a good tuber to survive the winter dormancy.

Winter Treatment Any green leaves re-tained by the end of October can then be removed, but the stems must not be forcibly pulled off. Stop watering as soon as all green leaves have dropped, or been removed, and the stems should drop off within a few days. The tubers can then be taken from the pots and cleaned up, but be careful not to damage the 'eyes' (axillary buds) on the top of the tuber as next year's growth will start from these. Store the tubers in dry peat in a frost-proof place until the following spring when they can be restarted. Plants in the garden should be lifted in early October with a ball of soil round the roots, placed on the floor of the greenhouse until all stems have dropped, then stored in dry peat.

(For begonias as house plants see the part of this work dealing with Indoor Plants).

Recommended Begonia Varieties

Tuberous doubles: 'Roy Hartley', and 'Judy Langdon', pink; 'Diana Wynyard' and 'Avalanche', white; 'Crown Prince', crimson; 'Guardsman', red; 'Harlequin', white ground picotee; 'Midas', yellow. Of the hundreds of different varieties of *B. semperflorens* 'Muse Rose' and 'Pink Avalanche', are well worth growing.

Fuchsias

Fuchsias are shrubs and in mild districts the hardiest kinds, such as *F. magellanica* and its variety *riccartonii*, are used for hedges. But most of the hybrid forms grown are not so hardy and are treated as disposable bedding plants or plants for a cool green-house. They are readily trained as bushes, cascades, standards and other more elabor-ate shapes. Their interesting hanging flowers are varied in size, form and colour and there is a multitude of varieties, varying in habit.

Propagation Soft wood cuttings root readily. Those of hardy kinds are taken in spring, as are also those of greenhouse ones needed for making standards or pyramids or small plants to flower later the same year, but the bulk of greenhouse ones are made in mid-summer for growing through the winter in a minimum temperature of $55°F$ ($13°C$) to flower from May onwards. Soft wood cut-tings are made by removing the top few inches of soft growing shoots. Ideally such a shoot should not have flower buds, but as the tip will be pinched out (stopped) soon after rooting this is not essential. The stem is cut with a razor blade straight across just below a node (leaf joint) and the bottom two pairs of leaves are carefully removed. The base is dipped in a hormone rooting powder and pushed into the cutting bed or pot, con-taining pure sand or a mixture of two parts of sand and one of peat, which gives better results as the brittle roots are less liable to be broken when removed for potting. Cut-tings will normally root in 3 to 4 weeks and should be potted singly into 3-in. pots of JIP1 or a soilless compost. As soon as they are growing again freely the top of each plant is removed, leaving only the two bottom pairs of leaves.

After-care When the pots are full of roots the plants are moved into a larger size with a richer mixture, until by the end of the winter the summer-rooted plants will have reached their flowering size pots and be in JIP3. Standards and other top heavy plants must be in a loam-based compost to help keep them stable.

Stopping During the summer shoots may be shortened to two nodes again and again to make a bushy plant. However, as it takes six weeks from stopping to flowering on a side shoot, do not go on stopping too long. Cuttings destined to be trained as standards should be stopped once. The best side shoots are then tied to a cane, the others removed.

Far left: 'Rosanna', a double-flowered tuberous begonia
Centre above: Varieties of *Begonia semperflorens*. *Centre below:* 'Judy Langdon', another popular double-flowered tuberous begonia
Left: Fuchsia 'Display', a single-flowered kind suitable for bedding out
Right: Fuchsia 'Mrs Popple', an outdoor variety

Recommended Fuchsia Varieties

The sepal colour is given before that of the petals. S=single, SD=semi-double, D=double.
Hardy
For hedges: *F. magellanica riccartonii*, erect, branching, [S] scarlet, purple.
For rock gardens or window boxes: 'Alice Hoffman', cerise and scarlet; 'Tom Thumb', carmine and mauve; 'Lady Thumb', carmine and white; 'Peter Pan', red and purple; *pumila*, very small, scarlet and mauve.
For borders: 'Brilliant', very erect, [S or SD] scarlet and magenta; 'Chillerton Beauty', upright, [S] rose, violet; *corallina*, spreading, [S] scarlet and deep violet; 'Brutus', erect, [S or SD] cerise, carmine and purple; 'Lena', arching, [D] flesh pink, rosy purple; 'Madame Cornelissen', upright, [SD] scarlet and white, long buds; 'Margaret', erect, [SD] carmine and purple, very long flowering; 'Mrs Popple', erect, [S] scarlet and dark violet; 'Peggy King', erect [S] carmine and purple, large flowers; 'Susan Travis', erect, [S] rose pink.
Greenhouse
For bedding out: Singles: 'Bon Accord', white, lilac, held upright; 'Caroline', cream, pale magenta; 'Display', self pink, extended petals; 'Dutch Mill', rose and violet, curling sepals; 'Falling Stars', pale scarlet, brick-red; 'Forget-me-not', flesh-pink, light blue; 'Golden Dawn', flesh-pink, orange; 'Hindu Belle', flesh-pink, plum-purple; 'Lady Heytesbury', white, rose; 'Leonora', self pink; 'Major Heaphy', brick-red, scarlet; 'Marin Glow', white, purple to magenta; 'Mission Bells', red, dark violet, extended petals; 'Mrs Pearson', red, dark violet, large flower; 'Queen Mary', pink, rose, large flower; 'Rose of Castille Improved', flesh-pink, violet; 'Rufus the Red', turkey-red self; 'Sleigh Bells', all white, 'Ting-a-ling', all white, extended petals; 'Tolling Bell', scarlet, white, large bell.
Semi-doubles: 'Abbé Farges', carmine, light purple; 'Pink Flamingo', deep pink, curling sepals, pale pink; 'Satellite', white, shades of red; 'Snow Cap', red, white; 'Tennessee Waltz', rose, Parma violet.
Doubles: 'Emile de Wildeman' ('Fascination'), waxy red, pink veined red; 'King's Ransom', crêpe white, purple; 'Lilac Lustre', carmine, lilac; 'Peppermint Stick', rose, striped white, purple, edged carmine; 'Prelude', white, purple, petaloids white striped purple; 'Royal Velvet', crimson, deep purple; 'Santa Cruz', crimson, dark crimson; 'Swingtime', red, white, veined pink; 'Tahoe', white, pink, mauve and blue; 'Torch', cream flushed salmon, salmon shading to red.
For foliage: 'Avalanche', bright yellowish green; 'Autumnale', coppery red; 'Golden Marinka', golden variegated; 'Sunray', cream and pink variegated; 'Thalia', red bronze.
For standards: 'Cascade', [S] white, carmine; 'Coachman', [S] salmon, orange red; 'Flying Cloud', [D] white, veined pink; 'Jack Acland', [S] pink, rose, pointed buds; 'Mrs Marshall', [S] white, cerise; 'Native Dancer', [D] red and purple; 'Pink Galore', [D] self pink; 'Red Ribbons', [D] long red, white; 'The Tarns', [S] pink and lavender; 'White Spider', [S] white flushed pink, white.
Greenhouse necessary for good flowering: 'Billy Green', salmon self, olive foliage; 'Candlelight', [D] white, light purple to carmine: 'Carmen', [D] carmine, magenta; 'Chang', [S] orange tipped red, orange; 'Citation', [S] rose, white, petals extended; 'Curtain Call', [D] cream, rose to crimson; 'Gartenmeister Bonstedt', orange self, blue green foliage; 'Sophisticated Lady', [D] pale pink, white; 'Texas Longhorn', [D] very long, carmine, white; 'Winston Churchill', [D] pink, silvery blue, compact.

Standards The best standards are not made from the stiff upright types but from the vigorous growing pendulous ones, therefore the trunk of the standard needs to be tied in straight at all stages. To make a head on top of a given length of trunk grow the stem at least two or three further nodes and then rub out the top. The growths from these make branches from which the head is formed as if it were a bush, Side shoots which appear lower down should be rubbed out at once, but the leaves growing from the trunk should be left to make food for growth.

Half standards make good table decorations in a sun parlour, but fuchsias do not like being moved into overheated, draughty or poorly lit places and usually drop their flower buds. They are fine in window boxes and on terraces and patios, as well as bedded out, preferably in beds by themselves.

Hanging Baskets The pendulous varieties, known as basket or cascade forms, are stopped as for bushes, but put the pots on other inverted ones to keep the growth above the bench. Or the plants can be grown in hanging baskets suspended from greenhouse rafters, or from the rafters of patio, porch or pergola or a bracket from a wall.

Planting The soft growth of even the hardy fuchsias will be killed by frost, but new shoots will usually shoot up from below ground the following spring. When planting scoop out a shallow depression in which to put the plant and after it is growing well gradually return the earth so that the base of the stem becomes covered, then in autumn put on a good top dressing. The small mound will help to protect the basal buds.

Housing Plants to be housed during the winter in a frost-proof place should be lifted immediately frost has cut the leaves, and stored almost dry until March when they will start into growth if moved into warmth and watered.

Fuchsia 'Golden Marinka', a variegated kind

❧ Gladioli ❧

The gladiolus (correct plural gladioli in Britain, gladiolus in North America and elsewhere), is named from the bud-tip that breaks through the foliage and resembles the short broad blade of the Roman soldier's and gladiator's sword.

What is planted is not a bulb, but a corm, in which all parts of the eventual plant are present in embryo. Choose, therefore, large high-crowned corms feeling heavy for their width and with a small basal plate (root scar) underneath, indicating that they are young and vigorous. Ensure that these get a good start and are well fed from the beginning, since the number of buds to a spike is determined quite early. Grown mainly as cut flowers and for garden decoration, they vary from little over 1 in. to about 7 in. across the bloom.

Soils and Situations Gladioli will grow on most soils, but prefer a medium to light well-drained loam with plenty of humus and some rich, moisture-retaining material from 1½–2 ft. beneath the surface.

Preferably, they should be sited where there will be full sun for most of the day and not close to trees or hedges.

Where to Grow In the herbaceous border they make good tall plants, not merely for the back, but to vary the centre. Here the foliage-fans create useful green verticals, even when the plant is not in flower. Attractive patterns may be made by placing one central corm with a circle of from five to nine around it on a 6–9-in. radius. Diamonds of from three to five corms a side are effective; a small diamond inside a larger is even better. For continuous planting, avoid the straight line in favour of a zigzag of three to five corms to each 'tack'. Where there is sufficient room, three zigzags consisting of tall large-flowered at the back, medium-flowered 'Butterflies' and ruffled in the middle, and the dainty primulinus hybrids and 'Face-ups' in front would give more continuity of colour.

Tubs or small beds may be planted with circles and diamonds, but tubs should be at least 15 in. deep. Underplanting with the usual range of low summer-flowering bedding plants works well, as they feed at a different level. Never let the tubs dry out, but ensure there is ample drainage.

For Cutting For cut flowers, gladioli are best grown in rows in the vegetable garden. Early saladings can be sown between corms (radishes, globe beets, cos lettuce, spring onions, short carrots). These are harvested before the gladioli need all the space between them.

Preparing the Site Dig in the autumn, working plenty of water-holding material into the second spit or immediately below it. Rotted farmyard manure is best; but mature compost, leaf-mould, sedge-peat, or anything organic and moisture-retentive will do. Gladioli like good drainage about the corms, but plenty of moisture at the roots. For the

smaller types, heavy feeding is not required.

Gladioli grow best in neutral or slightly acid soil, so do not over-lime. In March make holes about 3 ft. apart throughout the patch, sprinkle a little naphthalene in, and cover immediately. The fumes will drive out wireworms. Avoid planting where potato ellworm is known to be present, as these attack the corms and their roots. Douse the whole area with a weak solution of disinfectant, to which a liquid slug-killer may be added. Then sprinkle dry slug-bait around the pot.

Planting Grow your gladioli in blocks of three or four rows each, with a 2-ft. path between for ease of access. The spacing between rows should be sufficient for easy hoeing, not less than 7 in. Larger-flowered kinds should be set about 9 in. apart, medium-flowered 6 in., small-flowered, primulinus, and nanus hybrids, 4 in. Plant throughout April and May. For the closely placed ones, dig a narrow trench about 6 in. deep. For the widely spaced ones it is quicker to trowel out holes; never use a pointed dibber that will create an air-pocket beneath the corm, as well as compacting the soil. On medium soils there should be 4½–5 in. of soil above each full-sized corm, on light soils 5–5½ in., on heavy soils 4 in.

Have a bucket of sharp fine sand to hand, into which has been thoroughly mixed a fungicide and an insecticidal dust. Dust trenches or holes with bonemeal or steamed boneflour to promote root development. Then place a handful of the sand mixture where each corm is to sit, press the corm firmly into this, and pour a second handful over it. This ensures good drainage around the corm, easy, dry lifting, and a protective barrier against below-soil pests and fungus growths. Fill the hole with crumbled, stone-free soil.

Before planting each corm, strip any remaining leaf-husks and examine the top. If you want the maximum number of spikes with a multiplication of corms harvested, leave all the little growing 'eyes' intact and be careful not to damage them when pressing the corm into the sand. If you want one straight spike, especially for exhibition purposes, rub out all but the most central 'eye'. NEVER plant corms that are stone-hard, or squashy, or with large patches of brown, or with concentric circles of black where the old leaves joined. These will infect other stock with disease.

After-care Hand weed close to the plants in moist conditions; hoe between the rows in dry weather. Mulching will reduce this labour, help the soil to retain heat and moisture, and suppress weeds. Mulch after the plants are showing and the larger-flowered kinds have been given a side-dressing of an organically-based fertilizer. Uproot entirely and destroy any gladioli showing yellow leaves with still-green veins. These are harbouring *Fusarium oxysporum*, which is incurable.

Watch for budtips to appear and see these grow clear of the foliage without

Recommended Gladiolus Varieties

The main types are primulinus hybrids (dainty hooded flowers on strong stems) and primulinus x nanus hybrids (less hooded, attractive throat-marks), both suited to windswept sites; small- and medium-flowered, such as the 'Rufmins' and 'Butterfly' range (attractive as cut-flowers); and the large and giant-flowered (best suited for mixed borders and large displays).

1. Peacock and Coronado Nanus Hybrids in Mixture; Miniglads: 'Berta', lime-yellow, striped red; 'Celeste', lilac, blotched purple-green, picoteed purple; 'Lipstick', purple with violet lip-petals; 'Orla', tiny, pink tipped red, blotched strawberry; 'Tampa', smoky brown, striped grey.

2. Primulinus Hybrids: 'Comic, reddish brown, lined yellow; 'Essex', bright red; 'Frank's Perfection', orange-scarlet; 'Hastings', light coffee; 'Pageboy', scarlet, picoteed gold; 'Pegasus', cream, darted rose-purple; 'Salmon Star'; 'Red Star'.

3. Ruffled small-flowered: 'Argus, grey-brown, veined red; 'Bluebird', blue-violet, blotched white; 'Camelot', pink; 'Greenwich', green-yellow; 'Foxfire', deep scarlet; 'Goldilocks' deep golden yellow; 'Little Slam', bright red; 'Mirth', pink; 'Parfait', salmon, red throat-marks; 'Rosy Posy', deep rose, plain-petalled, tall; 'Smidgen', dark red, picoteed gold; 'Statuette', yellow, red throat-marks; 'Tidbit', cream, flushed lavender, blotched purple on yellow; 'Towhead', creamy yellow, tall; 'Troika', lavender yellow rose.

4. Medium-flowered: 'Angel Eyes', white blotched blue-violet; 'Amusing', cherry red; 'Blondine', ivory, blotched white; 'Clio', deep purple; 'Confetti', scarlet, blotched yellow; 'Daily Sketch', cream, blotched biscuit-buff; 'Dream Castle', pale yellow, edged pink, blotched carmine; 'Madrilene', light apricot, red blotch on yellow; 'Sweet Fairy', mimosa yellow; 'Storiette', salmon-pink, blotched yellow; 'Sweet Song', bronzy-salmon, blotched apricot; 'Zenith', strawberry pink.

5. Larger-flowered: 'American Beauty', deep rose; 'Aurora', golden yellow; 'Blonde Beauty', pinkish buff, yellow throat; 'Cameo', creamy yellow, picoteed pink; 'Blue Smoke', mulberry salmon, smoky; 'Frostee Pink', pink and cream, sparkling; 'Isle of Capri', salmon-orange, tall; 'La France', pink and white; 'Landmark', cream, blotched dull yellow; 'Limelight', lemon; 'Mount Everest', white, tall; 'Orange Chiffon', robust, salmon-orange; 'Orchid Queen', pale rose-pink, blotched white; 'Pink Prospector', flesh-pink and yellow; 'Pompeii', deep pink, lavender smoky, silvery overlay, white throat; 'Salmon Queen', salmon and creamy white; 'Simplicity', tall, white; 'Spring Song', light salmon, blotched rich yellow; 'Green Woodpecker', green-yellow, red throat-marks; 'Thunderbird', deep salmon; 'Winnebago Chief', deep red; 'King David', blue-purple, picoteed white; 'Chintz Blue', pale blue violet.

Above: The medium-flowered gladiolus 'Daily Sketch'. *Below:* A typical gladiolus corm, showing the base plate, the new corm and the cormlets, which may be grown on for propagation purposes. *Right: Gladiolus* 'Green Woodpecker'

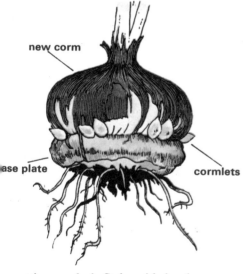

new corm

base plate

cormlets

getting crooked. Stake with bamboo canes in wind-swept areas and always for the larger-flowered varieties, as soon as the direction of facing can be determined by the forward bend of the flowerhead. Tie in with *soft* material.

Cutting Cut in the early morning when the first bloom is partly or fully open, using a sharp knife down inside the foliage and then slanting it through the stem, to leave at least four leaves intact. Treat the plant as a growing entity, so that about six weeks later you may lift the new corm plump and healthy.

Lifting Trim off all roots and foliage immediately and dry the corms thoroughly and quickly. A fortnight later the old corms will pull cleanly away from the new ones, which should be cleaned, further dried, dusted with an insecticide and fungicide mixture, and stored cool (but above freezing-point) where there is air circulation (dry) and preferably in the dark.

Irises

Of the large and varied family of irises cultivated today the bearded iris of the *germanica* type is the one most commonly grown. The original bearded iris, *I. germanica*, had purple flowers with a purple beard and 'falls' that hung down with rather a sad effect, but beautiful modern cultivars have come a long way since then and are available in a rainbow of colours. The poise and elegance of the bearded iris, its sword-like leaves that are excellent contrast for the soft foliage of other plants, and its wide range of colourings, make it a perfect gap-filler when tulips are over and border plants not yet at their best.

Colours These range from snowy white through cream to shell-pink and apricot, from butter yellow to flax blue, from deep sapphire to ruby red and purple. There are also browns, tans and near blacks as well as bicolours, and the plicatas have markings of another colour etched on a paler ground. The upstanding portion of the flower, known as the 'standard' and the drooping tongue-like petal, known as the 'falls' are often different again, so that every conceivable combination of colour exists somewhere in a named cultivar.

Heights The plants vary in height, from dwarfs a few inches high, through the intermediate irises, 16–24 in., to 4 ft. tall kinds. Dwarf bearded irises, forms of *I. pumila* or of *I. chamaeiris* and of many beautiful hybrids, can be used with great effect on rock gardens, in pockets in paving, on dry walls or in sinks and troughs. Their flowers, on stalks a few inches high, resemble the tall flags. They flower during late March and April. They are vigorous and need re-vitalizing by division and replanting every year or two.

Intermediate Irises These, the result of crossing the dwarfs and the tall kinds, increase quickly and are less susceptible to rhizome-rot than the tall irises. Named cultivars come in a wide variety of colours. Though tall flags are better planted apart from other perennials which prevent the sun from reaching and baking their rhizomes, the intermediate irises are happy at the front of the border. Flowering in May, they prolong the season. They are rarely more than 2 ft. tall.

Tall Bearded Irises The tall bearded irises flower in late May and June. Though the blooms are individually short-lived, a succession of flower-buds ensures weeks of colour. The modern kinds branch out, the better to display their numerous flowers.

Requirements Bearded irises are the most good-natured of hardy plants, provided their modest requirements are met. These are: 1. Proper preparation of the ground before planting. 2. A sunny site. 3. A well-drained soil containing lime, which should be deeply dug, and some humus-forming material incorporated before planting (on no account use animal manure).

Planting Always plant shallowly but firmly, barely covering the rhizome so that the sun can bake it. Artificial fertilizers are not necessary if the soil is fertile; excess of nitrogen tends to lush leaf growth and loss of flower. Plants must be hand-weeded, since hoeing can damage the rhizomes. Flower-stems should be removed as close to the ground as possible, but sound leaves should not be shortened until they die down naturally.

The best time for planting or dividing is soon after the flowers are finished, when congested clumps should be split up and only the young vigorous fans, each with a rhizome and strong roots, replanted. Space the tall irises 2 ft. apart; the dwarfs and intermediate kinds should be planted more closely. The most effective way for *all* bearded irises is to plant in blocks of one colour; they look their loveliest grouped together, in island beds or standing alone, surrounded by stone paving, a perfect setting for their beautiful flowers.

Left: 'Enchanted Violet', a tall-bearded iris. *Below:* The parts of an iris flower. *Bottom:* Dividing an iris rhizome. *Right:* Tall-bearded iris 'Summer Song'

Bulbous Irises Dwarf bulbous iris provide some of the most striking splashes of colour in the winter garden. *I. danfordiae*, canary-yellow, and *I. histrio aintabensis*, blue, flower during January and look well planted together. The brilliant blue *I. histrioides* 'Major', with flowers 4 in. across on short stems, flowers before the leaves appear. The bulbs of these tend to split up into tiny bulblets so that it is best to renew annually, potting on the little offsets until they reach flowering size. In February and March flower the sweetly scented, violet-purple *I. reticulata* and its cultivars, pale blue 'Cantab', reddish-purple 'J. S. Dijt' and dark blue 'Royal Blue'.

The Spanish, Dutch and English irises make good clumps in the border. The Dutch, at 2 ft., flower in May and June. The colours are white, yellow, mauve and blue. They are followed by the Spanish irises, *I. xiphium*, in a similar colour range. Both are excellent cut flowers. Bulbs are so cheap that it is worth planting annually, though many will flower each year in a dry soil. The English irises, *I. xiphioides*, flower in June and July.

Recommended Iris Varieties
(height in inches)

Tall bearded irises: 'Big Day' (36), medium blue, white beard; 'Canary Bird' (38), lemon-yellow, white markings; 'Forest Hills' (36), blue-black; 'Golden Planet' (34), golden-yellow; 'Green Ice' (34), greenish-cream; 'Lady River' (30), apricot, falls bronze-violet, beard tangerine; 'My Smoky' (34), white, marked plum-purple; 'Happy Birthday' (34), pink, ruffled petals; 'Karachi' (33), purple-red, falls splashed white; 'Islander' (37), gentian-blue, ruffled petals; 'Foamy Wave' (32), sky blue.
Intermediate irises: 'Langport Honey' (26), orange, reddish falls, beard gold; 'Langport Chief' (16), purple-blue, beard gold; 'Langport Finch' (18), medium blue; 'Langport Lady' (20), apricot-pink, tangerine beard.
Dwarf irises: 'Green Spot' (9), waxy-white, green spot on falls; 'Royal Contrast' (12), dark purple, white beard; 'Tinkerbell' (9), lobelia-blue; 'Path of Gold' (6), golden-yellow.

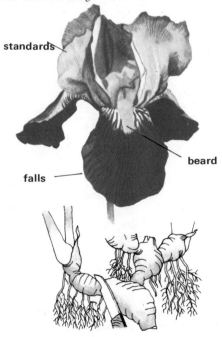

standards

falls

beard

Right: Delphinium 'Mrs F. Bishop'

Sweet Peas, Pelargoniums, Delphiniums

Sweet Peas

A most popular annual, the sweet pea (*Lathyrus odoratus*) is not difficult to grow, though the richer the soil the better the results. Given good cultivation it will produce stems 2 ft. long bearing four, five or more florets. Elegant, graceful and fragrant, with the exception of yellow, it will provide every colour of the spectrum and dozens of different tones or shades. It is a 'cut-and-come-again' annual; indeed, every other day blooms should be gathered to keep the plants in full production.

The 'Spencer' type, trained up canes in 'cordon fashion', will grow to a height of 14 ft. though this means that all side shoots need to be removed during the growing season and every few days there is the business of tying or ringing the thick haulms (stems), and once or twice during the summer kneeing, or layering is called for. On the other hand, if the sweet pea is allowed to go its own way brushwood or wire to the height of 8 ft. will not be too tall.

Soils Land enriched with farmyard manure at the rate of one barrowful to each strip of 15 ft. by 4 ft., dug in autumn or early winter into the second spit of soil and fortified by $\frac{1}{2}$ lb. of bonemeal, will give the best results, or good garden compost at the same rate will serve. Failing that peat may be used. A big bucketful to the square yard, fortified by a $\frac{1}{4}$ lb. of artificial fertilizer containing nitrogen, phosphates and potash in the ratio of 20. 10.10, obtainable in granular form, has proved a very good substitute.

The whole area where the sweet peas are to be grown should be double-dug and the bottom spit treated as suggested. If the soil has been used the previous year for a crop that has been manured, nothing at all need be added. Acid soils should be given a light dusting of lime in January or February. Sweet peas revel in sunshine and dislike draughts, so give them a sheltered place.

When to Sow In the North sow from late September to 7th October. In the Midlands and the South, from the 5th to the 21st October. It is best to sow in a shallow frame, otherwise the plants tend to get drawn; the aim is short, stocky plants.

Sowing Six seeds to a 6-in. pot, sown an inch from the edge is ideal; or if boxes are used sow the seeds 2 in. apart each way. Sow $\frac{3}{4}$ in. deep. Use a moist compost of 3 parts of sieved loam, 1 part of peat and 1 part of coarse sand. Cover the pots or boxes with thick layers of paper to prevent drying out; replace the framelights after placing slug pellets between the pots or boxes. Set a couple of mouse traps, for mice find the seeds irresistible. Inspect after a week and as soon as the shoots appear remove the paper. Water if necessary, and after a day or two open up the frames and do not replace the lights unless frost is threatened.

In hard or severe frosts keep the lights down and cover them with old carpets or sacks. Never let the sun shine on pots and boxes if the soil within them is frozen, since a quick thaw does great damage to the plants.

Springtime sowing will require a greenhouse. When the plants have four leaves pinch out the growing points to induce side shoots. When these are $1\frac{1}{2}$ in. long, harden off the plants by placing the pots or boxes in a frame or under the south wall of the greenhouse.

For a late spring sowing the seeds may be sown $\frac{3}{4}$ in. deep, like garden peas. Always put down slug killer.

Planting Never plant out until the soil on the plot has been reduced to a fine tilth. Then erect the canes if the plants are to be grown cordon style. A strong support at each end of each row will be necessary, with a cross-bar at a height of 5 ft. Double rows, 2 ft. apart, are best, as this helps when it is time to layer. Stretch strong wire from the end of each cross-bar, insert 8 ft. tall canes, 7 in. apart and secure them to the wire.

Using a trowel, make holes to receive the plants *on the outside* of each cane, to facilitate layering. If the plants are to be in circles, they should be planted *inside* the circle of hazel sticks or brushwood. If a circle of netting is to be made, plant first and surround with the netting. Spread the roots and return the soil, so that it just covers the white collar of the plant. If a plant has a brown collar, reject it. It may grow to a height of 3 or 4 ft. and then collapse. Always surround each plant with small twigs. Black cotton stretched across the twigs will deter sparrows.

The Climbing Plants May is a month of vigorous growth. The cordon plants by now will have been restricted to a solitary stem by removing the weaker of the side shoots, of which there may be three or more. Tie in the early stages, very loosely, using raffia. At 1 ft. in height the big sweet pea metal rings may be used. Pinch out side shoots and tendrils to channel the sap into the one stem.

When the plants are grown 'naturally' side shoots are left alone and the tendrils are not removed.

Watering Never allow the land or the plants to become dry. Water the former and spray the latter.

Left: Mixed sweet peas, Spencer type
Above: Sweet Pea 'Legend'
Right: Sweet Pea 'Bijou Mixed'

Bud-drop Early in the season buds which should develop into flowers sometimes assume a frozen appearance and drop off. This is not a disease and eventually nature will correct the trouble. It will even occur, on occasion, in the middle of the flowering season. It is caused by hot days and cold nights, or excessive rain, and there is nothing to worry about.

Kneeing or Layering This is a task only for the cordon-growers, and a somewhat bewildering one for those who tackle it for the first time. If possible, it is best to visit a local grower and help him layer his plants. Broadly speaking, when the plants are 5 or 6 ft. tall, in mid-June, six plants are detached from their canes and drawn out at an angle of 45°, the next six, in order, are placed where the first six have been and so on right to the end of the double row, until there are six vacant canes left, for the first six detached to fill. This means turning the corners at the two ends of the row and great care is needed. But the growing point of each plant should rest near the cane up which you require it to climb.

The stems are laid in a row close to the line of canes. Each plant will lift up its head within a few hours and within three days it will be possible to start the tying process again. Flower stems at first will be twisted and should be cut off, but once the plants have grown a foot or so up the canes, if they are kept tied, the stems will be just as straight as previously, and there is still another 6 ft. or more of cane for them to climb.

The Natural Method Since only exhibitors require flowers with very long stems, the easiest method is to grow the plants much as garden peas are grown, with brushwood or netting for support. Four or five times as many blooms may be cut. Keep the plants weed-free, kill the aphids and, above all, keep cutting the flowers.

Feeding If the land was well prepared in the winter, feeding should hardly be necessary. However, if the flower stems are short, give the plants a liquid feed.

Exhibiting Special vases are filled to the brim, quite firmly, with thick bulrushes. The vase is thoroughly soaked in a bucketful of water. The stems of sweet peas are arranged in the shape of a fan. Exhibition sweet peas are straight of stem, and with four, five or six florets evenly placed. Gappy blooms should be avoided, as should any that have been marked.

Choosing Varieties The most popular sweet pea is the 'Spencer' which grows tall, has exceptionally long stems, and carries 4–6 florets per stem. 'Galaxy Hybrids' also tall-growing, will carry as many as nine or more florets per stem, but they are not so nicely placed. The shorter type known as 'Knee-Hi' grows into a nice bush, needs little support, and will reach a height of 4½ ft. with stems about 1 ft. long. Some dwarf types are less useful if cut-blooms are required; 'Little Sweetheart' varieties grow to 1 ft. and 'Bijou' will sometimes grow to a height of 3 ft. but the flower stems are usually fairly short.

The following is a list of 'Spencer' sweet peas, good exhibition varieties and also splendid for decorative purposes, chosen from hundreds of named varieties. Where two or three of the same colour are named there is not much to choose between them.
White: 'White Leamington'; 'White Ensign'; 'Majesty'. **Cream:** 'Hunter's Moon'; 'Margot'. **Picotee:** 'Selana'; 'Tell Tale'. **Pale Blue:** 'Cambridge'; 'Larkspur'. **Mid-Blue:** 'Noel Sutton'. **Deep Blue:** 'Blue Velvet'. **Lavender:** 'Leamington'; 'Harmony'. **Mauve:** 'Mauve Leamington'; 'Reward'. **Salmon Pink** *(white ground):* 'Splendour'; 'Superfine'. **Salmon Pink** *(cream ground):* 'Royal Flush'; 'Philip Simons'. **Almond-blossom Pink:** 'Southbourne'. **Orange-Cerise:** 'Herald'; 'Clarion'; 'Alice Hardwick'. **Scarlet:** 'Firebrand'. **Crimson:** 'Gipsy Queen'. **Maroon:** 'Milestone'. **Carmine:** 'Rosemary Govan'.
There are not many 'Galaxy' or more dwarf varieties from which to choose; their colours are generally indicated by their names.

Pelargoniums

The pelargonium was introduced into Europe from South Africa towards the beginning of the 17th century; today it is one of the most popular of flowers. It is native to South Africa, Australia and Turkey, but is now widely grown in the temperate areas of the world.

Of the several sub-divisions of the genus the following six are the most popular.

1. **Zonals** *(P. hortorum)* Commonly but incorrectly known as 'geraniums', these are widely grown in beds, greenhouses, tubs, urns, borders, etc. Foliage may be zoned or plain, flowers single, double or semi-double, colours ranging from white through all shades of salmon and pink to reds and purples. Included in this section are Irenes, Deacons, Rosebuds, Cactus and Stellar varieties, detailed as follows:

IRENES This vigorous strain was raised in California and produces larger flower-heads in greater abundance than older varieties. Flowers are produced on long stems making them particularly suitable for arrangements and cut flowers, and are all semi-double. Spaced at not less than 18-in. intervals for correct development in beds and borders, the best results are obtained by planting first into 5-in. clay pots and sinking the pots into the ground. The following is a selection: 'Springtime', light salmon-pink; 'Trull's Hatch', coral-pink with paler centre; 'Penny', neon-pink with blue overtones; 'Electra', deep red with blue overtones; 'Surprise', powder-pink; 'Modesty', pure white.

DEACONS (often known as Floribunda Geraaniums) Derived from a cross between an ivy-leaf and a miniature, these are more compact than Irenes and produce many more smaller flowerheads. The development of the plant may be controlled by the pot size: for instance a plant in a 5-in. pot will grow to about 1 ft. in diameter, whereas one in a 15-in. pot may develop to about 4 ft. in diameter. Six of the most popular varieties, all double, are: 'Deacon Bonanza', neon-pink; 'D. Coral Reef', coral-pink; 'D. Mandarin', orange; 'D. Fireball', bright red; 'D. Lilac Mist', pale lilac-pink; 'D. Romance', purple-mauve with blue tinge.

ROSEBUD AND CACTUS VARIETIES The former bear relatively small flowers and the petals never fully open, thus looking like rosebuds. There are five varieties, three shades of red, one medium purple and one white with pink edges to the petals and a green centre. Cactus varieties have narrow twisted petals rather like quills. Colours range through white, salmon and pink to red, orange and purple.

STELLAR VARIETIES, available in both single and double varieties, originated in Australia. The foliage is star-shaped (hence the name), sometimes zoned but often unmarked, and the flowers are carried on long stems. Plants seldom reach more than 18 in. in height in Britain but will grow to over 5 ft. in Australia and California.

2. **Fancyleaf Zonals** These are mainly grown for their unusual leaf colouring, the

flowers often (but not always) being insignificant, usually red, single and sparsely produced. Popular for bedding schemes, they are also widely used for edging borders and to add variety to mixed groups. Leaf colouring ranges from green-and-black, various shades of green, yellow and bronze to red and copper in a variety of combinations. Because they are seldom as bushy as the Irenes or Deacons, a more impressive effect is produced by spacing them 8–9 in. apart. The following six will give an idea of the colourings available: 'A Happy Thought', mid-green leaves with cream butterfly mark in the centre, flowers red, single; 'Mrs Pollock', red single flowers, leaves red, cream and bronze; 'Mrs Quilter', pea-green leaves with broad bronze zone, salmon-pink single flowers; 'Caroline Schmidt', silver-edged deep green foliage, flowers turkey-red, double; 'Bridesmaid', peach-pink double flowers, foliage golden-green; 'Daydream', rose-crimson double flowers, pea-green foliage with copper zone.

3. Regals *(P. domesticum)* These are commonly known in Britain and Australia as pelargoniums and in USA as show or Lady Washington geraniums. They are mainly grown in this country as pot plants and greenhouse plants but they are suitable for outside beds, borders and tubs in sheltered but sunny positions. The older English varieties flower for only two or three months of the year but the modern hybrids will continue to flower for at least ten months if grown under correct conditions. Flowering depends upon light to a large extent; if the quality of winter light is sufficient they can be flowered throughout the year; if the light is poor they will rest. In their natural environment pelargoniums have no dormant period nor do they need one; dormancy is unnatural to them and is produced by adverse conditions.

Colours range from white to near-black through every possible shade and combination of shades (many being multi-coloured), except yellow and pure blue. The flowers are usually larger than those of the zonals and the leaves are unzoned. However, there are now at least two varieties with coloured foliage. 'Miss Australia' has silver-edged foliage and deep-pink flowers; 'Golden Princess', has gold and green foliage and white flowers. The following are among the most suitable for greenhouse or outside use: 'Georgia Peach', peach-pink with frilled petals (USA); 'Geronimo', blood-red with frilled petals (USA); 'Aztec', strawberry, white and chocolate with maroon markings (USA); 'Grandma Fischer', bright orange with brown marks on most petals (USA); 'Nhulunbuy', cerise, edged with white, very ruffled (Australia); 'South American Bronze', chocolate-maroon with white edge to petals (USA).

4. Ivyleaf varieties *(P. peltatum)* The fleshy leaves of these are shield-shaped. Flowers may be single, semi-double or double. These trailing varieties are mainly used in Britain for hanging baskets, tubs and urns, but are widely planted in other countries in bedding schemes for ground cover. Foliage may be zoned or plain, and there are a few fancy-leaved varieties, including 'Crocodile', with a mesh-like pattern over the foliage in white or cream. Colours range through white, salmon and pink to reds and purple. The six modern varieties listed below are a vast improvement on the older ones: 'Sybil Holmes' ('Ailsa Garland'), rose-pink, double (USA); 'Blue Springs', mauve-pink double, upright habit (Continental); 'Cliff House', white rosettes with a touch of pink in the centre (USA): 'Jack of Hearts', bright pink semi-double with scarlet mark on each petal, upright habit (USA); 'Malibu', crimson-cerise with maroon marks and orange flash, double (USA).

5. Scented-leaf varieties There are hundreds of these since they seed readily and produce many forms with only slight variations. The aroma is released when the foliage is brushed or gently pinched with the fingers. In California and South Africa they can make bushes up to several feet in diameter, but in Britain they are normally grown as pot plants or in the greenhouse and seldom reach more than 2 ft. in height, although plants of 'Mabel Grey' have been grown to nearly 6 ft. Flowers are usually insignificant, white or pale mauve. The following six will serve as the basis for a collection: 'Attar of Roses', rose-scented, pink flowers; 'Crispum Minor', lemon-scented, small pale-mauve flowers; a variegated strain of this is 'C. variegatum'; 'Fragrans', small velvety leaves with spicy perfume and tiny white flowers; 'Prince of Orange', orange scented with small pale-mauve flowers; 'Royal Oak', peppermint perfume, mauve flowers; 'Mabel Grey', strongest of all the scents, sharp citron perfume, small mauve flowers.

6. Miniatures and Dwarfs These are mostly zonals, double, semi-double and single varieties in colours ranging from white through salmon and pink to reds and purples. This classification covers mature plants normally less than 8 in. high, chiefly grown as greenhouse pot plants but they can be used very effectively in bedding schemes, wall pockets and borders. Cultivation is as for other groups but over-potting should be avoided if maximum flower is desired. They can be flowered throughout the year under the correct conditions. The colour range is as for zonals. There are a few miniature regals all with mauve or purple-and-white flowers, and two miniature ivy leaves – 'Gay Baby' with tiny white flowers, and 'Sugar Baby' with pink flowers.

Among fancy leaf miniatures are: 'Fantasie', white, double; 'Fleurette', deep-pink, double; 'Jane Eyre', deep-lavender, double; 'Miss Wackles', deep-red, double; 'Petite Blanche', very pale pink, double, with white areas; 'Sun Rocket', orange-scarlet, double.

General Culture All pelargoniums prefer a sunny position, medium loam and shelter from north and north-east winds. They will withstand temperatures between 34°F (1°C) and 120°F (49°C), but will not survive frost.

Top left: 'Mrs Quilter', a fancyleaf pelargonium
Top right: The scarlet-flowered zonal pelargonium 'Gustav Emich'
Above: Pelargonium 'Maréchal McMahon', a fancyleaf variety
Taking pelargonium cuttings. 1. A suitable shoot is cut from the parent plant. 2. It is cut cleanly below a leaf joint with a razor blade. 3. Prepared cuttings are inserted round the edge of a pot of cutting compost
Right: Delphiniums in the summer border
Far right: Delphinium 'Ann Miller'

Propagation is by cuttings, 3–4 in. long, taken from green shoots, preferably in late July or early August (cuttings from miniatures will be shorter). Over watering should be avoided; plants can easily be killed by an excess of water. Regular feeding with a balanced fertilizer is beneficial, but avoid high-nitrogen feeds including animal manures, which will result in lush growth and few flowers.

are so pure a blue; there are also many varieties with mauve, purple, violet, lilac or white flowers. Early in the 1960s the first hybrid reds, pinks and yellows were bred by Dr R. A. H. Legro in Holland.

Generally described as hybrids of *D. elatum*, modern delphiniums are a mixture of more than half-a-dozen species. *D. belladonna* and its varieties are not so widely grown today. They produce several spikes on each main stem. *D. belladonna* tolerates light shade, but other delphiniums demand open, sunny positions, sheltered if possible from wind.

Soil Although a good garden loam is ideal, sandy or clay soils can be improved by digging in plenty of rotted manure, peat, leafmould, rotted compost or spent mushroom compost. Dig 18–20 in. deep, mix in 4 oz. per square yard of a general fertilizer and let the ground settle for at least a month before planting.

Planting July to October, or March, are the best times to plant, except in heavy, wet ground or where slugs abound, when spring is preferable. A space 2½ ft. across each way is sufficient in a border, but plants intended to produce spikes of exhibition quality deserve spaces 3–3½ ft. across. Young plants knocked from pots can be set with a trowel; those from open ground often arrive with their roots 'balled' in soil and then the roots must be spread out, keeping the crowns of the plants at surface level. Firm planting is essential.

Propagation Delphiniums are increased by seed, division and cuttings. Seed does not come true; that from a blue-flowered plant may produce seedlings with mauve, purple and white flowers. However, the best quality seed produces excellent plants cheaply. Preferably sow freshly harvested seed in August or early September, in seed boxes filled with J.I. seed compost. Stand the boxes in a frame, greenhouse or sheltered spot outdoors. By late April or May seedlings are big enough to plant 1 ft. apart in a nursery bed outdoors and

are moved later to their permanent positions.

Named varieties will come true only when propagated by dividing clumps in early spring, when the shoots are 3–4 in. high, or by cuttings. The roots are teased apart and the crown served with a knife so each new portion has roots and one or two shoots. Cuttings generally produce sturdier plants. They are made by choosing healthy shoots 3–4 in. high, scraping soil from around them before cutting them off close to the crown. Strip off their lower leaves, dip the lower ends of the stems in water, then in hormone rooting powder and set them with a dibber, about five in a 4½-in. pot of cutting compost. Bury one third of each stem, water the cuttings, and place them in a propagating case, or on a shaded greenhouse bench. They root in six to eight weeks and then are potted up singly in 3½-in. pots of J.I.P.1.

Cultivation In early spring crowns should be covered with ashes or coarse grit to keep slugs off the young shoots. Thin these out to leave the strongest four to six per plant, when 6 in. tall. Knock in a 6–8 ft. cane beside each shoot; tie the stems to the canes as they grow. Feed each plant with a heaped trowelful of dried blood in May, the same amount of general fertilizer in early June, and a tablespoon of sulphate of potash as the flower buds show colour, watering in these plant foods. Keep the soil damp. Dead flower spikes should be cut back; secondary spikes sometimes develop and bloom in early autumn.

Ten Reliable Delphiniums
'Betty Hay': pale sky-blue, white eye, tall. 'Blue Tit': indigo-blue, black eye, dwarf. 'Butterball': creamy yellow, yellow eye, medium. 'Daily Express': bright blue, black eye, tall. 'Great Scot': pale mauve, black eye, tall. 'Page Boy': mid blue, white eye, dwarf. 'Purple Ruffles': purple, double, tall. 'Silver Moon': silvery-mauve, white eye, tall. 'Strawberry Fair': rosy lilac, white eye, medium. 'Swanlake': white, black eye, tall.

❧ Delphiniums ☙

July brings the delphinium flowers on towering spikes 5 to 7 ft. high, and the modern, shorter 4 ft. varieties which need little or no support. These hardy plants die to the ground in autumn and produce new shoots the following spring. They are used most frequently in herbaceous borders, mixed borders and in front of shrubs. Few flowers

ᏋᏋᏒ Dahlias ᏒᏒᏋ

Dahlias are half-hardy perennials, originally from Mexico, introduced into the British Isles about 1789. Very adaptable, they grow well in any type of soil. They are versatile, being used for garden decoration, cut flowers, floral art and exhibition. Few flowers can match them for their wide range of brilliant colours, their wide variety of shapes and sizes, and their long flowering period. They tolerate extremes of climate and, even in a poor season, some kinds will produce over one hundred flowers.

Classification In height dahlias range from the Lilliput type, 1 ft. high, to the more normal types which can reach a height of over 5 ft., although the average is about 3½ ft. The sizes of the blooms vary tremendously, from about 1 in. across to over 14 in. There are ten groups as follows:

DECORATIVE Fully double, the petals are broad and usually flat with rounded tips.

CACTUS Narrow petals rolled or quilled backwards half their length or more, sometimes curving inwards, sharply pointed.

SEMI-CACTUS Halfway between the previous two, the petals broad at the base and rolled for less than half their length.

(*Size:* These three groups are divided into bloom sizes as follows: Giant, over 10 in., large, 8–10 in., medium, 6–8 in., small, 4–6 in. miniature, not exceeding 4 in.)

BALL AND MINIATURE BALL These have a tight honeycomb formation with short petals rolling inwards for half their length or more and rounded at the tips. Ball dahlias range from 4–6 in., miniature ball dahlias are 4 in. or less.

POMPON Smaller more perfect than the ball dahlias and 2 in. or less in size.

SINGLE-FLOWERED A single row of petals surround an open centre.

ANEMONE-FLOWERED In these the flowers have numerous tubular petals surrounded by a single row of flat petals.

COLLERETTES These have a single inner row of small petals, usually of a different colour

from the larger outer row of petals.

PAEONY-FLOWERED These resemble the singles with an open centre but have two or more rows of petals.

MISCELLANEOUS In this group are those bizarre dahlias which as far as shape is concerned cannot be put in any of the other groups.

DWARF BEDDING DAHLIAS These belong to any of the ten groups but must not exceed 24 in. in height.

Site Dahlias prefer an open sunny position but will still grow well in a partially shaded spot, away from trees. They look glorious when massed in a bed or border by themselves. They also fit in well with other plants in the herbaceous border, if they are placed carefully to use their various heights and colours to best effect. The 1-ft. tall dwarf kinds will add summer colour to the rock garden, or can be planted in a bed in a retaining wall or even in a window box. Planted in tubs or other containers, they will brighten up a patio, terrace or other paved area.

Soil Cultivation Single digging is all that is necessary. This should be done in late autumn or early winter on heavy soil, leaving the ground rough for the snow and frost to break it down; light soils can be left until early spring. Every soil benefits from the addition of humus-forming material such as farmyard manure, peat, horse manure, leaf mould, compost, straw, hop manure, seaweed, etc., dug into the top few inches.

A month or so before planting, the soil should be broken down to a reasonable tilth and a top dressing of either bonemeal or a general fertilizer should be raked into the top couple of inches of soil.

Planting Out Dahlias can be grown either from tubers or green plants. Tubers are the roots which have formed at the base of a plant grown the previous season. They can be planted from mid-April onwards. Space the tall types about 2½ ft. apart the dwarf bedding types 1½ ft. apart, and the Lilliput types 1 ft. A stout 4 ft. stake or cane is needed for the taller types and these are put in position first. Plant the tubers 6-in. deep, just in front of the cane. On poor soil put in a couple of handfuls of a mixture of peat and a little general fertilizer, into the hole and put the tuber on this, stem upwards, and fill in the hole with fine soil. Once the shoots appear above ground they are treated exactly as green plants.

Green plants are planted as soon as all danger of frost is over. Canes are put in position first and a hole slightly larger than the plant rootball is taken out just in front of the cane. A planting mixture of peat and fertilizer will help to get the plants away to a flying start on poor soil. Place the plant in the hole and fill it in with soil. Tie the plant loosely to the cane with soft twine then water the plants in well. Place a few slug pellets round each plant.

Summer Management For the first three or four weeks after planting, hoe the soil between the plants to keep down the weeds. When the plants have developed five or six pairs of leaves, pinch out the growing tip to promote bushy growth. As the side shoots develop after this stopping they will need to be kept tied in to the cane.

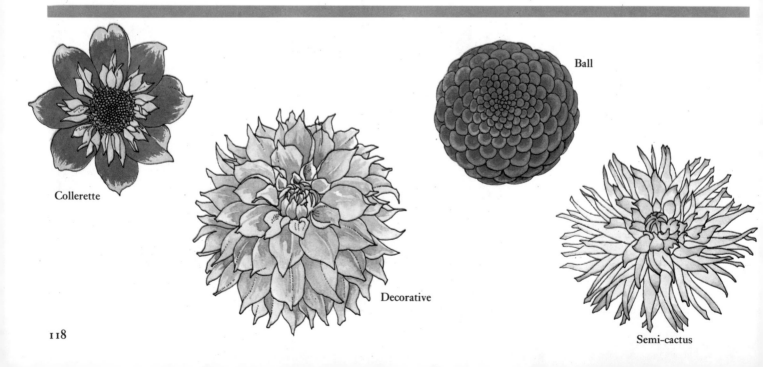

Collerette

Decorative

Ball

Semi-cactus

The soil around the plants should never be allowed to dry out. Dahlias benefit greatly from the application of a mulch which will lessen the need for watering. Apply this in early July to a depth of about 4 in., completely covering the soil around the plants.

Flowering The first flowers should begin to appear about mid or late July. Better quality flowers can be obtained by disbudding, which means removing the two small side buds which appear either side of the main or terminal bud. Also remove the two side shoots which appear at the joint of the pair of leaves below the flowering bud. Left to themselves dahlias produce dozens of small poor quality flowers on short stems; a little light disbudding and de-shooting makes an amazing difference.

Faded blooms should be removed to ensure continuation of flowering. This is particularly important with the single-flowering types which form seed heads very quickly. When cutting blooms for the house use a sharp knife, make a long slanting cut and plunge the stem immediately in deep water; cut in this way, dahlias should easily last a week. Cut as many blooms as you like, as often as you like.

Give the plants an occasional foliar feed. Make sure that all the plants to be saved for next year are clearly labelled with their name (if known), or type and colour.

Lifting and Storing

Lifting The tubers which have formed at the base of the plants will need to be lifted and stored for the winter. After the frost has killed the foliage cut through the main stem about 6 in. above soil level. With a fork loosen the soil round the tuber then push the fork underneath and lift the tuber.

Remove surplus soil from the roots and place them stem downwards in a greenhouse, shed, garage, or spare room for about ten days to dry. While they are drying the tubers can be prepared for storage. Trim off the thin stringy roots from the ends of the tubers

and cut the stem down to about 2 in. Any damaged ends of the roots should be trimmed away and the cut surface dusted with either green sulphur or a mixture of lime and flowers of sulphur in equal parts. Tie the label securely to the stem.

Storing If a frost-free garage, shed or spare room is available, place the tubers in shallow boxes of peat or dry soil. A cool cellar makes an ideal storage place. Where frost protection cannot be guaranteed, protect the tubers by placing them in stout wooden or cardboard boxes filled with an insulating material such as dry soil, sand, ashes, straw or sawdust.

Inspect the tubers once or twice while they are in store to make sure they are sound. Feel each tuber; if any parts are soft and brown this indicates rot which will have to be trimmed away and the cut surface dusted with sulphur/lime powder. Any tubers with a white fluffy deposit (mildew) will need to be wiped clean with a dry cloth and dusted with sulphur/lime.

Propagation

Dahlias are very easy to propagate, whether from seed, division of tubers, or by cuttings.
Sowing seed Plants will not reproduce true to type or colour from seed, except for the single Coltness type and the semi-double dwarf bedders.

Sow the seed in March in a heated greenhouse, thinly, in pans or boxes of John Innes seed compost or one of the soilless seed composts, covering the seed with $\frac{1}{4}$ in. of compost. Once they germinate they should be pricked out 24 to a box. Grow the plants on coolly and in April move them to a cold frame to harden off before planting them out in late May or early June.

Dividing tubers A dahlia tuber consists of a stem which is attached to the crown or collar where the eyes or buds are situated; swollen, potato-like tubers are attached to the crown. There are two types of tuber; the ground tuber is usually quite large and is formed at the base of a plant grown outdoors

without restriction; the pot tuber is small and compact and is formed at the base of cuttings grown throughout the season in pots.

Before dividing the tuber the eyes must be visible and are coaxed into life by placing the tubers in moist peat or compost in late March or early April in shallow boxes which are placed either in a greenhouse or cold frame or on a sunny windowsill in the house. Once the eyes are visible, cut down the centre of the stem between the buds, right through the tuber. Further division may be possible, depending on the size of tuber and the position of the eyes, but each piece to be planted must contain a portion of stem attached to a piece of the crown bearing an eye, and at least one portion of swollen root or tuber. The divisions can either be planted out in mid-April or grown on in boxes in the greenhouse and planted out in late May.
Taking Cuttings Large numbers of cuttings can be taken from dahlia tubers; they root easily in a warm greenhouse in a minimum temperature of 60°F (16°C). If any tubers show signs of rot or mildew, treat them as described earlier. The tubers are boxed up in moist peat or compost, or they can be bedded down on the open greenhouse bench, if possible, over some form of bottom heat. Keep the compost moist.

The cuttings are taken when the shoots are 3-4 in. long and are normally placed round the sides of a pot or pan or placed in a seed box in rows.

With a clean sharp knife cut through the shoot just below the lowest leaf joint. Trim off the lower leaves, dip the end of the cutting in a hormone rooting powder then place the cutting 1 in. deep in the compost. Space the cuttings so that the leaves are just clear of each other and water lightly. Place the cuttings in a propagating frame, or bed the pots in moist peat on the open bench and provide shade.

Spray the cuttings with a fungicide to prevent damping off and after a day or so allow them a free flow of air. To lessen the risk of flagging, spray the cuttings with tepid

Pompon

Cactus

Single-flowered

Anemone-flowered

water twice daily until rooting takes place in about 14 days.

Pot the rooted cuttings singly into 3½-in. pots of JIP1 or a peat-based compost. Keep the plants in a shady spot in the greenhouse for a day or so before placing them on a shelf near the glass, keeping the greenhouse well ventilated. In April remove the plants to a cold frame, keep the lights closed for a couple of days then progressively allow more ventilation until, towards planting out time in late May or, in the colder areas, in early June, the lights can be left off completely. At all times protect the plants from frost.

Top left: 'Pink Joy', a good example of a medium decorative dahlia variety
Above left: A typical pompon dahlia, with perfectly formed, ball-like flowers, under 2 in. in diameter
Above right: 'Twiggy', a good small decorative dahlia for cutting purposes. The blooms are reminiscent of those of water-lilies

Recommended Dahlia Varieties

The giant and large varieties are more suited for exhibition than garden decoration; the medium varieties are suitable for the back of the border as well as for exhibition; the small and miniature dahlias make excellent cut flowers, garden plants, as well as show blooms or are suitable for flower decoration purposes. The heights given are approximate.

Decorative Dahlias
Giant: 'Alvas Supreme', lovely sulphur yellow, 5 ft.; 'Hamari Girl', lavender pink, easy to grow, 4 ft.; 'Holland Festival', orange with white tips, 4½ ft.; 'Lavengro', deep lavender overlaid bronze, 4½ ft.
Large: 'Polyand', unusual lavender, almost blue, 4½ ft.; 'Shirley Jane', lemon-yellow suffusing to mauve, 4 ft.; 'Silver City', white, 4 ft.
Medium: 'Alloway Cottage', lemon-yellow with a lilac tinge, 4½ ft.; 'Cyclone', cylamen pink, 4 ft.; 'Evelyn Foster', a fine white, reflexed shape, 4 ft. 'Golden Turban', 4 ft.; 'Rustig', lemon-yellow, 4½ ft.; 'Suffolk Spectacular', glistening white, 4½ ft.; 'Thames Valley', bold yellow, 4 ft.
Small: 'Angora', white, split petal ends, 3½ ft.; 'Amethyst', pale bluish lavender, 4 ft.; 'Dedham', lilac and white blend, early 3½ ft.; 'Edinburgh', purple with white tips, 3½ ft.; 'Rothesay Robin', magenta, the outstanding show dahlia, 4 ft.; 'Twiggy', rose pink, waterlily shape, for cutting, 3½ ft.
Miniature: 'David Howard', bronze with dark foliage, outstanding, 3½ ft.; 'Jo's Choice',

brilliant red, good show form, 3 ft.; 'Newchurch', salmon, free-flowering, 3½ ft.
Cactus Dahlias
Giant: 'Polar Sight', white with ivory centre, twisted petals, 5 ft.
Large: 'Drakenberg', salmon, mauve and orange blend, 5 ft.; 'Paul Critchley', dark pink, 4 ft.
Medium: 'Arthur Lashlie', vivid blood-red, compact, 3½ ft.; 'Banker', orange-red, quilled petals, 4 ft.; 'Raiser's Pride', light salmon-pink, 4 ft.; 'Yellow Galator', yellow, 4 ft.
Small: 'Alvas Doris', deep blood red, 3½ ft.; 'Klankstad Kerkrade', sulphur yellow, perfect, 3½–4 ft.; 'Paul Chester', orange on lemon, base, early, 3–3½ ft.; 'Richard Marc', pink and yellow pastel shades, 4 ft.; 'Tradition', antique rose on orange-yellow base, 4 ft.; 'White Kerkrade', perfect sport from 'Klankstad', 3½–4 ft.
Semi-Cactus Dahlias
Giant: 'Arab Queen', coral pink, yellow centre, 4½ ft.; 'Inca Dambuster', lemon-yellow, 5 ft.; 'Respectable', golden amber on long stem, 4 ft.
Medium: 'Autumn Fire', apricot orange on yellow base, 3½–4 ft.; 'Hamari Bride', beautiful glistening white, 4 ft.; 'Hamari Sunset', orange gold blend, outstanding, 3½ ft.; 'Rotterdam', dark velvety red, 4 ft.; 'Symbol', salmon apricot overlaid bronze, 4 ft.; 'Yellow Spiky', sport from 'Symbol', 4 ft.
Small: 'Cheerio', cerise with white tips, 3½ ft.; 'Hoek's Yellow', 3½ ft.; 'Mariner's Light', yellow, 3½ ft.; 'Tyros', brilliant red,

4 ft.; 'White Swallow', popular show and garden bloom, 3½ ft.; 'Wootton Wedding', pure white, good for exhibition, 4 ft.
Ball Dahlias: 'Highgate Robbie', very dark red, large, 4 ft.; 'Mrs Anderson', lilac cup winner, 3½ ft.; 'Rev. Colwyn Vale', deep purple, 4½ ft.
Miniature Ball: 'Connoisseur's Choice', brilliant red, 3½ ft.; 'Dr John Grainger', deep golden orange, 3½ ft.; 'Nettie', perfectly formed yellow, 3½ ft.; 'Rothesay Superb', bright red for show and garden, 4 ft.
Pompon: 'Hallmark', a good exhibition pink, 3½ ft.; 'Moorplace', deep purple, 3½ ft.; 'Rhonda', light lavender, 3½ ft.; 'Willo's Violet', deep purple on lighter ground, 3½ ft.
Miscellaneous: All of these are very good for flower arrangements: 'Andrie's Wonder', salmon, yellow and lavender, 4 ft.; 'Giraffe', maize-yellow with bronze stripes, 3 ft.; 'Lilac Lace', narrow split petals, 2½ ft.; 'Pink Giraffe', 3 ft.
Anemone-flowered: 'Comet', deep velvet blood red, 3½ ft.; 'Honey', bronzy pink with yellow middle, 2 ft.; 'Roulette', pink with apricot-pink centre, 1½ ft.
Collerettes: 'Chimborazo', dark maroon with yellow collar, 4 ft.; 'Easter Sunday', creamy white, 3½ ft.; 'Grand Duc', scarlet with yellow tip and collar, 3 ft.
Paeony-flowered: 'Bishop of Landaff', scarlet with dark foliage, 2½ ft.
Single-flowered: 'Little Drummer Boy', blood red, 1 ft.; 'Princess Marie Jose', pink, 1½ ft.; 'Yellow Hammer', yellow with dark almost black foliage, 1½ ft.

Carnations and Pinks

The genus *Dianthus* is large, but the popular garden flowers are border carnations, growing about 2½ ft. tall, with exquisitely formed blooms and smooth-edged petals, and pinks in a wide variety of shapes, sizes and heights.

Carnations and pinks have evergreen, blue-grey narrow leaves with a waxy covering; their habit is more like a shrub than a herbaceous plant, so that they should not be cut down.

They need a sunny, well-drained position. Any soil suits them, so long as it is not very acid, and they are very tolerant of lime. They can be planted in open weather from October to the first half of April, setting them firmly but not deeply, burying the roots but not the stem, securing to a 6-in. stake if necessary. Planting distance for border carnations is about 12 in. and for pinks about 10 in.

To improve soil before planting, dig compost or well-rotted manure below the first spit, and hoe bonemeal at 4 oz. per sq. yd. into the top spit. In spring a side-dressing of sulphate of potash at 2 oz., or bonfire ashes at 8 oz., per sq. yd. is good, but potash fertilizers should not be given in autumn as they make the stems brittle in winter. Plants in their second and subsequent years should have a side dressing of a balanced fertilizer.

Border carnations need staking with a 3-ft. cane, and they should be disbudded to leave one bud on the central stem and one on each side stem, removing the others when about the size of a small pea. Pinks are not disbudded, and rarely require staking.

Border carnations flower in July and August, and old-fashioned pinks in June, and apart from snapping off the old flower stems no special treatment is needed. Most modern pinks flower a second time, and should be thoroughly watered and then given a dressing of complete fertilizer.

Border carnations are propagated by layering in July and August. Select a good side stem and strip off all the leaves from the lower part, leaving five fully developed pairs at the top. Push a thin-bladed knife into the stem just below the lowest joint with leaves on. Cut downwards through the joint below and turn the knife away from the centre of the plant so as to bring it out just below the joint. This leaves a tongue which opens out as the stem is bent down to the ground. If the stem is too stiff to bend down without snapping, bruise it between the joints with the thumbnail or a pair of thin pliers. Push the open tongue into the ground and secure it in position with a loop of wire. Prepare the ground beforehand by working in a mixture of equal parts of sharp sand and peat.

After enough layers are put down, they are watered in and not allowed to become dry while rooting, which takes about six weeks. They are then cut away from the parent plant and left another week when they can be lifted. They can be planted out directly, or potted up for a fortnight before planting.

Pinks can be propagated in the same way, but usually cuttings are taken from late June to early August. Select strong side shoots for cuttings, and leave four or five fully developed pairs of leaves at the tip. Strip off the pair of leaves below this with a downward pull, exposing the joint. Cut just below the joint with a sharp knife or razor blade. The cutting is inserted in sandy soil up to but not above the next joint, in a pot in a cold frame, exposed to the sky but not the sun, watered and kept in a close atmosphere for three to four weeks, when top growth shows that it has rooted. The cuttings are then hardened off and either potted up into 3½-in. pots and grown on for a month or so before planting.

Modern pinks sometimes send up the central stem to flower before proper side growth has been made, and if so they must be stopped. This is done when the plants have made ten to twelve joints. Hold the seventh or eighth joint in one hand, and bend the top sharply sideways when it should snap off, or cut it off cleanly just above the joint.

Border carnations should never be stopped, and stopping may delay the flowering of old-fashioned pinks for a season. However, a pink should never be allowed to flower unless it has good side growth.

Below: Pink 'Gran's Favourite'

Recommended Varieties of Carnations and Pinks

The following varieties are easy to grow. All the pinks listed are scented; the scented border carnations are marked Sc.

Border Carnations: 'Robin Thain', Sc. white; 'Merlin Clove', Sc. white, marked purple; 'Mendip Hills', pink, flaked red; 'Catherine Glover', 'Thomas Lee', yellow, marked red; 'Leslie Rennison', Sc., rosy mauve; 'Harmony', grey, flaked red; 'Alice Forbes', white, marked pink; 'Fair Maiden', white with red picotee edge; 'Marvel Clove', Sc., violet; 'Gipsy Clove', Sc., crimson; 'Salmon Clove', Sc., salmon pink; 'Lavender Clove', Sc., lavender; 'Beauty of Cambridge', 'Mary Murray', yellow.

Modern Pinks: (A laced pink is one in which a dark centre zone or eye is extended to form a loop of colour near the edge of the petal). 'Cherryripe', bright pink; 'Doris', salmon-pink, red eye; 'Constance', bright pink, paler edge; 'Laced Joy', pink, laced crimson; 'London Poppet', palest pink, laced ruby red; 'Timothy', 'Freckles', pink with red flecks; 'Show Aristocrat', pale pink, buff eye; 'Prudence', palest pink, laced dark red; 'Swanlake', white, 'Show Portrait', crimson; 'Show Beauty', deep pink, maroon eye; 'Winsome', deep pink.

Old-fashioned Pinks: 'Whiteladies', white, better now than 'Mrs Sinkins'; 'Excelsior', pink with dark eye, often called 'Pink Mrs Sinkins'; 'Inchmery', pale pink; 'Dad's Favourite', white, laced purple.

Above: Pinks: varieties 'Doris', 'Ideal', 'Cherry Ripe', 'Portrait', 'Bouquet', 'Gaiety', 'Rosalie'

Some Definitions

Today, many people begin gardening, which often means tree and shrub planting, without the slightest previous practical experience. Therefore, terms and phrases of whose meanings they may be entirely ignorant are found regularly, even in the popular press.

A *deciduous* tree or shrub is one that is bare of leaves in winter, then sprouts them in spring and loses them in autumn (often after they have turned gorgeous colours). For quite a time, therefore, such plants are relatively dormant, giving a long period during which they may be transplanted with safety.

The individual leaves on an *evergreen* tree or shrub have a life of more than a year, even up to three of four, before they fall. This means that the plant always carries a lot of leaves. These leaves are, however, to some extent always active; an activity that may be reflected in the need for root action. Thus expeditious handling when transplanting is essential so that root action is not unduly checked. Further, to prevent this, planting in early autumn or middle to late spring is desirable as the soil is then warm and natural root action is taking place. This applies to such plants as hollies, rhododendrons and laurels. Conifers, botanically different from these, and for the most part carrying their seeds in cones or adaptations of cones, are also evergreens. Pines, cypresses and firs must have the same treatment.

Standards Most deciduous trees such as crab-apples, cherries and rowans are supplied as standards. That is, in the nursery they are trained up on single bare stems (or legs) with a bunch of shoots at the top. The stems are about 5 ft. high, and are kept clean by pruning away side growths. Among the cluster of branches there should be one somewhere near its centre which is growing vigorously and is forming a *leader*. This branch should not be cut back, as it is the key to a well-formed crown or head to the young tree.

Half-standards Trees on a stem about half the length of a standard, are sometimes produced and can be most useful.

Bushes These are quite simply the very numerous woody plants, deciduous or evergreen, which it is virtually impossible to train as standards. They grow naturally from the ground upwards with a number, indeed often, a tangle of shoots.

Trees and Shrubs on a New Property

As a first step, it is essential to make sure that there are not preservation orders on existing trees; such trees must not be touched. The local authority (usually its Planning Officer) will give information on this matter.

There may also be restrictions placed on the felling or even planting of trees by the owner or seller of the land which will be a condition mentioned in any contract. This point will be dealt with by the solicitor.

Placing Trees Of a more general and practical nature, the planter should study the placing of his trees to ensure that:

(1) The eventual size will not block his view, or overhang his house.

(2) Overhang a neighbouring property or a road, or interfere with electric or telephone lines.

(3) Be planted so that the root system will not interfere with proposed or existing drains.

(4) Carefully consider the eventual size of any tree planted to ensure that it is proportionate to the size of the property and will not occupy too much space.

(5) Should there be trees already present on the site, examine them carefully. If any seem to be unsound, consult a qualified tree surgeon or at least someone with a knowledge of trees, as for example a member of the local Parks department's staff, if this can be arranged.

It cannot be over-emphasized that attention to these matters at an early stage may possibly save a great deal of trouble in the years to come. The smaller the garden, the more important it is.

Soil A great many of our woodlands, such as those of oak, ash and beech among deciduous trees and even more so evergreen conifers, grow on the sides of hills and mountains. This means that the rich, fertile soils of the valleys are not essential for their growth, but suggests that they do like good drainage. In other words most trees and shrubs on the market are well suited by the usual soil conditions on a modern housing estate.

Camellia chandleri 'elegans' is an old but still popular variety

There is one important qualification to this. There are certain trees and shrubs that will not grow where there is above a certain quantity of lime present in the soil, particularly if the situation is chalky.

In practice, if rhododendrons or azaleas are growing in or around the new garden and the leaves do not look yellow, then you can grow all the trees and shrubs listed as lime haters.

Even so, you can grow some of these when lime is present—for example, you can make a raised bed of peat into which water from the surrounding soil does not drain, and water it with rain water. Or you can treat plants with a chemical, sequestrene, which helps to overcome the effects of the lime, but the effect of this is not permanent.

Planting Assuming that you have decided where to plant your trees or shrubs, you may obtain them in two ways:

First, if they are ordered from a nurseryman they will arrive carefully packed during the dormant season—that is at any time when the leaves have fallen, if they are deciduous trees or shrubs. If they are evergreen trees or shrubs, say conifers or rhododendrons, they will come when growth has apparently ceased—preferably in autumn or early spring.

That is still the most usual method followed in supplying trees; the plant is very carefully lifted from the ground by skilled labour and packed so that it will stand the rigours and delays of modern transport on its way to the recipient.

There is now another method, that of 'instant' trees (or shrubs) when the buyer selects his plants in the nursery and takes them home to plant without delay.

To start with standard trees, if a decision has been made, not necessarily of the kinds to be used but as to their position, a start can be made in the autumn. If they are to be in grass, then an area of up to a yard in diameter may be sprayed with a weedkiller. When, in due course, the grass has been killed and has gone straw-coloured, it should be skimmed off. The ground can then be deeply forked over and such things as the roots of nettles and docks, which will not have been killed, pulled out. If the ground is very light, compost may be forked in; if it is heavy, some peat will do good.

For the actual planting, you will need to have some moist peat ready and a good, stout pointed stake, say from 4–5 ft. long, with a supply of the specially designed tree-ties and some string.

If the tree arrives by rail or road, loosen the packing. But do not attempt to plant if there is *any* frost in the ground, or if the ground is saturated. Leave the package in an unheated shed. If conditions for planting are suitable, completely unpack the tree. If deciduous, disentangle the roots, cutting off cleanly any that are broken; if it is a conifer, the roots will be in a ball of soil and do not disturb this too much. Then in the prepared spot of ground, dig a hole wide enough to take the roots spread out, and deep enough

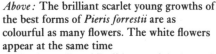

Above: The brilliant scarlet young growths of the best forms of *Pieris forrestii* are as colourful as many flowers. The white flowers appear at the same time
Right above: 'Royal Red' is one of the best of the *Buddleia davidii* varieties
Right centre: Genista cinerea, a good broom for dry soils and sunny places
Below: The 'japonica' (Chaenomeles) is one of the most brilliant of spring-flowering shrubs

for the previous depth of planting, easily identified on the stem by the soil mark, to be as near as possible to that of the present level of the surface. Now drive a stake in, carefully avoiding damage to the roots, as near to the stem of the tree as possible and loosely tie the stem to it. Then start filling in the hole; it is a good thing to sprinkle plenty of moist peat on the roots. Firm the soil by treading gently on it, and before the hole is full, give the tree a good soaking. Then use a tree tie to replace the string. This can be done single-handed, but a second person to hold the young tree in place, is a great help.

Firmness and stability are the secrets of tree and shrub planting. Nurserymen must benefit enormously from the number of trees one sees flopping about because they are not securely staked and the roots fail to get a hold in the soil. The adjustable tree ties must be examined, say, twice a year. The stake can be removed when it is obvious that the trees are firmly anchored.

The treatment for 'instant' trees and conifers is much the same, but here you have the roots carefully grown in a ball, which must not be broken. Staking is just as important, if indeed not more so. Regular watering for at least the first season after planting is essential, for it is easy for the ball of roots to dry out and it is difficult to wet it properly once this has happened.

The planting of shrubs, which is usually done in beds, follows exactly the same principles. But these branch down by the ground, and usually very little staking if any is necessary as they do not blow about except, for example, in windy sea-side districts.

Pruning

We hear a great deal about pruning, so much, indeed, that the subject often sounds very perplexing. Let us try to simplify it, first by explaining the reasons why we prune.

Pruning Trees As far as the pruning of ornamental trees is concerned the objective is to produce nice, shapely specimens that look attractive even when bare of leaves. We grow these to become standards, that is, to have a crown of branches on top of a clean stem or trunk, perhaps 6 ft. or more tall. All side shoots on this stem must, therefore, be removed. But the leading shoot, the natural growing point, must not be cut back. We want to aim for a stem – eventually the trunk – arising from ground level and carrying through gracefully to the top of the tree. It is an aim that admittedly cannot always be fulfilled, as, for example, the upper part of crab apples generally and unavoidably becomes a bit of a tangle. But this should always spread from the top of a clean stem.

As to the actual operation of pruning, the main objective is to make as clean a cut as possible, close up to the stem (but not damaging it) so that the bark can gradually spread over and heal the wound. Do not let the piece you are cutting off come away and tear bark with it. If the shoot you are cutting off is stout and heavy, shorten it first so as to avoid its weight tearing it away. If the wound you leave is large – say an inch or more in diameter – it is as well to paint it with one of the special proprietary paints. Infection can quickly take hold, particularly in the growing season.

Suckers coming up from the bottom of a tree must always be removed; it is quite possible that they come from the quite different stock on which your tree was grafted or budded.

So much for young trees – except perhaps when two branches have grown together so that they rub, which is undesirable. The least important must be removed.

When it comes to dealing with large branches on big trees, it is essential to leave this to a qualified tree surgeon. It needs most careful judgement to effect a good job and can be dangerous to an unskilled operator as well as, perhaps, causing damage to passers-by or neighbouring property.

Pruning Shrubs When we come to the pruning of shrubs, to some extent the main principles apply. But the essence of a shrub is its growth which rarely arises from a leader but normally from a cluster of shoots at the base. There is the matter of pruning just to

tidy up the shoots when they have become untidy – mere commonsense, bearing in mind that most shrubs send up new shoots naturally from the base.

There are, however, two underlying rules to follow when shrub pruning.

Firstly, some kinds flower mostly on wood that was produced and ripened in the past year; that wood must be retained.

Secondly, a considerable number flower on shoots that have grown during the current year – that is, you cut them hard back early in the spring.

These peculiarities are mentioned in the individual descriptions of shrubs and trees.

The craft of pruning is mostly easily learned by seeing examples of it that have been well done. Today, so often (but not always) this is carried out in local parks, visits to which are always worth while.

Always use sharp secateurs and well sharpened pruning saws.

The Waste Corner

Many gardens have awkward bits of land, often sloping and dry, perhaps shaded by trees when the sun shines and which drip when it rains. They are spots in which practically none of the ordinary run of garden plants, except a few snowdrops – will thrive.

However, there are several shrubby plants not exciting enough for the garden itself, that will grow quite happily in such places, spreading when once established, and giving quite a lot of interest.

Generally, in such places, all that grows naturally is rough grass. To establish plants, good patches of this are killed by spraying with one of the herbicides. As soon as the grass is killed, this ground is dug over and clumps of the following plants established. As this spot is sure to be dry, water them well until they have taken hold.

First, one would choose the Oregon grape, *Mahonia aquifolium*. This was brought here in 1823 from California, by the plant collector David Douglas. With the typical prickly leaves, which colour well in autumn, its spikes of yellow flowers opening in earliest spring followed by little purple grape-like fruit with a grey bloom, it so excited gardeners that for a few years after its arrival plants were sold at ten guineas a time. Then it was found that it would grow anywhere, spreading freely, and though the plant was just as beautiful, the price tumbled.

Rose of Sharon, *Hypericum calycinum*, is a low growing evergreen shrub that steadily spreads around by means of runners. Because it will thrive anywhere, under any conditions, it has been pushed into waste corners. If it was a new plant, the large yellow flowers which open at about midsummer, would cause it to be all the rage.

In wild, rough places, and often in neglected hedgerows, another shrub, the snowberry, *Symphoricarpos albus* (sometimes called *S. racemosa*) will be found. This, an erect growing, slender, suckering, shrub of about 6 ft., is ideal for wasteland. It is quite common for the reason that pheasants are reputed to

Basic Pruning Tools

Grecian saw

secateurs

pruning saw

pruning knife

1. Using notched shears to cut through thicker branches. 2. Right and wrong pruning cuts (a) is correct (b) the cut is too slanting and the top bud will be killed (c) the cut is too far away from the top bud and the snag left will die back (d) a ragged cut caused by blunt secateurs (e) the cut is too close to the top bud which will die. 3. A typical branch showing the terminal, lateral and dormant buds. 4. A *Buddleia davidii* in full flower before pruning. 5. The same bush after hard pruning. 6. Light pruning. 7. Harder pruning. 8. A typical tree. The 'feathers' on the trunk should be cut off as they form and the suckers on the right should be pulled off the roots. 9. Before cutting off a large branch make an undercut with the saw. 10. Then cut off the branch close to the trunk. 11. Failure to make an undercut will result in the branch tearing the bark of the main trunk. 12. Paint the wound with a fungicidal paint to prevent the entry of disease spores.

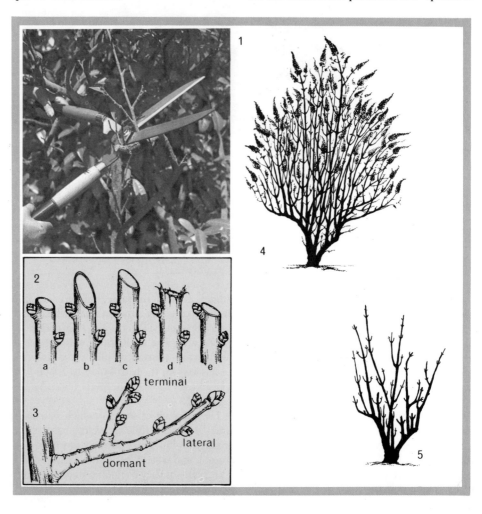

like the berries. These are fleshy, oval and white, $\frac{1}{2}$ in. or so long, with a sparkling crystalline surface. They are a joy to flower arrangers in autumn, and follow the tiny pink flowers in June and July which one usually notices because of the myriads of bees collecting their nectar.

The dwarf *Cotoneaster dammeri* (*humifusa*) needs a certain amount of light. This is an evergreen, of dense, twiggy growth with glossy green leaves about $\frac{1}{2}$ in. long; self-sown seedlings often arise. But its value for the garden wasteland is that it lies flat on the ground, its shoots curving to conform with the contours. One plant will very soon cover a square yard and more.

Topiary For The Small Garden

In olden times the cutting of evergreen trees and shrubs into every kind of fanciful shape was an important part of gardening. During the last years of the reign of Queen Anne, Peter Collinson, the naturalist, described how as a boy he used to visit the small gardens of his relations at Peckham which were remarkable for their ornamentally cut 'greens', yews in the shape of birds, dogs, men and ships.

The fashion went out in the 18th century and has never really returned. It is as a rule only in the small gardens of old houses in the country, and particularly of inns, that today we see the pleasing entertainments of clipped yews coming to life in a variety of forms, from the simple or even elaborate geometric, to the horse and jockey with the hounds.

It is surely more fun to have the homemade, living frivolities than the many mass-produced plastic vases and bowls.

Traditionally, yew has long been the material from which British topiary is formed. It long ago replaced the Mediterranean cypress from which the topiary of the ancients was formed for this tree is only hardy in the mild parts of Britain. The basis for a sizable piece of topiary may well be a mature yew in a garden, for yews will stand the most murderous pruning if it is not all done at once but spread over two or even three years.

Pyramids In this way a sizable tree can first be cut to form a pyramidal shape. A wooden template is easily knocked up to press against the tree as a guide for working. Another step can be taken by cutting slices into this pyramid, right back to the trunk, so as to form a series of layers.

Finials Smaller yews can, again with the aid of a semi-circular template, be gradually cut to form balls that rest at the end of close-clipped yew hedges as finials. Or these may stand, as they do at Levens Hall, Cumbria, on solid blocks of yew, a simple and very effective design for a small garden.

Corkscrews Most ingenious and perplexing in its origin is the yew corkscrew, also a device suitable for a small garden. It takes the form of a yew spiral, broad at the bottom narrowing to a point at the top. The mystery of its construction is quite simple. A young yew is placed beside a stout stake; all the side shoots are cut off or pinched out so that it grows on a single shoot. This shoot is, as it

extends, wound spirally round the stake. Every side shoot is removed. So, as it thickens, it becomes rigid; the stake is removed and the centre is, like a cork-screw, hollow.

Arches Fanciful topiary arches can be made. They too, are trained to wood frames which are eventually removed as the branches of the yew become rigid. Perfectly simple, rectangular, massive frames for elaborate wrought iron gateways are also very effective. The top consists of two leading shoots trained on a cross bar until they meet and thereafter thicken out.

Figures It is when we come to representation of living creatures – the peacock or the huntsman on his horse, that we become really excited. It is usually the result of some years of work by the owner of the cottage outside which such marvels are displayed. A young vigorous yew is trained on bamboos. First, a branch is selected to form a bird's tail and two more trained to sticks placed fanwise for the tail. Consistently, all shoots extraneous to the design are pruned away; those that are to take part in it are led onwards as far as they are needed and allowed to thicken as required. The body is allowed to swell and clipped to form its final shape.

Box is sometimes used for topiary, but now not so often as formerly. *Lonicera nitida* can also be used for small works; it needs frequent clipping.

Topiary work does not, as is sometimes suspected, take many years to reach completion. Yews, if well fed, grow surprisingly quickly.

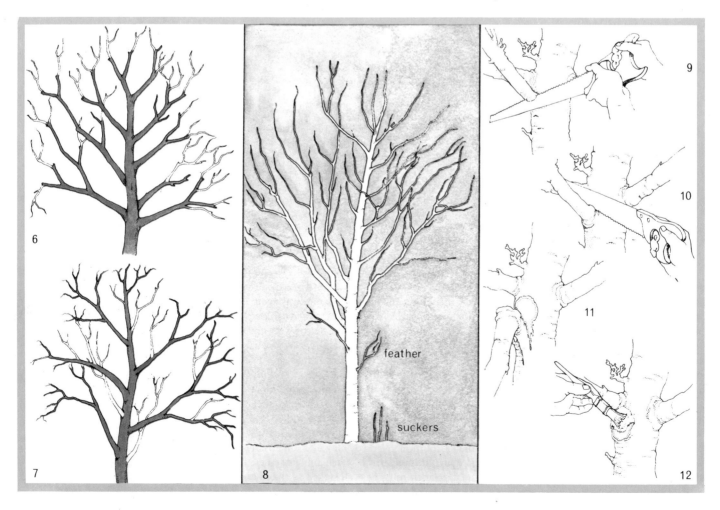

feather

suckers

6 7 8 9 10 11 12

Propagation Hedges; Conifers

Raising Your Own Shrubs And Trees

Shrubs, and still more so trees, are the most expensive items in the plant world of the gardener. This is principally because they take much longer to produce than, for example, bedding out plants or perennials. Furthermore, the nurseryman, for commercial reasons, raises only things for which there is a regular popular demand, whereas the gardener may want something, say a tree, that he has seen in a friend's garden which he cannot find in any nurseryman's list or displayed at any garden centre.

Propagation by Seed In autumn, the tree may be scattering (and wasting) large numbers of its seeds on the surrounding ground. Why not try raising the tree from seed? The general impression is that it takes too long. Yet, for example, from seed of a fine maple, it is possible to have a specimen 20 ft. tall, in ten years.

Sow the seed in a pot of seed compost, transfer the seedling after a couple of years into a bigger pot and then at about 2 ft. high plant it out in the garden. For the small garden, the Japanese maples are ideal. Lots of seed is usually produced. If you sow some of it, you can expect to get seedlings in two years 2 ft. high, big enough to plant out in a rock garden. A similar plant bought from a nursery may cost £5 or more.

The usual way of sowing seeds of trees and shrubs is in pans of John Innes seed compost, standing them in a shaded cold frame. There is now a more effective way of doing it. You remove the husk or acorn cups, cut off the wings of maple seeds and, as soon as they are ripe, put them in a plastic bag, mixed with damp peat. You then tie the neck of the bag with a bow of thin string. Put the bag in a dark, unheated shed. When spring comes, at regular intervals, untie the bow, tip the contents, seeds and peat, on to a sheet of newspaper. You may find that some of the seeds have produced a small rootlet. If so, very carefully you put these seeds, with the rootlet pointing downwards, in a small pot of John Innes seed compost, which you water and put in a shady place. You treat it as any seedling and in due course the leaves (with a bit of luck!) will appear. After extracting any seeds which have sprouted, or as it is called 'chitted', you put the remainder, peat and all (making sure that it is still damp) back into its plastic bag.

This operation can be repeated, going through all the bags say once a fortnight. Great care must be taken not to damage the rootlet.

In due course, those seedlings that grow should be put into large pots as soon as they have filled the smaller pots with roots and eventually planted in a nursery bed until they are big enough to go into their permanent positions. Usually one nearly always raises too many for one's own garden but the surplus is very welcome to friends and for charity sales.

Propagation by Layering Few shrubs are more desirable or more expensive than magnolias. These are quite easily reproduced by layering—as are rhododendrons. As it does little harm to an established plant, you can generally get a friend to let you operate on one that you covet. Spring is the best time to carry out the operation but any time of the year will do. You choose a low-lying shoot and remove the leaves from its base. You then lightly fork the soil below it, working in some peat. Then scrape away the soil and gently pull down the shoot into the hollow. When it is firmly embedded, you either by means of a stout wire hook driven into the ground or a good heavy stone laid on it, fix the shoot, firmly pressing it into the ground. And firm it must be, for your next operation is to bend the free end upwards as steeply as you can and tie it firmly to a stout stake that has been driven in beside it. Then cover the base of the shoot with peaty soil and press it down firmly.

Next you wait for a season's growth to take place, i.e., for a year after the layering. Then cut through the junction of your layered shoot with the main plant and then, after cutting the ties to the stake, very carefully, with a fork, remove the layer, which should have produced roots which must not be broken.

Sometimes the layered plant will have grown bigger and will be so well rooted that it can go into its final place at once. Otherwise it should be planted in a nursery bed and left there for a further year before it is again lifted and planted in its permanent position.

Most shrubs that have low-sweeping branches—particularly, as already mentioned, rhododendrons, can be propagated in this way. In fact, if you look and feel carefully round the base of an old rhododendron bush you may find naturally self-layered pieces which can be carefully cut away, forked up, and planted (preferably in autumn) with plenty of peat worked into the fine root system. Layered plants when put into their final position must be well staked as the fine roots formed are only surface roots.

Propagation by Cuttings A great many trees and shrubs can be quite easily propagated from cuttings. All poplars (*populus*) and all willows and sallows (*salix*) grow freely from stout shoots cut in winter when they are dormant. Once the ground where they are to grow permanently has been cleaned and dug, they are driven in and the soil round them firmed, a crowbar or some similar tool being used to make a hole to receive them. They should be firmly staked. The shoots from the lower part of the sett—for this is what these stout cuttings are called—should be cut clean back to the stem. Very considerable branches of the popular weeping willow can be propagated in this way and a substantial tree can be produced in a few years. As a general rule willow cuttings need a moist situation.

Heaths (ericas and callunas) can also be propagated by cuttings quite easily, but in a quite different manner. The short, current year's growths are pulled gently off in July or August and dibbled into sandy soil in pans in a frame standing in a shady place. In a year many of them will have made tufts of roots and can be repotted in the following spring.

There is a number of trees the propagation of which is beyond the scope of the amateur unless he is capable of the skilled crafts of budding or grafting. These include apples, pears, cherries, apricots, quinces, medlars, damsons and other members of the rose family. Many of these produce fertile seed which will germinate but they are of hybrid origin and the sedlings will differ from their parent. Very, very rarely a seedling will arise that is better than its parent, but the chances are very much against this happening.

For the same reason, many modern shrubs do not come true from seed, but with the fine, dust-like seed of rhododendrons, which should be sown on a mixture of peat and sand and kept carefully watered, there is a chance that something good may arise.

Propagating a rhododendron by layering a branch is not a difficult process, although it may be a year before the layered branch has formed sufficient roots for it to be detached from the parent plant and replanted. The

Willows are among the easiest of all trees to root from cuttings. Even quite stout branches will root, if they are removed in winter when the tree is dormant. A suitable branch is shown at (1). Cut the branch below a bud (2). Then make a hole with a crowbar or similar instrument (3) and insert the cutting or 'sett' as it is known, firming the soil round it afterwards. To prevent wind rock, tie the cutting firmly to a stake (4)
Right: Berberis thunbergii, a good hedging plant

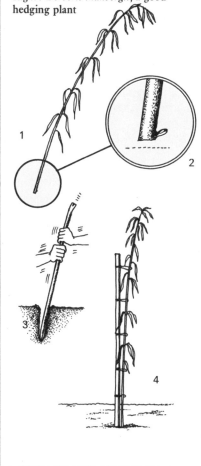

branch to be layered is bent down to the ground and held in place with a strong wire hook or a heavy stone. The free end of the branch should be tied to a stout stake, driven firmly into the ground beside it

✿ Hedges ✿

The countryside, in the interests of more efficient agriculture, is gradually being stripped of its hedges. Building estates and road making often obliterate many miles more.

Nothing gives a more finished, indeed cosy appearance, to a small garden than a hedge, or even hedges–not of any great length or height but placed to give the appearance of an enclosed space making the garden a world of its own.

This is surprisingly easy to do with quite short lengths of hedging rightly placed. Do not in your enthusiasm have too much, as hedge-clipping (unless you have a mechanical trimmer) is tiring work (a good quality pair of shears is a splendid investment).

So many gardeners unfortunately get no further than the indestructible and deadly dull privet. But all sorts of plants, naturally of a variety of sizes and an even greater variety of shape, leaf colour and in many instances of flower can be used; some of them are described in the list that follows. Privet (*ligustrum*) is omitted as not being worthy of the space it takes.

There are one or two rules that the hedge planter should learn.

The Site First must be the suitability of the plants used for the site. Most of the usual hedging plants and most of the unusual ones will tolerate a wide range of soil, provided they are well drained. Some are better when lime and chalk is present than others. Near the seaside plants that will stand the salt-laden gales and protect the choicer plants that they shield are essential; several of these will not stand the harder frosts of inland districts.

When deciding to plant a hedge, apart from considering its position from the point of view of appearance, remember that a hedge has to be cut on two sides and make sure you are going to leave plenty of room on both sides, not only the one you will be looking at, to give easy access for this clipping.

Hedging plants are like other garden plants: the better their soil conditions the better they grow.

Planting A strip about a yard wide should be marked out where the plants are to grow and should be dug–it is a good idea to work in some compost.

A line should be stretched down the centre and the young trees planted carefully against it. A wiggle in the hedge will take a lot of hiding later.

Except in really wet weather, always keep the young hedge well watered until it is established. The use of lawn mowings as a mulch is a valuable help to the young trees.

Clipping Then, an important rule about clipping; always trim a hedge so that the bottom is wider than the top, that is, so that it tapers slightly from the base to the apex.

Never cut the leading shoots at the top of the hedge until they have reached the final height that you intend. The top will look untidy for a year or two, but do not worry about that.

The planting distances given below are approximate only; if the plants are a little wider apart, they will probably fill up in due course.

No suggestion is given of the height of the plants you should buy. Tell your nurseryman the purpose for which you will require them and remember that small plants will soon catch up the bigger and more expensive ones.

Old Favourites

Hawthorn (*Crataegus oxyacantha*) forms most of the field hedges in this country. The shoots are stout and springy, and it is still unsurpassed for a boundary. It should be planted close, about 1 ft. apart. Winter is the usual time for pruning.

Beech The common beech (*Fagus sylvatica*), is one of the most attractive and decorative of hedging plants. Happy on any kind of soil, including chalk, provided it is well drained, it is a fresh green throughout the late spring and summer. Then in autumn the leaves turn russet colour and hang on until May when the fresh new leaves break and push them off. If the young trees are planted about 1½–2 ft. apart, a good hedge soon results. The best time to clip the hedge is in summer when the leaves are fully unfolded. It can be clipped very hard and close so as to make, if so desired, a very narrow hedge, the growth being so twiggy that it becomes very dense.

To make a vari-coloured beech hedge, seedlings of the copper and purple kinds may be mixed in a random way with the normal form.

Hornbeam Rather similar and particularly good on chalk soils, is hornbeam (*Carpinus betulus*).

Yew The yew (*Taxus baccata*), is another widely used hedging plant, but seldom used as a purely protective hedge for outer boundaries but as an internal, formal division, its sombre green making a fine background for flowers.

Young plants should be set about 2 ft. apart in October or April and during dry weather in spring watered freely. It is particularly important not to cut the leading shoot until it has reached the final required height. The sides should be clipped back hard on a slight slope so that the base of the hedge is broader than the top. Pruning can be done after the spring growth has finished.

Yew can be poisonous to animals, particularly the prunings, which should never be thrown where stock can get at them.

Box Another old favourite for evergreen hedges was box (*Buxus sempervirens*). This is not an ideal material; it is subject to disease and has a wide-spreading, greedy root system. This is not the same as the dwarf kind, *B. suffruticosa* used for edging, which must be placed close. The roots of this also rob the beds which it surrounds. Shrubs such as lavender are better.

Some Newer Kinds

The following are of comparatively recent introduction and are also suitable for hedges, particularly those that are informal.

Berberis Several of these prickly shrubs are quite often used for hedging. *B. stenophylla* and *B. thunbergii* are generally recommended. Neither stand pruning and in time become thin at the base.

Cotoneaster Various species are particularly useful as informal, decorative hedges that need no more than trimming to keep them tidy. All carry red or orange berries, eventually enjoyed by birds. *C. simonsii* is a

semi-evergreen of close, erect growth which if pruned hard in spring will eventually form a quite rigid hedge some 5 ft. tall. As a contrast the evergreen *C. franchetii* is of close, bushy growth with arching branches which can be lightly pruned to keep it at about 7 or 8 ft. The leaves are green above, grey below. Both may be planted about 2 ft. apart.

Euonymus *E. japonica* is an evergreen shrub with glossy leaves, reaching about 10 or 12 ft., which is a valuable and fairly common hedging plant virtually restricted to sea-side gardens where it withstands the salt-laden gales. Generally, it is not generally hardy inland. Plant at about 18 in.

Griselinia The large, leathery, evergreen leaves of *G. littoralis* can stand strong winds and salt spray but the shrub is hardy only in mild districts inland. It is often used for hedges, when plants are set about 3 ft. apart. It will grow about 8 ft. tall and needs little pruning. It will grow on chalk.

Lavandula The grey-leaved, fragrant lavender, *L. spica* has for centuries been used as a low hedge reaching 3 ft. It must have sun, likes lime and should be kept lightly clipped. It will grow by the sea. Plant 18 in. apart.

Lonicera *L. nitida* a very small-leaved evergreen honeysuckle (though no one would guess its relationship to the honeysuckle of our hedgerows), is quick growing and suitable for low hedges. It should be planted about 1 ft. apart and cut back hard afterwards. It needs good soil. It may be damaged in severe weather. Prune in summer at fairly frequent intervals.

Rosmarinus Rosemary (*R. officinalis*) is

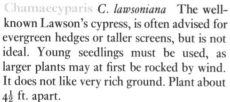

Far left: Lonicera nitida 'Baggeson's Gold' makes a colourful hedge. *Left:* The golden-leaved form of Lawson's cypress, *Chamaecyparis lawsoniana lutea*, is sometimes used for making a tall screen. *Above:* 'Tapestry' hedges are both colourful and interesting: this one is made up of *Prunus pissardii* (*P. cerasifera atropurpurea*) 'Purple Flash' and *Prunus cerasifera* 'Green Glow'. *Right:* An example of a 'battlemented' yew hedge at Knightshayes Court, Devon. *Bottom:* Although not an ideal hedging plant, the box (*Buxus sempervirens*) is readily clipped to shape

another famous old garden plant which stands clipping well, September being the best month. It will grow well on lime and by the seaside. Treat it in the same way as lavender (Lavandula), setting plants about 18 in. apart and keeping them lightly clipped.

Evergreen Conifers

Chamaecyparis *C. lawsoniana* The well-known Lawson's cypress, is often advised for evergreen hedges or taller screens, but is not ideal. Young seedlings must be used, as larger plants may at first be rocked by wind. It does not like very rich ground. Plant about $4\frac{1}{2}$ ft. apart.

Cupressocyparis The Leyland cypress, *C. leylandii*, is a splendid, hardy and adaptable tree. It is often recommended for hedges, but its rate of growth is so rapid that it will need cutting twice or more in a year, the last time in autumn. It is ideally suited for screens and windbreaks. Set the plants out 4–5 ft. apart.

Cupressus The Monterey cypress, *C. macrocarpa* has often been planted for hedges in the mildest districts. On all soils it is good. But even so, a particularly hard winter will kill isolated plants in a well established hedge, so destroying its appearance.

Thuya *T. plicata*, the western red cedar in its native habitat, is a large western American forest tree. However, it stands clipping extremely well and is a hedge plant of great merit with glossy-green fragrant leaves in fern-like sprays. Plants should be set out at about $4\frac{1}{2}$ ft. apart.

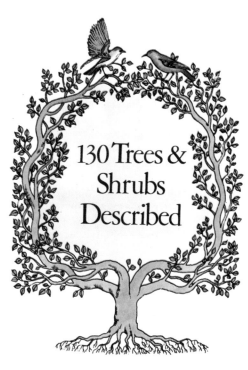

130 Trees & Shrubs Described

The following key letters will help you to pick out the different types.

D   Deciduous
E   Evergreen
F   Valuable for decorative foliage
FL Valuable for decorative flowers
FR Valuable for decorative fruit
H   High growing
L   Low growing
M   Medium growing
NC Will not grow on chalk
S   Shrub
T   Tree

Omitted from the list are some highly popular trees which are unfortunately far too often planted in small gardens. Seen as attractive young nursery stock, they will, alas, in a few years occupy so much space that they will have to be removed. For instance, a common weeping willow, 3 ft. in diameter when planted, will cover a circle 18 ft. in diameter in 10 years. Conifers are described in a later section of this work.

Acer   Most acers grow far too large for the average, let alone small garden. But a small, slow-growing form of the sycamore makes an excellent, striking standard tree. It is *A. pseudoplatanus* 'Brilliantissimum' (T.M.D.F.). The leaves in spring are shrimp-pink, changing to pale yellow green and finally green.

Of the shrubby maples, *A. palmatum* (S.M.F.), the Japanese maple, with lobed leaves, is very decorative. It forms a low, rounded bush which after many years grows into a small tree. The form 'Atropurpureum' with purplish-bronze leaves is the most effective. Like all the *palmatum* maples, it does better in some shade and shelter from wind.

Amelanchier   The snowy mespilus, *A. lamarckii* (D.FL.M.) (sometimes catalogued as *A. laevis* and *A. canadensis*) can be grown as a large round bush or small tree from 20 ft. to 30 ft. tall, and eventually about the same across. It is densely covered with spikes of small white, scented flowers in spring which appear among the bronzy pink opening leaves. The autumn colour of the leaves is also good. It will grow on any well-drained soil.

Arbutus   The strawberry tree, *A. unedo* (S.E.FL.FR.) is a slow-growing evergreen shrub, or eventually a tree, with leathery, deep green leaves. The flowers, rather like those of lily-of-the-valley, appear in late summer and autumn at the same time as the round fruit produced from the previous year's flowers ripen and turn scarlet. It is good in stony districts near the seaside and is happy on chalk soils.

Berberis   Of the many barberries, *B. stenophylla* (E.FL.S.H.) is one of the best. The dense, arching slender stems, up to 10 ft. tall, are covered with small orange flowers in April–May. It is excellent for tall, informal hedges. Prune in winter, only to restrict size as required.

Betula   The native birches (D.H.T.) with their white trunks and fine twiggy growth, are suitable for moderately sized gardens, particularly if grown in grass. If set in flower beds their greedy roots take the nature out of the soil. The weeping birch, *B. pendula youngii*, with shoots that fall vertically, is one of the best weeping trees, slowly reaching about 20 ft. high. It needs careful pruning when in leaf, only to ensure a good shape.

Buddleia   *B. davidii* (D.FL.S.) grows to 10 ft. tall and the long spikes of small, sweetly scented flowers attract butterflies during July and August. The long shoots should be cut hard back in winter to encourage the production of new, flowering shoots. There are cultivars with purple, violet, pink and white flowers.

Calluna   (E.L.NC.) The Scottish heathers or lings (see also *Erica*) are varieties of the wild plant with mostly purple, pink and white flowers. There are many kinds, often grown with ericas to form heath gardens. Callunas must have light sandy soil without lime, to thrive, and benefit from leaf-mould or peat worked in around their roots at planting time. Shear them over lightly in April to maintain a close, tufty growth, otherwise they tend to sprawl. They should always be obtained in and planted from pots. Foliage colour varies from gold to deep green.

Camellia   (E.F.FL.M.NC.) The difficulty of growing these choice shrubs with rich glossy green foliage and ornate flowers in spring is often exaggerated. Many are not easy, but 'Donation' can be grown in most gardens on lime-free soil, giving a good crop of its semi-double pink flowers from March to April. Some shade is needed and protection from wind. Plenty of leaf-mould or peat should be placed around the roots, and in very dry weather the shrubs should be watered. The only pruning needed is to keep the bush to a good shape. Camellias make very good house shrubs if grown in pots. The soil should have plenty of peat mixed with it and at all times be kept well watered. During the winter months and while flowering they can be stood in the house and later stand in a shady spot in the garden.

Caryopteris   *C. clandonensis* (D.FL.L.), the blue spiraea, is a shrub with attractive grey foliage, which carries masses of small blue flowers from September onwards. It does well on light, sandy soils. Cut the bushes back hard in April, when growth is just beginning.

Ceanothus   These are the Californian lilacs, a group of shrubs, some evergreen and others deciduous. Many are liable to damage or may be killed in severe winters and so are often grown against walls. The hardiest and most reliable is 'Gloire de Versailles' (S.D.M.FL.). This bears many clusters of powder-blue flowers in late summer. In about April all the shoots that flowered the previous year should be cut out to their base. It will usually grow well in the open, but is splendid when trained against a wall, where it may eventually reach 10 ft. The evergreen kinds, which flower in spring or early summer, need little pruning.

Chaenomeles   This is the shrub well known as 'japonica'. Of the various kinds, one of the best is 'Knap Hill Scarlet' (D.S.FL.L.), noted for its brilliant flowers in March and April. Other named kinds have white, pink and double flowers. All like a sunny position and do well in any fertile soil and on chalk. Pruning, after flowering, consists in thinning out some of the long, slender shoots to provide a framework of branches, and shortening the side-shoots on those that are left to leave two or three buds to provide flowering 'spurs'. The quince-like fruits that are sometimes formed may be left on until they ripen and made into jelly.

Choisya   (S.M.F.FL.), the Mexican orange, *C. ternata*, is an evergreen, rounded shrub reaching 6 ft. or more. The 5-petalled white flowers, sweetly scented like hawthorn, about 1 in. in diameter, are produced freely in spring and occasionally at other times. It is occasionally damaged by unseasonable frosts but is often unharmed in severe cold winters.

Cistus   (E.FL.M.S.) The sun roses are sun-loving shrubs, about 3 ft. tall, flowering in June or July, thriving on lime and chalk and not always hardy. The flowers are numerous, mostly white or pink, with golden stamens; the leaves of some kinds glossy green and sometimes sticky, while others have soft grey foliage. Most are easily raised from seed. Prune only to remove dead branches.

Cistus, the sun rose

Left: One of the forms of the Japanese maple, *Acer palmatum*

Above : One of the best of all small, slow-growing trees, *Acer pseudoplatanus brilliantissimum* has pinkish leaves in spring
Right : Erica carnea, a winter-flowering heather, is one of the few which will thrive on soils containing chalk or lime. 'Springwood Pink' is one of its varieties
Below : Deutzia 'Magician', one of a number of beautiful hybrids which flower in late spring or early summer
Far right : Eucryphia nymansensis makes an upright tree with beautiful white flowers in late summer

Self-sown seedlings often appear and are best left where they arise. One of the strongest is *C. laurifolius*, with leathery dark green leaves, and white flowers up to 4 in. across.

Cornus (D.F.FL.M.S. and T.) The dogwoods are of two distinct kinds, those that are shrubby with decorative twigs and those that form small trees. Of the former, *C. alba* produces a mass of red stems, up to 9 ft. tall, very striking in winter. It thrives in wet or dry positions, and should be hard pruned in alternate years in March.

Of the small trees *Cornus mas*, the cornelian cherry, is densely covered with small yellow flowers in February before the leaves open, followed by small red fruit; its form 'Variegata', the leaves margined with white, is attractive. It needs little pruning.

Cotinus (D.F.FL.M.S.) The Venetian sumachs or smoke trees are large, sprawling shrubs flowering in June and July and giving good autumn leaf colour. They grow and flower better in poor soil, need little pruning, and grow 8–12 ft. tall. Probably the best is *C. coggygria* (syn. *Rhus cotinus*). The many large flower spikes are pinkish, turning smoky grey later.

Cotoneaster This genus provides a wide range of shrubs of varying sizes and forms, notable for their berries which follow very numerous small white flowers. They are adaptable for all soils and situations. Two contrasting kinds are *C. franchetii* (E.FR.L.S. M.) and *C. horizontalis* (D.FR.L.S.). The former has arching sprays up to 8 ft. tall and makes a fairly wide bush with greyish-green leaves and brilliant red berries in autumn. The latter, a close-growing, spreading shrub with her-ringbone twigs and small leaves, usually grows pressed against the ground or a wall, with small green leaves which colour well in autumn, and bright red berries.

Crataegus The common white hawthorn (*C. monogyna*) and the red hawthorn (*C. oxyacantha* 'Coccinea Plena') the double red may, are common throughout the British Isles. One of the best small garden thorn trees is the plum-leaved thorn, *C. prunifolia* (D.FL.FR.N. T.). This has a broad rounded head, its leaves turn brilliant crimson in autumn. The flowers, larger than those of our native thorn, open in mid-June and the scarlet haws likewise are much larger. It needs pruning only to keep it in shape.

Cytisus The brooms are deciduous shrubs, mostly with insignificant leaves on slender stems, with pea-like flowers. All need full sun and thrive on light or peaty soils, growing well with heaths. Prune back the shoots that have flowered by about two-thirds after the blossoms fade—or they can be left unpruned if tall, leggy bushes are not objected to. The several kinds, some low and spreading, are excellent for furnishing a new garden. *C. albus*, the white Portugal broom (D.FL.M.S.) with white flowers in May on arching 7 ft. sprays of grey-green foliage, is good. *C. praecox*, which blooms earlier, on 6 ft. shoots with deep yellow and cream flowers, is another well tried kind.

Daphne *D. mezereum* (D.FL.L.S.) with small pink flowers is grown for its strong, sweet scent in earliest spring. The flowers are followed by red berries in summer. It likes some shade in summer and moist but well-drained soil. Several other kinds are attractive, but are often difficult to grow. Do not prune.

Deutzia (D.FL.M.S.) These are easy to grow and reliable on all but the poorest soils. The numerous small pink and white flowers are produced on young plants from May to June. The heights range from 5–7 ft. Cut out a proportion of the shoots after they have flowered. One of the best is *D. elegantissima*, with deep rose flowers in May or June, on arching shoots reaching 6–7 ft.

Elaeagnus (E.F.M.S.) These valuable and hardy shrubs, eventually reaching 10–12 ft., have insignificant but scented flowers and handsome leathery leaves. They will grow in windy situations and beside the sea. No pruning is needed unless it is necessary to reduce their size, when it can be done in spring. *E. pungens maculata* with leaves splashed with gold is one of the finest of all variegated shrubs, less tall and more spreading than other kinds. Shoots that revert to green should be cut out.

Enkianthus (D.FL.M.NC.S.) Related to the heaths, *E. campanulatus*, an erect-growing hardy shrub will thrive on any lime-free soil, reaching 6 or 7 ft. In May it carries masses of hanging, small bell-shaped cream flowers with red veins. In autumn the leaves turn fiery red. No pruning is needed.

Erica There are many species and almost countless garden forms of the heaths. All like open situations and do best in lighter soils. They may be lightly clipped over after flowering. Kinds can be had to flower in almost every month of the year. Some will grow on light, acid soil only, while a few others will grow where lime is present.

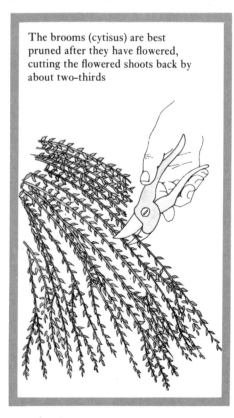

The brooms (cytisus) are best pruned after they have flowered, cutting the flowered shoots back by about two-thirds

The principal species, of which well-known variants are cultivated, are: *E. carnea* (E.FL.L.S.), lime tolerant, flowering from early winter to early spring. The colours range from white through pink to purple; *E. cinerea* (E.L.NC.S.) the native purple bell heather with flowers mostly ranging from white through pink to purple, from June to September.

The numerous forms of these will be more than adequate for most gardens and will provide colour throughout the year. Those who wish to make a heath garden, will find that many other kinds are available.

Escallonia These close-growing, bushy small-leaved shrubs, often with arching branches, bear numerous small flowers, from white through pink to crimson over a long period, but at their best in June and July. They are most useful as isolated plants or as free-growing hedges in any type of soil and will thrive in windy conditions. Prune by shortening the flowered branches in July or allow them to make sizable bushes up to 7 ft. or so and prune only to give the requisite size. 'Apple Blossom' (E.FL.L.S.) with pink flowers is one of the best.

Eucryphia (E.FL.H.NC.S.) Tall, narrow growing shrubs or small trees, these have large white flowers, with central bosses of golden stamens, in late summer. They like fertile, fairly moist soil and some shelter. The most striking is 'Nymansay', flowering in August and September.

Euonymus Of the numerous kinds some carry the scarlet, fleshy fruit from which, when they ripen, the orange seeds dangle. Of these our native spindle-tree (*E. europaeus*) is well known in hedgerows, particularly on chalk soils; a fine form, 'Red Cascade' (D.FR.M.S.), about 8 ft., is well worth a place in any garden on account of its heavy fruiting on the arching branches. In contrast, the richly gold and silver-leaved (with some red in winter) *E. fortunei variegata* (E.F.L.S.) will grow flat against a rock or a wall and make a striking sheet of colour throughout the year. It bears no berries.

Forsythia (D.FL.M.S.) This invaluable shrub, with its mass of bright yellow flowers in March and April, prefers sun, and will thrive on any reasonable soil. In some districts bullfinches destroy the flower buds; black cotton intertwined in the bush or one of the proprietary bird repellents may do good. Cut out a few of the oldest branches after they have flowered. The best form is *F. intermedia* 'Lynwood', reaching about 5–6 ft. *F. suspensa* has paler flowers but a lax drooping branching system which enables it to be trained against screens or walls where it will grow much taller.

Fuchsia The genus includes many shrubs, a few quite hardy. The most reliable out of doors is *F. riccartonii* (D.S.M.FL.), erect growing, to 4 ft., which carries scarlet and purple flowers from June to October. Plant so that the point from which the buds arise is 1–2 in. below the surface. In late spring cut back shoots now showing bud to near ground level.

Garrya *G. elliptica* (E.S.M.FL.) should be planted in any soil, in a sheltered spot to protect the jade coloured catkins borne in trails up to 9 in. long over a long period in winter. These are valuable for flower arranging. Prune after flowering only to shape the plant.

Genista (D.S.M. to L.FL.). The brooms are attractive, floriferous yellow-flowered shrubs which thrive in light soils even when lime is present. Many are quick growing and for their first two years staking and cutting back will help to get them firmly established; this does not apply to dwarf kinds such as *G. pilosa*. One of the best for display is *G. cinerea*, 6–10 ft., with masses of sweetly scented golden-yellow flowers in June and July.

Hamamelis The Chinese witch hazel is *H. mollis* (D.FL.M.S.), one of the most delightful of winter flowering shrubs with many yellow flowers consisting of narrow, twisted petals, set in a crimson cup and scented like cowslips. These open from December to February on the bare shoots. The leaves colour a good yellow in autumn. The bushes, up to about 10 ft. high, need no pruning other than to keep them shapely.

Hebe These shrubs (E.FL.L.S.), known as shrubby veronicas and still sometimes listed under *Veronica*, will grow in any conditions, provided the situation is open, sunny and not wet. The small flowers range from white through violets and lavenders to purple. Clip the shrubs back in spring to keep them compact and tidy. One of the best is 'Autumn Glory', violet, flowering from June to August.

Hydrangea (D.FL.M.S.) All hydrangeas like rich, fairly moist but well-drained soil, and prefer light shade. Though ideal for pots and greenhouse culture, or in tubs, most are quite hardy. In general, blue kinds will only come true to that colour in acid soil or when watered with a special blueing mixture. The pink and red kinds do best on slightly alkaline soil.

In the most popular kinds of cultivated hydrangeas, the 'Hortensia' varieties, only showy infertile flowers are present, built up into globular large heads. There is a wide range of colours and sizes.

In the lace-cap hydrangeas the flower head is flat, with an outer ring of false petals at the centre of which are small florets. One of the best and hardiest is 'Blue Wave', 4 ft. or 5 ft., the outer ring pink on soils where any lime is present, rich blue on acid soils. The central florets are always purplish blue.

Hypericum *H. calycinum* (D.FL.L.S.) The rose of Sharon, a low, rapidly spreading shrub with yellow flowers at mid-summer is invaluable for carpeting dry shady situations. The best decorative St John's wort is *H. patulum* 'Hidcote', reaching 5 ft., bearing golden saucer-shaped flowers in August; this needs full sun. Cut hard back in winter.

Kalmia The calico bush, *K. latifolia* (E.FL. M.NC.S.), thrives in conditions suitable for rhododendrons, but in full sun. It slowly reaches 6 ft. and bears prettily shaped small pink flowers in June. No pruning is needed.

Kerria *K. japonica pleniflora* (D.FL.M.S.) is known as bachelor's buttons from the small yellow pompon-like flowers carried on the slender, arching, bright green stems in spring and early summer. It will grow in most soils and situations and needs pruning only to train it.

Laburnum (D.FL.M.T.) This well-known tree often called golden rain, tolerant of most conditions, is grown for its small, golden pea-shaped flowers hanging in long chains during May and June. It can be grown as a bush or a standard and needs only the minimum of pruning to shape it. By far the best kind for gardens is the hybrid *L. vossii*, with very long trails of flowers.

Lavandula (E.F.FL.L.S.) The lavender, fragrant in all its parts, can be grown as a dwarf hedge or individually. Some give the name to the colour lavender, others are shades of blue, purple, pink, or white. Heights range from 1–2 ft.; they flower in July. All need full sun and thrive in poor, light soil and like lime. Clip them over in autumn to remove the old flower spikes and again in spring for the sake of tidiness, but the old wood should not be cut. One of the best is *L. spica* 'Hidcote' with purple-blue flowers.

Leycesteria The flowering nutmeg, *L. formosa* (D.FL.M.S.) will reach 5–6 ft. in almost any position or soil and is notable for its bright green stems from which hang reddish-purple leafy catkin-like growths containing small, pale pink flowers in late summer and autumn. Cut out a few of the oldest stems in early spring.

Lonicera The winter flowering honeysuckle, *L. purpusii* (D.FL.M.S.) is valuable for its scent and use in flower arrangements. In a sunny sheltered spot, the bare arching branches 6–7 ft. tall, are covered with creamy white flowers from January to February.

Left: Belonging to the same family as the rhododendrons, *Kalmia latifolia*, the calico bush, needs a lime-free, peaty soil
Above: The shrubby veronicas, correctly known as hebes, flower over long periods in summer and autumn. This is 'Midsummer Beauty' with long trails of flowers
Right: *Cotoneaster glabrata*, a hardy, evergreen garden shrub which grows from 10 to 15 feet in height

Magnolia All magnolias do best in moist, slightly acid soils, though many will do well when some lime is present. All prefer sunny, sheltered positions but several are tough and extremely hardy. All have fleshy roots and are best planted just before growth begins in spring, using plenty of peat around the roots and watering well and staking firmly until they are established. The most reliable for a small garden is *M. soulangeana* (D.FL.M.S.). This bears large, white cup-shaped flowers with claret coloured bases, from April to May; a pure white form ('Alba') and one with purplish flowers ('Rubra') are available. All have spreading, stout branching systems. They will flower when 3 ft. or so high and under ideal conditions will become small trees. Little pruning other than to shape the bushes is needed. None likes root disturbance – e.g. the forking of ground underneath them.

M. stellata is the smallest magnolia; it forms a compact shrub with very numerous white many-petalled flowers about 3 in. across in March and April. It is suitable for the smallest garden.

Mahonia The Oregon grape, *M. aquifolium*, 3 ft. tall, with prickly leaves and small yellow flowers followed by small purple berries, is used effectively as a dense, decorative evergreen carpet under trees.

M. japonica (E.F.FL.M.S.) is similar but on a much more magnificent scale with long, drooping spikes of small lemon-yellow flowers with the scent of lilies-of-the-valley, and is one of the finest late winter flowering shrubs. In a sheltered corner it may reach 5 ft., and will thrive in any reasonably good soil. Prune only to shape it.

Malus One of the best and most reliable decorative crab apples, 'John Downie' produces a heavy crop of fruit, bright golden-yellow flushed with vermilion, which makes excellent jelly. The flowers in late May or early June are snow-white. The tree is erect, reaches perhaps 25 ft. on a standard and needs little pruning.

M. 'Profusion' has coppery-crimson young leaves, red flowers and small blood-red fruit. *M.* 'Golden Hornet' has white flowers and heavy crops of bright yellow fruit which hang late on the tree. Both make smaller, spreading trees. All are deciduous.

Olearia The daisy bush, *O. haastii* (E.FL. M.S.), is a rounded evergreen with small, leathery leaves, sometimes reaching 6 ft., which is covered with small white daisies in July and August. It will stand seaside gales and town conditions; sometimes used as a hedge, it needs no pruning.

Osmanthus *O. delavayi* (E.FL.M.S.) makes a most attractive rounded plant reaching 6 or 7 ft., with small, neat glossy leaves, that is thickly covered with small, sweetly scented white flowers over a long period in April. It is not particular about soil or situation and need not be pruned unless to keep it small, when shearing over after flowering does little to prevent subsequent bloom.

Parrotia *P. persica* (D.F.FL.M.NC.T.) is a small tree, eventually reaching 20 ft., of slender, open growth. In February and March the bare twigs may be covered with flowers in which the tassel-like clusters of anthers are crimson. In autumn the leaves turn a mixture of pinks, crimson, gold and orange. As the tree ages the bark becomes boldly marked like that of a London plane. It is at its best in a sunny, sheltered spot on lime-free soil.

Philadelphus This is commonly called mock orange and sometimes incorrectly syringa (which is the lilac) (D.S.M.FL.). Most kinds have stout, erect or arching shoots, covered with usually white, strongly scented flowers in June and July. All will thrive in any normal soils. Prune some of the oldest shoots from the base when flowering is over, which should be done annually when bushes are established. 'Beauclerk' has large flowers with a pale purple blotch in the centre. 'Virginal' is a vigorous, erect growing form with white double flowers. There are many others.

Pieris (E.S.M.NC.F.FL.) These evergreen shrubs must have acid soils. Their attractive flowers, borne in April and May, are like small lilies-of-the-valley, but the main feature is the brilliant scarlet young foliage. 'Forest Flame' is among the hardiest and most showy, the leaves passing from flame colour through pinks and cream to green. It will reach about 7 ft. and needs no pruning.

Potentilla (D.S.L.FL.) The shrubby cinquefoils are most useful shrubs. Their brightly coloured flowers like small single roses, in shades of yellow and white appear over a long period. They are tolerant of position and soil as long as drainage is good. In March some of the oldest twigs should be cut away at the base. *P. beesii*, 1½ ft., has silver leaves and buttercup yellow flowers from late summer to autumn; 'Tangerine', 1½ ft., has yellowish-red flowers in late summer; 'Mandschurica', also dwarf, has grey leaves and white flowers.

Prunus (D.T.M.FL.) Under this name botanists and so, alas, nurserymen have to include trees and shrubs which the innocent gardener considers, particularly on examining their fruit, to be quite different. These are in alphabetical order: almonds, apricots, bird cherries, cherries (including the wealth of Japanese kinds), laurels (not included here) and peaches.

All like open, well-drained situations with plenty of sun and, except where stated, lime in the soil. The minimum of pruning is desirable. This should be done about midsummer or just after, otherwise the trees will 'bleed' their gum-like sap so that the wounds will hot heal and fungal diseases may enter.

ALMOND *P. dulcis (amygdalus)* is a small, rather gauntly branched tree, with large pink flowers on the bare stems in March or April. The large fruit with its downy skin does not contain edible almonds.

APRICOT *P. armeniaca*, the kind usually grown for garden ornament, is a small tree opening its thickly clustered carmine buds in March and April to show the pink flowers. This does not produce fruit.

BIRD CHERRY *P. padus* is a medium-sized tree with narrow spikes, 5 in. or more long, of small white almond scented flowers in May after the leaves open. Small black berries follow. The form *watereri* has spikes 8 in. long.

ORNAMENTAL CHERRIES (including the Japanese kinds of which there are many); none normally produces fruit. A representative selection would include:

'Accolade', a small graceful tree with very numerous semi-double, large pale pink flowers hanging in clusters during April or even earlier in very mild weather. In autumn the leaves turn a rich yellow.

'Amanogawa' is a tightly erect-growing Japanese cherry of narrow outline, like a dwarf Lombardy poplar. It has semi-double pale pink flowers in April or May. A little pruning to remove spreading branches may be necessary. It will occasionally and very slowly reach 20 ft.

P. avium 'Plena' is a form of our native cherry making a handsome specimen larger

Left: One of the most reliable of all the beautiful magnolias for the small garden is *M. soulangeana*, of which various colour forms are available

Above: 'Blue Diamond', a dwarf rhododendron, suitable for the larger rock garden or the front of a border

Right: One of the tall-growing hybrid rhododendrons derived from *R. fortunei*

Far left: The silver birches (*Betula pendula*) are among some of the best small trees for growing in grass

than the Japanese cherries, which in mid-May is heavily laden with double white, long-lasting flowers. In autumn the leaves often turn crimson.

'Kanzan' is the most popular and reliable of pink-flowered Japanese cherries. When young the branches are stiffly erect but later spread. The large, purplish-pink double flowers open in April–May. The unfolding leaves are somewhat copper-coloured; before falling, they turn a dull yellow.

P. sargentii is a round-headed tree. The opening leaves are bronzy-red, the flowers in March are single, pink in colour and not as showy as in many kinds. Its principal feature is the brilliant red colouring of the leaves in autumn, often as early as September, and long-lasting.

'Tai-haku' is a vigorous Japanese cherry notable for its very large, dazzling white flowers opening among the copper coloured young leaves in April–May. In autumn the leaves hang on late into the autumn turning yellow and vermilion.

137

Pyracantha (E.S.M.FL.FR.) The firethorns are valuable thorny shrubs, with narrow evergreen leaves and hawthorn-like flowers in June, followed by red or yellow berries. They will thrive in any type of soil or situation including shade, and are thus often used for training against shady walls. They may be reduced in size by pruning when the berries are set, leaving untouched as many berry bearing shoots as possible. *P. atalantoides* has scarlet berries; its form 'Aurea' has yellow fruit. *P. coccinea lalandei* is of vigorous, rather erect growth, with orange-red berries.

Pyrus The orchard pears are large and beautiful trees but the kind most suited to gardens is the weeping willow-leaved pear *P. salicifolia* 'Pendula' (D.T.H.F.FL.). A broad spreading tree, it reaches 25 ft. or more. The leaves are narrow, silvery green in colour and quite unlike those of an ordinary pear. The clusters of small creamy-white flowers which open in late March or early April, have prominent crimson anthers. The fruit is insignificant. The only pruning needed is to keep the tree shapely. This can be done in winter.

Rhododendron (E.D.M.NC.FL.) In many modern catalogues, under this name (according to botanical rules) are included what we usually call azaleas (which are often, but not always, deciduous). Those we have long known as rhododendrons are evergreens.

None will tolerate lime and prefer sandy and peaty soils. Many appreciate some shade and in general all dislike drought, particularly the evergreen kinds. All prefer protection from strong winds.

The roots are fine and fibrous, and naturally form balls, making them easy to plant and transplant. Plenty of peat should be worked in round this ball when planting, and the young plants should be well soaked. If, when planted, the bush shows a tendency to rock, it should be tied to a stake for a year or so.

One of the best azaleas is *R. luteum* (*Azalea pontica*), a medium sized shrub covered with very sweetly scented yellow flowers in mid-May, the leaves turning a rich red in autumn. Smaller growing, with a much wider variation in colour, are the Mollis hybrids, and the

Exbury and Ghent hybrids, usually flowering in May and also giving good autumn leaf colour. There are also the much smaller evergreen Japanese azaleas, mostly in pinks and reds and some white, opening from April to June. All these of the azalea group are suitable for moderate and small gardens.

The true rhododendrons are even more numerous and vary in size from trees to little shrubs. The common *R. ponticum* (not to be confused with the so-called *Azalea pontica* mentioned above) is a large shrub with mauve to pink flowers. It is very common and is naturalized in places: there are many better kinds for gardens. A few well-known and reliable kinds are 'Pink Pearl', large rose-pink flowers, April–May; 'Fastuosum flore-pleno' semi-double flowers of an unusual bluish-mauve colour, May–June; 'Cynthia', deep rose with dark crimson markings, April–May; 'Britannia' fiery red flowers, April–May, and 'Mrs Furnival', soft-pink flowers with crimson blotches, May–June. These are all reliable and suitable for most gardens.

There are many other dwarf kinds suitable for the edge of borders or rock gardens, including 'Blue Tit' (April–May) with blue flowers; *R. racemosum*, thickly covered with small rose-pink flowers at the same season; 'Blue Diamond' of erect growth with blue flowers in May and *R. campylocarpum*, also May-flowering with yellow blooms.

R. praecox is an erect shrub up to 3 ft. tall, with pink flowers opening in February if the weather is mild, but which may be frosted unless protected.

Rhus (D.T. or S.M.F.) The stag's horn sumach, *R. typhina*, is a small tree or large shrub of sprawling growths which suggest the antlers of a stag. They are covered with thick, close down when young. It is grown

---

Above left : Santolina chamaecyparissus 'Neopolitana', is grown for its finely divided foliage and its yellow, button-like flower heads
Above right : Sorbus pohuashanensis is a Chinese mountain ash with very large clusters of scarlet fruits. It is one of the best of this group for the smaller garden
Below : The pink flowers of the evergreen *Skimmia japonica* are followed by bright crimson berries

for its large, very handsome fern-like leaves which turn orange and red in autumn. There is a cut-leaved form, 'Laciniata'. Any old dead wood should be cut out. It needs sun and will thrive on poor, light soils.

Ribes (D.S.M.FL.) The flowering currants are very hardy and will grow almost anywhere. Their flowers are borne in tassels early in the year. The best known is *R. sanguineum* 'King Edward VII', 6 ft. with deep crimson flowers in March or April. Prune by cutting out a few old shoots from the base from time to time.

Robinia (D.T.M.FL.F.) The false acacia, *R. pseudoacacia*, with delicate foliage and pealike flowers at mid-summer, is a quick growing tree that thrives in light sandy soils, but is too large for the small garden; its form 'Frisia' is smaller and has golden foliage which becomes paler in autumn before it falls.

Romneya The Californian tree poppy, *R. trichocalyx* (D.S.M.FL.), is a remarkable shrub with white flowers of up to 5 in. in diameter with crinkled petals and a great boss of golden stamens at their centre. These open from late July until early autumn. The deeply cut leaves are silvery grey. It will reach 5 ft. and needs a sunny situation. Often slow to establish, the chances are that after apparently dying back at first it will recover. It likes a position adjoining paving or large stones under which the roots can run. Cut the shrubs down to ground level in spring.

Rosmarinus *R. officinalis* (E.S.M.F.) Rosemary, with its greyish, scented leaves and blue flowers in late spring, is one of our oldest garden plants. A sunny spot is essential and it is at its best on light soils. It can be used for low hedges. Under good conditions it will reach 6 ft. A form with paler blue flowers and erect growth is 'Miss Jessop's Upright'. Plants should be clipped over lightly after flowering to retain a good shape.

Ruta Rue (*R. graveolens*) (E.S.L.F.) is an old favourite evergreen grown for its blue foliage rather than its yellow flowers which open from mid-summer to August. It reaches 2 ft. or so. It prefers a light soil and sunny posi-

Above: The large fragrant white flowers of
Romneya trichocalyx, the Californian tree
poppy, are produced from July
to September

tion. Some gardeners prefer to remove the
flower spikes before they open. Otherwise,
the previous year's shoots should be clipped
back in spring.

Salix (D.T.M.FL.) The willows range from
large trees, such as the white willow (*S. alba*),
crack willow (*S. fragilis*) and the yellow-
twigged weeping willow (*S. chrysocoma*), all
too large for most gardens, through the
bushes known as sallows, to dwarf shrubs
suitable for rock gardens. The flowers are
borne in catkins, the sexes normally on different trees. The males are showy, as they
consist of the anthers covered with golden
pollen. One of the best small trees is the male
form of our native sallow or goat willow (*S.
caprea*) which is widely cut as 'palm' at
Eastertide. As far as propagation is concerned,
a tree having been marked as of the right sex
when in flower, a stout, leafless shoot, 3–4 ft.
long is cut from it during winter and the
lower twigs entirely removed. The lower foot
or so is then firmly planted in the ground.

This method can be used to propagate almost
any willow.

Of similar size is the violet willow, *S.
daphnoides*, with purple-violet shoots covered
with an almost white bloom. The large
catkins open in late March.

One form of the white willow, *S. alba*
'Chermesina' has bright orange-scarlet shoots
and makes a fine show in winter; it should be
treated as a shrub and cut back hard every
other year, in order to produce the colourful
shoots.

Santolina *S. chamaecyparissus* (E.S.L.F.)
The lavender cotton is a dwarf shrub grown
for its silvery thread-like foliage. It bears
yellow flowers in late summer. It needs sun
and prefers poor, dry soils. If cut over in
April to remove the previous year's growth
this both keeps it tidy and prevents flowering,
thus preserving its silvery appearance.

Sarcococca (E.S.M.F.FL.) The sweet box is
a narrow-leaved shrub with small sweetly
scented flowers in very early spring. *S.
hookeriana digyna* is the best kind. It grows
about 3½ ft. high and will cover the barest,
completely shaded ground by means of
suckers. It has purple stems.

Senecio *S. laxifolius* (E.F.FL.L.S.) is a grey

leaved, bushy, evergreen spreading shrub up
to about 3 ft. high with clusters of bright
yellow daisy-like flowers in June and July,
or even later. It must have sun and is a good
plant for a bank, as it needs sharp drainage.

Skimmia *S. japonica* (E.S.L.F.FR.) grows
from 2–3 ft. high. It needs shade but dislikes
lime. It is grown for its foliage and bright
crimson berries which last into winter. Male
and female flowers grow on separate bushes
and to achieve berries both must grow together. There is an exception, however; *S.
japonica foremanii* which carries both sexes of
flowers and usually produces some berries.

Sorbus (D.T.M.FR.FL.) This genus includes
the rowans or mountain ashes with leaves
consisting of numerous leaflets and the whitebeams with entire (simple, undivided) leaves.
All are moderate sized trees particularly suitable for gardens, with clusters of small white
flowers followed by red (or sometimes yellow)
berries. The leaves usually colour well in
autumn. All tolerate a wide range of soils,
provided they are well drained, the whitebeams being good on chalk. Prune only to
keep the stem clean. Young trees should be
firmly staked after planting but are good in
exposed places. All may be attacked by fire-

blight where this is widely present on pear and other members of the rose family and it is advisable not to plant them in such districts.

ROWANS *S. aucuparia* 'Asplenifolia', the fern-leaved form of the rowan, has deeply cut leaves and makes a very attractive small tree reaching about 25 ft. *S. cashmiriana* is another small rowan, with pink flowers in late May, followed by large, sparkling white berries that hang on far into the winter; it looks well if allowed to branch low and form two or three stems. *S. hupehensis* has rather large leaves with a distinctive bluish sheen, often turning a good yellow or sometimes red in autumn. Large hanging bunches of small white or sometimes pinkish berries follow the numerous flower clusters. *S.* 'Joseph Rock' is a beautiful erect-growing tree, eventually reaching about 30 ft., which produces striking yellow, long-lasting berries amidst autumnal leaf colouring in rich variety.

WHITEBEAMS *S. aria* 'Lutescens' is a fine form of the common whitebeam which makes a stout tree reaching about 30 ft. The leaves are silvery when young and on developing become green above and grey below. The white flowers in June are followed by scarlet berries larger than in the rowan group. *S. intermedia*, the Swedish whitebeam, is similar but with toothed leaves. It is very hardy.

Spartium The Spanish broom, *S. junceum* (D.S.H.FL.), is one of the few brooms that will thrive on limy soils, and in any sunny situation. Reaching as much as 9 ft. it carries large, bright yellow pea-like flowers on the rush-like shoots from June until as late as October. Occasionally shorten some of the branches in April.

Spiraea (D.S.M.FL.) These useful shrubs do well under most normal conditions and carry large numbers of small flowers. *S. arguta*, the bridal wreath, about 6 ft., is covered with small white flowers in late April. On estab-

lished plants, cut out some of the old shoots when flowering is ended. *S.* 'Anthony Waterer' is a dwarf shrub with flat clusters of crimson flowers from mid to late summer. Cut the stems back hard in spring.

Syringa (D.S.H.FL.) The lilacs provide a wide range of colour in their sweetly scented flowers opening from mid to late May. All prefer sun and good fertile soil, particularly if lime is present, but are tolerant of conditions. Newly planted bushes should be cut hard back to vigorous buds. When plants become dense and thicket-like, a few stout stems should be cut out down to the base as growth starts. It is worth removing the faded flower spikes for the first year or two.

Single flowers: 'Esther Staley', pink, mid-May; 'Maud Notcutt', white, late May; 'Souvenir de Louis Spath', reddish purple, late May.

Double flowers: 'Mme Antoine Buchner', rosy mauve, late May; 'Mme Lemoine', double white, late May; 'Paul Thirion', rosy red, early June.

Tamarix (D.S.H.F.FL.) The long, slender shoots are covered with minute flowers. The plants are quick growing and thrive in wind-swept places and by the seaside but will grow almost anywhere. To give their most graceful effect they should be cut almost to ground level in spring; unpruned they will form straggling, picturesque small trees. *T. pentandra* has rosy-pink flowers in July and August.

Ulex (E.S.L.NC.FL.) The double form of the common gorse, *U. europaeus* 'Plenus', is covered with rich yellow flowers in April and May. It is good on poor, sandy soils in full sun, and should be clipped over after flowering to keep it tidy.

Viburnum (D. and E.S.M.FL.) These decorative shrubs, with clusters of small white or pinkish scented florets, thrive in any garden

soil and are good on lime. Some are notable for flowering in winter; the remainder bloom in spring and early summer:

WINTER FLOWERING *V. fragrans* (*V. farreri*) is an upright deciduous shrub with fragrant, white, pink-flushed florets opening from November onwards to February. The young leaves are a rich bronze colour. Pruning is not needed. A sheltered, sunny position is desirable.

V. tinus, the laurustinus, a rounded evergreen shrub, reaches 10–15 ft. and carries bosses of white flowers from October or November into spring. It is a fine, solid-looking specimen and is often grown in hedges.

SPRING FLOWERING *V. burkwoodii* has large heads of white, scented flowers in April and is one of the showiest of all viburnums. It will reach 6 ft. or more. Some of the rich green leaves may remain during the winter.

V. opulus has two forms, both valuable garden shrubs. The native guelder rose, *V. opulus*, a deciduous shrub to 10 ft. tall, will thrive under any conditions, with scented white flowers in May and June, followed by red translucent berries hanging among the red autumn leaves. *V. opulus sterile*, the snowball bush, is an abnormal form in which all the flowers are large and infertile, giving a solid effect, at first greenish and then white like a snowball. The leaves colour brilliantly.

Weigela These (also sometimes known as diervilla) (D.S.M.FL.) are shrubs heavily laden in May and June with flowers shaped like small foxgloves. They will grow under practically any conditions, including shade. Prune only to remove old, twiggy, worn out shoots after flowering. *W. florida variegata*, one of the best, reaches 6 ft. with leaves edged with creamy white, and pink flowers – a most effective colour scheme; 'Bristol Ruby' has ruby red flowers; 'Eva Rathke' is an old favourite with bright red-crimson flowers.

Above: The translucent red fruits and colourful autumn foliage of the guelder rose, *Viburnum opulus*
Left: Syringa 'Sensation' has purplish-red white edged flowers

The Rock Garden & Garden Pool

Rock Garden Plants

Traditionally, a rock garden is a place in which to grow alpine plants. Way back in Victorian days and before, such a place was usually referred to as a 'rockery', a word which, in these more enlightened times is very much out of favour with devotees of alpine gardening, who even eschew the word 'rock' and more often than not describe it as an alpine garden.

Even the word 'alpine' is suspect in this context, since many of the plants most fitted to be grown on a rock garden are far from having alpine origins. One must, however, have a brief collective description for plants which serve a specific purpose and it is convenient, and sufficiently accurate, to refer to all plants which one would associate with rocks and stones in the open air, as alpines.

There are more amateur gardeners today than there have ever been and the general interest in gardening is very evidently increasing, but it is gardening on a different scale from that to which our fathers and grandfathers were accustomed. It is much more a 'do-it-yourself' affair and this is good as it encourages a closer and more personal interest in plants.

Gardens are small and labour either unobtainable or too expensive. On the other hand, alpine plants are yearly increasing in popularity. So many of them can be grown in a limited space, and they respond so eagerly to individual attention that they offer an ideal form of gardening to those who come to love their jewel-like beauty and wish to grow as many of them as possible in surroundings which are often very restricted indeed.

That alpines are temperamental and difficult plants, needing very special care and attention is a myth going back to the bad old days, when 'rockeries' were made of ugly piles of stone heaped in unsuitable places–under the drip of overhanging trees, or in shaded and draughty corners. These were death traps for most plants and it is small wonder that alpines died in them and created the illusion that they were difficult to grow.

A select minority of alpine plants, mostly the true 'alpines' which come from great elevations and dwell in the rarified air and austere conditions of high mountains, demand skilled and knowledgeable care. It is to the cultivation of these that the novice progresses in gradual stages.

Although it is tempting to the beginner to attempt such plants as the delicious and exciting domes of alpine androsaces, or to 'have a go' at the exasperating but supremely beautiful *Eritrichium nanum*, wisdom should prevail and these delights postponed until the necessary skill has been acquired after experience with the many easy and lovely plants which are available.

One of the reasons for the avoidance of alpine plants by a few gardeners may well be the result of starting at the wrong end and trying to grow the rare and difficult minority. Failure with these will lead to discouragement and a disinclination to take further steps along what can be one of the most delightful paths into specialized gardening.

Those who are new to alpine gardening should start by growing the easier plants; those which will provide colour and interest over as long a period as possible. Another criticism which has been aimed at rock gardens is that they are supremely beautiful and colourful in the spring and early summer, but deadly dull thereafter.

This is untrue; by choosing carefully from the immense variety of plants available a rock garden can be colourful from earliest spring until winter. There is, and always has been, a tendency to plant too many aubrietas, alyssums and arabis. These all blossom in the spring and are invaluable for providing masses of colour, but if they are too generously used, there are wide blank spaces for the rest of the year.

Any such vigorous and space devouring plants must be employed in moderation and ample space left for later flowering specimens. The beginner would do well to seek among such genera as *Dianthus, Campanula, Phlox, Gentiana, Primula, Helianthemum, Achillea, Saxifraga, Geranium, Iris, Lewisia, Ranunculus, Polygonum, Sedum* and *Sempervivum* in order to secure a succession of flowers throughout the summer and autumn.

A few really dwarf evergreen shrubs should also be grown. For this purpose none is better than the genuinely pygmy conifers. There is a trap here for the unwary however. Too often conifers are sold as dwarfs which will ultimately grow much too large for any rock garden.

It is fatally easy to be misled by the dainty and miniature appearance of such conifers as *Chamaecyparis lawsoniana fletcheri* when seen as young, immature plants and only guaranteed dwarfs should be planted. Ideal examples are the little Noah's Ark juniper, *Juniperus communis* 'Compressa', any of the several pygmy forms of *Chamaecyparis obtusa*, and some of the tight, cushion-forming varieties of *Picea abies*.

One of the functions of the tiny trees is to create a sense of scale and proportion in the miniature mountainscape. The shape of the trees should be borne in mind when they are placed. Those of upright, columnar habit, such as the little juniper quoted above, should never be planted on high points. Place them lower down, against a small 'cliff' and reserve the prostrate kinds for the heights.

Plants for Special Purposes

The Alpine House Yet another aspect of alpine gardening is the cultivation of plants in an alpine house. There is a general impression that only the rarest and most tricky plants may be grown in such a structure. It is true that skilled growers keep their choicest specimens in such a house, but there is no reason why an alpine house, or a cold greenhouse, should not form a valuable adjunct to the rock garden.

There are many weeks during the year when gardening out of doors is far from being a pleasurable occupation and a select collection of plants grown in an alpine house can provide pleasure and interest at a time when other gardening activities are impossible and plants can be admired and cared for in comparative comfort.

There are specially designed alpine houses which differ from conventional greenhouses in having a lower pitched roof, and more ventilators. This is the ideal but is not essential. An ordinary house can easily be adapted and the only major modification likely to be needed is the provision of extra ventilation. No artificial heating is necessary, or even desirable and this is an economy.

By growing a number of alpine plants in pots and pans a constant succession of interest can be obtained. When not in flower the containers can be stood out of doors, preferably plunged to the rims in ashes or sand. Very early flowering alpine bulbs make a splendid beginning to the year and for this one would choose from the tiny narcissi, crocuses, snowdrops, snowflakes, winter aconites (eranthis), fritillaries, erythroniums etc.

The gentianella, *Gentiana acaulis*

Above: A miniature waterfall will help to provide the right conditions for water-side plants. *Right: Caltha palustris* 'Plena', the double-flowered kingcup

After these come the early flowering saxifragas, particularly such kinds as *S. irvingii, S. kellereri, S. apiculata, S.* 'Cranbourne' and *S. burseriana.* Then come all the spring-flowering alpines of dwarf, compact habit, with campanulas and dianthus to follow on and some of the choicer sedums and late-flowering gentians.

The staging on which the pots and pans stand is best made of a solid base, not spaced wooden slats. If a layer of sharp shingle or ashes is spread over the staging this will help to keep the soil in the containers moist and cool and avoid the constant drying out to which the plants object.

In the summer, with some pots and pans outside those in the house can be spaced more widely. In the winter the entire population can be brought inside and stood more closely together. Autumn potted bulbs can be stored on the floor beneath the staging until they begin to grow.

Pond and waterside plants The addition of water, and especially moving water, to a rock garden has several advantages. Not only does it widen the variety of plants which can be grown, but it adds life to the scene. There are now available several inexpensive types of submersible pump which can be used to circulate water from a pond at the lowest level to another higher up, from which it can be made to flow in a small stream, or a succession of small pools, back to its origin.

Pools and streams can be constructed with modern fibre-glass materials and with plastic sheeting, or they can be made more conventionally with concrete. Anyone with moderate abilities as a handyman can construct streams and pools without difficulty and at little expense. (See also Handyman Gardener article on Water Garden features.)

Left: 'Escarboucle', a free-flowering water-lily

By arranging for small overflows here and there moist areas can be contrived by the pool or streamside in which to accommodate some of the plants which relish having their roots in wet soil. Do not ever imagine that, without making deliberate moist areas, the plants which enjoy them can be made happy by merely planting them at the waterside. The very edge of a stream or pond creates the illusion of dampness but can be very dry.

Appropriate plants for such damp situations would be all kinds of mimulus, moisture-loving primulus, for example *P. rosea, P. denticulata, P. frondosa* and, of course, all the candelabra primulas such as *P. japonica.* The double kingcup, *Caltha palustris* 'Plena' hangs its golden flowers attractively over the water and such plants as tiarella, astilbe, *Saxifraga aizoides* and the double ladies smock, *Cardamine pratensis* 'Plena' would help to create a pretty scene.

The Site Whatever one does in a garden it is well to have an ideal at which to aim. It is not always possible to achieve perfection, but the very act of striving to attain it is rewarding and is certain to provide better results than aimless attempts.

The ideal site for a rock garden would be a gentle slope, on well-drained soil, falling to the south or west. Not many gardens will be able to provide such a perfect position, but there is no need to despair; many alternative situations will be quite satisfactory. Avoid if at all possible a due east aspect.

A sloping position is better than a flat one, but a rock garden built on the flat can be perfectly successful. The absolutely essential thing is good drainage. It is quite useless to construct a rock garden on soil which is likely to be flooded and waterlogged in the winter.

Alpine plants on the whole are extremely tolerant of widely varying conditions of soil, aspect and climate but they will not, under any circumstances, endure having their roots surrounded by sodden soil. Water they love, and need, and it does not matter how much there is, as long as it flows readily through and past their roots. The positions in which many

of them grow naturally may appear to be dry, but water from melting snows flows constantly below the surface.

If the natural drainage is adequate little more preparation is necessary than deeply digging the area and removing all perennial weeds. It is a good idea to leave the area alone for a few weeks after it has been cleared and dug to allow weed seeds to germinate. These can then be destroyed by applying a post-emergence weedkiller. This will save a lot of later laborious weeding. Weedkillers which leave a residue in the soil and prohibit planting for some weeks or even months after application, should be avoided.

Site the rock garden right out in the open and never, if it can possibly be avoided beneath overhanging trees, or in narrow alleyways between adjacent buildings. The first will ensure a detested dripping of water from

The sort of compost to use is described below in the section devoted to cultivation, but make sure before you begin to build that you have available enough mixed soil. It always takes more than you expect and nothing is more annoying than to run out of compost halfway through the construction. Very roughly, you may estimate that, on a flat site, one cubic yard of soil will be needed for every ton of stone. A sloping site may need rather less as you can cut into the hillside to help fill the pockets.

If, after reading the above you feel that there is no possible position for a rock garden on your property, and if you still wish to grow rock plants, do not throw up your hands in despair and abandon the project. It may be a heretical statement, but it must be said that the great majority of rock plants can be grown very successfully without the aid of a rock

built up in brick, stone or even planks or old railway sleepers, to a convenient height. Many who find the ground getting a long way away as the years advance discover in such raised beds a delightfully easy form of gardening. A good height to aim at is from 2–2½ ft. Fill the bottom half with good roughage for drainage and top up with compost and a perfect home is provided for alpine plants.

Cultivation There are two main divisions in the requirements of alpine plants. There are those which either like or will tolerate a soil containing chalk or lime and there is another, smaller but quite intolerant section, which cannot abide lime in any form.

The lime lovers will grow in limefree soil, but the lime-haters will not put up with alkaline soil. If, therefore, the natural soil is chalky, you must either refrain from growing the lime-haters, or make special provision for

Left: One of the many desirable forms of aubrieta. *Below*: A well-planted rock garden. *Below centre left*: After excavating the site for a plastic pool, put down a layer of sand. *Below centre right*: The plastic sheet is held in place temporarily by bricks, while water is gently run in from a hose. *Bottom*: The pool complete

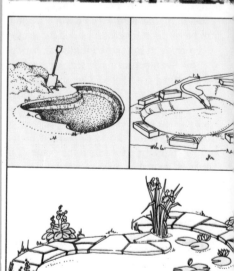

branches above and the latter will be draughty, and all plants hate draughts. Positions for plants which relish some shade can always be contrived in the construction of the rock garden. An outcrop of rocks running east and west will provide a warm south face and a cool north aspect on the other side.

Construction A detailed, stone-by-stone description of the making of a rock garden is almost impossible to write and quite impossible to follow in practice. So much depends upon each individual rock, the site, and what sort of scene it is desirable to create. One can really only set down some basic rules, which amount to a series of 'do's' and 'dont's'.

Do not set the stones in isolation over a mound of soil, This only creates a Victorian 'rockery' and there will be constant erosion of soil from higher to lower levels. Do not set stones up on edge so that they erupt from the soil like fangs. Instead lay them on their longest edge and make sure that they join in pleasant complexes or outcrops much as they would in nature on a hillside.

garden; a rock garden is the ideal setting for them, but it is not essential.

Possible situations for alpine plants are between the cracks of paving stones. In fact, such a position provides everything that they like, such as a cool root run which does not dry out, their heads in the light and their collars protected from too much wet by the closely adjacent paving stones.

Retaining or free-standing walls provide excellent homes for alpines. Here too, they find perfect conditions. If all else fails, you have only to dig out a depth of soil in an open, sunny position, ensure good drainage and fill in with suitable compost and you have a bed which will grow a wide variety of them to perfection.

Many of the smaller plants will do well in old stone troughs and sinks. These little gardens are invaluable where space is really limited and it is astonishing how many different plants can be gathered into a small sink.

Finally, some people resort to a specially constructed raised bed. The sides can be

them. Unless you particularly desire to grow the lime-haters, many of which are very lovely plants, you need not be too sorrowful, for most alpines are tolerant. It is only the minority whose idiosyncrasies must be pandered to.

If you insist upon growing the lime-haters in spite of the lime in your soil, then you must make a special part of the rock garden for them. This should be on one of the higher places, so that lime-impregnated water does not soak into the soil from above. Many of the lime-haters are also plants which appreciate some shade so try to organize their special situation so that it is protected from full sun.

Dig out the natural soil to a depth of at least 1 ft. and fill in with prepared lime-free soil. This can be a mixture of lime-free loam, leaf-mould or peat, and sharp sand in the pro-

portions, by bulk, of 3-2-1. Make sure if leaf-mould is used that it is really lime-free. If made from the leaves of trees which have been growing on chalk it is likely to have a lime-content. Peat is safer, and it should be fine grade moss peat. If there is any doubt about the lime-content of any ingredient test it with one of the inexpensive soil-testing outfits which are available.

Plants likely to demand this treatment are most heathers (except the lime-loving, winter-flowering forms of *Erica carnea*), cassiopes, andromedas, gaultherias, pernettyas, autumn-flowering gentians such as *G. sino-ornata* and its allies, and most members of the family *Ericaceae* (which includes all rhododendrons). Most good catalogues quote the family to which plants belong and this can be a guide to their needs.

Drainage The first and most important basic need of alpine plants is perfect drainage and no time or trouble expended in ensuring this is wasted. Once you are certain that water will pass rapidly through the soil and will not linger around the plant roots you are more than halfway to success. On a naturally gravelly or sharply draining soil, little preparation will be necessary, but if you have to contend with a heavy, sticky clay, then some preliminary work is essential to provide the necessary drainage.

If the site on which the rock garden is to stand, or indeed, any position where alpines are to be grown, is flat, and if the soil is clay, or has a hard pan beneath, causing water to stand in puddles instead of draining away, then a deep sump must be excavated in the centre of the site and filled with old clinker, rough stones, ashes, gravel, or any good draining material. The sump cannot be too deep and a minimum depth of 5 or 6 ft. should be the objective. Its width will depend to some extent upon the area of the site. A large area may demand two or even three sumps, but a small space, say 200 square feet, would be sufficiently served by one such excavation approximately 2 ft. in width. If it is decided to manage with only one sump on a larger site, it should be twice that width.

On a sloping site drainage is more simply provided. If necessary surplus water can be led away down the slope by a series of narrow trenches, in which land-drains can be laid, or the trenches filled with clinker or other rough material.

Soil mixtures Simplicity should be the aim of the beginner. Experts who delight in accepting the challenge offered by really rare and difficult plants will have 'cookery-books' of complicated soil recipes with which to pander to the tastes of individual plants, but 90 per cent of alpine plants (excluding the line-haters) can be successfully grown in one basic soil mixture.

The three main ingredients of a desirable compost are loam, a good organic material and sharp sand or grit. Loam is either rotted turves or good top-spit soil containing an appreciable amount of fibre. Good, friable, well-nourished garden soil will serve very well.

The organic material will consist of either moss peat, leafsoil or well-decayed compost: peat should be of the finer grade, and sedge peat should be avoided; leafsoil should be nicely rotted and broken down into a dark, friable material.

Sand is an important ingredient; its primary purpose is to ensure an open, freely draining compost. The soft yellow sand used for mixing mortar or cement is quite useless for alpines. The sand must be sharp in texture. If such sand is not available locally it should be replaced with any form of fine but sharp grit.

Measuring by bulk, the proportions of the three ingredients should be 3 parts of loam, 2 parts of organic material and 1½ parts of sand or grit. These must all be thoroughly mixed together, adding at the same time bonemeal in the proportion of 5 lb. to each cubic yard of compost.

Such a compost is ideal for the great majority of plants and no form of artificial fertilizer will be needed for at least the first two years. After that, a spring topdressing with similar compost is desirable and an additional light dressing of bonemeal in autumn and spring, scattered on the soil and gently forked into the top inch or so.

When filling the pockets and joints between the stones of the rock garden during its construction press the soil down firmly, using a blunt-ended wooden rammer to pack it well under and around the rocks. When building is completed leave the whole area unplanted for a week or two, to allow the soil to settle, which it will do after rain, or a thorough soaking. Some compost should be kept in reserve to top-up where necessary. It is better to do this first rather than have settlement after planting has been done.

Great care should be taken to ensure that all spaces and crevices between the rocks are well filled with soil. These are the crannies into which alpines delight in delving with their roots in search of the cool, moist conditions they need. Should they emerge into a soilless vacuum they may perish.

Above right: Hypericum polyphyllum growing in a crevice. *Below:* Rocks should be placed in the mound of soil built up over a deep sump to ensure adequate drainage (important if the site is level). *Inset:* The wrong way to lay rocks. *Below right:* Rocks laid correctly, sloping slightly backwards

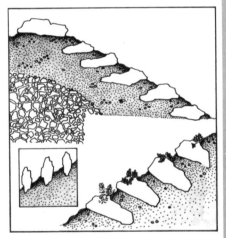

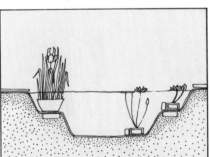

Above: A section through a pool. If marginal plants are grown, make raised 'platforms', on which such plants can be grown in containers. *Below:* The roots of plants to be grown on the bottom of the pool can be contained between bricks (or in baskets) to anchor them

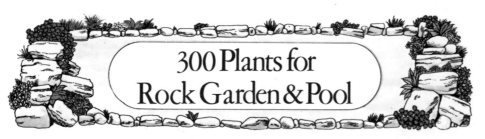

300 Plants for Rock Garden & Pool

Planting The two main planting periods are spring and autumn. There are certain advantages in early autumn planting if it can be done while the soil is still warm. The plants can make growth and become well established, thus ensuring a reasonable display in the first spring and summer after planting. If it cannot be done before the soil becomes wet and cold it is as well to delay until the spring.

Alpine plants supplied by nurseries are always pot-grown and, if necessary, planting can continue during the summer months, although it will be necessary to water them and even shade them from the fiercest sunshine until they begin to take root and are able to seek their own moisture.

When alpines are knocked out of the pots or other containers for planting they will be found to have a firm rootball, If this is hard it should be gently pressed and loosened, without breaking it to pieces, before it is planted. Plant very firmly. Ideally the soil in which to plant should be just moist but not really wet. Do not plant in dust-dry compost, or in any which is saturated. After planting give the plants a really thorough soaking, using a fine-rosed can. This settles the soil nicely around them and provides them with moisture until the roots begin to seek for it further afield.

Watering Once plants in the open are firmly established watering should never be done unless it is absolutely necessary but, if, in a prolonged drought it has to be done, then do it very thoroughly; preferably in the evening.

Top dressing When areas have been completely planted, and especially those occupied by the smaller, possibly cushion-forming plants, it is a good plan to top dress the whole area with small stone chippings, ensuring that the chippings are inserted beneath the foliage and close against the collar of the plants. This top dressing retains moisture in the soil, discourages the ravaging slugs and imparts a nicely finished appearance to the rock garden.

Cutting back Plants such as the cushion phloxes, helianthemums, aubrietas, arabis, alyssums, dianthus, veronicas, hypericums, iberis and geraniums benefit from being cut back quite severely after they finish flowering. This encourages new growth and often results in a further flush of late season blossom. It also maintains a tidy habit and prolongs the life of the plants.

Maintenance Normal maintenance and cultivation consists of controlling weeds, slugs and snails, and limiting the growth of the more vigorous plants which may tend to swamp smaller neighbours.

Winter care The average alpine plants with which a collection is started need no special winter care if they have been planted in suitable conditions as described above. If, during periods of excessive rainfall any which have very soft and hairy leaves seem to be suffering, they may be protected by a sheet of glass placed over them and held in position by easily contrived wire clips, but this is seldom necessary. The enemy of alpine plants is not cold, but wet. Most of them are accustomed to spend their resting period beneath a covering of snow.

Propagation Alpine plants can be increased by various methods. The usual means of propagation are seeds or cuttings but old plants may often be divided, usually in early spring or early autumn, and a few plants may be increased by root cuttings.

The seeds of alpine plants germinate more readily if they are sown as soon as convenient after ripening. If they cannot be sown at once they should be cleaned and dried and stored in a cool, dry place until sowing can take place.

Sow the seeds in pans, pots or boxes, on a surface of finely sieved, rather gritty soil. Just cover the seeds with similar compost, stand the containers in a cold frame or greenhouse, or in a box out of doors and cover them with paper over which a sheet of glass is placed. As soon as they germinate they must be brought into the light.

The seedlings are ready for pricking-off separately as soon as they make the first true leaves which differ from the first, or cotyledon leaves. John Innes seed compost is suitable, especially if a little extra fine grit is added.

Cuttings of most alpine plants are made from soft tips of young growth which do not contain flower buds. They should be from $\frac{1}{2}$–$1\frac{1}{2}$ in. long. Trim off the lower leaves and, with a very sharp knife sever the cutting immediately below a node (leaf joint) and insert into pure gritty sand in pots or pans. Keep shaded and moist until the cuttings root, when they can be separately potted and grown on until well enough rooted to be planted out.

Divisions should be potted and treated in the same way as potted cuttings. Make sure that all portions have some root. It is often possible to detach rooted pieces of old plants without digging up the entire plant.

1: Sowing seeds of alpines in a seedbox
2: They may also be sown in pans. Before seedlings become overcrowded, they should be pricked out into a box (3) spaced out well
4: Dianthus may be propagated from 'pipings', strip off the lower leaves first. 5: Then insert the 'pipings' in a pot of cutting compost

Above right: Androsace sarmentosa chumbyi
Right: A variety of *Armeria caespitosa*

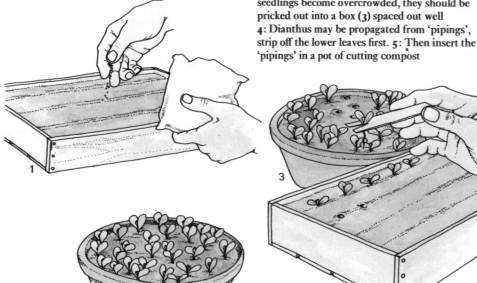

Three Hundred Rock Plants Described

Acaena (*Rosaceae*) (New Zealand burr) Carpeting plants native, mostly, to New Zealand, these are invasive but ornamental and are useful for crevices of paving and to clothe areas of poor soil where little else will flourish. All are sun-lovers. Their small flowers are carried in dense heads on very short stems and are often accompanied by brightly coloured spines. They also make good ground-cover for dwarf bulbs. *A. buchananii* has pea-green leaves and yellow-brown flower heads; *A. glauca* has silky, blue-grey foliage; *A. microphylla* has bronze leaves and innumerable scarlet burr-like flower heads.

Achillea (*Compositae*) (yarrow) Many of these sun-loving plants are suitable for the rock garden. They flower in spring and early summer and possess beauty both of leaf and flower. They are easily grown in any well-drained soil. The following are unlikely to exceed 6 in. when in flower. *A. argentea* has intensely silver leaves and white flowers; *A. chrysocoma* has grey leaves and yellow flowers; *A.* 'King Edward' has soft grey-green leaves and lemon yellow flowers, and *A. tomentosa* green leaves and bright yellow flowers.

Aethionema (*Cruciferae*) (stonecress) Valuable dwarf, shrubby plants for places in full sun and any good garden soil, these flower from early summer onward. Propagate by seed or cuttings. *A. grandiflorum* makes a 9 in. bush of grey-green small leaves and has large heads of rose-pink flowers; *A. pulchellum*, similar but not so tall, has flowers the colour of pink coconut-ice. *A.* 'Warley Rose' is a lovely, daphne-like shrub 6 in. tall with innumerable heads of rich rose-red flowers. As it is a sterile hybrid it has to be propagated by soft tip cuttings.

Allium (*Liliaceae*) This genus contains several fine rock garden plants; they mostly relish full sun and have no special soil requirements. *A. karataviense*, 9 in., has huge, handsome grey-green leaves and large 'drum-stick' heads of grey-white flowers in spring; *A. moly*, 9 in., is invasive but lovely. It has large heads of bright yellow flowers in spring; *A. narcissiflorum* has large, nodding wine-red flowers on 4-in. stems in spring.

Alyssum (*Cruciferae*) These easy-going, sun and lime-loving plants are very decorative in the early spring. They benefit from being cut back after flowering and can be increased from seeds and cuttings. They are splendid wall plants, especially when associated with arabis and aubrieta. They are mostly forms of *A. saxatile*, which has grey-green leaves and many heads of yellow flowers on 9–12 in.

stems; 'Compactum' is dwarfer and more compact; 'Citrinum' has sulphur-yellow flowers, and 'Dudley Neville' orange-buff flowers.

A. spinosum (*Ptilotrichum spinosum*) though not strictly an alyssum is usually included in the family. It is a 9 in. tall spiny bush smothered with white or soft pink flowers in summer.

Anacyclus (*Compositae*) (Mount Atlas daisy) *A. depressus* makes prostrate mats of grey, ferny leaves and radiating stems carrying large daisy-shaped flowers, crimson on the back of the petals and white in front. It is a plant for full sun and very well-drained soil. Propagate from seeds.

Androsace (*Primulaceae*) (rock jasmine) This large genus contains some of the most desirable rock garden and alpine house plants. They are all sun-lovers and, as most of them have densely hairy leaves they may appreciate some protection against winter wet. Propagate by seeds or by detaching rooted rosettes or by cuttings. All are spring and early summer flowering. *A. lanuginosa* should be planted in crevices from which it can hang its trailing stems, which end in heads of pale pink, crimson-eyed flowers; *A. primuloides* (*sarmentosa*) 'Chumbyi', 'Watkinsii' and 'Salmon's Variety' have neat, rounded, hairy-leaved rosettes and heads of deep pink flowers on 6-in. stems.

Anemone (*Ranunculaceae*) (windflower) Several species are admirable rock garden plants. They like well-drained, gritty soil, rich in humus and are increased by division or by seeds. All are sun lovers except where otherwise stated. *A.* 'Lesseri', a sterile hybrid has glowing rose-red flowers on 1 ft. stems in spring; *A. magellanica* has creamy flowers in loose heads on 6-in. stems in spring and early summer; *A. nemorosa*, the wood anemone, likes partial shade and cool soil. The species has white flowers; the cultivars 'Allenii' and 'Robinsoniana' are blue. There is also a form with pretty, double white flowers; *A. vernalis* is one of the most beautiful of all alpines. It has huge opalescent flowers on 6-in. stems. It needs very gritty soil and sun.

Antennaria (*Compositae*) These easy little carpeting plants for sunny positions in any soil are invaluable for planting in crevices between paving stones. Propagate by division or seed. *A. dioica* has tiny grey leaves and fluffy heads of pink flowers on 3-in. stems in spring.

Aquilegia (*Ranunculaceae*) (columbine) Some of these are good rock garden plants. Few of them come entirely true from seed. They like sun and well-drained soil and flower in spring and early summer. *A. ecalcarata* has flights of elegant red-purple, spurless flowers on stems 9 in. tall. It comes true from seed; in *A. flabellata*, 9–12 in. tall, the large flowers may be blue or ivory-white; *A. glandulosa* has large blue and white flowers on 15-in. stems.

Arabis (*Cruciferae*) (rock cress) These sun and lime-loving spring flowering plants are easily grown in ordinary soil. Propagate by cuttings or seeds. Cut hard back after flowering. *A. albida* 'Coccinea' is the double white arabis, a valuable and showy spring flower; 'Snowflake' has large single, snow-white flowers; *A. blepharophylla* is very early flowering. It has pink blossoms on 6-in. stems.

Arenaria (*Caryophyllaceae*) (sandwort) These spring-flowering plants are easily grown. *A. balearica* loves shade. It has a mere

film of tiny leaves and clouds of dainty, tiny white flowers on 1-in. stems; *A. montana* is a spreading, sun-loving plant about 9 in. high, with innumerable large pure white flowers.

Armeria (*Plumbaginaceae*) (thrift) These decorative sun lovers will grow in any soil. All flower in spring. Propagate by division or cuttings. *A. caespitosa* has tight tufts of closely packed deep green leaves and almost stemless heads of rich pink flowers; of *A. maritima* the best forms are 'Vindictive' deep red, 'Laucheana', crimson, and 'Alba', white.

Asperula (*Rubiaceae*) These flower in spring and have clustered heads of pink or white flowers. Propagate by division, seeds and cuttings. *A. gussonii* makes mats of dark green foliage and pink flowers. It will grow in any good soil; *A. odorata*, the woodruff, likes shade and cool soil. It has leafy 9-in. stems and heads of small white fragrant flowers; *A. suberosa* is an especially beautiful plant, but it needs gritty soil and a warm, sunny position. It produces soft carpets of grey leaves and clusters of tubular pink flowers. In wet areas it will appreciate shelter from winter rain.

Aster (*Compositae*) Those species suitable for rock gardens do well in open, sunny positions and in any good, well-drained soil. They may be increased by seeds or by division of old plants. Most flower in mid to late summer. *A. alpinus* has large blue and gold aster flowers on 9-in. stems. There is a nice white form and 'Beechwood' has large, more richly coloured flowers but is a little less 'alpine' in appearance; *A. natalensis* has flowers of gentian-blue on 6-in. stems.

Astilbe (*Saxifragaceae*) There are a few dwarf astilbes for cool, semi-shaded positions. Propagate by division of old plants. *A. chinensis* 'Pumila', 9–12 in., has stiff, dense spires of flowers the colour of crushed raspberries, in August and September; *A. glaberrima* 'Saxosa' has dainty spikes of pink flowers on very short stems in late summer.

Aubrieta (*Cruciferae*) (rock cress) Aubrietas can be raised from seed and provide a mixture of colours. The best kinds are named and are propagated by cuttings or division. They are sun and lime-lovers and need to be heavily trimmed immediately after flowering to maintain their tidy habit and increase the length of their life. They flower in early spring. Any alpine plant catalogue will provide a list of names and colours, but the following may be regarded as a selection of the best kinds:
'Bressingham Pink', very large double flowers of rich pink; 'Bressingham Red', large flowers, deep glowing red; 'Dream', light mauve-blue; 'Dr Mules', one of the oldest and still a good one. Violet blue; 'Godstone', vivid violet-purple; 'Gurgedyke', deep rich purple; 'Joan Allen', double, deep red; 'Mrs Rodewald', very large bright red flowers; 'Variegata', silver and green variegated foliage. Very compact and neat.

Calamintha (*Labiatae*) These are pretty plants with aromatic foliage and worthwhile flowers, easily grown in any good

soil and full sun. All flower in summer. Propagate from seeds or by cuttings. *C. alpina* bears violet, white-tipped tubular flowers on 4-in. stems; *C. grandiflora* is a slightly larger plant with border pink flowers.

Campanula (*Campanulaceae*) (bellflower) Many campanulas are invaluable for the rock garden. Most flower in summer and late summer and are easily grown in good, well-drained soil and sunny positions. Those mentioned may be regarded as the essential nucleus of a collection. Propagate by seeds, division or cuttings. *C. carpatica* has large, saucer-shaped flowers on 9–12 in. stems, its forms vary in colour from white to blue and rich purple; *C. cochleariifolia* (*pusilla*) is a tiny gem with blue or white bells on 3-in. stems; *C. garganica* is a splendid crevice and wall plant. The spreading stems cling closely to the stones and carry multitudes of blue, white-centred starry flowers; *C. portenschlagiana* (*muralis*), 6–9 in., is one of the very best. It has sheets of rich purple flowers in dense masses and will grow and flower in light shade; *C. poscharskyana* is semi-prostrate, invasive but very handsome and flowers for a long period. It has star-shaped blue flowers on long stems.

Cerastium (*Caryophyllaceae*) The common snow-in-summer, *C. tomentosum* is too invasive to be permitted in any rock garden although it is a decorative plant for wild places. There is at least one well-behaved, easily grown species however. This is *C. alpinum* 'Lanatum', which has dense pads of woolly grey leaves and small white flowers in summer. Grow in poor, gritty soil. Propagate by seed, division or cuttings.

Cheiranthus (*Cruciferae*) (wallflower) Wallflowers suitable for the rock garden like dry conditions, lime in the soil and a sunny place. Propagate by cuttings. *C. cheiri* 'Harpur Crewe' is the old double yellow Scotch wallflower with fragrant flowers in short spikes on stiff 15-in. bushes; *C.* 'Moonlight' is a deliciously fragrant dwarf plant with soft yellow flowers.

Chiastophyllum (*Crassulaceae*) In *C. oppositifolium* (*Cotyledon simplicifolia*) the golden flowers hang in slender chains from short leafy stems in spring. It likes a cool spot or light shade.

Chrysogonum (*Compositae*) *C. virginianum* is an easy plant for a not too hot place. It flowers the summer through. It has leafy stems and star-shaped yellow flowers. Propagate by division.

Cortusa (*Primulaceae*) *C. matthiolii* likes a cool position with moist soil. It has rounded lobed, softly hairy leaves and heads of pendent pink tubular flowers on 9-in. stems in summer. Propagate by seeds.

Cotula (*Compositae*) These are invasive but useful for paving and poor, stony soil. The flowers are inconspicuous but the foliage is pretty. They are invaluable ground-coverers. *C. potentillina* has deeply divided bronze-green leaves in dense prostrate mats; *C. squalida* has green, almost fern-like tiny leaves in close mats.

Crepis (*Compositae*) These showy easy plants for sunny positions in any good soil flower in summer. Propagate by seeds. *C. aurea* has leaves like those of a dandelion and copper-red flowers on 4–6 in. stems; in *C. incana*, 9 in., the leaves are ash-grey and it has showers of soft pink flowers.

Cyclamen (*Primulaceae*) The hardy cyclamen are invaluable tuberous-rooted plants for cool positions in the rock garden. Of the many cultivated species the three described are of outstanding virtue. They love lime but do not demand it. Plant them as growing tubers, not stored and dried ones which take a long time to grow. Plant 3–4 in. deep in soil rich in humus. Propagate by seeds. *C. europaeum* has marbled rounded leaves and pink fragrant flowers in summer; *C. neapolitanum* has beautifully shaped and marked leaves and

Above: The blue flowers are those of *Campanula portenschlagiana*, a vigorous bellflower for the rock garden. *Left:* Dwarf forms of the wallflower (*Cheiranthus cheiri*) provide colour and fragrance in spring. *Below: Dianthus deltoides*, the maiden pink, a fine rock garden plant. Note how the surface soil is mulched with stone chippings which help to keep it cool and moist and discourage slugs. *Above right:* Many colourful alpines may be grown in the crevices of a dry stone wall

deep pink – sometimes white – flowers in the autumn; *C. repandum* bears long-petalled rose-pink flowers in early spring. The dark green leaves are marbled with white.

Daphne (*Thymeliaceae*) This genus contains some of the most beautiful dwarf rock garden shrubs. They like sunny places but not dry conditions. The soil should be gritty and rich in peat or leafsoil. They are sometimes slow to establish but are long-lived. Propagate by cuttings and seeds. *D. cneorum* is a low bush smothered in summer with heads of rich pink, intensely fragrant flowers. If the stems become bare, fill up the plant with leafy soil; *D. collina* has red-purple fragrant flowers in spring and often again in late summer, on rounded 15-in. bushes; *D. retusa* makes a stiff, upright 2-ft., bush with sweetly scented purple flowers followed by large red berries.

Dianthus (*Caryophyllaceae*) (pink) This is a large and valuable genus of easily grown, lime and sun-loving plants. Their colourful, often sweetly scented flowers are borne in summer. Propagate by division, cuttings, and seeds of those which are not hybrids. Many are fertile hybrids; seedlings of these will not come true but may produce some worth-while plants. *D. alpinus* makes low pads of dark green leaves and huge, almost stemless, rich pink flowers; *D. arvernensis* consists of ash-

grey hummocks of leaves and 4-in. stems carrying rounded pink flowers. There is also a lovely white form; *D. caesius*, the Cheddar pink, has narrow grey leaves and large pink flowers on 6–9 in. stems; *D. deltoides*, the maiden pink, 9 in., makes sheets of flowers varying from light to dark pink; there is also a white form; *D.* 'Pike's Pink' is very dwarf with large pink flowers over flat cushions of grey-green leaves; *D. subacaulis* forms green mats and has slender 4-in. stems carrying neat rose-red flowers.

Dodecatheon (*Primulaceae*) *D. meadia* likes a moist position or cool shade. It has pink and white, cyclamen-shaped flowers on 9–12 stems in spring.

Draba (*Cruciferae*) These spring-flowering plants are easily grown in sun and any good soil. Propagate by seeds. *D. aizoides* forms tufts of deep green pointed leaves and many yellow flowers in small clusters, on 3-in. stems; *D. dedeana* has grey-green leaves in huddled rosettes, and white flowers on 1-in. stems.

Dryas (*Rosaceae*) *D. octopetala* is a woody plant with trailing stems and tiny dark green leaves. The large white flowers are abundantly produced in summer on short stems. Plant in full sun. Propagate by division or by cuttings.

Epilobium (*Onagraceae*) *E. glabellum* is a sun-loving plant which flowers from May until autumn. It has showers of large white flowers on branching, slightly arching 1 ft. high stems and bronze-green foliage. Propagate by cuttings.

Erigeron (*Compositae*) There are a few dwarf erigerons suitable for the rock garden. They are easily grown and like open, sunny positions. They flower in spring and summer. Propagate by seed or division. *E. aurantiacus* has rich orange flowers on 12 in. stems; *E. compositus*, 3 in. has tiny tufts of greyish leaves and soft lavender flowers; *E. mucronatus* (*Vitadenis triloba*) bears profusions of white, pale and deep pink flowers from spring until winter, on 9 in. stems. It likes dry, poor soil.

Erinus (*Scrophulariaceae*) *E. alpinus*, 3 in., is an easy plant for sun or light shade, flowering in spring and delightful in rocky chinks. Propagate by seeds. It has soft pink flowers. There is a nice white form and several named forms of which 'Dr Hanelle', deep red, and 'Mrs Charles Boyle', rich pink, are the best. All naturalize freely but never objectionably.

Erodium (*Geraniaceae*) (heron's bill) These important rock garden plants flower over a long summer period, are long-lived and easily grown in sunny positions, and any soil. Propagate by seeds or cuttings. *E. chamae-drioides* makes prostrate mats of dark green leaves studded with short-stemmed white, pink-veined flowers. The cultivar 'Roseum' has rich pink blossoms; *E. chrysanthum* has tufts of ferny, silver-grey leaves and sprays of sulphur-yellow flowers on 9-in. stems; *E. corsicum* has grey, hairy leaves in neat 4 in. high tufts and rich pink flowers. It loves a sunny crevice.

Euryops (*Compositae*) *E. acraeus* is a good dwarf silver-leaved bush of about 15 in., studded in summer with multitudes of golden, daisy-shaped flowers. It needs a hot, dry place. Propagate by cuttings.

Festuca (*Gramineae*) A few small alpine grasses are invaluable for filling chinks and crannies in the rock garden. Those described make neat, dwarf tufts, will grow in sun or shade and are propagated by division. *F. glacialis*, 3–4 in., has fine, grey-green leaves; *F. glauca*, 9 in., has ornamental silver-grey foliage; *F. viridis*, 4 in., has bright emerald-green leaves.

Frankenia (*Frankeniaceae*) *F. laevis* our native sea heath, is worthy of cultivation, but *F. thymifolia*, a better garden plant, forms prostrate mats of grey-green leaves and sheets of bright pink flowers in summer. It needs a sunny, but not dry position. Propagate by division or cuttings.

Genista (*Leguminosae*) (broom) These dwarf shrubs are essential in any rock garden. They relish open, sunny positions and dry soil. Propagate by seeds or cuttings. *G. hispanica* 'Compacta' is a spiky 1 ft. high bush covered in summer with golden flowers; *G. lydia* rather large for the rock garden, at 2 ft. high and 3 ft. in diameter, provides a sheet of rich yellow flowers; *G. pilosa* has prostrate woody stems covered with golden flowers in summer; *G. sagittalis* has curiously 'winged' stems which make low mats concealed in summer by yellow flowers.

Gentiana (*Gentianaceae*) (gentian) This is one of the most important genera of rock garden plants. They are too numerous to describe in detail and only a representative list of the most useful can be given. Their needs vary considerably and are suggested in the descriptions. Most of them are increased from seeds. *G. acaulis* is the ever-popular spring and summer flowering blue trumpet gentian. Plant very firmly in good loamy soil and sun; *G. asclepiadea*, the willow gentian, likes a cool position. Its 3-ft. stems carry many pendent, tubular blue flowers in mid to late summer; *G. septemfida*, the 'everyman's' gentian, will grow in almost any soil and open, sunny places. Sheets of blue flowers are borne in clustered heads on 9-in. stems in mid-summer; *G. sino-ornata* demands lime-free soil and a cool spot. It makes sheets of azure flowers from late August until winter; *G. verna* has clear blue star-shaped flowers on 3-in. stems in early spring. Grow in gritty soil, rich in humus, and full sun. Raise fresh seedlings every two or three years.

Above: The azure flowers of *Gentiana sino-ornata* are produced from late summer onwards for many weeks. It must have a lime-free soil

Geranium (*Geraniaceae*) (crane's bill) Of this large genus several are admirable for the rock garden, in any good, well-drained soil and sunny positions. Propagate by division, seeds and cuttings. *G.* 'Ballerina', 6 in., has sprays of rounded pink flowers, veined with deeper colour the summer through; *G. dalmaticum*, has erect 4 in. stems which carry shapely pink flowers in summer. The foliage assumes rich autumn tints; *G. renardii*, 9 in., has lovely lobed leaves and pastel-lavender flowers; *G. sanguineum* 'Lancastriense' makes prostrate mats of deep green studded with large, saucer-shaped salmon-pink flowers; *G. subcaulescens*, 6 in., bears carmine, dark-eyed flowers all summer.

Geum (*Rosaceae*) (avens) At least one geum is an easily grown and showy alpine species, for full sun and any soil. Propagate by division or seed. *G. montanum* has large lobed leaves and huge golden, rounded flowers on 6-in. stems in summer.

Globularia (*Globulariaceae*) (globe daisy) These are sun-loving woody plants. Propagate by division, seeds and cuttings. *G. cordifolia*, a prostrate plant has tiny leathery dark green leaves and blue powder-puff heads of flowers on very short stems; *G. trichosantha* is larger in all its parts. It has quite large heads of blue flowers on 9-in. stems. Both flower in summer.

Below: Erinus alpinus is a first-class plant for sun or light shade. It grows particularly well in the crevices between stones in the rock garden or dry wall. *Right: Geranium sanguineum lancastriense*, one of the most popular of the dwarf crane's bills, makes prostrate mats surmounted by salmon-pink flowers

Gypsophila (*Caryophyllaceae*) (chalk plant) These easy and very showy plants trail effectively from walls and ledges. They are spring and early summer flowering. Propagate by cuttings. *G. dubia* has showers of clear pink flowers; *G. fratensis* bears rosy flowers in profusion; *G. repens* is best in the variety 'Letchworth Rose' which provides a mist of rich pink flowers on 1 ft. high stems.

Haberlea (*Gesneriaceae*) *H. rhodopensis*, 4 in., is a plant for cool, shady or north facing crevices. It has rosettes of deep green leaves and tubular lavender, gold-flecked flowers in spring.

Hebe (*Scrophulariaceae*) (veronica) This is the correct name for most of the evergreen shrubby plants often known as veronicas. It is a large genus and contains a number of valuable summer-flowering rock garden shrublets. They are easily grown in any good soil and sun, but some are slightly frost tender and should be placed in warm positions sheltered from early morning sun. Propagate by cuttings. *H.* 'Carl Teschner' is a 9-in. tall bush sheeted with purple-blue flowers; *H. macrantha*, 18 in. tall is covered with very large pure white flowers. *H. pinguifolia* 'Pagei', 6 in., has grey leaves and myriads of small white flowers.

Helianthemum (*Cistaceae*) (sun rose) For a summer-long display of brilliant flowers the sun roses are unequalled. They appreciate full sun and sharply drained soil and it is essential to trim them quite severely as soon as the flowers are finished. This not only keeps them in good and tidy health but usually provokes a second display of blossom in the late summer. Propagate by cuttings. There is a multitude of named varieties of *H. nummularium*: *H.* 'Amy Baring', 6 in. with orange-bronze flowers, is the dwarf of the race. Others range in height from 6 to 12 in.; *H.* 'Ben Hope', carmine flowers with an orange centre; *H.* 'Broughty Beacon', large flame-red flowers; *H.* 'Croftianum', silver foliage and apricot flowers; *H.* 'Golden Queen', rich yellow blossoms; *H.* 'Henfield Brilliant', glistening brick-red flowers, splendid new variety; *H.* 'Jubilee', double yellow flowers; *H.* 'Mrs Earle', double red flowers; *H.* 'Red Orient', glowing deep red flowers; *H.* 'Snowball', double white flowers; *H.* 'Wisley Pink', large soft clear pink flowers.

Helichrysum (*Compositae*) (everlasting, Immortelle) These are sun-loving plants, some shrubby, others compact tufts. They have attractive grey or silver foliage and showy flowers. Propagate by division, seeds or cuttings *H. bellidioides* forms grey mats of foliage and has white flowers in summer; *H. frigidum* has tiny silver tufts and daisy-shaped, golden-eyed white flowers in summer; *H. milfordae* has mats of glistening silver leaves and white, scarlet-backed flowers in spring and summer.

Hepatica (*Ranunculaceae*) These delightful early spring flowering plants do best in cool positions and light shade. They like soil rich in humus and can be increased by seeds or division of old plants, although old plants should only be lifted when really necessary as they resent disturbance. *H. nobilis* (*triloba*), 4 in., has dainty clear blue flowers; *H. transsylvanica* (*angulosa*) has larger leaves and larger flowers of equally vivid blue. Both are sometimes included in the genus *Anemone*.

Hieraceum (*Compositae*) (hawkweed) This genus contains a few good rock garden plants. They are invasive and should be planted with this in mind. They do best in poor soil and full sun. Propagate by division or seeds. *H. aurantiacum*, 1 ft., has handsome heads of brilliant orange flowers in spring and summer; *H. villosum*, 1 ft., has lovely silver hairy leaves and yellow flowers from June to August.

Hippocrepis (*Leguminosae*) *H. comosus* 'E.R. Janes' is a delightful creeping, sun-loving plant which covers its carpets of green leaves with countless lemon-yellow flowers in spring and early summer. Increase by division or cuttings. It flowers more freely in well-drained poor soil.

Houstonia (*Rubiaceae*) (bluetts) *H. caerulea* has myriads of small clear blue flowers on 3-in. stems in spring. It loves cool shade and moist soil and should be divided and replanted every two or three years.

Hutchinsia (*Cruciferae*) *H. alpina* is a pretty little plant for a position where it is shielded from full sun. Tufts of dark green leaves are enlivened by clouds of snow-white flowers on 3-in. stems in spring. Propagate by seeds.

Hypericum (*Guttiferae*) (St John's Wort) These are semi-shrubby, summer-flowering, sun-loving plants. They flourish in any good well-drained soil. Their flowers provide brilliant colour and they are long-lived, especially if trimmed fairly severely after flowering. *H. olympicum* has brilliant golden flowers on 9-in. bushes. There is a delightful form with lemon-yellow flowers; *H. polyphyllum* is a neat, 6-in. bush with bright green leaves covered beneath multitudes of rich yellow flowers; *H. reptans* is completely prostrate with trailing, leafy stems set with orange-yellow flowers; *H. rhodopaeum*, 9 in., has softly hairy grey-green leaves and soft yellow flowers.

Hypsela (*Campanulaceae*) *H. longiflora* is a prostrate plant, excellent for crannies between paving stones. It bears small lilac and white flowers in summer, likes a cool position and soil which does not parch. Increase by division.

Iberis (*Cruciferae*) (candytuft) These sun-loving, spring and summer flowering plants are easy to grow in any good soil. *I. gibraltarica* has flat heads of white, lilac-tinted flowers on 9-in. stems; *I. jucunda*, 6 in., bears large heads of white flowers turning to soft lilac as they age. It will flower until autumn; *I. sempervirens* 'Snowflake' is a spreading evergreen 9-in. bushlet, smothered with snow-white flowers. It makes a magnificent display.

Iris (*Iridaceae*) There are various dwarf species and varieties which are invaluable rock garden plants for various positions. They are best increased by division after flowering. Unless otherwise stated all those described are sun lovers and do best in a lime-rich soil. *I. chamaeiris* 'Campbellii' has large indigo-blue flowers on 4-in. stems in May-June; *I. innominata*, 9 in. has stiff, narrow leaves in dense tufts and, in summer, flowers which may be golden, pencilled with chocolate, or a variety of pastel shades; *I. pumila* is grown in a variety of named forms, all usually less than 9 in. tall. The flower colour varies from white to all shades of blue and purple. It flowers in early summer; *I. gracillipes* likes shade and lime-free soil. It has dainty lilac and gold flowers on branching 6-in. stems; *I. cristata* has lavender and gold flowers on 4-in. stems in late spring. It prefers a cool position.

Jasione (*Campanulaceae*) *J. perennis* is a pretty, blue-flowered plant but even better is *J. jankae*, which has large heads of clear blue flowers on 1-ft. stems from mid to late summer. It is an easy plant for any soil or situation. Increase by seed or division of old plants.

Leontopodium (*Compositae*) *L. alpinum* 6–9 in., is the famous edelweiss. It will succeed in any good and well-drained soil and a sunny place. The tufts of narrow grey leaves are surmounted in summer by the characteristic heads of flowers which look as if they have been cut out of grey flannel. Propagation is by seeds.

Leucanthemum (*Compositae*) *L. osmarense*, 9–12 in., is an alpine chrysanthemum of great merit. It requires a warm, sunny position in gritty but good soil, where it will make foaming masses of silver filigree foliage and carry innumerable large, white, golden-eyed daisy flowers throughout the summer. Increase by cuttings or seeds.

Lewisia (*Portulacaceae*) These are splendid spring and summer flowering rock garden plants. They prefer lime-free soil but will grow in alkaline soil if it is enriched with peat. They like sun and prefer to grow in crevices or on slopes rather than on the flat. Propagate by seeds and cuttings of side-rosettes. Keep plants dry after they finish flowering. They all have fleshy-leaved rosettes and when in flower vary from 9 to 15 in. in height. *L.* 'Birch Hybrids' range in colour from pink to deep salmon and crimson; in *L. columbiana* 'Rosea' the wiry stems carry flights of red-purple flowers in abundance; *L.* 'George Henley' is a hybrid of great merit. It flowers from May until October with short, branching stems bedecked with brick-red blossoms;

L. 'Rose Splendour' is another hybrid strain with very large flowers in which pale and deep pink predominate; *L. tweedyi* is perhaps the most splendid of the genus. It has lax rosettes of fleshy leaves and many large opalescent pink and salmon flowers carried singly on short stems.

Linnaea (*Caprifoliaceae*) *L. borealis* is the famous twin flower of the botanist (Carolus Linnaeus) whose name it commemorates. It is a woodland plant and creeps at soil level with wiry stems clad in tiny leathery leaves. The exquisite flowers, borne in spring, are clear pink bells carried two to each 1-in. high stem. It needs lime-free soil and shade or a north aspect. Increase by cuttings.

Linum (*Linaceae*) (flax) This genus contains dwarf shrubby plants and elegant perennials with tall stems and blue, yellow or white flowers. They all flower in summer and need sunny positions in good, perfectly drained soil. Propagate by cuttings or seeds. *L. flavum* is a stiff, 9–12 in. tall bush, with clouds of rich golden flowers; *L. monogynum*, 12–15 in., has large pure white flowers; *L. narbonense* bears huge funnel-shaped lovely flowers of gentian-blue on slender, arching 18-in. stems. *L. salsaloides* 'Nanum' makes prostrate mats of tiny leaves on woody stems and large white flowers on very short stems.

Lithospermum (*Boraginaceae*) The most widely grown and popular is *L. diffusum* and its forms. They are all lovers of hot, dry positions in full sun. They are propagated by

cuttings. 'Grace Ward' has sprawling stems which carry myriads of vividly blue flowers throughout the summer. It makes a wide, semi-prostrate mat and must be given lime-free soil. With age the stems become bare, and then the plant should be liberally top-dressed with leafy soil.

Lotus (*Leguminosae*) *L. corniculatus* is our pretty native wildflower, lady-buckle-my-shoe, which is too rampant a weed to be planted on the rock garden. The double form 'Plena', a desirable plant, makes a wide, flat mat, covered with golden flowers in the spring. It likes sun and sharp drainage and may be increased by cuttings.

Lychnis (*Caryophyllaceae*) (catchfly) Several species are excellent plants for the rock garden, easily grown in any good soil and sunny positions. Propagation is by division or seed. *L. alpina* is a tiny tuft of glossy leaves above which are carried, on 3-in. stems, clusters of small pink flowers early in the year. It is not long-lived and seeds should be sown every two or three years; *L. flos-jovis* has grey hairy leaves and large carmine-red flowers on 1-ft. stems; *L. viscaria* 'Splendens Plena' 18 in., is too large for a very small rock garden, though it is a fine plant which deserves a place for the sake of its intense carmine-red flowers carried on 18-in. stems.

Maianthemum (*Liliaceae*) *M. bifolium* is a shade-lover and grows best in lime-free soil. It is a pretty plant, 3-4 in. tall, a rare native, delightful in a cool corner of the rock garden. It creeps by underground stems and erupts into dense clusters of heart-shaped green leaves and fluffy heads of tiny white flowers in spring.

Margyricarpus (*Rosaceae*) *M. setosus* is a semi-prostrate shrub, 12-15 in. tall, its stems densely covered by small, pointed dark green leaves. The inconspicuous flowers are followed by myriads of round, translucent white berries. It grows in any good soil and sun, but should not have a parched position. Propagate by seeds or cuttings.

Mazus (*Scrophulariaceae*) These dwarf carpeting plants do best in cool rather than hot positions. They flower in mid to late summer

and grow in ordinary garden soil. Propagate by division. *M. pumilio* makes green carpets studded with stemless blue and white flowers. It should be lifted, divided and replanted in fresh soil every so often; *M. reptans* has bronze-green leaves and flowers of mauve, white and gold. It is rampant and must be given room to spread.

Mentha (*Labiatae*) (mint) There are a few mints which find a place among the alpines. They flower in summer and are increased by division or cutting. *M. requienii*, the Corsican mint, makes a mere film of soft green which spreads over the ground in moist or cool places and displays countless tiny, stemless lavender flowers. The whole plant is intensely peppermint-scented.

Micromeria (*Labiatae*) All the plants in this genus give forth a pungent but pleasant odour when the leaves or stems are handled. *M. corsica* likes a really hot, dry and sunny place. It makes 6-in, spiky bushes of sharp twigs and tiny grey leaves and carries many small pink flowers in summer. Propagate by seed or cuttings.

Mimulus (*Scrophulariaceae*) (musk) These easily grown and showy plants like moist or cool position shaded from full sunlight. Several are invaluable for places by the sides of pools or streams. They flower in early summer and are increased by seeds, cuttings or division. Most are fairly short-lived and should be re-propagated every two or three years. *M. burnetii* has red-brown, mottled

Left: Lewisias are among those plants which grow best in the crevices between rocks, or in cracks in a dry wall
Top: A relative of the anemones, *Hepatica transsylvanica* bears vivid blue flowers in early spring
Above: The bright yellow flowers of *Hypericum olympicum*, a 9-in. high semi-shrubby plant for the rock garden. *Right*: Helianthemums benefit from being clipped over quite severely after they have flowered
Far right: There are many named varieties of the sun rose *(Helianthemum nummularium)*, in a good colour range, including 'Pink Beauty' illustrated here

Left: *Leucanthemum osmarense*, a free-flowering dwarf chrysanthemum relative, covered with large, daisy-like flowers for many weeks in summer
Above: Trailing plants are always useful on rock gardens. *Oenothera missouriensis*, a relative of the evening primrose, produces its golden-yellow flowers over a long period

flowers on 9-in. stems; cut down after flowering to produce a second blossoming the same year; in *M. cupreus* 'Whitecroft Scarlet' the brilliant flowers are carried in abundance on 6-in. stems. Cut back after flowering; *M. primuloides* is a choice, tiny plant for a cool but not boggy position in the rock garden. It has gay yellow flowers on 2-in. stems. Divide and replant frequently; *M. radicans* likes a cool but not boggy position. It makes flat carpets of bronze leaves studded with stemless white and violet flowers all summer.

Minuartia (*Caryophyllaceae*) *M. verna* makes a delightfully neat little tuft of emerald green with gleaming white flowers on thread-like stems in spring. It is a splendid companion for *Gentiana verna*, which dislikes living in solitude. Grow it in full sun, in gritty soil and propagate by seeds.

Mitchella (*Rubiaceae*) *M. repens*, the partridge berry, is a plant for cool shade and lime-free soil. A prostrate shrub, it makes a dense mat of interlaced slender woody stems. The pink bell flowers are followed by bright red fruits. Increase by means of cuttings or seeds.

Nierembergia (*Solanaceae*) *N. repens* (*rivularis*) is entirely herbaceous and disappears below ground in the winter. Its underground creeping stems erupt in summer into bright green leaves amidst which nestle large, white stemless funnel-shaped flowers; it likes poor gritty soil and will flourish in a gravel path. Propagate by division in spring.

Oenothera (*Onagraceae*) (evening primrose) Several species are suitable for the rock garden. They are all sun-lovers with no special soil preferences as long as it is well drained. They have a long flowering season from late spring onward and, although the flowers of many last for one day only, there is a constant succession to continue the display Propagate by seeds and cuttings. *O. acaulis* forms tufts of jagged-edged bright green leaves and has stemless clusters of white flowers which become pink as they age; *A. fremontii*, 9 in., has slender grey-green leaves and large bright yellow flowers; *O. missouriensis*, 9–12 in., a sprawling plant, provides an endless succession of enormous deep yellow flowers; *O. pumila* (*perennis*), makes small tufts of shining green leaves and bears neat, cup-shaped yellow flowers in profusion on 6-in. stems over a period of many weeks.

Omphalodes (*Boraginaceae*) These are very early flowering plants for light shade or a cool north aspect. They are not fussy about soil. Propagation is by division. *O. cappadocica* has fresh green leaves and showers of clear blue forget-me-not flowers on 9-in. stems in March–April; *O. verna* flowers earlier, is not quite so tall and the flowers are of a paler blue. There is a delightful white-flowered form.

Oxalis (*Oxalidaceae*) Most of the species suitable for the rock garden are lovers of sun and warmth and good, well-drained soils. Propagation is by seeds or division. *O. acetosella*, the native wood sorrel, is one of the species which prefers a cool position. The cultivated form 'Rosea' rambles about in light shade and woodland soil, producing many rich pink flowers on very short stems in spring and summer; *O. adenophylla*, 4 in., has deeply cut silver leaves and countless funnel-shaped pink flowers in spring; *O. enneaphylla* produces grey leaves and large pink, or sometimes white, cup-shaped flowers in spring. *O. inops*, 4 in., can be a weed, but it is a lovely one and should be spared a space where an invader is welcome. The large beautiful rose-red flowers are produced abundantly in summer; *O. lobata* sends up, from tiny, hairy bulbs, in early spring, clusters of emerald-green leaves. These soon die down, to reappear in the autumn, accompanied by delicious golden flowers on 3-in. stems. It needs a warm corner and light soil; *O. magellanica* is a delightful plant for a cool position. Its minute dark green leaves make close mats and are studded with flat, pearl-white flowers in summer.

Right: One of the colourful varieties of *Phlox subulata*

The alpine poppy, *Papaver alpinum*, provides a display of miniature poppy flowers throughout the summer

Papaver (*Papaveraceae*) (poppy) *P. alpinum*, the charming alpine poppy, is a short-lived plant but it perpetuates itself by means of self-sown seedlings in sunny places and light, gritty soil. The leaves appear in tiny tufts, surmounted throughout the summer by miniature poppy flowers which may be white, yellow, cream or shades of pink and red, on 4-in. stems.

Parochetus (*Leguminosae*) *P. communis* is a particularly lovely creeping plant which is hardy in a warm, moist position. The leaves are clover-like and the plant spreads by trailing stems and carries, during late summer and autumn, and often on into the winter, pea-shaped flowers of gentian-blue. Propagate by division or rooted runners.

Penstemon (*Scrophulariaceae*) These dwarf shrubs like warm positions and protection from east winds. A lime-free soil is preferable but not essential. They flower from spring until mid-summer, Propagation is by cuttings of soft tips taken early in the year. *P. davidsonii* (*rupicola*), 4 in. has leathery grey-green leaves and ruby-red flowers; *P. heterophyllus*, 1–1½ ft., has spires of blue flowers; *P. menziesii*, 1 ft. has small, thick and fleshy, toothed leaves and violet-purple flowers; *P. pinifolius* 9–12 in., bears scarlet flowers in profusion; *P. pulchellus* is quite prostrate and bears blue flowers on 3-in. stems; *P. roezlii*, 9 in., makes a stiff bush covered with red flowers; *P.* 'Weald Beacon' is a lovely hybrid with glowing crimson flowers.

Phlox (*Polemoniaceae*) In this large genus there are many important rock garden plants. The species, selections and hybrids, loosely grouped as 'cushion phloxes' provide invaluable colour early in the year, are of neat habit, easily grown in any good, well-drained soil and benefit from being closely trimmed after they have flowered. Propagate by cuttings or division of old plants in spring or autumn. The most popular are the forms of *P. subulata*. All are sun-lovers and, although they will grow in light shade, they do not as a rule flower freely unless given full light. *P. adsurgens* is an exception in that it prefers a slightly shaded position. Its 3–4 in. mats are decorated by large, salmon-pink flowers; *P. amoena* has 6-in. stems which carry heads of purple flowers. There is a form with pretty, variegated foliage; *P. divaricata* is of rather loose, untidy habit but the large lilac flowers are carried in loose heads on 12–15-in. stems; the forms of *P. douglasii* are of close, cushion-forming habit and carry carpets of almost stemless flowers. Among the best are 'Boothman's Variety', with clear mauve flowers, 'Rosea', rich pink, and 'Snow Queen', pure white; *P. stolonifera* 'Blue Ridge', 12 in. is a lovely phlox with heads of clear blue flowers; *P. subulata* has several forms and it should be plentifully represented on every rock garden. They are also excellent plants for growing in walls, crazy paving, or for tumbling over a path-edge. They all make wide, low cushions covered with flowers: 'Appleblossom', soft pink; 'Fairy', small, neat flowers of lavender with deeper colour marking the base of the petals; 'G. F. Wilson', one of the oldest and still one of the best with mauve flowers; 'Model', rose-coloured flowers; 'Pink Chintz', clear soft pink blossoms; 'Temiscaming', brilliant magenta-red, are excellent varieties.

Phyteuma (*Campanulaceae*) Several species are worth growing in the rock garden in any good soil and an open position. Propagate by seeds. They flower in mid-summer. *P. hemisphaericum* has grassy leaves and heads of clear blue flowers on 6-in. stems; in *P. nigrum* the intense dark violet flowers are borne on 12-in. stems; *P. scheuchzeri* has rounded heads of deep purple-blue flowers on 12-in. stems.

Pimelia (*Myrtaceae*) *P. coarctata* is a completely prostrate woody shrub whose ground-hugging stems are clothed in tiny grey leaves. The plant is sheeted with small white flowers followed by translucent white berries. Propagate by cuttings or seeds. It needs very gritty soil and full sun.

Platycodon (*Campanulaceae*) (balloon bell-flower) This handsome plant, valuable for mid-summer flowering, needs only full sun and any good soil. Propagate by seeds. *P. grandiflorum* 'Mariesii' is the most usually planted form. On 12–15-in. stems it carries huge, inflated buds which expand into rich purple saucer-shaped flowers. The variety 'Apoyana', 6 in., is suitable for the small rock garden. There are also forms with white or soft pink flowers.

Polygala (*Polygalaceae*) (milkwort). *P. calcarea* loves chalky soil and sunny places. It has tiny tufts of slender stems and 3-in. spikes of deep blue flowers in the spring; *P. chamaebuxus* likes a cool north aspect. It is a 6-in. evergreen shrub with clusters of cream and yellow tipped purple, fragrant flowers. Propagate by division in spring.

Polygonum (*Polygonaceae*) (knotweed) Two species at least are desirable: *P. tenuicaule* flowers in the very early spring, with short spikes of white flowers on 3-in. stems. Propagate by division; *P. vacciniifolium* is at its best from August until October. It forms dense mats of bronze-tinted green leaves on woody stems and has short spikes of heather-pink flowers. Propagate by cuttings.

Above: A view of a small part of the famous rock garden in the Royal Horticultural Society's Gardens at Wisley, Surrey
Below: Plants of *Potentilla aurea* are almost hidden by the golden flowers in late spring and summer
Right: *Penstemon menziesii microphylla*, a dwarf kind suitable for the rock garden

Potentilla (*Rosaceae*) (cinquefoil) Some of these showy, easily grown sun-lovers should be on any well-planned rock garden. All flowers in spring and summer. Increase by seeds or division. *P. alba* is a sprawling plant, good for ground cover, with white flowers; *P. aurea* has sheets of golden flowers on prostrate mats of foliage. There is also a good form with double flowers; *P. megalantha* makes bold clumps of large, velvety leaves and huge golden flowers on 6-in. stems; *P. nitida* makes carpets of silvery foliage over which are set on very short stems pretty pink flowers. It needs very gritty soil; *P. verna* 'Nana', a prostrate plant continues to produce its golden flowers throughout the summer and well into the autumn.

Primula (*Primulaceae*) These are mostly spring and early summer flowering. Propagate by seeds or division. The latter operation yields the best results if carried out soon after flowering. Seeds should be sown soon after ripening. *P. acaulis* is the primrose, of which there are many double flowered and coloured forms, all good rock garden plants. They all like a cool position and deep, rich soil; *P. auricula*, 4 in., the alpine auricula, loves a sunny crevice from which to display its charming yellow, fragrant flowers; *P. denticulata* is a plant for a moist place. It has great heads of purple, crimson or white flowers on 1-ft stems; *P. frondosa* makes tufts of soft, meal-covered leaves and has rounded heads of pink flowers on 4-in. stems; *P. minima*, one of the smallest, has tufts of glossy leaves and large pink flowers on 1-in. stems. It needs gritty soil; *P. marginata*, 6 in., is a fine crevice plant with white powdered leaves and heads of lavender flowers; *P. rosea* loves a really wet position such as a bog garden or by the edge of a stream. In early March it produces vivid carmine-red flowers on 6–9 in. stems.

Pulsatilla (*Ranunculaceae*) (pasque flower) The spring flowering *P. vulgaris* (syn. *Anemone pulsatilla*) loves full sun and chalky soil. There are many desirable forms, varying in colour from white through shades of purple to pink and deep red. The finely divided leaves make a handsome foil to the large flowers carried boldly on 1-ft. stems. Propagate by seed, sown as soon as it is ripe in late summer, in light soil in an unheated frame.

Ramonda (*Gesneriaceae*) *R. myconii* demands a tight crevice between rocks with a cool, preferably north aspect. It has flat rosettes of leathery, wrinkled leaves and deep lavender, golden centred, flowers on 4-in. stems. Propagate by seeds or by very careful division.

Ranunculus (*Ranunculaceae*) (buttercup) Many species are valuable for the rock garden. They flower in spring and summer, thrive in sunny places and, in general are not at all fussy about the soil in which they grow as long as it is well drained. Propagate by seeds or division. *P. amplexicaulis* has large, flat-faced white flowers on 9-in. stems; *R. ficaria*, the lesser celandine is a pernicious weed but there are some good trustworthy cultivated forms, notably 'Aurantiacus' which has coppery-orange flowers on 4-in. stems; *R. gouanii* has huge, saucer-shaped golden flowers on short stems; *R. gramineus* has narrow, grassy leaves and elegant, branching 12-in. stems carrying golden buttercups; *R. montanus* 'Molten Gold', a gem of a plant, very easily grown, makes low mounds of large golden flowers on very short stems, seldom more than 3-in. high.

Raoulia (*Compositae*) These are completely prostrate plants with minute leaves. They make good ground cover for tiny bulbs or for carpeting the soil beneath pygmy columnar conifers. Plant them in full sun. Increase by division. *R. australis* forms mats of intense silver leaves and has stemless golden flowers in the early summer; *R. glabra* makes green mats and has cream flower heads; *R. lutescens* is the tiniest of all, a mere film of grey-green which becomes golden with massed tiny flowers in early summer.

Salix (*Salicaceae*) (willow) Several delightful pygmy willows make entrancing little shrubs for the rock garden. They do not mind full sun, but like cool root conditions and will grow in light shade if necessary. They have fascinating gnarled woody stems and many of them bear pretty silver catkins in the spring. Propagate by cuttings. *R. arbuscula* a prostrate plant, has tangled woody stems and dark green foliage. It will spread over a considerable area; *S. reticulata*, another prostrate species, has lovely rounded leaves netted with conspicuous veins, and silver-grey catkins.

Saponaria (*Caryophyllaceae*) (soapwort) *S. ocymoides* is a useful and decorative plant to trail down from a high ledge or crevice. The long leafy stems carry, in spring, sheets of bright pink flowers. It is easily grown in sun or light shade and any soil. Propagate by cuttings.

Saxifraga (*Saxifragaceae*) (saxifrage) This is one of the largest and most important genera of rock garden plants. The number of species, hybrids and forms is legion and there are kinds for many different soils and situations. They vary from 1 in. to 1 ft. or more in height. Unless otherwise stated they like open, sunny positions and sharply gritty soil. According to their kind they can be increased by seeds, division and cuttings; each will suggest by its habit and appearance the appropriate method. Most of them flower in spring and early summer. Space permits mention of only a representative few of each of the many groups. *S. aizoon* is a large complex of slightly varying plants; the two most desirable varieties are 'Lutea' with soft yellow flowers and 'Rosea', soft pink. Both are about 6 in. tall; *S. apiculata* makes flat green cushions and has yellow flowers on 6-in. stems. There is also a good white form; *S. burseriana* is a choice plant of which there are many varieties. One of the best is 'Gloria' which has red stems and large white flowers on 3-in. stems

over spiny cushions of grey leaves; *S. cochlearis* makes hard, humped cushions of congested grey rosettes and 9-in. pink stems carrying white flowers in summer; *S. fortunei* has large lobed leaves, red on the reverse, and 18-in. stems carrying flights of white flowers in autumn; *S. granulata* 'Plena' is the double meadow saxifrage. It dies down in winter but bears massed double white flowers in spring on 9-in. stems; *S. irvingii* makes hummocks of minute grey-green rosettes and stemless pink flowers in great profusion; *S. longifolia* forms magnificent rosettes of symmetrical grey leaves and very long spikes of innumerable white flowers; *S. oppositifolia* flowers in very early spring. It makes prostrate carpets of dark foliage and bears stemless red flowers; *S. urbium* (*umbrosa*), London pride, is an old garden plant, still a deservedly popular favourite. It also has some attractive miniature forms.

The so-called 'mossy' saxifrages are a separate group. They like a little shade or a cool aspect. They all make compact mats and vary in height when in flower from 3–6 in. Such kinds as 'Sanguinea Superba', deep red; 'Peter Pan', pink; 'Pearly King', creamwhite; 'Winston Churchill', deep pink and 'Four Winds' rich red, are all excellent.

Sedum (*Crassulaceae*) (stone crop) Many of these easy, sun-loving plants are extremely decorative plants for the rock garden. Some species, of which *S. acre* and *S. album* are examples, are handsome but so weedy that

Left: Saxifrages are among the best of all dwarf plants for the rock garden. *Saxifraga apiculata* bears its yellow flowers on 6-in. stems in spring and early summer
Above: The Pasque flower, *Pulsatilla vulgaris*, has many different colour forms. This is 'Rubra'
Right: 'Jersey Gem', a distinctive variety of the horned violet, *Viola cornuta*
Far right: One of the coloured forms of the native primrose, *Primula acaulis*, which make a fine display on the rock garden in early spring

they should be excluded from all but the wildest places. The few named below may be regarded as a nucleus of the best kinds. Propagate by division or cuttings. All are spring and early summer flowering unless otherwise stated. *S. album* 'Coral Carpet' makes flat mats of fleshy coral-pink leaves and soft pink flowers; *S. cauticolum* produces large heads of crimson red flowers on 6-in. trailing stems in late summer. *S. lydium* has tufts of small fleshy leaves, red in summer, green in winter. It bears white flowers in profusion, on 3-in. stems; *S. spathulifolium* has several good varieties of which the most decorative is 'Purpureum', with purple fleshy leaves and golden flowers on 3-in. stems. In 'Cappa Blanca' the leaves are densely covered with white 'meal'.

Sempervivum (*Crassulaceae*) (houseleek) These sun-lovers are best grown in poor, gritty soil. Very decorative and trouble-free, they carry quite good flowers but are valued most highly for the rosettes of fleshy leaves, often brightly coloured. Propagation is by division; few of them breed true from seed. One hundred or more species, forms and hybrids are available. *S. arachnoideum* is the cobweb houseleek; the green and red rosettes are spangled with tangled white 'spiders-webs' of fine threads; *S.* 'Commander Hay' has large deep red-purple leaf rosettes; *S. tectorum*, the common houseleek, is often seen in great clumps on cottage roofs. It is very variable and various forms are available. The species has green, purple-tipped leaves.

Silene (*Caryophyllaceae*) (catchfly) These are easy plants for sunny positions, variable in colour of flower and ranging from high alpine cushion plants to tall border plants. Propagate by seeds or division. They flower in spring and summer. *S. acaulis* makes hard humps of tightly packed tiny rosettes and stemless pink flowers. It needs very gritty soil; *S. schafta* produces sheets of pink flowers on 6-in. stems.

Sisyrinchium (*Iridaceae*) These sun loving, summer flowering, plants have tufts of narrow, grass-like leaves. They are increased by seeds or division. *S. brachypus*, 6 in. has bright yellow flowers; *S. angustifolium* bears bright blue flowers on 6-in. stems.

Soldanella (*Primulaceae*) These lovely, typical alpine plants like cool positions and gritty soil, rich in humus. They flower in earliest spring. Propagate by seeds or by very careful division. Guard from slugs. *S. alpina* has tiny rounded, leathery, dark green leaves and fringed lavender bells on 3-in. stems; *S. montana* has larger leaves and wider flowers of purple-blue, on 4–6-in. stems.

Thymus (*Labiatae*) (thyme) These summer-flowering aromatic plants present no cultural problems in sun and well-drained soil. *T. citriodorus* 'Silver Queen', a variety of the lemon thyme, makes an upright, 6-in. bush of green and silver leaves; *T. herba-barona* is prostrate, its leaves strongly scented of caraway. It has pink flowers. *T. drucei* (*serpyllum*) has many named forms, all invaluable carpeters. Flower colour varies from white to deep crimson.

Tiarella (*Saxifragaceae*) *T. cordifolia* is a dainty, shade-loving spring and early summer flowering plant. It has elegant soft green leaves in neat tufts and fluffy spikes of white flowers on 9-in. stems. Increase by division.

Veronica (*Scrophulariaceae*) This is a large genus varying from dwarf kinds for the rock garden to tall plants best suited to flower borders. They all love full sun and grow well in any good garden soil. Propagate by seeds, division or cuttings. All flower in spring and early summer. *V. cinerea*, 1 ft., has grey leaves and long spikes of blue flowers; *V. prostrata*, a low-growing plant, has several named forms providing low mounds of white, pink or blue flowers according to kind; *V. teucrium* 'Royal Blue' has deep blue flowers on 1-ft. tall stems.

Viola (*Violaceae*) *V. cornuta*, the horned violet, bears graceful long-spurred lavender-mauve flowers on 6-in. stems. Grow from cuttings or seed. It grows in any good soil and sunny place; *V. cucullata*, 4 in. loves shade and carries large white, lilac-veined 'violet' flowers in spring. Increase by division every two or three years.

Zauschneria (*Onagraceae*) (Californian fuchsia) *Z. californica*, 9–12 in., is a plant for the hottest, driest available position, where it produces a riot of intense scarlet flowers over grey leaves in late summer and autumn. Increase by cuttings of soft tips.

Fruit in Your Garden

Fruit should find a place in every garden. In the very smallest there must surely be room for a tree or two to be trained against walls of the house; even in the paved town garden or patio a few fruits may be grown in pots.

Fruit-growing is a part of gardening with a fascination all its own. As with vegetable-growing one has a useful end-product but in achieving that end one has quite different problems to solve and the interest of a quite different mode of growth. As a by-product, too, one is rewarded by beauty of spring blossom, summer fruit and autumn leaf colour, which can add much to the general decorative effect of the garden.

The nutritional value of a plentiful supply of fresh fruit cannot be over-estimated and in these inflationary days an investment in fruit trees and bushes will make an ever-growing saving to your pocket.

For many gardeners, however, the greatest joy of home fruit-growing lies not so much in cash-saving, horticultural interest or visual effect, as in the enhanced flavour of fresh fruit eaten direct from the plant. One has to remember that all produce in a greengrocer's shop is relatively stale as it began to lose flavour from the moment it was harvested. Moreover, commercial growers have to select the varieties they grow for the size of their yield, their ease of culture and their ability to withstand the rigours of handling, grading and transport, rather than for their flavour. The home grower can enjoy varieties of different kinds of fruit which are quite un-economic to grow commercially – fruits he will never see in any shop – and he can indulge his own personal preferences.

Choice of Site

Possible sites for fruit may be divided into three areas: (1) in a clean-cultivated area specially dug for the purpose just as a special plot may be provided for vegetables; (2) in the decorative part of the garden, e.g. beds cut out of the lawn; (3) against house or garage walls, or boundary fences or walls.

A Special Plot   The provision of a special plot reserved entirely for fruit is the ideal. This enables you to group together fruits having similar manurial needs – gooseberries and red currants close to the apples, for instance, as these all call for much potash, and blackcurrants next to plums and pears, these three requiring more nitrogen than the first trio.

Having all your fruit in one place also simplifies spraying and makes it easier to provide protection from birds.

Although the fruit plot often has to border the vegetables it is unwise to mix the two if you can avoid it. Vegetables frequently have fertilizer needs that are not suited to fruit and dotting fruit trees among vegetable crops leads to complications when spraying with toxic or leaf-damaging sprays.

In the Flower Garden   These same objections hold when fruit trees are planted in the flower garden. Perhaps the least objectionable is cutting out beds from the turf and planting trees in the lawn. When a grass-spoiling chemical is sprayed the adjoining turf can be temporarily covered with plastic sheets or old sacks.

Trained trees (espaliers or cordons, see below) can be planted on either side of a pathway to form an avenue or arch and make

Left: Pear 'Williams' Bon Chrétien' is a popular dessert variety, at its best in September
Right: 'Blenheim Orange', a late apple, for both dessert and culinary purposes
Above right: Autumn harvest from the fruit garden

a picturesque feature, the attractiveness of which quite compensates for any spraying or feeding problems with the adjoining plants.
Against Walls or Fences   The third possible site – against walls or fences – is one much too often neglected. A wall provides shelter and warmth and, therefore, sometimes enables less hardy fruits to be grown successfully. A tree trained against a wall can be more easily given temporary covering in the event of spring frost and can very easily be netted over to keep off birds. A tree growing against a house wall, being so close at hand, often receives better attention than those at the other end of the garden.

There are, however, certain points about the wall-training of fruits which must be borne in mind. This is an extremely dry situation and regular attention will always have to be given to watering. When planting, set the stem 9 in. away from the foot of the wall. In summer, red spider mites which thrive in the dry, may be a nuisance: occasional syringeing with clear water will discourage these pests.

If you are planting against a solid fence or boundary wall, think of the ultimate height of your tree. A fan-trained tree can soon reach 10 ft. and an espalier, restricted to the number of tiers for which there is space, may be a much better proposition especially for apples and pears.

If you intend planting against an open fence, remember that there are no protective benefits and if the fence forms a boundary, the pruning, spraying and picking of the fruit may put a strain on good neighbourly relations.

Any kind of fruit tree may be grown against a wall if desired but to make the best possible use of this privileged position one should reserve it for as choice a fruit as may be grown outdoors in your particular district. In the south it would be a waste to grow apples against a wall (and red spider mites would certainly be a worry) where figs, peaches or nectarines might flourish. In some of the less clement parts of eastern Scotland and the north-east of England, using wall protection may be the only way to be assured of a good apple crop.

The selection of fruits to grow against a wall should depend not only on the geographical situation but also on the aspect of the wall itself. House walls seldom face the cardinal points of the compass exactly, but the following recommendations may be used as a guide:

For east-facing walls: Early plums and pears. These are also suitable for north-east and north-west walls in the south, the fruits advised for north walls being a safer choice in the north.

For south-facing walls: Apricots, figs, gages, peaches and nectarines, pears sweet cherries and grape vines. In northern and very exposed areas use such sites for pears and plums.

For west-facing walls: Apricots, early peaches and nectarines, south of the Thames. North of that river to the Tees, plant plums, early gages and pears.

For north-facing walls: Morello cherries, blackberries and loganberries, and, grown as cordons, gooseberries and red and white currants. These fruits, grown against a north wall, will ripen their crops later than the same varieties grown in a sunny position in the open garden and thus lengthen the season.

Fruit trees and bushes need sunshine for healthy growth. It is the action of sunlight upon the leaves which enables them to convert carbon dioxide and oxygen from the air and various minerals in solution absorbed by the roots into new tissue, including eventually the fruits which are your aim. Insufficient sunshine can result in weak growth, poor colour in the fruit and indifferent flavour.

In small gardens it is not always possible to allot an ideal situation to all the fruit. Some, however, can tolerate partial shade better than others—the cane fruits (raspberries, blackberries, loganberries and other hybrid berries), gooseberries and red, white and blackcurrants—but these will crop later than those in full sun.

Remember that the trees you plant will themselves cast shadows and so the tallest specimens should be on the north side of the plot.

Shelter from wind is valuable but never plant close to a hedge or tree whose roots will spread into the soil and rob it of nutriment intended for the fruit. Exposure to biting east winds in the spring can result in frost damage to blossom but, much more likely, this will be the cause of poor setting because the pollinating insects have been discouraged from flying.

What to Grow

Fruits are normally divided into two main classes:

(1) The soft fruits which include herbaceous plants such as strawberries, the shrubby ones, such as blackcurrants and gooseberries, and the cane fruits, such as raspberries and blackberries. All these are grown on their own roots.

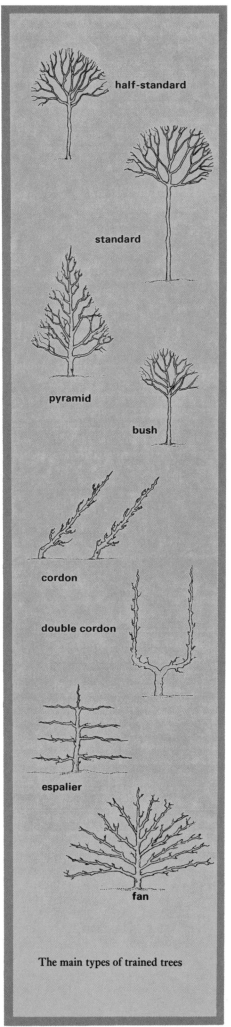

The main types of trained trees

(2) The top or tree fruits. Apples, pears and plums are common examples. The named varieties you buy at a nursery have all been budded or grafted (mostly, the former) on to roots (known as the rootstock) raised separately and designed to impart certain desired characteristics to the behaviour of the tree. Thus for garden planting apples are frequently budded on a weak-growing rootstock which will result in the tree starting to fruit early in life and never growing too big. See table of rootstocks.

Tree fruits may be pruned or trained to various different shapes or forms, e.g.

Standard This is the old-fashioned bushy-topped tree with a vertical stem of 6 ft. before the lowest branches arise.

Half-standard As above, but with a stem of only 4 ft. A half-standard, therefore, is only 2 ft. shorter than a full standard and both types are too large for most gardens. Not only do such trees eventually take up much space (30–40 ft. each way) but a ladder is essential for spraying, pruning and picking, and a good crop (possibly over 200 lb. of apples) is probably greater than any one family wants of one variety. Half-standard plums of the varieties whose branches tend to 'weep' downwards (such as 'Warwickshire Drooper') are sometimes planted in gardens but such a tree still requires from 15–20 ft. each way according to rootstock (see below).

Bush This is the most common form of tree, with a clear stem of from 1½ to 3 ft. below the branches. Soft fruits are also grown as bushes, the clear stem of red and white currants and gooseberries being about 6 in. Blackcurrants are grown as bushes but with no leg, the branches being encouraged to grow from as low down as possible. Apples are sometimes grafted or budded on weak-growing rootstocks which result in quite a small tree (see 'rootstocks' below). Dwarf bushes are very suitable for garden planting.

Cordon A single-stemmed tree without branches, fruiting spurs arising directly from the main stem. To induce early fruiting, cordons are frequently planted at an angle of 45° and are then referred to as oblique cordons. This is a useful type for the small garden and enables a range of different varieties to be planted in a small space, thus spreading the season of use and reducing the risk of poor cropping because of inadequate cross-pollination. Single vertical cordons are useful for growing against house walls, filling in comparatively narrow spaces between windows etc. Pears do well in such places.

Double Cordon This is formed by training the stem horizontally on both sides of the short vertical stem and then training up a single vertical stem or cordon from the extremity of each 'arm' so that the tree is U-shaped. In a similar way a triple cordon can be trained with three main vertical stems. The double or triple cordon shape is most often used with gooseberries and red currants.

Espalier A tree with a central vertical stem from which horizontal branches spring in pairs, one on each side. Apples and pears are often grown in this form along-side paths but espaliers are also useful for training against walls particularly where space for upward extension is limited.

Fan From a short vertical leg the branches are trained like the ribs of a fan, all in one plane. Fans are often trained against walls but they can equally well be freestanding but fastened to horizontal wires. Fans are most usually formed from peaches, nectarines, apricots, pears and plums, but apples can be trained in this form, against horizontal wires.

Pyramid A Christmas-tree shaped tree, with a central vertical stem from which the branches radiate. Apple and pear pyramids on dwarfing rootstocks are excellent for the small garden. Although there are no dwarfing rootstocks for plums, pyramid-training is gaining in popularity for keeping garden plum trees within bounds.

Family Tree This is not a shape but means that several varieties have been grafted together to form one tree. The 'family trees' sold commercially are usually in the form of bushes but this is not essential.

❧ Preparing the Site ❧

If your soil does not happen to be ideal for fruit-growing, you can do something to improve it and you can choose for planting the fruits least likely to be adversely affected.

Drainage The first and most important point of all is drainage. All fruits need good drainage for waterlogged conditions in winter kill the roots by drowning.

Sometimes it is possible to lay field drains in the direction of the fall of the land or to dig trenches at least 30 in. deep, spread 9 in. of rubble in the bottom and cover with inverted turves before returning the soil. Unfortunately this procedure is seldom possible in gardens because there is no outfall without which no drain can function.

Deep digging, however, will improve surface drainage and this should be carried out over as much of the garden as possible. If you only prepare individual sites for the trees, these become miniature sumps collecting surface water from their immediate vicinity.

It is also possible to mitigate the effects of bad drainage by planting on mounds or raised beds (see Planting).

Clay soil is, naturally, much more likely to collect water in winter than a light, sandy soil. To open up a clay soil, work in sandy or gritty material and vegetable matter such as well-rotted dung, peat, garden compost, spent hops, composted seaweed or leafmould. These same materials that will open a heavy soil will give 'body' to a very light soil.

As a general rule when preparing for fruit a piece of previously cultivated garden it will be quite unnecessary to add any manure. Over-rich soil will only encourage lush growth at the expense of fruiting. Some soft fruits require a richer soil initially than the tree fruits and a soil containing plenty of well-rotted vegetable matter which retains moisture well in summer is most desirable.

Weeds Whether you are preparing a previously cultivated site or a piece of virgin meadowland, it is important to eradicate all perennial weeds. These can be a considerable nuisance in a fruit plot later and not easy to deal with when their roots are intertwined with those of the fruit. Where severely weed-ridden areas are concerned, it may be advisable to defer planting for a year to devote a whole growing season to fallowing the land and eliminating every weed to appear. Annual weeds can be easily dealt with by the application of a contact weedkiller. A total weedkiller such as sodium chlorate will make short work of all weeds but it will render the soil sterile for as long as a year, during which time it would be unsafe to plant anything. One based on glyphosate overcomes this problem.

Soil Acidity The degree of acidity of the soil is of much importance to the fruit-grower. All the fruits we grow, but two, flourish best in a slightly acid soil. The two exceptions are blueberries and cranberries which like very acid conditions.

Because chalk is alkaline, chalk-land areas

Above: The strawberry variety 'Red Gauntlet' crops heavily, bearing large fruits
Right: 'Victoria' is still deservedly one of the most popular of all plums
Below: Peach 'Dymond', a hardy, free bearing variety, ripens in late August

are not noted for fruit-growing. Nevertheless one often sees quite flourishing garden fruit trees and bushes in these districts – it all depends on the depth of slightly acid soil lying on top of the chalk. Provided no deep digging is practised, to stir up the chalk lumps and bring them near the surface, the natural action of rain and drainage wash the alkaline chalk particles downwards rather than up. Some fruits will tolerate a certain degree of chalkiness better than others (see below).

When preparing ground for fruit it is prudent to test it for acidity or otherwise. Testing outfits for garden use are quite inexpensive. Make several tests, using distilled and *not* tap water, and average the results.

One cannot in the garden control acidity within fine limits, nor is it necessary. Ideally we should like the test to show a *p*H scale reading between 6·0 and 6·5. But if the test shows a reading under 5·5 spread a 3 oz. per sq. yd. dressing of hydrated lime over the surface and lightly prick it into the topsoil. (The *p*H scale indicates the acidity or alkalinity of the soil. *p*H 7·0 indicates neutrality,

readings below this indicate the degree of acidity, those above 7·0 indicate the degree of alkalinity. The scale is logarithmic, i.e. a reading of *p*H 5 shows that the soil is 10 times as acid as a soil which has a reading of *p*H 6 and one which has a reading of *p*H 4 is 100 times as acid as a soil with a *p*H 6 reading.)

It is not so easy to rectify matters if the test shows an alkaline reaction (over 7·0 *p*H scale). If the alkalinity is the result of over-liming in the past (old vegetable plots often suffer in this way), then of course you should not add any more lime. The addition of any humus-making material – farmyard or stable manure, garden compost or peat – will all help to reduce the alkalinity. Refrain from using old mushroom compost manure because this usually contains chalk and is slightly alkaline. In future years fertilizers of an acid nature (e.g. sulphate of ammonia) should be preferred for the provision of nitrogen.

The reason why an alkaline soil is unfavourable for fruit-growing is that in such conditions certain trace elements – quite essential but required in tiny amounts only –

become chemically unavailable to the roots. The minerals chiefly concerned are magnesium, iron and manganese and in chalky land top and soft fruit soon show deficiency symptoms – yellowing, loss of leaf colour between the leaf-veins and die-back.

Simply feeding extra iron and manganese is no remedy because the ordinary fertilizers soon become locked up, too. Chemists have circumvented this by producing these minerals in a form known as chelates or sequestrenes and one can now buy fertilizer mixtures containing both chelated iron and manganese for application as a liquid from the watering can or as a foliage spray. The use of chelated fertilizers has made fruit thrive in gardens where it has never flourished before.

Soil preparation should be completed several weeks before planting so that the disturbed ground can settle properly. Early digging is important where manure has to be worked in (no manure should ever come into contact with the roots at planting time). Shuffling your feet over the dug soil will break up surface lumps and help to settle it.

Soil Needs of Individual Fruits

Apples These are tolerant fruits but they do not like bad drainage. They do best in deep, medium loam; on light soils they may suffer from potash deficiency. Their nitrogen requirements are moderate. They are liable to show serious signs of magnesium, iron and manganese shortage on chalky soils. The varieties 'Charles Ross' (Oct.–Dec.) and Gascoyne's Scarlet' (Sept.–Jan.), both dual-purpose apples, best withstand chalky conditions.
Apricots These thrive in a deep marly topsoil (marl is a mixture of lime and clay) over limestone. Any well-drained, moisture-retentive loam should suit them.
Blackberries The stronger varieties will succeed in almost any soil but the weaker ones need a deep, well-worked moderately heavy loam for best results.
Blackcurrants These may be grown on most soils including chalky kinds. A deep medium loam is best. Light soils should be enriched with plenty of bulky manure.
Cherries Cherries flourish best in deep medium loam as typified by the brick-earth soil found in parts of Kent. They will also prosper on a deep heavy loam, but will not tolerate poor drainage and soon show mineral deficiencies on a chalk soil.
Figs Too good a soil results in growth rather than fruit and for that reason figs do well in a shallow loam overlaying chalk, the latter checking extensive root development. A light, sandy soil should be strengthened by the addition of peat, to aid moisture-retention, rather than by manure or compost.
Gooseberries These do best on a deep loam rich in organic matter. They are very susceptible to poor drainage. They often show potash deficiency on light sandy soils. Shallow and light soils should be well enriched to improve moisture retention. They are most

likely of all fruits to succeed in chalky soil.
Loganberries (and other hybrid berries) As for blackberries (see above).
Peaches (and nectarines) As these are usually on plum rootstocks they have the same soil requirements as plums (see below).
Pears These have requirements generally similar to those of apples but flourish best in a somewhat richer and moister soil. They are slightly more tolerant of indifferent drainage. When on quince rootstock they are very susceptible to iron deficiency on chalky soil.
Plums (and damsons and gages) These do best on a deep heavy loam; they will also succeed on a clay soil but it must be well-drained. Ex-vegetable plot soil (rich in nitrogen) is excellent. Light soil results in poor fruit quality, brittle branches and a short life. Plums are very susceptible to iron deficiency on chalky soil.
Raspberries A well-drained deep loam is the ideal but raspberries will also flourish in a light soil if top and second spit have been liberally enriched with mositure-holding vegetable matter and the soil never allowed to dry out in drought. Good drainage is essential. Iron and manganese deficiencies can be serious on chalky soil.
Red and White Currants These are tolerant of most soils. They do best on a light loam but may show potash deficiency signs on a light sandy soil. They are less in need of rich humus content than other soft fruits and prefer only slight acidity. They are liable to iron deficiency on very chalky soil.
Strawberries A rich, well-drained medium loam is best. Light soils need the addition of plenty of vegetable matter to improve moisture-retention. Clay soils need plenty of vegetable matter worked in to lighten them and improve drainage. Winter waterlogging can cause serious losses. Iron deficiency is very liable to appear on a chalky soil.

Planting; Feeding; Growing Apples

The planting season for fruits other than strawberries (a special case and dealt with separately) extends from leaf-fall, usually early in November, until the resumption of growth in March or early April but always slightly later in the north.

For rapid re-establishment close contact is necessary between the particles of moist soil and the tiny root hairs. This is more likely to be achieved early in the autumn than in the winter when the soil is sticky. Another reason for early planting is that the soil then still retains sufficient warmth to encourage immediate root growth.

Early planting is particularly valuable for the fruits which start first into growth in spring–the apricots, peaches and nectarines.

It is one thing to plan to plant early, quite another to accomplish this. October and November rains may make the soil unsuitable, transport difficulties may hold up your new trees, the nurseryman may not have immediately just what you want or may be slow to deliver or frost may freeze the soil solid or the planting site may be deep in snow.

Should the fruit trees or canes arrive before you are immediately ready to plant them, heel them in temporarily. For this take out a slit trench with the spade with one face at an angle of 45°. The trench must be deep enough to take the roots when roughly spread out and so that they will be covered to the same depth as they were in the nursery (notice the soil mark on the stem). Lay the trees along the sloping side of the trench, return the soil, covering all the roots and firm it.

If the trees arrive during hard frost or snow so that planting is impracticable, unfasten the bundle and place the plants in the garage or a shed. Cover them and protect them from mice. If, when it comes to planting, the roots look dry, soak them in water for a couple of hours.

Staking and Tying Finally, stakes and tying materials should be obtained and prepared. In light land all posts should be sunk at least 2 ft; in heavy soil 18 in. is sufficient. Above ground the stake must extend to just below the lowest branches. Strong stakes are necessary because they may have to do duty for many years. Peeled chestnut is excellent, so is 3 in. x 3 in. hardwood. The underground part of the stake and at least a few inches above should be thoroughly soaked (not merely painted) in a copper-based preservative.

All tree fruits need to be staked on planting and those on dwarfing rootstock will need support for the whole of their life.

If a single vertical stake is to be used, this should be inserted before planting to obviate root damage. Some growers prefer a longer, oblique stake which is inserted at an angle of about 45° and pointing towards the prevailing wind. Such a stake must be long enough to cross the tree's trunk just below the lowest branches. Another method is to drive in two vertical stakes, one each side of the tree and at least a foot apart, then fix a crosspiece to these to which the stem will be fastened.

Apple or pear trees to be grown as oblique cordons require a system of horizontal wires. Preferably these should run from south to north and be 2, 4 and 6 ft. above the ground. Use gauge 12 galvanized wire and insert an adjustable straining bolt at one end of each wire to keep it taut. The end posts must be really stout (concrete or angle iron posts are often used) and should have angle struts facing down the row to take the strain.

Whether grown in the open or against a wall, fan-trained trees will require a system of horizontal wires about 6 in. apart.

Soft fruits such as currants and gooseberries do not require any support except where they are grown as cordons. Blackberries, loganberries and other hybrid berries need four horizontal wires at heights of 3, 4, 5 and 6 ft.

These preparations completed, planting may be carried out, provided that the soil is quite friable.

Take out a planting hole wide and deep enough for the roots of the tree, bush or cane to be spread out to their natural length. Clip off with the secateurs any damaged roots and shorten any one root which is substantially longer and stronger than the rest.

Break up the soil at the bottom of the hole with a fork and draw in a little topsoil to form a slight mound at the centre so that the tree 'sits' on this. At this stage of the proceedings, an assistant to hold the tree is most helpful. When planting is completed and the soil firmed down, the tree should be at the same depth as it was in the nursery (the soil mark on the stem will probably be visible). Where tree fruits which do not grow on their own roots are concerned, it is essential that the join (known as the 'union') between the top part (the 'scion') and the rootstock should be quite clear of the soil, at least 4 in. above it. Most soft fruits should be at their previous, nursery, depth, except blackcurrants which should be slightly deeper than before.

Now, your helper holding the tree at the right depth (a stick laid across the planting hole will indicate the final soil level), begin to replace the topsoil round the roots. A little moist peat mixed with this soil as you proceed will aid rapid new root growth. Never add manure. Use your fingers to work the

Planting Distances for Tree Fruits
(All figures in feet)

	Standard or half-standard	Bush	Dwarf bush	Pyramid	Cordon	Fan	Espalier
Apple	30–40	15	9	3½×7	2½×6	15	10–15
Apricot						12	
Cherry (Sweet)	30–40	30–40				20	
Cherry (Morello)	20	15				10–15	
Fig		12–18				12–18	
Nectarine		Not recommended				12–15	
Peach		18				12–15	
Pear	30–40	15	12	3×6	2½×6	12–15	12–15
Plum (including Gages)	15–20	12–20		10×10		12	

soil well in beneath and around every root. Firm it occasionally as you work. When ground level is reached firm with your feet and then just rake over the surface.

In spring, spread over the root area a 2 in. deep mulch of rotted manure, compost or peat to conserve moisture.

Immediately after planting fasten the tree temporarily to its stake. Permanent fastening should only be done a few months later when the soil has had time to settle. Inspect and adjust the fastenings of all newly-planted trees frequently in their early years.

Patent plastic straps are excellent for fastening fruit trees because these incorporate a plastic buffer which prevents the stem from chafing against the stake and because they are so easily adjustable as the tree grows.

Alternatively, use soft string for tying a newly-planted tree, first wrapping a piece of sacking, old rubber inner tube or something similar round the bark.

Cordons should be tied with soft string or plastic tying tape to canes which, in turn, are tied to the horizontal wires. Similarly, espaliers and fan-trained trees should have their 'arms' tied to canes which are then fastened to the wires.

Oblique cordons should be planted at an angle of 45°, pointing to the north and with the scion part of the union on top of the rootstock part so that when the tree is bent down to a more acute angle this will tend to press the two parts of the union together rather than tear them apart.

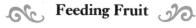

Feeding Fruit

Like all other plants, fruits have special need for three major nutrient elements—nitrogen, potassium and phosphorus followed by magnesium. Many other minerals are needed in lesser amounts, some quite minute.

In the following pages the 'straight' fertilizers are recommended for the provision of the three major elements—sulphate of ammonia and Nitro-chalk for nitrogen, sulphate of potash for potassium and superphosphate for phosphorus. Natural manure provides all these three and all the minor elements.

Many excellent proprietary mixed manures are now on the market and these may be used with every confidence according to the makers' instructions.

The Care of Apples

Most gardeners plant two- or three-year-old trees which have already been pruned by the nurseryman into the required shape—bush, cordon, pyramid, espalier or fan. It is more interesting to start with a one-year-old tree (a 'maiden') and carry out the shaping yourself: this is cheaper, but it means you have to wait longer before you can pick fruit.

As soon as a new tree has been planted you must consider what pruning is necessary, according to the age of the tree. Winter pruning, carried out while the tree is dormant, promotes growth and in the early years, when the framework of the tree is being built up,

can be fairly drastic. Later, when the branches to carry the crop have been developed, winter pruning should be more restrained, the aim now being to stimulate fruit bud formation rather than much more growth. Summer pruning encourages fruit bud formation and keeps trees within bounds.

Pruning Bush Trees FIRST WINTER: If a maiden has been planted, the first pruning consists of beheading it at a point immediately above a growth bud about 18 to 24 in. above soil level. This cut determines the length of stem below the main branches.

SECOND WINTER: Select the three or four sturdiest of the resultant shoots made during the first summer. These should be evenly spaced round the tree and will form the main branches from which other branches will spring. The aim should be a goblet shape with an open centre. Shorten each of the selected branches to between a third and a half of its length, making the cut beyond and close to a bud pointing to the desired direction.

Cut back any other shoots, not needed as main branches, according to vigour, the weakest to one bud and the strongest to five buds.

THIRD WINTER: Each of the three or four main branches will have produced one extension growth and a number of laterals. Cut back the leader by a half. Choose two or three of the strongest and best-placed laterals as new branches and cut these, too, back by half. Cut back other laterals over 5 in. long to the fourth bud and any laterals pruned in the second winter to one bud of the new growth.

Pruner's Terms

Branch: A primary branch arises directly from the main trunk of the tree. A secondary branch grows from a primary branch. All branches end in leaders (see below).
Buds: Buds are of two kinds—growth buds and fruit buds (i.e. those which develop into blossom). The former are thinner and more pointed, the latter plumper and more rounded. Growth buds can remain dormant for years.
Feather: A sideshoot on a maiden tree.
Lateral: A sideshoot from a branch. A sublateral is a sideshoot from a lateral.
Leader: The new growth from the extremity of a branch or, in a pyramid or cordon, from the tip of the central stem.
Maiden: A tree in its first year.
Notching: The cutting of a tiny wedge of bark immediately above a bud. This will stimulate its growth.
Spur: A short sideshoot bearing one or more fruit buds. A spur may develop naturally or be induced by pruning. One or more spurs may grow out of another and this is called a spur system.
Tip-bearer: A variety which tends to produce fruit buds at the tips of laterals rather than on spurs.

Far left (top): A six-year-old fan-trained apple 'Sunset' on M.7 rootstock
Far left (bottom): Apple 'Ellison's Orange', espalier trained, on M.7 rootstock
Left: Apple 'Worcester Pearmain'

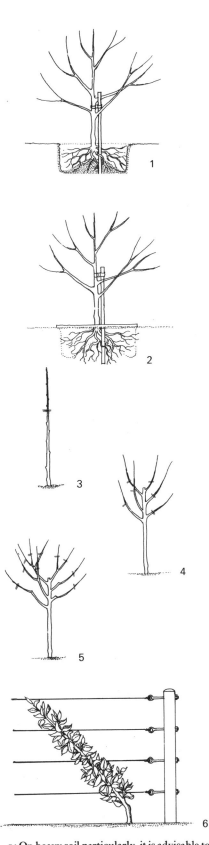

1: On heavy soil particularly, it is advisable to plant fruit trees on a mound of soil in the centre of the planting hole, as shown. 2: A stick laid across the rim of the planting hole will enable you to ensure that the tree is planted at the right depth, according to the soil mark on the stem. 3: A maiden tree is beheaded above a growth bud, about 1½–2 ft. above the ground, during the first winter after planting.
4: Branches will develop and these should be shortened during the second winter, as indicated. 5: Further growths which develop will need to be pruned in subsequent winters.
6: The system of wires, posts and straining bolts used for cordon and espalier trained fruit trees.

Left: Apple 'Ellison's Orange', a dessert variety

Any feathers growing from the main stem of the tree should be removed entirely.

FOURTH WINTER: The stage has now been reached when, to encourage fruit production, pruning may be substantially less drastic. Subsequent treatment will depend upon the habit of growth of the tree in question. Most apples form fruiting spurs naturally or when their laterals are cut hard back. Some varieties, however, tend to make their fruit buds at the tips of young shoots and at or near the tips of older shoots. These are called tip-bearers. Examples are 'Bramley's Seedling', 'Cornish Gilliflower', 'Irish Peach', 'Lady Sudeley', 'Mr Gladstone', 'Tydeman's Early Worcester' and 'Worcester Pearmain'. A few –'George Cave' for one, 'Crispin' ('Mutsu') is another–bear their fruit terminally and on spurs. If tip-bearing varieties have all their leaders and laterals cut back, few if any fruit buds will be formed.

For the spur-forming majority of varieties only tip the leaders, removing about 2 in. and cut back new laterals to three buds and previously pruned laterals to one bud of new wood. Eventually the spur systems will become overlong and possibly congested. Remove a few entirely and shorten others by a half. Should growth be weak cut back branch leaders more than usual–by a half, even three-quarters of the new growth.

With all systems of pruning, a first step is to cut out entirely any dead or diseased wood and any shoots growing in an undesirable direction (e.g. congesting the centre of a bush tree, directly towards the wall of a wall-trained tree) or crossing or chafing against another shoot.

If a shoot on a tip-bearing variety is left unpruned, it should develop a fruit bud at its end during the next year which, if still left unpruned, will produce fruit in the third year. If a tip-bearer is to crop well a good proportion of shoots must be left unpruned and the system known as renewal pruning is suitable.

Each year some fruited laterals are shortened to two buds so that two new shoots are produced the next summer. The remaining laterals are left unpruned to make fruit buds.

When a tip-bearer has begun cropping the tipping of leaders may cease.

Pruning Oblique Cordons FIRST WINTER: If a maiden spur-bearer is planted, no winter pruning is necessary. Prune tip-bearers back by a quarter. Should there be any feathers of more than 4 in. cut these back to three buds. MID-JULY: Cut back mature laterals (those which are becoming woody at the base and are more than 9 in. long) to the third leaf after the basal cluster. Leave immature laterals for similar treatment at mid-September. If, by mid-September there has been secondary growth from your first cuts, prune this back to one bud from the point of origin. SECOND JULY AND SUBSEQUENT YEARS: Cut back mature laterals as in previous summer. Where sub-laterals have formed, and are mature, cut back to one leaf after the basal cluster. Deal with previously immature laterals and sub-laterals in September.

The leader of a cordon does not usually need to be cut until further height has to be restricted and then it should be shortened, as necessary, in May. Before that, however, greater length can be accommodated by unfastening the cane to which the tree is tied and pressing it down to a more acute angle before refastening to the wires.

In time the fruiting spurs may become overlong and congested. They may be shortened or thinned out in winter.

Pruning Dwarf Pyramids The laterals and sub-laterals along the branches of a pyramid are pruned in summer in the same way as those on cordons and, accordingly, the spur-bearing varieties are much easier to deal with than those inclined to tip-bearing. FIRST WINTER: Behead the maiden at about 20 in. above soil level, just above a bud which will grow to provide further upward extension. Rub out the next bud below this (its growth would tend to compete with the leader). The next three or four buds should point out evenly round the stem. Rub out any buds pointing in the wrong direction (i.e. too close to their neighbour). The aim is a central leader growing vertically with three or four branches evenly spaced below it. The bottom three of these buds will be stimulated if you take a notch out of the bark immediately above each bud (see definitions). Feathers more than 9 in. from the ground but less than 12 may be used to form the first branches: cut them back to about 6 in., to a bud pointing downwards.

FIRST SUMMER: Tie the leader to a bamboo cane if necessary to make it grow vertically. If more than four sideshoots have appeared, cut the surplus back to four leaves after the basal cluster in mid-July.

SECOND WINTER: Pruning now is designed to provide a second tier of branches to fill the gaps between the branches of the tier below.

Cut the central leader to a bud 12 to 18 in. above the previous winter's cut and to keep the central stem vertical, on the opposite side. Select suitable buds to form the branches, rubbing out unwanted ones and notching the two lowest. Prune back the leaders of the first tier of branches to downward-pointing buds about 9 in. from the point of origin.

SECOND SUMMER AND SUBSEQUENT YEARS: Treat laterals and sub-laterals as those on a cordon. THIRD WINTER: Prune as in second winter. When the desired height limit has been reached defer pruning of the central leader

Apple 'Newton Wonder'

Rootstocks for Apples

M.27 The most dwarfing rootstock available. Suitable for very vigorous varieties such as Bramley's Seedling.

M.9 Very dwarfing. A good stock for cordons and dwarf bushes. Usually too dwarfing for espaliers and pyramids.

M.26 Less dwarfing than M.9. For small espaliers, dwarf pyramids and for cordons and dwarf bushes where soil is not rich.

M.7 & MM.106 Semi-dwarfing, producing trees of moderate size on good soil, often used for pyramids. Will produce dwarf trees on poorish soil. Recommended for cordons or varieties which do not spur freely.

M.2 & MM.111 Vigorous stocks which make big trees on good soil. May be used for espaliers where there is plenty of space and good for cordons and pyramids where the soil is definitely poor.

Notes The letters refer to the research stations originally responsible for them. M=Malling; MM=Malling-Merton.

Apples for Every Season

July–August: Emneth Early (2) C, B-B.
July–October: Arthur Turner (2) C.
August: George Cave (2) D; Stark Earliest (2) D.
August–September: Bakers Delicious (3) D; Epicure (3) D, F; Tydeman's Early Worcester (3) D.
September–October: James Grieve (3) D; Merton Charm (3) D.
September–November: Ellison's Orange (4) D, B-B; Rev. W. Wilks (2) C, B-B.
September–January: Golden Noble (4) C, F.
October–December: Egremont Russet (2) D, F; Sunset (3) D, F.
November–January: Cox's Orange Pippin (3) D, F; Holstein (3) D, F; Ribston Pippin (2) D, F, T; Spartan (3) D.
November–February: Golden Delicious (4) D; Laxtons Superb (4) D, F, B-B.
November–April: Newton Wonder (5) D-P, F; Idared (3) D-P.
December–February: Crispin (4) D, T.
December–March: Boston Russet (1) D; Crawley Beauty (6 but self-fertile), C.
December–April: Edward VII (5) C.
December–May: Ontario (3) C, B-B.
December–June: Annie Elizabeth (5) C.
January–February: Orleans Reinette (4) D, F.
January–April: Winston (5) D.
February–March: Duke of Devonshire (4) D.
March–May: Tydeman's Late Orange (3) D, F, B-B.

Notes (1) (2) (3) (4) (5) (6) These figures indicate flowering time. Another variety in the same group is likely to be the best pollinator but a few blossoms from one group may well overlap the adjoining group. C=Cooker; D=Dessert; D-P=Dual-purpose; F=Recommended for fine flavour; B-B= Biennial bearer (this unfortunate habit can sometimes be corrected by drastic blossom thinning in the good years). T=Triploid (such varieties will not pollinate others and it is necessary to plant two other non-triploid, diploid, varieties in the same flowering group, one to pollinate the triploid, the other to fertilize the pollinator). *Note that Cox's Orange Pippin will not pollinate Holstein, and Golden Delicious will not pollinate Crispin.*

until May and then cut it back by half. Thereafter cut new growth back to ½ in.

Pruning Espaliers Espaliers are usually sold ready-trained with two or three pairs of horizontal branches. There is no reason, however, why you should not plant a maiden tree and train your own espalier. Then you can have a single pair of branches or, if you wish, four, five or more tiers.

There is no rule as to the height of the first pair of branches or the space between subsequent tiers–usually about 15 in. is convenient. For preference plant an unfeathered maiden and cut back to a bud just above the lowest horizontal support wire. This bud will provide vertical growth to carry the second tier of branches 15 in. higher in a year's time. Below the top bud look for a pair of buds as nearly as possible opposite each other. The growths from these will form the lowest pair of horizontal branches and to stimulate the lowest bud make a small notch just above it. Rub out any unwanted buds.

Tie the resultant shoots from the two lower buds to canes fastened to the wires at an angle of 45°. If one shoot grows more strongly than the other, lower it slightly to a more acute angle and raise its partner slightly, nearer to the vertical. Try thus to get equal growth in the two shoots. At the end of the first season lower both canes half way to the horizontal, then down to their permanent horizontal position at the end of the second season.

Treat any laterals and sub-laterals arising from these horizontal branches as those on a cordon. Year by year a further pair of new branches can be made as desired. Leaders need not be pruned until the limit of available space is reached unless growth is unsatisfactory–in which case in winter cut back the new growth of leaders by a half or more.

Pruning Fans Except in the coldest districts, apples are not satisfactory when trained against a wall. However, an apple can be fan-trained, the ribs of the fan being fastened to horizontal wires.

The initial training follows the method adopted with peaches (see Peaches). Once established treat each rib as if it were a cordon, though when it reaches the limit of available space it cannot be bent down to a more acute angle and so the leader must be cut.

Fruit Thinning In good years failure to thin may result in a glut of undersized apples and put such a strain on the tree that it can produce little fruit the next year. In this way a habit of biennial bearing may be induced. Certain varieties are notorious for this alternate good and bad crop habit.

Timely fruit thinning will often check a tendency towards biennial bearing. Start thinning as soon as the fruitlets have set and you can form an idea of the possible crop.

With most varieties the central apple in each cluster (usually larger and hence known as the king) does not in the end prove the best. So begin by removing any obviously blemished fruitlets and then all the kings (an exception here being 'Worcester Pearmain').

Thin in about three stages, first reducing each cluster to one apple. Then continue until finally about one fruit remains for every 25 to 30 leaves. Dessert varieties should not be closer than 4 in. apart, cookers 6 in.

Watering Never wait until signs of distress are noticeable. Watering is particularly desirable in the spring for newly-planted and young trees and an equable moisture supply in the soil is always important.

Mulch trees in early spring with a 2-in. layer of rotted manure, garden compost or peat to help conserve soil moisture.

Picking An apple is ready for picking as soon as it will easily part company with the tree, the stalk remaining on the apple. Pick by taking an apple in the palm of the hand, lift it to a horizontal position and give a very slight twist. If ready, the apple will come away quite easily. The picking season begins in late July and extends into November for late kinds. Early varieties of apple should be eaten quite soon after picking.

Storing Mid-season and late apples will only keep to their proper season (by which time only will their full flavour have developed) if they have not been picked too soon (which results in premature shrivelling) and if they have been stored in good atmospheric conditions and a low temperature.

A cellar provides the nearest to ideal conditions–moist air, adequate ventilation, darkness and an even temperature as near as possible to 40°F (4.5°C). If a shed has to be used, do not worry about an occasional drop in temperature to a few degrees below freezing but never handle the apples at such a time.

If you have a cellar or an insulated hut or shed, space the apples out, stalk uppermost on clean shelves. If space is short, wrap the apples separately in squares of newspaper or oiled apple wraps and put carefully into boxes.

Feeding Where apples have been planted on cultivated garden soil of reasonable fertility they are likely to need little feeding in their early years beyond an annual spring mulch of rotted manure or compost.

Always watch for signs of potash deficiency: fruits may drop excessively or be small, leaves may assume a bluish-green shade, developing paleness between the veins and eventually looking scorched at the edges. Dress with 1 oz. per sq. yd. of sulphate of potash.

In normal circumstances a suitable annual spring fertilizer dressing for established trees would be ½ oz. of superphosphate and ¾ oz. of sulphate of potash per sq. yd. If no natural manure or compost is available for mulching, use peat and add 1 oz. per sq. yd. of sulphate of ammonia to the fertilizer. If growth is sluggish, increase the sulphate of ammonia to 2 oz. per sq. yd.

Over-vigorous growth can be checked by sowing fine grasses up to within a foot or so of the trunk. Mow the grass several times during the growing season but always leave the mowings to rot *in situ*. When growth has steadied down the grass will need feeding with an annual dose of 2–4 oz. of sulphate of ammonia and ½–1 oz. of sulphate of potash with ½ oz. of superphosphate per sq. yd.

Various Fruits

The Care of Apricots

Apricots flower even earlier than peaches so that some kind of covering (hessian, old curtains etc.) should be held in readiness for evenings when frost threatens. They are self-fertile but unless flying insects are plentiful hand pollination is helpful (distributing the pollen with a camel's-hair brush or wisp of cottonwool).

Two comparatively new varieties are thought to be an improvement on older kinds – 'Farmingdale' and, a few days later and a little more vigorous, 'Alfred', both ripening in late July or early August.

In the warmest parts apricots may be grown as bushes but more often they are trained as fans (see peaches) against walls. The habit of fruiting resembles that of the plum. Keep the pruning of mature specimens to a minimum, cutting back leaders where necessary immediately after picking, rubbing out misplaced sideshoots as they appear and pinching the growing points from other laterals after the first flush of spring growth.

Apricots may be grown in the greenhouse but there should be no attempt to force growth, using the glass merely to safeguard from frost. Ventilate freely whenever possible.

The Care of Blackberries

Blackberries and the other berry fruits are all very easy to grow. They fruit on canes produced during the previous year. After planting, cut down to a sound bud about 9 in. above the ground. Shoots which grow during the first summer will fruit in the second year. After picking, cut old canes to ground level and tie the new season's canes against the horizontal support wires. It is sound practice either to spread out the old canes all to one side of the plant, tying the new ones in on the other side or to spread out the fruiting canes on both sides, but fairly low down, and fasten the new canes to the centre and along the top. These schemes, by keeping the new canes separate or above the old ones prevent them from becoming disease infected by drip from above.

Recommended Varieties: Blackberries Bedford Giant (late July), earliest and largest berries; Himalaya Giant (Aug.–Sept.) Extremely vigorous, large berries; Oregon Thornless (Aug.–Sept.), less vigorous. The absence of thorns is a great asset.

Hybrid berries: Loganberry (second half July). The LY 59 strain is the best cropper. Thornless Loganberry, as above but smooth canes. Phenomenal Berry (Aug), similar. Japanese Wineberry (Aug). Very sweet, crimson berries; Malling Hybrid 53-16. Dark purple berries the pips of which are less trouble than raspberry pips in jam; Youngberry (late July–Aug.) Large purplish-black berries. Very vigorous, thornless.

Blackberries and their related hybrids are all self-fertile.

The Care of Blackcurrants

Plant slightly deeper than the bushes were in the nursery, put down a 2-in. mulch of rotted manure, compost or peat and at once cut all shoots down to within an inch of the mulch. The next winter cut down half of the new shoots; those which remain will give you your first crop. In subsequent years prune as soon as the crop has been picked, removing entirely about one third of the shoots which have just fruited. Blackcurrants yield most heavily on the young wood of the previous summer's growth but also on two-year-old and older wood. Try to keep the centre of the bush from becoming congested.

Feeding Blackcurrants are gross feeders. Liberal dressings (5 lb. per sq. yd.) in winter or early spring with rotted farm or stable manure are best. Also scatter $\frac{3}{4}$ oz. of sulphate of potash and 2 oz. of sulphate of ammonia per sq. yd. in spring. Every third year add 1 oz. of superphosphate per sq. yd. Where no natural dung is available mulch freely with garden compost, lawn mowings or peat, and double the sulphate of potash and treble the sulphate of ammonia dressings.

Recommended Varieties: For succession: Mendip Cross (very early); Blacksmith (mid-season); Baldwin (late); Amos Black (very late). All are self-fertile.

The Care of Cherries

Sweet cherries were not grown much in gardens because until recently there was no dwarfing rootstock and no self-fertile variety. This has changed with the introduction of a self-fertile variety (Stella) and a dwarfing rootstock (Colt).

The Morello sour cherry is a different proposition because it is self-fertile and less vigorous. It can be grown as a bush or be fan-trained and as most fruit is borne on the previous year's growth pruning (in spring after the buds have broken) should be directed towards stimulating new growths, as with peaches, old fruited shoots being cut out and a few complete old branches being taken out each year from established trees.

Left: 'Baldwin', a late-fruiting blackcurrant variety. *Below:* Pruning a blackcurrant bush by removing about one third of the stems that have fruited after the crop has been picked

Planting Distances for Soft Fruits
(All figures in feet)

	Between plants	Between rows
Blackberry		
Himalaya Giant	12	6
Other varieties	10	6
Blackcurrant	5	6
Gooseberry (bushes)	5	6
Gooseberry (cordons)	$1\frac{1}{4}$	5
Loganberry and other hybrid berries	12	6
Raspberry	$1\frac{1}{2}$	6
Red & White Currant (bushes)	5	6
Red & White Currant (cordons)	$1\frac{1}{4}$	5
Strawberry	$1\frac{1}{2}$	$2\frac{1}{2}$

The Care of Gooseberries

The most usual way of growing a gooseberry is as a bush. The lowest branches should not be too low, however, or they may soon droop to the ground ('Leveller' and 'Careless' are notable offenders in this respect) and if shoot tips take root, a tangle of growth results. To prevent this, start with a leg of at least 6 in. and prune branch leaders to upward-pointing buds.

Pruning Bushes

Gooseberries bear their fruit both on wood of the previous year's growth and on spurs arising from older wood. The first few years' pruning should be fairly hard, directed to forming a good open framework of branches: cut branch leaders to half their length and laterals to three or four buds.

After three years confine winter pruning to removing crossing branches, those congesting the centre and those drooping down to the ground. New upward growing laterals will then have to be selected to replace the old branches and these should be cut back half way to encourage growth. All laterals should be shortened to five leaves in late June.

Pruning could be done in autumn, as soon as the leaves fall, but it is often deferred until spring to discourage the birds which, in some districts, can do much damage pecking out the growth buds.

Protection against birds can, of course, be provided during the winter and in some areas may prove essential. It is not normally necessary to protect the berries while they are unripe but once ripening begins it is.

Trained Forms

Gooseberries can be trained as standards as well as espaliers, fans or single or double cordons.

In pruning cordons cut back in winter the new growth of the vertical leader by a third (but never leaving an extension of more than 10 in.). In the second half of June cut back laterals to four leaves and in winter shorten these laterals to two or three buds.

Feeding

Give an annual early spring dressing of $\frac{1}{2}$ oz. sulphate of ammonia and 1 oz. each of sulphate of potash and super-phosphate, per sq. yd. Then follow this with a liberal mulch of farmyard manure.

Recommended Varieties: Gooseberries are self-fertile and there are many varieties.
EARLY: Keepsake. Early for picking green. Rich flavour. Pale green.
MID-SEASON: Leveller. Best flavour but must have good soil. Greenish-yellow. Whinham's Industry. Red, large, upright.
LATE: Lancer. Excellent flavour. Good for bottling and dessert. Greenish-yellow.

The Care of Peaches and Nectarines

Peaches and nectarines (which are simply a smooth-skinned type of peach) are usually fan-trained against a sunny wall but in the eastern and drier parts of the country peaches (but not nectarines) may be grown as bushes.

Most peaches and nectarines are self-fertile and so a single specimen can be quite successful. However, as they flower very early when the weather may be unpropitious for pollinating insects a little pollinating by hand (see Apricots) will assist a good set.

Pruning Bush Trees

In forming a bush peach tree the aim should be an open-centred goblet-shaped tree, as with apples. Pruning should be carried out early in May.

At the first pruning of a maiden cut the central stem about 2 ft. above soil level. If any of the remaining feathers have failed to break into growth at the extremity or have a dormant patch between the tip and point of origin, cut back to an outward-pointing shoot on the lower part where buds have broken vigorously into growth. The strongest of any feathers, if well placed, may be selected to form main branches, the others being cut back to one bud.

In subsequent years pruning follows similar lines. Cut back any branch which shows die-back at the tip or down its length to a point immediately above the second strong lateral. You have to remember with peaches (and nectarines) that blossom is carried only on wood made the previous year. Therefore your cutting is directed towards stimulating a continual supply of new laterals and, happily, the peach is naturally extremely vigorous. Any completely dead branches should be cut out at source and some may have to be removed or shortened to a sound bud because they cross others or cause congestion at the centre.

Where a three- or four-year-old tree (bush or fan) is planted, remove any blossom the first season, and allow only a token crop to develop the second year.

Pruning Fans

Although bush peaches have become quite popular in recent years the most common way of training them both against walls in the open and in the greenhouse is as fans. You can buy trees ready-trained as fans with anything from five to twelve shoots but the nurseryman is apt to take a short-cut by tying in every single feather produced in the maiden year which can possibly be twisted round to a cane fastened obliquely to the horizontal supporting wires. The method described here takes more time but results in a more robust tree, which is more likely to fruit evenly.

Plant the maiden as early in autumn as possible and in early spring just before growth starts cut it back to a sound bud 2 ft. or slightly less from the ground. It is necessary to note carefully the difference between pointed growth buds and the rounded blossom buds. The cutting must be to a growth bud. If you are in doubt, cut to a triple bud—one of the three is always a growth bud.

Select, some 9–12 in. above the ground, a growth bud on either side of the main stem: from these the first two ribs of the fan will spring. Rub out all other buds and cut off any laterals flush with the stem. As a result of these operations the top bud will produce a vertical shoot and below it there will be a lateral on either side. When these two laterals are about 18 in. long tie each to a cane fastened to the horizontal wires at an angle of 45°. As in forming an espalier (see 'Pruning Espaliers' under 'The Care of Apples') lift or lower these arms to stimulate or check growth and keep the development of the

Left: Gooseberry 'Leveller'. *Right:* Morello cherries

A wall-trained peach showing the fruits well spaced out

two branches equal. On tying in these two main branches, cut out the central, vertical leader entirely.

In the second winter, in February, cut back these two branches to good buds 12–18 in. from the vertical leg. The buds to which you cut must be pointing either upwards or downwards, never towards the wall or away from it and from them further extension growth will be produced. As growth begins select two promising shoots from the top of each branch and one from below: allow these to grow on and form three more ribs of the fan on either side. Rub out all other shoots. When these six new shoots attain a length of about 18 in. they in their turn can be fastened to slanting canes fastened to the wires.

This process of trebling the number of branches or fan-ribs can be repeated year by year until the whole wall space available has been filled. Frequently this is achieved in three years and then fruit production may begin, laterals being allowed to develop along the branches, these fruiting the following year. Rub out any laterals which start growing towards the wall or directly away from it. Select suitable laterals at intervals of about 6 in., rubbing out all others, tying the chosen shoots in and pinching out their growing points when some 18 in. long. In subsequent years allow one or two replacement shoots to grow out from close to the base of the fruiting lateral. Rub out all others. Let the fruiting lateral grow until eight more leaves have appeared, then cut back to the fourth. After harvest, cut back the fruited lateral to the best replacement shoot.

Fruit Thinning Thinning is essential with wall-trained peaches to prevent overcropping and secure good fruit size. When the fruits are the size of marbles reduce all pairs to singles and then when walnut size has been reached remove further fruits until none is closer than a foot from its neighbour. Thinning is less essential with bush trees.

Feeding Mulch lightly with rotted farmyard manure or garden compost in early spring and fork this into the top few inches of soil in autumn. Only if growth seems to lag, and after cropping has begun, give an annual February dressing of 1 oz. of Nitro-chalk and ½ oz. of sulphate of potash per sq. yd. with an extra 1 oz. per sq. yd. of superphosphate every third year. If peat replaces the manure or compost, double the quantity of Nitro-chalk.

Greenhouse Culture Fan-trained peaches or nectarines are popular fruits for the greenhouse, particularly suited to growing against the back wall of a lean-to. Do not coddle the peach, but give free ventilation after harvest until growth is started in January. Aim at a temperature of 40°F (4·5°C), 50°F (10°C) in February, using the glass and heat, if any, to protect the blossom from frost rather than to force growth. Give plenty of water when growth begins.

Recommended Varieties: Peaches Amsden June. The earliest, but in fact does not ripen until mid-July. White flesh; Duke of York. Mid-July. Pale greenish-yellow flesh. Good for greenhouse or outdoor culture; Hale's Early. July–Aug. Needs a pollinator. Pale yellow flesh. Hardy; *Peregrine. Early to mid-Aug. White flesh. Most reliable variety for the open; Rochester. Mid-Aug. Yellow flesh. Reliable variety for the open.

The last two are the best varieties for growing as bushes.

Nectarines: *Early Rivers. Mid to end July. Pale yellow flesh. Good for greenhouse culture; John Rivers. Late July. Yellowish flesh; Lord Napier. Early Aug. White flesh. Good for greenhouse culture; Elruge. Late Aug. White flesh. One of the hardiest; *Pine Apple. Early Sept. Yellow flesh. Good for greenhouse culture.

All the above peaches and nectarines have good flavour but those with an asterisk are outstanding. For rootstocks see under The Care of Plums.

The Care of Pears
Pears blossom a little earlier than apples and therefore there is a slightly higher risk of damage by frost or inadequate pollination because the weather discourages the pollinating insects from flying. They often take somewhat longer than apples to settle down and start fruiting. Pears may be grown in any of the forms in which apples are grown.

Pruning Bush Trees At first prune as for apples but more lightly, but when regular cropping starts, pruning needs to be harder than for apples, leaders being reduced by two-thirds to three-quarters, laterals to three buds and sub-laterals to one. Pears form natural spurs more readily than do apples but a few varieties–notably 'Jargonelle', 'Joséphine de Malines' and 'Packham's Triumph' –are tip-bearers and these must be pruned much more lightly with all short laterals left uncut to form a terminal fruit bud.

Pruning Cordons, Dwarf Pyramids, Espaliers and Fans As for apples, except that the new shoots will mature earlier.

Fruit Thinning Generally less thinning of

pears is required than for apples. Size of fruit will be improved and regularity of cropping aided if glut crops are thinned to one or, occasionally, two fruitlets per spur.

Watering In dry weather watering will be necessary, particularly when the trees are young. A spring mulch will help.

Picking The test for readiness to pick is the same as for apples, but pears need to be handled with even more caution as they bruise remarkably easily and the spurs are very brittle. The earliest varieties will be ready in late July or early August and should be eaten at once. Do not wait for pears to become soft before picking. Williams' Bon Chrétien, for example, should be picked when still quite hard but will soon ripen.

Storing Polythene bag storage is not so successful with pears but they will keep indoors in a slightly drier atmosphere and higher temperature than apples. Be careful not to pick the late-keeping varieties too soon. They are better laid out separately on shelves rather than wrapped and stored in boxes. When almost ripe they should be brought into a living room to finish.

Feeding Pears often need more nitrogen

Above: 'Louise Bonne of Jersey' is an early flowering dessert pear
Below: Pears in a fruit store

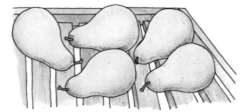

than do apples and are less liable to suffer from potash shortage. Normally the ground around them should be clean cultivated and mulched in spring with rotted farmyard manure or garden compost. Where no natural manure or compost is available, mulch with peat after first dressing with $1\frac{1}{2}$ oz. of sulphate of ammonia, 2 oz. of superphosphate and $\frac{3}{4}$ oz. of sulphate of potash per sq. yd.

The Care of Plums and Gages

Plums and gages may be grown as standards, half-standards, bushes, pyramids and fans. They are unsatisfactory as cordons or espaliers. They do best on deep heavy loam or on a well-drained clay soil. Ex-vegetable plot soil (rich in nitrogen) is excellent. Light soil results in poor fruit quality, brittle branches and a short life.

Plums are extremely susceptible to a fungoid disease known as silver leaf which is most infectious during the winter months. Pruning should be carried out during the summer, in spring or in early autumn immediately after the crop has been picked.

Pruning Bush Trees FIRST YEAR: If a maiden is planted, behead it at about 3 ft. from soil level in spring just before growth starts. Existing feathers may be selected for the fruit branches if well spaced. Plums are very liable to branch breakage and it is important to select as branches laterals with a wide angle to the main trunk, these being much stronger than those which are more nearly vertical and make an acute angle with the stem.

SECOND YEAR: In early spring cut back the selected branch leaders by a half.

THIRD YEAR: Again cut leaders by a half of the previous season's growth.

SUBSEQUENT YEARS: Between June and August remove crossing branches to open up the centre of the tree. Cut out any dead wood before mid-July. Some laterals may have to be cut out or shortened in summer to avoid overcrowding but otherwise plum pruning is best kept to a minimum. Should growth be poor, cut back some laterals drastically to encourage new wood. Plums fruit on second-year wood and on spurs which will develop without your assistance on older wood.

Pruning Pyramids The pyramid is the best form for plums in most gardens because it only needs 10 ft. of lateral space and can be restricted to a height of little more than 9 ft. You cannot buy plum trees already trained as pyramids so you must start with a maiden which should be on St Julien A rootstock. Apart from size a great benefit with this type of tree is that branch breakage is substantially reduced and, with it, there is less possibility of silver leaf infection.

FIRST YEAR: In late March behead the maiden 5 ft. above the ground. Cut off at source any feathers up to a height of 18 in, and reduce those above that point to half their length. When the growth of new shoots ceases (about the third week in July) cut back branch leaders to 8 in., pruning just beyond a bud pointing downwards or outwards. Shorten laterals to 6 in.

SUBSEQUENT YEARS: In April cut off two-thirds of the central leader's new growth. To keep the trees straight, cut to buds on opposite sides of the tree each year. When new growth ceases about the third week of July cut branch leaders to 8 in. and laterals to 6 in. Once the tree has reached 9 ft. cut the central leader to an inch or less of new growth each May. Should a new vertical shoot grow up to replace the central leader, remove it at source.

Pruning Fans Form the framework of the fan in the manner described for peaches. When the tree reaches fruiting age, however, the treatment has to be slightly different as

Rootstocks for Plums, Peaches and Nectarines

St Julien A: Semi-dwarfing (there is no satisfactory dwarfing rootstock for plums). This stock is the most widely used for garden plums (bushes, pyramids or fan-trained) and peaches.

Common Mussel: Semi-dwarfing. In dry districts trees on this stock may lose vigour early and start throwing up many suckers. This stock is also used for apricots, peaches, nectarines and ornamental prunus.

Common Plum: Semi-dwarfing. Sometimes used for garden plums but all varieties are not compatible with it.

Myrobalan B: Vigorous. Only suitable for large trees. Unsuitable for gages or peaches.

The Brompton: Vigorous. Suitable for all large trees, plum and peach. Seldom makes suckers.

Rootstocks for Pears

Years ago pears were grown on their own roots or on a seedling pear rootstock. These made very large trees and sometimes took 20 years or more to start fruiting—hence the phrase 'plant pears for your heirs'. Pear stocks are only used nowadays for standards and half-standards. For garden culture pears are now budded on quince rootstocks which restrict growth and induce early fruiting. Unfortunately some varieties of pear are not compatible with quince and in such cases the stock is 'double-worked', budded or grafted first with a variety which is compatible and then with the desired variety.

Malling Quince C: Most dwarfing (although not so markedly dwarfing as M.IX used for apple). May be used for bush trees, cordons or dwarf pyramids.

Malling Quince A: More vigorous than Quince C and should be used for bush trees, cordons or dwarf pyramids where the soil is poor, and, on good soil, where a larger tree is required.

Pears for Every Season
(From August to April)

August: Jargonelle (2) D, T.
September: Gorham (3) D; Williams' Bon Chrétien (2) D, F.
September–October: Bristol Cross (3) D, N P; Fertility Improved (*), D-P; Merton Pride (2) D, F, T.
October: Beurré Hardy (3) D; Beurré Superfin (2) D, F; Fondante d'Automne (2) D, F; Louise Bonne of Jersey (1) D.
October–November: Conference (2) D; Emile d'Heyst (1) D; Marie Louise (1) D; Seckle (1) D, F; Thompsons (2) D, F.
November–December: Doyenne du Comice (3) D, F; Packhams Triumph (2) D, F.
November–January: Winter Nelis (3) D,F.
December–January: Blickling (2) D, F; Josephine de Malines (2) D, F; Vicar of Winkfield (1) C, T.
January–March: Passe Crassane (2) D, F.
February–April: Easter Beurré (1) D.

Notes
(1) (2) (3) These figures indicate flowering time. C=Cooker; D=Dessert; D-P= Dual-purpose; F=Recommended for fine flavour; T=Triploid. Such varieties will not pollinate others and it is necessary to plant two other non-triploid (diploid) varieties in the same flowering group, one to pollinate the triploid, the other to fertilize the pollinator. N P=Has no good pollen and cannot pollinate others. (*) This is a tetraploid, a special case and self-fertile.

Note that Fondante d'Automne, Louise Bonne of Jersey, Seckle and Williams' Bon Chrétien will not pollinate each other.

Below: 'Denniston's Superb' is a good plum variety for the small garden as it crops regularly and can be grown as a pyramid

Above: A fan-trained plum, 'Early Laxton', on St Julien A rootstock. Note the use of bamboo canes for training the ribs of the fan

the plum fruits on old and new wood and one does not, therefore, have to cut back a lateral as soon as it has fruited. Any new laterals not required to extend the tree or to replace old laterals should be stopped when they have made six or seven leaves. It may be necessary to 'go over' the tree several times during the growing season for this pinching. Also rub out entirely any shoots pointing at the wall or directly away from it, doing this as soon as these unwanted growths are noticed.

As soon as the crop has been picked cut back by half all the laterals previously stopped and either tie down towards the horizontal any vigorous shoots growing verti-cally or cut them out entirely.

Fruit Thinning With glut crops on bush or pyramid trees, the thinning of plums not only increases fruit size but reduces the risk of branch breakage and the entry of silver leaf disease. Proper thinning also promotes regular cropping.

Thin gradually in two stages–early in June and, later, after the natural drop during stone formation. Break or cut the fruitlets off so that stalks remain on the tree, eventually reducing dessert plums to a minimum spacing of 2 in. Cooking plums may be slightly closer.

Feeding As advised for peaches.

Choice for the One-plum Garden

In many gardens there is room only for one plum tree and that must, therefore, be a self-fertile variety needing no other plum to pollinate it. Here are some of the best, all self-fertile, all dessert plums unless otherwise stated:

Name	Ready to pick	Colour	Comment
Czar	Early Aug.	Red-purple	Cooker. On small side but very heavy cropper. Reliable. Will grow on north wall.
Denniston's Superb	Mid Aug.	Greenish yellow, red flush	Good regular cropper, fair gage flavour. Succeeds as a pyramid.
Early Transparent Gage	Mid Aug.	Pale greenish yellow with red dots	Very sweet and superb flavour but also makes first-class jam. Crops heavily and often needs thinning. One of the best.
Oullin's Golden Gage	Mid Aug.	Straw-yellow, with red dots	Large fruit, fair flavour. Also good for cooking, jam and bottling.
Victoria	Second half Aug.	Carmine-rose with deeper red dots and pale blue bloom	Large fruits with good flavour when really ripe. Very heavy and regular cropper. Also first-class for all cooking or preserving.
Thames Cross	First half Sept.	Golden yellow	Very large fruits. Fair flavour when ripe. Good for jam.
Merryweather	Second half Sept.	Black	Cooker. Large fruit of damson flavour. Very good for bottling.
Severn Cross	Second half Sept.	Golden yellow, pink flush, tiny red dots	Very large fruit. Sweet, fair flavour. Crops well.
Marjorie's Seedling	Late Sept.–Oct.	Blue-black, deep blue bloom	Primarily cooker. Passable for dessert when ripe. Large fruits. Good and regular cropper.
Reine Claude de Bavay	Late Sept.–Oct.	Pale lemon yellow, with white and sometimes red dots	Rich, gage flavour. Reliable cropper, sometimes heavy.

More Soft Fruits

The Care of Raspberries

Summer-fruiting raspberries bear their berries on new canes made the previous summer. On planting cut back the canes to 2 ft. and then in spring, when growth shows, cut back farther to a live bud about 10 in. above soil level. This means you will get no crop the first summer but give the plants a chance to develop a good root system. No pruning will be necessary in the autumn following planting and the canes produced during that summer will give you your first crop in the second summer after planting. Thereafter, prune as soon as the crop has been picked, cutting all fruited canes to ground level, tying in up to six of the strongest new canes and removing any others. In February tip the canes, reducing them to about 4 ft. 6 in.

Autumn-fruiting varieties crop on the new canes which grew during the summer. Thus new plants cut down in April will try to fruit on the new canes the first year. This will put too much strain on the plants so be hard-hearted and cut off all blossom the first year. Subsequently delay pruning until February and then cut all fruited canes to ground level (and in the first winter after planting that means cutting down the deblossomed canes).

The summer-fruiting varieties must be protected from birds and netting over the whole row is most satisfactory. By the autumn the birds have sometimes lost interest in this type of food and, in some areas at least,

netting is unnecessary. Apart from this, and the time of pruning, summer and autumn raspberries need similar treatment. Methods of support were described earlier under Staking and Tying.

Feeding Raspberries need a steady supply of nitrogen and potash. In the first year a mulch of farmyard or stable manure (5 lb. per sq. yd.) put down in March will be sufficient but in subsequent years also give a dressing of 2 oz. of sulphate of ammonia and 1 oz. of sulphate of potash per sq. yd. in February. Every third year add 2 oz. per sq. yd. of superphosphate.

Plenty of moisture is essential throughout the growing period and the hose may well have to be used in June. Keep weeds down but try not to disturb the surface soil more than is essential because this damages surface roots, for which reason a paraquat/diquat weedkiller is excellent. Such a weedkiller may also be used to destroy unwanted suckers which spring up away from the row.

Recommended Varieties. Summer-fruiting: Malling Promise (early). Very heavy cropper and very vigorous. Good flavour; Lloyd George (early). Best for flavour. Has long picking season. Not very vigorous and may well be planted at half usual spacing. This variety tends to produce a small second crop in autumn and may be grown as an autumn variety by cutting down old canes in February; Malling Jewel (mid-season). Flowers late and often misses

frost. Very popular in Scotland. Crops well but not very vigorous and this, too, may be planted at half usual spacing; Norfolk Giant (late). Somewhat acid but extends the season. Autumn fruiting: September. Large berries, excellent flavour. More likely to ripen in October than September; Zeva. Possibly better flavour and larger berries than September; Fall Crop. A promising new variety.

Raspberries are self-fertile.

The Care of Red and White Currants

These are both grown in the same way and there are also but seldom seen, pink varieties. Their fruiting habit is quite different from the blackcurrant's and they, therefore, need quite different pruning. Red currants produce most of their fruit on short spurs on old wood and at the base of new growths. Little is borne on the new wood. As with gooseberries, birds can be a nuisance in winter pecking out the buds. Where this occurs it is preferable to give protection (see under 'Pests'): otherwise delay pruning until early spring when, after first signs of growth are visible, you can make sure of pruning to sound buds.

Pruning Bushes If a one-year-old bush is planted there may be three or four branches. Cut all back by two-thirds, to outward-pointing buds so as to secure an open-centred bush.

In the second winter again cut back hard, by two-thirds, and remove entirely any ill-placed laterals. Shorten other laterals, not required as branches, to one bud.

By the third winter the bush should have sufficient main branches. In this and subsequent years shorten branch leaders by a half, always to outward-pointing buds. Shorten laterals to one bud. If in later years growth continues to be vigorous the leaders need only be tipped; if growth is weak, cut back harder.

Left: Mixed soft fruit. *Above:* Raspberry 'Lloyd George'. *Right:* Raspberry 'Malling Exploit'

Trained Forms Red currants grow well as cordons and are often used as single or double vertical cordons for filling odd spaces against walls or fences. The pruning is as for cordon gooseberries except that the laterals should be cut even more severely in winter – to one or two buds.

Picking It is easiest to use scissors, cutting off complete bunches at a time.

Feeding Give a February dressing of 1 oz. per sq. yd. of sulphate of potash and every third year add superphosphate at 1 oz. per sq. yd. Follow this dressing in late March with 1-in. deep mulch of rotted manure or compost. If the mulching materials are likely to be unavailable include 1 oz. per sq. yd. of sulphate of ammonia in the February dressing and mulch in March with peat.

Recommended Varieties. Red Currants: *Very early:* Jonkheer Van Tets; *Early:* Laxton's No. 1; *Mid-season:* Red Lake; *Late:* Wilson's Long Bunch.

White Currants: *Early:* White Versailles; *Mid-season:* White Dutch.

Below: Strawberry 'Royal Sovereign', one of the most popular varieties. It bears fruit in early or mid-summer, but does not crop heavily. This 'Rolls-Royce' of strawberries is good for forcing
Right: Summer pruning a red currant bush, by shortening the new growth
By following the pruning instructions on page 175, an established, well-shaped bush should be obtained in 3 years

The Care of Strawberries

Weeds must be kept down in the strawberry bed but any hoeing must be very shallow to avoid root damage: it is better to use paraquat/diquat weedkiller as much as possible, being very careful not to let it touch the leaves of the strawberry plants.

When the berries begin to swell take steps to prevent soil-splashes spoiling them. There are three ways, the traditional one being to spread a little clean straw over the soil and beneath the fruit trusses. Alternatively buy proprietary strawberry mats and lay one of these round each plant, or put down black polythene tucking it into the soil or weighting it down with stones to prevent the wind getting beneath it. Never put straw or other mulches down too early as they may increase the risk of frost damage to open flowers.

Quite early in the season summer-fruiting strawberries start trying to propagate their kind by producing runners – cord-like growths on which tiny plants develop. These should always be cut off as soon as seen unless you wish to raise new plants. Unless you are very sure that your strawberries are quite free from virus disease infection (to which they are extremely prone) it is wiser to leave this job to the experts and buy new plants as required. It is never advisable to keep a strawberry bed for more than three seasons.

If you decide to raise your own plants, simply sink a 3-in. pot of good growing compost (John Innes potting compost or soilless compost) into the ground by the parent plant where the plantlet on the runner can be bent down. Hold the runner in place with a stone or 'hairpin' of galvanized wire and pinch out the tip of the runner to prevent further growth. At the end of July the new plant can be separated from its parent and a week or two later lifted and replanted.

As soon as picking is finished, cut all the old leaves off with shears and deal with any weeds. In early autumn rake in ½ oz. per sq. yd. each of sulphate of ammonia and sulphate of potash and put down a mulch of well-rotted farm or stable manure or garden compost (about 5 lb. per sq. yd.).

Greenhouse Culture The strawberry season can begin very much sooner if you force a few pots in the greenhouse. 'Royal Sovereign' and 'Tamella' are good varieties for this. Early-rooted runners are needed for this – late July if possible. Plant singly in 6-in. pots using JIP 2 potting compost. Stand the pots in the open on a sheet of polythene until mid-November and then either turn them on their sides (to prevent over-watering) or put them in a cold frame. Towards the end of January transfer to the unheated greenhouse. When fresh growth becomes visible, start watering cautiously and turn on the artificial heat. A night temperature of 45°F (7°C) will be quite sufficient at first. Let this rise gradually to 50°F (10°C) when the blossom trusses are seen. Pollinate the flowers by hand, dusting their centres with a camel's-hair brush. When the blossom has fallen the night temperature may be permitted to rise another five degrees (F) to 13°C and gentle liquid feeding should begin and be continued until the berries colour.

Cloches and Tunnels The strawberry season can also be advanced two or three weeks by covering first-year plants with cloches or polythene tunnels at the end of February. Deal with all weeds before covering. Keep closed until the blossom opens and

then open cloches or pull them apart slightly and open tunnels fully by day to allow entry of pollinating insects. Close tunnels and cloches again by 4 p.m. In April and May ventilate in sunny weather to prevent a dangerously high build-up of temperature. In dry weather watering may be necessary. Do this in the morning to let the plants dry before ventilation is closed again.

Perpetual-fruiting Kinds These need slightly different treatment. In the first season, nip off all flower trusses which appear before June. In subsequent years all blossom may be allowed to develop. Some do not produce runners freely; where new plantlets appear they may be allowed to root and may flower and fruit the same season. After fruiting the first year cut off all old leaves but in subsequent years leave them to fall naturally. Always burn strawberry leaves after removal.

Your Strawberry Choice
Summer-fruiting varieties
Cambridge Vigour (First-early): Very early in maiden year, thereafter mid-season. Good for cloching in first year. Good cropper. Juicy berries with good flavour.
Cambridge Rival (First-early): Good for cloching. Erect foliage suits wet land. Good flavour.
Cambridge Favourite (Second early): Good for cloching. Very heavy cropper. Little flavour.
Gorella (Second early): Very heavy cropper. Berries large but uneven shape. Not very sweet. Moderate flavour.
Royal Sovereign (Early mid-season): The 'Rolls-Royce' of strawberries but does not crop heavily and very susceptible to disease. Good for forcing.
Hapil (Mid season): Large size and good flavour.
Tamella (Second early in first season, mid season to late subsequently): Very heavy yield and fruits of good size and flavour. All-round variety for dessert, freezing, bottling and jam.
Red Gauntlet (Late mid-season): Heavy cropper. Large, dark crimson berries. Little flavour.
Cambridge Late Pine (Late): Frost-resistant. Fair cropper. Very good flavour and recommended for bottling.
Talisman (Late): Heavy cropper and very vigorous. Good flavour. May produce second crop in October.

Perpetual-fruiting variety
Gento: Now thought by many to be the best of this class. First trusses may ripen in June. Yields well with heaviest crop between August and October. Large berries of very good flavour.

Alpine varieties
Baron Solemacher: Larger berries than wild strawberries and less acid than the cultivated summer strawberries. Does not produce runners. Rich flavour.
Alexandria and **Delicious:** Improved strains of Baron Solemacher with larger berries and better disease resistance.
Alpine Yellow: Golden yellow berries with excellent flavour.

Above: 'Gento', the best of the 'perpetual-fruiting' strawberries, will yield fruit between June and October
Below: A cage made from wire-netting, will protect various soft fruits from birds
Right: To save space and to provide decorative value, strawberries may be grown in a barrel

Fruit Pests

Birds Pests are, alas, always with us but thanks to modern specifics there is generally no reason why they should cause serious damage to our trees or crops. There is, however, one exception against which no easy defence has yet been discovered–the birds which, it must be admitted, often add much to the enjoyment of our gardens but can rob us of our reward for a year's care in a few hours.

As they begin to ripen, nearly all fruits are subject to bird attack but, worse than that, our chances of any crop at all can be destroyed the previous winter when birds turn to the dormant buds on gooseberries, currants, plums and other tree fruits as a source of food in hard weather. Which fruits are most liable to be attacked probably depends on the balance between the trees available and the local bird population.

To protect the buds one can apply a proprietary bird repellent spray. This can work well, for a time, but frequent renewal can be expensive and is a task easily forgotten. More lasting protection is provided by rayon web, the fine gossamer strands of which are teased out over the tree or bush. The birds hate this material but the individual threads are so fine and fragile they cause no injuries as cotton and, particularly, nylon thread can.

The only absolute protection against birds is provided by small mesh netting carefully draped over permanent or temporary supports. Plastic netting is available in many sizes and is rot-proof and very light in weight.

Both rayon web and netting will, of course, protect the ripening crops as well as the buds in winter.

Aphids Like birds, aphids (the greenfly tribe) always make an appearance sooner or later. If unchecked they can do serious damage to the tree fruits. Although they do little apparent harm to strawberries and raspberries, their sap sucking introduces virus disease which can be fatal. Aphids tend to attack growing points first and their activities frequently cause leaves to curl. Aphid eggs over-winter on the trees.

Woolly aphid

Caterpillars A number, notably the leaf and fruit-eating tortrix caterpillars and those of the winter moths (known as 'loopers') feed on fruit trees, particularly apples, pears, plums and gooseberries. The parent moths lay their eggs in bark crevices between October and March.

Capsids These bugs hatch in spring from eggs over-wintered on the tree. They first eat the leaves and then start on the fruitlets.

Apples are the most common sufferers but currants and gooseberries are attacked by related species.

Sawflies These creatures lay their eggs in the flower of the apple or, less frequently, pear. The larva bores into the fruitlet. It will pass from one to another, spoiling each, and then fall to the ground. A mass of sticky frass (excreta) exudes from the hole where the pest enters the fruit.

Codling Moths This moth lays its eggs in early summer on leaves or fruit, and the grubs bore into the fruit to feed. These are the creatures you may find near the core when you come to eat the apple. Pears are less commonly attacked.

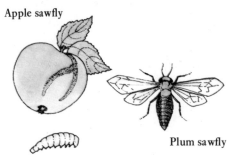
Apple sawfly

Plum sawfly

Spraying Programme There are many other pests to spoil our fruit but the above-mentioned are those which do most damage. A drenching of the dormant trees and bushes in winter with tar-oil will do much to kill over wintering eggs but should only be resorted to about one winter in three because it also kills friendly insects which prey on red spider mites which may then become a menace.

A minimum spray programme starts at the green cluster stage of apples and pears to kill caterpillars and greenfly. Give a second spraying at the pink bud stage (apples) or white bud stage (pears), to deal with capsids, and a third spraying as soon as 90% of the blossom petals have fallen, to kill sawfly and tortrix caterpillars. In mid-June spray to deal with codling moth and tortrix caterpillars, repeating this a fortnight later. Two sprayings are essential for plums–between bud burst and the white bud stage, to control aphids and caterpillars, when the petals have fallen and the fruitlets set, against sawfly.

Further sprayings, of course, must be given if pests are seen. Aphids may appear at any time and if the fruit is shortly to be eaten it is essential to spray with something which is non-toxic to humans–derris, for example.

There are dozens of pesticides on offer in the garden shops. The labels on the bottles or packets will tell you what pests they are intended for and when and how to apply them. The important thing is to follow those directions exactly.

Brown rot

Fruit Diseases

Careful attention at all times to garden hygiene will do much to keep disease to a minimum. Indeed, one cannot 'cure' plant diseases and prevention must always be the policy. Always cut out any dead branches or shoots as soon as you notice them and burn them. Also burn any rotting fruits.

Scab This fungoid disease disfigures the skin of many apples and pears, especially in wetter and more humid districts. It is not likely to cause much harm if you spray regularly with captan at the green cluster, pink (or white) bud and petal fall stages.

Brown Rot Concentric rings of small pustules on ripe or ripening fruit are the outward signs of this fungus. It is very contagious. Burn all infected fruit and wash your hands immediately after touching them.

Silver Leaf This may attack all stone fruits (and sometimes apples) but is particularly virulent on plums. The leaves assume a silvery tinge and the diagnosis is confirmed by a brown stain inside the wood of infected branches or shoots. The disease is spread by spores entering wounds or cuts in the bark, usually between September and May. Do not, therefore, prune in winter and cut out any dead or infected wood in midsummer. Pare all wounds smooth and cover with a protective tree-pruning paint.

Leaf Curl A very common trouble with apricots, peaches and nectarines, causing the young leaves to become puckered and curled. Such leaves become yellow, then reddish and develop 'blisters'. New growth is distorted.

For control, spray with a fungicide such as mancozeb or benomyl in mid to late February and again about a fortnight later, while growth is still dormant and just before the buds swell. Repeat in the autumn, just before leaf-fall.

Codling moth

Virus Diseases Of recent years a number of fruit troubles have been found to be of virus origin. Those most likely to come to the amateur grower's notice are those which attack strawberries and raspberries, drastically reducing crop yields. To avoid virus troubles only buy new stock from a nurseryman who takes part in the Government Certification Scheme, and spray against aphids.

Early symptoms include various leaf markings but these can easily be mistaken for those caused by mineral deficiency. If you see abnormal markings on the leaves of strawberries or raspberries, give first-aid in the shape of foliar watering with a foliar feed containing chelated trace minerals just in case the trouble is due only to a lack of iron or magnesium or other trace element. Never use suspected plants for propagation. If cropping fails, dig up and burn the offenders.

Right: A yellow-fruited variety of the sweet pepper (capsicum)

178

Vegetables and Salads

The Seed Order

When deciding what to grow and when preparing your seed order consider what space you may have in your garden for each crop. Drawing a plan to scale is of help. It can prevent over-ordering. When planning for vegetables take into account the site of your kitchen garden. Few vegetables tolerate shade nor do they grow well if the roots of fruit trees and hedges rob the soil of nourishment. Plan so that your vegetables grow in good soil and where the plants receive lots of sunshine.

Potatoes This is a useful crop to grow if you are starting from scratch. Potato plants are spreading in habit and smother weeds. A potato crop is often referred to as a 'cleaning crop' because the spreading habit and the cultivation carried out can eradicate many weeds.

Cauliflowers are greedy plants. Do not order cauliflower seeds unless you know your soil is very fertile. Planting cauliflowers in poor soil is a waste of time and garden space.

Onions are easy – from sets. A good crop of good-storing, maincrop onions is easily obtained if you start off with sets rather than by sowing seeds.

Vegetable marrow Seed catalogues show varieties as *Bush* or *Trailing*. A bush plant is compact. Trailing plants may be trained on a wire mesh garden fence or on nylon netting.

Cucumbers For the greenhouse you have a choice of varieties which bear male and female flowers or of all-female flowerers. For outdoors there are ridge kinds which roam over the ground and there are trellis cucumbers which need supports.

'Alicante' is outstanding for indoors and outside. 'Sigmabush F_1' is excellent for quality, earliness and yield. Tomatoes not only come in very large, medium and small reds; there are also yellow, gold and striped tomatoes. The yellows and golds are excellent for mixed salads.

Less usual vegetables There are many other vegetables not included in this seed list. You will find something about them under the heading *Fifty Vegetables and Salads*. Few are difficult to grow. If you have room in the garden why not order seeds of a few of them?

Some Useful Kitchen Garden Practices

Intercropping This is of great use in the small kitchen garden. A quick-to-grow and mature vegetable is grown between two rows of a slower-growing vegetable. A good example is radish sown between two rows of peas. Two somewhat slower-growing vegetables may be grown alongside each other.

Thus lettuces may be grown in the vacant spaces left between two rows of peas. A later-to-mature vegetable may be planted in between or alongside rows of another vegetable which will shortly be harvested. Examples: cabbage plants set out among lettuces about to be cut for use; Brussels sprouts set out alongside rows of peas; broccoli planted between rows of dwarf French beans.

Mulching Mulches are soil covers. Their use saves time in watering and weeding. All mulches are laid down when the soil is moist. They prevent a loss of soil moisture by evaporation. They also smother weed seedlings and usually inhibit the growth of more weeds. Most mulches disintegrate slowly and improve the garden soil. One only does not. This is black polythene sheeting.

Garden compost acts as a plant food as well as a mulch. The food is immediately available to plants mulched with compost. It may itself contain weed seeds. Well-rotted farmyard manure is excellent as a mulch for cucumbers, but must not be used as freely as garden compost around most vegetables. Granulated sedge peat contains little plant food but is the neatest mulching material. Lawn mowings are the most commonly used mulching material, but can attract slugs. Autumn leaves should be partially rotted before being applied. Several sheets of newspaper make a useful but unsightly mulch. It is best covered with a little straw. Straw should not be used around seedlings because loose straw may blow over and on to them causing damage. Well-rotted or raw sawdust may be used only if the garden soil is highly fertile. Sawdust robs a soil of some nitrogen during decomposition. Wood shavings are liable to blow around at first. Use them only on very fertile soil. They are rather unattractive to the eye. Black polythene sheeting is ugly when laid in position but is camouflaged rapidly by growing vegetables.

Rotation A rotation of crops is very necessary in the vegetable garden. The main aim of rotation is as a preventive against pests and diseases. If cabbages and their kin are grown regularly in the same patch of ground there is the likelihood of the soil becoming cabbage-sick and infected with club root disease. Should onions be grown often in the same bed an outbreak of onion white rot may occur making the whole garden unfit for onion growing for several years. Where potatoes are frequently grown in the same patch or very near to it a build up of keeled slugs may be expected. A secondary reason for crop rotation has more bearing on a less fertile rather than on a highly fertile soil. The theory is that because all vegetables do not utilize the same

amounts of plant food in the soil it pays to rotate crops each season. The tomato is noted for its need of sufficient potash and lettuce plants need a lot of nitrogen. By rotating beans and peas in the garden the soil in which they grow is enriched with nitrogen.

For the medium-sized garden, the following three-year rotation is suggested.

Potatoes. Give these priority for supplies of manure or compost, to be applied in autumn, winter or early spring.

Second Season: *Cabbages and their kin.* Soil limed if necessary in winter or early spring. Where available apply manure or garden compost later. Alternatively, apply manure during late autumn or winter when digging the garden. Apply lime where necessary in early spring.

Third Season: *Other vegetables.* No manure or garden compost need be applied for most other vegetables apart from such greedy feeders as cucumbers, marrows and sweet corn.

The bounty of autumn from a well-planned kitchen garden

In a larger garden the rotation may be based on a four-year plan. For this the garden is divided into four sections with planting as follows: *Section A:* potatoes. *Section B:* cabbages and their kin. *Section C:* peas and beans. *Section D:* root crops and other vegetables.

For the second season section A is used for root crops and other vegetables, potatoes are grown in section B, cabbages and their kin in section C, and peas and beans in section D. After the fourth season the rotation is complete and section A is used again for the potato crop.
Successional cropping This term covers two different aspects of vegetable growing. Successional sowings of the quick growing radish and fairly quick growing lettuce are made on and off between April and August. Successional planting means that no ground is left vacant throughout the summer. As soon as one crop has been harvested, the soil is prepared at once for a follow-on crop.

Examples of successional cropping

Vegetable	Sown or Planted	Ground Cleared	Sown or Planted
Broad beans Peas (first early) Lettuce Spring cabbage	Late summer and autumn	June	Winter cabbage, Broccoli
Broad beans Peas (first early) Lettuce Potatoes (first early)	March or April	July	French beans, Beet-root, Carrots, Lettuce, Winter radish
Potatoes (second early and maincrop)	March or April	September	Spring cabbage

Right: Plan for a 4-year crop rotation

Certain vegetables have varieties which are earlier to mature than other varieties. The good gardener chooses, if he knows there will be available garden space for them, early and later varieties. There is then a succession of the same vegetable for use over a longer period than there would be were only either an early or a later variety grown.

In addition to choosing early and late varieties a greenhouse, an unheated garden frame or a set of cloches can be put to use to extend the season itself. This leads to earlier than usual spring and summer vegetables and a greater choice of fresh vegetables from the garden in late autumn.

F₁ Hybrid This term frequently appears on seed packets and in seed catalogues. It signifies that the variety is produced by crossing two selected parents. Plants of the two selected parents are grown in separate blocks. Pollen from the male flowers of one parent is transferred to flowers of the second parent. Self-fertilization of the flowers of the second (female) parent is prevented. Seed has to be produced afresh each year and the cross pollination is effected by hand. F₁ hybrid seeds are, therefore, usually dearer. In favour of F₁ hybrids is their outstanding vigour. The plants also have striking uniformity. This fact is worth noting if you exhibit at local or national shows. With ordinary, non-hybrids it is not easy to find several vegetables which are almost identical and just what is wanted for the show bench.

Pelleted Seeds These make sowing easier because the pellets may be handled separately and placed at a distance from each other in the seed drill. This replaces the old method of mixing such small vegetable seeds as carrots and lettuce with sand. Because pelleted seeds

are evenly spaced, each seedling has room for good development. For the gardener there is far less tedious thinning of seedlings to be done.

Moisture must be present for the germination of all vegetable seeds. Where pelleted seeds are sown, even more moisture must be present to encourage the clay of the pellets to disintegrate quickly and permit rapid germination. Unless the soil is already very wet, always soak seed drills with water before sowing pelleted seeds.

Peas

Soil These vegetables need well-drained soil which is not at all acidic. Should a soil test show acidity, apply lime (ground chalk) at the rate indicated as a result of the test, after winter digging. Simply sprinkle the lime over the dug soil. No manure or garden compost need be applied to the sites where peas and beans are to grow. Choose a site which was enriched with manure or garden compost for a different crop grown in the previous summer. Land in which potatoes or winter cabbage was grown is suitable.

Sorts of Peas There are two main groups of garden peas. Hardiest are round-seeded; slightly less hardy but with a reputation for their superior flavour are varieties with wrinkled seeds. These are known as 'marrowfats'. There are many different pea varieties. These are divided into three sections: First Early; Second Early; Maincrop.

When to Sow

FIRST EARLY. *Late October:* in colder parts cover the row with cloches and keep cloches in position until late April. *Early February:*

in large pots in a warm greenhouse. *March:* outdoors or under cloches. Remove cloches in late April. *Early April:* outdoors. *Late June:* outdoors and always keep well-watered in dry weather.

SECOND EARLY. *April:* outdoors.

MAINCROP. *Late April/May:* outdoors.

Some Popular Garden Peas The height given is the average for the plant.

FIRST EARLY: Early Onward 2 ft; Feltham First 1½ ft; Gradus 3 ft; Hurst Beagle 1½ ft; Kelvedon Viscount 2 ft; Kelvedon Wonder (q.f.) 1½ ft; Little Marvel (q.f.) 1¼ ft; Meteor 1½ ft; Progress 1½ ft; Sleaford Phoenix 1½ ft; Sweetness 3 ft; Winfrida 2 ft.

SECOND EARLY: Achievement 5 ft; Giant Stride 2 ft; Hurst Green Shaft 2½ ft; Kelvedon Climax 2½ ft; Kelvedon Monarch (q.f.) (syn. Victoria Freezer) 2½ ft; Miracle (q.f.) 4½ ft; Onward (q.f.) 2 ft; Shasta (q.f.) 2½ ft; Show Perfection (q.f.) 5 ft.

MAINCROP: Alderman 5 ft; Dwarf Greensleeves 3 ft; Giant Stride 2½ ft; Lincoln 2 ft; Lord Chancellor 3 ft; Rentpayer 2 ft; Senator 3 ft; Trio (q.f.) 2½ ft.

q.f.=Suitable for the quick-freeze, should you have a surplus.

How to Sow Garden peas are sown where the plants are to grow. Before sowing rake the soil surface level, removing all large stones and clods. A popular way of sowing peas is to take out an 8-in. wide furrow, using a draw hoe. Use a garden line to have a straight row and make the furrow no more than 1 in. deep in heavier soils; 2 in. deep, but no more, in light soils. Should the soil not be wet, flood the furrow with water. Start sowing after the water has drained away. Pea seeds are quite large. Sprinkle them fairly evenly on to the flat bottom of the furrow so that

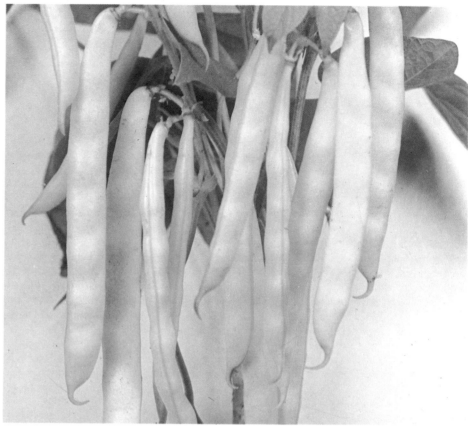

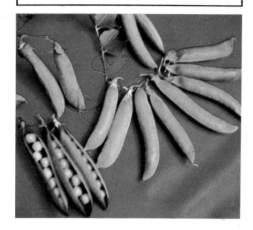

Successional sowing chart

Vegetable	When sown or planted	Where sown or planted	Season of Use
Broad beans	November	In pots in unheated greenhouse, in pots in a cold frame, under cloches, in the open.	Late May/June
	January	Under cloches	June
	March/early April	In the open	July
French beans	April	In pots or boxes in slightly heated or unheated greenhouse, under cloches	July/August
	May	Outdoors	August
	Late June/early July	Outdoors	September/October
Runner beans	April	In pots or boxes in slightly heated or unheated greenhouse, under cloches	Late July/August and September
	May	Outdoors	August and September
	Early June	Outdoors	Late August to mid-October
Peas (first early)	February	Under cloches	Mid-June and July
	March or early April	Open garden	Late June and July
	Late June	Outdoors	October
(second early)	Late April	Outdoors	July
(maincrop)	Mid-May	Outdoors	August
Cabbage (spring)	Early August	Outdoors	April to July
(summer)	March	Under cloches	Late June to August
	April	Outdoors	Mid-July to September
(autumn)	April	Outdoors	September to November
(winter)	April	Outdoors	November to February
Lettuce	February	Heated greenhouse for planting under cloches in mid-March	May
	March	Under cloches	June
	April	Outdoors	July
	May	Outdoors	August
	June	Outdoors	September
	July	Outdoors	September to October
	August	Outdoors for cloching in late September	November and December
Potatoes (first early)	March/April	Outdoors	Mid-June to August
(second early)	March/April	Outdoors	July to August
(maincrop)	March/April	Outdoors	Dig and store for winter use in September

each seed is about 2½ in. from the next. After sowing use a rake to draw soil over the seeds and to fill the furrow at the same time gently firming the soil.

Some birds will take pea seeds and will hunt for them after they have been sown; other birds peck at pea seedlings. Cloches give automatic protection against bird attacks. For open garden sowings, several strands of black cotton stretched around and over the rows immediately after sowing provide full protection. Secure the cotton to short bamboo canes on either side of the rows.

A rough, ready and fairly accurate guide to the distance between rows is to space them to the height of the variety.

Do not waste large spaces between pea rows; grow lettuces or various members of the cabbage tribe in them.

Cultivation Where black cotton is used to prevent bird damage the cotton also serves as an excellent support for short growing (dwarf) peas. For varieties growing taller than 3 ft. augment the black cotton with brushwood or with strings tied to tall canes. Hoe between rows to prevent weeds. Pull out weeds growing in the rows by hand when the pea plants are young. In dry weather water often and water well. Pea plants which are short of water are prone to several disorders. The worst pest of garden peas is the pea moth. This is attracted to pea plants weakened by lack of moisture at the roots. Mulching pea rows with straw can reduce the amount of watering necessary in hot, dry summer weather.

Pick pods before they are drum-tight and cook the peas as soon as possible. Peas quickly lose their sugary flavour after harvesting. Pick peas regularly.

 Beans

Broad Bean This is the only hardy garden bean. It is still common to place broad bean varieties into two groups—*Windsors* and *Longpods*. But newer varieties often have mixed ancestry. A true Windsor has short pods containing about four large seeds. A Longpod has longer pods with more but smaller seeds. Most broad beans are tall growers. There is one true dwarf—'The Sutton'.

When to Sow *November*: give cloche protection in colder areas, elsewhere protect rows with small mesh chicken wire or with small mesh nylon netting to prevent birds from pecking seedlings.

February: sow a single seed in each 3½-in. pot in a warm greenhouse. Peat pots are excellent for this sowing. Set plants outdoors in April—preferably with cloche protection.

March/early April: outdoors where plants are to grow.

Some Popular Broad Beans Aquadulce; Aquadulce Claudia; Conqueror (syns. Colossal and Exhibition Longpod); Express; Giant Windsor (syn. Giant Four Seeded White Windsor); Imperial Green Longpod; Imperial White Longpod; Imperial White Windsor; Masterpiece Green Longpod; The Sutton; Unrivalled Green Windsor (syn. Giant Four Seeded Green Windsor).

How to Sow Use a draw hoe to make an 8-in. wide, 1½–2 in. deep furrow. Sow seeds in a double staggered way (see diagram) at 9 in. apart. Sow a few seeds quite close together at the end of the row; the seedlings may come in handy should any seeds in the row fail to germinate. The dwarf 'The Sutton' needs less space and seeds may be sown 6 in. apart. Leave 2½–3 ft. between rows of tall varieties and 18 in. between rows of 'The Sutton'.

Pot-raised plants should be set at these distances at planting out time.

Cultivation Keep the plants free from weeds by hoeing. Water often and generously in warm, dry weather. Bean plants, particularly broad beans, are prone to an attack of black bean aphis. This pest favours bean plants which are short of moisture.

As well as watering when necessary, thwart black bean aphis by:

(1) Sowing in late autumn or in February; early sowings usually miss an aphis attack.

(2) Pinching out the growing point as soon as flowers have set and small pods are forming.

(3) Cutting off all tender young shoots around the base of plant.

(4) Spraying with derris, pyrethrum or malathion in May before aphids appear.

Continue spraying weekly. Spray in the late evening so that bees are not harmed. Do not spray at all if you see ladybird larvae devouring the aphids.

(5) Destroying any weeds which harbour the aphis. Docks and fat hen are often infested with it.

In very exposed areas it helps to give tall growers supports of some kind so that plants are not blown down when cropping.

Harvest broad beans when the pods are well filled but before the seeds inside them are leathery and tough.

French Beans There are two forms—dwarf bush and climbing. The bush form is the most popular. Although the pods of most varieties are green some bear yellow or mauve pods.

When to Sow At any time between late April and early June. It is advisable to prewarm the soil with cloches if sowing in April. Just leave cloches in position over the soil for a week or so. Then sow and cover with cloches. Keep cloches in position for as long as possible.

Seeds may also be sown in small pots in a warm greenhouse during April. The plants must not be set out in the open garden until all risk of a late spring frost has passed.

Some Popular French Beans

DWARF BUSH: Canadian Wonder; Canadian Marvel; Chevrier Vert; Glamis; Cordon; Kinghorn Waxpod; Mont D'Or Golden Butter; Pencil Pod Black Wax; Royalty; Sprite; The Prince.

CLIMBING: Blue Lake White Seeded; Earliest of All; Garrafal Oro; Veitch's Climbing (syn. Guernsey Runner); Violet Podded Stringless.

How to Sow Dwarf beans are sown 6 in. apart and 2 in. deep in drills 18 in. apart. Sow climbing kinds allowing 6 in. between each seed in a single row.

Set out pot-raised plants at these distances. Leave 3 ft. between double rows of dwarf beans; 5 ft between rows of climbers.

Cultivation Keep down weeds and water often and well in dry weather from late May onwards. Healthy plants are seldom attacked by black bean aphis. Spray with derris, pyrethrum or malathion should this pest appear on the undersides of the leaves. If dwarf plants topple under the weight of crop push brushwood alongside the plants to support them. Alternatively, provide strings tied to short bamboo canes. Climbing French beans attain a height of about 4 ft. Tall brushwood was the traditional form of supports. Plastic garden mesh or wire mesh or plastic mesh fencing are modern supports.

Harvest French beans before the pods toughen. Many older varieties have pods which tend to be stringy when they age. Newer varieties such as 'Glamis' are stringless. Pick pods often and when of full size. Cropping continues over a period of about six weeks.

Runner Beans Most runner beans bear scarlet flowers; a few have white flowers and the seeds are white. The flowers of 'Painted Lady' are red and white.

When to Sow Sow between early May and mid June in the open garden. A sowing in April may be made under cloches. Seeds may also be sown in pots in a warm greenhouse during April. The tender plants must not be set out in the open garden until all danger of frost has passed.

Some Popular Runner Beans Achievement; Best of All (syn. Streamline); Crusader; Czar; Enorma; Fry; Hammond's Dwarf Scarlet; Hammond's Dwarf White; Kelvedon Marvel (syn. Kelvedon Wonder); Mergoles; Prizetaker (syn. Goliath); Painted Lady; Prizewinner; Red Knight; Scarlet Emperor; White Achievement; White Emergo (syn. Erecta).

How to Sow The two dwarf 'runner' beans—'Hammond's Dwarf Scarlet' and 'Hammond's Dwarf White'—are sown and cultivated as dwarf French beans.

Other varieties may be grown in two different ways. The best method is to provide the plants with tall supports. These may be traditional bean poles or bean netting. Plastic or wire fencing is also very suitable. In very windy gardens runner beans may be grown as dwarfed plants.

Where plants are to have supports sow seeds at from 6–8 in. alongside them in a 1½–2 in. narrow furrow made with a draw hoe. If plants are to be dwarfed sow as for broad beans. Leave from 4–5 ft. between rows of runner beans. Pot-raised plants should be set out at these distances.

Cultivation Hoe to prevent weeds and water well and often in dry weather. Spray with derris, pyrethrum or malathion should black bean aphis show on the stems or on the undersides of the leaves. Permit plants on supports to reach the top of them. Then pinch out the growing point at the top of each plant.

Plants to be grown dwarfed are pinched back by a few inches when the plants are 1 ft. or so high. Lots of side growths are then made. Nip these back occasionally until the row of bean plants resembles a low, bushy hedge. If dwarfed plants topple, support them with brushwood or with strings tied to bamboo canes.

Soil which is enriched with manure or garden compost periodically is suitable. Where the soil is not highly fertile plants may be fed with very weak liquid manure water. Alternatively, side dress the rows with organic fertilizers.

Harvest pods often and when they are young and tender. Never allow seeds inside the pods to plump up. Cropping should continue for two months.

Salads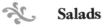

Lettuce There are three principal types lettuce: cabbage, cos and loose leaf. Cabbage lettuces are divided into two groups: *Butterhead*, e.g. 'Unrivalled', 'May King'. *Crisphead*, e.g. 'Webb's Wonderful', 'Windermere'.

Sowing The sowing times are linked closely with varieties. The table shows when to sow for successional crops.

Sow fairly thickly in 1-in. deep drills, 9 in. apart if all the seedlings are to be dug up and the stronger plants transplanted. If the seedlings are to be thinned to leave strong plants at 1 ft. apart in the row, rows should be 1 ft. apart. Sow pelleted seeds 1 in. apart. Keep down weeds and water well in dry weather. Cos make quicker, tighter hearts if tied loosely with string or raffia just when hearting starts.

When to sow	Where to sow	When to transplant	Suggested varieties	When to harvest
Feb/Mar	frames or cloches	April under cloches	Unrivalled; Premier	May and June
Early April	cloches or open garden	late April or early May	Unrivalled	late June and July
Mid to late April	open garden	mid to late May	Webbs Wonderful; Little Gem	July
May	open garden where the plants are to grow	late May or early June	Little Gem; Buttercrunch; Continuity	July and August
June/July	open garden where plants are to grow	July or August	Windermere; Continuity; Avondefiance; Little Gem	August and September
Early August	open garden where plants are to grow	do not transplant	Avondefiance; Continuity; Salad Bowl	September and October
Mid August	open garden. Give cloche cover in early October	do not transplant	Avondefiance; Unrivalled	November
Late August	open garden	late September. Give cloche cover in October in colder areas	Imperial Winter (syn. Winter Crop); Valdor	late April and May
Mid October	unheated or slightly heated greenhouse	thin seedlings, do not transplant	Kloek	April

Above: 'Crusader' is a good variety of runner bean. It produces excellent pods for exhibition as well as for culinary purposes. *Above right:* Cos lettuces produce crisper leaves and whiter hearts if the plants are tied with soft string or raffia as they develop. *Right:* There are various ways of growing and training runner beans. The 'standard' method (1) consists in placing bean 'poles' on each side of a double row of beans. The same principle is employed in (2) where the plants are grown up strings, or netting. Where space in the vegetable garden is limited, the plants may be grown up a 'wigwam' (3) of strings or stakes, surrounding a central support

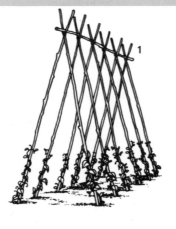

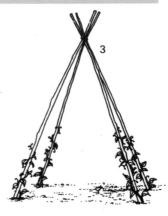

Radishes Those grown for summer salads vary in shape from round, 'tankard' and long. Varieties are: 'Scarlet Globe', round; 'French Breakfast', tankard; and 'Long White Icicle', long. Autumn/winter radishes are large; 'China Rose' and 'Black Spanish' are grated for salad use.

Sowing Sow in late March; for sowing under cloches choose a variety like 'Saxerre'. For open ground sowings between late March and late July all summer varieties are suitable. Sow winter radish in mid to late July. Sow in fairly fertile soil, keep the plants moist and thin seedlings to 1 in. apart each way. Sow the large seeds of winter radishes 1 in. apart in 1 in. deep seed drills. Thin seedlings to 8 in. apart. Pull summer radishes as soon as some are sufficiently large for use. Pull winter radishes for use in autumn. Harvest those remaining in late October. Cut back the foliage to an inch from the radish and store the roots in sand in a shed or garage.

Three modern ways of growing tomatoes in the greenhouse. *Left:* The 'Tom-Bag' system, in which a single plant is grown in each section of the bag of compost. *Centre:* The 'ring culture' method, in which the plants are grown in whalehide, plastic or clay 'rings'. *Right:* Plants grown in straw bales, previously partially rotted down. *Below right:* Tomato 'Outdoor Girl' and various kinds of round radishes

Tomatoes These vary very much in shape and size. 'Big Boy' averages from 8–12 oz. each; 'Small Fry' and 'Gardener's Delight' measure no more than 1 in. in diameter. Most varieties produce tomatoes weighing 8 or 9 to the pound. Red is the usual colour; white is rare, but yellow tomatoes, e.g. 'Tangella', are liked by some gardeners. 'Tigerella' is a red tomato with yellow striping.

Most standard varieties like Alicante are grown as single cordons; the self-stopping Sleaford Abundance, the Amateur and other dwarf bush types are primarily suited for outdoor growing. Golden Sunrise, yellow, Alicante and Outdoor Girl, both red, are standard types for indoor or outdoor cultivation.

Sowing Sow seeds in the greenhouse in late February or March in a temperature of 65°F (18°C). After germination maintain day temperatures of 60°F (15°C), dropping a few degrees lower at night. In the south of England sow seeds in an unheated greenhouse in early April. Slight heat is needed elsewhere. For plants to be moved into the garden later, sow in early April.

Sow seeds about 1 in. apart in JI seed compost or soilless compost and cover with more compost. Firm gently, water thoroughly and cover with a sheet of glass and lay a sheet of brown paper over it. Turn the glass daily to rid it of excess moisture. As soon as germination is seen, remove the glass and paper. Two to three weeks later pot the seedlings into 3½-in. pots. Always hold seedlings by a seed leaf, never by the stem. A night temperature of at least 56°F (13°C) is best.

In the greenhouse border space the plants 18 in. apart and tie them as they grow to stout bamboo canes. The soil should be clean, well drained and enriched with partially-rotted strawy manure or peat. Plants must never be short of water. Good ventilation is necessary. Side shoots must be pinched out frequently, when they are small. When the plants have attained their full height, nip out the growing point.

There are four other ways of growing tomatoes in a greenhouse:

1. IN POTS Plants may be grown successfully in large pots filled with a suitable compost, housed on the greenhouse staging.

2. RING CULTURE Soil in the borders is removed to a depth of 6in. and replaced by an aggregate (sieved clinker, ash or screened, washed, coarse gravel). Plants are grown in clay, plastic or whalehide 'rings', which allow the roots to grow easily into the aggregate.

3. STRAW BALE A 56 lb. bale of wheat straw will take two tomato plants. Lay bales in position on the greenhouse border and sprinkle a gallon of water on to each bale every day for 12 days. Then apply to each bale: 1 lb. of Nitro-chalk, 1 lb. of potassium nitrate, ½ lb. of triple superphosphate of lime, ¼ lb. of magnesium sulphate (Epsom salts), 3 oz. of sulphate of iron. Water these chemicals in well. Fermentation of the straw occurs in a heated greenhouse and plants are set out in the fermenting straw when the temperature within the bales falls to 100°F (37°C).

4. THE TOM-BAG SYSTEM Bags filled with a suitable compost are laid down and panels of the bag are removed and one plant is set in each of the spacings. Using any of these methods it is necessary to feed with a tomato fertilizer.

Although many varieties are capable of ripening fruits in gardens of Southern England, gardeners elsewhere should choose a hardy variety such as 'Outdoor Girl' or 'The Amateur'. Harden off plants before moving them from a greenhouse to the open garden. Plants to be grown under cloches may be moved directly from the greenhouse to where they are to grow. Plant standard tomatoes 15 in. apart with 30 in. between rows and push a bamboo cane alongside each one or erect a simple wire trellis to which plants may be tied periodically. Allow bush plants 2 sq. ft. of soil surface; no staking is necessary Keep plants watered in dry weather, hoe to keep down weeds, de-shoot standard plants and stop them during the first week of August by pinching out the growing point.

Always leave tomatoes on the plants until they are really ripe. Pick unripe fruits on outdoor plants in late September; the larger fruits will ripen quickly in a warm room indoors. Small green tomatoes are excellent for chutney.

Tomato leaf mould, a fungal disease, is common on greenhouse tomato plants. Yellowish spots appear on the leaves with a pale greyish mould on the underside of the leaves. The foliage dies and the disease passes from plant to plant rapidly. Hot, moist conditions favour the disease. Take care not to over-water, and provide ample ventilation. Never water in the evening. Pick off and burn infected leaves. If the outbreak is severe spray with a copper-based fungicide. Many new varieties resist this disease.

Tomato plants can suffer from several different disorders. Almost always they are caused by faulty cultivation. Should flowers fall without fruits setting it may be that the plants are not receiving sufficient water. Over-watering or irregular watering are two possible causes of blossom end rot, which shows as a dark green patch at the blossom end of the fruit. The patch changes to brown or black and has a leathery texture. If the greenhouse temperature is very high but the soil itself is on the cold side the tomatoes may not ripen well, a condition known as blotchy ripening. Very strong sunlight can lead to a disorder known as greenback. The stalk end stays green or yellow but the rest of the tomato ripens well. Some varieties never suffer from greenback. These are catalogued as 'greenback-free'. Potato blight can attack outdoor-grown tomato plants, more often in the wetter, western half of Britain. If, because of blight, the growing of outdoor tomatoes is difficult, be prepared to spray regularly from July to September with Bordeaux mixture or a copper-based fungicide.

Cucumber Cucumbers grown in the greenhouse or frame are tender plants. There are varieties which bear both male and female flowers and new, all-female flowering kinds. Older, ridge sorts bear short cucumbers and the plants roam over the ground. Some newer varieties need a trellis to which plants may be tied; these are very suited to unheated greenhouses in the midlands and north.

Cucumber Varieties:

1. *Suitable for heated and unheated greenhouses* (F)=all-female flowerer: 'Butcher's Disease-resisting'; 'Conqueror'; 'Famdan' (F_1) (F); 'Femspot' (F_1) (F); 'Improved Telegraph'; 'Landora' (F_1) (F); 'Pepinex 69' (F_1) (F); 'Rocket' (F_1).

2. *Suitable for the unheated frame in warmer areas*: 'Conqueror'; 'Improved Telegraph'.

3. *Suitable for the unheated frame or for outdoors – ridge sorts*: 'Burpee Hybrid' (F_1); 'Crystal Apple'; 'Long Green Ridge'; 'Nadir' (F_1).

4. *Suitable for the unheated greenhouse in most parts and for the open garden in the south – trellis sorts*: 'Chinese Long Green'.

5. *Suitable for growing on a windowsill indoors*: 'Fembaby' (F_1).

Sowing For greenhouse cultivation sow in late March. Otherwise, wait until late April. A temperature of 75°F (24°C) is needed for rapid germination. Sow two seeds in a $3\frac{1}{2}$-in. pot. Later pinch off the weaker seedling.

The border soil must drain well and should be rich in organic matter. A framework of wires or of canes and wires is needed, to which plants may be tied. Set out plants 2 ft. apart and do not plant deeply. Stop the plants when they reach the top of the supports. Prevent fruits from setting on the main stems by pinching off flower buds. Tie side shoots to horizontal wires and prune back these shoots to the second leaf beyond the first small cucumber on each of them. Cucumber plants like a warm, moist atmo-sphere so keep plants well watered and spray with tepid water each evening in hot, sunny weather. In late July mulch the bed with a 1-in. layer of garden compost or strawy horse manure.

Frame Cultivation When plants have made four true leaves pinch out the growing point. As side shoots develop pinch these out too, at four leaves. Stop all fruit-bearing shoots at one leaf beyond each swelling cucumber and stop main lateral shoots when they reach the sides of the frame.

Ridge Cucumbers Plant these in early June, 18 in. apart. When plants have made seven leaves nip out the central growing point to induce branching.

Trellis Cucumbers Plant 1 ft. apart alongside a trellis 4–6 ft. high; a wire mesh garden fence or bean netting is suitable. Pinch out growing points of plants when they reach the top of the supports. Water often in dry weather.

The Onion Family

Onions do best in a medium loam or reasonably light soil, provided that it does not dry out excessively.

Onions from Sets An easy way of growing maincrop onions is by planting 'sets' (small immature onions) during the second half of March. After digging rake the site level and press or trowel plant the sets in loose soil 9 in. apart with 1 ft. between rows.

Onions from Seed In late August sow seeds thickly in a 1-in. drill. It pays to protect with cloches from October to early March. Dig up all the young plants in March and transplant them 9 in. apart in good rich soil. Do not plant deeply. Use 'Kaizuka Extra Early' and 'Express Yellow' for August sowing. Alternatively, in late March/early April sow seeds fairly thickly in 1-in. deep drills, 1 ft. apart.

Varieties 'Ailsa Craig'; 'A.1'; 'Autumn Queen'; 'Bedfordshire Champion'; 'Big Ben'; 'Cranston's Excelsior'; 'Express Yellow'; 'Kaizuka Extra Early'; 'Rijnsburger Yellow Globe'; 'Solidity'; 'Stuttgart Giant'; 'Unwins Reliance'; 'Wijbo'.

Hoe and hand weed. Start thinning spring sown seedlings in June and continue doing so until mid-July. Plants left to bulb up should be around 9 in. apart.

The maggots of the onion fly burrow into young onions. The foliage withers and the plants die. Autumn-sown onions and those grown from sets are unlikely to be affected, spring-sown seedlings are likely to be damaged in June and July. Female onion flies find onion plants by their odour. Prevent broken roots and foliage during thinning by watering beforehand if the soil is dry. Bury unwanted thinnings in the compost heap or the ground. Avoid breaking onion foliage when hoeing.

Hoe occasionally to keep down weeds. Water generously in dry weather. Liquid feeds may be given weekly when bulbs are swelling, but over-feeding will lead to onions which will not store well.

When in August the foliage yellows and topples over on to the soil, stop watering and feeding. When the foliage is brown, dry and brittle, just lift the onions off the ground. Hang the onions in bunches in full sun for a week when they are quite dry, rub off dead roots, dry soil and very loose scales. Store in a cold place such as an unheated greenhouse, a garden shed or a garage, in trays or, better still, roped.

Salad Onions Although thinnings of spring-sown onions are of use in early summer salads, 'White Lisbon' is grown solely for salad use. Sow seeds in August or March, quite thickly. Use thinnings as soon as they are large enough.

Pickling Onions (Shallots) These are generally grown for pickling, although they may be used in soups and stews. As soon as the soil dries somewhat in March, push bulbs into it, 9 in. apart, in rows 1 ft. apart. Keep the rows weed free. Lft the clumps in July, separate the bulbs and spread them out to dry. Store in a cool place. There are also brown-skinned and white-skinned ('Paris', syn. 'Paris Silver Skin') onions for pickling. Sow seeds quite thickly in March in a $\frac{1}{2}$-in. deep drill. Keep down weeds and dig the crop when the foliage withers.

Garlic Plant 'cloves' (segments of garlic bulbs) 6 in. apart, 1 in. deep in a sunny site during February or March. Dig the crop when the foliage dies. Hang clusters of bulbs to dry before storing them in string nets.

Leeks Sow seeds late March/early April; keep down weeds and water well in dry weather. Dig up all the seedlings in late June and replant at once. Use a dibber to make holes 4 in. deep about 8 in. apart in rows 1 ft. apart. Drop a seedling into each hole and pour in a little water. Weed when necessary. Dig leeks for use at any time between November and late April.

For Tree Onion and Welsh Onion see Fifty Vegetables and Salads; Chives see Herbs.

Cabbage Family; Root Vegetables; Marrows

These do best in fertile, well-drained, alkaline soil. On acid soils spread lime at from ½–1 lb. per sq. yd., after the ground has been dug in winter or early spring. However, over-liming is dangerous; sufficient lime is added to most soils when garden compost is dug in or spread on to them; it is useful to sprinkle a little lime over layers of waste when a compost heap is being built. In a kitchen garden rotation (see Some Useful Kitchen Garden Practices) the plot where cabbages etc., are to be grown should be dressed with manure or garden compost.

Sow brassica seeds in a special bed of fertile soil, which, after it has been dug, should be raked level and firmed with the feet. Make 1-in. deep seed drills, 8 in. apart. If the soil is dry, fill the seed drills with water; allow the water to drain away before sowing fairly thickly. The seedlings will not remain in the bed for very long so that the ill effects of overcrowding will be minimal.

Varieties

Brussels Sprouts: 'Peer Gynt' (F_1); 'Citadel' (F_1); 'Zid' (F_1); 'Achilles' (F_1); 'Rampart' (F_1); 'Predora' (F_1); 'Fortress' (F_1).
Cabbage (Summer): 'Babyhead'; 'Grey-hound'; 'Primata' (F_1); 'Princess' (syn. 'JuneStar')(F_1); 'GoldenAcre'(syn.'Primo').
Cabbage (Autumn): 'Autumn Monarch' (F_1); 'Autumn Pride' (F_1).
Cabbage (Winter): 'Christmas Drumhead'; 'January King'; 'Winter Monarch' (F_1).
Cabbage (Spring): 'April'; 'Harbinger'.
Cabbage (Savoy for Winter): 'Ormskirk–Ormskirk Late'; 'Best Of All'.
Cauliflower (Spring): 'All the Year Round'; 'Mechelse–Arcturus'.
Cauliflower (Summer): 'All the Year Round'.
Cauliflower (Autumn): 'Canberra'.
Cauliflower Broccoli: 'English Winter–Reading Giant'.
Sprouting Broccoli: Calabrese, 'Green Comet' (F_1). Purple Sprouting Broccoli. White Sprouting Broccoli.
Kale 'Pentland Brig'

Weed and water when necessary. In a frame or beneath clothes you may have to water frequently. Remove the frame light and take off cloches in May.

Brassica plants do best in firm fertile soil. The evening before transplanting water the seed bed well if it is dry.

Make holes with a dibber. If the soil is dry fill the holes with water and allow it to soak away. Pull seedlings out of the seed bed, choosing sturdy, straight specimens. Lower a plant into each hole until the lowest leaf is level with the surrounding soil. Push the dibber into the ground alongside, to press soil against the root and stem of the plant. Plant cauliflowers only to the depth at which the seedling was growing in the seed bed.

Cabbage root maggot is a fairly common pest. Eggs are laid alongside brassica plants often after they have been transplanted. The maggots bore into the roots. Plants are dwarfed or may wilt and usually die. The female flies find the plants by sense of smell. The scent from newly-planted brassica seedlings can be masked by setting out plants in firm ground mulched with garden compost.

Club root is a common and serious disease. Affected plants make poor growth and are often stunted, the roots are badly swollen and may smell nasty. Badly drained and acid soils favour the fungus. Regular heavy dressings of compost lower soil acidity and improve drainage. Dressing with lime also counteracts acidity.

Hoe and water often; plants weakened by drought are particularly prone to attack by caterpillars of the cabbage moth and cabbage white butterflies. Strong, healthy brassica plants may be visited by cabbage white butterflies and by the cabbage moth. They

are rarely a nuisance to plants making good, steady growth. If you spot any small caterpillars, pick them off. Spray with a weak solution of table salt and water. The best preventive measure is to ensure that the soil is fertile and that plants are never short of water in summer.

Start picking Brussels sprouts near the base of the stem in late autumn/early winter. Continue harvesting until the top of the stem is reached. Cut tops of the plant in February and March for use as 'Spring greens'.

Harvest cabbages when they are firm and tight. Cut cauliflowers and cauliflower broccoli when heads are well formed and snowy white.

Pick side shoots of sprouting broccoli in winter and spring. Finally cut and use the central head, a loose collection of shoots. Cut the central, loose heads of kale for use in late winter or early spring. Side shoots will develop; pick these when they are still young and tender.

Calabrese This appears in catalogues as 'Green Sprouting Broccoli', 'Italian Sprouting Broccoli' or simply as 'Calabrese'. It is a winter/autumn vegetable. Sow in April and set out plants in June. A green central head will form on each plant in August or September. Cut and use this as cauliflower. Thick side shoots are then produced; these may be cooked as asparagus, after removing the leaves and peeling the stems.

Red Cabbage This is often grown for pickling. Sow seeds in August and give the seedlings cloche protection until they are planted out at 18 in. apart each way in late March/early April. Seeds may also be sown in early spring and seedlings transplanted in June.

Transplanting dates and distances

Vegetable	Date	Between rows Inches	Between plants in the rows Inches
Brussels Sprouts	May/June	30	30
Cabbage—summer	May/June	15–18	15–18
autumn, winter	June		
spring	September/October		
Cauliflower—spring	Move plants to cold frame in October. Transplant to final positions in spring.	18–24	18
summer, autumn	June		
Cauliflower Broccoli (Winter Cauliflower)	June	24–30	18–24
Sprouting Broccoli	June/July	24–30	18–24
Kale (Borecole)	June/July	24–30	18–24

When to sow	Cloche or cold frame	Outdoors
Brussels Sprouts	March	early April
Cabbage—early summer	March	early April
late summer	–	mid April
autumn	–	mid April
winter	–	mid April
spring	–	late July/ early August
Cauliflower—spring	–	August*
summer	–	early April
autumn	–	mid April/May
Cauliflower Broccoli	–	mid April
Sprouting Broccoli	–	mid April
Kale	–	mid April/May

*Overwinter plants in cold frame or cloches.

Far left: Cabbage 'Primata', a F₁ hybrid variety
Centre left: Club root of brassicas
Left: a clean root. *Right*: a root affected by club root disease. *Left*: Planting brassica seedlings. Use a dibber to make the hole, then push the dibber into the soil by the side of the seedling to firm it. *Above*: A red cabbage
Below: Purple sprouting broccoli
Right: Cabbage 'June Star', a F₁ hybrid

Root Vegetables

Root vegetables do well in fertile garden soil but there should be no hard band of gravel or clay beneath the top spit nor should the top soil contain a high percentage of large stones. Often some deep digging is necessary to prepare a garden soil initially for first-class root vegetables. No manure or garden compost should be applied to spots in the garden where root crops are to be grown that season. Grow root crops in soil to which manure or garden compost was applied for a different crop in the previous season. Where peas and beans or cabbage were grown are suitable sites for root crops. After the digging of the whole kitchen garden in winter or early spring just rake level and remove any large stones before sowing root vegetables.

Beetroot Beets may be round, cylindrical or long. Quick-to-mature beets for summer salads are round. 'Detroit' is an example. Newer is 'Boltardy'. 'Cheltenham Green Top' may be grown for summer beet and also for storing. Long beets are not now in favour among gardeners. Beetroot is usually deep red in colour. Very new to Britain is 'Burpee's Golden' with orange red skin and yellow flesh.

Sowing Beet seedlings are noted for 'bolting' if seed is sown too early. The introduction of 'Boltardy' now permits seed to be sown as early as the first half of April. In the north cloches come in handy for this early sowing. Other beets should not be sown until the second half of April or early May. Sowings of a quick maturing round beet may be sown again in late May and in June.

Sow seeds thinly in 1-in. deep seed drills spaced at 12 in. apart. If you sow under cloches leave only 8 in. between rows.

Hoe between rows to keep down weeds. If you have sown too thickly pull out some seedlings when the soil is wet. Do not thin seedlings too drastically. Pull young beets for summer salads in July just as soon as they are large enough to cook. Continue to pull roots as and when wanted in the kitchen.

Lift beet for storing during October. Twist off the foliage and rub off any dry soil adhering to the roots. Store, sandwich fashion, in dry sand or peat. Apple and orange boxes are useful storage containers. House them in a cool but frost-free place.

Carrots For summer use a quick-to-mature stump-rooted carrot such as 'Amsterdam Forcing' which is popular. The best-known maincrop is 'James Scarlet Intermediate', but stump-rooted 'Scarla' seems even better.

Varieties such as 'Early Scarlet Horn', 'Amsterdam Forcing' and 'Early Nantes' may be sown in a frame or under cloches in March. Pre-warm the soil by having the light on the frame and cloches in position for a week or so before you sow. These early varieties may be sown outdoors during April, May and June. Sow maincrop carrots in early May.

If you are sowing in a frame or under cloches make 1-in. deep seed drills at 6 in.

apart. In the open garden allow 12 in. between rows. Do not sow too thickly. Mixing the small seeds with some dry sand or dry soil prevents a thick sowing. Carrot seeds are also offered in pellet form. Pellets can be sown at $\frac{1}{2}$–1 in. apart. When sowing pelleted seeds the soil of the seed drill must always be quite wet. Flood seed drills with water should the soil be dry. Sow when the water has drained away.

Prevent weeds from developing by hoeing. Pull young carrots for use as soon as they are large enough. Maincrop carrots are thinned in July. Spread this job over several weeks, thinning so that finally carrots are about 4 in. apart.

Carrot flies can cause much damage. The female flies are guided to carrots by the odour emitted from the foliage. Eggs are laid and the maggots tunnel into the roots. The foliage yellows and plants die. To prevent a strong carrot smell attracting the female flies always thin carrots when the ground is moist, try not to break any carrot foliage when hoeing or thinning and always bury young foliage inside a compost heap or in a hole in the ground.

Dig carrots on a dry day in October. Cut back the foliage to 1 in. from the crown of each carrot. Store carrots in a pit or in boxes sandwich-fashion between damp sand. Keep boxes in a cool place such as an out-house, shed or garage.

Parsnip Most gardeners favour a long rooted parsnip such as 'Hollow Crown Improved' and 'Tender and True' (Sutton's). Shallow-rooted sorts like 'White Gem' are better for shallow soils. The new 'Avonresister' has short, thick roots.

Sowing Parsnip seed may be sown as soon as the soil is workable in March or in April. Sow fairly thinly in 1-in. deep seed drills

spaced at 12 in. apart. Pelleted seed is on offer. Sow pellets at 1 in. apart.

Hoe to keep down weeds. Thin parsnip seedlings twice, first in April, to leave seedlings at about 1 in. apart and again in late June when each plant left to grow on should be about 8 in. from its neighbours in the row.

Dig parsnips for use as and when wanted during winter and early spring. Any parsnips still in the ground in March may be dug up and heeled in a trench.

Parsnip canker is a common physiological disorder of parsnips, not a disease. Brown patches occur on the parsnip skin. A bad attack leads to rot. If this is your problem in parsnip growing change to 'Tender and True' or 'Avonresister'. Both show resistance to canker.

Swede 'Purple-Top' is a popular swede. A new variety noted for resistance to club root (see The Cabbage Tribe) is 'Marian'. Sow seed in early June.

Sowing Sow thinly in 1-in. deep drills spaced at 18 in. apart. Hoe to prevent weeds from developing. Thin seedlings to 1 ft. apart.

Pull swedes for use in autumn/early winter. Any swedes not used by Christmas should be pulled up and stored in the same way as carrots.

Turnip There are two main classes. Early turnips for summer and autumn use are quick growers but do not store well. Examples are 'Snowball', 'White Milan', 'Purple Top Milan' and 'Tokyo Cross'. 'Manchester Market' is a good storing maincrop turnip. 'Imperial Green Globe' is the turnip to choose for an abundant supply of 'turnip tops'.

Sowing Sow quick growers at any time between mid-March and July, sow maincrop

Below: Stump-rooted carrots mature quickly for use in summer

in mid-July and to have turnip tops in winter and the following spring, sow seeds in August. Sow seeds in 1-in. deep seed drills spaced at 1 ft. apart. Try not to sow too thickly. Weed and water often in hot, dry weather. Thin seedlings of summer turnips to leave strong plant at from 4–6 in. apart; thin maincrop turnips to 9 in. apart. Do not thin seedlings of turnips being grown solely for the edible foliage ('tops').

Flea beetles make holes in leaves of many seedlings – cabbage, radish, cauliflower, wallflower, alyssum, iberis and turnip. Damage is usually serious if seedlings are left to become dry at the roots. Frequent waterings lead to quicker growth and the seedlings recover from beetle damage. Dusting with derris at weekly intervals helps to control this pest. Strong growing seedlings, although holed by these beetles, do not appear inconvenienced.

Pull summer turnips when they are quite young and tender. Leave winter turnips in the ground and harvest as and when wanted.

Below: After the leaves have been twisted off, lay the beetroots on sand in a box and cover them with more sand

If you wish, you may lift all remaining turnips in December and store as carrots. When pulling turnip tops try not to take more than a couple of leaves at any one time from each plant.

For Hamburgh Parsley, Salsify, Scorzonera *see* Fifty Vegetables and Salads.

Potatoes The potato plant needs a well-drained soil, but one which retains moisture in dry summer weather. For potato growing the texture of both light and heavy soils is greatly improved by regular dressings of strawy manure or garden compost. The site chosen for potatoes should always be dressed with either of these plant food-rich soil improvers during winter digging, but never limed.

Planting Seed potato tubers should be bought in winter and stood in trays to sprout. House the trays in a frostproof, light, cool, airy place. Good Friday is the traditional planting time but delay planting for up to a fortnight if the soil is too wet and cold.

Varieties Potato varieties are divided into three groups: First Early; Second Early; Maincrop. All are planted at the same time. FIRST EARLY: Arran Pilot*; Duke of York; Epicure; Foremost*; Home Guard*; Ulster Chieftain*; Maris Bard*.
SECOND EARLY: Craig's Royal*; Maris Peer*.
MAINCROP: Arran Banner*; Golden Wonder*; Kerr's Pink*; King Edward; Majestic*; Pentland Crown*; Dr McIntosh*; Great Scot*; Maris Piper*; Pentland Dell*.

*= Immune against wart disease.

Only *immune* varieties should be planted in soils known to be infected with wart disease fungus. Never accept a gift of potatoes for planting in your garden if there is any chance

Above: 'Golden Ball' is a popular turnip variety

that they were grown in soil infected with wart disease. Buy Ministry of Agriculture certified seed potatoes each season.

Use a garden line to make straight rows and use a draw hoe to make 6-in. deep furrows.

Planting Distances	Distance between seed tubers in a row	Distance between rows
First Early	12 in.	2 ft.
Second Early and Maincrop	15 in.	2½ ft.

Discard any tubers which have not sprouted or which show decay. Plant so that the end of the tuber where most shoots are is uppermost. Rake soil over the tubers to fill the furrows.

Hoe between rows to keep down weeds. When the plants are 9 in. or so high, use a draw hoe to draw up soil around them. This practice is known as earthing-up. Some gardeners earth up again a few weeks later. After earthing up your potatoes do not use a hoe to remove weeds. Remove the few weeds which may appear by hand. In the drier, eastern half of the country the potato bed should be drenched with water off and on in dry summer weather.

Apart from wart disease, potato blight is the most feared disease among potato growers. This fungus is unlikely to be troublesome in a dry summer and is a greater worry in western parts of the country than in the drier east. Where blight is a normal hazard of potato growing, fortnightly sprayings with Bordeaux mixture or mancozeb are often necessary between early July and mid-September. A power sprayer is needed to ensure that all of the foliage is well-coated with one of these fungicides. A first early potato, such as 'Arran Pilot' is seldom affected by blight. Among maincrop potatoes, the new 'Pentland Crown' appears to resist blight.

Before harvesting first early varieties wait until flowers die and fall. The popular 'Arran Pilot' seldom blooms but imperfect flower buds form and fall. The digging of first earlies usually starts in late June. Dig only sufficient roots for immediate use. Continue digging on and off as and when potatoes are required in the kitchen.

By mid-August all first earlies may have been dug. Second earlies may then be dug as and when potatoes are wanted. Lift the rest of second earlies along with maincrop in September.

Do not dig maincrop potatoes until the plants are brown, dry and shrivelled. Choose a dry, sunny day for digging the entire crop. Leave the tubers on top of the ground for an hour or so to allow them to dry.

Examine each tuber and put aside for immediate use any which are damaged. Store undamaged tubers only in boxes or trays in a dry, cool but frostproof place. Drape black polythene sheeting over the storage containers to prevent the potatoes from greening. Green potatoes are not edible.

Below: 'Tender and True', a bush variety of marrow. *Right:* 'Long Green', one of several trailing marrow varieties

Melon, Marrow & Pumpkin

Fertile, well-drained soil is necessary for the good growth of these plants as they are greedy feeders.

Sowing Sow melon seeds in a warm greenhouse in early April. Wait until the last week of April or the first week of May before sowing seeds of vegetable marrow and pumpkin. In the south of England there is sufficient sun heat in the greenhouse for seed of vegetable marrow and pumpkin to germinate well. In other parts of the country it is an advantage to have some form of heating so that night temperatures do not fall below 50°F (10°C).

Fill 3½-in. pots with the potting compost of your choice. Make sure the compost is moist. Then press two seeds into the compost in each pot. Water lightly, with a fine rose on the water can. Keep the pots moist but not over-wet. Germination takes about a week. When seedlings are forming the first true (triangular) leaf, pinch off the second, weaker seedling in each pot. Do not pull out this unwanted seedling. If you do, you may disturb the roots of the seedling you wish to retain. From now on until planting time keep the seedlings moist. Growth is very rapid.

Melon Varieties Those suitable for a greenhouse, cold frame or for cloche growing are 'Dutch Net', 'No Name', 'Sweetheart', 'Charentais'.

For greenhouse cultivation set out plants at 2 ft. apart. Erect a framework of bamboo canes and soft wires to which the plants may be tied loosely. Stop all side shoots when they are 1 ft. long and tie them to the horizontal wires. When the plants reach the top of the supports, pinch out the central growing points. To have a good set of fruits it pays to hand pollinate. You can transfer pollen from male flowers to females with a dry, clean camel's hair brush. Do this at around midday on bright sunny days. When four fruits have set on each plant cut off any surplus foliage and surplus fruitlets. Start feeding with liquid manure and keep the plants well watered. Allow plenty of ventilation. Stop all watering and feeding when it appears to you that the melons have stopped swelling. To prevent

them from falling off the plants ripening melons are tied in string net bags. Knowing when the first melon is ripe is easy. A ripe melon emits a delicious aroma.

Various bacteria cause foot rot, a severe and killing disease of melon and cucumber plants. The soft rot occurs at or just above soil level. The trouble is caused by water collecting and remaining near the base of the stem. Prevent this from happening by setting out melon and cucumber plants on a slight mound. Ensure, too, that the soil ball is just above the surrounding soil after melon and cucumber plants have been planted out.

If you grow melons in frames each plant requires at least 2 sq. ft. of room. Plant during the second half of May and pinch off the growing point of each plant. Within a short time lateral shoots will be made. Retain four of them only. Pinch off the shoots when they reach the sides or corners of the frame. In July the plants will have made much growth. Prop up the frame light in warm weather to permit bees and other insects entry for pollinating the female flowers. As soon as you see that three melons (on plants of larger varieties) or four (on small varieties) have set, each on a sub-lateral shoot from a different main lateral, prune off surplus sub-laterals and surplus fruitlets. Place the melons you are retaining on to pieces of slate, tile or wood to prevent slug damage. Water often and apply liquid feeds occasionally. Stop watering and feeding when the fruits are of full size and ripening has started.

When growing melons under cloches two lateral shoots only are retained on plants set out at 2 ft. apart. Otherwise, cultivation is as for frame-melons. During flowering, stand cloches somewhat apart to allow bees to enter.

Marrow Varieties Some varieties produce plants which are low, compact bushes, other varieties make long, trailing stems. These varieties are known as 'trailers'. Popular varieties are:

BUSH: Gold Nugget; Golden Zucchini; Green Bush (F_1); Green Bush Improved; Prokor (F_1); Green Bush–Smallpak; Tender and True; White Bush; White Custard; Yellow Custard; Zucchini (F_1).

TRAILERS: Long Green; Long Green Striped; Long White; Table Dainty; Vegetable Spaghetti.

Sowing Although seeds may be sown outdoors in mid-May where the plants are to grow it is more customary to give them an earlier start by sowing under glass. Plants must not be set outdoors (unless cloche protection is given) until all danger of a night spring frost has passed. Early June is usually the right time to set marrow plants out in the garden. A bush plant needs 2½ sq. ft. of room; a trailer needs much more if permitted to roam over the ground. Plants of trailing varieties may be planted at 15 in. apart alongside a 6-ft. high trellis. This may be a wire mesh fence, plastic or wire garden netting or nylon bean netting. Trailers also grow well on 'wigwams' made by pushing four strong poles or bamboo canes in the soil, tying them near the apex and winding soft wire or string around the structure. Marrow plants need no pruning apart from the removal of the central growing point of the main leader of trailers when the leaders reach the top of the supports. Keep down weeds, water often in dry weather and if the soil is not very rich apply liquid manure feeds when marrows are swelling. Fertilization of female marrow flowers is usually carried out by pollinating insects. Some gardeners like to make sure of fertilization by doing the job themselves. To hand pollinate wait until midday. Then pick a male flower, strip off the petals and twist the single 'core' of the male flower into the divided 'core' of a female flower. Female flowers have small marrows at their rear. Always cut marrows when young and tender and when the thumb nail pierces the skin easily.

Pumpkin Treat pumpkin plants as if they are plants of trailing vegetable marrows. Each plant will set and swell one or two fruits. Large pumpkins are obtained by giving liquid manure feeds generously and often.

Harvest pumpkins on a sunny day in late September when the skins are firm. Store them in a cool, dry place.

For Courgettes and Squashes *see* Fifty Vegetables and Salads.

Right: Aubergine 'Black Pekin', a variety of the egg plant

Artichoke (Globe) A decorative, grey-leaved thistle-like plant, this grows 4–6 ft. tall. Plants can be raised from seed but superior varieties such as 'Vert de Laon' and 'Grand Vert de Camus' are propagated from suckers. Cut flower buds for use before the bud scales are fully open.

Artichoke (Jerusalem) This hardy perennial resembles a sunflower plant and reaches a height of 10 ft. Plant tubers 1 ft. apart and 6 in. deep, in February. Lift roots as and when tubers are wanted in the kitchen between November and February.

Asparagus Plant two-year-old plants in April. 'Superior' is a recommended F_1 hybrid. Set plants on a ridge at the bottom of a 9-in. deep trench so that the crowns are 5 in. below the soil surface. Apply a 1-in. thick mulch of compost to the bed each spring. Do not harvest asparagus until the second season and when plants are well established. Sever the thick shoots well below soil level, using a sharp knife, during May and early June. Allow the foliage to grow naturally all summer but cut it down in late October.

Aubergine (Egg Plant) Sow seeds in pots in a warm greenhouse in late April. Plant out in the greenhouse border in late May, or grow the plants in large pots in a greenhouse or cold frame. Pinch out the central growing point of established plants to encourage sub-lateral shoots. Water well and spray with tepid water occasionally to prevent red spider infestation.

Harvest the purple, egg-shaped fruits when they are glossy and softening.

Beans (Haricots) A small white haricot such as 'Comtesse de Chambord' is sown and grown as French dwarf beans. For large haricots choose 'White Wonder' and sow and cultivate as scarlet runner beans. Allow pods to remain on the plants until late summer or early autumn. After harvesting the dry pods place them in a sunny position to ripen off; when perfectly dry, shell them. Store the beans indoors in glass jars without lids.

Beans (Ornamental) Scarlet-podded ornamental beans such as the robin bean or robin's egg, and the speckled cranberry are grown as French climbing beans. The pods may be picked for use when young and tender or allowed to dry off and the beans are then shelled for use as haricots.

Cabbage (Chinese) 'Pe-Tsai' and 'Sampan' (F_1) are the best known. Sow seeds in 1-in. deep drills 1 ft. apart in June or July. Thin young plants to 1 ft. apart. Do not transplant any seedlings. The foliage is a lettuce substitute in salads, or it may be

cooked as cabbage. The mid-ribs may be cooked and served as asparagus.

Cabbage (Portugal) Sow seeds in April. Set out plants 3 ft. apart in early June. The edible portions are the thick, white mid-ribs of the leaves.

Capsicum or Sweet Pepper Sow in small pots in a greenhouse at a minimum temperature of 60°F (15°C) in March or April. Plants may be grown in a greenhouse, either in the border or in large pots, or transferred to cold frames. Allow 18 in. between plants. Keep them well watered. Gather peppers when of full size and bright green.

Cardoon The plant is a 3-ft. high thistle-like plant. Sow seeds in a heated greenhouse in late March. Harden off plants before transferring them to the open garden, 18 in. apart. Keep them well watered. In October remove all yellowing leaves and tie the plants at the top. Then pile earth up and around them to blanch the stems, which takes about a month. Plants may also be grown in trenches in the same way as celery, but the earthing up is done in one operation.

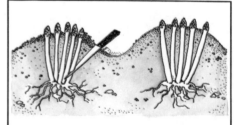

Left: 'Bull Nosed Red', one of several kinds of capsicum or sweet pepper. Some kinds are bright green when ripe
Above: Cut asparagus shoots well below soil level
Below: The thick white midribs are the edible portions of the leaves of Portugal cabbage

Celeriac or Turnip-Rooted Celery Sow seeds in heat in March or April, harden off the plants and plant them 1 ft. apart in the garden in May. Remove all suckers. Lift and store the roots in October. Store as carrots.

Celery There are three sorts – blanched, self-blanching and green. Sow seeds in trays or pots in a heated greenhouse in March. Harden off plants in a cold frame before planting outdoors in early June. Those which need blanching are set out in a trench; earth up plants slightly in mid-August, continue the operation two weeks later and finish it a fortnight afterwards. Start digging blanched celery in November. A good place for self-blanching celery is a cold frame. Plant 9 in. apart. Remove the frame light in late June and in mid-July tuck straw around the plants to assist blanching. Lift plants for use in August and September. Green (American Green) celery is grown in the same way as self-blanching celery but because it is eaten green there is no blanching to be done at all and plants may be grown in the open.

Celtuce Sow and cultivate as lettuce. The plants reach a height of 2 ft. The thick stem is the edible part of the vegetable. Peel stems before use.

Chervil (Turnip-Rooted Chervil) Sow in April and cultivate as parsnips. Dig the roots as and when required in winter, or lift and store in moist sand in October.

Chicory Sow seeds 1 in. deep in early June and thin seedlings to 9 in. apart. In November dig up the parsnip-like roots and heel them in a trench over which a little straw should be spread. Take small batches for chicon production now and then during the winter. Trim roots back by a few inches and reduce the foliage to within 1 in. of the crown. Plant roots closely in the greenhouse border and cover with straw weighed down with dry soil. Inspect for chicons after a month or so. Alternatively, plant prepared roots in pails or pots and force chicons indoors or in a garage or shed. It is important that all light be excluded.

Chopsuy Green (or Shungiku) Sow seeds of this edible chrysanthemum in spring or in late summer. Cultivate as spinach. Harvest plants for use when they are from 4–5 in. high. It is used in Chinese dishes.

Corn Salad or Lamb's Lettuce Sow this useful lettuce substitute in August or in September in very shallow drills. Thin seedlings to 6 in. apart. Plants are ready for use when young so that thinnings may be added to salads. Pick leaves as and when required all winter.

Courgettes These are small immature vegetable marrows. 'Zucchini' and 'Courgette' are excellent varieties. Sow and cultivate as bush type marrows. Cut courgettes regularly when they are a few inches long.

Cress (Landcress or American Cress) Sow seeds between August and October in ½-in. deep, damp drills. Thin seedlings to 6 in. apart. It is helpful if plants are protected by cloches between November and March. It is a substitute for watercress.

Dandelion The cultivated dandelion is a selected French plant. Seeds are sown in April and the seedlings thinned to 9 in. apart. Roots are dug in November and are stored in sand. Batches of roots are taken out of store for forced, blanched foliage for winter salads. A heated greenhouse encourages the rapid production of blanched foliage.

Endive Sow and cultivate as lettuce. Hearts may be partially blanched by tying the plants with string. Full blanching is achieved by covering the plants with large pots so that all light is excluded.

Finocchio or Florence Fennel Sow seeds in shallow seed drills, 1 ft. apart in April. Thin seedlings to 9 in. apart. The swollen stem bases are ready for use in late summer or early autumn.

Garlic Plant cloves (segments stripped from garlic bulbs) 2 in. deep and 6 in. apart during March. Dig the crop in summer when the foliage yellows. Dry off the bulbs in a sunny place before storing them in a dry, cool but frost-proof place.

Gherkin For pickling gherkins sow and grow a few plants of a ridge cucumber solely for this purpose. 'Venlo Pickling' is a suitable variety.

Good King Henry (Mercury, Lincolnshire Asparagus) Sow seeds in April and thin the seedlings to 1 ft. apart. The leaves are a substitute for spinach. Young shoots poking through the soil in March or April may be cut when 4 in. long and used in the same way as asparagus.

Left: 'Gold Nugget', a winter squash variety grown for summer use or for storing
Above: Celery 'Giant Red'

Horseradish Plant root cuttings 1 ft. apart in late autumn. Dig up plants when required in the following autumn and winter. Keep a few pieces of root for replanting elsewhere in the garden.

Kohlrabi Sow at any time between March and August. Thin seedlings to 9 in. apart. The thinnings may be transplanted. Harvest when the turnip-like swollen stems are no larger than a tennis ball.

The edible swollen stems of kohlrabi

Mustard (Chinese Mustard) Sow seeds between April and July in a shallow drill. Thin seedlings to 8 in. apart. Water well in hot, dry weather. Use as a lettuce substitute in salads.

Okra or Gumbo Sow seeds in small pots in heat during April and plant out the seedlings 18 in. apart in the greenhouse border. Alternatively, transfer each pot-raised plant to a large pot in the greenhouse. The yellow flowers are followed by the edible pods which are harvested when still soft.

Onion (Potato Onion) Plant and cultivate as shallots.

Onion (Tree Onion) Plant small bulbs 1 in. deep and 18 in. apart between November and March. The tall stems need supporting. Clusters of small onions form at various levels on the stems. Harvest them for use between August and March.

Onion (Welsh Onion) Plant pieces taken from clumps at any time of the year, 12–18 in. apart. Lift clumps in winter and early spring for use in salads and cooked dishes.

Orach (Mountain Spinach) There are green, white and red forms. Sow seeds thinly in shallow drills between March and July. Thin seedlings to 15 in. apart. Use young leaves as a spinach substitute.

Parsley Sow in April in ½-in. deep drills. Thin the seedlings to 6 in. apart. 'Moss Curled' is a popular variety.

Parsley (Hamburgh Parsley) Sow and cultivate as parsnips. Cook roots as parsnips and use the foliage as parsley.

Pea (Asparagus Pea) Sow in a shallow drill in late May. Space the seeds at 6 in. apart and thin the young plants to 1 ft. apart. Give the plants some twiggy brushwood supports. Gather the pods when they are about 1 in. long

Pea (Mangetout or Sugar Pea) Sow and cultivate as garden peas and provide the plants with supports. Harvest pods before the seeds inside them start to swell.

Pea (Pea Bean) Grow as French climbing beans but allow seeds in the pods to plump up. Pods may be gathered when green and the beans cooked as peas or the pods may be left to ripen and shelled for dry haricots for winter use.

Pea (Petits Pois) Sow and cultivate as garden peas. Pick pods when very young and tender.

Popcorn Sow and cultivate as sweet corn but do not harvest cobs until they are dry and brittle, in early autumn.

Rhubarb The best variety is 'Timperley Early'. Plant stools in late autumn, 4 ft. apart. Do not pull sticks until the second season and always stop pulling at the end of June. Mulch the bed with compost or well-rotted manure each autumn.

Salsify Sow seeds thinly in shallow drills in April. From then on cultivate and harvest as parsnips.

Scorzonera (Black Salsify) Sow, cultivate and harvest as salsify.

Seakale Plant thongs (root cuttings) 18 in. apart in March. Mulch with well-rotted manure or compost in May. Allow the foliage to die before lifting roots for blanching in winter. Plant roots in the greenhouse border and cover with dry straw weighed down with dry soil. Cut blanched seakale just below soil level with a small piece of the root attached.

Seakale Beet (Swiss Chard, Silver Beet) Sow seeds in shallow drills 12 in. apart between April and July. Thin seedlings to 12 in. apart. When plants are fully grown pick leaves as required. The thick white midribs may be cooked as a substitute for seakale and the green parts as spinach. There is a red form known as rhubarb chard or ruby chard.

Ruby chard, a red form of seakale beet

Spinach (Summer Spinach) (Round-seeded Spinach) Sow seeds in mid-March and make successional sowings until July.
Sow in 1-in. deep drills, 1 ft. apart and thin seedlings to 3 in. Keep plants well watered in dry weather. Harvest but a few leaves from each plant at any one picking.

Spinach (Winter Spinach) (Prickly-seeded Spinach) Sow and cultivate as summer spinach but wait until July or August before sowing. Cloches come in handy for protecting the plants during the winter.

Spinach (New Zealand Spinach) Sow in a greenhouse or cold frame in early April. No artificial heat is necessary. Plant out 3 ft. apart in early June. Pick the tender side shoots as and when wanted. The leaves may be cooked as spinach or eaten raw.

Spinach (Perpetual Spinach) (Spinach Beet) Sow seeds in shallow drills 1 ft. apart in early April. Thin seedlings to 8–12 in. apart. Pick leaves as with summer and winter spinach, between July and winter.

Squash (Summer Squash) In American English the vegetable marrow is a summer squash. In Britain seedsmen and gardeners generally consider such differently shaped marrows as 'Patty Pan' (the custard marrow), 'Crooknecks' and 'Straightnecks' as summer squashes. Cultivate these as bush type vegetable marrows.

Squash (Winter Squash) Examples are 'Hubbard' and 'Golden Delicious'. 'Gold Nugget' is dual purpose and may be grown for summer use or for storing. Cultivate as bush or trailing marrows and harvest for storing in the autmn.

Inspecting sweet corn for ripeness

Sweet Corn (Corn on the Cob) Sow two or three seeds in 3½-in. pots in a greenhouse or cold frame in late April. Thin the seedlings to leave one only in each pot. Plant out in early June in blocks consisting of several plants about 1 ft. apart. Harvest cobs when the grains are full but immature in August. At that stage the 'silks' hanging from the cobs are dark brown to black in colour and brittle.

Tomatoes (Ornamental) These are excellent in salads and are attractive in the garden, too. Grow as ordinary standard tomatoes. Ornamentals include Red and Yellow Cherries, Red and Yellow Plums, Red and Yellow Pears.

Watercress Choose a damp, shady spot and dig in plenty of peat to retain moisture, leaving the surface of the bed a little lower than the surrounding soil. Sow in April and in August, protecting August-sown plants with a frame light between November and March.

Water Melon Sow in pots at a temperature of around 80°F (27°C) in late March and plant out in the greenhouse border in early May, 5 ft. apart. Do not prune the rambling plants at all. Hand pollinate the female flowers and retain two fruits only on each plant. Water freely and apply liquid feeds. Maintain a night temperature of 70°F (21°C). Harvest fruits when the tendrils on the fruit-bearing shoot are dry and almost black in colour.

Common Pests and Diseases

Vegetables growing in fertile, well-drained and well-cultivated gardens seldom suffer greatly from pests and diseases. The modern gardener accepts that all wildlife has a right to live. It is only when things get out of hand that any living creature causing damage to garden plants can be rated as a pest. It is up to the gardener to use his superior intelligence to outwit possibly harmful small creatures instead of polluting the environment surrounding his home. The labels of packaged pesticides should be read carefully. If the contents are dangerous to you, your children and your family pets consider carefully before you buy such substances. Always lock dangerous pesticides quite safely away from children. Do *not* mix dangerous pesticides with water and store them in beer or lemonade bottles. Your child may drink the stuff and be poisoned. As for chemical weed killers the long term effect of some modern kinds is as yet unknown. The older weedkiller, sodium chlorate, is liable to explode; it also runs in the soil and may not only kill your own choice plants but may kill plants in your neighbours' gardens. Many sprays and powders contain derris or pyrethrum. These are natural insecticides prepared from plants. They are harmless to all warm-blooded creatures but derris can kill fish. If you use derris pesticides, keep sprays and dusts away from your garden pool. Encourage natural predators, e.g. the hedgehog, toad, frog, ladybird, wasps (in spring but not in summer) and lacewing flies. Learn to distinguish between the helpful centipede, the less helpful millepede and the unpleasant wireworm. Most moths, butterflies and their caterpillars are on your side. The caterpillars of cabbage white butterflies and of the cabbage moth are not!

The following list gives some of the most common pests and diseases, the chief vegetables affected, the damage done, and lastly the control measures available.

Aphids (greenfly, mealy aphis, blackfly). *Vegetable:* all. *Damage:* they are sap suckers. Plants are weakened, leaves die and flower buds may be ruined. *Control:* allow plants sufficient space and do not grow vegetables in shade. Water well and often in dry, summer weather. Keep down weeds. Encourage ladybirds. Spray with derris, pyrethrum, or pirimicarb.

Birds *Vegetable:* seed beds and the seedlings of several vegetables. *Damage:* seeds are sought for and devoured; seedlings are pecked. *Control:* net or protect with black cotton. A scarecrow or strips of tinfoil may be tried.

Cabbage Root Fly *Vegetable:* the cabbage tribe. *Damage:* grubs burrow into the roots; plants wilt and die. *Control:* use cardboard or foil collars, or dust ground with bromophos or diazinon.

Carrot Root Fly *Vegetable:* carrot. *Damage:* grubs eat roots; plants yellow and die. *Control:* thin seedlings only when soil is moist. Bury unwanted thinnings and broken foliage.

Caterpillars *Vegetable:* the cabbage tribe. *Damage:* leaves are eaten. *Control:* pick off caterpillars. Dust with derris or spray with malathion.

Celery Fly *Vegetable:* celery. *Damage:* maggots burrow into the leaves which appear blistered. A bad attack can lead to dead leaves and a poor crop. *Control:* hand pick and burn 'blistered' leaves. Spray seedlings with derris in May and June.

Club Root *Vegetable:* the cabbage tribe. *Damage:* the fungus causes swellings on the roots which decay. Plants are stunted and may die. *Control:* do not raise plants in soil known to be infected with the fungus. Rotate crops. Feed the soil with plenty of compost. Lime where necessary. Burn roots of affected plants. Calomel offers some control.

Common Scab *Vegetable:* potato. *Damage:* scabby marks on the skin; seldom serious and the flesh of potatoes is rarely damaged. *Control:* do not lime ground in which potatoes are to be planted. Rotate crops. Where this trouble is common surround seed tubers with peat, leaf mould or lawn mowings at planting time.

Cutworms *Vegetable:* many. *Damage:* these soil caterpillars eat stems, leaves and roots. They often cut stems of seedlings at soil level. *Control:* destroy any found when digging. Hoe frequently and destroy any seen. Keep down weeds. Diazinon and bromophos will control.

cutworm

Damping Off *Vegetable:* many at seedling stage in greenhouse and in frames. *Damage:* a fungus which causes stems to shrivel. Seedlings topple over and die. *Control:* use sterile composts when sowing seeds. Sow thinly. Do not over-water, prick out early, ventilate freely. Cheshunt Compound is a chemical control.

Grey Mould *Vegetable:* lettuce, marrow, melon, cucumber, tomato. *Damage:* a fungal disease. Softening of plant tissue is followed by decay. Outgrowths of grey mould appear. *Control:* ventilate well. Clear away any debris. Remove side shoots when quite small. Prune cleanly so that no jagged stems are left. Allow plants sufficient room. Do not splash plants when watering. Dust with flowers of sulphur or spray with colloidal sulphur or benomyl.

Leaf Mould *Vegetable:* tomato (in greenhouse). *Damage:* this fungus shows as yellow spots on upper surfaces of leaves with pale greyish mould on undersides. *Control:* ventilate well. Give plants adequate space. Do not over-water. Remove and burn infected foliage. Spray with mancozeb or a copper-based fungicide.

Leather Jackets *Vegetable:* many. *Damage:* grubs feed on plant roots just below ground level. *Control:* as for cutworms.

Mildew *Vegetable:* many. *Damage:* the fungus shows as a grey/white powder on foliage. *Control:* ensure that plants have sufficient moisture and ventilate frames and greenhouses well. Dust with flowers of sulphur. Spray with mancozeb.

Millepedes *Vegetable:* all. *Damage:* roots are eaten. *Control:* destroy any found when

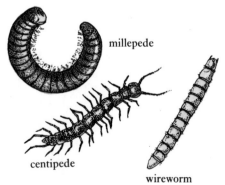

millepede

centipede

wireworm

digging and cultivating. Remove all rubbish to the compost heap. Trap by burying pieces of sliced potato or carrot on skewers in the soil. This pest prefers roots already decaying. Do not confuse with beneficial centipedes.

Mosaic Virus *Vegetable:* vegetable marrow. *Damage:* leaves show mottling and distortion. Plants are dwarfed. Crop is poor. Plants die. *Control:* prevent by spraying plants with derris or pyrethrum to deter aphids which spread the disease. Destroy plants of white bryony. Pull up and burn affected plants.

Onion Fly *Vegetable:* onion, sometimes leek and shallots. *Damage:* grubs eat roots and below ground portion of plants. *Control:* avoid breaking or bruising onion foliage. Thin onion seedlings only when soil is damp. Bury broken onion foliage and unwanted thinnings. Bromophos or diazinon will control.

Parsnip Canker *Vegetable:* parsnip. *Damage:* brown patches occur on the parsnips. Rots may also occur; seldom serious. *Control:* Grow resistant parsnips, e.g. 'Avonresister'.

Pea and Bean Weevils *Vegetable:* peas, beans. *Damage:* Leaves of seedlings are eaten. The bites show as 'U'-shaped notches. *Control:* hoe regularly around seedlings to disturb the pests. Break down clods under which they hide. Remove all rubbish to the compost heap. Dust or spray with derris.

Pea Moth *Vegetable:* peas. *Damage:* grubs eat peas in the pods. *Control:* rotate crops. Hoe frequently around plants to expose pupae in the ground to birds. Spray with fenitrothion just as the flowers are opening. Early sowings often escape this pest.

Potato Blight *Vegetable:* potatoes, tomatoes. *Damage:* the fungus shows as brown/black markings on foliage. Potatoes and tomatoes decay. Plants rot and smell. *Control:* where this disease makes potato growing hazardous grow only first early varieties. Some newer varieties appear to resist blight. 'Pentland Crown' is an example. 'Maris Peer' foliage can suffer from the disease but the tubers may not be harmed. It seldom occurs on tomato plants in the greenhouse. Spray or dust with Bordeaux mixture or mancozeb from early July onwards.

Saddleback *Vegetable:* onion. *Damage:* underside of bulb splits. *Control:* never permit plants to become dry at the roots when bulbs are swelling.

Slugs and Snails *Vegetable:* all. *Damage:* these pests eat foliage, roots, tubers and fruits. *Control:* remove all rubbish. Search for possible hiding places and destroy the pests. Bait slugs by leaving cabbage and lettuce leaves on the soil at night. Use proprietary slug killers with care. Some are harmful to pets and wild life. Encourage hedgehogs, toads, frogs, slow worms and song birds.

Turnip Flea Beetles *Vegetable:* the cabbage tribe, radish, swede, turnip. *Damage:* holes show in younger leaves. *Control:* Prepare seed beds properly. Remove all rubbish. Keep seedlings well-watered in dry spring and summer weather. Dust seedlings with derris. The damage usually looks nastier than it is.

Turnip Gall Weevil *Vegetable:* the cabbage tribe, swede, turnip. *Damage:* grubs occur in galls on roots and stems just below soil surface. *Control:* Very common but causes little if any damage. Unsightly. Burn badly infested roots. Do not confuse with club root.

Wireworm *Vegetable:* all. *Damage:* grubs eat roots. *Control:* Trap by burying cut pieces of potato or carrot on skewers. Diazinon or bromophos will control. Grow less vulnerable vegetables such as broad beans and members of the cabbage family if this pest is present in quantity in a new garden.

The Greenhouse & Garden Frame

The Greenhouse

Apart from the three standard types of green-house – the span or ridge, three-quarter span, and lean-to, recent years have seen the introduction of the circular house and the modification of the span types, often producing irregular designs.

The span type is an independent structure standing alone and the best for all-round purposes. Many of these are now produced with glass to the ground, instead of the traditional style with low walls of brick, concrete or wood. These walls help to preserve heat and do not allow the same violent changes of temperature as the all-glass house. Plastics are increasingly used as glass substitutes, but these materials have at present a short life only.

Wood Apart from cost, an important decision to make is whether the framework should be wood or metal. Wood is warmer, easier to repair and better for fitting shelves. Against this, wood needs to be painted or oiled if red cedar is used. Type of wood is also

important. Teak is strong and durable but expensive. Redwood or red deal is much used and is easier to work.

Whitewood is cheaper but it is not fully weather resistant and sometimes splits. Western red cedar is particularly durable. If used unpainted, it should be dressed annually with linseed oil.

Straight grained oak is very durable and to lessen expense, it is now often used in conjunction with steel. The use of white lead paint inside helps to preserve wood and reflects light.

Metal Steel and aluminium greenhouses are quite widely used, the latter material being easier to shape. Aluminium alloys are reasonably strong and provided they are well and firmly sited, they are satisfactory and in spite of their light weight, will stand firm. Points to watch for when selecting a metal greenhouse are absolute rigidity and provision for expansion and contraction without glass breaking or air leakage. Metal sashes are not glazed with putty; they need an elastic sealing compound. Steel needs painting, aluminium does not.

Concrete Concrete greenhouses are only rarely, if ever made now. Less elegant than wood or metal, they are strong and heavy since the concrete is usually reinforced with rods or frames.

Whatever type of greenhouse you decide to buy, make sure that all parts work properly, for ill-fitting joints, doors or ventilators can lead to trouble.

Guttering and down pipes should be provided to prevent water pouring off the roof and down the wide panes, as well as making it possible to store rain water in butts or cisterns.

Choosing your Greenhouse Buying a greenhouse is an investment, not only because it increases the value of your property but because of the all the year round pleasure it will give.

Since there are many kinds of greenhouse available, in various sizes and made of different materials it is important to choose the one that will best suit your needs. This will depend on a number of factors, including the site available, the plants you intend to grow and the price. Price will govern the

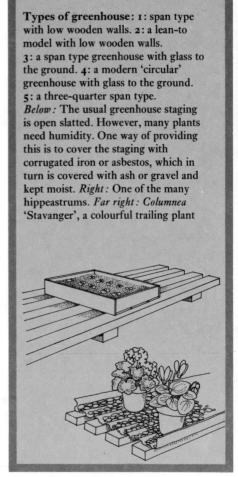

Types of greenhouse: 1: span type with low wooden walls. 2: a lean-to model with low wooden walls.
3: a span type greenhouse with glass to the ground. 4: a modern 'circular' greenhouse with glass to the ground.
5: a three-quarter span type.
Below: The usual greenhouse staging is open slatted. However, many plants need humidity. One way of providing this is to cover the staging with corrugated iron or asbestos, which in turn is covered with ash or gravel and kept moist. *Right:* One of the many hippeastrums. *Far right: Columnea* 'Stavanger', a colourful trailing plant

size, although it is wise to buy the largest house you can afford to begin with.

It is a mistake to buy a greenhouse without first deciding on what plants are to be grown in it. If you want to grow grapes or peaches well as ornamental plants it is no use choosing an 8 × 6 ft. greenhouse. The so-called Dutch light houses provide plenty of light and, in summer, they can accomodate tomatoes followed by chrysanthemums in autumn. Winter lettuce can follow and other forced vegetable crops could succeed the lettuce.

For pot plants such as cyclamen and primulas and for raising bedding plants, the usual span roof greenhouse is ideal. A structure with a brick or wood wall allows for staging but if you want to grow tomatoes or chrysanthemums, or lettuce on one side where they will need full light, it is possible to buy a type with glass to ground level – or to have one side with staging and one with glass to the base.

If you are concentrating on orchids there are special houses for these plants. They are fitted with extra ventilators and often with two-tier staging, the idea being to stand the plants on the top lath staging, covering the lower staging with pebbles or old coarse ashes which are kept moist to provide the required humidity. A lean-to house is useful for a vine, peach, or nectarine, while staging can be erected to accommodate colourful plants.

Make sure whatever type of greenhouse you buy is provided with ample ventilators of the right size. Ensure there are ventilators on both sides of a span greenhouse so that there is always one side against the leeward wind.

Siting the Greenhouse   It is advisable to put the structure where it receives the maximum amount of sunshine, especially in winter. Avoid overhanging trees, because they cast shadows, and shed leaves and other deposits which can easily dirty the glass. Ideally the situation should be within easy reach of a water supply.

Avoid ground which becomes wet in winter and, wherever possible, choose a site where good paths can be made and which is not too far from your house.

The traditional alignment for a greenhouse is north to south, since in this position plants on both sides of the house receive direct sunlight. Some gardeners prefer an east to west siting to have a warmer and cooler side to the house. At all costs avoid windy situations, especially those exposed to north or east winds for these will bring draughts and some loss of heat, especially if north winds blow directly into the door. For preference, a lean-to should face south.

Erecting the Greenhouse: The Foundation   A proper and permanent foundation is of paramount importance. Most greenhouse manufacturers supply a ground plan which must be strictly adhered to. A simple way of making a satisfactory foundation is to take out a 10-in. deep trench 1 ft. wide, with vertical sides. In to this is built a brick footing. Concrete blocks for footings and walls are also satisfactory. Cultivated ground needs stronger foundations since it is more likely to sink.

If the superstructure is to rest on brick walls the top of the concrete foundation must be 6 in. below ground level. If electricity is to be used lay the cables before the concrete is put in.

A solid or concrete floor can be made, but a soil base is an advantage, as it allows some crops to be grown in the 'floor'. In winter the soil can dry out, in summer it will help to maintain a humid atmosphere.

Glazing   When putting in the glass, it is advisable to use putty for bedding it on the glazing bars. If the structure needs a coat of paint or preservative, put it on before the framework is glazed.

Glass should be dry when used. If wet, the panes stick together and they break more easily in cold weather. Make sure the woodwork can be securely fastened to the foundations so that subsequently, there is no movement as could occur in windy, exposed positions.

Plastics are often used as a substitute for glass and are improving steadily in quality. Glass is easier to clean, but is heavy and requires strong structures. Polythene or plastic houses are useful for providing summer protection and giving dappled light. While it does not break in the same way as glass, plastic needs renewing from time to time.

 Heating Methods

Greenhouses can be heated by electricity; solid fuel; gas and oil fired burners. The warmth is distributed by means of hot water pipes; electric heaters; blowers and warming cables or convector heaters. Efficiency, cost and ease of operation will influence the choice of system.

Electricity   Electrical heating is time and labour saving and requires no boiler or fuel storage. With thermostatic control a predetermined temperature can be maintained, provided the right heaters have been chosen and there are no power cuts. There are various ways of using electricity for heating:

(1) By a wire grid over which air is blown by a fan.

(2) By a convector heater designed to produce warm air without a fan. Rapid warmth is produced, although distribution is not so even.

(3) By radiating tubes, plates or strips.

(4) By immersion heater used for hot-water pipes.

Soil warmth can also be produced by electric cables. This is used to provide bottom heat for propagating seeds or rooting cuttings and does not substantially increase air temperature.

Paraffin These heaters are widely used and, provided high quality heating oils are used, there is little danger of poisonous fumes. This means keeping the burners clean so that incomplete combustion does not release harmful gases. For large houses, heaters with outside chimneys should be used. For small houses there are several portable models available which need little attention other than refilling. Choose one producing a blue flame which results from complete combustion of the oil.

Manufacturers usually indicate how long a heater will burn with one filling. More important, is how much heat is produced. Heat is lost through ventilation, but stagnant air encourages fungoid diseases and other disorders, and particularly with paraffin heating, a crack of ventilation is always needed, except during the severest weather.

What can be grown in a greenhouse largely depends on the temperature that can be maintained. At one time, in large private gardens, a range of houses was to be found, starting from the cold house and passing from the cool to the intermediate and hot or stove house. Today few gardeners can afford more than one greenhouse.

While many greenhouse owners like to specialize in particular types of plant, those less experienced, usually prefer to cultivate a range of plants. This means that one has to grow plants which need similar conditions.

Types of Greenhouse

The Cold Greenhouse This is one which is never heated by anything but the sun and a colourful display can be had without any artificial heat. In extra cold weather, some protection can be given by blinds which can be pulled down or let up at will. Outdoors, many plants are killed by winter dampness but if taken indoors they come through bad weather unscathed.

Where space is scarce the staging can be erected in tiers. Slatted wood is useful in that it allows air to circulate round the pots, helping to avoid atmospheric dampness in winter. Unfortunately, it also encourages pots to dry out quickly in summer.

The best plan is to place corrugated or asbestos sheeting over the staging and cover it with small shingle or stone chips. In summer the shingle can be kept damp to provide humidity, while from late autumn onwards, through winter it can be allowed to dry.

The Cool Greenhouse This is one where a minimum night temperature of 40°–45°F (4°–7°C) can be maintained. This must be controlled, which means adequate ventilation. It is, perhaps, plants in smaller greenhouses that suffer most when air conditioning is wrong, especially if sufficient ventilators have not been provided. Fresh air is important but when the air vents are opened, this naturally lowers the temperature but equally important, it moves the stagnant dank air, leading to the buoyant atmosphere so vital for plant health.

The Intermediate or Warm House A winter night temperature above 48°F (8°–9°C) will allow a wider range of exotic plants to be cultivated. Such houses are usually sited where the benefit of all available sun is felt.

It pays to install automatic ventilation which acts according to outside weather conditions and inside temperature. Costing nothing to run, it is easily fitted.

A Hot (or Stove) House This is one where the winter temperature never falls below 60°F (16°C). As it is fairly expensive to run not many amateur gardeners can afford a house of this type. Except for the temperature difference and the fact that a wider range of tender plants, including many orchids, can be grown, the inside arrangements and attention needed, are the same as for the warm greenhouse.

Plants to Grow

In the Cold Greenhouse The success of plants in the cold greenhouse largely depends on the choice of the right kinds and the way they are looked after. There are distinct advantages in being able to provide just enough heat to keep the temperature falling below freezing point in winter. Failures are often due to overwatering in winter. In frosty weather, plants should be kept on the dry side.

Many alpine plants can be grown successfully in the cold house, where they can be raised from seed. These include: *Aster alpinus*, aethionemas, aubrietas, campanulas, dianthus, gentians, primulas, saxifrages and miniature cupressus.

Many bulbs do well as the protection provided leads to unblemished blooms. Among these treasures are crocuses, irises, including the Dutch varieties 'Wedgwood', lavender; and 'Princess Beatrix', yellow.

Dwarf irises are specially good, including *I. danfordiae*, yellow; and *I. reticulata*, violet, and its many forms. Narcissus, early tulips, fritillarias, liliums, scillas, tritonia and the early gladiolus produce a bright display. *Cypripedium calceolus* is handsome in flower. It likes a limey soil. Early flowering shrubs grown in pots taken in the greenhouse in December or January, soon produce a showy display. They include daphne, *Erica carnea*, forsythia, prunus and spiraea, while *Helleborus niger*, the Christmas rose, responds well.

In the Cool Greenhouse It is fascinating to see how quickly many exotic plants become acclimatized and grow in a cool greenhouse.

Left: Brunsfelsia calycina produces its flowers freely
Above: The wax flower, or honey plant, *Hoya carnosa*. It is a greenhouse climber
Right: the flowers and fruits of the Passion flower, *Passiflora caerulea*, another climber
Right above: Clivia miniata, a striking South African bulbous plant suitable for a warm greenhouse

Daisy-flowered plants raised easily from seeds, such as arctotis, dimorphotheca, gazania and ursinia, will bloom continuously. *Gerbera jamesonii* has long lasting huge brilliant orange-amber flowers.

Erica hyemalis the Cape heath has long, white-tipped pink bells, while there are species with red, orange and yellow flowers. Gardenias, daphnes, epacris and daturas are handsome shrubs.

Hoya bella, the wax flower, is flesh-pink. Ipomoea or morning glory, easily raised from seed, is in shades of blue. *Jasminum primulinum*, yellow; *Lapageria rosea*, rich pink waxy bells; *Passiflora caerulea*, the Passion flower; and *Thunbergia alata*, orange with a black throat are all interesting.

Foliage plants are indispensable. They include *Lippia citriodora*, the lemon-scented verbena, caladiums with beautifully spotted and veined leaves; *Eucalyptus globulus* with grey-green foliage; *Grevillea robusta*; *Maranta leuconeura*, with leaves curiously marked and spotted; *Saxifraga sarmentosa*, fine for hanging baskets. Ferns and palms can be grown

for temporary use in the living room.

Climbing plants can be grown in pots or planted in the greenhouse border. Among these are bougainvillea with brightly coloured mauve bracts in summer; *Clematis armandii*, an evergreen with white flowers; *Cobaea scandens*, a fast climber of which seed is sown in March.

Carnations are among the important cool greenhouse flowers. Their cultivation is described later.

Fruit in the Greenhouse Although there are specially constructed greenhouses for the cultivation of fruit, few amateur gardeners are likely to buy a greenhouse solely for this purpose.

What can be grown depends on the space available and the amount of time that can be spared. For further details see Fruit in Your Garden elsewhere in this work.

Propagation

Greenhouse and frame plants are progagated from seed or various types of cuttings. Seed sowing is often the easiest method although many plants must be propagated by cuttings, division, or off-sets.

By seeds The majority of seeds germinate in a temperature of 60°–65°F (15°–18°C) but it is not necessary to keep the whole greenhouse to this required minimum. A propagator heated independently, can be used for seeds and cuttings.

Many seed failures are due to the use of unsuitable compost. Destructive damping-off diseases frequently result from the use of poor soil. This is why the John Innes seed compost has proved such a blessing.

Whether trays, pans or boxes are used the compost should be evenly compacted without

being made hard. Thin sowing is essential. Very fine seeds such as those of begonias and gloxinias need not be covered but merely pressed into the surface soil. Larger seeds should be lightly covered. After watering place the boxes or pots in a propagator and cover them with glass and paper. Once the seedlings appear remove the paper and glass, taking care to keep the surface soil just moist.

Early pricking out of seedlings is necessary. Keep the pricked out seedlings shaded for a few days until they are established. As the seedlings develop they will need potting up.

Stem cuttings Many plants raised from seed can be increased from stem cuttings. These are usually made from young shoots or shoot tips. Only really healthy plants should be propagated and the cuttings should have two or three joints. Remove the lowest leaves and sever the stem cleanly just below a joint. The best results are obtained when the cuttings are inserted around the edge of pots filled with a moisture-retaining but fairly open mixture. Water in the cuttings, then place them in a heated propagator or in a polythene bag, closing it with a rubber band, but keep the plastic off the cuttings.

When the plants have rooted the propagating case should be gradually ventilated so that they become accustomed to greenhouse temperatures. Cuttings with hairy leaves are liable to damp off and should be rooted on the open bench where they should be shaded to reduce transpiration.

Leaf Cuttings Some plants, notably peperomias and saintpaulias, can be increased by leaf cuttings. Use healthy mature leaves and trim them so that the stalk is up to 1 in. long. Insert them in compost so that the leaf blades just touch the soil.

Rex begonias are treated rather differently. Slit the main veins in several places. Then weight or peg down the leaves. Roots and plantlets will develop where the cuts are made.

Stem Sections Ficus, dracaenas and some other plants can be propagated from stem sections. The dormant bud in the leaf joint will develop into a good plant.

Leaf-bud Cuttings These consist simply of a leaf situated centrally on a piece of stem about $\frac{3}{4}$ in. long complete with a dormant bud. August and September are good months for the job since plants will be in full growth. Among plants that respond to this treatment are aphelandra, pilea and ficus.

Division Some plants such as chlorophytum and maranta can be divided in spring. Many bulbous plants multiply naturally by forming offsets which can be detached and potted separately.

Using Frames for Propagation Garden frames can, where required, be supplied with soil warming equipment. This will allow seeds and cuttings to be started as well as bringing chrysanthemums, carnations and other flowering plants through cold periods. When used without heat, frames are useful for blanching endive and for growing a number of vegetable crops and salad plants.

The Garden Frame

Types There are four standard patterns of frames, determined by the size of the glass or light. The English frame is 6 ft. long × 4 ft. wide, usually glazed with four sheets of glass. Next is the 4 ft. × 4 ft. pit light usually fitted to the sides of greenhouses. The Dutch frame measures 59 in. × 31¾ in. and is glazed with a single pane of glass. The French frame measures 4 ft. 4 in. × 4 ft. 5 in.

Sectional frames of cast aluminium or steel are on the market, and there are many satisfactory portable frames with single or span roof, with sliding tops easily removed for ready access.

The size of frame you buy or make will depend on the purpose for which it is to be used, although the aim should be to have one as large, as space and pocket allow. Many frames are made with 4 ft. extensions, so that as with cloches, any length of run can be achieved.

Position Where possible face the frames due south and not under or too near trees. If it can be backed on to the greenhouse or other building to give protection from north winds, so much the better.

The body of the frame can be of tongued and grooved timber, brick, breeze blocks or metal. Where frames are not permanent constructions make sure they are on a proper draught and damp-proof base. Provide a firm path round the structure, otherwise it will be difficult to attend to plants in winter or wet weather.

Keep the glass clean and free from cracks with puttying so efficient that rain drips cannot penetrate. Make sure the frame will open and shut properly without water getting between the panes or hinge joints.

Water with care to avoid excess moisture in the frame. An old-fashioned remedy for keeping out dampness is to place a lump of quicklime under each light. This takes up air moisture in winter and lasts for several weeks.

Heat escapes through the bottom of the frame into the surrounding soil. A 2–3-in. deep bed of cinders placed under the frame area before soil is added, greatly reduces the loss.

Propagating frames are used exclusively for raising plants from seed or cuttings. They can be a simple arrangement, such as a box on which a sheet of glass is placed, or a more elaborate structure with a wooden or metal base.

Use A garden frame can become an introduction to greenhouse culture, for with a frame you look after the plants from the outside, with a greenhouse you tend them from within, whatever the weather.

In summer greenhouse temperatures are likely to fluctuate rapidly; in a frame, plants can be kept cool easily, for as necessary, the glass can be completely removed.

Many small frames are available but none less than 4 ft. × 3 ft. gives much scope for growing worthwhile quantities of edible crops. An ideal internal height is up to 2 ft. at the front, 2½ ft. or more at the back.

Hardening off Frames are invaluable for hardening off greenhouse-raised plants, summer bedding plants, which must be gradually acclimatized to outdoor conditions. At times greenhouses become overcrowded and the frame can be used to accommodate plants in different stages of development—an important matter when they are being grown for living room decoration.

Heating Frames can be electrically heated by soil cables which should be laid on 2 in. of sand and covered with another 2 in. before loamy soil is put on. Make sure there is no crossing or touching by different sections of the same heating element.

Ventilation Damp and draughts cannot be kept out simply by keeping the top closed. Without air, mildew and rotting will occur. Ventilation is needed daily excepting in very cold or frosty weather. Never let cold winds blow into a frame; sliding lights are better than the hinged type since they can always be kept open away from the wind by using little blocks. Protective mats are valuable during frosty periods but should not be used when they are wet. It is an advantage to have duplicate mats so that the wet ones can be dried.

Forcing With heat you can force chicory, rhubarb and seakale, and in January, early potatoes 'Home Guard' and 'Arran Pilot' can be planted. Lettuce sown in September will heart by Christmas, while partially grown lettuce, cauliflower and endive plants can be placed in frames to mature. Parsley transferred to frames in October will give winter pickings. Continuous supplies of mustard and cress may be had by successional sowings.

Drying Frames can be used for drying onions, potatoes and haricot beans, while they keep dry the ripening seed heads of onions and leeks.

Catch Cropping You can use the frame for catch cropping; for instance early tulips planted 4 in. deep in November over-planted with October-sown lettuce 'Premier' or 'Kloek'; 'Early French Breakfast' radish sown between the plants in January, will mature before the lettuce or tulips are very large.

A Greenhouse Annexe Frames can serve as an annexe to a greenhouse to accommodate flowering plants out of bloom and those for which the greenhouse would be too warm in summer.

What to Grow

Garden frames need never be vacant for they can be used to grow a great variety of edible and ornamental plants.

Cuttings of hardy plants and seedlings of autumn sown sweet peas will benefit if covered with frames in winter, while frame-grown violets are always appreciated.

Bulbs Spring flowering bulbs in pots and

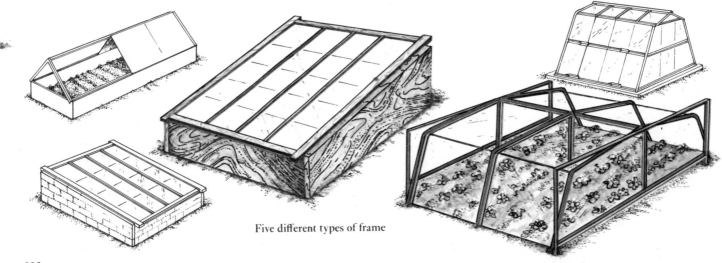

Five different types of frame

bowls can be kept in the frame before being taken a few at a time into the living room thus ensuring a succession of bloom. Bulbs or tubers such as hippeastrum, begonias, gloxinias and freesias can be placed in the frame in summer to ripen off properly before being stored for winter.

Bulbs in pots and bowls plunged in the frame in peat or leaf mould will make good roots before much top growth.

Greenhouse Plants Some popular plants

Provided the frame is properly ventilated, it may be used to house pot plants which would otherwise take up greenhouse space. *Right :* The range of plants for the cool greenhouse is very wide. Coleus dominate the foreground here

used for greenhouse display can be sown in pots or boxes in early summer and kept in a cool frame until September. These include calceolarias, cinerarias and primulas.

In strongly made brick or wooden frames half-hardy plants such as geraniums, heliotrope and fuchsias can be over-wintered if there is just enough heat to keep the air buoyant and free from dampness.

Beans and Peas Dwarf French beans 'The Prince' sown in pots at intervals of three weeks from March to August will be ready for picking about 12 weeks after sowing.

For early peas such as 'Feltham First', glass covering without heat gives protection from cold winds and wet soil as well as keeping away mice.

Cucumbers Cucumbers are an ideal frame crop. To provide the high temperature and humidity this crop requires, make an 8 in. or 9 in. deep hot bed of fresh manure in March. Greenhouse raised seedlings will be ready for planting on the hot bed in April.

Alternatively, frame cucumbers may be grown by making in early May, a trench 6–9 in. deep along the centre of the frame and filling it with fresh grass mowings, old leaves and fermenting straw. Plants raised in a heated propagator can be set in the trench in early June.

The frame soil should consist of fibrous loam, old manure and leaf mould or material from the compost heap. One strong plant is sufficient for a frame of 6 ft. × 4 ft. Maintain a humid atmosphere and provide shade. Stop side-shoots when there are four leaves. Spread the resultant growth evenly over the frame area. Remove male flowers, otherwise fruits taste bitter.

Melons Dutch Net or Cantaloupe melons can be grown in frames. For each plant, prepare a trench a foot deep and wide. Fill this with fermenting manure over which place a mound of soil on which plant the melon. Apply water and keep the frame closed for four or five days. Shade from hot sun and avoid excess moisture. Hand pollinate female flowers (those with an embryo fruit behind the flower) and spray with water in early mornings. Give liquid manure each week. Cut the fruit when a circular crack appears at the base of the stem.

Tomatoes Single, lean-to or double span roofed frames can be used for tomatoes. Fill the frame with a mixture of four parts of loam, and one part each of well-rotted manure (or compost), silver sand and mortar rubble or hydrated lime, plus a 3-in. potful of tomato fertilizer to every bushel of the other ingredients. If the frames are shallow excavate soil before adding the mixture so there is up to a foot of headroom. In mid-March set the plants 15–18 in. apart. Provide supports and keep side-shoots removed.

Year Round Interest

While a garden frame and a greenhouse used separately, will provide much interest and allow the production of many ornamental and edible crops, their value is greatly enhanced if they are used together. Whatever the size of one's greenhouse there never seems room enough to take in everything, which is why it is almost essential to use one or two frames in conjunction with the larger structures.

Many ornamental plants regarded as greenhouse specimens, can be placed outdoors in summer, in fact, they benefit from such treat-

ment by making a better display the following season. It will not do to stand them in the open, or even in a sheltered position; they must have a place unexposed to winds and where water requirements can be met.

A frame is ideal for this purpose since pots can be plunged and the glass kept off the frames in reasonable weather. This applies to winter flowering plants such as azaleas, poinsettias and hydrangeas.

Frames are invaluable for propagating from seeds, cuttings, offsets and division, many highly decorative plants which will subsequently live in the greenhouse. Half-hardy bedding plants such as asters, antirrhinums, petunias, sweet peas and zinnias can be hardened off.

Viola cuttings can be overwintered, while bulbs in pots or bowls can be plunged in the frame for making a good root system before being moved to the greenhouse. In summer frames can be used for greenhouse plants that do not like high temperatures, while a shaded frame will hold calceolarias, cyclamen and primulas such as *P. obconica, P. malacoides* and *P. sinensis.*

Regal pelargoniums and perpetual flowering carnations will benefit from being placed in sunny frames from June to mid-September. The lights can be taken off or the sides of the frames raised for tall plants.

Pans of alpines kept in the frame in summer can be transferred to the greenhouse for autumn and winter display.

The use of a greenhouse and frames means that a kind of shuttle service is operated. Many young plants may be started in the greenhouse early in the year, moved to the frame in summer, and taken back into the greenhouse again in autumn.

One Hundred Greenhouse Plants

Abutilon Half-hardy evergreen shrubs, the abutilons have several common names including Indian mallow, flowering maple, false maple and lantern flower.

Propagate in autumn or spring by cuttings of young wood, 4–5 in. long placed in trays of sandy compost in a temperature of 60°F (16°C). Cuttings of half-ripened wood can be taken in July and rooted under a bell-glass or in a frame. Use a compost of two parts of fibrous loam and one part each of peat and silver sand. Sow seeds in pans in a warm greenhouse in March.

A temperature of 60–65°F (17°C) in summer and 40°F (4°C) in winter is suitable.

Species include *A. darwinii*, 4 ft., orange; *A. megapotamicum*, orange-pink, 2½ ft.; *A. striatum* var. *thomsonii*, 6–10 ft., mottled green and yellow foliage.

Acacia With their showy yellow flowers in spring, these shrubs or small trees, are often referred to as wattles or mimosas. Simple to grow, they need a minimum winter temperature of 45°F (7°C). Pot plants can stand outdoors in a sunny position from June to September, making sure the roots remain moist. Pruning and potting can be done after flowering. Cuttings of young shoots root well in a propagating frame during the summer.

A. dealbata is the most commonly grown species. Others are *A. armata*, 9–10 ft., and *A. drummondii*, which grows well in large pots.

Achimenes These belong to the same family as gloxinias and are first-class in hanging baskets, indoor window boxes, pots and tubs. If the shoots are stopped periodically, good bushy plants develop.

Plant the small tubers from the end of January in a peaty compost, in a temperature of 65–70°F (18–21°C). Provide a close, humid atmosphere, giving more ventilation once flower buds develop. After flowering is over dry off the tubers, keeping them in a light airy place, where the temperature does not fall below 50°F (10°C).

Seed provides a cheap and easy method of building up stock. In pans or boxes of fine compost sprinkle the seed on the surface, lightly firming it. In a temperature of around 70°F (21°C) germination occurs within a fortnight. Move the plants into small pots and then into larger sizes as growth develops. A mixture of leaf mould, peat, silver sand and some old manure, or JIP 2 are satisfactory. Leaf and stem cuttings root easily.

Anthurium These are often known as flamingo plants, on account of their ornamental foliage and brightly coloured flowers which appear on long stems from April to August.

They flourish in a well-drained compost of equal parts of rough peat and sphagnum moss. Shade them from direct sunlight and provide a minimum winter temperature of 60°F (16°C). A moist atmosphere is essential, and plenty of water is needed in spring and summer. Repot in March.

Species include: *A. andreanum* with heart-shaped leaves and orange-red flowers. There are forms with red, pale pink, rose and white flowers. *A. scherzerianum* produces scarlet flowers which show up well against the deep green leaves.

Propagate by division in March, or by seed sown in a temperature of 70°F (21°C).

Anthurium scherzerianum

Aphelandra *A. squarrosa louisae* is a shrubby evergreen plant with handsome leaves and showy flowers and bracts. It does well in pots of peaty loam and likes warms conditions, although after flowering it succeeds in a temperature of 50°F (10°C), needing little water until spring. At that time, badly placed and weak growths should be removed.

Some of the resultant new shoots can be used as cuttings, especially if taken with a heel and placed in the propagating frame. When rooted, cuttings can be moved to 4- or 5-in. pots where, if left unstopped, they will produce flower heads the first year.

Asparagus These are invaluable for providing cut 'fern' and make attractive pot plants. They are not real ferns, but belong to the lily family. Use a compost such as JIP 1 and keep the plant well watered, or the foliage becomes discoloured. Sow seed in spring or summer in a temperature of 60°F (16°C). Move the seedlings to 3-in. pots, discarding those of slow or irregular growth.

A. plumosus nanus has long trails of fine foliage, ideal for cutting and useful for making up buttonholes in conjunction with various flowers. *A. sprengeri* is valuable for hanging baskets as it produces bright green sprays 1–2½ ft. long.

Azalea One of the most popular winter flowering greenhouse plants, *A. indica* is correctly *Rhododendron simsii*, but is still widely known and sold as an azalea. Colours include shades of pink, red and white.

Make sure the roots remain moist. Plants are grown in a peaty mixture which is difficult to moisten if it dries out. Remove faded flowers to encourage the following season's flower buds. Repot as necessary in May and stand the plants outdoors in a sheltered place or bury the pots to their rims in the garden. Bring them into the greenhouse in September, maintaining a moist atmosphere. Frequent syringeings of water encourage the flower buds to develop. Avoid lime in the compost or in the water; it is best to water with rainwater.

Propagation is by cuttings of young shoots in summer or early autumn, rooted in a propagating frame.

Begonia This beautiful genus consists of a number of groups each with distinguishing features. All like moist, peaty leafy compost, good light with liquid feeding when in growth. See Favourite Garden Flowers for further details.

Beloperone Known as the shrimp plant, *B. guttata* is an evergreen, shrubby plant from South America. It has inconspicuous pink flowers concealed by decorative pink bracts which colour best when the plant is kept in the sun. Too much warmth hinders full colouring. They need fairly rich soil. Encourage a winter rest by keeping them dry and cool.

Cut plants back early in the year and ensure good drainage. Over-watering causes leaf drop. Propagate by cuttings of young growths in spring. They will root better if bottom heat is provided.

Boronia *B. megastigma*, a sweet-scented plant comes from Australia. Sow seed thinly and evenly in sandy compost in seed trays or directly into small pots in a temperature of not less than 55–60°F (13–16°C). Germination is slow, sometimes taking four to six weeks depending on temperature. When the seedlings are 1 in. high move them to 2½-in. pots and give more room as growth develops. Use lime-free, sandy loam. Occasional top dressings of leaf mould are helpful. Prune established specimens in spring, although if the blooms are cut this can be part of the pruning procedure. The maroon and yellow flowers are produced over a long period.

Bougainvillea These sub-tropical shrubs or small trees depend on their gaily coloured flower bracts for their decorative value. Sun and good drainage with room to climb are necessary if there is to be a lasting summer display. Moisture and frequent liquid feeds are needed but avoid over-potting. After flowering, prune back side shoots to two buds, removing weak shoots. *B. glabra* and its form *sanderiana*, both pink, are free flowering, while *B. spectabilis* has mauve-pink bracts. Propagate by cuttings of young shoots in February in a temperature of not less than 75°F (23°C).

Boussingaultia The Madeira vine, *B. baselloides*, a native of Equador and Peru, is a quick-growing, half-hardy perennial climber. The reddish stems bear wavy, heart-shaped fleshy leaves and scented white flowers in branched sprays in autumn.

Use sandy loam and peat with plenty of moisture in summer. Dry off the tuberous roots in winter, leaving them in the soil, or lift and store as for dahlias. Seed or division of the tuberous roots and tubercles are means of increasing stock. Sowing and planting time is in spring, although seed-raised plants are slow to reach flowering size.

Bouvardia These evergreen plants provide a splendid display from September to January. They can be grown in small pots which should be watered and fed well in summer to build the following season's flower buds. Plenty of light, but shade from direct sun suits these plants. If growths are kept pinched out bushy specimens develop. Prune after the plants have been rested for a few weeks. Flowers form on new shoots.

Propagation is by cuttings in spring, preferably in a temperature of 65–70°F (18–21°C).

Reliable species and varieties include: *B. humboldtii*, white and *B. triphylla*, scarlet.

Bromeliads The majority of these interesting greenhouse plants originate from Central and South America and have decorative foliage and in some instances colourful flowers. There are two main groups (1) the epiphytes, which live on boughs of trees, (2) the terrestrial kinds which grow on the ground or on rocks.

The leaves of most epiphytes form a rosette making a central depression or cup which collects water. If this cup is filled with water at greenhouse temperature, the plants will stand long periods of dryness. Keep the roots just moist. Liquid fertilizer in spring is all the feeding required.

The easiest bromeliads to grow include *Aechmea rhodocyanea*, *Billbergia nutans* (Queen's tears) and *Neoregelia caroliniae tricolor*. *Cryptanthus bivittatus* is one of the best of the smaller kinds. It forms a star-shaped rosette of leaves which lie flat on the soil. These are prettily striped in shades of green and have crumpled edges. Sideshoots can be used for propagation. *C. zonatus* is broader leaved with silvery or yellow markings on a maroon-green background. *Vriesea splendens* flourishes in a temperature of 50°F (10°C). The pale green leaves are banded maroon. It likes semi-shade in summer; offshoots can be used for propagation.

Brunfelsia These evergreen shrubs freely produce scented flowers in spring and summer. Good light, but not prolonged sunshine is helpful and they need well-drained rich soil. Cut out weak shoots in February and once growth is fully active, give plenty of moisture. A warm, moist atmosphere is best when the plants are growing. Propagate by cuttings of half-ripe shoots in a warm frame.

Species include: *B. americana*, white; *B. calycina*, purple passing to white.

Top: A group of colourful foliage house plants. In front are examples of the so-called 'vase plants' or bromeliads. In nature, water collects in the central cup or 'vase' formed by the leaves. This should always be kept full, preferably with tepid rainwater. *Left: Bouvardia* 'Mary', one of the plants which provide colour in the greenhouse in autumn and early winter. *Below:* One of the many colour forms of achimenes, the hot-water plant

Cacti and other Succulents These bizarre plants are very popular and widely grown in greenhouses. Easy to cultivate, their extensive range of shape and habit plus in many species showy flowers, make them attractive. For fuller descriptions see INDOOR PLANTS elsewhere in this work.

Caladium These are tuberous-rooted perennials grown for their richly coloured ornamental foliage. They like warmth, and $55°F$ ($13°C$) should be regarded as the minimum winter temperature.

Start tubers in March, in boxes of peaty soil, giving frequent overhead syringeings. When the plants are growing well, move them to 5-in. pots of two parts of loam and one part each of peat, decayed manure and silver sand. Water regularly while the plants are growing, but when leaves discolour, dry off the roots, keeping them in the warm. Propagation is by division in spring, occasionally from seed. Species to grow are *C. bicolor* and *C. humboldtii* and their forms.

Calceolaria These easily grown plants succeed in a temperature of $50–65°F$ ($16–18°C$). They form bushy plants with pouch-like flowers in yellow, red or brown, many being prettily freckled.

Sow seed in June and July, prick out seedlings early and pot on according to growth. The plants like light, rich soil which should be pressed firmly. The weakest looking seedlings often produce the best blooms. Keep the plants cool and shaded. Overhead sprayings produce the right atmosphere. If the pots are placed on a base of moist gravel or shingle, growth develops evenly. A winter temperature of $45–50°F$ ($8–10°C$) is sufficient and less moisture is needed then. As the flower buds develop, a rather drier atmosphere is required. It takes between eight and nine months for flowering sized plants to develop.

C. multiflora nana hybrids grow to 9 in. tall and the large-flowered 'Albert Kent' hybrids 15 in. There are newer strains including F_1 hybrids, as well as the shrubby *C. integrifolia* (*C. rugosa*), 3–4 ft. tall.

Callistemon A native of Australia, *C. citrinus*, the bottle brush, has leathery, greyish green leaves and dense, highly decorative spikes of yellow flowers near the end of the shoots. In the form *splendens* the flowers are bright crimson. The plants need ample sun, light and air. Use well-drained pots of peaty loam. Cut back shoots after flowering and give overhead syringeings of water. Repot every third year. Stand the pots outdoors during summer but never expose the plants to low temperatures. Propagation is by cuttings of ripe wood rooted in a propagating frame in late spring or summer.

Camellia These shrubby plants are much easier to grow than is often supposed. They flourish in a temperature of $60–65°F$ ($16–18°C$) and like plenty of light and sun. Keep them in the same position, for when moved around the buds fail to open or fall prematurely. Sandy loam and leaf mould suits them. Frequent overhead syringeings from the time the buds begin to swell until colour shows are helpful. Repotting with good drainage should be done after flowering. Do not feed until spring. As necessary, shorten long, badly placed shoots after flowering. Many named single and double varieties are available in shades of red, pink and white.

Propagation is by seed or by cuttings rooted in late summer in a warm propagating frame.

Campanula *C. isophylla*, an almost hardy, blue-flowered trailing plant is valuable for hanging baskets and pots, giving a fine display from spring to autumn. Specially useful for the cooler parts of the greenhouse, it can be grown outdoors in summer. Remove faded flowers. Cuttings of young growths root easily in spring or plants can be divided. Any good soil mixture is suitable. *C.i. alba* has white flowers.

Canna see Bulbs, Corms and Tubers.

Cantua *C. buxifolia* is a branching flowering shrub of easy cultivation. Treat it as a bush, or train the growth to the roof or greenhouse pillar. Clusters of six to eight large funnel-shaped flowers are produced in April and May. The bright red buds open a showy rosy-red, suffused yellow.

A compost of turfy loam, leaf mould and silver sand is suitable. Propagation is by cuttings made from half-ripened shoots placed in sandy soil in a temperature of $50–55°F$ ($10–13°C$), in summer.

Carex *C. morrowii variegata* is an attractive, decorative grass; the narrow green leaves have white edges. Keep the plants moist and away from bright sun, or they will dry out quickly. Peaty loam with a little bonemeal suits them, and they do best kept in small pots. Propagate by division in spring.

Carnation These can be grown with other plants, but are best by themselves. There are two main groups for growing under glass, the Perpetual Flowering and Perpetual Malmaison. A start can be made in spring by buying rooted cuttings or better still, established plants in 5- or 6-in. pots. Essentials for success include good ventilation and a fairly dry cool atmosphere; even in frosty weather

A beautiful form of the Australian bottle-brush, *Callistemon citrinus splendens*. Plants grown in pots in the greenhouse may be stood out of doors in summer

Left: A sweetly scented bloom of the gardenia (*Gardenia jasminoides*), an evergreen shrub for the greenhouse, which blooms intermittently over a long period

Right: Some of the wide range of colours to be found in the cinerarias, which flower from December through to April. For the earliest show, sow in May, with further sowings at 14-day intervals

a temperature of around 45°F (7°C) is sufficient. Avoid overwatering. For periodic feeding, use a carnation fertilizer. Catalogues of specialist growers list a wide range of varieties and also describe the stopping process.

Propagation is from cuttings or pipings taken in spring.

Celosia   see Annuals and Biennials.

Ceropegia   These fleshy-rooted plants of twining or semi-climbing habit grow best in full light with shading from direct sun. The finest results come from plants which have restricted roots. Use well-drained compost with plenty of peat and some old manure or bonemeal. Free ventilation and a slight winter rest will prove beneficial. Propagation is by short cuttings, preferably rooted in a propagating case.

C. woodii is the most reliable species. Often known as hearts entangled because of its manner of growth, it has small heart-shaped foliage and freely produced pinkish-purple flowers. It is ideal for hanging baskets.

Chrysanthemum   No collection of autumn and winter flowering greenhouse plants is complete without chrysanthemums. The range of varieties and their cultivation is described in FAVOURITE GARDEN FLOWERS.

Cineraria   These are indispensable for a colourful display from December to April. For the earliest show, sow in May, with further sowings at 14-day intervals. Transplant seedlings to small pots and keep them

away from direct sunshine. Stand the plants in a shaded cold frame. Plant firmly, not bruising the stems or burying the crowns. Cinerarias flower well in 5-in. pots. In September move them to a temperature of 50°F (10°C). When flowering stems show, feed with liquid manure. Watch for white and green fly; use derris insecticide to deal with these pests.

Good strains include *C. multiflora maxima nana*, 1 ft., compact and uniform; *C.* 'Moll' Strain, 1 ft., enormous heads on compact plants; *C. stellata*, star-shaped flowers in immense clusters. 'Gubler's Mixed' produces up to 70% double and semi-double flowers.

Citrus   *C. mitis*, the calamondin, makes a branching shrub about 18 in. high with small oval, dark green leaves. The fragrant white flowers are followed by oranges up to 1½ in. in diameter. Specimens in fruit are attractive from December to April.

A minimum winter temperature of about 50°F (10°C) is suitable. If the pots are plunged in soil outdoors in a sheltered sunny situation, the wood will ripen and flower buds for the following season will develop. A moist atmosphere encourages fruit to set. Propagation is by cuttings rooted in spring in a propagating frame.

Clivia   see Bulbs, Corms and Tubers.

Codiaeum   see Indoor Plants.

Coleus   see Annuals and Biennials.

Columnea   These evergreen trailing plants grow successfully where the winter temperature remains above 55°F (13°C). Use a compost of equal parts of peat, sphagnum moss and coarse sand with a little charcoal. Water, warmth and a moist atmosphere are needed in summer, with regular applications of liquid manure. In winter keep plants cool and dry to encourage a resting period.

Left in the same containers for a few years they produce a striking effect in hanging baskets or cascading over greenhouse pillars.

Propagation is by rooting 2–3-in. cuttings of half-ripened shoots in a propagating frame in spring. Stop rooted plants a couple of times to ensure bushy growth and trailing stems 2–3 ft. long.

Species include *C. gloriosa*, scarlet and yellow, and *C. glabra*, orange-scarlet.

Cordyline   see Indoor Plants.

Cuphea   Although it can be grown outdoors in a sheltered spot *C. ignea* (*C. platycentra*), the cigar plant, makes a delightful pot plant. The red tube the flowers form, has a dark ring at the end which, with the wide mouth, produces an effect resembling a cigar. Flowers appear freely on 12–15-in. stems from July to September. Sow seed in boxes or pans during March and prick out the seedlings into boxes or small pots.

Cyclamen   see Bulbs, Corms and Tubers.

Cypripedium   This is one of the easier orchids which can be grown with other plants. A minimum winter temperature of 45°F (7°C) is needed. Avoid draughts and keep the plants from direct sunshine. Provide a humid atmosphere during spring and summer at which times the pots should be soaked every five or six days.

Use an orchid compost of which the base is osmunda fibre or sphagnum moss. Good drainage should be provided and the pots placed on gravel covered staging or inverted pots. Sphagnum moss round the plants is helpful. Necessary potting can be done from March to July.

C. insigne, with white, purple and brown flowers, and its many hybrids are especially reliable.

Datura   The angels' trumpet, *D. suaveolens*, an impressive shrubby plant, is invaluable for cool greenhouse decoration with its large white pendulous trumpet-shaped blooms in late summer.

Give plenty of water in summer, but keep almost dry in winter and as growth develops keep from direct sun. Propagate by 6-in. long cuttings inserted in pots of light soil. The plant will grow 9 or 10 ft. high in time, but may be kept smaller by hard pruning after it has flowered.

Dipladenia   This attractive twining plant likes a minimum winter temperature of 55°F (13°C). A moist atmosphere and plenty of water in summer are needed. Propagate by cuttings of young shoots in spring, inserted in a peaty, sandy mixture in a warm frame.

The flowers are trumpet-shaped; in *D. brearleyana* pinkish-red, and in *D. splendens* pink, in large heads which open one flower at a time.

Dizygotheca see Indoor Plants (under Aralia).

Dracaena These splendid foliage plants thrive in a minimum winter temperature of 55°F (13°C). The species vary greatly in shape and colour and should be grown in pots of rough peaty loam. Full light ensures that the leaves colour well. Propagation is by pieces of stem placed in sandy peat in a propagating frame, with bottom heat. Species include, *D. deremensis*, with silvery stripes; *D. godseffiana* with cream-spotted leaves; and *D. sanderiana*, the glossy leaves edged ivory.

Eranthemum A beautiful winter and spring flowering shrub for the warm green-house, *E. pulchellum* (*macrocephalum*), 2–2½ ft., grows easily in a mixture of fibrous loam, leaf mould and sand. The flowers are an attractive bright blue, a colour uncommon in winter-flowering plants.

Specimens reserved for propagation should be cut back after flowering. They then produce strong basal shoots suitable for cuttings. These soon root if inserted in pots of a mixture of equal parts of loam, leaf mould and silver sand, or JIP 2. Once growing well, move them singly into 3-in. pots of a similar compost. Keep them in a temperature of not less than 60°F (16°C) and maintain a moist atmosphere. Once established and growing freely, plentiful supplies of moisture will be beneficial, with occasional applications of liquid manure.

Erica This very large genus, the heaths or heathers, contains the Cape heaths, excellent winter-flowering plants for the cool green-house. They require lime-free compost, regular pinching in early stages to ensure bushy growth, and a constant supply of moisture. Trim off the dead flowers and in summer stand the plants in a sheltered place outdoors.

Propagation is from cuttings of new growth taken in early November and inserted in a mixture of peat and sand in a temperature of 60°F (16°C), preferably with bottom heat. Pot on and pinch out as necessary. *E. gracilis* and *E. hyemalis* and their varieties are the easiest kinds.

Eucalyptus Many species make excellent pot plants when young, the foliage assuming an attractive silvery shade. They flourish in rich open compost and like plenty of water in summer but should be kept drier in winter. Propagate by seed sown in warmth in spring or by cuttings of side-shoots rooted in June in a propagating frame.

Eucharis These bulbous plants produce fragrant flowers in winter. Plenty of water is needed from March to September, less at other times, and a temperature of 60–70°F (16–21°C). Pot in a compost containing well-rotted manure, bonemeal and charcoal.

Propagation is by division. If necessary, pot the bulbs after flowering, although they can be left in the same pot for three years if top-dressed annually. Liquid feeding can begin once the flower buds begin to unfold. Gradually dry off as foliage discolours.

E. grandiflora amazonica, the Amazon lily has white flowers; *E. sanderi*, white and yellow.

Euphorbia The most popular and widely grown greenhouse species is *E. pulcherrima*, the poinsettia, which is so showy in autumn and winter. The large scarlet or pink bracts are very decorative.

Keep plants in full light and moderately watered. A temperature of 60–65°F (16–18°C) is ideal. Once the bracts expand less moisture is needed. After flowering gradually dry off the plants. At the end of April, soak the roots and cut back stems to 4 in. From these will develop three or four shoots, which can be used as cuttings. Dip the cut ends in powdered charcoal before inserting in a mixture of loam, peat and sand. Provide a temperature of about 60°F (16°C) and when plenty of roots have formed, feed with liquid manure.

The 'Mikkelsen' strain has shorter, bushier growth and the bracts remain in showy condition for a long time.

Eurya *E. japonica*, a splendid foliage plant

for the cool greenhouse, has large leathery green leaves prettily edged with yellowish-scarlet. The flowers are insignificant. The plant has no special cultural requirements but will benefit if placed outdoors in a sheltered place in summer. Propagation is by cuttings taken in spring or summer, rooting them in a propagating frame.

Exacum These biennials will flourish in a winter temperature of 55°F (13°C).

Sow seed in early August in pots or boxes of sandy compost. Little water is needed from November to February, when the plants should be moved to 5-in. pots.

E. affine, 6 in., with scented lilac flowers is the best known species; *E. macranthum*, 1½ ft. has deeper blue flowers.

Fatzhedera *F. lizei* is a hybrid between fatsia and hedera. Tall-growing, it has five-lobed dark green leaves. There is a variegated form, *variegata*. Cultivation is as for Fatsia (below), except that propagation must be by stem cuttings rooted in spring.

Fatsia *F. japonica*, the false castor oil plant, is a tall shrub with large, dark green, 7- to 9-lobed leaves. It can be grown outdoors in sheltered places but looks impressive in large pots. Propagation is by seed or by cuttings which root easily. The form *variegata*, with white leaf tips *must* be propagated from cuttings.

Ferns Ferns like occasional overhead sprayings of tepid rain water, but do not spray those species with hairy foliage. Moist, well-drained compost containing plenty of leaf mould plus some bonemeal, is suitable.

Dust-like spores form on the undersides of the fronds; when sown these form a prothallus, which contains male and female organs,

Little water is necessary in winter, but plenty during spring and summer.

Freesia see Bulbs, Corms and Tubers.

Fuchsia see Favourite Garden Flowers.

Gardenia *G. jasminoides* and its varieties, with fragrant white flowers, are splendid evergreen shrubs, worth a place in any greenhouse with a minimum winter temperature of 50°F (10°C). Watering plays a crucial part in obtaining good results. Too much or too little will cause the buds to fall before they develop. Syringe frequently in spring and summer, except when the plants are in bloom. Prune into shape in February, when repotting can be done. Plant them in well-drained pots or beds of equal parts of loam,

Wijks' strain cannot be surpassed for size of flower, colour range and constitution.

Gloriosa The glory flower, *G. superba* is a tuberous-rooted climbing plant. Its cultivation is described in Bulbs, Corms and Tubers.

Gloxinia see Bulbs, Corms and Tubers.

Grevillea *G. robusta*, the silk-bark oak, an evergreen foliage plant, is easily grown in the average greenhouse. It has attractive, fern-like foliage in shades of green, bronze and almost red. It likes well-drained soil, free ventilation and plenty of water in summer. Repotting should be done in March or April. Plants are raised from seed sown in spring in a temperature of 65°F (18°C).

Far left: The angel's trumpet (*Datura suaveolens*), a fine plant for the cool greenhouse, has long, trumpet-shaped flowers in late summer
Left: Twining plants are always valuable in the greenhouse as they can be trained up into the rafters to give height to the display. This one is *Dipladenia sanderi*
Below: One of the many bright colour forms of the Barberton daisy, *Gerbera jamesonii*
Right: The poinsettia (*Euphorbia pulcherrima*) is one of the most colourful of greenhouse plants. It does well in a living room, provided it is not too cold, and is at its best in winter

which, in a temperature of 50–55°F (10–13°C), fertilize to produce the first leaf.

Specimens for the cool greenhouse include: *Adiantum cuneatum*, the maidenhair fern; *Nephrolepis exaltata* – for hanging baskets; *Pteris cristata* and *Davallia dissecta*.

Ficus see Indoor Plants.

Francoa A native of Chile, *F. ramosa*, the bridal wreath, has a stiff, erect main spike 2–3 ft. high, with numerous small subsidiary shoots, especially if the main stem is cut back after flowering. These are clothed with white or pinkish-red flowers throughout late summer. It succeeds in the cool greenhouse where the temperature is about 60°F (16°C) in summer and not less than 45°F (7°C) in winter.

Sow seed in March, preferably with bottom heat. Prick off and pot up the young plants, in a compost of equal parts of sandy loam and leaf mould. Provide cool, airy conditions such as in a frame during summer, and bring the plants into the greenhouse in early autumn.

peat and decayed manure (or leaf mould) with a little charcoal, and shade them from direct sunshine.

Propagation is by cuttings of firm side-shoots taken from February to March, in a temperature of 70–75°F (21–23°C).

Gerbera The Barberton daisy (*G. jamesonii*) will flourish in a sandy soil containing plenty of humus. Free drainage is needed, but the soil should never dry out. It is best to grow plants in large pots or boxes about 15–18 in. deep. Do not bury the crowns. Cover the surface soil with a layer of sand and shingle and plant so that the crown is just above soil level. Plenty of water is required in summer, but little during winter. Never cut the flowers; pull them from the crown. Propagation is from seed, as fresh as possible. Sow thinly in a temperature of 65°F (18°C), preferably with bottom heat. When the seedlings can be handled, prick them into a sandy compost, subsequently transferring them to pots.

Various strains are available, but the 'Van

Heliotropium see Annuals and Biennials.

Hippeastrum see Bulbs, Corms and Tubers.

Hoya *H. carnosa*, the wax flower, has heads of flesh-pink flowers; *H. bella*, less vigorous, has flowers with crimson centres. Both are showy evergreen climbers suitable for pots or a well-drained border. Water freely in summer, moderately in winter. Frequent overhead sprayings when in growth are beneficial. Pruning consists in cutting out weak, badly placed shoots. Do not remove the flower stalks, since secondary growths develop from the base for further flowering. Propagate by layers or by cuttings of the current season's growth.

Humea *H. elegans*, the incense plant, is best treated as a biennial and seed should be sown in sandy soil in spring. Water carefully during winter and grow the plants in rich soil containing lumpy peat. Well-grown plants may reach 4 or 5 ft. high. The feather-like flower plumes consist of many small pinkish florets.

Impatiens The balsams have fleshy stems growing 1–2 ft. high. Well-grown plants often remain in flower over a period of many months. *I. holstii* has reddish stems and pink flowers; its hybrids are in shades of pale rose, red and violet. *I. sultanii* has carmine and rose flowers. Both are known as busy Lizzie, because they flower so freely. The dwarf 'Scarlet Baby', which produces bright scarlet flowers, and 'General Guisan', growing 5–10 in. high with red and white blooms, are particularly useful pot plants.

Sow seed in boxes or pots from March to May in a temperature of around 60°F (16°C). Once the first rough leaf appears, prick out the seedlings and pot up singly, in a compost rich in peat or leaf mould.

Kalanchoë These useful succulent plants have interesting foliage and attractive flowers from March onwards. *K. blossfeldiana*, bright flame red, is the best known. It has a dwarf form, 'Tom Thumb', with bronze leaves. *K. carnea* is pink, and *K. flammea*, orange-scarlet.

A soil mixture of loam, leaf mould, silver sand and a little old manure or bonemeal is ideal. Keep plants in full light and water regularly. After flowering is over pinch back the growing points to a pair of good leaves. This will encourage bushy growth. If the plants are kept in a temperature of around 60°F (16°C) from the end of July, flower colour will show in October thus lengthening the time of flowering. Propagation is by seed sown in February and March or from summer cuttings.

Lantana These evergreen shrubs have large heads of verbena-like flowers over a long period from spring to autumn. Good species include *L. camara*, yellowish-red; *L. nivea*, white; and *L. selloviana*, mauve, of trailing habit. They flourish in a rich soil mixture, containing decayed manure or bonemeal. Pot plants should be cut back in February, to keep them bushy, shortening each shoot to 3 in. In a temperature of 60°F (16°C) new growths soon develop and, as necessary, some of these can be taken as cuttings. Bottom heat encourages rooting. Lantanas can also be raised from seed.

Lapageria *L. rosea*, with its bell-like, rosy-crimson flowers, is one of the best evergreen flowering climbers for the cool greenhouse, standing a winter temperature as low as 40–45°F (4–7°C). It can be grown in pots but is best planted out in a well-drained compost of very peaty loam plus a sprinkling of silver sand and charcoal. Shade from strong sunshine and give plenty of water in spring and summer with overhead syringeings until flower buds begin to break.

Propagation is by layering of shoots in summer. There are forms with white, rose or red flowers.

Lasiandra *L. macrantha*, a native of Brazil, produces large rich violet-blue flowers in summer. It is an evergreen climber, excellent for covering walls or pillars. The flowers are more freely produced when the plants have a free root run. Well-drained peaty soil is suitable. Trim the plants as necessary in February. Well-rooted specimens like plenty of water in summer. A winter temperature of 50°F (10°C) is needed. Propagation is by cuttings in spring or from soft growth in summer.

Lilium Many lilies make first-class pot plants. A suitable compost consists of three parts of fibrous loam, one part each of peat (or leaf mould), silver sand and decayed manure. Alternatively, JIP 3 is suitable. For forcing, plant bulbs in October and November. Use 6- or 7-in. pots and for stem-rooting varieties, leave space in the pots for top-dressing later. Plunge the pots in peat or sandy soil in the cold frame and bring them into a temperature of 40–50°F (4–10°C) early in the year, gradually raising the heat to 60–70°F (16–21°C). Top dress when growth is 5 or 6 in. high. Where little heat is available, plant bulbs in February for flowering from

May onwards. Good varieties for pots include *L. auratum* and *L. speciosum*, both stem rooting; *L. longiflorum*, the white Easter lily; *L. formosanum*, white; and *L. brownii*, creamy-white with brownish-red markings.

Maranta *M. leuconeura* and its varieties are handsome foliage plants which like warm conditions with a winter temperature of 60–65°F (16–18°C). Shade and humidity are aids to good development. While plenty of water is needed during spring and summer, drainage must be perfect.

Propagation is by division of crowns in spring. In the species the leaves have white veins; the form *kerchoveana* has emerald green leaves blotched red; it is known as the prayer plant since the leaves move to an upright position at night.

Mesembryanthemum This is the name of a group of widely differing plants, all of succulent habit. Some are tall and bushy, others prostrate or creeping. The lithops group is sometimes known as 'living stones' on account of their thick round or angular shape and colour.

There are many types to choose from as will be seen from the catalogues of specialists, and from the section of this work dealing with Indoor Plants.

Above: Easter lily 'Lilium longiflorum'
Left: Rehmannia angulosa

Mimosa Often known as the humble or sensitive plant, the common names of *M. pudica* refer to the fact that the leaflets droop at the slightest touch. Although little spikes of blue-purple flowers are produced it is the foliage which makes this plant worth growing, always creating interest, particularly among children. Plants are raised from seed sown thinly in pots of sandy compost. A temperature of 60–65°F (16–18°C) is quite sufficient.

Nerium An evergreen shrub with fragrant flowers, *N. oleander*, the oleander, thrives in pots, tubs or well-drained beds in the lightest and sunniest part of the greenhouse. A minimum winter temperature of 45°F (7°C) is needed. Repotting is done in February. Prune after flowering by shortening shoots of previous season's growth to 3 or 4 in. from the base. Propagation is from cuttings of firm shoots in early summer, placed in a temperature of 60–65°F (16–18°C).

The species has rosy-pink flowers; there are double white and red forms.

Opuntia These cacti are divided into several groups, those known as prickly pears being most decorative as pot plants. These have flat 'pads' which are really stem segments and not leaves. Opuntias are easy to grow, in sun and rich loamy soil with good drainage. Plenty of water is needed during the growing season but much less in winter. Propagation is easy by removing the pads and letting them dry for three days before potting them. Seeds can be sown in pots.

O. paraguyensis is a good flat padded species, with yellow flowers sometimes followed by purple fruits. See also Indoor Plants.

Palms There are several palms which can be grown successfully in the cool greenhouse. They flourish under cool conditions but during the growing season like warmth and moisture. They do well in a compost of fibrous loam, silver sand, old manure and if possible, brick dust. Avoid overpotting. Frequent overhead syringeings in summer help the fronds to develop properly. An occasional spongeing with weak soapy water will keep off scale insects.

Useful palms include: *Cocos weddelliana*, particularly reliable for small pots; *Howea* (*Kentia*) *balmoreana*, *Phoenix dactylifera*, the date palm, and *P. roebelinii*. The latter has arching fronds and looks well in the green-

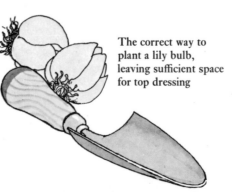

The correct way to plant a lily bulb, leaving sufficient space for top dressing

house or living room in 5- or 6-in. pots.

Pancratium These handsome bulbous plants are suitable for pots in the cool greenhouse. They flower most freely when established and slightly pot bound. Repotting in spring is rarely needed more than once in three years. The bulbs flourish in a mixture of three parts of loam, one part of decayed manure or bonemeal, with a little silver sand. Water freely in the growing season but give little in winter when a temperature of 45–50°F (7–10°C) will be ample. *P. illyricum* and *P. maritimum* grow 2 ft. high, and have fragrant pure white flowers.

Passiflora Vigorous climbers, the passion flowers will cover the rafters and walls of good sized greenhouses. They can be grown in tubs or large pots but are best in a well-drained border. A very rich soil encourages rampant growth at the expense of flowers and some form of root restriction is advisable. Transplant only in spring. A winter temperature of 45–50°F (7–10°C) is sufficient. Propagation is from cuttings of young shoots in spring.

P. caerulea, blue flowers and its white form, 'Constance Elliot' are best. *P. edulis* has bluish-purple flowers followed by fruits.

Pilea These plants form close mats of foliage and are useful for growing towards the front of the staging or for draping tubs or troughs. They thrive in semi-shade but are sensitive to gas fumes. Propagation is easy by spring cuttings. In a moist atmosphere and a temperature of 50–60°F (10–16°C) growth is freely made.

P. cadieri has small, green shiny leaves with red and silver markings. *P. microphylla* (*muscosa*) is the artillery plant, so named because of the way it discharges its pollen when shaken.

Pelargonium The so-called 'geraniums' are excellent greenhouse plants. Their cultivation is described in Favourite Garden Flowers.

Platycerium These fascinating ferns look well among the colourful cool greenhouse flowers. The common name stag's horn fern gives an idea of their shape. They are easy to cultivate in baskets or pots, but are a source of wonder when seen growing on a block of

1: Space for top dressing. 2: A layer of compost above the bulb. 3: The bulb surrounded by compost. 4: A good layer of compost below the bulb. 5: Rough compost or lumpy peat. 6: Broken crocks over the drainage hole.

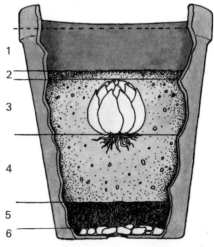

wood or a piece of bark which they encircle with their strong, infertile fronds. They can be grown in rough peat and sphagnum moss kept damp. Light and a moist atmosphere should be provided. Propagate by division.

P. bifurcatum often makes fronds of 2 ft. or more; *P. grande* requires rather more heat.

Primula In this large genus there are species which are invaluable for growing under glass from which frost can be excluded. All can be raised from seed sown in spring. For sowing and potting use a slightly acid compost.

P. obconica continuously produces clusters of large lilac, pink, crimson or white flowers. When some persons touch the foliage they are affected by a rash. The problem is overcome by wearing gloves. Sow from February to April. *P. malacoides* has dainty flowers produced in tiers. The colour varies from lavender to deep rose or white, some strains being double. Sow in June. *P. sinensis* has large single purplish-rose or white flowers. When potting do not bury the centres of the plants or they will decay. Sow in spring. *P. × kewensis* has fragrant yellow flowers in winter or early spring. Sow in March or April.

Do not leave the plants in small pots too long or they will starve, resulting in irregular development. Keep the soil in the pots firm

but not hard. Cool summer treatment, shade from strong sunshine, ample ventilation with no over watering and freedom from pests, encourage the plants to give a long-lasting display.

Rehmannia A half-hardy herbaceous perennial from China, *R. angulosa* grows 2–4 ft. high. Its large drooping pink flowers are somewhat like those of the foxglove.

Sow seed thinly from the end of May until August, using well-drained pans or boxes, just covering the seed with fine compost. Prick out seedlings as soon as they can be handled and pot on gradually until the 6- or 7-in. size pot is reached.

Keep them in a cool greenhouse or frost-proof frame during winter. Water regularly in spring and summer, giving occasional feeds of liquid manure. As cut flowers, they are long lasting. Specially good plants can be used for propagation, taking basal cuttings in autumn.

Rochea These succulent plants have at various times been listed under crassula, kalosanthes and cotyledon. The 12-in. stems produce long, thickly arranged leathery leaves. In summer these stems are crowned with tubular scarlet flowers. Easily grown, a winter temperature of 45°F (7°C) is suffi-

Above: 'Constant Nymph', one of the many varieties of the Cape primrose (streptocarpus), which enjoy cool greenhouse conditions
Below: A variety of colourful plants in a cool greenhouse, where many exotic plants quickly become acclimatized and grow successfully
For these plants to flourish, a minimum night temperature of 4°-7°C should be maintained, with good ventilation

Above: Brazilian spider-flower
Tibouchina semidecandra

Saintpaulia
leaf cuttings

cient. Rich, well-drained compost is needed and plenty of water during spring and summer–much less for the rest of the year. After flowering, cut back the stems to keep the plants shapely. Propagation is by cuttings rooted in warmth in spring.

Roses Where sufficient space is available bush and climbing roses can be grown in the cool greenhouse, either in the border or in pots. Use a well-drained compost containing a good proportion of decayed manure with fibrous loam and bonemeal to ensure that food is available when needed.

Except where climbers are grown against the pillars or walls of the house, they should be potted in November and kept in the open until February and then be taken into a temperature of 45°F (7°C), given plenty of light and ventilation. In subsequent years, prune well before they start into growth.

Good hybrid tea varieties include older sorts such as 'Ophelia', 'Mme Butterfly', 'Richmond'. 'Maréchal Niel', 'Niphetos' and 'W. A. Richardson' are reliable climbers.

The dainty, small-flowered red and pink Garnette roses are very long lasting, and are suitable for buttonholes or other decorative purposes.

Saintpaulia The African violet is not among the easiest of flowers to grow, but once its likes and dislikes are understood and acted upon, it responds generously. Light is important and plants should have all possible winter sunshine. Lack of blooms is caused by too little light, while anaemic-looking foliage and short stems, are an indication of too much.

Temperatures are important. The aim should be to maintain warmth at 60–70°F (18–21°C) and at night 55°F (13°C) should be the minimum. Avoid draughts and stagnant air, but maintain humidity round the plant. Never attempt to grow saintpaulias where gas is used. Water with care; always use tepid water. Cold water splashes lead to leaf spotting.

Leaf cuttings are a ready means of increasing stock. Plants can also be raised from seed sown in a temperature of 70°F (21°C). While there is no need to cover seed with compost but merely to press it in, a little silver sand sprinkled over the surface helps to prevent damping off. Prick off and pot up in the usual way. Repot from February to May.

The only species grown, *S. ionantha*, has violet-blue flowers, but many single and double hybrids are available in shades of blue, pink and white.

Salpiglossis The netted and veined funnel-shaped flowers of *S. sinuata* are to be had in colours ranging from brown to deep violet, through to orange, yellow and white.

Sow seeds in late August for winter and spring display, and in February for summer colour. JI seed compost is suitable. Sow the seed thinly, in a temperature of 55–60°F (13–16°C). Cover with paper to prevent the soil from drying out.

Once the seedlings have made three rough leaves thin them to 2 in. apart or move them straight into small pots. Pot on as growth proceeds. Light supports are useful, also shade from direct sunshine. August sowings can be moved into the cold frame and the plants brought indoors when the cold weather comes.

'Superbissima' is a fine mixed strain and the F_1 strain 'Splash', is most free flowering.

Sansevieria Often known as mother-in-law's tongue this favourite foliage plant for the cool greenhouse or living room has narrow erect, pointed fleshy leaves. For details of cultivation see Indoor Plants.

Schizanthus The butterfly flower or poor man's orchid is a showy, easily-grown cool greenhouse plant. It is raised from seed sown in August and September in pots of JI seed compost placed in the cold frame. Once the seedlings can be handled move them singly to small pots and transfer to the cool greenhouse before frosts come. They like plenty of air and light but little water in winter. Pot in spring using 5- or 6-in. pots according to size of plants. Pinch out growing points as necessary and provide slender supports. Seed can also be sown in spring.

The hybrid *S.* × *wisetonensis*, 1½–2 ft., has large flowers on compact bushes; in the strain 'Dwarf Bouquet Mixed', 1 ft., colours range from crimson to apple-blossom pink.

Smithiana Once known as naegelia, this makes a beautiful pot plant. The rich velvety foliage is attractively marked or veined in contrasting colours. The flowers, like small foxgloves, are produced in spikes well above the foliage. Many named cultivars are obtainable in a good colour range, including cream, pink, rose and salmon. Strong plants make a number of rhizomes which can be separated and used for increasing stock. Seed-raised plants take seven or eight months to come into flower. Sow seed in spring in a temperature of 75–80°F (24–27°C).

Start dormant tubers in spring in a temperature of 60–65°F (16–18°C) using pots of peaty compost, but do not bury them deeply. When flower spikes show, give liquid feeds at ten-day intervals. Keep water off the foliage or it will become marked.

After flowering, gradually dry off the rhizomes and store in a cool frost-proof place for the winter.

Solanum The bright orange-scarlet berries of the winter cherry, *S. capsicastrum*, make it popular at Christmas time. From January onwards sow at 10 to 14-day intervals to provide a succession. Keep the boxes or pans, in a temperature of 60–65°F (16–18°C) and cover them with glass and paper. Move the seedlings to other boxes or pans before potting them separately. This encourages bushy growth. Plants should be ready for 3-in. pots by early May and later for bigger sizes according to growth. Keep them under cool condi-

Right: Camellia reticulata 'Noble Pearl'

Above: The fragrant, white, wax-like flowers of *Stephanotis floribunda*, an evergreen climber for the warm greenhouse
Right: The orange-red flowers of *Streptosolen jamesonii*, an evergreen climbing plant for the cool greenhouse

tions and subsequently move them outdoors to a sheltered place. Once the flowers begin opening overhead sprayings of clear water will encourage a good set of berries. Several dilute liquid feeds will encourage the berries to swell.

Take the plants indoors in September, shortening long growths. Avoid a dry atmosphere and if aphis or red spiders are seen, spray with insecticide to keep the foliage clean and fresh looking.

Stephanotis Sometimes known as the clustered wax flower, *S. floribunda* is a choice evergreen climber for the warm house, with white fragrant flowers. A minimum winter temperature of 55°F (13°C) is required. Not one of the easiest plants to manage it is, however, well worth any trouble. In the greenhouse border it will grow tall, but in a large tub or pot it can be restricted to 8 or 9 ft. It likes a peaty compost and plenty of moisture in summer but should be kept almost dry in winter.

Cut out weak shoots in spring and apply a top dressing of rich soil. Propagation is by cuttings of the previous season's growth taken in spring; a temperature of 75°F (24°C) is needed for good rooting, preferably with bottom heat.

Strelitzia *S. reginae*, the bird of paradise flower, is a showy plant with handsome, long-stemmed leaves and in summer, large purple and orange flowers resembling a bird's head. A well-drained loamy compost containing peat and coarse sand is suitable. This should be kept moist in summer but little water is needed in winter when a temperature of 50°F (10°C) is quite sufficient.

Propagation is by detaching and planting up suckers. This is best done in late winter or early spring.

Streptocarpus The Cape primrose likes cool, humid conditions and the greenhouse should be ventilated on all reasonable occasions. The plants remain in growth well into October when watering should be reduced

so that the soil is on the dry side during winter but not dust dry. Repot in March, using a porous, moisture-retentive compost, plus decayed manure. Established plants benefit from feeds of liquid manure.

Propagation is by seed sown in succession to prolong the flowering period. From a December or January sowing, flowers appear between June and September, while from seed sown in June and July and over-wintered in a temperature of 50°F (10°C), plants will bloom from April onwards.

Various hybrid selections are available, many having flowers with unique throat markings contrasting with the dominant colour, usually purple, violet and pink shades, or white, the large bell-like blooms measuring 2 in. at the mouth.

Streptosolen Evergreen climbers for the frost-proof greenhouse are always of value. *S. jamesonii* is doubly useful because of its showy clusters of orange-red flowers in summer. It grows well in pots or tubs or can be planted out in rich, well-drained soil in the greenhouse border. Regular watering and syringeing in summer help to maintain good growth. Prune as necessary when growth is dormant.

Propagation is by cuttings of young growth placed in the propagating frame.

Tibouchina The Brazilian spider-flower, *T. semidecandra*, is an interesting evergreen shrubby climber for the cool greenhouse where it can be grown in pots of rich compost, although it does best in the greenhouse border. It bears clusters of rich purple flowers, individually 4–5 in. across.

Use a mixture of equal parts of loam and peat with a little silver sand. Keep the plants in full light and water and feed well in summer, with little moisture in winter. Prune established plants in February.

Propagate by half ripe shoots, preferably in a propagating case.

Torenia Usually treated as an annual, *T. fournieri*, 1 ft., is a charming, free-flowering

pot plant which thrives in a temperature of 60°F (16°C). It produces during July and August, large blue, antirrhinum-like flowers with a deeper blue and gold blotch.

Sow seed in March or April. Move seedlings to small pots and provide thin canes or sticks as support.

Trachelium *T. caerulea*, a half-hardy, shrubby perennial, known as the throatwort, is best treated as a biennial. Young plants are much more floriferous than older specimens. It likes light and sun and a compost of sandy loam and leaf mould. Heads of fragrant blue flowers on 18-in. stems appear from June to August.

From February to June, sow seeds thinly in boxes of beds in the greenhouse or sheltered frame. Prick out seedlings early. Fairly slow growth ensures bushy specimens. Pot firmly and when plants are growing well, pinch out the leading shoots. In late September transfer plants to 5-in. pots and maintain a minimum winter temperature of 45°F (7°C).

Zantedeschia This popular plant has several names including calla lily, and arum lily and is sometimes listed botanically under *Richardia*.

Pot the roots in July, one in a 6-in. pot or several in larger receptacles, in a compost of equal parts of loam, sharp sand and well-rotted manure. Keep them outdoors until mid-September and water sparingly. As growth is seen, increase moisture with overhead syringeings. In the greenhouse, give free ventilation and keep the compost moist. A temperature of 45°F (7°C) is sufficient, but more heat brings earlier flowering. Once the flowers are over and foliage discolours the roots can be dried off. Propagate by suckers detached at planting time.

Z. aethiopica, the lily of the Nile, has white flowers; *Z. elliottiana* yellow. The latter requires a temperature of 55°F (13°C) and should be planted in spring. Both grow 3 ft. or so tall.

House plants are those plants that can be expected to spend all their life in a dwelling house. If you have a greenhouse you can grow a very large number of plants for decorating your rooms, but, once they have spent a certain time indoors, they are then returned to the greenhouse and kept there to recover. These are not house plants in the sense in which we shall be discussing them. Here we shall confine ourselves to plants that can be expected to thrive in the rather difficult conditions of a dwelling house.

Humidity Conditions in rooms are difficult for plants mainly because the atmosphere is very dry. The majority of house plants are evergreens from tropical countries and in the tropics you are only liable to find evergreens where the atmosphere is damp. In many parts of the tropics the atmosphere tends to be so wet that a number of plants have evolved, known as epiphytes, which can get all their nourishment from the atmosphere and have more or less dispensed with a root system. We do not want a moist atmosphere in our rooms, but it is possible to create a moist zone around our plants, by standing the pot or pots in some container, which will either contain water or will contain some substance such as peat, which can be kept moist. You can put pebbles in a dish, nearly cover them with water and stand the pot on the pebbles, or you can get rather a deep bowl, plunge the pot in some moisture-retaining material, which can be peat, or sand or moss and keep this surround always rather moist. Both these methods will ensure that water vapour will always be rising around the plant and the warmer it is the more vapour will rise, which is just what the plant likes. If the pot is stood on pebbles you should make certain that the base of the pot is clear of water.

Light Compared to even a rather shady situation outside the light in rooms is not very satisfactory. It is, naturally, at its best on the window sill and gets down to near impossible conditions in corridors and halls. Some plants have evolved to grow in extremely poor light conditions, but it is only in the very densest forests that you will find the dark conditions of parts of our houses. Apart from a few ferns, not much will grow in these very shaded conditions and even these will not grow so well as they do where it is lighter. This means that the choice of plants for these murky places is extremely limited and it is probably easiest to forgo plants altogether in this sort of situation, rather than to put plants in and see them slowly deteriorate. In reasonably lit situations, it is probable that the light will be

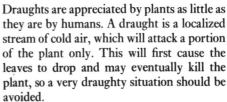
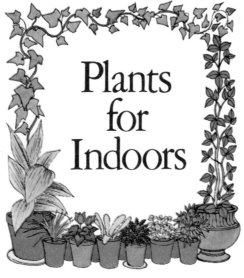

Plants for Indoors

House Plants

coming from one direction only, unless you have a room with windows on all sides. Plants tend to grow towards the light, so if your plant is lit from one window only, turn it slightly every week, so that all parts of the plant will be illuminated in turn. This will not only ensure that all the leaves receive ample light (and without ample light the leaves will not function properly), but it will also mean that the plant stays symmetrical and does not grow twice as fast from the side nearest the light source. This should be done whether the plant is on the window sill or whether it is in the centre of the room.

Leaves and Roots Most plants have two main feeding organs, the leaves and the roots. The leaves can take in plenty of nourishment and syringeing them with a foliar feed will have surprising results, but their main function is to make food for the plant. The roots will take up moisture and various chemicals from the soil. Normally neither can subsist without the other, but some plants do dispense with roots to a greater or lesser extent. A very few flowering plants dispense with leaves, but they can only do this by robbing other plants. Most plants require air, water and soil before they can function.

Air Apart from increasing the humidity of the air, there are other considerations.

Draughts are appreciated by plants as little as they are by humans. A draught is a localized stream of cold air, which will attack a portion of the plant only. This will first cause the leaves to drop and may eventually kill the plant, so a very draughty situation should be avoided.

Fumes from various forms of heating are another problem. Paraffin oil burners are normally fairly innocuous, although a few plants will shed leaves if placed near them, but if something goes wrong and the appliance smokes, you may well find many of your house plants dying. The fumes from gas fires used to be harmful to many plants, but the fumes of North Sea gas do not seem to damage plants. Coal fires seem to be harmless and, of course, central heating which maintains a more or less even temperature, is the ideal.

In the open air it is a safe assumption that the temperature will be lower at night than during the daylight hours. If you are out at work all day, and you do not have central heating, you will not light your fires until you come home, so that you may get the appalling conditions, from the plant's point of view, of a cold day and a hot evening. Many plants are very tolerant and can survive these unnatural conditions, but bear in mind that it is the daytime temperature that is the important figure to watch, as it is during the daylight hours that most of the growth is made. The fact that your room at night may be at a temperature of 70°F (21°C) does not mean that you can grow the plants that require this temperature, if it is liable to fall to 45°F (9°C) at midday. Minimum winter temperatures refer to the daytime readings, and these may fall a few degrees at night without any harm being done, so that you can air the room at night without qualms. During very frosty weather plants that are on the window sills should be brought further into the room, as it is quite possible for the window panes to be freezing, even though the rest of the room is quite comfortable and frost will certainly damage any house plants on window sills and will probably kill them.

Apart from frost many plants from warm climates will survive at temperatures that are lower than they require to make growth. For example, the popular *Philodendron scandens* will go through the winter quite happily with the temperature as low as 45°F (9°C), but it will be in a state of suspended animation. Not until the temperature reaches 60°F (15°C) will it start to make any growth. The re-

Left: To provide local humidity, place pebbles in the base of a bowl
Centre: Cover the pebbles with water and stand the plant pot on the pebbles
Right: Or place the pot inside a larger one, filling the space between with peat, kept damp

Codiaeum 'Mrs Iceton', one of the colourful crotons, which must be kept in a constant temperature, away from draughts

commended winter temperatures for house plants are usually about 10°F (5½°C) below the growth temperature, which means that if they are adhered to the plant will survive perfectly well, but will not be making any growth. The point of this is that growth made during the short daylight hours of winter is usually not very decorative. The stems are liable to become spindly and drawn, while the leaves will be small and a bad colour. Indeed with foliage plants it is usual in the spring to nip out all the growing points and any bad growth that has been made in the winter, so that when the plant does start into growth again, the growth will be well-leaved and the plant will become bushy rather than drawn. However, there are available enclosed glass boxes with their own heating and illumination and in these it is possible to keep tropical plants growing evenly throughout the year.

It is customary to put house plants into three categories, Cool, Intermediate and Warm. The Cool group need a winter temperature of from 45°F–50°F (7°–10°C), while a few, notably ivies and fatshedera will tolerate even lower temperatures. The Intermediate group need winter temperatures around 55°F (13°C), while the Warm group need a temperature around 65°–70°F (18°–21°C). During the summer they will need at least 10°F (5½°C) more. Few people can manage to maintain the higher temperatures and plants needing them are not discussed here.

Soil Nowadays one has a choice of two sorts of compost, those containing loam and those without loam, known as soilless composts. The most popular compost containing loam is the John Innes Potting compost, usually referred to as J.I.P. This is probably the best compost that one can purchase ready mixed, (see also Gardener's Glossary under Compost). J.I.P. 1 is used for plants in 3-in. pots, J.I.P. 2 is used for plants in 5- and 6-in. pots. For larger pots use J.I.P.3.

Good quality loam is hard to come by in large quantities and so the peat-based composts are now being increasingly used. These are mixtures of peat and sand with added chemicals. Peat and sand contain no nutrients so that when the plant has used all the chemicals in the soilless compost it will starve. With plants that are only going to be kept for a single season, for example, *Primula malacoides* this does not matter, but with plants that are going to be grown on from year to year, it is necessary to start replacing the chemicals as soon as the plant starts to use those already there.

Feeding Most house plants make their main growth between the end of March and the middle of September and this is the time to replace the chemicals by some form of feeding. There are various proprietary feeds, all of equal value, but it is necessary to follow the directions as to the amount and frequency of application. As the plant can take up only a limited amount at a time, little and often is better than large quantities at long intervals. Moreover any food not available to the plant is liable to be washed out during subsequent waterings, so it is not only potentially dangerous, but also wasteful to give too much food in any single application. Most of the feeds are applied to the soil dissolved in water

and these should not be given when the plant is completely dry, otherwise the chemicals could damage the roots. Feeds are best applied about two days after the normal watering, when the soil will not be completely dry, but equally will not be sodden. It is also possible to apply foliar feeds to the leaves, by syringeing the plant with a foliar feed solution. This is one of the best ways of feeding a plant, but it may not be convenient to syringe plants in your rooms. It is, however, usually possible to remove all the plants to your draining board and syringe them there.

Repotting As the plants grow, so do their roots and after a time it is necessary to move the plant to a larger pot. Most plants will want potting on yearly for the first few years.

The usual progression is from a 3-in. pot into a 5-in. pot and thence into a 6-in., 7-in. and finally an 8-in., in which pot it will probably remain, as plants in larger pots tend to be very large and unwieldy. Usually once you reach the 6-in. pot, it will probably suffice to pot on only every other year, so that it will be six years before you reach the 8-in. pot. Potting on should only be done when the plant is in full growth, so that May is usually the best month. If you tip the plant out of its pot (which is best done a day or so after watering) you can see if there are plenty of roots and if these are showing white tips. If the pot appears to be full of roots and these have their white growing tips, the plant is ready for potting on. This is best done when the plant is on the dry side, although it should not be dust dry, the soil may fall away from the roots when you take it out of its pot.

Take the plant out of its pot and lay it on the potting bench, or on the draining board.

Right: Aphelandra squarrosa 'Silver Queen'

If you are using a loamy compost, put some coarse grit or broken crocks at the base of the new pot; with loamless composts this can be dispensed with. Now place some of the compost in the base of the pot and stand the old plant in the middle to see if you have enough in. In pots up to 3-in. there should be a gap of ½ in. between the soil level and the rim of the pot, while for larger pots the gap should be an inch. If the level is too high, you will not get all the soil moistened when you water, if it is too low, you will get too much water and also the plant will not have all the soil that it could have, so this is a matter worth paying attention to. When you have the right level, fill in around the old soil ball with the new compost, firming it down with your thumbs fairly heavily, otherwise you will find that after watering there will be a gap between the old soil ball and the new soil. The new soil you are using should be on the dry side and crumbly, but not dust dry.

Once repotting has been completed, give the plant a good watering, after which it should be allowed to dry out and only watered sparingly for the next week or so. Putting the plant in a warmer situation will encourage the roots to grow more rapidly into the new soil. No feeding is necessary until this new soil has been occupied by fresh roots.

Watering The most essential part in the successful growing of house plants is in the correct use of the water can and more plants are lost through drowning than through any other cause. When you do water, you should do it properly. Fill the pot to the brim. If you give less it may well not moisten the whole of the soil ball. It does no harm to make sure of this and to turn out a plant a few hours after watering to see if the whole soil ball has been watered. If it has not, the only thing to do, if the plant is not in a state to be repotted, is to give two applications each time you water.

If you have some method of catching and keeping it, rain water is much to be preferred to tap water, but it is not always possible to obtain this. During the winter, very cold water will lower the temperature of the soil in the pot, perhaps to an excessive degree. Ideally the water should be at the same temperature as your room. You can get this either by mixing some hot water with the cold water, or by storing some water in your room for at least 24 hours before you use it. With most plants the temperature of the water is not very critical, but as far as African violets (saintpaulias), are concerned, if the temperature of the water is lower than 53°F (13°C) or higher than 60°F (15.5°C) you are liable to get unsightly blotches on the leaves. Always, during cold weather particularly, avoid using very cold water, or water that is more than luke warm, otherwise you can again damage the roots. Having watered the plant, give it no more water until it has used up all the water you have applied. The smaller the pot, the sooner the soil will dry out, so that plants of the same species in 3-in. pots will require rewatering sooner than plants in 5-in. pots. Plastic pots, not being porous, retain water for longer than clay pots. During the spring and summer the plant will absorb water much more rapidly than during the autumn and winter, when growth is almost stationary and all the plant requires to do is to replace any water it may have lost through its leaves. It will lose more in high temperatures than in lower ones, so the room temperature in autumn and winter is also a factor.

There can be no hard and fast rules for watering plants, as, for example, once a week or once a fortnight, but if you inspect your plants daily, you will notice when the soil dries out. Soil at the top of the pot may well be dry while the lower portion is still reasonably moist, so wait for 24 hours after the top soil looks dry and then water. In this way there is little risk of overwatering.

If, when you water, the water runs straight through the pot and out at the bottom, the soil must have become over dry and shrunk. This can usually be cured by firming the soil around the edge of the pot with your thumbs, but if this is not effective fill a bucket with water to the level of the pot and stand the pot in this water and leave it there for 2 or 3 hours, then remove it and firm down around the edge of the pot. Mother-in-law's tongue (*Sansevieria trifasciata laurentii*) is only watered once a month during the winter and this could well be excessively dried out when you want to give more water in the spring, so for this and similar plants the bucket treatment may be necessary.

Leaves wilting is usually a sign of a plant needing water, but it is not a certain sign. If a plant is dying as a result of overwatering, the

Above: Repotting a house plant, using a loamless, peat-based compost. *Right: Cordyline terminalis*, one of the most colourful of all foliage plants. *Far right: Begonia rex* leaves are more colourful than many flowers; the colour range is very wide

leaves may well wilt, so that if you see wilting with a wet soil ball, you can be fairly sure that you have over-watered and that you must let the plant dry out (although your chances of getting it to recover are pretty slim). Also leaves may wilt if they are in burning sunlight. They will immediately recover if placed in the shade or if they are given a light spray with cool water and this phenomenon is, in any case, only temporary; the leaves wilt to prevent excessive lack of water. If the leaves are wilting, inspect the plant and if it is dry, then watering is the answer, but do not water wilting plants unless you have made sure that they are dry.

Cleaning Leaves   In towns and industrial districts, the air is liable to be polluted and some attention must be paid to the plant's hygiene. The plant 'breathes' through its leaves and if these get clogged up with dust, the plant will not grow well. It is, therefore, advisable to sponge the leaves once a week. Use a piece of cotton wool and luke warm water, but sponge the mature leaves only, as the young leaves are very soft and could easily be damaged.

Pest Control   Insect pests are uncommon on house plants, but can be prevented from spreading by means of this weekly spongeing; even greenfly can be removed in this manner. Aerosol insecticides are available to deal with any serious infection, but these are often poisonous, so they should be kept away from children and the aerosol should not be applied in the house, but in the open air or in an outhouse or garage in inclement weather.

Stopping   Many house plants have a stem from which side branches emerge. With such plants, it is usually good policy to remove the growing point, as well as any unsatisfactory winter-made growth in the spring. This is known as stopping. Stopping will encourage the production of sideshoots, so that you have a nice bushy plant as opposed to a rather thin lanky one. However, there is no use in stopping a plant unless it is well-rooted and making good growth. If it is not, all you will do is to get another growing point to replace the one you have removed and the plant will not bush out. With some very vigorous plants, such as the tradescantias, it may be necessary to stop two or three times during the growing season and sometimes with such plants not only the main growing point is removed, but the side shoots are also stopped when they have elongated sufficiently. Further details about whether or not to stop will be found under the descriptions of individual plants.

Propagation   Some house plants can be easily propagated from tip cuttings in the home without any elaborate paraphernalia. For these you take a piece of the plant with the growing tip and some 2–4 in. of stem, depending on the ultimate size of the plant; low growing plants will not have much stem. Now make a clean cut with a razor blade at the lowest leaf joint. Then remove most of the lower leaves, if your cutting is very leafy, leaving only about a third of the leaves. Fill a small pot either with a ready purchased cutting compost (the soilless ones are very satisfactory) or with a mixture of equal parts (by

The leaves of house plants should be cleaned from time to time to keep them healthy. Stiff, hard leaves may be washed to remove dust and grime; softer leaves must be treated very gently. *Below*: Calatheas and marantas

bulk) of peat and sharp sand, and then insert your cuttings to a depth of about $\frac{1}{2}$ in. Water them in and then enclose the pot in a polythene bag (or invert a large glass jar over the pot). The pot should be stood in a shady situation.

The best time to take cuttings is between mid-May and mid-August and the worst possible time is during the winter when rooting will probably not take place at all. Rooting usually takes place between 3 and 6 weeks after taking the cuttings. If you see new leaves being produced, that is a fairly reliable sign of rooting. Another method is to give a very gentle tug to the cutting; if there is some resistance it is probably rooted, but if it just comes out, it must be reinserted and you must wait longer. Once the cuttings are rooted, remove the polythene bag or glass jar, and wait a week. Then knock the potful of cuttings out and pot each one up separately, taking care to damage the roots as little as possible. The newly potted-up plants should be put in a warm situation for a week or so and then they can be placed in their permanent situations. One or two plants require special treatment, but this is noted below. Some plants will root faster if the pot is placed in the airing cupboard; cuttings do not seem to mind being in darkness while they are making their roots, but once these are made, the cuttings must be brought out into the light and it is probably better to be patient and keep the pots outside.

Beloperone guttata,
the shrimp plant

House Plants Described

Flowering Plants There are two flowering plants that will do well under the coolest conditions; these are the geranium (*Pelargonium × hortorum*) and the fuchsia.

These are such popular plants that their cultivation is fully described in Favourite Garden Flowers, elsewhere in this work. When grown in the house, pelargoniums should be given as much light as possible, preferably on sunny windowsills. Fuchsias like a well-lit, but not sunny situation and will do perfectly well in the centre of the room. They do not mind shade, provided it is not dark shade.

Busy Lizzie (*Impatiens walleriana*) is a popular flowering plant for rooms, but the purple-leaved *Impatiens petersiana* is better. This is like the old busy Lizzie with its scarlet flowers, which are produced freely in quite shady situations as well as in well-lit ones, but its dark purple leaves make it attractive even when it is not in flower. Cuttings root so easily, that all you have to do is to put them in water and roots will soon start to appear. As the season advances the plants tend to become leggy and the lower leaves drop off, so it is best to renew the plants at frequent intervals, with the last cuttings, that you intend to overwinter, taken at the beginning of September. If you do not want to start them in water, you can insert them in the usual cutting mixture, but there is no need to cover this with a polythene bag. It is practically impossible to overwater these plants during the spring and summer, and they require plenty during this period. During the autumn and winter they must be kept just moist and they also require to be fairly warm, preferably around 55°F (13°C), although they will survive at 50°F (10°C). Stopping may encourage bushy growth, but they seem to do quite well without any encouragement. Since the plants are normally only kept for the one season, soilless composts will be quite satisfactory without additional feeding.

One of the best and most easily grown house plants for continuous flowering is the Barbados heather (*Cuphea hyssopifolia*). This makes a small, twiggy shrub with every twig covered with leaves, about 1 in. long and $\frac{1}{4}$ in. across. From the axils of these leaves emerge innumerable small purple trumpet-shaped flowers. Flowering starts in April or early May and will go on non-stop until November. During the winter a temperature of 55°F (13°C) is advisable, but if it falls below this occasionally, no harm seems to occur. Tip cuttings, which should not be too soft, root rather slowly in warm conditions, which probably means that you cannot take them until June, unless you have a heated propagating case. The plant should be grown on year after year, but when it is three years old it may be rather too large (although in this case you can prune harder) so occasional propagation is a good thing. At the end of March it should be pruned, shortening all the main shoots by about 2 in., but otherwise no stopping is necessary. The plant should be potted on every year in April and regular feeding from June until September will encourage more growth and flowers. It likes a well-lit situation and does not mind some direct sunlight, so long as it is not excessively burning, while during the winter it should be given a well-lit situation.

The shrimp plant (*Beloperone guttata*) is another small soft-leaved twiggy shrub, with heads of flowers at the ends of the branches. The flowers are concealed in the bracts, which form a shape like the body of a prawn and are either maroon-purple or, in the form known as 'lutea', a pale yellow. These are produced fairly continuously throughout the summer and autumn and, if conditions are warm enough, well into the winter.

During the winter the temperature should be 55°F (13°C) and the plants should be given as much light as possible. In the spring all the main growths should be cut back by a third, or the plant will tend to become rather leggy with a bare base. Once in a 5-in. pot it can remain there for two years, provided it is fed between mid-May and mid-September and the same period when it is potted on into a 6-in. pot. The plant should be kept moist all the year round, although it will require far less water during the winter months and it should be in a well-lit position that does not receive much direct sunlight.

If you keep your house very warm in the winter, beloperones may produce a lot of weak spindly growth, which looks unhealthy. Remove this in early spring. The plants should be fairly warm, around 65°F (18°C) between the spring pruning and the appearance of the first flowers and higher temperatures will do no harm. Once the flowers have appeared they will persist for longer under cooler conditions, but this sort of temperature adjustment is not very easy in the home and the plant will grow quite happily whatever the temperature is, within reason.

Foliage Plants There is a much larger range of plants with attractive foliage. Many of these plants are variegated. This variegation tends to be more marked in well-lit situations and most variegated plants need more light than the normal green-leaved forms. On the other hand many green-leaved plants will thrive in shady conditions which would be unsuitable for either flowering or variegated plants, so they have definite advantages. The only plant that will survive in very dark shade is the aspidistra. However, there are numerous situations where foliage plants will grow happily, although they would be too dark for flowering plants. Foliage plants also have the advantage that they look attractive throughout the year, while even the best flowering plants have some period when they are not flowering, so in many ways the foliage plant gives you better value for your money.

Impatiens walleriana variegata, the variegated Busy Lizzie

Right: Stapelia hirsuta, one of the 'carrion plants'

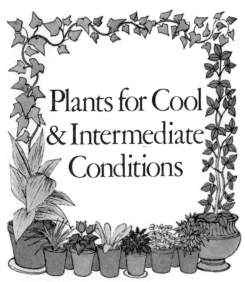

Plants for Cool & Intermediate Conditions

Plants for Cool Conditions

Some plants like cool conditions, with the winter temperature ranging between 45° and 50°F (7°–10°C). These plants will not enjoy higher temperatures, although many of those in the next group, needing a temperature of 55°–60°F (13°–16°C) will survive a winter either with lower or higher temperatures, without any ill effects. Plants that thrive in cool conditions will not necessarily like to be warm in winter, so choose other plants for your warm rooms.

The most notable cool-growing plants are the various ivies, the tradescantias, eucalyptus, chlorophytum, *Ficus pumila* and *Araucaria excelsa*.

The ivies are either small-leaved variants of the common ivy, *Hedera helix*, or of the larger leaved Irish ivy, *H. hibernica*, or of the large-leaved vigorous ivy, *H. canariensis*.

Both *H. hibernica* and *H. canariensis* are climbing plants and do best if they are trained up a stake or on trellis work. There are two forms of *H. canariensis* generally available, of which the most popular is the one with variegated leaves, with a wide silver margin and a dark green centre. The other, 'Golden Leaf' has bright glossy green leaves with a yellowish patch in the centre. Although from the Canary Islands, these plants are quite hardy out of doors, They do not make their best impression until they are quite large. On the other hand many of the forms of the common ivy are satisfactory as small plants. They can be divided into two main sections, those that are self-branching and tend to make erect little bushy plants and those that are either trailers or climbers. The latter either have to be trained up some support or put in a hanging container, which may well look effective, but is a nuisance to water. The self-branching ivies will branch without any stopping, while the trailing forms require to be stopped in order to produce sideshoots and will only do this if they are quite sizeable plants; smaller plants will just replace the original growing points and then grow on.

Among the self-branching ivies are 'Pittsburgh', 'Chicago', 'Minima', 'Minigreen', and 'Green Ripple', with plain green leaves, while among those variegated with silver are the 'Variegated Chicago', 'Little Diamond', 'Heisse', and 'Goldchild', which is more cream than silver. Among the trailers some good plants are 'Glacier', 'Eva' (sometimes called 'Little Eva'), and 'Maculata'. An unusual plant is 'Golden Jubilee', also known as 'Goldheart'. This has the centre of the leaf a deep yellow and a dark green margin. Unlike the other ivies it needs as much light as possible and has the disconcerting habit of making a lot of new stem without any leaves; however patience is all that is required as eventually the leaves form. The other ivies will grow happily in quite shaded conditions, although the variegated forms look better in well-lit situations. During the winter you may get some unvariegated leaves coming at the end of the branches. These should be removed at the beginning of March. Ivies should be kept on the dry side at all times.

The so-called German ivy is in reality a climbing groundsel (*Senecio macroglossus variegata*). It has roughly triangular leaves of dark green and cream and is one of the few house plants that do not require spongeing, as the leaves are covered with a waxy secretion. It is a vigorous climber that will need frequent stopping and it is a greedy plant needing ample feeding.

The tradescantias and zebrinas are trailing plants with variegated leaves about $1\frac{1}{2}$ in. long and $\frac{3}{4}$ in. across. Some of the tradescantias are liable to revert to unvariegated leaves and any unvariegated shoot should be removed as detected, as otherwise they will grow so much faster than the variegated portions that they will eventually swamp the plant. This danger does not apply to the tradescantia known as 'Rochford's Quicksilver', nor to the zebrinas. Too deep a shade may suppress the variegation, otherwise they will thrive in any situation. Trails will root if placed in water and can be put several to a pot and watered in to make new potfuls. The plants soon become rather leggy and are best replaced every one or two years. You must make a hole in which to insert your cutting (which should be about 2 in. long) as they are rather brittle and might break if you just pushed them in. The compost must be kept fairly moist until the cuttings have rooted, which takes about a fortnight. Tradescantias like plenty of water, but if kept dry the leaves will come small but quite well-coloured. Sideshoots appear whether you stop the plants or no, but, they will appear sooner, if you stop the main growths.

The eucalyptus most commonly grown as a house plant is *E. cinerea*, which could eventually make a small tree. It is very attractive with its white branches and blue-green leaves, which are nearly circular in young plants and lance-shaped when adult. To keep the plant within reasonable bounds it must be pruned hard every spring and the leading shoots that emerge at the top of the plant, must then be stopped, otherwise they will continue to grow and no lower growths will be formed. The plant should have a well-

Top left : Zebrina pendula

Above left : Tradescantia 'Rochford's Quicksilver'

A colourful group of house plants, grown for their foliage, though the aphelandra at the bottom right will also flower

Top right: Tradescantia fluminensis variegata

Above right: Tradescantia purpurea

lit situation and be kept reasonably cool during the winter. Once in a 6-in. pot, it is advisable to keep it there, as otherwise the resultant plant might become too unwieldy. This entails regular feeding.

Chlorophytum comosum variegatum is sometimes known as the spider plant. It throws up a clump of grassy leaves, which are nearly a foot long, but which reflex to give a fountain-like effect. They are either cream coloured with a thin green margin or else they have green margins and a cream centre. The small white flowers are often replaced with a tuft of leaves and if this is pinned down into a pot, it will soon take root and the stem can then be severed, giving you a fresh plant. Keep these young plants somewhat on the dry side until they are well rooted, but well-rooted plants can take plenty of water during their growing season, although they are kept fairly dry from October until March. Small plants look rather grassy, but they grow rapidly and large plants are very impressive. They should be got into 5-in. pots as soon as possible and then potted on every other year.

Ficus pumila is a low creeping plant, producing aerial roots like an ivy and it can be trained up walls in the same way. The leaves are small, about 1 in. long and $\frac{1}{2}$ in. across, heart-shaped, and they completely cover the thin wiry stems. This plant thrives in shade and must, indeed, never be exposed to bright sunlight and similarly it must never be allowed to dry out completely, otherwise the leaves may shrivel and drop off. Overwatering is possible, particularly during the winter, but some moisture is essential even during this period. In mild parts of the country it will grow outside on a north-facing wall, so it has no objection to quite low temperatures.

Araucaria excelsa, the Norfolk Island pine is in nature a very large tree, but it is very slow-growing as a house plant. It makes a perfectly symmetrical pyramid, with a central stem, from which, after every year's growth, four branches radiate horizontally from the central stem and, in their turn, produce symmetrical sideshoots, which are produced in opposite pairs all along these side branches. All these main and side branches are densely clothed with bright green needles. The plant must be rotated at regular intervals, so as to preserve its symmetry. The plant should never be pruned nor stopped and once in a 5-in. pot needs potting on every two or three years, and should be fed during the intervening period. The plant can be stood outside during the summer in a somewhat shaded situation, to great advantage. The plant must not dry out at any time, but on the other hand it does not require much water at any period, although more will be required when the new growths are elongating.

Other house plants that will thrive under cool conditions are two vine-like climbers, *Cissus antarctica*, the kangaroo vine, and *Rhoicissus rhomboidea*, while an attractive trailing plant is *Plectranthus oertendahlii*, with leaves that have the principal veins picked out in silver.

Chlorophytum comosum variegatum, known as the spider plant, is grown mainly for the sake of its cream-variegated, grass-like leaves

Hedera helix 'Eva' ('Little Eva'), one of a number of trailing forms of the common ivy, with small, variegated leaves

Plants for Intermediate Temperatures

With a constant winter temperature of from 55° to 60°F (13°–16°C), the choice is very much wider and many more colourful specimens may be grown. Perhaps the most gorgeous of all are the plants known in the U.S.A. as the Ti tree, *Cordyline terminalis*. These are small palm-like plants with leaves up to a foot in length and 4 in. across, which first unfurl with the most brilliant colours in cerise, pink, or cream and pink and which gradually age to a purplish brown or a medium green with a red margin, but practically any combination of red, pink, cream and green can be found in the various cultivars. Since they grow more or less continuously, the appearance of the plant is constantly changing. Unfortunately, these gorgeous colours do not appear until the plant has been growing some three years, so that they are not cheap to purchase. They are greedy feeders requiring a rich soil mixture and ample feeding. They should be potted on every two years. They must have a well-lit situation, but not in direct sunlight for too long and they require ample water, but should not be over-watered. Since the leaves are more brightly coloured than a good many flowers, it can be appreciated that this is a fairly striking plant. It is never stopped.

The croton, *Codiaeum variegatum*, is equally colourful, but not quite so easy as it is very sensitive to draughts, which can cause the leaves to fall, and also to any violent fluctuations in temperature, which can also have bad results. If the temperature can be kept constant, the plant will thrive. The leaves vary in shape from nearly circular to almost grass-like and are in various combinations of brilliant colours. This can be kept somewhat on the dry side during the winter, but will take plenty of water during the summer. The plant contains a milky juice, which spurts out whenever the plant is damaged in any way, so this should be avoided and the plant is never stopped. It requires ample light at all times and has no objection to direct sunlight. It is by no means one of the easiest of house plants, but it is very showy. Potting on should take place every other year.

Very much easier are the rex begonias. These have roughly triangular leaves, which may be fairly regular or which may have very jagged edges and these leaves are gorgeously coloured in varying shades; some are deep or rosy purple, others varying shades of green and silver; the choice is very large. They have no objection to shady conditions and will still keep their gorgeous colours in such situations. Begonias have very fine roots and are usually grown in a mixture composed mainly of leaf mould and sand, with only a little loam so that soilless mixtures will prove very satisfactory. They must not dry out at any time, but they do not require to much water either and should be watered regularly. Rex begonias spread outwards rather than upwards and they can be divided, if the plant is getting

too large. The plants should be fed during the summer, but rather sparingly. The 'Iron Cross' begonia (*B. masoniana*) needs rather warmer conditions than the rex group and has bright green leaves with a maroon 'Iron Cross' in the centre.

The zebra plant, *Aphelandra squarrosa louisae*, has an upright stem from which spring pairs of leaves, which may be 9 in. long and half as wide. These are a dark green, with the main veins picked out in bold ivory stripes. The original plants used to produce pyramidal heads of yellow flowers, but the later forms, known as 'Brockfeld' and 'Dania' flower very rarely. The plant needs repotting yearly and takes ample water during the summer and a certain amount in the winter. Sideshoots can be detached and rooted in the summer, but a temperature of at least 65°F

(18°C) is necessary and preferably somewhat higher. These plants need a reasonable amount of light, but will grow in partly shaded conditions quite satisfactorily.

The various ficus are not particularly colourful, but they are impressive. The most popular is the indiarubber tree, *F. elastica*, which is offered either as var. *decora*, which has the immature leaf covered with a red sheath, or as var. *robusta*, which has very large leaves, somewhat rounder than those of *decora*. There are also some handsome variegated forms known as 'Schryveriana' and 'Tricolor', with their leaves blotched with cream, light and dark green, which are somewhat more decorative. The indiarubber plant can eventually make an enormous tree, so it is kept to reasonable dimensions by keeping it in a small pot, 5 or 6 in. in diameter, and feeding it during the summer to get the leaves a good size, but not to encourage much stem elongation. Their large leathery leaves must be sponged regularly on both squrfaces

to keep them glossy and to stop any possible infection with scale insect. They can be kept fairly dry in the winter and watered normally during the summer, when they will much appreciate the leaves being syringed during very hot spells. They will grow equally well in shade or sun, although they should be in the shade when the new leaves are unfurling, otherwise these will not be a good size. Ordinarily you do not stop at all, but if the plant gets too tall, it can be cut back in spring to about 6 in., when it will break again from the base. This is a messy job as the plants are full of milky latex (from which rubber can be obtained) and this will gush out and stain the plant. The cut surface should be sprinkled with powdered charcoal immediately to stop excessive bleeding. *Ficus benjamina* is another member of this genus, which makes a branch-

ing, thickly-leaved tree with long narrow leaves giving something of the effect of a weeping willow. Some of these leaves will be shed in the winter whatever you do, as it is their natural habit, but many more will be produced in the following spring and summer. This needs a well-lit but shady position and will take rather more water than *F. elastica*.

There are many philodendrons used as house plants; most of them are climbers, producing aerial roots, but one striking plant, *P. bipinnatifidum*, does not climb, but forms a rosette of long-stemmed very jagged leaves, which get larger as the plant grows and can end up a yard across. The leaves also get more jagged as the plant matures; the first leaves are heart-shaped. As the larger plants are handsomer, they are potted on yearly until they are in a 7- or 8-in. pot, in which they can then stay, being fed regularly each season. With these larger sized plants clay pots are better than the plastic ones, that are so light that a large plant makes them top heavy. This plant is never stopped. On the other hand the climbing species are stopped from time to time, although not necessarily every year. These climbers all require shady conditions, although these should not be too dark, whereas *P. bipinnatifidum*, will grow either in shade or in full light, although the leaves seem to be larger in the shade. Ideally the climbing forms should have a very damp atmosphere from which their aerial roots can obtain nourishment, but they are often tolerant of quite dry conditions. They are sometimes trained on blocks of cork bark, to which the roots adhere and which is quite easy to moisten. The most attractive, but a delicate, rather difficult plant, is *P. melanochryson*, with heart-shaped, dark green, iridescent leaves, 5 or 6 in. long. Much easier are the

popular *P. scandens*, with green heart-shaped leaves, and two very similar species, *P. hastatum* and a plant called *P.* 'Tuxla', both of which have spear-shaped leaves about 7 in. long and 4 in. wide. They are a shining dark green, with some coppery sheen in the young leaves. These latter are fairly slow growers, whereas *P. scandens* is quite fast and benefits from a yearly stopping. If it becomes too tall you can bend the flexible main stem right over and tie it in at the base of the plant, whence it will start to climb anew. A plant needing similar treatment to the climbing philodendrons is *Monstera deliciosa borsigiana*. This has large serrated leaves, which are perforated with holes, giving a very exotic outline. In dark shade these perforations will not develop. It is best trained upright and the aerial roots carefully guided down into the soil in the pot. Stopping is not recommended unless the plant is getting too large, as it is slow to break again. Similar to *P. scandens*, but with gold variegated leaves is *Scindapsus*

aureus, which needs more light than the philodendrons and requires a yearly stopping.

Aralia (Dizygotheca) elegantissima makes a slow-growing shrub with leaves like those of a horse-chestnut in shape, but the leaflets are extremely thin in young plants, becoming wider as the plant ages. They are coppery red when they emerge but become very dark maroon, almost black. This may not sound very attractive, but the plant has enormous grace and charm, as much from its elegant habit as from its light, graceful leaves. It requires a well-lit position, but shade from much direct sunlight and the leaves should be syringed frequently during the summer and occasionally during the winter to discourage red spider. On the other hand the soil is always watered somewhat sparingly, particularly in the winter.

Far left: Ficus elastica variegata and *Ficus benjamina* are two excellent but very different members of the fig family which make good house plants. *Left:* The striped leaves of *Calathea zebrina*, a plant which needs a warm, moist atmosphere and shady conditions. *Below: Philodendron* 'Burgundy', a large-leaved kind grows fairly slowly as a house plant

Mother-in-law's tongue, *Sansevieria trifasciata laurentii*, makes an upright plant, with its stiff, fleshy leaves, which are mottled in light and dark green with a golden margin.

The plant usually produces only one extra leaf each year and this may turn up some way from the rest of the plant. There is a temptation to cut this out to form another plant, but this should only be done the year after it has appeared, as it does not produce any roots the first year and the plantlet would probably die. If, when the leaf is about 8 in. long, you can find the underground stem from which it rises and cut this half-way through with a knife, this seems to encourage rooting. This plant needs ample light and very little water. In the winter one watering a month is sufficient and even in the summer it should be allowed to dry out thoroughly between waterings. The new leaves are somewhat rolled in to start with and water should not be allowed to lodge in this hollow, otherwise the root could rot. Otherwise they are tough resilient

plants, which will put up with almost any conditions and tolerate oil or gas fumes.

Peperomias are low plants, with a very small root system. Some have trailing stems, but the most attractive throw up a tuft of leaves from a central point. The best are probably *P. hederaefolia*, *P. caperata* and *P. sandersii*. *P. hederaefolia* has heart-shaped leaves some 2½ in. long and 2 in. across, which have a quilted effect from the undulating surface. They are pale grey with olive green main veins. In the autumn it produces flowers that look like white mouse tails. If a leaf is removed and inserted shallowly in a cutting mixture with the temperature not below 65°F (18°C) a small plant will arise from the base of the leaf. *P. caperata* has smaller corrugated leaves, the peaks appearing greyish, while the valleys have a purple tinge. The flowers are pure white. It is propagated the same way as *P. hederaefolia*, but the stalk can be inserted a little deeper. Both these plants like shady conditions and never a great deal of water around the roots, although they revel in a moist atmosphere. The rugby football plant, *P. sandersii*, is the most handsome of all the peperomias, but is not very easy, requiring a winter temperature of 60°F (16°C) and great care in its placing as it is very sensitive to even mild draughts. The striking leaves, shaped like a rugby football, are silver with green zones around the main veins. Keep the plant as dry as possible in the winter; the leaves can flag before you need apply water as they come back without damage.

The calatheas and marantas all have very attractive leaves. They must have moist, shady conditions and the plants need ample feeding during the summer. They will probably need potting on yearly. If plants get very large, they can be divided. Although they will pass the winter happily at the temperatures recommended, they need about 10° (5½°C) more during the summer to make proper growth. Direct sunlight can shrivel the leaves, so should be avoided. The plants are sometimes known as prayer plants, as they raise their leaves at night. *Calathea insignis* has elongated oval leaves, 4–9 in. long; they are yellowish green darkening towards the leaf margin and with dark green blotches along the midrib, while the underside of the leaf is a deep claret colour. *C. makoyana* is very striking with rounder leaves, about 6 in. long and 4 in. across. The main portion of the leaf is silvery in colour with dark green blotches, underside rosy purple, so that the plant has a rosy glow. *Maranta leuconeura* is a variable plant, rather lower than the calatheas, its leaves usually about 4 in. long and 2½ in. across. The var. *massangeana* has leaves of soft green with the main veins picked out in white to give a herring-bone effect, while the var. *kerchoveana* has leaves that when young are emerald green with red blotches between the veins, while in older leaves the colours are dark green and maroon. The var. *erythrophylla (tricolor)* has larger, very dark green leaves, the main veins bright red, with yellowish-green blotches between them.

Cacti and other Succulents

Succulent plants are the camels of the vegetable world, storing up food and water to be used not on a rainy day, but during a period of prolonged drought. This may last for a few weeks or, in extreme cases, plants have survived without rainfall for over a year. This water can be stored in either the leaves or the stems of the plants, depending on the type. This gives rise to two distinct types of succulent plant, leaf succulents and stem succulents. The stem succulents usually have no leaves (except sometimes very small ones on young growth, soon falling off), and the green tissue of the stems takes over the work of the leaves to manufacture the food. Without leaves, the plants can reduce much of the water loss. The stems are usually very thick and full of water storage tissue, and are mostly either cylindrical or spherical in shape, sometimes being deeply ribbed. The ribs enable the plant to expand or contract as it absorbs or loses water.

Leaf succulents have plump, rounded leaves full of water storage tissue. They are often coated with wax, meal or hairs, helping to reduce water loss from their surfaces. Often these succulents have fleshy stems as well, but the leaves play the most important part in food manufacture.

The cacti, all belonging to one family, are the most popular group of succulent plants, but many other plant families have succulent members. Among the families whose succulent species are grown are the *Crassulaceae, Aizoaceae, Euphorbiaceae, Asclepiadaceae, Liliaceae*, and *Agavaceae*.

ᏇᏇ Cacti ᏇᏇ

The cactus family is native to America; plants found in Europe and elsewhere have been introduced at some time in the past. There are three distinct types of plant, the pereskias, the epiphytes and the desert cacti, and these require different treatment because of their differing 'home' conditions. Except for the pereskias, they are stem succulents, having either no leaves or small temporary ones. Cacti are not all spiny plants,

some being strongly armed while others are quite spineless. All cacti have areoles, small pincushion-like structures scattered over the stems, Spines, when present, off-shoots, and branches come from these areoles. This is the way to distinguish a cactus from another stem succulent, such as a euphorbia, which does not have areoles. Also all cactus flowers have the same general design, while those of other succulents differ enormously between the various families.

Pereskias The pereskias must have a brief mention here, as they are so different from other cacti. They are obtainable from the specialist nurseries, but not likely to be found in the local florist. They are interesting in that they are the only cacti which are not really succulents, and have normal leaves, rather like those of a privet, but possess spines and, of course, the characteristic areoles. The flowers bear a superficial resemblance to the wild rose. They are bushes and climbers from the tropical regions of north and central America, where they are used as hedging plants, and can be grown as pot plants, but to be really successful they need to be bedded out in a large greenhouse, where they can scramble up a wall or over a support. They need a winter temperature of about 50°F (10°C) and to be kept moist all the year round. Most growers regard them as curiosities, and they are not very common in collections.

Epiphytic Cacti By contrast, the epiphytes are grown in this country very commonly, many being sold as florists' plants. In their native American tropical rain forests, the epiphytic cacti are found growing in the

debris caught up in the branches of trees. They grow among the other epiphytes, ferns, bromeliads, and orchids, which festoon the trees in these tropical regions. Although there is no shortage of water where the plants are found, the pockets of humus they are growing in dry out very quickly. Epiphytic cacti have no leaves, but flattened, slightly succulent stems, sometimes incorrectly called 'leaves'. These stems may consist of short segments, as in the familiar 'Christmas cactus' (schlumbergera), the flowers appearing on the ends of the segments, or the stems may be long and strap-like, as in the epiphyllums. In these latter, the flowers are usually carried on the sides of the stems. Owing to the beauty of their flowers, epiphyllums have received a lot of attention from the horticulturists. There are enormous numbers of beautiful hybrids on the market, in all colours except blue, while the wild species are not often grown as greenhouse plants owing to their large size and the difficulty of flowering them in cultivation. These hybrid epiphyllums, together with the short stemmed rhipsalidopsis and schlumbergeras are the ones in this group most often grown as pot plants. All require the same basic treatment.

They need a good, porous soil; J.I.P.2 with some additional leaf mould or peat and grit is suitable. Leaf mould is ideal if it can be obtained as it more closely resembles the natural soil of the forests. The soilless composts are also very suitable for these and other cacti, but for the epiphytes, the lime-free type of compost is best. It helps to add a teaspoon of bonemeal to each pot of compost.

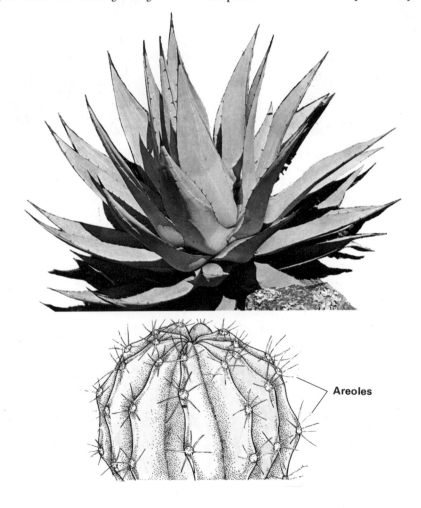

Areoles

Re-potting should be done annually. These cacti will survive winter temperatures as low as 41°F (5°C), but flower much better if kept a little warmer. They should be kept moist all the year round. In fact, it is best to forget that they are cacti and treat them as normal pot plants. When in bud, epiphytes can be fed once a fortnight with a tomato-type potassium fertilizer.

Because these epiphytic cacti grow among trees, they do not need full sunlight. They make very successful house plants if grown on an east-facing window-ledge, where they will receive the early morning sun, but are in shade during the heat of the day. They grow rapidly, and when a plant outgrows a 6-in. pot, it should be re-started. A stem is cut from an epiphyllum, or a few segments from the schlumbergeras and rhipsalidopsis. The cutting is allowed to dry for two or three days, and then potted up. This drying period for cactus and other succulent cuttings is always carried out to prevent rot from spreading into the fleshy stems. As they are succulents, they do not wilt during this period as other plants would. The best time of the year for taking cuttings is April-May, although it is quite possible at any time during spring and summer.

Desert Cacti The desert cacti are the spiny tall or round plants that we associate with the American deserts. Actually many are found growing on rocky mountain sides and in grassy areas, as well as in the sandy regions of Mexico and South America. They all need the maximum amount of sunlight to flourish and flower freely. For this reason they do not

Left above: Agave hauchacensis
Left below: Areoles are distinctive features of a cactus plant
Below: Succulent-leaved aeoniums
Above right: Rhipsalidopsis 'Electra'
Right: A selection of succulent plants in the subtropical garden of Tresco Abbey, Isles of Scilly

make such good house plants as the epiphytes. If a greenhouse is not available, they should be kept on a south-facing window-sill, and preferably stood outdoors from May to September.

A minimum winter temperature of 41°F (5°C) is adequate for most desert cacti. A well-drained compost is essential. If about a third extra grit or sharp sand is added to J.I.P.2, this will make a suitable compost. Even the grit is not essential if the compost is not allowed to cake. Alternatively, a soilless compost may be used. Since the food content of the soil does not last forever, the plants should be repotted annually.

Many people seem to think that cacti need no water! This is far from the truth, although they will certainly survive a period of dryness (after all they are adapted to do just this). This means that it is not necessary to worry too much while you are on holiday (although seedlings will suffer). But without water they will just survive, not grow, and the plants should be kept more or less continually moist between April and October. The watering should be reduced after this and they should be left dry during December and January, if kept in a greenhouse. Watering can be re-started gradually as the light improves in February. If the plants are wintered in a heated house with a very dry atmosphere, more water will be needed during winter to prevent excessive shrivelling. Indoors, the ideal winter spot is an unheated room, but this may not always be possible. The reason for keeping them dry at this time is that if they grow in the poor light of winter, they are likely to become distorted and may well rot the following year. Also, flowering is very much affected by the previous winter's treatment.

Desert cacti are mostly very easily reproduced from cuttings. Some plants form offsets which can be removed and potted up, after the usual few days drying period. Some clustering plants will have rooted 'pups' (offsets) around the base of the parent; these can be removed and potted up directly. If the plant does not form offsets, a section of stem can be cut off and potted up after drying for about a week. The base of the parent plant can be kept as it will often sprout again, forming a number of offsets around the cut top. The best time to do all this is, as before, between April and June.

Other Succulents

As mentioned earlier, the other succulents fall into several different families, and since the cultivation varies somewhat for each, it is best to give a brief description of them.

Crassulaceae This family is very large, consisting of leaf succulents with almost world-wide distribution. The most beautiful members of the family are the echeverias of the New World and the crassulas of South Africa. Other attractive plants are the aeoniums and sedums, with plump, often highly coloured leaves, arranged in rosettes. All should be kept slightly moist all the year round. Seed of these plants is difficult to obtain, but they can mostly be easily reproduced from cuttings which need little or no drying before potting up. Some species can even be grown from leaves, just laid on the soil, when they will root, and send out new shoots.

Aizoaceae This is a family of leaf succulents found mainly in Africa. They vary from small shrubs to plants about 1 in. high consisting of one pair of very succulent leaves. One of the main characteristics of this group is that most of them have distinct resting periods, corresponding to the dry season of their native lands. During this period, from about October to March, they must be kept completely dry. The old leaves will gradually shrivel away. Watering should not be re-started until the new leaves appear in spring. Popular plants are the autumn growing conophytums, glottiphyllums and pleiospilos and the summer growing lithops and faucarias. This group is quite easily raised from seed, or heads of clustering plants may be removed, dried for a few days and potted up. June to July is a good time for this.

Euphorbiaceae This contains only one group, the euphorbias, commonly grown, but this is an immense group of world-wide distribution, many of which are not succulents. The succulent plants are most commonly found on the African continent. These are stem succulents, although during the growing period some species produce leaves on the new growth. Euphorbias vary enormously in size, some reaching tree-like proportions, closely resembling the giant cacti. Others are small, clustering plants only a few inches high. All have one thing in common, an irritating, sometimes poisonous, milky sap. Euphorbia flowers are usually small and insignificant, but often have a sweet lime-like scent. In some species the male and female flowers are on separate plants. Euphorbias are difficult to propagate from cuttings, but may be readily raised from seed, although it needs to be fresh for success.

Asclepiadaceae This family contains a large number of leafless stem succulents from the dry regions of the Old World. Where they occur, there are no bees and the flowers are pollinated by flies. To be attractive to flies, the flowers often have an unpleasant smell to us. However, the flowers are usually large (sometimes immense) in shades of reddish-brown or yellow, often covered with hairs. Stapelias are probably the best known in this group. We also have duvalias and carallumas. They are easily raised from seed, which germinates quickly but has a tendency to damp off equally quickly. Cuttings may be taken from June to August. They are best just laid on the soil and may be watered after about a week.

Liliaceae This family contains not only the lily bulbs of our gardens but a group of leaf succulent plants which are found mainly on the African continent. The most interesting plants are the aloes, gasterias and haworthias.

Aloes can reach a large size and bear a superficial resemblance to the American agaves, with their long strap-like leaves. There are also a number of small plants which are very attractive and will survive on a window-sill. Aloes have long flower stems, but the rosette does not die after flowering.

Gasterias and haworthias are found growing in the shade of grasses and small shrubs in their native land. This makes them useful small plants for growing on window sills or under the greenhouse staging.

All the plants which form clusters may be reproduced by removing off-sets. Otherwise they must be raised from seed.

Agavaceae This last family dealt with here, includes yuccas, sansevierias and agaves. It is the agaves that interest the grower of succulents. These are rosette-shaped plants with tough, strap-like leaves. Although many are far too large for the average grower, there are small species that are ideal for the living-room, because the very tough leaves enable these plants to withstand the dry atmosphere. Many people are familiar with the large, rather coarse specimens of *Agave americana* found growing along the Mediterranean coast. These plants have at some time been introduced; the agaves are native to the southern U.S.A., Mexico, Central America, the West Indies, and northern South America.

Agave flowers are borne on stems many feet long, but only on very old specimens, and after flowering, the rosette dies, but by then there are usually offsets growing around the base of the plant. These can be removed and used for propagation. Agaves are very easily raised from seed.

Cultivation The cultivation of the other succulents is very similar to that of the desert cacti; any differences have been mentioned. They should be given plenty of water in summer and kept either dry or slightly moist in winter, depending on where they are kept. A suitable compost is J.I.P.2 plus about a third extra grit or sharp sand, with the exception of the *Aizoaceae* which are better with rather more grit, up to 50%. They all need the maximum amount of sunlight, particularly the *Aizoaceae*, which are not really suitable as house plants, but need the sunniest part of the greenhouse. A minimum winter temperature of 41°F (5°C) is adequate for most succulents although the stapelias and other *Asclepiadaceae* appreciate a little more.

Raising from seed Cacti and other succulents can be raised from seed in much the same manner as any other greenhouse plants. A good seed compost should be used; either J.I. or soilless. After thoroughly moistening the compost, the seeds are just scattered on the surface. The container is placed in a plastic bag to conserve moisture. A temperature of 70°–80°F (21°–27°C) is needed for germination. If a propagator is available, early spring is the best time to sow, otherwise it is necessary to wait until later when the weather warms up.

Bowl gardens Small cacti and other succulents can be used to make attractive bowl gardens, but care should be taken to include plants with the same growing and resting periods and light requirements. Bowl gardens are not merely ornaments, but contain living plants, and must be given the light and water needed.

Pests and diseases Cacti and other succulents do not suffer greatly from these, if they are carefully looked after. Small cotton-wool-like patches indicate mealy bugs which can be controlled with a malathion spray (but do not use malathion on *Crassulaceae*). Brown spots on stems (particularly epiphyllums) are usually due to too low winter temperatures, too much nitrogen in the compost, or otherwise faulty cultivation. Cold, damp conditions can cause plants to rot.

25 Cacti and Other Succulents

Chamaecereus silvestrii (peanut cactus) is found growing among grass and low bushes in Western Argentina. The short, prostrate stems are freely branching, and covered with short, stiff white spines. The stems are pale green in winter, but turn violet in the hot sun. The furry brown buds open in May or June to large scarlet flowers. This cactus is hardy if kept dry, and may be wintered in an unheated cold frame. Propagation is particularly easy by removing branches and rooting them.

Cleistocactus strausii from Bolivia, forms a tall, silvery column, which may reach a height of 5 ft. With age it branches from the base. The stems are covered with short white spines. Old specimens will flower; the narrow flowers are red and are formed at the top of the stem. However, if confined to a pot it will be many years before this plant becomes too large. It is hardy if kept dry in winter.

Echinocactus grusonii (golden barrel cactus) comes from the deserts of central Mexico. Young seedlings have tubercles which carry stout golden spines. As the plant gets larger the tubercles merge into ribs. Mature specimens of this cactus are about a yard across, but are very ancient as it takes about ten years for a specimen in cultivation to make a diameter of 6 in. The small yellow flowers are seldom produced in this country, due to poor light intensity.

Echinocereus knippelianus is native to Mexico. The dark green, almost globular stem is about 2 in. across. It is divided by five ribs which carry weak, white spines. The pink flowers are produced profusely in May. This is a slow-growing plant and should be watered with care. Like most echinocereus, it is hardy if kept dry.

Echinocereus pectinatus is found growing in central Mexico. It has a thick stem about 3 in. in diameter, branching from the base, and covered very neatly with short white spines, arranged in a comb-like pattern. The pink flowers are 3–4 in. across and in some specimens are sweetly scented. The flowering period is about June. This is a slow growing cactus which is hardy in winter if kept dry; it needs particularly good drainage.

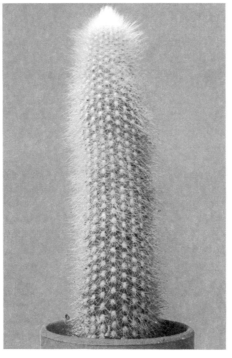

Facing page: Echinocereus knippelianus, a cactus from Mexico. Below left: Echinocactus grusonii, the golden barrel cactus. Above: Cleistocactus strausii, an easily grown cactus from Bolivia. Below: One of the many beautiful epiphyllum hybrids. These are available in a good colour range and often make large plants

Echinopsis rhodotricha from Argentina, is an oval plant which in the wild can reach a height of 32 in. In cultivation it will flower when 6 in. high; the long-tubed, white fragrant flowers are about 6 in. long and 3 in. across. They are produced freely during the summer. They open in the evening. The stem is dark green, divided into ribs with stout brown spines. This is a fast growing plant and is hardy if kept dry. The best known is *E. eyrieseii*, but most specimens on the market are probably hybrids.

Echinopsis 'Golden Dream' is a *Lobivia* × *Echinopsis* hybrid, a vigorous and hardy plant. It has a globular plant body, up to 6 in. across, divided into ribs with short brownish spines. Off-sets form around the base. The golden-yellow flowers appear in summer; they have long tubes and are 2 to 3 in. across and slightly scented.

Epiphyllum hybrids are examples of the 'jungle' type of cactus. They make largish plants with strap-like stems, often 2 or 3 ft. long. The flowers are 3 or 4 in. across, and appear on the edges of the stems, usually opening in the evening. Various un-named red hybrids are common; among the named specimens are 'Appeal' (red), 'Bliss' (orange), 'Cooperi' (white and scented), 'Exotique' (purplish), 'Gloria' (orange-red) and 'Sunburst' (orange).

Hamatocactus setispinus

Ferocactus acanthodes from southern California makes a cylindrical plant about 9 ft. high and 3 ft. across in nature. But such plants are very old. Seedlings and young plants make delightful pot plants; they are globular and have bright red spines, but are unlikely to reach flowering size in cultivation. The flowers, when produced are yellow and small for such a large plant, about 2 in. across.

Gymnocalycium bruchii is a miniature cactus from Argentina which eventually clusters from the base. The globular plant body is divided by twelve ribs, bearing neat white spines, covering the plant. The pale pink flowers open in May; these are over 1 in. long, and since the flowering plant may be less than 1 in. across, it often cannot be seen for flowers. This is a very easy plant to grow and flower.

Gymnocalycium baldianum is sometimes incorrectly named as *G. venturianum*. This native of Uruguay forms a plant body 3 in. across; it has nine ribs with yellowish spines. Old specimens form off-sets. The flowers, produced in May, are usually deep red but occasionally specimens are found with beautiful intense pink flowers.

Gymnocalycium platense, a native of Argentina, is a globular plant, eventually 3 in. or more in diameter. The plant body is greyish-green and is divided into twelve or fourteen ribs. These carry short whitish spines. White flowers are freely produced in early summer. This is a very hardy, easily grown plant.

Hamatocactus setispinus is native to Mexico and southern Texas. It is a globular plant which can be as much as 5 in. across. Very old specimens cluster from the base. The stem is dark green and divided into thirteen ribs. The large satiny flowers are borne on top of the plant continuously through the summer. The petals are deep yellow with a red base. Again a very easy plant to grow and flower.

Lobivia jajoiana grows in Argentina at altitudes of up to 10,000 ft. It is a cylindrical cactus, slow-growing, 2 or 3 in. thick forming a few off-sets. The plant body is dark green. The spines on the new growth are red but fade to brownish with age. The deep red flowers open during the summer; they are red with an almost black throat.

Mammillaria craigii is a native of Mexico. It is a globular plant, branching with age. Like all mammillarias, the plant body is covered with small protuberances (tubercles). These have yellowish-brown spines on their tips. The small, deep pink bell-like flowers form a circle around the top of the plant in spring.

Mammillaria spinosissima is a Mexican plant. It is very variable; the spines may be white, yellow, brown or red. One of the most attractive forms is the variety *sanguinea*, with red-tipped spines. The cylindrical stem is dark green; it may remain solitary, or cluster. The purplish-red flowers open during the summer, and may be followed by bright red berries.

Mammillaria prolifera is a widely distributed cactus, found in Texas, the West Indies and Mexico. It clusters freely, forming a 'cushion' of small heads about 1 in. across, covered with fine white spines. Creamy flowers appear in late spring and are often followed by orange-red berries, which are said to taste like strawberries. The heads are knocked off very easily, so the plant must be handled carefully.

Notocactus haselbergii grows wild in southern Brazil. It forms a silvery ball, about 4 in. across, covered with fine white spines. The tomato-red flowers are carried on top of the plant in early summer. This is a hardy cactus, easy to grow, but does not flower as a seedling. Flowering-size plants are about 2½ in. across.

Notocactus mammulosus, a native of Uruguay and Argentina, forms a large, globular plant, with stout yellowish spines. With age it forms off-sets from the base. White, woolly buds appear at the top of the plant and open to golden-yellow flowers in early summer. It flowers profusely and is hardy. The flowers are self-fertile and large quantities of dark brown seeds are formed.

Opuntia microdasys is a Mexican plant, and to keep it unmarked, the winter temperature should be at least 45°F (7°C). It has flat stem segments (or pads) up to about 6 in. long. These are dotted with little collections of fine barbed hairs (glochids), which may be white, yellow or dark reddish-brown, depending on the variety. These glochids (characteristic of the opuntias) can irritate the skin. This cactus is grown for the beauty of its form and rarely flowers as a pot-plant. Given a free root run in a greenhouse bed, it produces yellow flowers in May.

Opuntia basilaris spreads from northern Mexico to the southern U.S.A. It has pads about 8 in. long of a beautiful bluish colour, dotted with collections of dark brown glochids. Branches form from the base, producing a large clump. The flowers are red, but it rarely flowers as a pot plant. There is a particularly beautiful variety, *cordata*, with heart-shaped, bluish-purple pads. This mostly branches from the base and remains one or two pads high.

Rebutia calliantha var. Krainziana is an example of the compact, very free-flowering South American rebutias. It will bloom when only 1 in. across. The globular stems are dark green, neatly covered with short white spines. The large orange flowers are produced in rings around the base of the plant in May. This is one of the easiest of the small cacti to flower and quite an old plant will only fill a 4-in. pot, but will be covered with flowers.

Rebutia miniscula var. violaciflora, from Argentina, is found growing about 10,000 ft. above sea level. It is a small clustering plant, and will flower when about 1 in. across. It is a light green in colour with short ginger spines. The intense magenta pink flowers are produced from the base of the plant in April and May. They are self-fertile, and if left undisturbed, the plant will eventually be surrounded by dozens of little self-sown seedlings.

Rhipsalidopsis rosea is an epiphyte from the forests of southern Brazil. It is a small

Below: Euphorbia beaumieriana, a spiny, cactus-like succulent, from Morocco. In its native habitat it may reach 6 ft. in height; in cultivation it is much smaller

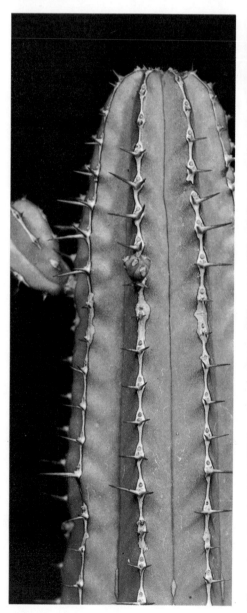

shrub about 9 in. high, consisting of dozens of stem segments about 1 in. long, with short bristles at the ends. The stems vary from green to dark red. The pale pink, bell-shaped flowers, about 1 in. across, cover the plant during May. After flowering the plant will look shrivelled, but after a few weeks it will come into growth again.

Schlumbergera 'Konigers Weihnachtsfreude' is one of the many schlumbergera hybrids flowering in the winter which are often called Christmas cactus. It is an epiphyte and forms a shrub, becoming pendent with age, and can reach massive proportions if not broken up and re-started. The glossy green stem segments are up to about $1\frac{1}{2}$ in. long. The intense cerise-pink flowers cover the plant in the winter months, but not necessarily at Christmas. The common Christmas cactus, formerly known as *Zygocactus truncatus*, is very similar. It is now correctly called *Schlumbergera* 'Buckleyi', though still often listed under *Zygocactus*.

Right: Ferocactus acanthodes, a colourful cactus from California, has bright red spines
Below: Glottiphyllum arrectum, a succulent from Cape Province, has large golden-yellow flowers in autumn

Other Succulent Plants

Aeonium domesticum (*Crassulaceae*) The aeoniums are native to the Canary Islands and are almost hardy. Beautiful specimens of these small shrubs may be found in the gardens of Cornwall. *A. domesticum* has almost circular leaves covered with fine hairs; the yellow flowers are produced in summer. Aeoniums may be grown permanently as pot plants or planted out in a rock garden for the summer, and repotted and stored under the greenhouse staging in winter.

Agave filifera (*Agavaceae*), a native of Mexico, is one of the smaller growing agaves suitable for pot cultivation. It forms a rosette about 2 ft. across, consisting of long, narrow dark green leaves, with white threads along the edges. Agaves only flower when old, and the flowering rosette dies. But new ones are formed at the base of the old plant. The flower stem is over 6 ft. high and the flowers are greenish.

Agave parviflora (*Agavaceae*) is a rare plant in the wild, found in a few localities in southern Arizona and Mexico only. It forms a rosette about 8 in. in diameter, ideal for a pot plant. The dark green leaves have white markings and marginal threads. The flower spike is about 3 ft. high and the flowers are reddish. New rosettes are formed at the base of the old plant after flowering.

Aloe jucunda (*Liliaceae*) is a miniature aloe, native to Somalia. The small, flat rosettes are about 4 in. across and the bright green leaves have attractive white spots, and small teeth along their edges. The pink flowers, carried on a long stem, open in spring. This aloe clusters freely and the individual heads can be used to start new plants.

Aloe variegata (*Liliaceae*) (partridge-breasted aloe) a native of Cape Province, South Africa, forms a stemless rosette, about 1 ft. high; the dark green leaves have attractive white markings. The plant produces many off-sets which are attached to the parent plant by underground stems. The small, orange, bell-shaped flowers are carried on a stout stem in March.

Caralluma europaea (*Asclepiadaceae*) is found around part of the Mediterranean coast, and also in South Africa. The thick leafless stems are greyish-green. This is a summer growing plant and the tiny flowers are stemless and produced in clusters. They are yellowish with brownish markings. The seeds are carried in long horn-shaped pods.

Conophytum flavum (*Aizoaceae*) comes from South Africa. The small plant bodies are green and rounded, freely clustering. The bright yellow flowers are usually produced in September or October, when they open in in the afternoon. The plant should be watered when the old leaves have shrivelled, usually about August, and watering should be continued until November.

Conophytum salmonicolor (*Aizoaceae*) is a native of Namaqualand, South Africa. The green plant body is about 1½ in. high and consists of a pair of united leaves. The plant clusters quite readily, and with age, a woody stem becomes evident. Its apricot-coloured flowers appear early in June. It should be watered when the old leaves have shrivelled (usually around the end of June) until the end of October.

Crassula falcata (*Crassulaceae*) spreads from Cape Province to Natal in South Africa. Because of its striking red flowers, it is a popular florist's plant. It is large, growing to about 1 ft., with bluish-grey leaves. The scarlet flowers are carried on a stout stem. It can be propagated from leaf cuttings.

Crassula teres (*Crassulaceae*) is a miniature plant from South-West Africa. The broad leaves are closely packed around the stem to form a short column. With age the plant clusters to form attractive groups. The tiny white flowers are stemless. It should be grown in a very open compost, placed in a sunny position and not over watered.

Duvalia radiata (*Asclepiadaceae*) is a smallish plant from Africa. The short, thick stem are prostrate and without leaves. The reddish-brown flowers are small and fleshy, but the horn-shaped seed pods are large and packed with numerous seeds, attached to tiny 'parachutes'. The growing and flowering period is summer.

Echeveria derenbergii (*Crassulaceae*) (the painted lady) is a dwarf plant from Mexico. It forms an almost stemless rosette about 3 in. across, which is soon surrounded by numerous off-sets. The leaves are plump and pale green with a white waxy coating. The reddish-yellow flowers open in the spring.

Echeveria hoveyi (*Crassulaceae*) from Mexico, forms a short-stemmed loose rosette which soon produces side shoots, making an attractive cluster. The long leaves are grey-green with pink and cream stripes. The colouring varies with the seasons; it is at its most vivid in the spring. Full sun and not too much water help to maintain a good colour.

Euphorbia aggregata (*Euphorbiaceae*) from Cape Province, is a shrub about 1 ft. high. It is a freely branching plant which soon clusters. The leafless stems are over 1 in. thick. The insignificant flowers are carried on thorn-like stalks which persist long after the flowers have died. This gives the whole plant a 'spiny' appearance, rather like a clustering cactus. The growing period is summer.

Euphorbia beaumieriana (*Euphorbiaceae*) comes from Morocco, where it can reach a height of 6 ft. It is, however much smaller in pots in collections. It is a cactus-like plant with ribs and spines. Like all euphorbias, it has milky sap, painful or even dangerous in the mouth or eyes.

Euphorbia obesa (*Euphorbiaceae*) is one of the more unusual plants from Cape Province, and is protected by the South African govern-

Haworthia limifolia, a South
African succulent

ment. It consists of a single spherical or slightly cylindrical stem, about 4 in. across, without leaves and reddish brown in colour. It is divided into blunt ribs. The small, stemless yellow flowers appear all the summer; they are sweetly scented. The male and female flowers are carried on separate plants.

Faucaria tuberculosa (*Aizoaceae*) is native to South Africa. Very young plants are stemless, but with age, a woody stem is formed. When this stem becomes too obvious the plant should be re-started from cuttings, leaving a small piece of stem to each rosette. The thick triangular dark green leaves have small teeth along their edges and small knobbly protuberances on the upper surface; they are about ¾ in. long. Golden flowers are produced in the autumn. The plant should be kept slightly moist throughout the year.

Gasteria maculata (*Liliaceae*) is a South African plant with long tongue-shaped leaves arranged in two rows. These are dark green in colour, with white markings. Off-sets are produced by the plant, and these can be left to form a group, or removed and potted up individually. The reddish flowers are carried on a long slender stem.

Glottiphyllum arrectum (*Aizoaceae*) is from Cape Province, South Africa. The soft, tongue-like leaves are bright green in colour and about 2 in. long. Young plants are almost stemless, but with age a woody stem appears. It is then best to cut up the clump, keeping a small piece of stem to each head. The large flowers are golden-yellow and almost hide the plant's body in September and October.

This plant has a short growing period and should only be watered from the beginning of July to the end of October.

Haworthia limifolia (*Liliaceae*) grows wild in South Africa. The stemless rosettes are about 4 in. across and consist of very dark green triangular leaves with ridges running across them. The plant forms many off-sets, attached to the main stem by underground runners. The tiny white flowers are shaped like narrow bells and are produced on a very long, slender flower stem in summer.

Lithops alpina (*Aizoaceae*) is one of the pebble plants. This little native of the Karroo, South Africa, closely resembles the stones among which it grows. The conical body is composed of one pair of stemless leaves with a fissure between them. These leaves are pale brown with dark brown markings. The bright yellow flowers appear from the fissure between the leaves, usually in June. Lithops are summer growing plants and should not be watered until the old pair of leaves has completely withered. The growing period is usually between April and September; the rest of the year the plants should be kept dry. The plant gradually clusters, forming a clump.

Lithops marmorata (*Aizoaceae*) is very similar to the above. The leaves are greyish-green with pale grey markings. The white flowers open in September.

Pleiospilos bolusii (*Aizoaceae*), from Cape Province, South Africa, is another of the mimicry plants, the thick, triangular leaves looking like pieces of granite. There is one

pair of thick purplish-green leaves, dotted with green. Old plants have woody stems, but younger plants are almost stemless. When the stem is obvious, it may be cut at about ¼ in. from the leaves and the plant re-started. The growing period is from late summer to autumn and the plant should be kept dry until the old pair of leaves has shrivelled completely. The large golden flowers open in October.

Sedum hintonii (*Crassulaceae*), like many of the beautiful tender sedums, comes from Mexico. It is a fairly recent discovery and consists of low rosettes, rapidly clustering. The furry leaves are egg-shaped and bluish grey in colour. The white flowers appear in the winter, and, although an easy plant to grow in summer, it is very prone to rot in the flowering period. It should not be watered at this time, and if possible should be wintered in the dry atmosphere of a room.

Stapelia hirsuta (*Asclepiadaceae*), a typical 'carrion plant' is found growing in Cape Province, South Africa. The thick velvety stems are leafless and about 9 in. high. This is a summer growing plant and the large flowers start to appear about mid-summer. These are five-petalled, yellowish and densely covered with brownish hairs. Although these flowers have little odour to us, they are most attractive to flies, which may lay their eggs in them. The maggots hatch out and promptly die, for although the flowers may look like carrion, the larvae cannot live on them. In nature, the flies cause pollination of the flowers. The seed pods are large and horn shaped.

The first of January may be the start of the Roman calendar year, but as far as gardening is concerned it is only the beginning of the end, spring being more commonly regarded as the start for gardeners. However, in January some plants begin to flower, snowdrops, winter aconites, the occasional primrose, and winter heliotrope with its delicious fragrance; others such as Christmas roses, winter jasmine and witch-hazel will be in full flower.

A wander round the garden on a sunny January day will point to seasonal jobs, in spite of its still being the close season for most plants. Bud pecking by birds, particularly of ornamental cherries, may be in full swing; one of the repellent sprays will help. Supporting stakes and ties of shrubs and trees may need renewal; snow should be shaken off branches, if possible, before they break; shelter and protection of small or tender plants may need strengthening. This is one of the worst times of the year for bark stripping by rabbits, hares, voles or mice, particularly in snowy weather, so make sure all is well. You can still plant woody specimens (shrubs and trees) when the soil is friable and crumbly, but not too cold nor too wet.

Borders can still be mulched. If you are a chrysanthemum fan, cuttings of winter flowering varieties need taking now, and of course will need some heat, in a propagating frame in the greenhouse; carnation cuttings can be put in as well. It is a good time to take root cuttings of phlox, anchusa, gaillardia, and perennial mullein (verbascum), which can all be increased in this convenient way.

Keep the greenhouse temperature up, the atmosphere not too damp, and ventilate slightly, even in severe cold; clean out rigorously all fallen vegetation, as botrytis (grey mould) thrives on this and is at its worst in cold, damp conditions.

But mostly the ornamental garden can be left to look after itself at this time of the year, and one can sit back in a comfortable chair by the fire and indulge one's self in dreams of sheets of colour, from perfectly grown plants, superbly blended and covering every inch of the ground. Seed for this spectacle should be ordered now from the new catalogues. Annuals, biennials and bedding plants can all be ordered; some of the more easily grown annuals for quick display are echium, godetia, calendula, (pot marigold), limnanthes (butter and eggs), annual chrysanthemum, cornflower, nigella (love-in-a-mist), night-scented stock, forget-me-not, nasturtium, larkspur and a variety of ornamental grasses, for sowing in March-April. Biennials for May and June sowing are foxgloves (the modern hybrids are delightful), sweet Williams, Canterbury bells and wallflowers (all good cottage garden plants). Pansies, honesty, sweet rocket and clary can be added, and a really striking and handsome plant is the mullein called *Verbascum bombyciferum*, with a rosette of great soft furry grey leaves, and a 5 or 6 ft. spire of white woolly buds unfolding to produce pale yellow flowers. The bedding plants can be started

Left: 'Hagley Hybrid', a clematis; hard prune in January or February

in February from seed – petunias, nemesias, ageratums, bedding dahlias, impatiens, lobelias, tobacco plants (nicotiana) and dwarf phlox are some to sow in a warm greenhouse.

Pruning of apples and pears can continue, so can that of cherries and plums, provided there are no diseases about such as silver leaf or bacterial canker; otherwise the wounds are very easily infected, and such trees are best left uncut until summer. Redcurrants and gooseberries can have their summer pruning completed by cutting the remains of the year's new lateral shoots back to 2-in. stubs, if this was not done in December. Raspberry canes should be tipped and ties renewed where necessary. Winter tar oil wash can be sprayed on to top fruit and soft fruit bushes to kill the over-wintering eggs of aphids, capsids and sap-suckers, spraying a drenching wash to run-off; it will clean off lichen and moss as well.

If peaches, almonds and nectarines are showing signs of bursting at the end of January, spray with a copper or sulphur fungicide to ward off leaf curl, again giving a drenching spray to run-off. Look for small mammal damage to bark of trunks; continue planting in suitable weather.

The vegetable front is the quietest, but even here there are jobs to be done. Digging and adding bulky organic materials such as well-rotted manure, compost and moist peat, especially if you have a sandy soil, is one and, on a cold, sunny winter's day, taken easily, this is a not unpleasant task, and one finishes glowing with virtue as well as exertion. Dress with lime, but only if the soil is very acid and, in any case, not at the same time as the working in of the bulky organic materials; allow an interval of at least six weeks between the two. Decide on your plan of cam-

Taking chrysanthemum cuttings

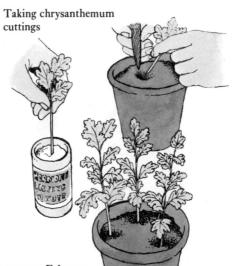

paign for rotating your vegetable crops; this enables use to be made of all nutrients in the soil and avoids the build-up of such troubles as eelworms, clubroot, scab and so on. Rotating means what is says; every year one of three (or four) different categories of vegetables is grown on a given piece of ground; the following year those types grown on plot (A) are grown on a second piece and their place of the previous year taken by a second (B) collection. In due course the vegetables in collection (C) are grown on the original piece of ground, and so sets revolve round, using three different soil sites.

In general, vegetables for this purpose are considered in the following categories: (1) brassicas such as cabbages, cauliflowers, sprouts, savoys, also lettuce mustard and cress, and radish; (2) potatoes; (3) legumes, e.g. peas and beans; (4) root crops – carrot, turnip, parsnip, beetroot. Onions are left to themselves and can safely be planted in the same piece of ground for many years, where they seem to do better than if moved about. If there is not much space they can, however, be grown with the roots and legumes.

In a rotation, potatoes can be followed the next season by the roots and legumes, and they in turn are succeeded by the leaf crops, brassicas and salads.

There is no need to manure before planting potatoes, since the ground will have been dressed early the previous winter for the brassicas which will have just preceded the potatoes; it is, however, a good idea in most instances to mix in a general compound powder fertilizer a week or so before putting out the sets. After the potatoes have been lifted, manure can be applied in autumn where peas and beans are to go in spring, but for the root crops potash only need be given, and that a few weeks before sowing or planting. For both again, a general fertilizer shortly before sowing or planting is advisable.

Tipping raspberry canes

In the third winter, compost or manure can be given before the brassicas, and by this time lime may also be necessary, allowing an interval of about two months between the two dressings. Since the leaf crops have such a large area of top growth, an application of a nitrogenous fertilizer while growing is advisable.

Tidying up vegetable refuse, such as old Brussels sprout plants and cabbage tops is very necessary to keep pests and diseases at bay. Some vegetables can be sown in heat in the greenhouse: these include tomatoes, carrots, onions, leeks, radishes and French beans, in a temperature of 60°F (15–16°C).

'February fill-dyke' is the old saying, and it can certainly be that in a good many parts of the country, either because of rain or melting snow. But the days have steadily begun to lengthen, and the extra light – and sometimes warmth – will start plants into growth towards the end of the month. Lawns may need topping, no more, on a mild day when the soil is not waterlogged or frozen. If it is very wet, spiking to a 4-in. depth with a garden fork is better treatment for the turf, and gives the grass roots a chance to breathe; later in the month worm casts may need sweeping off with a stiff broom.

In sheltered places roses showing signs of breaking into leaf should be pruned quickly before they do; this applies of course to the hybrid teas and floribundas, and those climbers not yet cut back. Clematis, similarly, may actually be bursting. The early summer flowering varieties should be tipped back only, the late summer flowering kinds need cutting back hard to leave 3, 4 or 5 ft. of growth from ground level. They grow exceedingly vigorously in the next four months and such hybrids as the blue-purple *C. jackmanii*, pink 'Hagley Hybrid', 'Étoile Violette' and white 'Huldine' relish such harsh treatment and reward it with an abundance of flower. As in January, keep a vigilant eye open for bud-pecking, wind-rocking, bark stripping and unsteady shrub and trees supports. After gales stakes and ties may need to be renewed, especially in exposed gardens. Be sure to firm the soil round wind-rocked plants.

Throughout the garden weeds may be starting to grow. Hoe them off or otherwise eradicate them before they get into their stride – it is so much easier to do and quicker, when they are at the seedling stage, or when they have only a weak winter hold on the soil. In the growing season it sometimes takes all one's strength to detach a well-grown weed from the ground.

Before the season really begins, a quick review of last year's pests and diseases will help in the battle against them this year. It is more than likely that some of the following will have appeared in the garden somewhere: white powdery mildew on roses, apple trees, chrysanthemums and herbaceous plants generally, grey mould throughout, rose black spot, scab on apples and pears, cankers on apple and rose shoots and branches, greenfly, and blackfly on practically everything, caterpillars of various sorts, earwigs, red spider mite, and sooty mould where greenfly have been feeding.

If so be prepared well in advance with such remedies as derris, malathion, gamma-HCH and trichlorphon insecticides, and benomyl, dinocap, sulphur and copper for fungi. Spray with the appropriate deterrent as soon as leaves unfold, if there was trouble last season, otherwise leave the plants alone but keep a vigilant eye on them.

Very cold snaps are another seasonal dismay, and the temperature may fall 20 or 30°F (10 or 15°C) below freezing, quite unexpectedly, so listen to weather forecasts, follow your own knowledge and experience of local weather conditions, and prepare to increase the greenhouse heat accordingly. Many precious plants are lost by just one night's severe cold. But, unless this kind of Arctic climate is expected, always ventilate the greenhouse, so that grey mould does not ravage the plants and be ready to spray if troubles appear.

At this time of the year the greenhouse can be very colourful, with cinerarias and freesias in full spate, lachenalias, crocus, narcissus and hyacinths brought on early, haemanthus and hippeastrum

The Gardener's Year
February

joining them, and some of the shrubs, camellias, jasmine, boronia, browallia, abutilon and the shrimp plant (beloperone), and azaleas still just in flower. Primulas such as *P. obconica, kewensis* and *malacoides* will be in flower and are charming, especially the Kew hybrid, in lemon yellow, with greyish-white leaves; it is fragrant as well. Many of these plants may be brought into the living room while they are in flower and returned to the greenhouse once their flowers are over.

Begonia, achimenes, dahlia and gloxinia (sinningia) corms and tubers will all start to produce shoots if put into a bed of moist peat. Another pleasant job for a dull February day is pruning

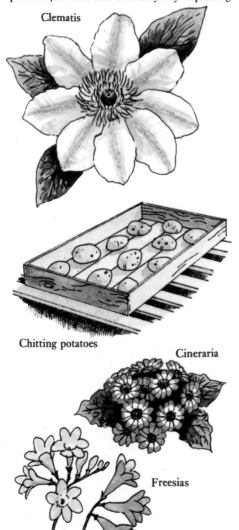

Clematis

Chitting potatoes

Cineraria

Freesias

many of the shrubby plants, for instance fuchsias, preparatory to topdressing or re-potting next month just as growth is starting. Flower seeds to sow are ageratum, impatiens, cobaea, canna, celosia, nemesia and petunia, in fact all sorts of half-hardy bedding plants for out of doors so that they can be brought on early and planted out at the end of May. Give them a temperature of 60°–70°F (16°–21°C); a propagating frame which can be heated will be needed if the greenhouse is a cool one. Sweet peas can be sown if missed out in the general rush in the autumn, and will flower in early July.

Hippeastrums, vallotas, clivias and lilies are some bulbs which can be started now, by watering a little and providing a little heat, to 50°F (10°C) or so. Watering of cyclamen, on the other hand, can be stopped, as flowers will have faded, the leaves will have fed the corms, and finished their useful life, and the plants can be gradually dried off and rested under the staging. More chrysanthemums can be footed from cuttings – the early-flowering kinds this month, as well as the winter ones, and so can perpetual flowering carnations.

Vegetables are an essential constituent of diet; home-grown ones are much better than shop sold (or soiled) ones for flavour and nutrient content, crispness and general deliciousness. Sowing vegetable seed now will give crops much earlier than usual; for instance, French beans, Brussels sprouts, cucumbers, carrots, radishes, tomatoes, leeks and lettuces, cauliflowers and broad beans will all germinate well in a temperature of 60°F (16°C) and more. Unusual vegetables are well worth considering; for instance celeriac seed can be sown inside, and Jerusalem artichokes and garlic can be planted in sheltered places and early gardens.

More run of the mill kinds for planting outside are spring cabbage, onion sets, shallots and chives. Parsnips which have been left in the ground, as good a way of keeping them as any, will not remain dormant any longer, and should be lifted and stored in dry sand before they start to grow again. Seed potatoes can be chitted, that is, put in single layers in shallow boxes in a light, frost-proof shed, so that the eyes start to sprout; the heel should be uppermost. Early varieties will then be ready for planting out in March in mild gardens.

Good vegetables must be grown well – they will not tolerate poor soil. A steady supply of moisture, as well as nutrients, is always necessary, otherwise they will not grow or will bolt. So, manuring and digging if not already done, can be completed this month.

If one's stomach rules one's gardening, then fruit growing is another branch which will take up a good deal of time. Pruning of apples and pears should finish this month; spraying with tar-oil winter wash is still possible; peaches and allied fruits may need protective spraying against leaf curl, with mancozeb or benomyl, timing the application for just before the buds begin to burst.

Raspberries can still be tipped and autumn fruiting kinds should have the old canes cut right out. Strawberries cloched late in the month will be ready for picking in early May. A tar-oil spray on blackcurrants now will save time later in spraying greenfly, since it will kill the over-wintering eggs. They can be a very real problem in that their attacks will severely stunt new growth on which next season's fruit will be produced. Gooseberry and red currant pruning should be completed.

Spring arrives officially this month, on the 21st, and by then the garden will be well on the way to a new season. The earliest shrubs will have started to bloom, *Mahonia japonica* with its bright yellow spikes of strongly scented flowers, the mezereon (*Daphne mezereum*), equally strongly scented but purplish-pink in flower, camellias, japonica, and that curious but attractively flowered shrub, *Corylopsis spicata*, in pale yellow, and acid-soil loving. These and other shrubs can be given a fertilizer dressing this month, watered in if the soil is dry; so, too, can herbaceous perennials, making the dressing relatively high in potash content if flowering is not all it might be. Rooted layers from shrubs can be detached and put in their permanent positions. Division of the border plants can also be undertaken successfully. Rose pruning will be in full swing; clematis pruning started last month should be finished by the middle of this one. Evergreens

cultivation one of the most satisfying and rewarding occupations. It needs a good deal of experience in gardening, on the whole; very well-drained composts are essential, and constant attention for most of the year. Small plants like these will be examined closely and need to be in first-class growth and flowering to be effective, so attention to detail is another 'must'. Some of the most easily grown and colourful plants for alpine houses, blooming in spring, are: the miniature narcissi, tulip species, scillas, *Aquilegia caerulea*, *Cyclamen orbiculatum*, *Anemone apennina*, grape hyacinths, primulas in variety, *Pulsatilla vulgaris* (the Pasque flower), iberis, *Gentiana acaulis*, and *Ramonda pyrenaica*.

In some parts of the country it is possible to sow seeds of herbs out of doors this month, but if the garden is a chilly one or the soil heavy, it is better to sow in the greenhouse. Parsley is always said to be slow to germinate, but in warm soil it

Left: Protecting a newly-planted conifer with sacking
Centre, above: Preparing and rooting dahlia cuttings

Right: Pans of colourful alpines
Centre, below: Dividing a clump of herbaceous perennials

can be planted this month, watered in well at the time of planting, and put in when the soil is moist. If in a windy position, give a temporary shelter of sacking, or polythene, while they establish, as wind is one of the main causes of browning of foliage, particularly conifers. Moisture vapour is literally blown off the surface of the leaf, and the roots do not replace this until they take hold of the soil. If dry weather follows planting, spraying overhead with a drenching spray of clear water once or twice a day will do much to mitigate the effects of desiccation.

Lawns can be given a spring clean, by first raking (provided there is no moss), then topping with razor-sharp mower blades, and following with spiking and the first feed. Where there is moss, spring is a good time to treat it with lawn sand, but a more long-lasting remedy is to improve the soil drainage or plant food content, so that the grass always grows strongly.

Lots of annuals can be grown out of doors, but do not be tempted too early in the month, and in cold gardens next month will be soon enough. Three or four very warm, sunny days often occur in March, deceiving one into thinking summer is on the way, but are followed by cold wet weather, when seeds rot in the ground. Annuals sown in patches, with some thought to colour blending, are highly satisfactory; for instance; one might have all the blues, purples, lavenders and pinks together; or a patch of different shades of yellow.

The corms and tubers started into growth last month in the greenhouse will be ready for potting; dahlias can have cuttings taken from them.

Rooted chrysanthemum and carnation cuttings will need potting in 3-in. pots; pelargoniums rooted from autumn cuttings will be growing and may need potting on. All sorts of pot plants can be turned out of their pots, the old compost removed, and replaced with fresh or, if they do not like root disturbance, the top 1½ in. can be scraped off and replaced with a topdressing.

Last month's seed sowings will need pricking out into boxes 2 in. apart each way; the plastic seed trays seem to give earlier and stronger growth. If the seedlings can be moved with the rounded root tip intact, they will 'take' practically without a check; try not to leave them too long in the seed-boxes. Once past a certain stage in their growth, even if pricked out they will never make good plants—they should be moved as soon as they are large enough to handle.

Tomatoes sown last month can be pricked out when the first true leaf shows, burying the stem so that the seed leaves are just above the soil surface. They will need warmth of at least 50°F (10°C) to keep them growing on; a check to growth either by cold or drought is disastrous at this stage, or when they are young plants. The sweet peas sown last month can be hardened off and planted out at the end of the month.

If alpine plants occupy a large part of the greenhouse, this and next month will be their hour of glory. A sunny, airy alpine house in the spring can be most colourful, and alpine plant

comes up just as quickly as the other herbs, and an out-of-doors sowing of it in April will produce more plants in the long run than a March one. Dill, coriander, sorrel, chives, sage, sweet marjoram and summer savory all germinate easily.

Parsnip can be sown in early March; it is very hardy and needs a good long season to develop. Most of the rest of the vegetables, summer spinach, broccoli, spinach beet, sprouts, cabbage, cauliflower, early carrots, leeks, onions, lettuce, peas, radish and spinach beet can be sown outside later this month. Celery, celeriac, cucumbers, melons and more tomatoes can be sown in heat.

Preparation of the soil for seed sowing will be the same as for annuals, broken down and raked to a crumb structure, and fed about 10 days before sowing. Seed is sown when conditions are moist, as warm as possible and preferably when rain is expected. Lining the drills with moist peat, or sieved compost helps germination and subsequent growth in difficult soils and poor weather. Maincrop potatoes should be put to sprout.

From vegetables to fruit—the earliest to break dormancy will be the blackcurrants, and they may need spraying before the end of the month if the greenfly hatch is early; malathion, derris, dimethoate or menazon are suitable controls. Bud pecking of gooseberries and blackcurrants must still be watched for, as it is easy to lose an entire potential crop at this stage as a result of bullfinch attacks. Cane spot of raspberries is a particularly deadly fungus disease, which reduces production of new growth, and depletes fruiting of the older canes. Spray with thiram to control this, if present, as the canes begin to shoot. Uncloched strawberries should be cleared of dead leaves, accumulated during winter.

The traditional sunshine and showers of April, and rising temperature, bring the garden to life with a vengeance; time is at a premium. The spring-flowering perennials begin to colour the border, blue lungwort with its white-spotted leaves; primroses and polyanthus, aquilegias in early gardens, aubrieta, alyssum, the Pasque flower, violets, brunnera, trollius and bergenia.

Below: Prick out seedlings carefully
Centre: Spring tulips in variety

The Gardener's Year
April

carefully prepared, well-drained compost.

The vegetable seeds sown last month in heat, such as celery, cucumber, marrow, aubergine and peppers, will need pricking out or potting. Runner beans can be sown inside for May planting out of doors and cropping in very early July; the dwarf runners can be cloched and brought on for June cropping. Outdoor vegetable

Below: Remove the cloches from strawberries on sunny days to enable the flowers to be pollinated

But the really blazing display is given by the bulbs, which have been growing away below the soil surface all through the winter and will have poked through in some places, and now burst out of their protective sheaths to unfold a rainbow of colour. An English garden in spring without daffodils is unthinkable–those shining yellow trumpets belong nowhere else–but there are so many other kinds that are lovely, in white, cream, combinations of white and yellow; some are double, some fragrant (the jonquils and narcissi), some with pink trumpets and petals, others orange-red, even some with trumpets split into three and doubled, the 'split corona', Dutch hybrids.

Then there is the 'blue' group of bulbs, the grape hyacinths, scillas, puschkinias, and chionodoxa, with the magenta *Cyclamen orbiculatum* to blend; there is the sturdy crown imperial orange fritillary (*Fritillaria imperialis*), and the species tulips, *kaufmanniana*, *greigii*, and *dasystemon*, charming with their brilliant red and yellow flowers, and purple streaked leaves. St Brigid and du Caen anemones in blue, red, purple, lilac, white and pink will flower with abandon now; the yellow pheasant's eye, *Adonis vernalis*, unfolds its round yellow petals in their nest of ruffled green calyces–sometimes the 'eye' is green. *Erythronium dens-canis*, the dog's tooth violet, in rose-pink, adds itself to the scene, and the strange snake's-head fritillaries quietly unfold in grassy places. Hyacinths and leucojums (snowflakes), so like a large snowdrop, complete the parade.

There are summer and autumn flowering bulbs, too and, provided there is good drainage, they will grow almost anywhere with little or no care; altogether it is rather difficult to fault the bulbs as garden plants. So make a mental note now, from what is seen in gardens, to order in time for planting in autumn; one of the arts of good gardening is to think ahead for next year.

All the annuals can be sown out of doors this month, and those that are best sown now and not earlier, can go in, nasturtiums, aster, tagetes, zinnia and salpiglossis. Border plants can still be put out, pansies, sweet peas, montbretia, gladioli and antirrhinums can be put in their flowering positions, and annuals pricked out last month in the greenhouse can be put out and gradually hardened off.

Shrub planting can continue, both of hardy kinds and those which are tender; pruning of the late-summer kinds should be completed this month, and the very early spring and winter flowering kinds can also be tidied now. If feeding was missed last month, shrubs and perennials can still be treated, roses can have their first feed and, later in the month, mulches can be put down on to moist soil. Spraying for rose black spot and mildew must be started, using mancozeb, dinocap, sulphur or a systemic fungicide which gives a month's protection. Lawn cutting can start in earnest, and grass seed for new lawns can be sown now.

Weed control is a priority, either by hoeing, forking and hand removal, mulching or chemical treatment. The modern range of herbicides is wide, and includes paraquat and diquat for annual and shallow rooted weeds; selective hormone weedkillers containing 2, 4-D, 2,4,5-T or mecoprop for application to the leaves of broad-leaved weeds, and dalapon for top growth of couch and other grasses; simazine, sodium chlorate or dichlobenil for root absorption, and propachlor to stop weed seeds germinating. Lawn weeds are best treated with hormone herbicides. Whatever is used, however, read the directions first, and then follow them.

The greenhouse will be crying out for attention, to prick out seedlings into trays and boxes, to put out and harden off bedding plants and half-hardy annuals, to pot on or plant in the greenhouse border, chrysanthemums, carnations and pelargoniums, also tomatoes (the first three will want stopping if it has not already been done), and to pot on corms started last month. Water will be required in increasing quantities by all plants; very careful management of heating and ventilation will be necessary, with night frosts still about, even snow, and bright sun during the day alternating with showers and strong winds. Freesia seed can be sown where it is to flower, eight to a 7-in. pot or deep box, for flowering next October onwards. Primula seed for next winter's display should be sown this month in

sowing can safely include autumn cabbage, maincrop carrots, lettuce, Brussels sprouts, peas, radish, savoy, spinach beet, beetroot, broccoli, cauliflower, globe artichoke, and all the herbs, including parsley at the end of the month, unless it is warmer than usual. Some of last month's vegetable sowing can be hardened off and planted out now, lettuce, leeks, onion and cauliflower. The spring cabbage sown last autumn will be the better for a fertilizer dressing, and chitted maincrop potatoes can be planted. Any earlies which have already gone out may need frost protection. Asparagus beds and Jerusalem artichokes from last year can be given a general compound fertilizer.

Pears, cherries and plums will blossom this month; blackcurrants begin to leaf and flower before the month is out, and should be sprayed with lime-sulphur if big bud is a trouble, when the leaves are about the size of a 10p piece. Otherwise a general greenfly spray over all the top fruit, and blackcurrants, will save a lot of trouble and work later on. Apple and pear scab are fungus diseases which may defoliate the trees later in the year, and will blemish the fruit with hard black spots which crack; in moist warm weather it spreads fast, and a protective covering of fungicide should be put on at fortnightly intervals until the end of June. Benomyl or bupirimate and triforine compound should achieve control. Spray apples at the green cluster, pink bud and petal fall stages in mid June and again in early July. For pears miss out the pink bud stage.

Strawberries will begin to come to life and should be weeded if not already done; the cloched ones will need ventilating on sunny days, and to allow the bees to pollinate them, and they may also need watering. Raspberries can be tied in, and both these and blackcurrants can be mulched. If all the soft fruit is clear of weeds, a good way of keeping them down for the rest of the season is to put down straw as a thick covering. The soil will remain moist, too, except in dry summers or if very sandy or gravelly, and by the autumn will be rotting in of its own accord. Moreover, it has the advantage of making picking easier and pleasanter. Peaches will have set, and may need frost protection; thinning can start towards the end of the month.

The warmth and wet of the last two months will, one hopes, have brought outdoor plants on fast, and flowering will really get under way. Border plants will shoot up and may need staking, particularly peonies. Annuals sown out of doors should be thinned. Dahlia cuttings or tubers which have sprouted can be planted out at the end of the month, when frost is unlikely, also tuberous and fibrous begonias which have started into growth, with the same reservation. Gladiolus corms can be planted in sandy soil and a sunny place. Chrysanthemums may be set out, in pots, or in the soil directly, from mid May onwards, and freesias grown from seed can be placed in a shady position in late May.

The April-flowering shrubs can be pruned, especially clematis, and those flowering in early May; included will be forsythia, kerria, *Spiraea arguta*, *S. thunbergii* and berberis. Rhododendrons, azaleas and lilacs should be deadheaded as soon as the blooms have finished. Evergreens and tender shrubs can still be planted; hibiscus is likely to remain apparently lifeless after planting, until July. Planting of water plants can start now that the water is beginning to warm up.

Grass cutting should continue at five-day intervals, and a combined feed and weed application will do much good if applied now, when weeds are at their highest rate of growth. Lawns sown from seed last month will need topping this month.

Mulching can still be done if missed last month. Biennials are sown this month for flowering next spring, e.g. wallflowers, Sweet Williams, Canterbury bells (*Campanula medium*) –the pink ones are unusual and pretty, and antirrhinums. Foxgloves, verbascums, pansies and polyanthus are also treated in this way.

This year's spring bedding will need clearing away, and spring-flowering bulbs can be lifted to make way for summer bedding. They are heeled in, that is, laid at an angle in a shallow trench, with the leaves exposed, but the bulbs covered with soil, to finish ripening, so that the embryo flower can form, ready for the next season. Sweet pea supporting and training, if grown as cordons, should start.

The compost heap will be growing daily; it is an essential to good gardening, and can consist of any green vegetative material, grass cuttings, weeds, soft shrub prunings, leaves and flower stems. Weeds should be pulled before they flower, otherwise the heap is likely to be full of weed seeds unkilled because of insufficient heat within the heap. A 6-in. layer of vegetation can be sprinkled with sulphate of ammonia, and the next layer dusted with lime. The heap can be built in this way with lime and ammonium sulphate alternating, or Nitro-chalk can be used to take

The Gardener's Year — May

both their places, at less frequent intervals. Quickly made heaps with plenty of green material in them will heat up high and fast, and kill weed seeds, fungus diseases and pests. Turning sides to middle is possible within a few weeks, and the heap can be ready to use in three months or less, but in any case not before it is dark and crumbly.

Capsids hatch at the beginning of the month and do great damage to dahlias, chrysanthemums, and all kinds of flowering shrubs by feeding on the growing points at the tips of the shoots and on embryo flower buds, the damage not being seen until at least a month later, when it is too late. So spray with a systemic or malathion insecticide in early May, and again 10 to 14 days later, treating the ground around plants at the same time, as these pests tend to drop to the ground.

Indoors, the greenhouse will be emptying of the half-hardy bedding plants, and pricked out seedlings, but tomatoes, pelargoniums, and chrysanthemums will be coming on fast. Tomatoes sown in heat in February will have been planted or potted last month and will now need regular training and sideshooting. Pelargoniums should be stopped as soon as possible; peppers and aubergines can be sown this month, so can primulas and cinerarias.

The greenhouse may need shading this month, particularly if tomatoes, begonias and gloxinias are grown; the increasing intensity of the sun will send the temperature very high very quickly, so give plenty of air during the day, but continue to close down to some extent at night, remembering that frost is still possible. Damping down greenhouse staging, and paths in the middle of the day, will begin to be a routine task, to maintain a humid atmosphere, and discourage red spider mite. Humidity is essential for setting fruit and prevent bud drop before blooms unfold; it also prevents browning of leaf tips and leaf margins. Cactus plants should be given as hot and sunny a corner as possible; they revel in heat and light.

Cucumbers, marrows, celery and melons

brought on and potted last month, can go out at the end of the month, into rich, well-prepared soils, though cucumbers and melons can also be grown in the greenhouse, and may do better there in cool seasons. They will need strong supports in that case, and regular training and tying in with removal of unneeded sideshoots.

Vegetable seed sowing can continue, of beetroot, ridge cucumbers, lettuce, radish, spinach, turnip, peas, runner beans and French beans.

Maincrop potatoes can still be planted out, and earlies will want ridging, unless grown on the flat, with a black polythene mulch. Weeds will need a good deal of keeping pace with, both among the vegetables and fruit, as well as ornamentals; they grow like wildfire this month. Broccoli will be finishing, so will spring cabbage, savoys, and late summer sown spinach, and the remains should be cleared off before they can provide homes for pests and diseases which can infect the new season's vegetables. The larvae of the flies which attack onion, carrot and cabbage seedlings should be warded off with diazinon or bromophos on the soil around the plants, or trapped with carrot or potato on skewers.

Quickly growing vegetables, e.g. the leafy kinds, will want a feed now, or regular weekly feeding with a liquid fertilizer; remember to water if the weather is dry, or to mulch on to moist soil so that the water supply is continuous throughout the life of the vegetables. If the district is a bird ridden one, protective matting is essential, both for vegetables and soft fruit. The fruit will probably not need protection until next month, unless it already is for bud pecking, but vegetables should be guarded sometime this month.

Strawberries will be flowering and setting; frosted flowers will have blackened centres, as will those of apples. Gooseberries and blackcurrants will finish setting early this month; if the flowering period is windy and cool, blackcurrants will 'run off', as bees will not work them in such conditions, and low temperatures inhibit pollination and fertilization. So give them a place sheltered from wind when planting, or put up a temporary barrier of sacking if the wind sets in from the north-east or south-west at flowering. There is still time to put straw on to clean ground. Spraying for greenfly, capsid, caterpillars, apple sawfly and mildew should continue. If dry weather occurs towards the end of the month, irrigate the raspberries, otherwise the new crop of canes will be severely depleted. Peaches will be stoning and should be thinned from the time they are about the size of marbles, spacing them eventually to about 1 ft. apart, and spreading the thinning over several weeks.

Left: Planting gladiolus corms
Centre: A selection of biennials
Below: A section through a compost heap

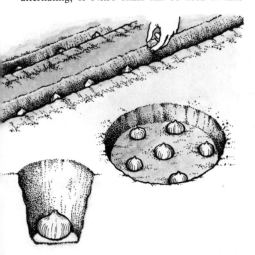

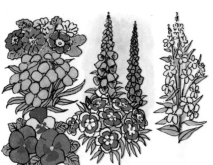

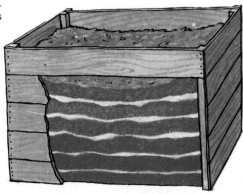

English gardens in June have only one equal – English gardens in April. The blend of the colours and fragrances of leaves and flowers is nowhere excelled; their tranquility, beauty, and splendour combine to make a scene found nowhere else and to which gardeners the world over return constantly for their inspiration.

Plants of all sorts spill over with blossom, scent and foliage in June; shrubs come into flower thick and fast – kalmia, ceanothus, cytisus, berberis, escallonia, deutzia, weigela, genista, philadelphus, spiraea, lilac, viburnum and roses of all kinds.

The climbing plants begin to make walls and fences and screens brilliant with flower; they include roses, whether they are climbers of the large-flowered kind such as 'Spek's Yellow' or the orange 'Schoolgirl', or ramblers of the small-flowered double 'Dorothy Perkins' kind, the tubular orange flowers of *Eccremocarpus scaber*, honeysuckle with its sweet scent, and white *Jasminum officinale*, sweeter still, and the large-flowered clematis, blue, red, purple, lavender, white and cream. All may want tying in and will need watering, particularly if they are growing up walls.

Perennials in bloom are delphiniums, campanulas, lupins, bearded iris, evening primrose, potentilla, poppies, peonies, verbascum, geranium, veronica, cimicifuga; the list is endless. But one can relax now that the first spring rush is over, and take time to wander round the garden, mark the gaps and note the plants doing badly, decide on new ones to fill them in or replace them; one sees clearly those that do not like their positions which will be the better for transplanting in autumn.

It is very important, this wandering round; it looks aimless, but in fact, the more one can do it the better. In the process a good gardener observes his plants and their reactions to his treatment and draws conclusions which result in better plants and an even more attractive interlocking of their habits of growth, colour, leaf shapes and flowering. He sees the beginning of pest and disease attack, and the onset of weed infestation, the need for water, the appearance of deadheads and the over-luxuriant growth that wants pruning away.

Jobs to do, if one must, are staking border plants, pruning early summer flowering shrubs, tying or ringing sweet peas, liquid feeding

annuals and bedding plants, mowing the lawn, spraying for rose mildew, black spot, greenfly and caterpillars. The last of the bedding plants should be out at the beginning of the month, together with dahlias and chrysanthemums. The latter should be stopped this month, in the first two weeks, and again at the end for second crown flowering, but if they are to flower at Christmas, stopping should be left until July.

Biennials can still be sown this month for next season's spring flowering. Watering is likely to be necessary constantly, particularly the lawn. The quick growing hedges can be given their first cut in early June, privet, *Lonicera nitida*, blackthorn, hawthorn and gorse.

Sweet peas may flower later this month, but in any case will be growing fast. They flower more prolifically if trained up supports, tied in, and their tendrils removed. Water copiously in hot weather as bud drop occurs when the soil is dry (and if they are growing on shallow soil); liquid feeding each week will help flower production.

Perhaps the plants most evocative of the English summer scene are the old-fashioned shrub roses, and this month and July are the times to see them in nurseries, if they are not already in the garden. They need very little care, will be recurrent flowering with the right choice, and are exceedingly free from diseases, though they can be rather heavily smitten with greenfly. They are loosely held together shrubs, of between 4 and 8 ft. tall, whose flowers range from single to very double, quartered blooms, in colours of white and yellow, pink and red to deep black-crimson, taking in red and white stripes on the way; they are mostly heavily fragrant, and have wildly romantic names; 'Belle de Crecy', 'Variegata di Bologna', 'Fantin Latour', 'Cuisse de Nymphe', 'Gloire des Mousseux', 'Tour de Malakoff', 'Zéphirine Drouhin' and 'Roseraie de l'Hay' are some of them. Deadheading is parti-

Far left: A climbing rose *Left:* Clematis. *Below left:* Rooting a soft tip shrub cutting. *Below:* Sweet peas grown on netting

cularly effective in encouraging continuous flowering from June to October, and it is even possible to pick the odd flower at Christmas.

The greenhouse will be almost too hot, but the cacti will be well suited, and so will the pelargoniums. Gloxinias, begonias, streptocarpus and achimenes must have shade, however, and frequent dampings down. Seedlings of cineraria and primula can be pricked out and potted, or sown this month, together with calceolarias. The big bulbs, hippeastrum, lily and clivia will be in flower and will need plenty of water; indeed watering will be a constant preoccupation, being necessary twice a day in really hot weather.

Soft tip cuttings of shrubs and greenhouse plants can be removed now and placed in sandy compost, three or four to a small pot, with a polythene bag over the top to keep the atmosphere moist and the cuttings shaded. The term 'soft' indicates that the top 3 in. of stem are used for the cutting, before the stem has time to ripen and harden.

Tomatoes which were sown in heat in February will be ripening this month under glass, and can be allowed to carry at least eight trusses before stopping, that is, breaking off the growing tip of the main stem just above a leaf. This prevents any more upward growth. Sideshooting and overhead damping should continue; if the yellow mottling of magnesium deficiency starts to show on the leaves, spray with Epsom salts at 2 oz. per gallon immediately the first faint yellowing begins to appear and repeat four or five times at two-week intervals. Cucumbers and melons will need further control of the excess sideshoots; the latter plants should be hand pollinated.

Marrows can still be planted out at the beginning of this month, also outdoor tomatoes, celery, leeks, cauliflower, savoy cabbages, sprouts, broccoli, and autumn-winter cabbage. Peppers and aubergines can be planted out in a sunny frame, or potted on in the greenhouse at least once, using a rich planting medium in both cases. Asparagus cutting should finish by mid June, early potatoes can be dug and maincrops will need earthing up. Vegetable seeds sown outside last month will need thinning, and more seed such as peas, lettuce, parsley, radish, summer spinach, spinach beet and shorthorn carrots can be sown outside.

The soft fruit season will start in about the middle of the month, and will continue for six weeks or so, with the earliest strawberries such as 'Cambridge Favourite', followed by 'Royal Sovereign', 'Grandee' and 'Gento', and finishing with 'Talisman' and 'Red Gauntlet' coming in at the end of June. Raspberries will be in full flower and should be sprayed with derris ten days after flowering starts, if raspberry maggot is likely to be a trouble. The first gooseberries may be ready at the end of the month. Blackcurrants may just be ready for picking in the last week, with a variety such as 'Boskoop Giant'.

Apples and pears will be suffering the June drop at the end of June, when they thin themselves naturally; spraying for mildew and scab should continue. Also spray for apple codling moth caterpillars in mid-June, repeating 2–3 weeks later. Make sure that plums and peaches against walls do not run short of water, and finish peach thinning. Strawberry runners should be removed and the plants netted. At the end of all this, spare yourself some time to enjoy the fruits (literally) of your labours with clotted cream and sugar.

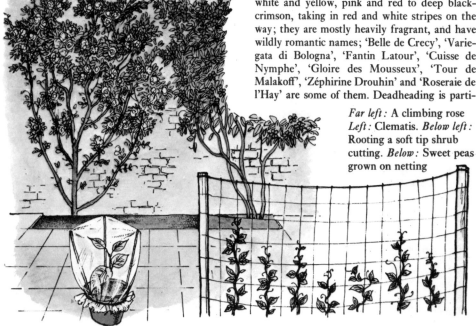

The herbaceous border comes into its own this month and, done well, carries a splendid display of colour. With careful choice and blending of plants, however, it can be highly decorative for most of the year. The use of plants which have coloured leaves, silver-grey, purple, and variegated, and using plants which are 'architectural' in form, so that their habit of growth and outline complements the flowering kinds, will make the border easy on the eye in or out of the flowering season.

Attention should be paid to the management of the soil, to provide a basis for good plants, and much of the work on this will be done in winter (see November, December). Then the choice of plants can come, and here it helps to note good plants at this time of year, in nurseries and other gardens, where one can see designs which need not necessarily be transferred complete, but can be modified to the pattern of one's own garden.

Herbaceous plants in flower are *Salvia haematodes*, kniphofias, hostas, day-lilies, veronicas, polemoniums, lilies, Shasta daisies, ligularias, rudbeckias, phlox, gaillardias, the blue thistle (eryngium) penstemons, and many, many others. The July gales will mean attention to staking; thunderstorms also often beat plants down and so it is doubly important to make sure that they are securely supported. Deadheading helps the appearance of the border.

Bedding plants and half-hardy annuals, such as petunias, ageratums, fibrous begonias, nemesias, impatiens, nasturtiums, zinnias, dwarf phlox, salvias and lobelias, will be at their best, and one begins to think they are worth the trouble of early sowing, coddling in the greenhouse in spring, pricking out, hardening off and finally planting out of doors. Sweet peas will continue to need training and layering by now. Chrysanthemums can be stopped the second time in mid July if flowering is wanted at Christmas. They will also need disbudding every few days, as will dahlias, if really large flowers are wanted. Both will be the better for spraying to control capsid bug and greenfly early in the month. Lawn watering should not be neglected; if no rain occurs for several days which are hot and sunny as well, start watering, as waiting until the lawn is obviously gasping for it is too late, and the grass will be irremediably weakened. Continue to mow, without the grassbox attached.

Cut the fast growing hedges again, privet, *Lonicera nitida* and the thorns, also start on most of those which grow at a more normal speed, such as beech, hornbeam, euonymus, hazel, holly and pyracantha. Conifer hedges can also be cut now, such as yew, thuja, juniper, cupressus and chamaecyparis. The pruning of early summer flowering shrubs should be completed; the late summer flowering kinds can be enjoyed, such as hydrangea, hypericum, fuchsia, clematis, late honeysuckle, some philadelphus, hebe, Californian tree poppy and cistus. Wisteria can be summer pruned this month or next, cutting back sideshoots to leave five buds or leaf joints. The rock roses (helianthemums) are much the better for having straggling shoots cut back after flowering. New shrubs can be ordered this month for November delivery.

Hybrid tea roses should be deadheaded regularly, unless heps are wanted, and it is during this month propagation of roses by budding can start, at any time when the bark lifts easily, but not during dry weather. Continue to spray for rose black spot, mildew, greenfly, red spider mite, caterpillars and thrips, especially the latter on gladioli.

The Gardener's Year
July

Bulbs, such as daffodils, tulips, bulbous iris, and hyacinth, can be lifted, cleaned, and stored. Biennials can still be sown, and seedlings of those sown last month should be transplanted to permanent positions or pricked out into boxes. Autumn flowering crocus, cyclamen, colchicum and sternbergia can be planted.

Greenhouse damping and watering are necessities; tomatoes will be ripening and feeding should continue. Primulas, cinerarias and calceolarias will need pricking out or potting on to 4-in. pots. Seeds of these can still be sown – it is not too late for flowering them next year. Freesias will want staking.

Soft tip cuttings of shrubs and perennials can be rooted in warmth, and half-ripe kinds will be rooted in a frame or cool greenhouse. Cyclamen can be retrieved from under the bench, so can Christmas cactus, watered and started into growth, and then repotted. Greenhouse plants in flower now are abutilons, achimenes, impatiens, begonias, bougainvilleas, calceolarias, *Campanula isophylla*, cannas, celosias, fuchsias, heliotropes, hoyas, ipomoeas, lantanas, lapagerias, neriums, passifloras, pelargoniums and crinums.

It is during July that the splendour of the lily is at its height; among the easiest to grow and the most magnificent is the regal lily, *Lilium regale*. Its great white trumpets, yellow-throated and centred with deep orange anthers, unfold in early July and waft a heavy fragrance over the garden. Once settled in well-drained, but not particularly fertile soil, provided it contains some leafmould, they will flower reliably every year without trouble. The Madonna lily, *L. candidum*, is another that is easily grown, and the clustered short white trumpets on stems 4 ft. tall were once seen in every cottage garden.

Others for this month are *L. amabile*, red; the 'Bellingham Hybrids', red, orange and yellow, with bell-shaped flowers; *L. martagon*, the Turk's-

Right: Lilium candidum
(the Madonna lily)
Centre right above: Lilium tigrinum (the tiger lily)
Centre right below: Lilium martagon (the martagon lily)
Far right: Strawberry layering (above) and Tip layering a blackberry

cap, in purple; *L. pardalinum*, orange and crimson; *L. tigrinum*, the orange tiger-lily and the 'Aurelian Hybrids' with such evocative names as 'Black Dragon', 'Golden Clarion', 'Green Magic', 'Limelight' and 'Pink Perfection'. All are easily grown in the soils that suit the regal lilies, except the Aurelians which mostly dislike lime in the soil and grow better in a slightly acid one. The lily fever is easily caught but not so easily lost.

Soft fruit picking will claim a good deal of time and with a deep freeze much of it can be preserved with its fresh flavour for winter; raspberries with cream or a blackcurrant pudding are particularly tasty out of season in the depths of winter. Strawberries will finish cropping this month; raspberries will come into ripening, and will finish by the end of July, and blackcurrants, redcurrants and gooseberries will also finish, although it has been known for all to continue to ripen into August, which is late for the south of the country.

Strawberry runners should be removed as they appear, unless wanted for a fresh bed next year; pegging them down directly into the soil, if it is done early, seems to produce as good plants as the pot-grown kinds. Blackberries can be tip layered, that is the tips of new shoots are pegged down into the soil, where they will send out roots. Melons will be swelling and superfluous growth should be removed; water copiously at this stage. Peaches, plums and cherries will begin to ripen; the first apples will be ready, such as 'Beauty of Bath', 'George Cave', and 'Emneth Early'.

Succession vegetables can be sown, lettuce, radish, parsley for winter, spring cabbage for next year, endive for blanching later in autumn. Winter vegetables to be planted out are cauliflower, broccoli, sprouts, cabbage, savoy and autumn celery – the self-blanching kind will begin to be ready at the end of this month. On potatoes blight may be a trouble, particularly in warm wet seasons, so spray the foliage with Bordeaux mixture or mancozeb to give a protective covering before the disease infects.

Onions will be maturing and the tops should be bent down, if they are not already doing it of their own accord. Early potato lifting can finish and that of second earlies start. Herbs can be gathered and dried this month, storing for winter use. Keep the hoe going and the weeds under; if ground empties as a crop is lifted, sow a quick maturing green crop such as mustard, rape or annual vetch, to be dug in early September, before it flowers.

The
Gardener's
Year
August

Left: The leaves of onions bent over to hasten ripening. Onions are often stored 'roped', the withered leaves plaited together as illustrated
Right: Most chrysanthemum plants, except spray varieties, are disbudded to obtain larger blooms

Traditionally the month for holidays and merry-making, August is, in fact, one of the quieter months in the gardener's year; the production of new growth has slowed down, and the process of ripening and maturing is evident. One can relax a little and the ornamental garden can be left to itself to a large extent, merely removing dead-heads, replacing supports, and spraying for mildew. This is a fungus disease, characterized by a white powdery coating on leaves, stems and buds, and at this time can be a great nuisance on ornamentals, particularly if the soil is dry or the garden rather stuffy. Dinocap or sulphur dust, or in solution, will restrain its increase. Watch for it also on apples, roses and hedge plants.

Mowing the lawn and irrigating it continue in hot weather. Hedge cutting can continue, or start, if missed last month. Shrubs which flower this month, as well as those which started in July, are hibiscus, more hebes, ceanothus, caryopteris, ceratostigma, buddleias, species clematis and more hydrangeas.

In late August Scotland comes to town, in that the heaths and heather bust into a purple glory and continue so for several months. It is not strictly accurate to confine the colour to purple as the modern hybrids and cultivars come in all shades of purple as well as pink, rose, and white, with foliage in grey, green, yellow, cream- or yellow-variegated, and red- or pink-tipped. Given an acid soil, preferably inclined to be peaty, but not fertile, heathers, once planted, will continue to be a carefree joy. Clipping the tops with shears when they have flowered, or in spring for those that bloom in late summer and autumn, is virtually all that need be done. For extra plants, pull down outside shoots to ground level and cover their stems with soil. Eventually, roots will form and new plants (layers) can be detached.

A border of heathers really is a patchwork of colour, and with the dwarf conifers in their equally varied foliage colours and silhouettes interspersed among them at suitable intervals, such a planting can only increase in beauty and effectiveness through the years. A heather collection could be started with the cultivars of *Calluna vulgaris*, which are in flower from August to October and later, such as 'Beoley Gold', acid yellow leaves and white flowers; 'Cuprea', copper-bronze leaves and purple flowers; rose-pink 'H. E. Beale', and purple 'Mrs Pat'; 'Silver Queen', lavender flowers and grey-white green leaves, and pink-lilac 'County Wicklow'.

Propagation of various plants by various methods can continue; semi-ripe cuttings can be taken, and at the end of the month pelargonium cuttings can be started, also conifer heel cuttings, 2 in. long, placed in a cold shady frame in pure sand or a sandy compost. It is still possible to root soft cuttings, and layering may be started at the end of August. Disbudding of chrysanthemums continues, and the top bud of the outdoor ones can be secured this month. Biennials to bloom next year can be planted out.

Freesia corms for December flowering can be planted early in the month, about 2 in. deep, in pots put out of doors in a shady place. So can prepared hyacinths for Christmas, but after potting they should be put in a cool dark place for three months. *Iris reticulata* for January flowering, and winter flowering begonias, can be potted; Christmas cactus and cyclamen can be started this month, if this has not already been done. Cyclamen will have spent the last two or three months out of doors in a shady place, and can now be moved to a lighter one, watering thoroughly to start them into growth. If new compost is required, they should be repotted before watering, using a slightly acid compost, and removing all the old. The corm is replaced so that it is only half buried.

Watering and damping down of pot plants should continue, and routine tidying of fallen leaves, flowers and dying vegetation generally.

Out of doors runner beans and self-blanching celery will be ready. Vegetable seeds which can still be sown outside include spring cabbage, lettuce, radish, spinach beet, winter spinach and endive; young plants of broccoli, winter cabbage and savoys can all be put in.

Herbs are still good for picking and drying, on a warm day when the foliage is dry. Second early potatoes will be ready, and onions can be lifted and spread out in the sun in single layers in boxes to dry before storing. Vegetables and salads in season this month are runner beans, cabbage, carrots, lettuce, onion, peas, potatoes, spinach, spinach beet, marrows (including courgettes), beetroot and garlic. Crops which have finished should be cleared out and the ground manured or not, depending on the rotation. Where broccoli, spring cabbage, savoy, onion and early summer lettuce are grown, manure helps.

August is the best time to clean up the soft fruit, removing the protective netting where this is temporary, as soon as the crop has been gathered. Strawberries can be burnt over if straw was used to keep the fruit clean, otherwise the top growth can be mown off and raked away, together with runners that are not wanted, old leaf and fruit debris, and the soil lightly hoed, fed and watered, and re-strawed. This will result in strong new growth, and probably a second crop of flowers which can be cloched for autumn fruiting; the variety 'Talisman' is very prone to flower a second time.

Old fruited canes of raspberries should be cut down to soil level and removed, also poor new cane growth. The remaining new canes are tied in, and thinned if still too plentiful. Blackcurrants are pruned so as to remove most of the old fruited branches, either to the ground or to a well-placed good new shoot. Branches close to the ground should be removed, strong or not, as they only get pulled down by the weight of fruit and trampled underfoot by pickers.

Gooseberries and redcurrants can be summer pruned, that is cut back to just above the fifth leaf from the base, not counting the basal cluster of leaves, of the new growth that season. The new leading growths are allowed to remain until winter. Clean up all weeds, leave the straw mulch until autumn, and renew where the soil is showing through.

Apples and pears trained as cordons and espaliers or other formal shapes can also be summer pruned in early August, finishing the job in winter. Remove the new sideshoots back to just above the fifth good leaf, excluding the basal cluster, when the shoot has started to become firm and brown at the base, but is still green at the tip; leaders are left uncut. If pruning is done too early, it will result in secondary growth, which will use up the tree's energy unnecessarily, and will be cut back by frost, so providing an entry for disease.

Some branches may be breaking or about to break under the increasing weight of ripening fruit, and branch propping may be a necessary job. Woolly aphis (American blight) may be apparent on apple trees, so spray with malathion under strong pressure, or scrub the patches with a wire brush dipped in methylated spirits if there is not too much of the pest and the trees are small.

This is the month of the plum and varieties in season include 'Victoria', 'Czar', 'Early Rivers', 'Denniston's Superb Gage', 'Oullin's Golden Gage', 'Cambridge Gage', 'Black Prince', and 'Bountiful'. The acid or Morello cherry will also be ripe in early August.

The Gardener's Year
September

Left: Repairing the broken edge of a lawn by reversing the turves. *Above right*: The correct way to pick an apple. *Right*: A modern device for spiking a lawn

The focus this month on work in the purely decorative part of the garden is on the lawn, as it is at this time that established lawns can be repaired and generally cared for, and seed can be sown to produce new ones.

Brushing, raking with a wire rake, and spiking all help to improve the penetration of air to the turf surface and the soil beneath. The mat of dead vegetation which is likely to form during summer is removed and so, too, are pests which may have been hiding in it, and fungus diseases which can damage the grass. Worm casts are brushed off at the same time.

Spiking can be done with an ordinary garden fork, at least 3½ in. deep, and at intervals of a few inches all over the lawn, but hollow-tined aerators are even better, as they remove soil instead of compressing it; a further variation is the use of slitting tines which will cut the turf and break up a vegetative mat.

This can be followed by an autumn feed with a compound lawn fertilizer high in potash and phosphate, and finally by a topdressing, made up of loam, peat and coarse sand, varying the proportions of the ingredients according to the basic soil type on which the lawn is growing. Apply this topdressing at 2–4 lb. per sq. yd. It should be applied dry and worked in with a stiff brush. Mowing can continue, but at less frequent intervals.

For new lawns, grass seed is best sown early in the month, in the second week for the south of the country, although in the north a spring sowing is preferable. Clean, weed-free soil and the application of a pre-seeding general fertilizer ten days or so before sowing are advisable; choose a day when the soil is moist and rain is likely to follow, make sure there is a good tilth, and sow the seed evenly at 1½ oz. per sq. yd. Patchy sowing leads to trouble with damping off disease.

Bald parts of established lawns should be scratched up to provide some sort of seedbed and sown with a seed mixture which matches the grasses already present. Breaking edges can be remedied by cutting the turf so that a piece a foot wide and of a convenient length is removed, to include the bad edge, turned round so that the edge is inside, and the turf replaced, filling in the gap now inside the lawn with compost and grass seed.

Autumn flowering border plants come in all the flaming colours, red, orange and yellow, for instance, dahlias are magnificent, rudbeckias, heliopsis, gaillardias, the early flowering chrysanthemums, and solidagos, but purples and pinks are by no means out of the picture. There

is a beautiful range of colour in the named varieties of Michaelmas daisy–'Marie Ballard' is a good blue, and 'Ernest Ballard' is an equally eye-catching crimson. Phlox, with their curious, slightly stuffy fragrance, the purple coneflower (echinacea), the magenta sedums, particularly the variety 'Brilliant', and liatris species (the Kansas gayfeather) all add a splendid burst of colour to the season's end. Autumn bulbs contributing to it will be *Cyclamen neapolitanum*, colchicum and autumn-flowering crocus, nerines, crocosmia and montbretia.

For early blooms in May and June next year, some of the annuals can be sown now, such as godetia, larkspur, nigella, calendula, Shirley poppies, annual scabious and coreopsis. They are sown in the open and should be well established by the time the cold weather comes. Sweet peas can also be sown now and over-wintered in a frame, for flowering in June next year or earlier. Mice can destroy them, however, so protect with small mesh wire netting.

Roses will be in bloom again, and the yellow flowered autumn clematis species, *C. orientalis* and *C. tangutica*, also *C. rehderiana*, tubular and cowslip scented. Rambler roses are pruned this month, cutting the flowered canes out completely and tying the new ones of this season in to take their place. Shrubs in flower are ceanothus, caryopteris, ceratostigma, hibiscus, perowskia, and *Hamamelis virginiana*, the witch hazel which is used to supply that refreshing substance. More heathers (calluna and daboecia) will be in flower, and all the berrying kinds of shrubs will be changing the colour of their fruit to red, orange, yellow, purple, blue and white.

Cuttings of half-ripe wood can still be taken and put in a cold frame; layers can be brought down to earth and encouraged to root, and planting of evergreen shrubs can be undertaken. Evergreen hedges are clipped now, and the fast growing kinds given their final trimming. Mildew on all sorts of plants should be watched for and sprayed against where necessary. Shrubs ordered now are not likely to arrive much before Christmas.

Frosts are possible before the end of the month, so plants which may have to be taken into the greenhouse are chrysanthemums, azaleas, carnations, fuchsias, heliotropes and pelargoniums, cyclamen and Christmas cactus. Freesias also can go in at the end of the month and, although they

would survive a light frost, it would slow up flowering.

Greenhouse tomatoes should be cleared of their remaining fruit, and pulled out, and sweet peas will also be finished. The shading should be cleaned off the glass and the inside of the greenhouse washed down and sterilized if possible, removing the plants temporarily to do this. Watering can be reduced and many pot plants can be gradually dried off. Cuttings of zonal pelargoniums can be taken and rooted now. Seeds can be sown to flower in late winter and spring, such as the annuals, schizanthus and salpiglossis.

Autumn-fruiting raspberries will be cropping so, too, will strawberries under cloches, and blackberries. Summer pruning of the soft fruit can be finished early this month, and strawberry runners may be planted.

Apple and pear picking will be in full swing; both are ready to pick if the stalk detaches easily when the fruit is lifted gently up in the palm of the hand. Pears to be stored should be picked just as the skin begins to turn yellow round the stalk but while the body of the fruit is still green, and then placed in single layers in a coolish room in the dark. The atmosphere should not be dry, otherwise they shrivel. Sometimes with late pears picking should be delayed until the weather deteriorates, but they must be picked then, even if the stalk has to be pulled quite hard to detach it. Apples will keep well in the same conditions, or can be put four or five in a polythene bag, with the opening closed, using fruit which is not injured and without signs of disease. Put in a dark, cool place, it will keep well, preserved in its own gases given off as maturing continues.

This time of the year is both an ending and beginning for the vegetable garden; potatoes, beetroot, carrots, turnip and celeriac are lifted for storing, and onions are finally cleaned and hung up. Blanching of celery and endive should continue. Aubergines and peppers will be in full cropping. Runner beans, cabbage and lettuce, peas, cucumbers, marrows and courgettes will be coming to an end. Once they have all been finished, the remains of the plants should be cleared away, and the ground cleaned of weeds. It is at this time that weeds seem to take on a new lease of life, and grow up behind one's back, just as the season seems to be over. If not cleaned off now, by the spring they will have gained control of the garden.

The atmosphere about the garden now is that of clearing up after the party; the guests have made their bow and graced the scene, they have been fed and watered and now they are leaving, and only the debris remains to be sorted and cleared away or used. The perennials will mostly have finished flowering and need cutting down, with the stakes and supports put away in a dry shed until next year. Now and next month are times to move and divide, and to act upon notes made during the season as to where plants should really be growing, and which ones will never do and can be thrown out. The large clumps can be split, and the best pieces from the outside replanted, the centre being thrown away.

Edges of beds and borders can be straightened and re-cut, and the last remnants of the annuals and bedding plants lifted and put on the compost heap. Dahlias should be cut down after they have been blackened by the first frost, the tubers dug up and shaken free of soil, then labelled and stored in a dry cool place through the winter. In mild winters, they will live in the soil without lifting, to shoot again without difficulty next spring. Tuberous rooted begonias and gladioli should also be lifted early in the month and cleaned, then stored in a dry, frostproof place.

This is the month for bulb planting, leaving it to the end, however, if the weather remains warm. Narcissi, hyacinths, scillas, snowdrops, crocus, grape hyacinths and chionodoxas (glory of the snow) can all go in. Leaves will need sweeping up everywhere, particularly from the lawn. Rambler rose pruning can continue. Tender shrubs, conifers and other evergreens, and hydrangeas can be planted this month, and propagation of most shrubs, including roses, by hardwood or fully ripened cuttings, can be started, as soon as the shoots are mature, putting them in a trench out of doors.

October is a suitable time to prepare the sites where shrubs are to be planted next month. This preparation is very important, and does a great deal towards ensuring that the new shrub will survive and thrive; so often it dies through being planted in badly drained soil that is starved of plant food, or short of humus, as well as being in all probability totally different to that in which it was growing in the nursery. The hole should be dug out two spade's depth deep and at least 4 ft. wide, the bottom forked up and well-rotted organic matter mixed with it. The excavated soil is then returned, making sure that the topsoil remains on top, and mixing with it all, more compost, manure and leafmould. A proportion of half and half is about right. Doing all this a month ahead gives the soil time to absorb the new material and settle after digging.

From now until late February, lawns can be made by laying turf, provided the soil is not too wet nor too cold. The spring bedding plants should be planted as soon as possible where they are to flower, for instance wallflowers, forget-me-nots, polyanthus and double daisies, perhaps

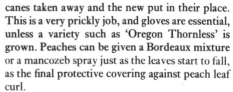

The Gardener's Year
October

leaving room among them for tulip planting in November.

By now most of the top fruit will be picked and in store, if not already eaten, and now is a good time to decide on possible new varieties to obtain a succession, and to grub up old, poorly fruiting trees, or those with fruit of poor flavour. Apples and pears can both be grown on dwarfing stocks, to produce small trees about 12–15 ft. tall and as much across. They can also be grown in restricted forms as cordons, pyramids, or espaliers. There is now a dwarf stock for cherries; plums and greengages do not grow very tall or large in any case, though they can be fan trained against walls. Peaches do well as fans on sunny south or west walls.

Fruit, like vegetables, is in a different class if eaten as soon as picked, rather than 24 or 48 hours later, as it so often is if shop bought. The production of one's own fruit also ensures that one knows exactly what was applied in the way of spray chemicals to ward off various pests and diseases. Choice of top fruit should be carefully made, as it will last twenty-five years on average; strawberry beds are replanted every three or four years, raspberries, gooseberries and currants every 10–15 years.

The ground can be prepared for the new fruit trees this month, as it is for shrubs. Strawberry runners can be planted, and the rooted tips of blackberries and loganberries can be separated from the parents, preparatory to planting next month. They should also have the old fruited

Left: Dahlia tubers lifted, dried, cleaned and being stored. *Centre:* Using a bulb planter to plant daffodil bulbs in turf. The planter removes a 'core' of turf which is replaced and firmed after the bulb has been planted. *Right:* The winter cherry, *Solanum capsicastrum*

canes taken away and the new put in their place. This is a very prickly job, and gloves are essential, unless a variety such as 'Oregon Thornless' is grown. Peaches can be given a Bordeaux mixture or a mancozeb spray just as the leaves start to fall, as the final protective covering against peach leaf curl.

Apples for picking, eating and storing this month are 'Bramley's Seedling', 'Charles Ross', 'Blenheim Orange', 'Egremont Russet', and 'Laxton's Superb'; Bramley's in particular can be kept without difficulty in a cool shed in boxes with lids on, provided they are not infected with rot or any kind of fungus in the first place, and will keep so until March and April of the following year. Similarly pears will keep for a good part of the winter, in particular such varieties as 'Louise Bonne of Jersey', 'Packham's Triumph', 'Pitmaston Duchess', 'Doyenné du Comice' and 'Joséphine de Malines'.

By this time the greenhouse will be filling up again, as plants come in early in the month for protection. These may include freesias, both from seed and corms – the former in flower by now – azaleas, cyclamen, Christmas cactus, poinsettias, orange and lemon trees, young plants of primula and cineraria, saintpaulias and the winter cherry, *Solanum capsicastrum*, and chrysanthemums for flowering in late November and December. Some good varieties for late flowering are 'Christmas Wine', and 'Christmas Red', 'Red Balcombe Perfection' and 'Yellow Balcombe Perfection' and the incurve 'Maylen White'. A little heat may be needed at the end of the month in the greenhouse if there is frost at night.

Carrots, potatoes, beetroot and celeriac can be lifted; good sized roots of the latter will be about 6 in. in diameter. The first of the parsnips may be ready, and the last of the marrows should be cut. Broccoli, Brussels sprouts, cauliflowers and leeks will be coming into season, also winter celery towards the end of the month; there may still be a few lettuces. Aubergines and peppers will come to the end of bearing. Cauliflowers should have the outer leaves bent over the curd to protect it.

Asparagus fern should be cut down to soil level, and the bed mulched with rotted manure or garden compost; if this is not available a light dressing of basic slag can be given. Asparagus does best in a limey soil, and if it is acid a dressing of lime in some form should be given every three or four years. Globe artichoke crowns should be protected with a heavy mulch after removing dead leaves.

Otherwise much of the work in the vegetable garden consists in clearing and cleaning of weeds, digging and rotavating, and manuring this month and next where brassicas, leaf vegetables and potatoes are to be planted next spring. Vegetable or animal manure should not be used where root crops are to follow, but for them wood ash can be forked in. Do not add lime at the same time as bulky organic material. Spring cabbage plants should be planted outside.

Shrubs and all sorts of hardwood plants will be arriving from nurseries in November, provided they were ordered in good time, back in the summer, and will need planting. The site will have been prepared last month, and now, about ten days before planting, a light dressing of bonemeal can be scattered over the area to which the roots are likely to extend, and forked into the top 4 or 5 in. of soil. When the plants arrive, put them in as soon as possible.

Planting can be undertaken, provided the soil is moist but not frozen or really sodden; if it is, then put the plants back in their wrappings with a little air and leave them for three or four days, or heel them in in a shallow trench in a place where they are sheltered from wind and least likely to be frozen, until the weather improves. They will be quite safe there for several weeks.

When they are planted, the roots should be spread out to their full length–they are not mobile, and will stay put in any position, so that if doubled up or bent backwards, they cannot extend normally and may never grow. A small hump at the bottom of the hole encourages the roots to spread out and downwards as they naturally would, and staking before planting avoids damage to the roots. Firmness is essential to prevent wind rocking and to avoid pockets in the soil. Water the plant in, and rake the soil surface so that it does not remain smooth and collect water, and all should be well, unless the winter is unusually cold.

Hardwood cuttings of shrubs, including roses can still be taken and put in a trench out of doors in a sheltered place, lining the bottom with sand, and stripping the lower leaves off the cutting. Climbing roses can be pruned, and ramblers should be given the finishing touches.

This is a good month for laying a new lawn. With the likelihood that rain will follow soon after turfing, there is every chance that the turves will unite strongly and the grass roots penetrate rapidly to the soil below. The soil is prepared as for sowing grass seed, though it is not essential to produce such a fine tilth. Turves are usually 3 × 1 ft. in size. Lay them as soon as they arrive, staggering them in the same way that bricks are for a wall, and stand on a plank on the already laid turf to place each successive row. Lay each turf slightly humped and then gently flatten them when the row has been completed; knock each row up against the preceding one as the work progresses. Finally, fill in the cracks with sand or sieved compost.

Established lawns will have their last cut, if they have not already had it, first sweeping off leaves; in fact leaves should be removed constantly as they encourage worms and suffocate the grass so that it turns yellow. They make good compost, except the leathery ones, such as laurel, bay and holly; beech, oak, elm, lime and fruit tree leaves are all good, however.

The Gardener's Year
November

Some plants will be coming into flower now, for instance *Mahonia* 'Charity' and *M. lomariifolia*, the autumn-flowering cherry (*Prunus subhirtella autumnalis*), some of the late varieties of *Calluna vulgaris* and *Erica carnea*, and *Jasminum nudiflorum* in sheltered places. Border digging and manuring can continue. Tulips can be planted, and there is still just time to plant narcissi and hyacinths. Outdoor chrysanthemums will now come to an end and the stems should be cut back to leave a few inches, lifted and boxed into compost, and placed in a cold frame until mid December. The grey-leaved plants and any with woolly leaves will come through the wet of the winter better if protected now, with a cloche or covering of some kind which keeps off the wet but lets in air.

Light becomes very short in November, and when it is there, is of poor quality, so the greenhouse glass should be as clean as possible, and should be scrubbed if necessary. Condensation should be avoided, as this cuts down light transmission, by adequate ventilation during the day. A little gentle heat will also dry things out and prevent too much humidity in which grey mould can thrive.

Young plants of primulas, cinerarias, polyanthus and calceolarias will need attention, and, in particular, should be watched for greenfly outbreaks. The late-flowering chrysanthemums will begin to flower in succession, and freesias will be in full bloom, scenting the greenhouse gloriously. Azaleas, cyclamen and poinsettias will be coming up to flowering, so that watering and liquid feeding will be required.

Many plants will have been dried off and put under the greenhouse staging for their winter rest, and cacti need only be watered once a month, if that. Pelargonium cuttings which have rooted will no longer be growing and will need only just enough water to keep the soil moist; the same applies to potted fuchsias, which do not appreciate dust-dry soil.

Left: Grey-leaved plants and those with woolly leaves benefit from cloche protection in winter.
Right: Heeling in a tree when the weather is unsuitable for planting out

As soon as the leaves have fallen, and the last of the crop is picked, the top fruit can be pruned this month and any time during the winter from now onwards, following with winter pest and disease spraying. Pruning is done to prevent shoots and branches becoming crowded and disease ridden, and to induce the production of new growth, which will crop well and regularly. Unpruned trees become a tangled jungle of growth, live and dead, full of pests and diseases, and bearing too much fruit which does not ripen or is too small when it does. Bud pecking by birds may start this month and proprietary bird repellents are advisable. Formally trained apples and pears can have the summer pruning finished now so as to leave stubs 2–3 in. long; the bush trees are better renewal pruned; be particularly careful to remove the shoot tips where mildew was a nuisance in the summer. Mulching can follow pruning and spraying.

If blackcurrant pruning was not done in August, it can be done now, and summer pruning of redcurrants and gooseberries can be completed as with top fruit. The old fruited canes of raspberries are cut out now, if not already done, together with those of the autumn fruiting kinds. Strawberries should be well established, and may be strawed to prevent weed growth. Established plants more than one year old may be treated with simazine as an alternative for weed control. Vegetable garden tidying can continue, together with digging and manuring. If lime is thought necessary, do not be too prodigal with it, and in any case time its application so that at least six weeks intervene between liming and manuring. Parsnips can be lifted now and stored in sand in a cool shed, though they will usually keep perfectly well through the winter if left in the ground, and dug up only when wanted for cooking. Celery can be lifted, leeks should be ready–they are a useful vegetable as they will go on right through the winter. Spinach and spinach beet are equally obliging. Lettuce sown in September, such as 'Winter Density', if cloched early this month, will survive the winter well and be ready for cutting in March. They have the further advantage that they have a very pleasant, nutty flavour. October lettuce sowings will need transplanting to their permanent positions and protecting.

Leatherjackets, the grubs of the cranefly (daddy-long-legs) may start to feed on grass roots this month, so that pale brown patches of dead grass appear on the lawn throughout the winter. gamma-HCH dust will control them. Worms can be killed or expelled with Mowrah meal, derris or chlordane; the best time to deal with them is the autumn and early winter, when the soil is moist and they have come close to the surface after the summer heat and dryness.

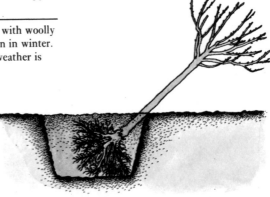

In the Christmas month, the garden will have one of two appearances: either it will be bare and clean, with branches and twigs silhouetted against the sky, the grass short and green and the soil borders and beds nicely brown, or it will be completely white, with only the evergreens and the red berries and haws of holly, thorn, rose and cotoneaster to colour it. Whichever it is, the gardener at any rate is now allowed a well-earned rest and a change as the end of the year and all its festivities comes. Indeed it is obligatory, however enthusiastic the gardener, that there should be some pause in the routine, otherwise the mind becomes set and the garden pattern reflects this and is static. Its owner needs to recharge his gardening outlook by letting it lie fallow, just as soil, left uncultivated for a season, builds up its food content and repairs its structure.

For the first fortnight or so there are small jobs to do, for instance planting of shrubs, trees, fruit and roses can be continued or finished as the weather allows. Pruning and spraying of fruit can continue; digging and manuring of borders and vegetable plots can finish. It is advisable to do this before Christmas to give the soil time to absorb the fresh material, and to allow sufficient time before spring for the breaking up of clay soil by frost.

Slug bait will be needed round delphiniums, lupins, pyrethrums and other succulent shooted border plants. Watch for bud pecking of fruit and ornamental trees, such as cherry and forsythia. There should not yet be trouble with bark stripping by rabbits and mice, but a wary eye can be kept open for this, particularly if the weather suddenly becomes very cold for a few days. Top the grass in the middle of the day when it is dry and the soil moist but not soaking.

One now has time to overhaul the machinery used during the year, such as rotavators, lawn mowers and hedge cutters, to sharpen all cutting blades and to clean and oil all hand tools.

The greenhouse will be the pleasantest and prettiest place, with chrysanthemums, freesias, azaleas, cyclamen, forced hyacinths and 'Soleil D'Or' narcissi, saintpaulias, poinsettias and Christmas cactus in full flower. Heat will be needed every night and sometimes during the day. Chrysanthemums boxed up and put in the frame last month can come in and be watered, in mid December, so that they start to grow and produce shoots for cuttings. It is the shoots that come from below soil level that will grow into the best plants; those which sprout from the old stems will not be strong. Sometimes chrysanthemum crowns or stools will produce a tremendous number of shoots tightly clustered round the old stems, and when this happens it is a sign that the plant is infected with a bacterial trouble called crown gall, and should be discarded.

Sweet peas passing the winter in frames should be stopped at the fourth leaf, and looked at occasionally in case they need further protection

Stopping sweet peas

The Gardener's Year
December

from mice. Fruit in store should also be examined occasionally, together with dahlia tubers and root vegetables, and rotting specimens should be removed.

This is a good time, while the bones of the garden show, to re-design unsatisfactory parts of it and to carry out new constructions, put up fruit cages and so on. Concrete paths can be laid (but not in frosty weather), ponds excavated before the soil becomes really wet, pergolas and arches built and paving laid for terraces and patios. Rock gardens can be established, or improved in their lay out, new borders cut and old ones turfed or planted with such ground cover plants as ajuga, periwinkle, lamium, *Rosa paulii*, violets, hypericums and saxifrages. A pattern for a herb garden can be laid down, or a fruit garden planned; dry stone walls built and planted. Colour groupings can be improved, planting a border with all the red tones or all the yellow ones, using leaves as well as flowers to give the effect. There is time to put any of these ideas into practice now, or to mull them over ready for carrying them out in the early spring.

Flowers for picking for Christmas celebrations will be in all the best gardens; there will be a few roses here and there, the hellebores (*Helleborus orientalis*) will be in bloom, so will laurustinus, winter jasmine, hamamelis, chimonanthus, ma-

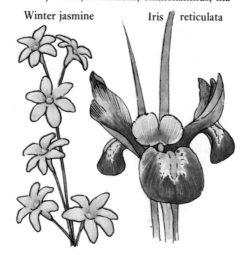

Winter jasmine   Iris reticulata

honia, *Erica cinerea* and its varieties, primroses and violets in sheltered places, the occasional precocious 'japonica' bloom, sedums, pansies, to say nothing of the greenhouse offerings. *Iris reticulata* may be showing bud towards the end of the month and if picked and put in a vase in the warmth, will unfold its dark purple-blue, fragrant flowers.

The plants in pots, both flowering and foliage can go into the home for the time being for extra decoration, and all sorts of berrying shrubs will add to their colour. The evergreens will retain their leaves, especially the conifers, if sprayed with the modern polyvinyl resin which lasts for several weeks, before or immediately after cutting, as it seals the pores and prevents the loss of water vapour.

Often, sadly, one of December's disasters is the death of expensive pot plants, acquired as Christmas gifts. Such plants include the azaleas, poinsettias, cyclamen, Christmas cactus and the zebra plant (*Aphelandra squarrosa*), at the height of their flowering season, covered in bloom and apparently in the best of health. They are in fact extremely fit, but the change from nursery greenhouse conditions to those of the home, particularly at Christmas time, is often too much for them. In no time, buds and flowers have dropped, leaves withered and fallen, and a few stark bare stems are all that is left of a once beautiful plant. One is so occupied at Christmas with other things that plants have all kinds of extreme and distasteful conditions to cope with, and it is no wonder that many succumb.

Smoky, dry atmospheres often predominate; although the temperature may be well up, it will be too high near radiators, electric or coal fires. Conversely, windowsills behind drawn curtains where pot plants are often put, can be death traps of freezing air, as the outside temperature drops swiftly to or below freezing, as it can easily do at this time.

In all the excitement nothing is more likely to be overlooked than watering, and an azalea in full bloom will want a big drink at least every day; cyclamen also flag extremely quickly with their leaves turning yellow, and the zebra plant will droop its leaves in no time, as it is another plant that must have a daily drink when flowering. Plants may also suffer from being given liquids other than water at this time of the year. Draughts are a further menace as doors constantly open with the arrival and departure of guests and family; one way and another, all pot plants have a hard time of it.

Try to remember at any rate, to review the water needs every day; bring the plants in from the windowsills when the curtains are drawn. Spray them lavishly every day with clear water, or pack really damp peat all round the container and keep it damp. Keep them somewhere out of the line of draughts and away from fierce heat.

Then leave the garden alone, except for the greenhouse, enjoy Christmas, hibernate a little as all sensible animals do in the short dark days, and come back to it with a refreshed mind in the New Year when the days begin to lengthen.

Aphelandra squarrosa

It is a pleasure for the housewife to walk out of the kitchen door to pick sprigs of mint and parsley as and when these herbs are required. Herb growing remains as simple as that in some gardens. But for many gardeners there is a special fascination about herbs and the collection increases until part of the garden is devoted exclusively to these plants.

Not all garden herbs are for use in cooking (for culinary purposes); some are used in medicine and others have cosmetic value. Examples are:

Medicinal Herbs

Alecost   Bistort   Catmint   Eyebright
Feverfew   Gentian   Horehound   Hyssop
Jacob's Ladder   Lady's Mantle   Mandrake
Pasque-Flower   Rue   Sweet Flag
Thorn Apple   Vervian

Culinary Herbs

Angelica   Basil   Carraway   Dill
Elecampane   Fennel   Garlic   Horseradish
Lemon Verbena   Lovage   Mace   Marjoram
Mint   Nasturtium   Parsley   Purslane
Rampion   Sage   Savory   Tarragon   Thyme
Tree Onion

Cosmetic Herbs

Camomile   Fennel   Lavender   Orris
Peppermint   Rosemary   Sweetbriar

Sometimes the groups overlap. Savory may be classed as a culinary herb in 'mixed herbs' but it may be considered as a medicinal herb if its value as an aid to digestion is taken into account. Fennel is culinary when used to flavour boiled fish but cosmetic if you use it to rid the face of a few wrinkles. Some herbs do not fit into these three groups. An example is woad at one time used both medicinally and to dye wool.

Some herbs may also be classed as vegetables if grown in the kitchen garden. Horseradish, garlic and tree onion are three examples. Not all herbs are similar to the better known sage, thyme and parsley. The elder is a tree, sweetbriar is a prickly shrub and bergamot (*Monarda didyma*) is a colourful, popular hardy herbaceous perennial. Herbs differ from vegetables in that a vegetable is eaten as a filling food, while a herb is added to a meal to give flavour. Although many herbs are also attractive flowering plants, herbs are distinct from flowers grown solely for their beauty. They may be equally beautiful but they also have a use either when fresh or dried. A herb may be a weed; wild plants such as the thorn apple, the red field poppy and sweet flag would be included in a fully representative collection of herbs. They are unlikely to feature in a small back garden collection

Above: Left, Pasque-flower
(Pulsatilla vulgaris). Right, Spring
gentian *(Gentiana verna).*
Above right: Left, Purslane.
Right, Creeping thyme
(Thymus serpyllum)

Herbs & their Uses

The Herb Garden

although two other weeds could. These are horseradish and fennel.

Some herbs are propagated from seeds; others from pieces of older plants. Some herbs are permanent (perennial or shrubs), some biennial and some annual. Mint is a perennial, angelica biennial, and summer savory an annual.

Herbs do best in a somewhat sheltered position and in the past, in the gardens of large houses, were invariably bounded by walls or hedges. The site was always a sunny one and, when you plan a small herb garden choose a place as warm and sunny as possible. One right out in the open is better than a site where a wall, tree or tall hedge casts shade.

The fortunate gardener starts off with the well-drained kitchen garden sort of soil in which most herbs thrive. Otherwise both drainage and fertility should be improved to provide the right conditions.

In planning a herb garden, however small or large it may be, reserve one square foot of ground space for each plant. Only when you have grown your own herbs and seen just how little or how much room each plant needs will you know for sure which of them can do with less than a square foot and which needs more. Where possible have your plants so spaced that barely an inch or so of soil can be seen between them in high summer. Sweet Basil will not need the complete square foot allotted to it but chives will as will the bushy

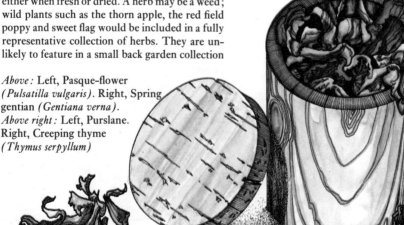

lemon balm. French and Russian tarragons will need a little more room after a couple of years.

Herbs vary a great deal in height. Bear this in mind in your planting. Fennel, angelica and lovage are tall and are best positioned to the rear of the bed. They can provide an excellent background to lower, bushier plants such as lavender, bergamot, St John's wort, lady's maid, old warrior and several of the sages. Near the front of the bed is the correct place for common thyme, lemon thyme, apple mint, white mint, purslane, chives, sorrel and other low growing kinds. The thymes and chives may be planted, if you wish, as a border alongside a garden path adjacent to your herb garden.

The mints never remain where they are planted; if you let them, they will try to take over the whole herb garden. Prevent this by planting them in large flower pots. Sink the pots to their rims in the soil. Cheaper than pots are old pails–plastic or metal. Make some drainage holes in the bottom of pails before planting mint in them.

Pot-Pourri

There are two kinds of pot-pourri–moist and dry. To make a moist pot-pourri take fresh or partially dry petals of such flowers as roses, violets, pinks and lily of the valley. Place the petals in layers in a jar after you have mixed them with scented herb leaves. Here you have a wide choice–scented geranium, peppermint, eau-de-Cologne mint, pineapple mint, citrus mint–even fennel or one of the sages if you like them. Cover each layer with ordinary salt. Add, if you wish to experiment, just a little all-spice, a few cloves and some powdered orris root. Some recipes suggest the addition of a little brandy as a preservative. Moist pot-pourris are best kept in special pot-pourri jars.

A dry pot-pourri is a mixture of dried flower petals and dried herbs. The herbs must be those noted for their aromatic quality and the petals from flowers of fine scent plus, for their colour effect in the mixture, petals from blue larkspurs and delphiniums. Do not try to dry petals of flowers, such as lilies, which although highly scented are far too fleshy for drying well. One part of scented leaves mixed with seven parts of flower petals is a favoured recipe. Small amounts of spices and a little grated orange or lemon peel may be mixed in, too. Make sure the peel is quite dry before adding it; after grating it will dry off well in a greenhouse or in a sunny window.

Herbs for a dry pot-pourri
(Leaves only–not stalks)

lavender*   marjoram   rosemary*
scented geranium   southernwood
sweet bay   verbena
*The dried, rubbed flowers may also be used.

Growing and Using Herbs

The herb garden should never be divorced from the rest of the garden. Trees and shrubs are good links to connect one part of the garden with another part. Visitors to large herb gardens should look for trees and shrubs in the vicinity. Some of them may be 'herbs' in their own right having culinary or medicinal properties. Other trees and shrubs near a herb garden may not be 'herbs' at all but may be grown for their highly aromatic foliage or flowers.

Examples of suitable trees and shrubs are: Balsam Poplar, Bay, Broom, Buddleia, Californian Laurel, Daphne, Elder, Eucalyptus, Juniper, Magnolia, Mahonia, Mountain Laurel, Myrtle, New Jersey Tea (*Ceanothus*), Rhododendron, *Roses*, St John's Wort (*Hypericum*), Hebe (Veronica), Witch Hazel.

Reference has already been made to the planning of a herb garden so that taller growers are planted towards the rear so that they neither hide nor shade shorter kinds. It is, therefore, important to have a knowledge of approximate heights of garden herbs.

The lists here show the majority of plants suited to herb garden growing. The heights are the maximum to which the herbs will grow but the ultimate height depends on several factors—soil, season, site and on the care you give your plants.

It should be noted that not all the plants listed below are described fully in the text. For further information the reader should refer to specialist books on the subject of herbs and their uses.

Very Short or Dwarf Herbs
(height up to 1 foot)

American Liverwort, American Mandrake, Bloodroot, Catmint, Chamomile (Roman Chamomile), Chives, Cowslip, Garlic, Heartsease, Indian Ginger, Lady's Mantle, Lily of the Valley, Lobelia, Mandrake, Marjoram (French Marjoram, Golden Marjoram), Micromeria, Mint (most mints), Nasturtium, Parsley (except when seeding), Pasque-Flower, Pennyroyal, Purslane, Pinks, Pimpernel, Sage, Samphire, Savory (Summer Savory), Scurvy Grass, Selfheal, Thyme, Wall Germander, Winter Green, Woodruff.

Short Growers
(from 1 to 2 feet)

Arnica, Betony (Wood Betony), Bistort, Burnet Saxifrage, Calamint, Chervil, Christmas Rose, Clary, Curry Plant, Dill, Geranium, Good King Henry, Henbane, Hounds Tongue, Lady's Maid, Lavender (dwarf lavenders), Lungwort, Marigold, Marjoram (French Marjoram), Old Lady, Pellitory of the Wall, Periwinkle, Sage (some sages), Savory (Winter Savory), Skullcap, Sorrel, Sweet Basil.

Semi-Tall Herbs
(from 1½ feet to 2½ feet)

Alkanet, Anise, Borage, Burnet Salad, Caraway, Celandine (Greater Celandine), Coriander, Horehound (White Horehound), Hyssop, Insect Powder Plant, Linseed, Marjoram (English

Herbs & their uses

Marjoram), Mint (some mints), Old Warrior, Orris, Poppy (Red Field Poppy), Sage (some sages), Santolina, Skirret, Vervain, Yarrow, Yellow Balsam.

Medium Tall Herbs
(from 2 feet to 3 feet)

Agrimony, Alecost, Balm of Gilead, Bergamot, Camphor Plant, Chamomile (German Chamomile), Clary, Comfrey (Blue Comfrey), Cotton Lavender, Feverfew, Grindelia, Jacob's Ladder, Lavender (some Lavenders), Lobelia (Scarlet Lobelia), Melilot, Motherwort, Old Woman, Opium Poppy, Rampion, Sage (some Sages), Soapwort, Solomon's Seal, Sweet Cicely, Tarragon (French Tarragon), Thorn Apple, Viper's Bugloss.

Tall Growers
(from 3 feet to 7 feet)

Aconite, Allspice, American Hellebore, American Spikenard, Angelica, Balm (Lemon Balm), Black Cohosh, Black Lovage (Alexanders), Caper Spurge, Camphor Plant, Chicory, Dyer's Green-

Left: Sorrel (Rumex scutatus)
Below: Plan for a herb garden enclosed by hedges *Right:* Marjoram (Origanum onites) *Far Right:* Hyssop (Hyssopus officinalis)

weed, Evening Primrose, Fennel, Foxglove, Fuller's Teasel, Goat's Rue, Gentian, Hemlock, Hemp, Incense Plant, Indian Physic, Jerusalem Sage, Jewel Weed, Labrador Tea, Lovage, Liquorice, Marsh Mallow, Meadowsweet, Mullein, Nettle, Old Man, Opium Poppy, Orach, Our Lady's Milk Thistle, Poke-root, Rhubarb, Rosemary, Russian Comfrey, Tarragon (Russian Tarragon), Tobacco, Tree Onion.

Weeds and Garden Herbs

Whereas the gardener usually rids his garden of weeds, the herb gardener often has several in the herb garden. Weed are plants out of place. In the herb garden a weed which has or has had a use in cookery, medicine or a folk craft may be included. Examples are: Good King Henry—at one time widely used as a vegetable; Foxglove—the source of the drug Digitalin; Woad—an ancient dyestuff.

Herbs and Blind People

A herb garden is often laid out with plant labels in Braille so that blind persons may recognize the herbs they smell. Do not be surprised if a blind visitor to your own herb garden is unable to distinguish the aroma of each of your aromatic herbs. Unfortunately, as soon as the juice of a highly aromatic herb like mint, sage or thyme is on the fingers, the aroma will linger for quite a time unless the hands are washed. Do not offer a blind person scented soap if the visitor wishes to wash off a plant aroma so that another may be 'sampled' for its scent.

The Publishers do not necessarily accept the claims made in the text for the uses of medicinal herbs described. Where poisonous herbs such as aconite, foxglove and thornapple are grown in the garden, care should be taken that children do not eat any part of the plants.

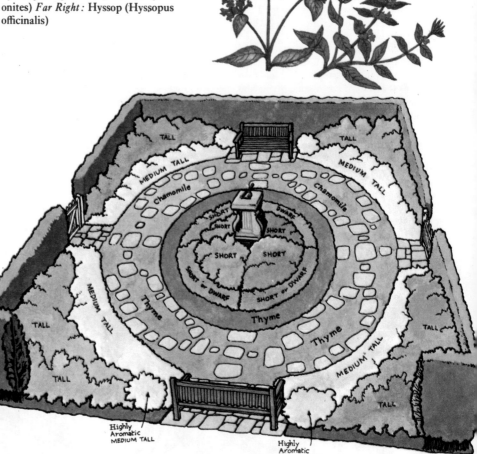

Man has made use of mint as a flavouring in food since time immemorial and a mention is made of this useful herb in the gospels of both Luke and Matthew. The Ancient Greeks used mint as a scent. The Romans added it to their baths. In Britain, where having a bath is more or less a novelty of recent times, mint was much used as a strewing herb over the floor.

Some Garden Mints Spearmint is the kind associated with new potatoes, green peas and mint sauce. Botanically, this is *Mentha spicata*, but mint plants vary from one garden to another. Whichever mint you already have in your own garden probably suits your palate because most of them are excellent. A selection of different mints suited to a herb garden is given along with, where it exists, the English garden name, though there is some confusion in mint names. *M. arvensis* var. *piperascens* (Japanese mint); *M. citrata* (bergamot mint, pineapple mint, citrus mint); *M. cordifolia*; *M. gattefossei*; *M. × gentilis* (ginger mint); *M. longifolia*; *M. piperita* (peppermint); *M. piperita* var. *officinalis* (white mint); *M. piperita crispula* (crisp-leafed form of peppermint); *M. pulegium* (pennyroyal); *M. requienii* (Spanish mint); *M. rotundifolia* 'Bowles' ('Bowles's mint', pea mint); *M. rotundifolia variegata* (apple mint); *M. spicata* (spearmint, common green mint); *M. spicata crispata* (curl-leafed mint); *M. sylvestris* (horsemint).

For culinary use there are no better forms than spearmint and 'Bowles's mint' and both or either should be included in a collection; white mint is also worth considering because of its attractive foliage colour. For something different in herb aromas, orange mint and pineapple mint are worth growing.

Plants vary in height according to variety; heights shown in seedsmen's lists refer to the maximum attained if plants are permitted to flower. The average height is 1–1½ ft., but there are exceptions. *M. requienii* is the smallest; it has very small leaves, but with typical, but minute mint flowers. 'Bowles's mint', on the other hand, will grow to almost 5 ft. Most mints may be planted in front of taller growing herbs, with *M. requienii* as an edging.

Mints are moisture-loving plants and although

often recommended for growing in window boxes, they do better if grown on their own in a window box or large pot, because the regular watering which they require in summer may not suit other herbs grown with it.

There is one drawback with mint in the herb garden. It can become an invasive weed. This can be prevented by planting in old pails. Holes are made in the bottom and they are then filled with good top soil. The pails are sunk in the ground to within an inch of the rim. Plastic pails or large pots may be used. Before plants are established, the colourful rims of plastic pails may be an eyesore. Hide them by spreading moist peat as a thick mulch around and just over them. When the mint has made lush growth, brush aside the peat so that mint roots do not run into the surrounding soil.

Although it needs adequate water in a hot, dry summer spell, garden mint is not a marsh plant and good drainage is essential. Both flavour and aroma are better where the plants receive all the sunshine possible, though plants will grow well in partial shade.

Young plants may be set out in spring or autumn, usually in small clumps, four or five small plants 6 in. apart. Propagation is easy. Just tear off a stem with a small piece of root attached and replant; keep the divisions well-watered until they are properly established.

In the first season do not rob young plants of foliage for use in the kitchen until they are about to flower. Tips may then be gathered for use. Side growths will develop and these may be pinched

off for use. Once established, pick as and when required for flavouring new potatoes and green peas in June and July.

It is a common practice to dig up the plants every three or four years and to replant roots 2 in. deep in another part of the herb garden after the soil has been dressed with garden compost.

Mint is susceptible to the fungal disease mint rust. This is more likely to affect spearmint than other mints. It shows as orange, rusty spots on leaves and stems. Dig up and burn affected plants.

The dwarf form of *M. pulegium*, with small oval leaves and numerous mauve flowers, may be used to make a mint lawn in a shady situation. Set out young plants 6–9 in. apart. Keep the site free from weeds until the plants have made a closely knit bed.

Drying Mint Choose a dry, sunny morning in July, before plants show signs of flowering. Cut stems about 9 in. long and hang them in small bunches on a clothes line. Rapid drying is important. The dry mint should be rubbed between the hands and stored in jars or boxes in a dry place indoors. Mint which is not dried rapidly tends to bleach. If rain falls during the drying process, browning occurs. A second cut may be taken and dried in September in dry, sunny weather.

Mint may be added in small quantities to salads. Dried or freshly cut, chopped mint may be sprinkled on pea soup and buttered, boiled new potatoes may also have a mint sprinkling. To give a mint flavour to new potatoes or green peas during boiling, add only two or four sprigs.

Mint Tea Spearmint and 'Bowles's mint' are of use in the preparation of mint tea which is made in a teapot and drunk as an aid to digestion.

Mint Sauce A simple recipe is to chop mint leaves very finely, sprinkle on a little sugar and add vinegar. If dried mint is used, 'reconstitute' the mint first by pouring a little boiling water over it before adding sugar and vinegar.

Mint Julep Mix ½ pint of ale, ¼ pint of water and ½ bottle of sherry. Add the juice of one lemon and float two bruised mint leaves on the surface for 15 minutes. If you use dried mint, allow this to soak in the mixture for 30 minutes and strain before pouring.

Mint Jelly Wash and slice 2 lb. of unpeeled, uncored tart green apples into 1 quart of cold water in a preserving pan. Add ½ teaspoon of citric acid and several sprigs of mint. Bring to the boil and cook till soft and pulpy. Then strain through a jelly bag and leave to drip over-night. Measure the juice and bring to the boil and to each pint of juice stir in 1 lb. of sugar. If you require a more minty flavour, hold a bunch of fresh, well-bruised mint in the liquor for a few minutes and continue to boil and test for setting. Pour into jars and cover with jam pot covers to exclude air.

1. For the town-dweller, one way of growing herbs is in separate pots, sunk into a window-box. 2. The roots of mint are so invasive that it is advisable to restrict their growth in a pail or something similar. 3. *Mentha spicata*, the spearmint, is the commonest kind of mint grown in gardens, though there are various other varieties and species. 4. Powdering mint after it has been dried.

Thyme along with sage, parsley and mint is one of the very few, very well known herbs but most people know it as one of the ingredients of proprietary mixtures rather than as a garden plant. Thyme has been used as a food flavouring for at least 2,000 years. It was also a noted medicinal herb with a reputation as a cough cure and for improving the digestion. The essential oil 'thymol' distilled from the flower heads is still used in medicines, scents and soaps. Thyme plants attract bees and honey derived from their nectar has a fine, aromatic flavour. Before houses were carpeted, thyme was included in strewing herbs.

There are numerous forms of thyme, but for kitchen use common thyme (*Thymus vulgaris*) is usually grown and, although it is of southern European origin, it is quite hardy in Britain. The plant is a 6–8 in. spreading bush with green to greyish-green leaves and light mauvish flowers. Established plants crop for many years. An easy way of propagating from established bushes is to dig up a plant, tear off rooted offsets and replant them 1 ft. apart. To have common thyme in the garden you may buy plants or seeds. Sow seeds fairly thinly in ½-in. deep seed drills 1 ft. apart. Thin the seedlings to 1 ft. apart. Spare seedlings may be transplanted elsewhere in the garden. There are two distinct forms – ordinary, narrow-leaved and broad-leaved. The broad-leaved is preferred by the housewife because the leaves are larger.

Above: Thyme is one of the herbs that can be dried easily and stored for future use. Once the leaves have been thoroughly dried they are crumbled between the fingers and stored in air-tight jars

Thyme plants stand up well to dry soil conditions and they need a sunny situation. The soil should not be rich and should drain well.

Fresh thyme may be picked for use from late spring until November. Take a sprig here and there from each plant. Wash the leaves well before use.

Dry Thyme Because the leaves are small and the stems woody, thyme dries quickly in high summer. Small bunches hung apart from each other on a garden line dry well in two or three days. Rub the foliage between the hands and store in covered containers in a very dry place indoors.

Use thyme sparingly because the aroma is very strong. For pot-pourri and for herb sachets, a lemon-scented and fragrant thyme are useful additions, although kitchen garden thyme also may be used.

The traditional *bouquet garni* is made up of a sprig of parsley, a bay leaf and two sprigs of thyme. The herbs are tied together and placed in soups or stews being boiled. Thyme is essential in the making of good faggots. Fresh or dried thyme may be sprinkled on to a soup, stirred into a thick gravy, or may be added to hash.

Herbs & their uses
The Thymes

Thyme Stuffing There are many recipes for this stuffing mixture for chicken and turkey. The following recipe is simple and the amount of thyme may be increased or decreased depending on the family's liking of its flavour.

INGREDIENTS 1 large loaf (1¼ lb.); ¾ oz. (roughly 1 heaped tablespoon) of dried thyme; 6 oz. of butter.

METHOD Remove the crust from the loaf and grate the white bread for fresh bread crumbs. Mix bread crumbs with the thyme and add pepper and salt to taste. Stir or spread the butter into the mixture so that it resembles a thick paste. It is now ready for use.

Thymus vulgaris, the thyme most commonly grown

For parsley and thyme stuffing mixture the following ingredients are suitable: Bread crumbs; beef suet; salt; dried parsley; dried thyme; grated lemon peel; spices.

Thyme Lawns Thyme lawns are more often come across in gardening books than in gardens. If a creeping form (any of the *T. serpyllum* varieties) is chosen a thyme lawn needs little attention and emits a delicious aroma when trodden on but such a lawn is more suited to see and smell rather than as a spot where the children and the pet dog may play. Prepare the site very carefully, removing every weed and its root. Dig in garden compost, rake level and sprinkle lime over the soil. Set out thyme plants 1 ft. apart. Pull out or hoe in all weed seedlings as soon as you spot them. Within a year the whole area will be covered with a mat-like growth of thyme.

A thyme path is best made by sinking paving stones here and there in the centre to take the tread and to plant *T. serpyllum* around them. The thyme will quickly clamber across the paving. A path of this sort should not be in frequent use; too much treading would damage the thyme.

Some Thymes for your garden Although for kitchen use common thyme is the widely grown variety, there are several other forms suitable for a herb collection or for other parts of the garden.

Thymus azoricus (Azores Island's thyme) (*syn. T. caespititius*). Native to Spain and Portugal, up to 3 in. high, flowers pale purple. There is a white-flowered form. Propagate by cuttings or offsets. The aroma is a combination of pine and orange.

T. x citriodorus (lemon thyme, lemon-scented thyme). Height from 4–12 in. Spreading and bushy. Var. 'aureus' (golden lemon thyme) similar to lemon thyme but the foliage has gold markings.

T. carnosus (erect thyme) (*syn. T. erectus*). Native to Portugal. Height up to 9 in. and often described as similar to a miniature, slow-growing yew. Useful for a rock garden. Narrow, green-grey leaves. Flowers white, June and July. Propagate by cuttings.

T. fragrantissimus (fragrant thyme) (probably a selection of *T. vulgaris*). The scent has a trace of orange. This thyme may be used in the kitchen and in pot-pourri.

T. herba-barona Native of Corsica and Sardinia and reasonably hardy in Britain, this is a semi-prostrate low shrub ideal for a rock garden or the front of a herb collection. It has small green leaves and mauve-rose flowers in June and July. It is said to have been used to flavour barons of beef.

T. hirsutus doerfleri. A native of the Balkans, this forms a woody, prostrate mat with grey foliage. The flowers are pink to purple.

Left: Stepping stones through a thyme pathway

T. hyemalis. A native of Spain, this is similar to common thyme and equally hardy. It may be used in cooking. It forms a straggly 6–12 in. bush with but few flowers.

T. nitidus. A native of the Mediterranean area, this forms a sprawling, shrubby bush with pale lilac flowers.

T. pallasianus (*syn. T. odoratissimus*). Prostrate in habit, this is a native of southern parts of the USSR. The purplish flowers have a 'fruity' thyme aroma.

T. serpyllum (wild thyme). A native of Britain, this forms a prostrate, mat habit, with 3–9 in. flower stems. The flowers are usually mauve, though there are white, pink and crimson-flowered garden forms. 'Annie Hall' pale pink, is a popular cultivar; *citri odorus* is a lemon-scented form; *coccineus* has little aroma. The foliage is a bronze-green and the flowers are crimson-purple; *albus* has small, bright green leaves and white flowers; *minus* is a very small-leaved form. The flowers are mauve.

T. zygis. This native of Spain and Portugal makes a bush up to 1 ft. high with whitish flowers in August.

Herbs & their uses
The Sages

Above: Golden sage provides colour in the herb garden

Old sage plants can be rejuvenated by layering the outer shoots, mounding soil over them, and eventually detaching and replanting the rooted layers

Above: The red or purple-leaved sage

The word 'sage' is an Anglo-Gallic corruption of the Latin 'salvia' which is derived from *salvere* meaning to be well or to be in good health. This indicates how highly the Romans thought of sage. Our ancestors thought likewise and we inherit from them the ditty 'Eat Sage in May and live for aye'.

Common sage (*Salvia officinalis*) is the form of sage most commonly met with in the kitchen garden. This short, bushy, evergreen perennial provides the foliage used in a stuffing for poultry. Some consider this shrub handsome; others complain that it is a straggly plant with a useful life of only three years. For those who want new, young bushes propagation is easy. Take cuttings in May of new wood with a portion of old wood attached. The cuttings need be no longer than 2 in. and they will root quickly in sandy soil kept well-watered in very dry spells. Cuttings may also be taken and planted in September and should be over-wintered in a cold frame or beneath a cloche. To induce bushiness, pinch out the growing point of each young plant when it is about 5 in. high. When it is seen that the young plants are making good growth, dig them up and replant at 18 in. apart in a sunny situation with well-drained soil. Although sage can withstand dry summer weather well, in their first season transplants benefit from waterings in dry spells.

There are several sorts of common sage. Broad-leaved sage seldom flowers and is much liked by those who claim that because no flowers are made all the strength of the plants goes into the highly aromatic foliage. Narrow-leaved sage has two forms – one with pinkish and the other with white flowers.

To have sage in the garden it is more usual to start off with nurserymen's plants and to propagate from them in due course. But narrow-leaved culinary sage may be propagated from seeds sown in shallow drills in the garden between late March and May. Thin the seedlings to 2 in. apart and move the plants to their final growing positions when they are growing well.

Red sage, *S.officinalis* var. *purpurea*, is more handsome than ordinary green sage and may be used, too, in the kitchen. There is a choice of a red sage (purple-leaved) which has flowers and of one

which bears none. Red variegated sage has purple flowers and is a favourite in a collection of herbs for its attractive foliage display. Golden sage rarely flowers but this, again, is an attractive foliage shrub for a herb garden.

Apart from its use in a stuffing mixture sage has no other modern uses in the kitchen. This herb should be added with discretion to stuffing mixtures because the flavour of sage can override that of other herbs. Sage tea is a medicinal herbal beverage to counter poor digestion.

Drying Sage Sprigs of sage for drying are taken just before flowering starts in May and further pickings may be made on and off throughout the summer. Quick drying is very important and the process must be completed within a week. In really hot summer weather small bunches dry rapidly outdoors. In dull and cool weather bunches may be hung above the cooker in the kitchen or spread out in a metal tray above the stove. Rub the dried leaves from the stalks and store in a very dry place.

Some Garden Sages

There are many other sages but apart from pine-apple sage which may be added sparingly to salads few are recommended for culinary use in lieu of common sage. The following sage varieties are, however, met with in herb collections and are worth considering if you aim at having a part of the garden devoted to garden herbs.

Salvia ambigens. Hardy perennial. Height 3 ft.– 5 ft. Deep blue flowers, in September–October.
S. glutinosa. Jupiter's Distaff. Perennial. Height about 3 ft. Pale yellow flowers with greenish black markings are produced in July.
S. grahami (syn. *S. neurepia*). Grow this in pots in colder parts of the country and sink the pots into the garden soil in May. Height 4 ft. or so. It bears red flowers from July until the autumn.
S. haematodes. Biennial. Height up to 4 ft. Heart-shaped leaves with light blue flowers from June to September.
S. involucrata bethellii. Height 2 ft.–4 ft. Rose-red flowers are borne in August and September. Not hardy in severe winters. In colder areas grow in pots as suggested for *S. grahami.*

S. lavandulifolia. Similar to *Salvia officinalis* but with narrow and longer greyish leaves and an aroma suggestive of a sage/lavender mixture. Height up to 1 ft. It bears a few mauve coloured flowers in early summer.
S. pratensis. Half-hardy perennial. Height about 30 in. Flowers blue to violet, borne in late summer.
S. pratensis rosea. A rosy-purple flowering form of *S. pratensis.*
S. rutilans. Pineapple sage. Half-hardy. Grow as a pot plant and house in a greenhouse at a temperature of 50°F (10°C) or more in winter. Move to the outdoor garden for the summer, in late May.
S. × superba (syn. *S. nemorosa, S. virgata nemorosa*). Perennial. Height up to 3 ft. Flowers violet with reddish bracts. July and August flowering. The variety *lubeca* is 1½ ft. tall, but otherwise similar.
S. uliginosa. Bog sage. Hardy perennial. Height up to 5 ft. Needs moister conditions than other herb garden sages. In very cold parts mulch around the plants with bracken or peat in November. Leaves are shiny green, flowers blue, borne from August to October.
S. verticillata. Perennial. Height up to 3 ft. Flowers mauve. July to August flowering.

Sage and Onion Stuffing

There are many recipes. The recipe given here is simple and the amount of sage used may vary depending on the strength of aroma of the sage. This will depend on the sage variety and on whether freshly chopped or dried sage is being used. Bear in mind, too, that sage is highly aromatic and a sage stuffing containing a high proportion of the herb may suit the family's palate but not that of guests. Fresh sage is more piquant than dried sage.

3 large onions;
2 level teaspoons of dried sage;
4 oz. of fresh breadcrumbs;
1 egg.

Parboil the peeled onions and chop finely. Mix with the sage and breadcrumbs and bind with the beaten egg.

Garlic

Nasturtium

Typical Herb Garden
Designs

Herbs & their uses
Other Culinary Herbs

Balm (lemon balm) (*Melissa officinalis*) This is a hardy perennial, bushy plant up to 4 ft. high. The white or pale yellow flowers are inconspicuous but are much visited by bees. Propagation is by seed sown in spring or by division of the roots at that time or in autumn. The leaves are nettle-like and have a pungent lemon aroma. Where dried lemon balm is wanted cut pieces of stem in August and dry quickly outdoors in full sun. Rub the dried leaves between the fingers and store in a dry place. Some like to pass rubbed, dried herbs through a sieve to have a more finely divided product. Fresh and dried leaves may be added to home-made stuffing mixtures for poultry. Chopped fresh leaves or dried leaves may be used sparingly in salads. Finely chopped fresh leaves or dried leaves may be added to a fish sauce where a lemon flavour is desired. Fresh or dried lemon balm may be used with Indian tea in the pot to give lemon-flavoured tea.

Basil (*Sweet Basil*) In Britain this herb (*Ocimum basilicum*) from the tropical areas of Africa and Asia, is treated as a half-hardy annual. Seed may be sown in boxes in gentle heat during late March or in April for plants to set out in the garden in early June. Alternatively, sow seeds in very shallow seed drills in the open garden during early to mid May. Seedlings raised under glass are moved to where the plants are to grow. The sowing in the open garden should be made where the plants are to grow. Thin these seedlings to 10 in. apart. If the seeds are broadcast thinly and covered with fine soil the seedlings may be thinned to leave a small clump of plants. The plants attain a height of about 2 ft. Flowers are creamy white. This is not an easy herb to dry and is therefore generally used fresh only. Pick the triangular shaped leaves as and when wanted between July and October.

The herb is used for flavouring soups and any recipes in which tomatoes are used. It is a flavouring for use when boiling vegetables or fish and especially when boiling shell fish. Sweet Basil may be one of the herbs chopped finely for *fines herbes* in omelettes.

Bergamot (Oswego tea) (*Monarda didyma*) Leaves of this hardy herbaceous perennial border plant, either fresh or dried, may be used in the teapot with or without tea. Sow seeds in a cool greenhouse or a cold frame in March or outdoors in April. Established plants may be divided in spring. To attain their height of from 2–3 ft. the plants require a richer soil than most herbs and they also need plenty of water in dry summer weather. This is one of the most attractive of all garden herbs and the brilliant carmine or pink flowers attract the eye immediately. The flowers or a few chopped leaves may be added to salads.

Borage (*Borago officinalis*) Sow outdoors in ½-in. deep seed drills in April, preferably where the plants are to grow but seedlings may be transplanted. Thin seedlings or space young plants at 10 in. apart. They form handsome plants with blue flowers which attract bees.

Young leaves may be added to a salad to give a cucumber flavour. This is especially useful to those who find cucumber does not agree with their digestion. Separate the calyces of the flowers from the petals which can then be floated on such drinks as cider and claret cups. Salads may also be garnished with the flowers.

Burnet (salad burnet) (*Poterium sanguisorba*) Of salad use, too, giving a flavour of cucumber without the possibility of the windy effects of that vegetable, salad burnet is a common wild plant in pasture land. Propagation is by seed or by division of established clumps.

Caraway (*Carum carvi*) A biennial plant, this herb flowers and sets seed in the season after sowing. Sow seeds thinly in April, where the plants are to grow and not more than ¼ in. deep. Thin seedlings to 6 in. apart. When in flower the plants closely resemble 'bolted' carrots. Seeds will be ripening in late June or early July. Cut the flower stems then and hang them in bunches in full sun and above a tray into which the ripe seeds may fall. The seeds may be used to flavour a seed cake or be sprinkled over home-made bread or buns before they are baked. On the Continent they are used to flavour certain cheeses; in Germany they are added to sauerkraut and used as a flavouring for kümmel.

Chervil (*Anthriscus cerefolius*) This hardy annual varies in height from 1–1½ ft. Sow at any time between April and June, in shallow drills where the plants are to grow. Thin seedlings to 6 in. apart. The soil should be rich and a shady position is better than the open, sunny site liked best by most garden herbs. It is the finely cut foliage which is used. Chervil is seldom dried. The flavour keeps better if the foliage is placed in a deep freezer. The French use this herb often and it should always be included in a French blend of *fines herbes*. The aroma is strongly aniseed and chervil must be used sparingly.

Chicory (*Cichorium intybus*) For the cultivation and use of chicory as a vegetable see *Fifty Vegetables and Salads*. It is mentioned here because it is so often included in public herbgardens where the plants are allowed to run up tall spikes on which are attractive blue flowers. The flowers tend to die in the early afternoon on sunny days. Witloof chicory is the kind grown in the vegetable garden. Magdeburg chicory is grown for its roots which are blended with coffee.

Chives (*Allium schoenoprasum*) This is a very useful flavouring herb. The most usually grown chives are low plants which form close clumps with mauve-purple flower heads in June. Chives are often recommended as a good edging plant for the herb and kitchen garden. Less usually grown are the taller, violet-flowered Great Chives. There is also Chinese Chives with white flowers on 15-in. stems, much grown for salad use in eastern Asia. Whereas the foliage of the better-known purple-flowered chives resembles onions in aroma and flavour, that of Chinese Chives has an onion-garlic aroma. Chives may be raised from seeds sown rather thickly, ½ in. deep. They may also be propagated by splitting up clumps and replanting off-sets. Allow at least 1 ft. between clumps. Cut foliage for use at any time between early May and October. Where clumps of chives are cut regularly in late spring and early summer no flowers will form. The small bulbs may be used to replace onions in soups, stews and salads but such uses are rare and usually only if the gardener has excess plants when he digs up the clumps to replant them when they grow overlarge. Chop chive leaves finely for the mild onion flavour much favoured in cream cheese, cream soups, in omelettes scrambled eggs and in salads. This is one of the few herbs which may be grown successfully in pots on a patio or in a window box.

Clary (clary sage) (*Salvia spp.*) There are two kinds—an annual and a perennial. The annual form is usually referred to as 'annual bluebeard'—a name it merits from its colourful display of purplish-blue bracts. Perennial clary is equally striking with its mauvish bracts and blue-mauve flowers. A white-flowered perennial clary is popular in herb gardens open to the public. The tall stems of both kinds look fine towards the rear of a herb border. Sow seeds in April, where the plants are to grow in clumps. The leaves may be used to flavour soups and were at one time much used to flavour home-made wine, ale and beer.

Coriander (*Coriandrum sativum*) This hardy annual reaches a height of 1½–2 ft. and has umbels of white, slightly mauve-tinted florets in high summer. Sow seeds thinly, ½ in. deep where the plants are to grow. Early May is a good time to sow for flowers in August. Thin seedlings to 4 in. apart. The foliage and unripe seeds have an unpleasant aroma. Only ripe seeds have the typical, pleasant aroma and flavour for which this herb is renowned. When the first seeds are ripe but before any fall, cut the flower stems and hang them in a sunny position over a tray into which the ripe seeds may fall. In Britain coriander is best known as a flavouring in liqueurs and confectionery. It may also be used to flavour curries and sausages.

Dandelion (*Taraxacum officinale*) For the use of this herb as a vegetable see *Fifty Vegetables and Salads*. The flowers only are used by the home wine maker. Dandelion roots may be roasted and then ground to make a coffee substitute for those who either cannot enjoy real coffee or for those who prefer a drink containing no stimulating drug such as caffeine.

Dill (*Anethum graveolens*) This hardy annual reaches a height of 1½–2 ft. and has grey-green stems, feathery leaves and typical umbels of the *Umbelliferae* family. The florets are greenish-yellow. Sow thinly ½ in. deep in April or May, where the plants are to grow. Thin the seedlings to 3 in. apart. Harvest the seeds in the manner described for Caraway and Coriander. The leaves may be used to flavour soups and sauces or be cooked with cabbage and cauliflower. In parts of northern continental Europe the foliage is used to flavour new potatoes and green peas in the way the British housewife uses mint. The dried seeds may be used in a seed cake. They are also popular as a flavouring for pickled cucumber and for flavouring vinegars for the pickling of other vegetables.

Fennel (*Foeniculum vulgare*) This is the wild or green fennel of the British countryside. There is a bronze or red form often chosen for herb garden planting. This herb is a perennial reaching a height of from 4–6 ft. The fern-like leaves are attractive foils to shorter, more colourful herb garden plants. Fennel may be raised from seeds sown in April or May where the plants are to grow. Thin the seedlings to 1 ft. apart and grow as a clump of several plants. When clumps get over-large, dig them up in the autumn, split them with a spade and replant offsets. The florets on the large umbels are yellow. Dry the seeds as suggested for Caraway and Coriander. The fresh leaves may be cooked with fish. Mackerel especially is said to have a better flavour if it is boiled with fennel. Leaves may also be chopped very finely and mixed into a white sauce for boiled fish. The dried seeds come in handy in winter to flavour fish and soups. Some consider fennel to have a liquorice aroma and flavour; other liken the aroma and flavour to a blend of aniseed and parsley. For *Florence Fennel* see *Fifty Vegetables and Salads*.

Garlic (*Allium sativum*) This herb is often seen in herb gardens open to the public where the plants are usually allowed to flower. For its cultivation see *Fifty Vegetables and Salads*. Although generally considered as a vegetable garlic must on no account be treated as one in the kitchen. Like many herbs it is very highly flavoured and a heavy hand with it spoils any meal. Cloves (segments of garlic bulbs) must be used very cautiously. Usually, unless a gargantuan meal is being prepared one clove only is needed for flavouring meat balls, rissoles and sausages. A saveloy should always contain garlic. For a salad it is sufficient simply to squeeze juice from a clove of garlic as one rubs it around the inside of the bowl before placing the mixed salad ingredients into it. Garlic vinegar is made by putting 2 oz. of finely chopped garlic into a quart of cold, boiled vinegar. Leave for two weeks, strain the garlic vinegar off the garlic remains and bottle.

Good King Henry (Good King Harry, Mercury, Lincolnshire Asparagus) (*Chenopodium bonus-henricus*) Although included in most books on herbs and herb growing and very often grown in herb gardens, Good King Henry is used by the cook as a vegetable. For its cultivation and uses see *Fifty Vegetables and Salads*.

Horehound (white horehound) (*Marrubium vulgare*) This perennial wild plant is no longer as common in eastern England as it once was. It was the base for the horehound ale of Norfolk and Suffolk. Plants may be raised from seed sown in early spring. It may also be propagated by root division or by cuttings. The crushed leaves have a very pleasant scent and with its woolly leaves and whorls of white flowers on stems 12–18 in. high, it is an attractive herb garden plant.

Lovage (*Ligusticum officinale*) A native of southern Europe; where it occurs as a local weed in Britain it could be the distant descendant of a monastery garden essape. Lovage was much grown by pre-Reformation monks and used by them in medicines. The flavour is likened to that of celery and leaves may be added sparingly to soups, stews and salads. It is a perennial and may be raised from seed sown in the open garden in April. The plants need fairly rich soil to attain a height of 4 ft. or more. With its tall, hollow stems and large umbels of small yellow florets lovage is an attractive plant for growing towards the back of a herb border.

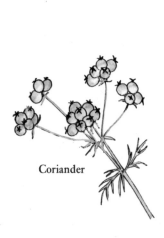

Coriander

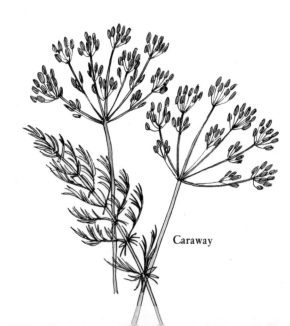

Caraway

Borage

Marigold (pot marigold) (*Calendula officinalis*) This is the old-fashioned marigold of cottage gardens. Once you have this herb it will always be with you, because it seeds itself freely and young plants appear all round the garden. It is a low-growing, bushy annual with yellow or orange disk flowers, a useful herb garden plant because the flowering period is spread over several months of summer and into late autumn. Sow seeds outdoors in April and thin the seedlings to where you want the plants to grow. A position near sage is ideal. The foliage is pungent, but for culinary purposes the flowers only are of use. They may be used when fresh in salads and either fresh or dried in soups.

Marjoram There are several marjorams all belonging to the genus *Origanum*. For the herb garden common, pot, English or wild marjoram (*Origanum vulgare*) and French marjoram (*Origanum onites*) are usually chosen because they are hardy plants. Wild marjoram has a form with yellowish foliage. French marjoram has a form with greenish-gold leaves. Common marjoram is a perennial, found in many parts of Britain, particularly on the chalk downs. Plants reach a height of 1–2 ft. The flowers are pale purple, French marjoram is a 1 ft. tall perennial, with pink-mauve flowers. Both marjorams may be raised from seed sown very thinly at a depth of no more than ¼ in. in the herb garden in April. Because the seeds are so small and the seedlings may be strangled by the quicker growing chickweed it is safer to raise marjoram in boxes of seed compost. House the boxes in a cold frame or beneath a cloche for quicker germination. Here again sow thinly and cover with very little compost sprinkled over them. Plant seedlings in the herb garden at 6 in. or so apart. Propagation is from established plants by division of the root-stocks in spring or in autumn.

Cut marjoram foliage just before the flowers open in July and hang to dry in a sunny place. When quite dry rub between the hands and store in dry jars in a very dry place indoors.

Marjoram, whether fresh or dried may be included in a home-made herb mixture for stuffing poultry or veal. This herb may also be used sparingly to flavour omelettes and salads.

Some herb enthusiasts consider the flavour of both common and French marjoram as coarse in comparison with the flavour of sweet or knotted marjoram (also referred to at times as Oregano

Marjoram). This is a rather tender plant and is treated as a half-hardy annual in Britain. Sow under glass in boxes or in peat in pots during late March or in April. Box-grown seedlings need pricking out into other boxes or into pots so that the plants have adequate room for steady, good growth. Set plants out in the herb garden, 6 in. apart in early June. Cut the flowering stems just before the flowers open and dry quickly in a sunny place.

Sweet marjoram is used as a seasoning for sausages in Germany and in Italy this herb is used to flavour sweet fritters made with spinach.

Nasturtium (*Tropaeolum majus cvs.*)   There are dwarf bush and trailing sorts. Both are excellent herb garden plants because, like marigold, the flowering period is long. There are many named varieties with a wide colour range varying from primrose yellow, orange to deep red. Poorish soil and a very sunny position suit this annual. Seeds may be sown in March in a greenhouse or cold frame for earlier flowering or sown in April or May where the plants are to grow. Flowers and leaves may be added to a mixed salad. The seeds, when at the unripe, green stage may be used in pickles.

Parsley (*Petroselinum crispum*)   This is a very well-known garden herb and is probably the most widely grown, apart from mint. There are several sorts of parsley. Plain-leaved Italian parsley is called French parsley by some. This sort is not popular in Britain where moss-curled kinds are preferred. These vary mainly in the length of stem and in the attractive curliness of the leaf. Length of stem is more important to the shop keeper who may wish to retain a bunch in a jar of water for sale to customers over a period. Much of the 'parsley' now used by butchers and fishmongers to decorate window displays is no longer the fresh herb but a plastic substitute.

In Ancient Greece parsley is said to have been in evidence at funerals although there is now some disagreement over this. Some say the herb was not parsley but celery. In Roman times parsley was added to vinegars. It was also added to a wine which had 'gone-off'. Presumably the parsley flavour masked off-flavours in the wine. In Britain there was a superstition that it was unlucky to take parsley from an old home to a new one. In America the superstition that a pregnant woman has a better chance of getting parsley seeds to germinate refers to the trouble germi-

nation can be at times. Parsley is a hardy biennial and it is treated as such in public herb gardens where the herb is usually permitted to run its course and to throw up flowering stems in the manner of all umbellifers.

In the garden where it grows for use rather than as a plant to be seen by visitors, parsley is treated as an annual. This herb will thrive in semi-shade, but will do equally well as an edging plant to the herb garden provided the plants receive adequate waterings in hot summer weather. The first sowing may be made in gentle heat in a greenhouse in February for plants to move outdoors in April. Sow seeds thinly, about ¼ in. deep. That germination of parsley seed can be very slow is well known among gardeners. An old dodge was to sow the seeds on a layer of peat, presumably the extra water-retention quality of peat kept the parsley seeds very moist and this encouraged quicker germination. Now with soil-less, peat-based seed compost on the market, adding peat to a compost mixture is unnecessary. Pouring 'boiling' water over containers or seed drills after parsley is sown is another gardener's way of hastening seed germination. It is doubtful whether the water is at boiling point by the time the kettle reaches the garden and the very hot water does not appear to damage parsley seeds.

A sowing may be made in the garden in late March and for parsley in winter sow again in July. This last sowing should, where possible, be given cloche protection throughout the winter. There will then be young foliage for use now and then, although winter growth is miserably slow. Plants from both March and July sowings will make seed heads in late spring and by that time another sowing should have been made for a continuous supply.

Because germination can be so slow it pays to sow a few radish seeds in the parsley seed drills. The quick-germinating radishes mark the row and enable the gardener to hoe and hand weed it without disturbing the slowly germinating parsley.

Early thinning of parsley seedlings is most important, leaving strong young plants at 6 in. apart. Never strip a plant of all its leaves. Just cut or pick off a leaf here and there at any one gathering. Where parsley is in regular demand the cook does not want to trudge up to the herb garden if that is at some distance from the kitchen. She wants parsley to hand and this accommodating herb

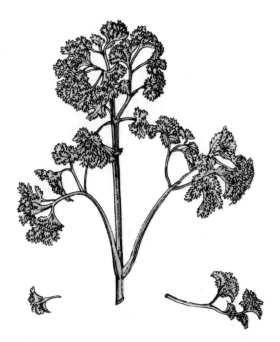

Left: Summer savory
Centre: Parsley
Below: Drying parsley over a low heat

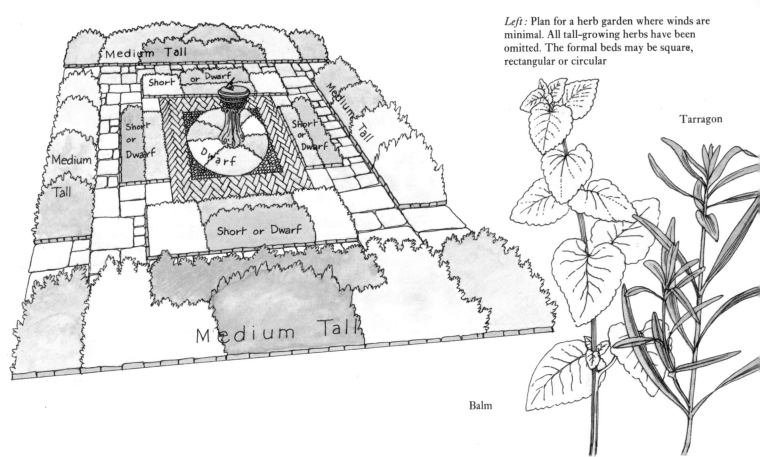

Tarragon

Balm

may be grown near the kitchen door in large pots or plastic pails and bowls as well as in a window box.

Parsley for drying should be gathered in late July or August. It is likely to lose its green colour during drying. As with all herbs the foliage must be quite dry when it is picked for drying and a greater heat is required than with herbs such as sage and thyme. Instead of hanging the leaves in full sun it is advisable to spread them out in a fire-proof tray above a cooker. Alternatively parsley foliage can be blanched in boiling water for five minutes; then cold water is poured over it and it is dried in a fairly cool oven for 20 minutes, by which time the leaves should feel crisp. Rub dried parsley between the fingers and bottle it at once. If it is left exposed it quickly re-absorbs moisture from the atmosphere.

Small quantities of chopped, fresh parsley or a little dried parsley may be added to soups and omelettes or to a home-made stuffing mixture. It may also be used to garnish meat and fish dishes. But in Britain it is used primarily to flavour parsley sauce.

Parsley Sauce (sufficient for four persons)
2 oz. of butter; 2 oz. of cornflour (approximately three heaped tablespoons); salt and pepper; ½ pint milk; chopped or dried parsley to taste.

(It is up to the cook to experiment with the ingredients so that a very thin, a reasonably thin or a thicker sauce results according to personal requirements.)

Place the butter in a saucepan and heat gently so that the butter does not brown. Remove from the heat and stir in the cornflour. Then gradually blend in the milk by stirring well. Return to the stove and bring to the boil slowly without great heat. As soon as the mixture starts to bubble, stir it several times, take it off the stove and continue to stir. The mixture will cohere. Now sprinkle on well-chopped or dried parsley to taste. Serve while still hot.

Purslane (*Portulaca oleracea*) There are two kinds: green purslane and golden purslane. Both are dwarf annual plants to be sown outdoors in May where the plants are to grow. Keep plants well watered in dry summer weather. For its more attractive looks golden purslane is usually chosen for herb garden growing. Young shoots may be added to a salad. The foliage is used as an ingredient of the well-known French soup *Bonne Femme*.

Savory There are two kinds of savory, summer savory (*Satureja hortensis*) and winter savory (*S. montana*). The Romans made a savory sauce rather as we now make mint sauce. This herb is well known by name but is now rather neglected. Summer savory is an annual and is sown in a shallow seed drill in April, where the plants are to grow. Thin plants to 1 ft. apart. Pick for use from July onwards. Winter savory is a perennial sub-shrub and is usually propagated by taking cuttings in spring or by root division. It may also be raised from seeds sown in April, preferably in a tray or pot in a greenhouse. Move seedlings to the herb garden when they show good growth. Both summer and winter savory are low growers and may be planted near the front of a herb border. For dried savory cut foliage in July before flowers show. This annual cut keeps winter savory well-trimmed. If older shrubs tend to make too much growth and to exceed their allotted space cut back all stems in spring to 4 in. long. Savory dries easily if the foliage is hung or spread out in full sun. The colour also stays well. Rub the dried herb between the hands and store in a dry place. Savory which is permitted to flower is attractive with its white and slightly pink, tiny blooms. When in flower the plants attract bees.

Savory has a pleasant spicy aroma and flavour which enhances a home-made stuffing mixture; it also improves the flavour of sausage meat. It may be added to sauerkraut and a sprig may be put in the pot when cabbage or peas are being boiled. In Britain savory is sometimes recommended as a flavouring for broad beans. Here again, use only a sprig or two during cooking.

Sorrel Here again there are two sorts of sorrel for a herb garden. The broad-leaved 1½–2-ft. high sorrel is a cultivated form of the native wild sorrel (*Rumex acetosa*). This form is sometimes called 'French sorrel' which complicates things somewhat for the gardener who knows the true French sorrel (*R. scutatus*) as a smaller, trailing plant. Both are closely related to docks and when seeding cultivated broad-leaved garden sorrel closely resembles a rather short dock. Use the foliage sparingly in salads or in soups.

Tarragon (*Artemisia dracunculus*) This herb is well known by name because of its connection with tarragon vinegar but few people would recognize the herb on sight. There are two sorts of tarragon, Russian tarragon and French tarragon. Of the two, French tarragon is superior for culinary use and has what is described as a mixed flavour of aniseed, balsam and pepper. A native of southern Europe, French tarragon is not as hardy as the Russian kind which is the one to choose if you live where winters are always very cold. Both tarragons are low, bushy, perennial shrubs with fine-cut grey foliage. Propagation is by division of the roots (pulling them apart) when new shoots are appearing in May. Each bush needs at least 1 ft. of soil surface area. If you want to dry tarragon harvest the tops of the shoots and the leaves in late July and August. Spread out the leaves in trays in full sun so that drying is rapid. Fresh leaves may be picked from plants throughout the summer.

Tarragon can be added to a home-made herb mixture for stuffing poultry. Before it is roasted a chicken may be rubbed well with this herb. If you add tarragon to a fish sauce, to omelettes or to salads, use it sparingly.

Tarragon vinegar (*a simple recipe*) Pick leaves or sprigs of tarragon or use the dried herb. How much tarragon you use is something to learn from experience. It depends on how much you like a strong tarragon flavour in the vinegar. Put the herb in a pickle or preserving jar and pour in white or wine vinegar so that the tarragon is well covered. Cork or seal with a screw cap and leave for ten days. Then strain and bottle your tarragon vinegar.

257

Few back garden herb enthusiasts grow medicinal herbs solely for their health-giving qualities. Instead, a few of the more attractive medicinals are included in most herb gardens.

The use of herbs in medicine goes back to pre-history. A Sumerian herbal of 650 B.C. records that it is a copy of a herbal made at around 2200 B.C. The ancient Egyptians used medicinal herbs as did the ancient Chinese. The herbalists of western Europe appear to have drawn on ancient Greek and on Arabic works for much of their knowledge. It may have come as a surprise to the Pilgrim Fathers to have found the 'Indians' of the New World using local herbs for the treatment of wounds and sickness.

Old-time herbalism was linked with astrology; Culpeper, for example, states which of the planets governs most of the herbs he describes; chervil being governed by Jupiter, marjoram by Mercury and sorrel by Venus.

The *Doctrine of Signatures* is another feature of old-time herbalism which has no appeal to our present thinking. Under this doctrine like heals like. The patches on leaves of lungwort appeared as similar to lungs to herbalists. They concluded that lungwort must, therefore, be of benefit to combat lung diseases. Culpeper was a great believer in the doctrine of signatures and advised his readers to dig up a root of pilewort (lesser celandine) and see for themselves 'the perfect image' of the disease they commonly call the piles.

Angelica

Modern British herbalism is in debt to Mrs C. F. Leyel (1880–1957). Mrs Leyel, a Life Governor of three London hospitals, not only grew and wrote about herbs but she also understood well the medicinal uses of many of them. The Society of Herbalists continues Mrs Leyel's useful work.

Herbal teas, as mentioned in the articles on culinary herbs, are often brewed with a medicinal value of one or more herbs in mind. Dandelion wine, too, is often made and drunk not solely for pleasure but for the medicinal value of the herb. Except for those who are knowledgable herbalists the preparation and the consumption of medicinal herbs is a practice fraught with possible dangers. Those who wish to know more about the uses of medicinal herbs are advised to write to The Society of Herbalists.

Angelica (*Angelica archangelica*) The herbalist Gerard recommended this herb garden plant as a 'singular remedy against poyson, and against the plague, and all infections taken by evil and corrupt air'. Angelica is one of the most widely grown herbs in public gardens. It is a very handsome biennial reaching a height of from 4–6 ft. Sow seeds in April where the plants are to grow, and thin seedlings to leave a clump of four or six plants 9–12 in. apart. At one time angelica was a popular culinary herb. The stems were blanched and eaten as celery. Pieces of stem were also stewed with rhubarb. Candied angelica stem is a French speciality.

Herbs & their uses

Medicinal Herbs

Autumn Crocus (meadow saffron) (*Colchicum autumnale*) Garden forms of this poisonous herb come in purple, white and rosy purple. The plant has no leaves when it flowers in autumn and has earned for itself the popular name of 'naked boys'. Grown from bulbs or from seeds, it is a useful herb garden plant, providing a patch of bright colour here and there at a time when all other herbs are drab.

Autumn crocus

Chamomile There are two sorts—German chamomile (*Matricaria chamomilla*) an annual, and Roman or common chamomile (*Anthemis nobilis*) a perennial. Both are popular garden plants, particularly a double-flowered form of Roman chamomile, a very short plant with creamy-white flowers. German chamomile grows to a height of from 2–3 ft. The flowers resemble daisies. Both may be raised from seeds sown in spring. Roman chamomile is the base for chamomile tea, said to relieve insomnia.

Foxglove (*Digitalis purpurea*) This poisonous herb is the source of the heart drug digitalin. It is a native wild plant with garden forms in a galaxy of flower colours. The cultivation of foxgloves is covered under Annuals and Biennials.

Goat's Rue (*Galega officinalis*) This hardy perennial with blue or white flowers reaches a height of from 3–5 ft. Propagation is from seed sown in spring. Choose a sunny site for this herb which was a popular flower in cottage gardens. Goat's rue was much used in time of plague.

Foxglove

Hyssop (*Hyssopus officinalis*) This short, semi-evergreen shrub may be raised from seed sown in April or May in the garden. Specialist seedsmen supply seeds of blue, white and pink forms; it is one of the most attractive flowering plants in a herb garden. It is mentioned in both the Old and New Testaments; medicinally its use was for relieving coughs, catarrh and rheumatism.

Jacob's Ladder (*Polemonium caeruleum*) This hardy perennial grows 2½ ft. tall. It is a popular herbaceous border plant. The spikes of light blue flowers appear in June. For cultivation see Hardy Perennials. Jacob's ladder was once used medicinally for the relief of fevers, headaches and nervous troubles.

Liquorice (*Glycyrrhiza glabra*) This hardy perennial, cultivated for its root, has yellow, pea-like flowers in late summer. Young liquorice plants are not so readily obtainable as they were when Yorkshire was a centre of liquorice growing. Most of the liquorice used in British medicines is now imported. A dose of liquorice as a purgative on a Friday night was a weekly ritual in some Victorian homes. This herb is cultivated for its root.

Lungwort (*Pulmonaria officinalis*) This perennial grows to 18 in. tall and has many popular names such as Adam and Eve, Joseph and Mary, Soldiers and Sailors. The flowers are pink in March and change through mauve to blue by May. Propagation is by division of the plants after flowering. It continues to be recommended by herbalists for lung troubles and other maladies.

Poke Root (Virginian poke, Red ink plant) (*Phytolacca americana*) A tall, hardy perennial, this has spikes of cream flowers followed by deep mauve to black berries. It can be raised from seed sown in spring. Preparations are used for skin troubles, rheumatism and catarrh.

Tansy (*Tanacetum vulgare*) A native wild plant, this is a perennial with green foliage and yellow button-like flowers. It is often included in a collection of herbs for its appearance and for its historical interest. Tansy was grown in the herb garden of Charlemagne; it was a popular strewing herb in the days of Elizabeth I and its medicinal uses were legion. In the kitchen it was used in tansy cakes and puddings and as a flavouring herb.

Tansy

Yarrow (milfoil) (*Achillea spp.*) Another of our wild plants with finely cut green foliage and clusters of white or pinkish-white flowers on 18-in. high stems. There are colourful garden forms of yarrow. Sow seeds in early summer. A shorter yarrow (*A. decolorans*), known as 'mace' among herbs growers, can be used to flavour soups and stews. But it was for its medicinal qualities that yarrow was famed. An old name was soldier's woundwort and for thousands of years this herb was of invaluable use in the dressing of wounds. Yarrow tea is said to be excellent for the treatment of a severe cold.

For us in the twentieth century with readily available perfumes, disinfectants and aerosols it is not easy to conjure up an olefactory image of the past with its smelly, filthy habitations and filthier city streets. Fragrant herbs played a vital part in ameliorating or disguising unpleasant odours caused by the absence of a sewage system and of refuse collection and the absence of a supply of piped water. True, the civilization of ancient Rome was noted for good supplies of water and for both private and public baths, but the habit of bathing and wearing clean clothes did not reach down to the masses.

Today we are reminded of the important part fragrant herbs played in the past when we see judges of the High Court carrying posies on ceremonial occasions.

Twentieth century man (and woman) continues to enjoy fragrant odours. They are supplied by cosmetic manufacturers. There is still, too, delight in naturally fragrant aromas and although some plant breeders appear to have forgotten it, most gardeners enjoy the natural fragrance of their roses, pinks and other flowers as well as the fine decorative use to which they may be put.

In the herb garden a good selection of fragrant herbs is always present. Even where culinary herbs predominate, there is always the pleasure of pinching and smelling a leaf of mint, sage and thyme. Several herbs, not already covered, noted for their fragrance are described below.

Jerusalem Sage

Camphor Plant (*Balsamita vulgaris*) This is not the tree from which real camphor is obtained but a hardy perennial reaching a height of from 3–4 ft. With greyish foliage and daisy-like flowers this is a handsome herbaceous plant for growing at the rear of a herb border or just in front of an even taller herb. Crush a leaf between the fingers and you have the pleasant odour of camphor. The dried leaves deter moths from woollens. Leaves may be placed in sachets either on their own or mixed with dried lavender.

Curry Plant (*Helichrysum angustifolium*) This is a low perennial sub-shrub with grey foliage and numerous small yellow flowers. The shrub emits a curry odour and this is more pronounced if a leaf is rubbed between the fingers. Sprigs of curry plant may be added to a curry after it has been made. Leaves may be dried but they do not have as strong a scent as fresh leaves.

Jerusalem Sage (*Phlomis fruticosa*) This hardy shrub is popular in herb gardens open to the public. With its grey foliage and yellow flowers Jerusalem sage is attractive in June and July. It is not a true sage and is grown only for the fragrance of its fresh or dried leaves.

Lavender (*Lavandula spp.* and *cvs.*) This is a 'must' for every herb garden, but choose carefully so that you select one or more varieties which fit in with your herb garden planning. There is a choice of dwarf and taller lavenders and of mauve, purple, white and rose coloured flowers. The cultivation of lavender is described under Trees and Shrubs.

Dried lavender continues to be used in many homes as a moth deterrent and also to give clothes in drawers and wardrobes a pleasant scent. The

Herbs & their uses
Fragrant Herbs

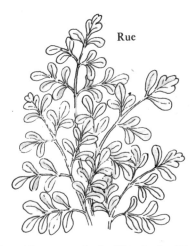

Lavender

flowers are very often used in pot-pourris. Deeper purplish-mauve lavenders are said to be the most highly perfumed. For dry lavender cut the flower stems when all of the flowers are in bloom and tie in small bunches. Always gather lavender for drying in dry, sunny weather. If bunches are to hang in a wardrobe, they will dry there quickly. For sachets and dry pot-pourris hang the bunches in a sunny place for a few hours before rubbing the dry flowers between the fingers.

Old Man (southernwood) (*Artemisia abrotanum*) This is the best known of the grey-leaved, hardy shrubs of the *Artemisia* genus. Apart from tarragon which continues to be used as a vinegar flavouring (see Tarragon) the *Artemisias* are not now included in the herb garden for their culinary or medicinal properties but for their handsome foliage effect among other herb garden plants. Do not allow old man bushes to become tall and straggly. Clip them back in March to keep them about 2 ft. tall. The foliage may be used in moist or dry pot-pourri but should be used with discretion as it is highly aromatic. This is an excellent shrub alongside a seat in a herb garden, or near a gate so that one can brush against or take a pinch of the fragrant foliage.

Old Man

Rosemary (*Rosmarinus officinalis*) Here is another 'must' for a herb garden, not so much for its culinary use as a garnish on lamb, veal and poultry nor for its cosmetic and medicinal uses, but solely for the pleasure a rosemary bush and its fragrant foliage give. Around 4 ft. is the height of an average bush but bushes can grow to 6 ft. Although a native of southern Europe, rosemary is hardy in Britain. Propagation may be from seed sown in spring, by cuttings taken in June or by pinning lower branches to the ground (layering) in summer. Rosemary may be used as a hedging plant. Trim such a hedge after flowering. Do not trim again in autumn. The clippings may be dried and the dry leaves stripped from them. Fresh or dried rosemary leaves may be mixed into a pot-pourri. Rosemary is among the nosegay of herbs offered to Her Majesty the Queen when she distributes Maundy Money at Westminster Abbey.

Rue

Rue (*Ruta graveolens*) This is the 'Herb of Grace', a name it certainly deserves if we believe all that Culpeper claimed for it. Among his claims were its use as an antidote against all dangerous medicines and poisons, its value as a cure for coughs 'and the tormenting pains of the sciatica and the joints' and for removing warts. Nowadays this hardy perennial shrub appears to be a feature of public herb gardens because visitors expect rue to be there. A form with bluish foliage is preferred ('Jackman's Blue'). Plants flower between June and September but the greenish-yellow flowers are not in any way beautiful. Flower arrangers like the young growth and visitors to herb gardens appear to enjoy plucking a leaf, rubbing it between the fingers and smelling the aroma. What they say varies greatly. Try it with your own rue and decide for yourself whether it reminds you of gorse scent, coconuts, a chemist's shop, a musty church or strong cheese! Propagation may be by seed sown in spring or by cuttings of young wood taken in summer.

Woodruff (*Asperula odorata*) The botanical name of this dwarf perennial gives a direct clue to the fragrance for which it is noted. Woodruff is a British wild plant with white, fragrant flowers in spring and is often recommended for garden cultivation. Propagation is by division of plants. In the Middle Ages bunches of fresh woodruff were hung in homes to mask unpleasant smells. Culpeper claimed that this herb was 'nourishing and restorative' but although there is a herbal use for it today, woodruff is more likely to be included in a herb garden for the fragrance of its dried leaves. They may be made up into sachets and placed among linen to give sheets and pillow cases the scent of 'new mown hay'.

A pergola is a feature which, basically, consists of a series of upright poles or lengths of wood which are linked together with a number of horizontal sections to form a pleasant pattern or design. Further variations can be achieved by the introduction of different types of materials such as brick or stone for the supporting pillars.

By itself, a well-designed and constructed pergola will add considerably to the appearance of the garden layout, and if it is clothed with suitable climbing or trailing plants, its appearance will be greatly enhanced.

When you contemplate making a pergola, it is important to consider its appearance in relation to the general layout or 'atmosphere' of the garden. The design, for example, could be a rustic affair or it could be 'contemporary'. What is its function to be? Will it have to divide or partition off part of the garden or will it be used as a decorative screen to provide privacy? Depending on the answers to these questions, so will the design be formulated.

The choice of materials for the construction of a pergola is comparatively limited. Larch or pine poles are ideal and can be used dressed or with the bark left on. Dressed poles have had the bark stripped off and the wood treated or varnished. Squared deal, oak or cedarwood are other suitable timbers which make up into very attractive pergolas. Oak is an extremely durable timber but rather difficult to work as it is so hard. It quickly blunts saws and is not easy to cut with a chisel. Cedarwood, on the other hand is a soft, easy-to-use wood which has a natural resistance to rot and insect attack. It will, however, weather to a grey colour unless treated every year or so with a suitable preparation which helps to retain its original beautiful warm colour. It should be used in fairly generous thickness as it is relatively weak – especially in the thinner sections. It is fairly expensive, but well worth the investment as far as appearance and durability are concerned.

Brick or stone can be introduced in the design of a pergola and for the main uprights or supports, these materials provide considerable strength and durability. If care is taken in selection, the appearance of a pergola can be enhanced, especially if rough textured and coloured stone is used. It takes longer to

The Handyman Gardener 1

How to Build a Pergola

build a pergola using these materials, but the result is well worth the time and effort expended.

There are several important points which *must* be observed during the design and construction of a pergola. Strength is of paramount importance. This is provided by the use of thick section timber and also by inserting the uprights or main pergola supports well into the ground.

The base of each upright should be thoroughly treated with a copper naphthenate wood preservative (1). Ideally, the bottom 2 ft. of the post should be immersed in a container of this solution for at least two to three hours. Ensure that the timber is treated for several inches above the soil level position.

Each upright or supporting post should be inserted at least 18 in. in the ground and for tall and large pergolas, this depth should be increased to 2 ft. Try to keep the excavation hole as narrow as possible as this ensures more compactness around the upright. When the

upright is in position check with a spirit level that it is vertical and at the same time pack a few large pieces of stone or brick around to keep it in place as some cement is poured in. Using a piece of wood, work the cement in place and make sure that there are no air pockets left. The top of the cement packing should finish an inch below the surface of the surrounding soil. When the concrete is dry, some soil can be pulled back over it to conceal it.

Another method is to insert the base of a pole in a land drain (2). This rather limits the selection of uprights to the thinner sections which can be inserted in this way but for lighter and smaller pergolas, the method is quite satisfactory. The pipe will protect the timber and cement, or stones and soil packed round it produce a good, secure installation. A tile or piece of flat stone or brick placed at the bottom of the hole on which the base of the pole and drain-pipe can rest, will reduce the effect of dampness on the timber.

Uprights should be at least 6 ft. above ground level to allow for adequate headroom and plant growth. Joints for cross pieces etc. *must* be kept as simple as possible to ensure strength and rigidity. The various important joints are illustrated in drawings (3), (4) and (5). Before the pieces are nailed or screwed together, the joint should be treated with wood preservative.

Where squared timber is used for uprights, the 'fill-in' wood which forms the design can be notched and joined as shown in drawing (6). Joining baulks of timber on brick or stone pillars is simply done with a long threaded bolt cemented into the top of each pillar (7).

With a little imagination, many different designs can be constructed, especially from larch or pine poles. Double pergolas (8) and (9) are very effective and form a covered walk. A simple line of woodwork (10) will provide an efficient screen or division in the garden. Squared timber can be used in the same way and is very effective when constructed as a covered walk (11). Timber thickness is important and should be in proportion to the size of the design. Larch or pine pole uprights should be about 4 in. diameter at the base and the design or fill-in sections about 3 in. in diameter. Thicker pieces can be used to advantage, especially in exposed districts. For

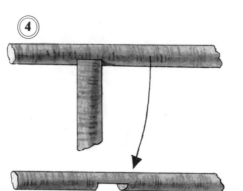

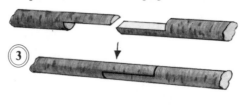

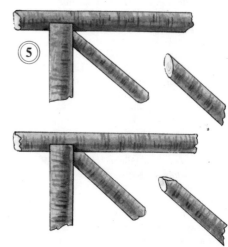

the squared timber, the uprights should be at least 4 in. square, preferably 5 in. for big designs. The design pieces can be cut from $1\frac{1}{2} \times 6$ or $1\frac{1}{2} \times 8$ in. timber. It is not necessary to use planed timber; the sawn finish will provide a more natural effect.

The more intricate designs should be carefully sketched out on paper so that, with the minimum number of pieces in the structure,

an eye-catching design is produced. Sometimes an unsightly view can be attractively concealed by 'closing-up' the number of pieces used in the design. Horizontal or vertical pieces of larch can be spaced about 2 in. apart between long, thick horizontal or vertical main supports.

This type of design should be built up slowly, taking care to keep the individual pieces as parallel as possible to each other. Although a reasonable amount of variation can be allowed for, blatant poor spacing will produce a rather unsightly and annoying finish.

Ingenuity will play a large part in the design and construction of a pergola feature and anyone who has reasonable skill with saw and hammer will be able to erect some fascinating patterns.

The Handyman Gardener 2

Making a Garden Frame

On its own, a garden frame is an invaluable accessory in a garden. Combined with a greenhouse, it provides a means of hardening off many plants which were raised in the greenhouse. A frame may be used to raise a wide variety of plants such as vegetable and flower plants for the garden, and cucumbers, melons or tomatoes as more permanent inhabitants in the summer. A reasonable amount of winter protection can be afforded to more tender plants by a frame.

The simplest frame to construct is a single light type which will provide a useful amount of growing room for average requirements. It is possible to extend the frame as growing requirements dictate, simply by removing an end section and adding on further front and back panels. These should have an occasional cross brace added from front to back to provide stability and strength.

Softwood is used throughout construction and deal or the more expensive and attractive cedarwood are suitable timbers which are easy to work. The main dimensions are—a height at the rear of 18 in., with headroom of 12 in. at the front. A width of 4 ft. 10 in. and a depth of about 4 ft. 1½ in. The frame light itself or the 'top' as it is usually called, is 4 ft. 10 in. wide with a depth of 4 ft. 3½ in.

Construction should begin with the body of the frame (1) which is cut from 6 in. wide timber, ¾ in. thick with corner posts of 1 × 1½ in. The back section requires three lengths of 6 × 1 in. timber which should be nailed to the two corner posts. Note that these are placed 1¾ in. in to accommodate the corner posts and thickness of the side sections. Before these corner posts are nailed in place, bolt holes should be drilled through them at top and bottom as illustrated.

The side sections are tapered from the back to the front and are cut from three lengths of 6 × ¾ in. timber. The top length must be sawn carefully to the required taper as illustrated in drawing (1) which is from a depth of 18 in. at the back to 12 in. at the front.

When shaped, the pieces of timber are nailed carefully to two corner posts which are placed right up to the outside edges of the side pieces. The top of these must be sawn to the angle of the timber side sections. Two bolt holes are then drilled at top and bottom right through these and out at the side panels also.

The front section is made up from two lengths of 6 × ¾ in. timber nailed to two corner posts which are 12 in. long. These must be placed 1¾ in. from each end. Bolt holes must be drilled through these also.

The body of the frame is assembled by eight ¼ in. thick threaded bolts about 3½–4 in. in length. Note how the end sections are located inside the back and front sections and hard up against the corner posts of these back and front sections. The frame light on top (2) has two side rails cut from 2 × 2 in. timber with a top rail of the same thickness. The bottom rail is cut from a piece of timber 3 in. wide and 1½ in. thick. A centre rail is cut from 2 × 2 in. and ½ in. square fillets or strips of wood serve as glazing bars or rebates.

The top rail can be joined to the side rails either by a mortise and tenon joint (3) or a simpler but slightly less rigid half-lap joint (4). Whichever method is used, the completed joint should be glued and screwed together.

The centre rail is half lapped into the centre of the top rail and half lapped at its base or bottom end so that, when screwed into the top of the bottom rail at its centre, the top of the centre rail sits 1 in. proud of the bottom rail (5). The bottom rail is joined to the two

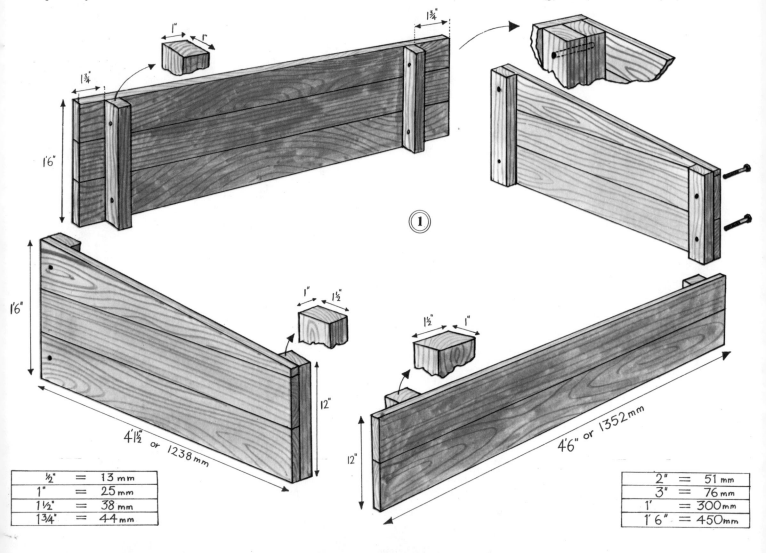

½"	=	13 mm
1"	=	25 mm
1½"	=	38 mm
1¾"	=	44 mm

2"	=	51 mm
3"	=	76 mm
1'	=	300 mm
1' 6"	=	450 mm

4′1½″ or 1238mm

4′6″ or 1352mm

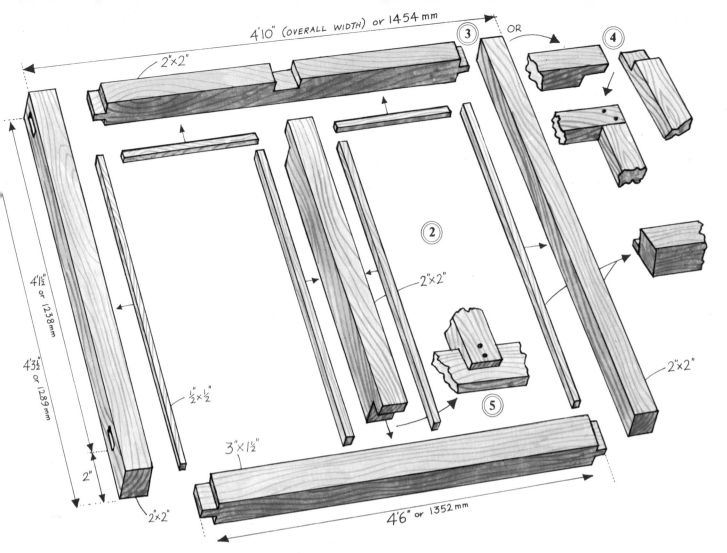

side rails by mortise and tenon joints which are made 2 in. in from the front end of these side rails. When in place (screw and glue again here) the two ends of these side rails should extend 2 in. past the bottom edge of the bottom rail. This provides a useful hand grip when the light is handled.

The thin ½ in. square pieces of timber are nailed in place along the inside faces of the top, side, and centre rails to provide a rest or rebate for the glass. They should be placed so that the bottom sheet of glass rests on top of the bottom rail.

Glazing is carried out with four sheets of 2 ft. × 2 ft. square panes of glass, using two pieces on each side of the centre rail (6). The panes should overlap by about ½ in. Bed well down in a generous layer of putty and retain in place by glazing sprigs. A side view section of the completed frame is shown in drawing

(7). The frame top should rest neatly on top of the base section and can be pushed back to allow for ventilation. In exposed gardens it would be a good idea to tie the front and back of the light to the body of the frame to prevent damage or movement by strong winds.

If deal is used, the timber must be liberally treated with a copper naphthenate wood preservative. Pay particular attention to all joints.

Another type of garden frame can be made easily and quickly from polythene and timber. The completed structure is light and particularly handy for the woman gardener. There is also the useful safety factor especially in a household of young children.

The sides of the frame can be made up as in the previous design but if necessary an 'all light' version can be made by using polythene or other plastic as the main filling in material for the sides instead of all timber. This will

allow even more light to enter the frame and will make it especially useful for the raising of plants from seed which require the maximum amount of light possible to prevent them from becoming drawn.

The sides are made up to the same dimensions as shown in drawing (7) with strips of wood used to fasten the plastic sheet to the framing. If the construction work needs to be even simpler, the four sides can be fastened together permanently. The complete structure will be light enough to carry about without difficulty. It is convenient, however, for storage purposes to have a frame which can be dismantled.

The frame top or light can be made up from a simple wooden support using 1½ × 1 in. timber. The corner should be reinforced either by plywood angle pieces or galvanized metal corner brackets.

The plastic covering should be stretched as tightly as possible across the framework and fastened in position by strips of wood. A double-glazed frame can be made simply by attaching a second layer of plastic to the inside faces of the frame light as well as the sides.

Good quality plastic should give a few seasons' good service but it will have to be renewed because it deteriorates.

This type of frame can be extended easily simply by constructing another set of three sides, removing and using one of the existing sides to form the other end of the new extension unit.

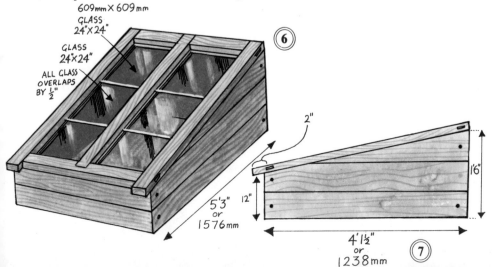

The Handyman Gardener 3

Making Fences

Fencing has an important role to play in the garden where it can be used to provide shelter from strong winds, privacy from neighbours and a means of dividing off or partitioning parts of the garden. Quite often, a suitably selected fence can add considerable character and interest in a garden and it is one possible solution to the problem of concealing an ugly view.

There are several different designs or patterns available and the choice of timber usually lies between cedar, pine or larch, and other materials are concrete and plastic. The type of pattern will have a bearing on the amount of protection or privacy afforded. For example, a solid or close-boarded fence with adequate overlaps will provide much more privacy than the more open interwoven design. Some fences have a special 'peep-proof' finish where extra intermediate battens are supplied which, when nailed to the overlap timber, prevents them opening up eventually. Adequate overlap of the timber used in the fill-in part of the fence also ensures privacy and very good protection from winds.

Fence height is a matter for personal decision. For complete privacy and shelter, the highest fence should be selected and this will usually be about 6 ft. The general range of heights is 6 ft., $5\frac{1}{2}$ ft., 5 ft., $4\frac{1}{2}$ ft., 4 ft., $3\frac{1}{2}$ ft. Sections are usually 6 ft. wide.

A fence is only as strong as its supports and the way in which they are inserted in the ground. They should, in most cases, be about 3 ft. taller than the fence if the fence is 6 ft. high. For lower fences the posts can be about 2 ft. taller. The posts must be inserted from about 2 to 3 ft. in the ground, allowing for the posts to extend about 3–4 in. above the top rail of the fence panel to accommodate the post cap.

The erection of a fence should start by placing a garden line along the site. Several posts should be laid down on the ground, close to this line, spacing them apart according to the width of the fence panels (1). The holes can then be excavated for the posts. Treat the bottom of each post with preservative to a position above soil level (2).

Place the first post in position and retain it in place with a few bricks etc. The exact position for the next post is now determined by fastening a fence panel to this first post (3). The next post can be placed in the hole and the panel fixed to this (4). Work proceeds in this way until the fence has been erected. When several posts are in place, they can be cemented in (5). Take the precaution of fixing a temporary stay or support to each post to prevent movement while the cement is setting.

Concrete posts will ensure a rot-proof fence erection and, in many cases, these can be ordered specially. Some firms can supply concrete spurs or stub-posts which are cemented in the hole first and then a length of wooden fence post is bolted onto this. The stub-posts stand above ground level and the base of the wooden post which is attached to it is kept off the soil.

Fence designs or patterns vary considerably and selection should be in accordance with the general 'atmosphere' of the garden. The wavy pattern (6) is very attractive and is particularly useful around a paved area where it will form a screen for seclusion. Interwoven fencing produces a pleasant design and combined with a trellis top as illustrated (7), a fence to suit most garden layouts can be had.

Close-boarded or solid fence panels (8) are very strong, rugged units and ideal for exposed gardens, in particular. They are quite heavy and very secure erection is essential.

Lighter types of fencing include the open rail fence (9) or the ranch type (10). These are useful for front garden boundaries or for enclosures round a terrace or even a swimming pool to give a measure of safety where there are children. The latest innovation is the plastic fencing material (11) which consists of hollow or box-like planking and hollow posts. Caps, end pieces and plank joining pieces are also available. Ranch type fences are made up with all these units.

Concrete fence units or panels can be used and these are available as individual sections which drop into place in specially slotted supporting posts (12), or a brick-faced outline panel (13) can be erected, which is also supported at regular intervals by special posts.

Concrete fences and walling have changed considerably in appearance recently and some very intriguing designs are now available. Some have a raised stone walling relief pattern which is very realistic and gives the appearance of a hand-built stone wall. Heights available are from about $2\frac{1}{2}$ ft. to about $6\frac{1}{2}$ ft. The panels are usually supplied in about 3 ft. to 6 ft. bays with suitable slotted concrete posts into which these panels are inserted.

There is a lot to be said for having a little consideration for one's neighbours and it is useful to know that there is one type of self-assemble concrete fencing or walling which has *both* sides equally attractive. The panels are finished in a warm coloured aggregate

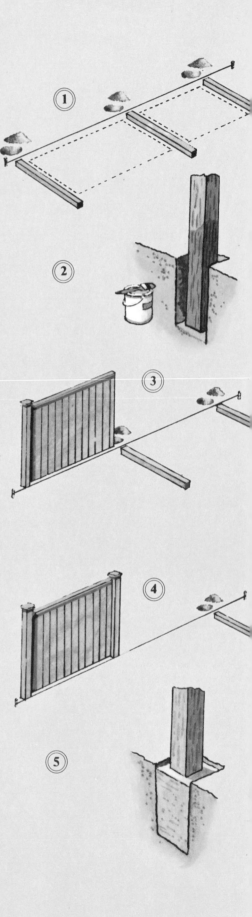

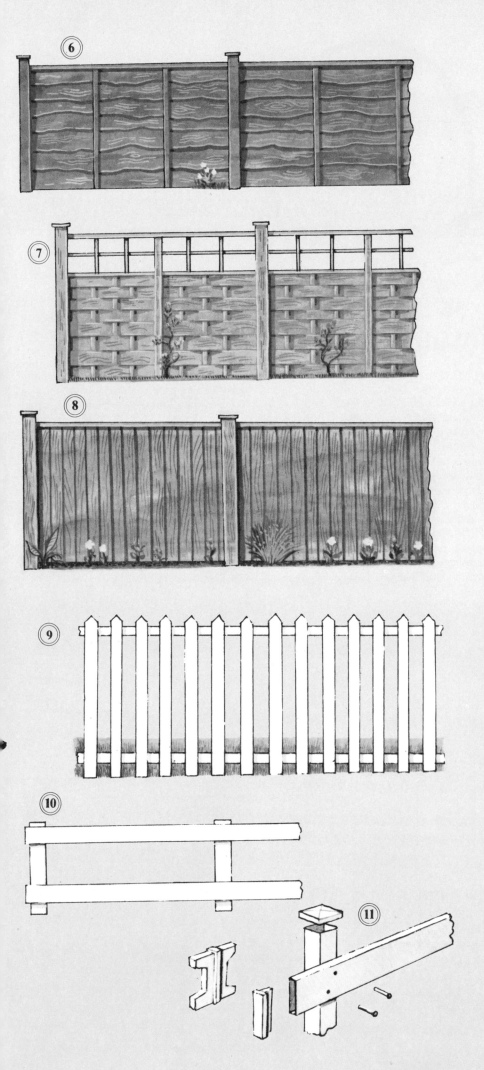

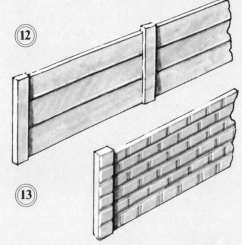

which provides a pleasant textured effect. One face of the supporting concrete posts also has this finish.

Sometimes a fence or boundary does not need to be 'solid'. This can apply particularly where the garden is being divided or partitioned off. It is also an idea to use an open fence where one does not want to blot out a neighbour's garden completely or where it might result in a great deal of light loss to a neighbour if one did erect a solid or filled-in fence design.

In these instances the trellis panels really come into their own. They can be either purchased as ready made units or can easily be made up at home. The timber used is about $1\frac{3}{8} \times \frac{3}{16}$ in. and is nailed together to form trellis gaps of about $4\frac{1}{2}$ in. square. The thin laths are attached to a main framing of $1\frac{1}{2} \times 1$ in. timber, with, if necessary, an intermediate piece of the same thickness about half-way along the panel, running vertically.

Attached to main posts the trellis makes a very attractive feature in the garden and if covered with climbing plants, can be quite colourful too. The panels can be used to enclose a terrace feature and are particularly useful as a screen between the ornamental garden and the vegetable garden.

A type of fence which is worth considering also is the extremely simple palisade design. This consists of a series of short upright lengths of timber which are pointed at their top end. The timber is about 4–6 in. wide and heights are from about 3–4$\frac{1}{2}$ ft. The series of pales are attached to two horizontal bars of substantial timber (about 1-in thick and 4-in. wide). Suitable short supporting posts link these together.

During construction it is very important to ensure that the pales are fixed level (vertical level), and a spacing block can be used between each as they are nailed in place. A gap between individual pales of about 6 in. is generally adequate. During all construction work it is essential that all timber is treated thoroughly with a suitable horticultural grade of preservative (copper naphthenate). Pay particular attention to all sawn edges and where posts are inserted in the soil. Galvanized nails must be used if rust effects are to be avoided.

The character and appearance of a garden can be enhanced considerably if features are constructed with decorative stone. Great strides have been made in recent years by manufacturers and a wide range of attractive stone is available for all purposes. Textured surfaces to several types of walling provide the gardener with an opportunity to create a layout which, after a comparatively short period, looks as though it has been established for many years and is, to a certain extent, a natural feature with its slightly uneven or irregular surface.

Several types of bricks for walling have a rough cut surface and give the appearance of having been hewn out of natural stone. Colour has been added to walling materials and this innovation certainly brightens up a patio or terrace–provided the colours are subtle.

Quality walling is expensive but is a very sound investment. It will add value to the property and will last for many years without the need for maintenance. Selection of sizes, texture and colours is easy because the leading manufacturers provide well-illustrated colour catalogues.

There are several types of walling stone. Some are similar to house bricks in size but much heavier as they are made from reconstituted stone. Screen walling blocks are available with either a solid face and a design in relief on it or with a delicate tracery of pattern. Random walling is also available in several different shapes or sizes. Used in various combinations, a very effective pattern can be built up although much more care and time is required during construction. Flat slabs of stone can be used for dry walling–an intriguing system of building walls, between the courses of which suitable plants can be established.

No matter what type of wall is built, the initial preparations are the most important and these include consolidation and levelling. To obtain a level, a master wooden peg should be driven in to the desired level and, using a straight piece of board and a spirit level, further pegs are driven into the level of this master peg and spaced along the trench according to the length of the level board. The master level should take into consideration the amount of soil excavation or movement necessary and this should be kept to the minimum. On lighter soils plenty of rubble must be rammed into the foundations which consist of a trench a little wider than the maximum width of the wall and about 6–8 in. deep. A layer of concrete 3–4 in. deep should be placed on top so that its surface is just at ground level (1).

One of the most attractive wall features can be made with screen blocks. Several components are required to make up this type of wall. There are the pilasters or pillars which are available in different designs such as the end pieces (2) and corner pieces (3). The centres are hollow and should be filled in with concrete and steel rods if a tall wall is built. Capping pieces (4) and (5) add the finishing touches to the wall at the top. Various screen block designs are available (6) and each, with its mortar joints, forms a 1-ft. square module.

On slopes, the wall can be stepped (7) or this treatment can be used on a level site to provide an attractive design. It is useful to use this system where a patio is constructed because the low section will provide shelter and will not obscure the view in the garden or from a house window.

Screen blocks can also be used to add patterns or relief to a brick wall (8). Panels or sections of the screen blocks can be built into the wall. The textured-faced bricks produce an attractive wall in a garden, and if the mortar courses are slightly scraped out where a profile type of brick is used, a three dimensional effect will be produced. Brick sizes are about 12 in. $\times$ 4 in. $\times$ $2\frac{1}{2}$ in.

Walls and Steps

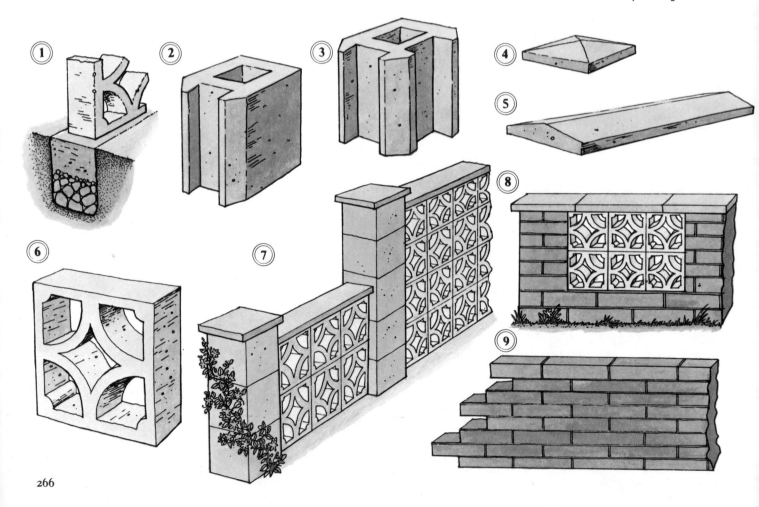

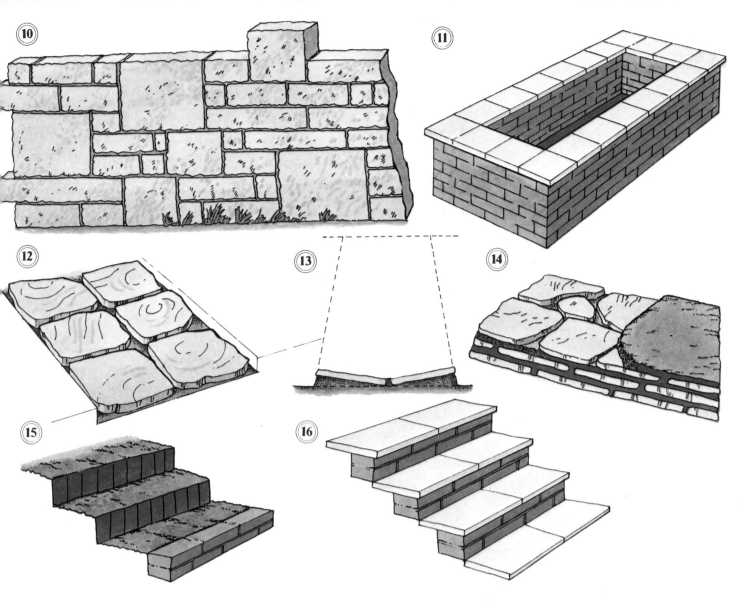

Blocks or bricks of various shapes and sizes can be built up to form a rather unusual wall pattern (10) and the extra effort and care required in its construction is worthwhile. This type of walling can be obtained in natural or coloured stone. Sizes range from about $8\frac{3}{4}$ in. $\times$ 4 in. $\times$ $2\frac{5}{8}$ in. to $17\frac{5}{8}$ in. $\times$ 4 in. $\times$ $5\frac{5}{8}$ in.

Raised beds add character to a garden design and rough or natural textured bricks and coping stones (11) can be used to construct this type of feature. A raised bed will be appreciated by the elderly or handicapped gardener as it will reduce stooping or bending to a minimum. Furthermore, such raised beds allow gardeners with sight problems to appreciate better the full beauty of the plants.

Another type of wall is a dry wall which is built up with flat broken paving stones. The base for such a wall should be excavated to a depth of about 6 in. and the base consolidated. The largest stones should be laid on the base and soil packed in between (12). These stones should be sloped slightly inwards and the wall should taper towards the top (13). As each layer of stone is placed in position it should be covered with about $\frac{1}{2}$–1 in. of fine soil (14). Smaller stones can be used in the centre of the wall to fill in any gaps. The top of the wall can be finished off with large pieces of slab.

Steps are essential in a garden which has pronounced levels or which slopes sharply. A combination of bricks and paving slabs will produce a neat effect. The steps should be dug out of the soil bank, allowing about 8 in. for the riser (the step face) and about 12 in. wide for the step tread. The front of the steps can be formed with one or two courses of bricks (15) and the treads of the steps with large precast paving stones (16). All must be securely mortared in position as the work proceeds.

Another very attractive way of constructing garden steps is to use a mixture of materials. For example, the face or riser of the steps can be built up with random stone, i.e. pieces of stone of different sizes. The individual pieces should not be too large otherwise you will be faced with the problem of having a rather high and somewhat uncomfortable step to negotiate.

Using this random size walling stone, about two courses are all that is usually required. These should be bedded securely on a layer of cement for the first course, making sure that each piece of stone is carefully levelled as it is laid. All pieces must be bonded well and a generous mortar joint allowed to ensure strength and rigidity. Natural coloured or coloured stone can be used for this type of step construction.

The tread or top of each step can be constructed from large slabs or, if the step is wide, several random size slabs can be laid. The latter plan is·most suitable where the riser is constructed with random stone. The tops or slabs should be bedded in a mortár mix made up of five parts of sand with one part of cement.

To avoid the possibility of wet mortar adhering to the face of the stonework as work proceeds (this can mark the stone unless removed immediately) the mortar mix should be on the dry side–never too wet when the joints are being pointed later.

There is no need to use a lot of mortar when the slabs are being laid as the 'spot' method is quite adequate. For the smaller slabs one central 'spot' or trowel-ful of mortar is sufficient and the slab is pressed evenly down on it. For larger slabs five spots of mortar are required–one at each corner and a central one.

Steps can be built with crazy paving to provide a rustic or natural finish, but a little care is necessary during the work to make sure that all the irregularly shaped pieces are securely seated in their mortar bed. Special care is necessary at the step edges to produce a reasonably smooth outline or edge without having too many pieces jutting out, which could be dangerous, especially in the dark.

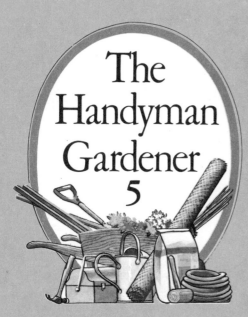

The Handyman Gardener 5

Building a Patio

One feature which should be included in most garden layouts is a paved area. There are several good reasons why this feature is worth consideration. Firstly it will provide a place for relaxation and leisure where garden furniture can be placed and where meals can be taken outdoors in the summer months. Secondly it will enhance the garden a great deal by its colour and texture. Finally, it will be quite a labour-saving part of the garden because a well-laid paved area is weed free.

There is, also of course, the considerable pleasure, interest and sense of achievement one gets from a do-it-yourself feature and this type of design can save quite a lot of money if it is constructed by the gardener himself.

A paved area can be, and indeed, should be as colourful as possible and this is quite easy to achieve with the modern pleasant shades which most manufacturers provide in their pre-cast paving slabs, though care should be taken to select only the subtle colours; the deeper colours are rather harsh and are apt to fade during the years. Texture, too, is important and there is much to recommend those paving slabs which have an exposed aggregate finish or a hewn look about them with their slightly irregular 'natural' surfaces.

The first important stage is the preparation of the site. This must be levelled carefully and to do this a master peg (1) (shaded peg in drawing) is driven in to the required level. This level should be one which will entail the least amount of work to level to all over the site. A straight edge or long piece of plank should be placed on top of this peg and another peg driven in at the other end of the plank. The true level is then checked by a spirit level which is placed on top of this plank (1). Levelling proceeds in this way all over the site, the distance between the pegs being the length of the level plank which is being used.

The mix for the mortar should be made up carefully. There are slight variations in the recommended formula but one which will give good results every time is made up of 1 part of cement and 5 parts of sand (3) both parts by volume. Make sure that the two ingredients are thoroughly mixed together in their dry state before any water is added. Avoid mixing up too much at a time. The right amount can only be ascertained by experience but this is quickly arrived at after the first few slabs have been laid. Keep the mix stiff and never wet or sloppy.

Not only will the colour and the texture of paving enhance the feature, but the use of various different sizes of slab can help to provide an intriguing pattern. Do not complicate things too much by having too many different sizes or a large number of small pieces. Design (4) is a typical example of a pleasing pattern which uses about four sizes of slabs. Another variation is shown at (5).

You can vary the appearance of the paved area by incorporating a 'panel' of pebbles here and there as shown at (6). These should be set in mortar and the stones graded for size. Keep these patterns towards the edge of the paved area with a few only here and there in the main area, because pebbles are not the best of materials to stand on, nor are they suitable to rest furniture legs on. They are, however, well worth using for effect. If there are trees or shrubs on the site to be paved, there is no need to remove these as it is quite a simple matter to pave round them as shown in the drawing (7).

Before you start work make a scale plan of the proposed layout, especially if it is a reasonably complex pattern. As the slabs are laid, they can be ticked off the plan (8). Then, if the work is interrupted, it is a simple matter to check where you left off and continue the pattern without mistakes.

There is no need to spread the mortar all over the area to be paved as work proceeds. The slabs can be bedded securely if a few dabs of mortar (9) are placed over the area which a slab will occupy. About five dabs will be sufficient for the large slabs; fewer for the small ones. Each slab should be carefully placed on top of the mortar and gently tapped in place. A frequent check should be made with a spirit level (10) as the work proceeds.

It is vital that these checks are made if the paved area is to be level and neat. The work must never be rushed and it is far better to lay a small section at a time, especially if large slabs are used. Check for level across several slabs after they have been laid, by placing a long level plank across them and checking with a spirit level.

Some slabs may have to be cut to fit. This is not the easiest of tasks but with a little practice, quite a neat finish can be achieved. The secret of success is to use a steel bolster chisel (11) and score the slab well round. Work on level ground, otherwise the slab will not break cleanly. If sizes are carefully selected for a difficult site the need for cutting will be reduced to the minimum.

PLAN of PAVING STONES

The soil should be levelled to the tops of all the pegs, taking care to see that where soil is added it is well compacted. Where the site is very uneven (2) it is a good idea to work with the levels. In other words a paved area may have to be stepped up in several places (2) allowing adequate room for chairs, tables, etc., in each area. Obviously the number of levels should be kept to the minimum and usually two only will be necessary.

In all the levelling operations, a slight slope to one side should be maintained to ensure adequate drainage. If the paved area is made against the house, the slope must always be *away* from the house walls. Where the soil is light a solid foundation of small rubble should be put down and rammed in. If this is not done, the paving may become loose or uneven.

The Handyman Gardener 6

Making Archways

One most attractive feature which can be constructed quite easily and relatively cheaply in the garden, is a decorative arch. This structure will provide an admirable support for choice climbing plants and will be a natural way of linking one part of the garden with another.

In a large garden, several archways can be erected to provide this linking system. An arch can form an integral part of a pergola which forms a division in the garden with the archway as an entrance and exit. In the small garden, an arch is not such an easy feature to incorporate and it is essential that its proportions are in relation to its site. For preference it should be made up from the thinner sections of timber and larch wood or poles are ideal for this situation.

Design is limited only by the artistic ability of the gardener. It should be borne in mind, however, that a lot of small bits and pieces should be avoided if the structure is to be kept as rigid and as strong as possible.

One of the simplest designs and one which is quite effective is that illustrated at (1). This consists of eight pieces of thick section timber. Deal, pine or cedarwood are suitable timbers and the minimum section should be about 4 in; 6×6 in. timber is ideal for a larger garden and where a tall, wide design is required.

The bottom parts of the posts must be thoroughly soaked in a copper naphthenate wood preservative to a few inches above soil level. Allow for at least 2 ft. of the bottom of each post to be inserted in the ground to ensure stability. Afterwards, each post should be cemented in place.

The width of an arch, i.e. the distance between the posts across the pathway, will depend on personal requirements to a certain extent, but ample clearance should be allowed for, say, the wheelbarrow. It is important, also, to look ahead to the time when the climbing plants trained over the archway are mature. Allowance must be made for clearance between the stems and leaves as one walks through the archway. Usually, a width of some 4–4½ ft. is adequate.

The same consideration about the plants is required when the height or headroom of the arch is being considered. A clearance of about 6 ft. is sufficient. Allowance for these measurements must be made when the upright or supporting posts are being ordered.

The length of the arch need not be more than approximately 8 ft.; usually about 6 ft. is adequate. In design (1), the roof of the arch is made by linking the side pieces with two shorter cross-pieces. The side top rails are notched (2) to fit over the ends of the four uprights. After this has been done, a long threaded bolt can be inserted through the side rails and when in place, the top cross rails can be secured to them by drilling a hole in them and, after inserting over the bolt, can be secured by a nut. Make sure that all joints and holes are thoroughly treated with wood preservative before assembly.

Another design (3) is made up from lengths of large poles. These can be used to fill in the structure as much as is required but the illustration shows how by the use of the minimum number of pieces, an attractive

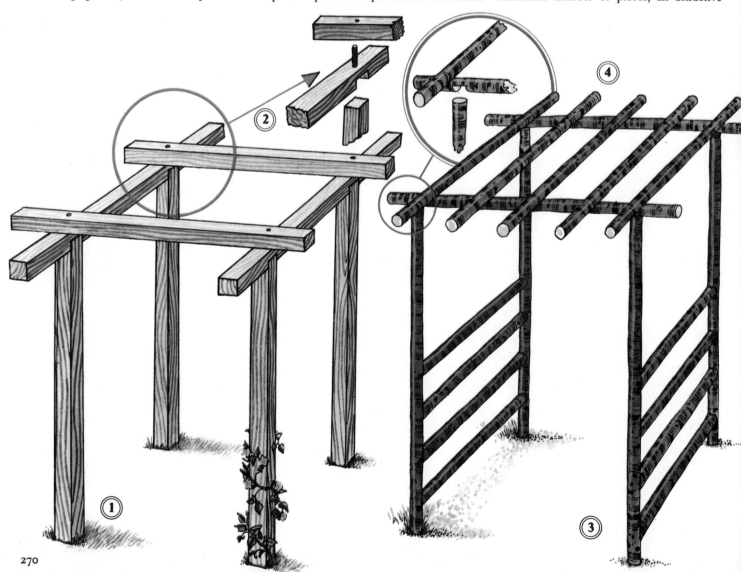

design can be built up. The lengths can be nailed into the main uprights and the two main top cross rails should be notched (4) to provide maximum strength. A reasonable number of fill-in pieces at the side and across the roof of the arch should be provided as a suitable framework for the covering climbing plants.

There are many versions which can be made up with larch poles and design (5) is another example. Still quite simple in construction, the finished appearance is very charming. Care should be taken when the joints for the angled roof supports are made (6). These must be carefully sawn so that they fit at the correct angles at the upright and top-cross piece sections. All timber is nailed in place. Variations on the design of the sides of the arches are shown at (10) and (11).

For a more ambitious construction, the design (7) can be tried. This entails a reasonable amount of stonework assembly but if a spirit level is used constantly, the main supporting pillars should be built completely true. Old bricks, pre-cast, rough-textured walling stone or random stone as shown can be used. A novel idea is to build short cavity walls either side of the archway (7) and fill these with gay flowers. The roof of this design is made up of lengths of thick baulks of treated timber notched into the two main long horizontal beams (8), which in turn

are secured to the tops of the wall pillars by a long threaded bolt which has been inserted through a thick piece of wood, which in turn is wedged and cemented inside the cavity of the pillar (9).

A reasonably skilled constructor can make up a variety of very attractive roofs to archways. A pent roof similar to a house roof, for example, can be built up with a series of thick larch poles.

A centre or top ridge piece should be constructed so that this runs for the depth of the archway. This ridge should be securely supported at each top end of the arch by a substantial piece of larch pole. The bottom edges of the roof structure are supported by two horizontal lengths of larch which are fixed to the tops of the archway uprights. Where these join the uprights they should be notched out to ensure a secure and rigid fixing. These notches should just take the size or diameter of the uprights to provide a wedge fit. Nailing or preferably screwing through afterwards must be carried out.

The roof itself can be formed by a series of larch poles which are fixed on either side of the horizontal ridge piece and the two horizontal pieces which are fixed to the archway uprights. The roof poles should butt up against each other as they are nailed in position.

It will be necessary to saw the tops of the roof pieces at an angle so that when they

meet at the ridge they butt up to each other neatly. This angle will depend on the width or span of the archway and should be checked carefully and marked before each piece is sawn.

An easier method of making the roof part is to cut and fix the ridge piece and two bottom pieces which are fastened to the tops of the archway uprights. Then join these at the two ends, only, with four pieces in all of larch pole, fixed in the form of a pent roof or triangle. The roof is then filled in by fastening lengths of larch to these four pieces, butting them up to each other on either side. These pieces run parallel to the ridge and bottom rails.

An attractive and unusual archway can be made of large section bamboo canes, which can be obtained from specialist firms. Sections are fastened together by carefully bolting them to each other, after drilling with an electric drill or hand brace and bit. Holes for the securing bolts should be made at least 3 in. away from the ends of the canes to avoid splitting them. This type of design is best kept as simple as possible and used as a 'delicate' archway in the garden. It could be used as a natural archway because the framework would be merely a support for climbing and trailing plants and, in the height of the season, would be completely concealed by well-established plants. It would, for example, be an ideal archway for the entrance to a rose garden.

The Handyman Gardener 7

Water Garden Features

There is no doubt that one of the most fascinating features which can be constructed in a garden is one which involves the use of water. Water has its own particular charm and there is a considerable therapeutic effect when one sits beside a pool and watches the antics of the fish or the movement of the water created by a fountain or waterfall.

Little artistry or constructional skill is needed in order to complete a very natural-looking effect. This is mainly due to the versatile range of accessories at the gardener's disposal. The simplest feature is a pool which can be of formal design (1) or informal (2). The former is either rectangular or square with straight sides or edges. It can be incorporated in many garden schemes and is particularly useful in a terrace or lawn setting. The informal design has an irregular outline and lends itself to the inclusion of other natural features such as a waterfall or stream which is designed to tumble into it. It is important, therefore, to decide at the outset, which type of pool is to be constructed.

Two ways in which a pool can be built are by using prefabricated pools or by using plastic liners. The costliest is by the use of prefabricated units (3) which are moulded in plastic or glass-fibre. Both formal and informal types are available in the larger sizes, but the latter are available in large numbers and in all shapes and sizes.

Installation is quite straightforward as all that is necessary is for a hole to be excavated just larger than the unit and, after stones have been removed, some of the excavated soil is used for backfilling when the unit is in place. Care must be taken to see that there are no large areas of unsupported unit which could be damaged or distorted when the water is added. Water is very heavy!

Plastic liner pools are very successful and if the tougher grades of plastic are used, many years of maintenance and replacement-free service should be provided. Some of these liners are coloured—usually a pleasant blue,

while others are reinforced with nylon. One of the toughest and most durable of the liners is Butyl, a rubber-based material of exceptional strength. As it is black in colour it looks more natural than the coloured liners.

None of the plastic or rubber-based liners is easy to use in formal pools if the contours of the pool are complex and to reduce the number of necessary folds and creases when the material is laid over the undulations, the number of contours should be kept to the minimum and should also be as gentle as possible.

A formal pool is quite easy to make from a liner (4) and a careful fold at the corners will be all that is necessary to maintain a reasonably crease-free surface all round the pool.

For all liners, an overlap of material must be allowed for so that it can be taken over the edges of the pool by about 6 in. Material for a pool can be calculated on the basis of length (overall length of the pool, plus twice the maximum depth); width (overall width of the pool, plus twice the maximum depth). Allow

about 6 in. at the sides and ends for the overlaps:.

Where ledges or shelves are required in the pool to provide different depths of water for the various aquatic plants these must be allowed for as extra measurements. Usually one shelf is adequate all round the sides, about 9–10 in. below the surface of the water. To avoid the necessity for shelves, plant containers can be raised on bricks.

Particular care should be exercised when the excavation for a liner pool is being undertaken, and all stones etc. must be removed to prevent damage to the liner. The base of the site should be lined with about 1 in. of sand which will serve as a cushion for the liner (5). The edges of the liner in a formal pool can be concealed very attractively if a row of paving slabs is laid all round (5). In an informal pool, crazy paving could be used or the edge of the plastic can be hidden or trapped by grass turves. The installation of a liner can be facilitated if, when it is in its approximate position, a *little* water is allowed to run into it. The weight of this water will pull and press

the plastic in place and it is a very useful method when an informal pool is being made (6). The edges of the liner can be retained by several pieces of stone as the water is run in.

Features such as a waterfall can be installed very quickly if a prefabricated unit (7) is used. These are finished in a simulated rock face with little rocks protruding in the 'run' to break up the water flow effectively. Several units can be linked to form a series of cascades. A stream course can also be introduced easily by the use of preformed units (8). Several can be arranged to form an intriguing course which could empty into a waterfall basin, which in turn finally empties into the main pool itself.

The movement of water from the pool to the top of a waterfall or stream course is provided by an electric pump. There are two types, a surface pump (9) which is installed outside the pool with a suction pipe connected to it and into the pool water. The submerged designs of pump (10) require less installation work as they are simply placed in the pool water. Several are connected to a transformer

which reduces mains voltage to a safe 24 volts or so.

By means of extra piping and gate valves, a powerful surface pump can be used to provide a fountain effect and a waterfall at the same time. The diagram (11) illustrates such a layout which uses a preformed stream course which runs into a waterfall basin.

The submerged pumps can operate a fountain and a waterfall simultaneously by means of an adaptor which is often supplied with the pump. For spectacular water effects it is necessary to select the more powerful electric pump.

Another most effective way of making a water feature in the garden is to construct a raised pool. This can easily be incorporated ideally in a terrace or patio feature. It is an excellent design for the elderly or infirm gardener because it reduces the need for stooping while the pool is being attended to.

Construction involves a little more work, but it is well worth the effort. The height of the pool above ground level is a matter for personal decision, but generally a height of

about $1\frac{1}{2}$ to $2\frac{1}{2}$ ft. is adequate. It is necessary to build an inner wall first, using breeze blocks or concrete blocks. This is the retaining wall which supports the liner and water. A firm footing or base of concrete should be provided in a 2 in. deep trench.

An outer wall is then built up about 3 in. distant from the retaining wall. For this wall, the decorative or rough textured walling stone is ideal. Again, a good foundation is essential for this wall. The tops of the two walls must, of course, be level. When set, the hollow between the two walls can be filled in with some of the excavated soil.

A plastic or, preferably, a Butyl liner, cut to size can then be used as a waterproof liner inside the retaining wall and the edges laid on top of the breeze or concrete retaining wall. To finish off the feature, suitable broad capping stones can be laid along the top of the walls and cemented in place. These capping stones also trap and retain the liner. Before this, partly fill the pool with water so that the liner is pulled into place and as many folds and wrinkles as possible are smoothed out.

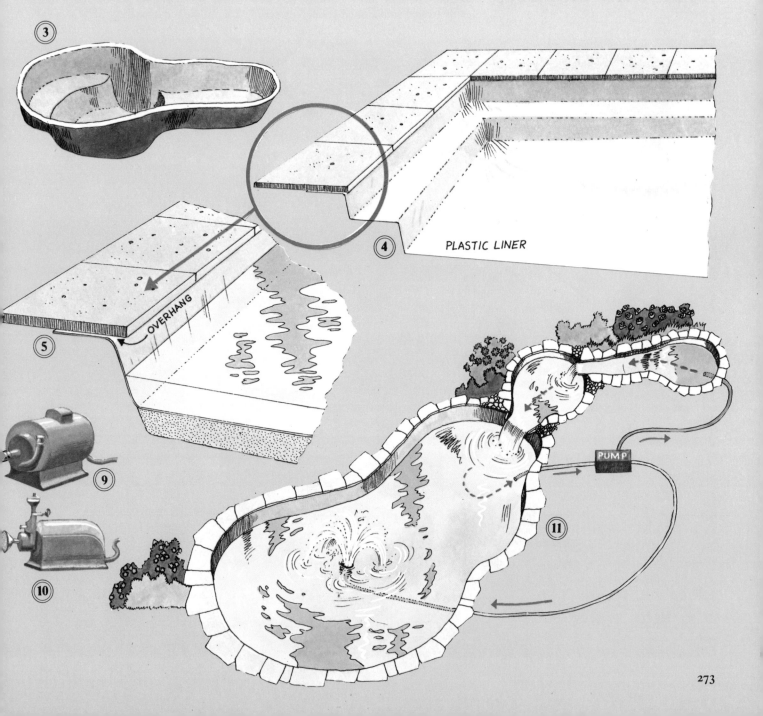

PLASTIC LINER

OVERHANG

PUMP

The Handyman Gardener 8

Marking out Beds and Borders

The various flower beds or borders play a very important part in the garden layout and these must be constructed as neatly as possible. This is especially important where the beds are sited in the lawn and neat outlines or edges are essential. In the smaller gardens, and the new gardens are getting much smaller these days unfortunately, good use of every available square foot of ground is important and careful marking out of the borders must be done.

It is irritating, for example, to see what is supposed to be a rectangular bed, the corners of which are not square. This can be avoided if care is taken to see that all the corners are true right angles. One of the easiest ways of ensuring this is to make yourself a device (1) which will give the correct angle at once.

This consists of a right-angled triangle made out of wood. The timber should be about 2 in. wide and at least 1 in. thick. Three lengths are required which, when fixed together form a triangle, with sides 3, 4 and 5 ft. long.

Before assembly the wood must be thoroughly treated with a suitable wood preserv-ative, making sure that the edges are painted also. Use screws to fix the joints together and check frequently with the tape measure as the work is carried out as an inaccurate joining together will result in incorrect marking out. In a long bed, an inaccuracy of only $\frac{1}{4}$ in. on the triangle will result in several inches of inaccuracy at the end of the bed.

The device is used by first driving in a peg at one corner of the bed and, after a line has been fixed to this, the line is run out to the far end where the bed will finish. The angle marker is then placed carefully by the first peg (2) and with one edge running against the line (2). The width line marker for the bed is then fixed to the first peg and run out so that it lies close up against the bottom edge of the angle measurer.

The angle thus formed by these two lines should be an accurate right angle. The same procedure is taken for the marking out of the other angle (see dotted line in drawing (2)). A line is used to mark out this edge of the bed. The width of the bed is then marked off on these two short lines and the remaining long edge of the bed is marked out by a line also. A

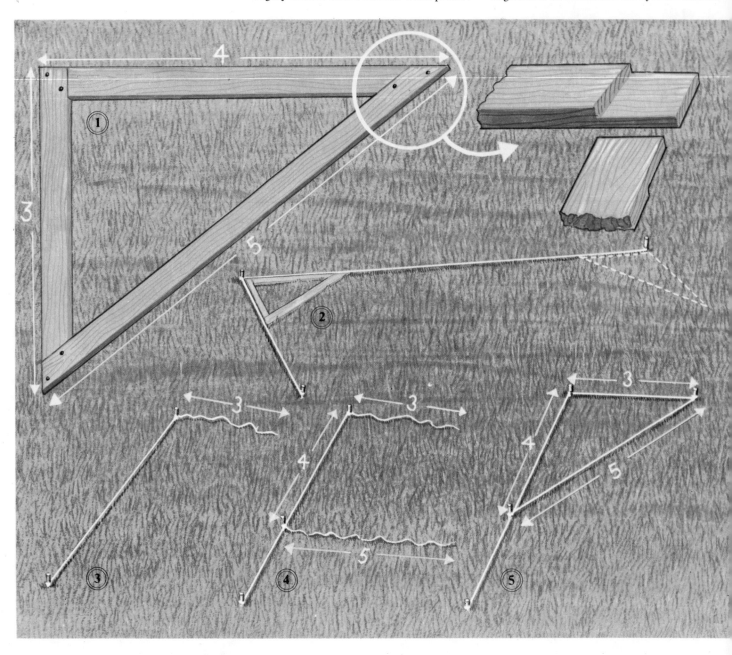

permanent marking out of the bed is then made by nicking out the soil or grass very carefully along the lines with either an edging iron or the spade.

Another method of marking out an accurate right angle is to use pieces of string. A long line is run out to the length of the bed and fixed to two stakes. At one stake a piece of string 3 ft. long is attached (3). Four ft. back from this stake, another stake is driven in and to it, another piece of string is fixed, this being 5 ft. long (4).

The 3 ft. long string and the 5 ft. string are then drawn together until their ends meet. At this point another peg or stake is driven into the ground (5). This will then form the right angle. This is not quite such an accurate method as the previous one suggested.

A popular shape for a flower bed is a circle. This is quite easy to mark out. All that is required is a strong stake which is driven into the ground at the exact centre of the bed to be marked out. A length of string is then attached to this stake and fixed to another pointed stake at its other end. This distance or length between the two stakes should be the radius

of the circle or in other words, half the width of the finished bed.

The circle is then marked out by scratching along the outer stake (6), keeping the string tight all the time. The tie of the string at the central stake should be in the form of a loose loop so that the string works freely round the stake as the string is used.

Marking out an oval bed is more complicated. Two lines should be laid out between two pegs (7). These indicate the length and width runs of the oval bed. Two 'focal' points or pegs have to be determined next. This is accomplished by attaching a piece of string, half the length of the oval, to one of these pegs which is marked out the width of the bed (this will be the maximum width).

The string should then be drawn out so that it touches the longer line first on one side (8) and then on the other side of the shorter line. Where it crosses two pegs should be inserted in the ground (9). A length of string or garden line should then be used which is twice the distance between one of these pegs and the furthest extremity of the bed. It is made into a secure loop and placed around

the two focal pegs (10). With a pointed stake and keeping the string taut, an oval can then be described on the ground (11).

There is much to be said for the informal bed outline. This is one which curves in and out gently and is particularly attractive in an informal garden and can look very eye-catching in the lawn setting. It is especially useful for island beds of herbaceous plants.

Marking out this type of bed is quite easy. A length of hose pipe can be laid down on the site for the bed and the various curves and sweeps can be made by moving the hose as necessary. An advantage of this method is that one can constantly step away from the work, and, if necessary, readjust.

Once the shape has been achieved, the edges can be either nicked out with the spade or the edging iron or a little lime or sand can be trickled along the edge of the hose (12).

Many varied shapes can be achieved in this way but it is wise to resist the temptation to make too complicated an outline, especially where the bed borders onto the lawn. It will be rather difficult and tedious to manoeuvre the lawn mower around a complex outline.

The Handyman Gardener 9

Making a Window Box

Colour and fragrance can be brought close to the home by the use of window boxes and troughs. With careful attention paid to planting schemes, a long period of colour and interest can be maintained, and a few fragrant plants will add the enjoyment of sweet aromas during the day and in the evenings.

Those people without a garden (e.g. flat dwellers) will welcome the opportunity of enjoying plant life by the use of window boxes. They are quite simple to construct and are well within the capabilities of the handyman. Also the amount of material required is quite modest and the costs are kept to the minimum.

The choice of timber lies between the ordinary softwoods such as pine or deal or the cedarwoods with their delightful warm brown colour and natural resistance to rot. Oak is a very durable timber, but rather difficult to use as it is so hard! If you think you can tackle it, then so much the better!

Timber thickness is important because a window box has to retain a reasonable weight of soil and thin wood tends to bend and warp. The timber used for a window box should be not less than $\frac{3}{4}$ in. when planed or prepared. Generally, a thickness of 1 in. is better. The length of the window box (1) should be about an inch or so less than the length of the window ledge. Very long ledges should have two or more window boxes made for them. The width of the box is rather critical and is usually about 10 or 12 in. Much will depend, of course, on the actual width of the cill itself but for adequate root room, a window box should not be less than 6 in. wide. Preferably, the window box should not overhang the cill but where necessary an overhang not exceeding 2 in. could be allowed for.

The construction of a window box (1) is quite basic. A start should be made with the base (2) which should have several holes drilled in it to provide adequate drainage for

the soil or compost. The holes should be about $\frac{1}{2}$ in. in diameter. The two end pieces (3) are cut out next. The sides (4) are the next sections to be made up. An average size for a window box would be a length of $2\frac{1}{2}$ ft., a width of 11 in. and a depth of 9 in., all wood 1 in. thick. In this case, the base and two sections should be 2 ft. 4 in. long. Assembly is as follows. The two side sections should be screwed through and into the base section (5). About four screws in each side should be adequate; $1\frac{1}{2}$ in. long galvanized screws should be selected. The two end pieces are then screwed into the ends of the side section.

To facilitate drainage, the window box should be raised slightly from the cill itself and for this purpose small blocks (6) can be screwed under the base. An alternative is to use wedge-shaped blocks (7) which are arranged to tilt the window box slightly back towards the window. This is a safety precaution and will prevent the box slipping off the cill. The box can be retained by chains or wires attached to the framework of the window frame. In high buildings this is essential.

The corner of the window box can be reinforced with angle-iron brackets which should be screwed into position. The face of the boxes can be made more attractive if they have thin strips of wood fixed to them to form a pattern as shown in drawings (13) and (14).

A Trough

A plant trough is virtually a window box on legs and is a very useful container to have especially where plants are required for a balcony or paved area. The illustration (8) shows quite a simple design which is easy to make up.

It is 3 ft. long and has ends (9) which taper from a 12 in. width at their base to a 10 in. width at their top. The base is a piece 3 ft. long and 12 in. wide with drainage holes drilled in it.

The two sides are 10 in. wide and 3 ft. long. The base or container is assembled by first screwing the two end pieces on to the ends of the base piece. The two side sections are then screwed to the bottom edges of the base piece and to the sloping edges of the two side sections.

The four legs (10) are cut from 4 in. wide and 1 in. thick timber and they should each be about 2 ft. long. The tops of each should be shaped (11) and then screwed into the sides of the container. Two cross braces should be cut from 2 in. by $\frac{3}{4}$ in. timber and attached to the legs by notching and screwing (12).

Both the window box and the trough should be thoroughly treated with the horticultural grade of a copper naphthenate wood preservative *before* assembly. Place them in position *before* planting; they may be too heavy to move when filled with soil. Cover the drainage holes with broken crocks.

Plant Suggestions

Spring Display: Plant one or two centre pieces of blue polyanthus and complete the remainder of the box with hyacinths and myosotis (forget-me-nots).

Summer Display: Use as centre pieces ivy-leaved pelargoniums with a plant of *Grevillea robusta* in between these. These plants will provide an attractive feathery foliage fill-in. The remainder of the box can be planted up with *Verbena venosa*. Another planting scheme can include petunias, *Campanula isophylla* and tuberous begonias. As dot or specimen plants for the centre of the box, use half-standard fuchsias.

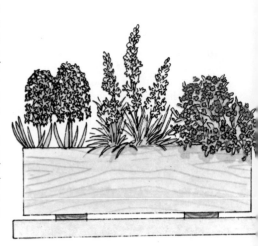

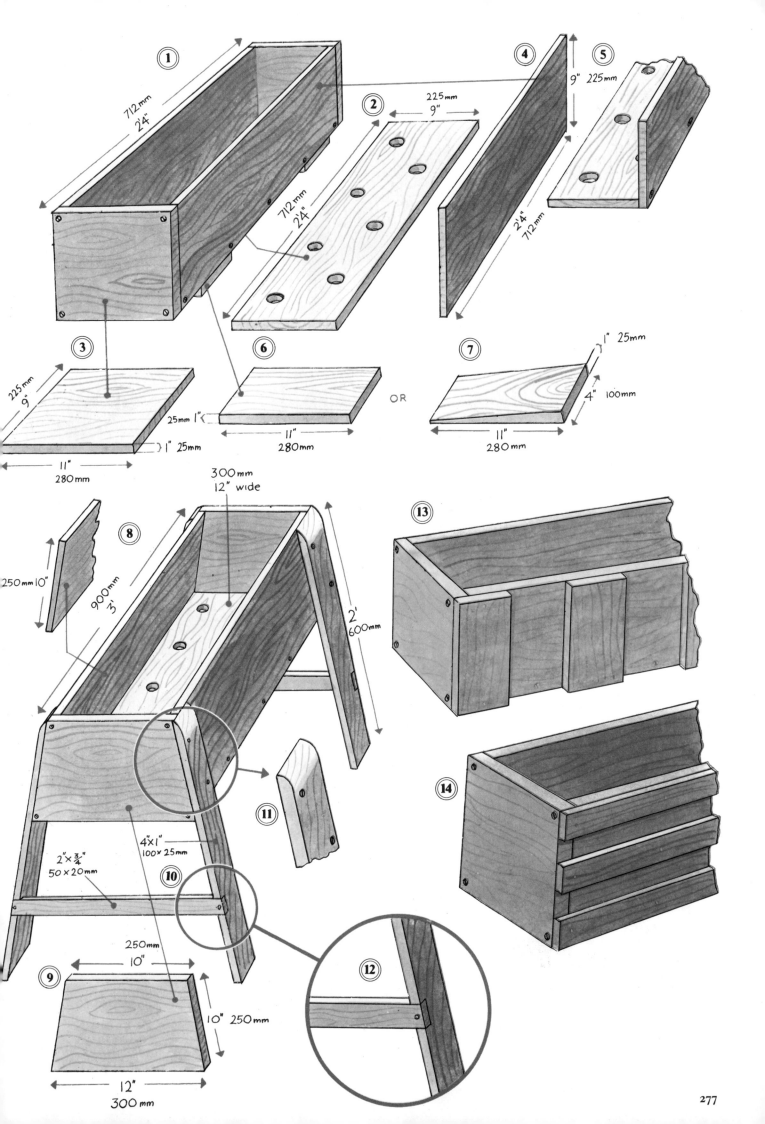

① 712mm 2'4"

② 225mm 9"
712mm 2'4"

③ 225mm 9"
11" 280mm
25mm 1"
1" 25mm

④ 9" 225mm
2'4" 712mm

⑤ 225mm

⑥ 25mm 1"
11" 280mm

⑦ 1" 25mm
4" 100mm
OR
11" 280mm

⑧ 300mm 12" wide
250mm 10"
900mm 3'
2' 600mm

⑨ 250mm 10"
10" 250mm
12" 300mm

⑩ 2" × ¾" 50 × 20mm
4"×1" 100 × 25mm

⑪

⑫

⑬

⑭

277

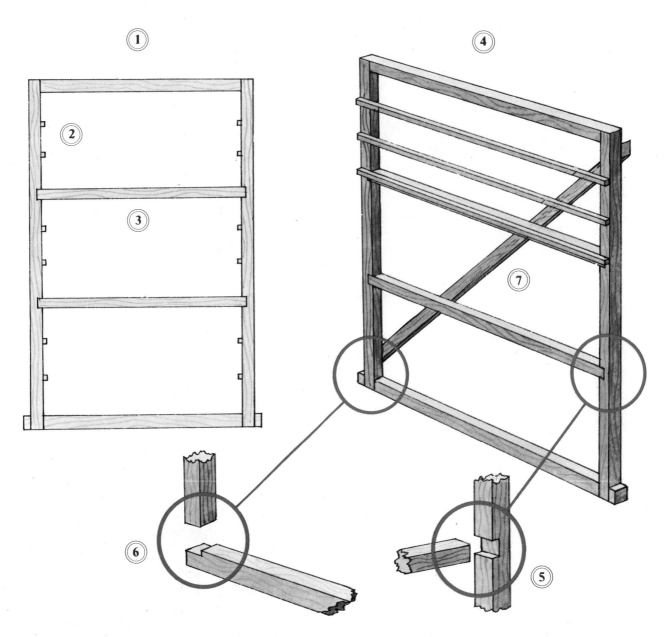

The Handyman Gardener 10

Making Fruit Racks

Correct storage of fruit is essential if the fruit is to last as long as possible during the out of season period. Even a modest number of top fruit trees such as apples and pears warrants the construction of a simple yet efficient fruit storage rack.

A fruit rack is important because it enables the gardener to keep a surprisingly large amount of fruit in a comparatively small area. It also ensures that the fruit is stored without damage by bruising. It also enables the fruit to be examined occasionally with the minimum of trouble and time so that a check can be kept on its condition. Any fruits which show signs of decay or rot may be removed to prevent the spread of storage diseases.

A sophisticated type of rack is one which has sliding trays and the main framework (1) is basically a frame to support a series of runners (2) on which the trays slide to and fro. Intermediate supports of timber (3) are essential in order to keep this frame rigid.

The side straining supports (7) should be 2-in. square timber (4) with simple cut out or half-lap joints (5)(6) for the individual pieces. These joints must be screwed and glued in place using galvanized screws.

The side straining supports (7) should be cut and screwed into the two side sections. These are important as they will help to maintain the rigidity of the whole structure; 2-in. square timber is ideal.

If necessary, metal brackets can be screwed into the inside faces of these joints. This will add to the strength and rigidity of the whole structure. The size of the framework must depend on individual requirements but a height of about 4 ft. would be adequate. The width should be kept to about 2 ft. so that the trays themselves are not too unwieldy.

About two intermediate bars will be required for a rack framework of these dimensions and these should be screwed and glued into position using screws at least 2½ in. long.

The runners for the trays can be cut from thin section timber which has been planed and sanded as smooth as possible so that the trays glide smoothly along as they are used. These runners can be about 1-in. square and must be screwed to the framework at intervals of about 6 in.

When the two side sections of the frame have been made up, they are joined by short lengths of 2-in. square timber which can be butt jointed to them or they can be let in slightly to ensure a more rigid structure. It is

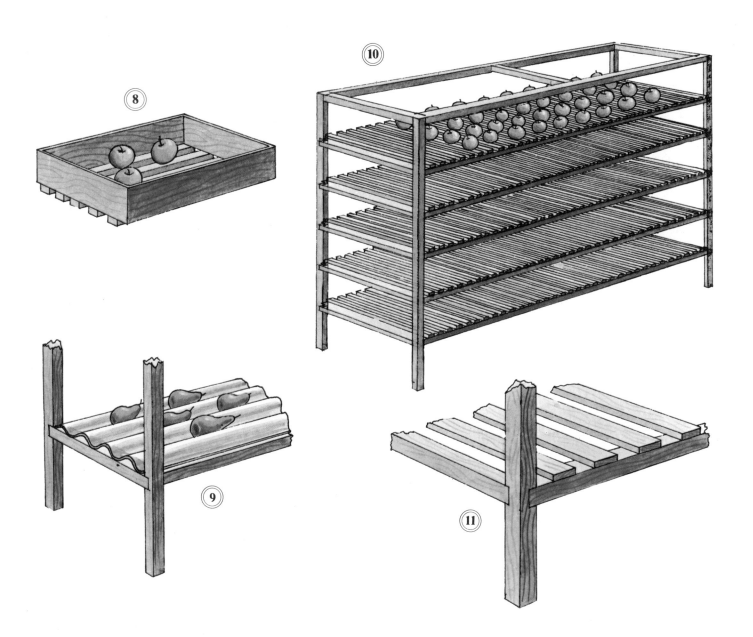

essential that at each joint, a metal angle bracket is screwed into place to make sure that the completed structure is strong and rigid.

The trays themselves (8) are made by using 2-in. wide timber about $\frac{1}{2}$ in. thick. These pieces form the sides and ends of the trays and they are nailed or screwed together at the corners.

The bottom of each tray consists of a series of thin laths cut from timber about $\frac{1}{2}$ in. thick and 1 in. wide. These pieces are then nailed to the two ends of the tray frame, making sure that the two pieces which run parallel to the two sides of the tray are set in about 1 in. or so to avoid catching on the runners of the rack framework. In other words, these trays will run on the bottom of the side sections.

The overall measurements of these trays should be such that they allow about $\frac{1}{4}$ in. clearance on the sides and ends of the rack framework to allow them to slide easily in and out when inserted in position on the runners.

Another simple fruit rack can be made up with PVC corrugated or box profile sheeting (9). This material forms the base of the rack and is screwed down onto a very simple

framework which consists of four corner legs of 2-in. square timber. The number of shelves required will determine the height of these legs but for general purposes a height of about 3 ft. will be adequate.

The individual trays of PVC can be spaced about 1 ft. apart above each other. The legs are joined together at the ends by short lengths of 2-in. square timber let into these legs in a similar way as for the previous structure. The width of the lengths must relate to the width of the PVC which is being used. They should be cut to length so that the PVC drops inside and between the two legs and rests on the timber as shown in the drawing (9).

Intermediate lengths will be required to support the PVC underneath and these should be screwed into the long horizontal timber pieces which join the legs at each end. These long horizontal pieces of timber should be 3 in. wide so that the edges of the PVC just rest on them. The outer face of this timber should finish flush with the outer face of the legs.

There should not be too much of a problem with condensation with the plastic, although most plastics do suffer from this.

One of the essential requirements of good fruit storage is the provision of adequate ventilation and the maintenance of a good circulation of air. If this is done, the amount of condensation should be reduced to the minimum. In any case, regular inspection is advised.

Another type of fruit storage rack can be made up with laths as a base for the fruit to rest on. The basic idea is to construct a strong framework of 2-in. square timber (10) with shelves formed of the laths (11). The joints should be half lapped and secured with long screws and metal angle brackets.

The width of the frame can be about 3 ft. and the length about 6 ft. It will be necessary to provide intermediate cross supports of 2-in. square timber if a long rack is required. These should be fixed between the long horizontal frame sections. The laths should be selected from 2-in. wide and $\frac{1}{2}$-in. thick timber nailed to the main framing (11).

The distance between the racks can be about 1 ft. and the laths which form the racks should be spaced not more than 1 in. apart in the rows. This will be adequate for most fruits and will ensure that air can circulate freely between the fruit at all times.

The Handyman Gardener 11

Paths and Path-making

Paths have a most important role in the garden to perform because they are a means of access to various parts of the garden and they should be used also to link interesting sections of the layout. For instance, a path could be laid in the lawn close by a flower border to link with one of the main paths.

Paths should be kept to the minimum however, especially in the smaller gardens. A firm clear pathway to the coal bunker or to the shed or greenhouse is essential in most gardens and there should be, if possible, a main path which extends the full length of the garden. This is important for wheeling things on, especially in a new garden where some construction work will be going on for several seasons. There is always the tidying up of the garden each autumn and the use of the wheelbarrow is facilitated if a good path is provided.

Paths need not be uninteresting–they should be as colourful as possible or laid with an interesting pattern. Try to sweep or curve paths in the garden to add a pleasing appearance but do not make them too complex in their routes. It is as well to remember that

straight paths have a tendency to narrow a garden. In the very small garden, there may not be sufficient room to have many meandering paths, so the design or layout should concentrate all the more on the use of texture, colour and slab size variation.

There are several interesting materials which can be used most successfully for path making. Slabs of one size (1) are very popular and a path can be made quite quickly with these. Paving of several different sizes (2) can be used to form an attractive design. Textured or 'natural-faced' surfaces (3) to paving adds a weathered touch and provides a path which has a good non-slip surface. Exposed aggregate surfaces (4) are available in the more expensive paving and these are very attractive indeed.

A curving or winding path is more easily constructed if specially shaped slabs (5) are laid. These can be quickly laid to form a very appropriate path in the natural or cottage garden type of garden setting.

Hexagonal paving (6) produces a very interesting pattern and is very easy to lay. Special

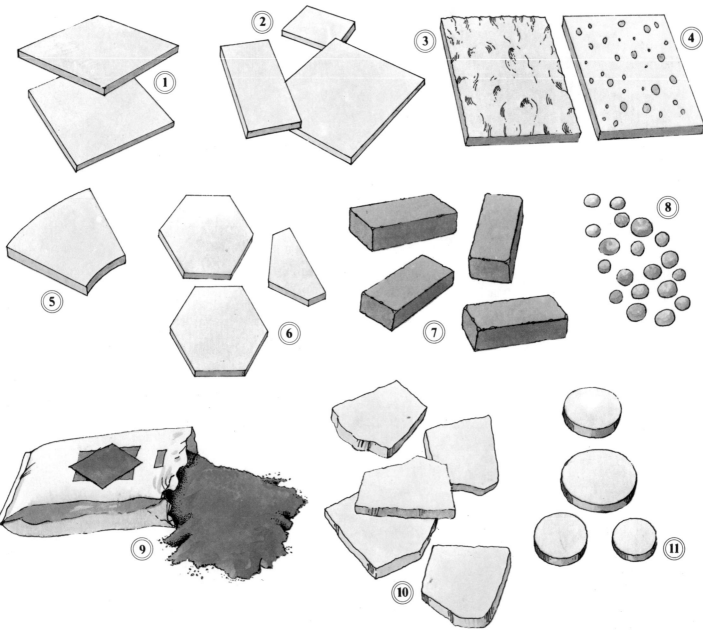

pieces are available so that a straight edge can be given to a path. This type of paving will produce a wider path than usual owing to the size of the slab and the need to use extra pieces to form the straight edge. Individually, these slabs form an interesting and unusual stepping stone path when set in a lawn.

Old bricks (7) can form a useful path although the work of construction will be somewhat slow because of the small size of the material used. Numerous different patterns can be created and the bricks blend in well with the informal type of garden layout.

Pebbles (8), unusual path-making materials are ideal for forming different patterns and textures. They are best laid in small blocks here and there in a path and should be placed where they will not be walked on as their surface is uneven.

Paths can be made from cold tarmacadam (9) which can be purchased in bags. This material forms a very useful path and is easy to lay. The material is difficult to use in cold weather, however, as it does not spread readily. Raked level to a depth of about ¼ in.

on a firm foundation, it is rolled afterwards and can be walked on immediately (16). Granite chippings are provided to form a pattern when they are scattered over the raked-over surface just before it is rolled (17).

Do not overlook the invaluable crazy-paving or broken paving (10); attractive paths may be made with this material and it is interesting to lay. Small pieces should only be used as fillers; always select the larger sections for the main work. The slabs are best laid on a mortar mix bed.

Round paving stones in various colours (11) are available and these can be used to form a stepping-stone path in the lawn.

When a path is made from concrete only it is a good idea to provide it with a slight curve or camber (12) so that water is shed to each side. Foundations for paths are most important and when a concrete path is to be laid, plenty of rubble should be rammed in the bottom of the shallow trench before the cement is placed over it. Where paving slabs are used (13) the rubble (a) should be topped with finer material (b), followed by a layer of

mortar (c) on which the slab (d) is bedded.

Mortar can be conserved if several lumps only (14) are placed on the foundations before a slab is laid on top. This provides a secure and stable path and enables the work to be done more quickly. The finished surface of the path should be slightly above the surrounding ground (15). This will prevent flooding or water holding in heavy rainfall.

It is surprising just how many attractive designs can be formed with paving materials. These range from the complex outlines of the crazy-paving path (18) to the simple pattern when slabs of one size only are laid (19). Extra interest in such a slab path can be created if several different sizes of slabs are used (20). Bricks set in several different patterns (21) will produce a restful path design with a matured effect, while the use of pebbles set occasionally in between paving slabs (22) forms quite an unusual path.

Hexagonal paving slabs when linked together (23) can transform a pathway into a feature which has an important role to play in the general design of a garden.

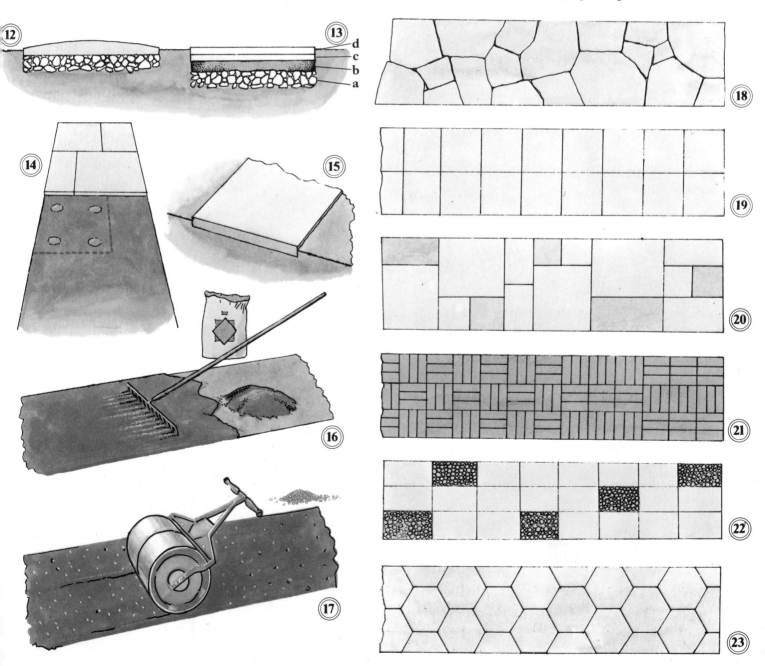

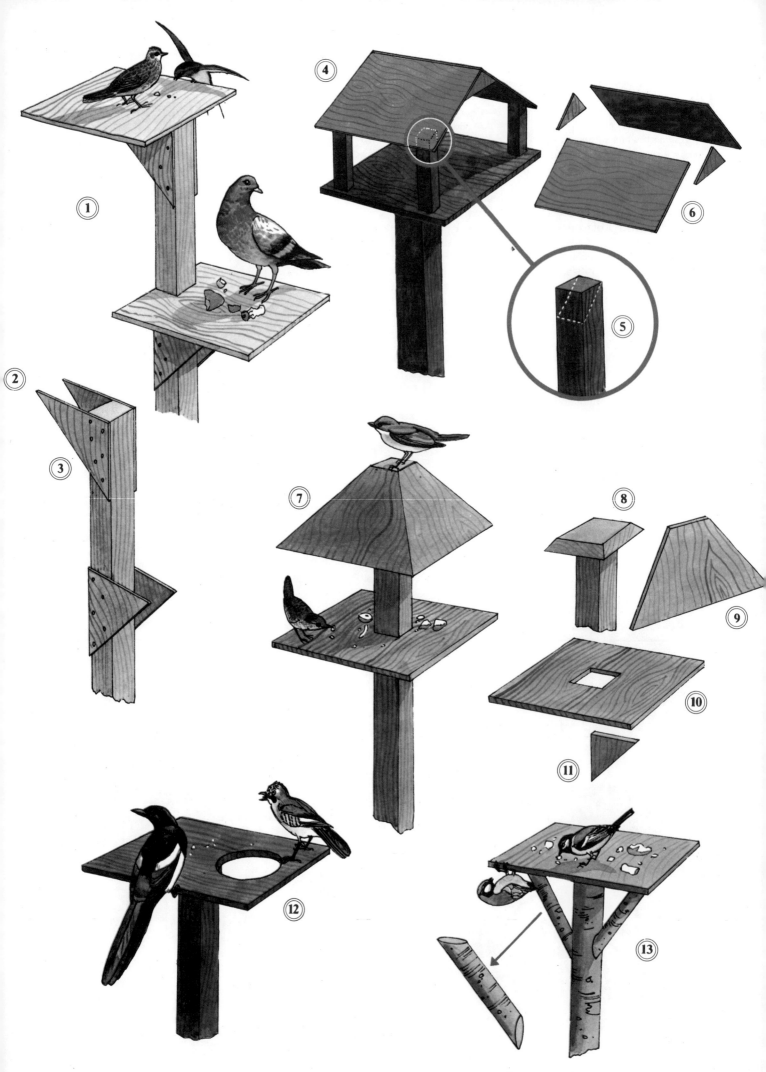

Bird Tables

There is no doubt that to encourage birds is one way of increasing the interest and fascination of a garden. There is a school of thought which says that birds do a lot of damage in the garden but the actual harm they do is relatively slight. A problem may arise if soft fruit is being grown but the modern garden cages or nets will reduce damage considerably.

One way of encouraging birds in the garden is to construct a bird table on which suitable bird food and scraps can be placed. It is always advisable to keep a bird table well above ground level so that cats cannot reach the birds as they feed.

The construction of a bird table is very simple and it is an ideal subject with which to start any form of garden carpentry. Deal or cedarwood can be used, the former being thoroughly treated with a suitable horticultural grade of copper naphthenate. A simple one which has quite an eye-catching design is shown in drawing (1).

Two platforms or feeding areas are provided, set off at opposite sides to each other. The main support for the bird table is a piece of timber about 3 in. square and from 2–4½ ft. above ground level, according to personal preference. About 2 ft. should be allowed for in the ground and this measurement should be *added* to the length suggested for the main support.

Both feeding platforms should be supported on triangular pieces of timber (2), (3). Birds are not at ease if they are not resting on something which is not reasonably secure. These triangular supports should be cut from timber at least ½ in. thick or strong plywood pieces could be used. The difficulty with the latter is the fixing to the platform itself as there is insufficient thickness for screws or nails to penetrate. A strong waterproof wood glue would be the best solution here.

The lower platform should be spaced about 1 ft. below the top one. The lower platform should have a section carefully cut out to accommodate the thickness of the main bird table support. Try to make this a good tight fit as this will add to the stability of the platform.

Preferably the triangular supports, of which there are four, should be screwed into the main support. Use rust-proof screws for this job.

A bird table with a little more interest can be constructed so that it has a miniature cover or roof over it (4). Again, this is a relatively simple design to make and one which requires the minimum of wood.

Basically, this bird table consists of a platform on which the roof is supported by four wooden corner posts. These should be about 10 in. high to give adequate clearance underneath for some of the larger birds such as thrushes and blackbirds. The supports for the roof can be cut from timber about 1 in. thick and 2 in. wide. They are fixed to the platform by screwing through from *underneath* the platform, which should be about 1½ ft. square.

The tops of the supports should be cut with an angle to suit the pitch or angle of the roof (5). This will depend, of course, on the width of the platform and also the height of the ridge on top of the roof. The construction of the roof is quite simple (6). Two end blocks should be cut from 2-in. thick timber and shaped to suit the slope of the roof sides. The latter are cut from resin-bonded plywood (exterior grade) or from ½-in. thick timber. One top edge of one of the roof pieces should be sloped or angled to take the angle or slope of the other section of roof when placed on it to form the ridge. The two roof sections are screwed down onto the four corner supports.

The main support for the completed bird table can be cut from 3-in. square timber. This should be attached to the platform of the bird table by strong screws.

Another design (7) has another type of roof which is built around a shaped wooden block (8) which, when suitably shaped along its edges, provides the angle or pitch for the four roof sections (9) when these are screwed in place.

The roof sections can be cut from similar wood to that for design (4). The shaped block (8) which also forms the top of the roof should be cut from timber which is at least 2 in. thick.

The platform (10) for this bird table should have a section cut out of its centre so that this can be slipped over the main bird table support, which should be sawn from 3-in. square wood. Small triangles of wood (11) should be cut to act as supports for the platform.

Birds should have clean water to drink and in many platforms a suitable hole can be cut out (12) so that a container of water can be supported by its rim. This can be used at times for a container of bird food and would help to contain the food better instead of having it scattered all over the platform.

A rustic type of bird table (13) can be made from larch poles which can be used to form the main support and to provide two small supporting arms for the platform. This can be cut from the same material as used for the other designs.

A small bird table can be attached to a suitable tree but it is very important that the table is well away from branches which might give access for cats. Try if possible to place the bird table away from prevailing winds.

A simple design (14) consists of a reasonably thick sheet of plywood which has had one side cut out to fit reasonably well round part of the tree trunk (15). The platform must be supported by a triangular piece of timber (16) cut from 1-in. thick timber. This should support *most* of the platform across its width. The triangular section should be nailed to the trunk and the platform screwed to it.

On suitable large trees, several of these small bird tables can be fastened to the trunks to provide interesting places to watch the birds from the house windows.

Sometimes a small old tree can be a problem. This can be used as a bird table with a large platform screwed to its top (17). Old tree branches can be sawn to length to provide unusual supports for bird table tops and if selected carefully, their graceful bends and twists will add considerably to their eye-appeal and general appearance.

(14) (15) (16) (17)

One could very quickly fill the garden shed with a massive array of garden tools and the very wide range of equipment which is available today is very tempting.

There are, however, several basic tools with which most of the essential and basic routine garden work can be carried out. To the new gardener this is an important point to note because, more often than not, expenditure on tools for the garden must be limited. It is a simple and convenient matter to add to a basic collection from time to time.

Tools for the tilling or cultivation of the soil are vital and the backbone of any collection of equipment is the digging spade and fork (1). Unless selected with a little care, these two tools can be uncomfortable and tiring to use. Look for a comfortable handle or grip. The latest designs are made from plastics which are smooth and very comfortable. If possible, go through the motions of digging, in the shop or garden centre and *do* select a spade or fork which is *not* heavy for you personally. Good balance is another useful buying point. Although the beautiful stainless steel tools reduce effort, especially in the wet or heavier soils, they are quite expensive and a good steel untreated design will prove just as useful–but do keep the tools clean.

There are smaller editions of the digging spade and fork known as the border spade and fork (2). The working heads (blade or tines) are much smaller and generally the two tools are lighter to handle. They can be used for general work but are especially useful for cultivating in between plants.

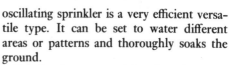

Garden Tools

a new garden is being created. There will be a lot of soil and rubble to move about and even in the established garden, the wheelbarrow can be kept busy throughout the year. There are autumn leaves to collect, not to mention all those grass mowings. Several types of wheelbarrow are available with large or small capacities. The lightweight yet strong design with two wheels (8) is highly manouverable. The sloping front and closeness to the ground enables the user to tip it forward and sweep debris into it.

A length of good quality hose will be required for watering in and around the garden. There are new designs available now with specially strengthened walls which withstand high water pressures. It is very important that a hose pipe is stored correctly, otherwise it becomes kinked and splits may occur. The purchase of a hose reel or holder (9) will be a sound investment.

oscillating sprinkler is a very efficient versatile type. It can be set to water different areas or patterns and thoroughly soaks the ground.

Pruning is an essential task and a good pair of secateurs is essential. There are heavy-duty models which will deal with quite tough wood as well as lightweight models which can be conveniently slipped into the pocket. Normally, a general purpose type (11) which is strong enough to deal with a wide variety of woods and thicknesses will be adequate.

For planting large specimens such as trees, shrubs etc, the spade can be used, but for smaller plants a hand trowel and fork (10) should be used. A stainless steel pair would be a good investment. Comfortable, smooth handles are important.

One of the most useful pieces of equipment is a lawn-mower. The range of machines is considerable and the choice will be conditioned by the area and type of grass which has to be cut. For the average lawn, a 12–14 in. cylinder mower is suitable, especially where a good close cut is desired. The rotary mower will cut reasonably rough, tough and tall grass as well as the normal domestic lawn, but it will give a close cut. For complete ease of starting the electric mower or the battery-powered types should be selected. The former are available in light, easy to manoeuvre designs or in larger and heavier forms for larger grass cutting requirements. The battery-powered mowers are heavy but are still ideal for the woman

Another essential tool is the rake (3). Try to purchase one which has at least 10 teeth. The more teeth there are the better the finish or break down of the soil which can be achieved. Many teeth will also ensure easier and better coverage of seeds and seed drills. Cross-raking of the soil surface (4) will produce a better break down of large soil particles and will ensure a finer finish.

There are many different hoe designs. A draw hoe (5) is very useful for taking out seed drills and for earthing-up operations. The Dutch hoe (6) is essential for keeping down weeds. A useful variant of the Dutch hoe is one which has two serrated cutting edges (7). This can be used with a push-pull action and deals with weeds very efficiently.

A wheelbarrow can play an essential part in the routine garden work, especially where

The correct application of water is important also and a sprinkler will ensure this. Many different versions are on the market and these provide coverages which will suit the small garden or the very large one. An

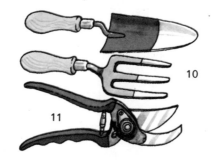

gardener, provided the machine has not to be negotiated over steps or other difficult places. Battery mowers are easy to recharge as they are supplied with a special charger. During the winter, an occasional charge should be given.

Grass-collection is a point worth considering when the rotary mowers are being looked at. Some of the cheaper models do not have this facility. Others have a simple yet efficient designed 'solid' box.

Pest and disease control depends a lot on efficient spraying equipment. The capacity of the sprayer should be closely considered and for the larger garden the compression or pressure sprayer is most suitable. Some of the simpler types have a suction hose with strainer which is placed in a container or bucket of spray. Long-reach lances with adjustable nozzles are other good buying points.

Anemone centred

Bract

Adventitious A plant growth, usually a root or shoot, that arises from an unexpected position. For example, aerial roots that appear at the base of a sweet-corn stem, or from branches of forsythia or willow that touch the ground. The leafy shoots that arise directly from the roots of raspberry and elm are further examples. Sometimes flowers are adventitious on older branches or from the trunk. Crab and culinary apples sometimes do this and it is usual in the Judas tree.

Aerial Root Any root that arises above ground, usually in an adventitious way from a stem. (See Adventitious.)

Air Layering (See Layering.).

Alpine In the strict sense, this refers to plants that are native to mountains, thriving only in the zone above where trees will not grow. In the garden, however, it covers all small-growing plants suitable for a rock garden or alpine house.

Alternate Referring to the arrangement of leaves on the stem. Leaves arise singly from a node (q.v.) and grow out on alternate sides of the stem, one above the other. Examples are elm, broad bean and the commoner species of ceanothus.

Anemone-Centred Usually referring to composite (q.v.) flowers in which the central florets are elongated and together form a prominent boss or cushion. Presumably the term arose in likeness to the double-flowered St Brigid anemones. A good example is the group of chrysanthemums known as anemone-centred. The term is also sometimes applied to certain varieties of ranunculus and peony in which the stamens are turned into narrow petaloids (q.v.).

Annual In the strict sense a plant which grows from seed, flowers and dies within a year. The term is also used for certain perennials, such as antirrhinum, gaillardia and *Cobaea scandens*, which can be grown and flowered from seeds in one growing season.

Anther (See Stamen.)

Axil The junction between a leaf stalk and the parent stem at a node (q.v.) and from where side-shoots or flowers appear in due course. In deciduous trees and shrubs resting buds are formed here which grow out the following spring.

Beard or Bearded A localized tuft or zone of hairs, usually on the petals of certain flowers. Examples are the central zone of yellow, blue or white hairs found on the lower petals (or falls, q.v.) of a tall bearded or flag iris and the tuft of hairs on the lower lip of certain penstemons. Certain grasses, notably barley and the ornamental squirrel-tail (*Hordeum jubatum*) are spoken of as bearded.

Bedding Plant Any plant used for a temporary massed display, being removed and often dis-

carded when its flowering period is finished. The best examples can be seen in the bedding schemes of our public parks. Many kinds of plants are used; annuals, both hardy and tender, bulbs, and even greenhouse perennials or shrubs.

Bell-Glass A bell-shaped glass cover originating in France and used to produce early vegetable crops. It can also be used to root cuttings and raise seedlings. The French name is cloche, which in Britain is now used to describe a structure of glass sheets or plastic. (See also Cloche.)

Berry In the true botanical sense a fleshy fruit with several small seeds embedded within. Examples are gooseberry, currant, grape, tomato

The Gardener's Glossary

and, although regarded as vegetables by many people, marrow and cucumber. The term is also used to describe any small fleshy fruit, notably blackberry and raspberry, each so-called fruit of which is really a collection of small drupes (q.v.).

Biennial In the strict sense, a plant which, raised from seeds, produces a rosette of leaves the first year, flowers the following year then dies. Examples are Canterbury bell, common foxglove and certain species of meconopsis and verbascum. (See also Monocarpic.)

Blind A term used when the growing point of a plant fails to develop properly or dies and there is no resumption of growth from that point. Seedling cabbages and cauliflowers often exhibit this state. Chrysanthemum, dahlia, tulip and other plants sometimes fail to mature flower buds and are then also described as blind.

Bolt, Bolting Usually referring to vegetables, such as lettuce, radish, beetroot and spinach that shoot up to flower before maturing properly. This is particularly likely to happen if the plants receive a severe check.

Bonsai A technique for producing miniature replicas of mature trees by careful root and stem pruning and training, originating in China and Japan. The most valuable bonsai are, however, originally collected as naturally gnarled and dwarfed specimens from exposed mountain sides which are further trained and improved.

Bottle Garden The using of closed glass containers for growing plants in the home. Large bottles such as carboys are ideal, though even smaller containers can house one or two plants. This method is ideal for growing the more delicate plants, particularly ferns, that require a humid, dust-free environment, though a wide range of house plants can be grown. Aquaria and terraria may also be used for the same purpose and are a near approach to the glazed boxes in-

vented early in the nineteenth century by Dr Nathaniel Ward. Known as Wardian cases, these containers were invaluable for transporting living plant material on long ocean voyages. Often in fancy shapes, they also became the rage in Victorian homes.

Bottom Heat The heating of the soil or other growing media from below, generally in propagating frames, but also in greenhouses, and sometimes even outside, for bringing plants along ahead of their normal season. Nowadays, this is usually done by means of electrically warmed wires. Before this invention it was usual either to place the propagating frame over the hot water pipes in a greenhouse or to use the natural heating of a manure bed – the hot-bed system.

Bract A reduced or modified leaf which takes various forms. In its most conspicuous form it acts as a petal and can be brightly coloured, for example the poinsettia flower head is made up of bright red bracts and small greenish flowers. The large white 'petals' of the dove or pocket handkerchief tree (*Davidia*) are also bracts as are the white or pink flushed 'petals' of the flowering dogwoods (*Cornus florida* and *C. nuttallii*). Bracts may also be small and scale-like, often protecting flower buds in their immature state.

Break A term mainly used to describe the branching which takes place after a young growing shoot has had the tip pinched or broken out to promote a bushy habit. In chrysanthemums, particularly certain varieties, the stem terminates in an abortive bud. This forces the stem to produce lateral or side shoots and is often called the break bud. Break is also used to describe the opening of flower buds. Tulips and wallflowers sometimes produce flowers with stripes and flakes of another colour. Some forms of tulip are even grown like this under variety names. The breaking of the colour is due to a virus and such blooms are spoken of as broken.

Broken (See Break.)

Bud A tightly closed immature flower or an embryo shoot. The latter is mainly restricted to deciduous trees and shrubs and appears as a small knob in the leaf axil towards the end of summer. It is protected by several, usually brown, sheathing scale leaves or bracts (q.v.). Similar buds appear on the crowns of such herbaceous perennials as peony and bugbane (*Cimicifuga*). These dormant, or winter, buds have characteristic shapes and on fruit trees, for example, it is possible to distinguish between the flower (or fruit) and leaf or growth buds. Apple flower buds are plump and cone shaped and are usually borne on short spur twigs, while the growth buds are much smaller and flattened against the twigs.

Bonsai

Bottle garden

The Gardener's Glossary

Budding A method of propagating fruit and ornamental trees and roses by inserting a single bud of a named variety or scion into a rootstock. (See Stock and Scion). During the summer plump buds are sliced from a healthy vigorous stem with a shield-shaped piece of bark and wood about 1 in. long attached. A T-shaped incision is next made low down on the stem of the stock and the two triangular flaps gently prised up. The bud is then slipped into this incision and any surplus length of shield cut level with the cross of the T. Finally the bud must be bound firmly with raffia or plastic tape. If the bud remains plump and firm at the end of three to four weeks after the operation, it has 'taken' and the binding material may be severed down the side opposite the bud, but not removed. The following spring as the buds are swelling, the stock growth above the bud is removed.

Bulb, Bulbil Essentially, a bulb is a type of bud with the outer scale leaves modified to fleshy storage organs. The base of the bulb is a very short flattened stem, in the centre of which are borne the immature leaves and flowers. These are fully formed by late summer and sit protected in the bulb until the warmth of spring brings about active cell expansion. The bulb is a resting and storage organ which tides a plant over an inclement season, usually a very dry or cold period. There are two main kinds of bulbs, those with leaf-like scales as in the lilies and those like the daffodil and tulip with very broad scale leaves that are wrapped around each other. Bulbs are generally underground, although some partially project above the soil surface. Bulbils are very small bulbs, usually occurring in the axils of leaves on the stems of certain lilies and dentarias. Many plants having a fleshy rootstock, which botanically may be a corm, tuber or rhizome are often spoken about as bulbous. Also, many epiphytic orchids have swollen stems which are known as pseudo-bulbs.

Callus A wound tissue of corky cells that form over any damaged stem, leaf-stalk or root. It originates from a thin layer of actively growing tissue just under the bark. Callus is particularly noticeable at the base of a cutting that is just about to root, forming a rounded whitish knob.

Calyx (See Sepal.)

Campanulate Bell-shaped, usually referring to the form of a flower, either corolla or calyx. Canterbury bell and shell-flower or bells of Ireland, are examples of a bell-shaped corolla and calyx respectively.

Campanulate flower

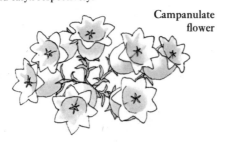

Chimaera It is not an uncommon sight to see flowers, chrysanthemum is one of the more frequent examples, with one or more petals of a different colour from the rest. Sometimes one or more complete blooms on a plant are so affected. This is technically a mutation or 'sport'. Mutations of this kind, where two kinds of dissimilar tissue are found side by side, are also known as chimaeras (also spelt chimera), from the legendary monster of this name with the body of a goat, the head of a lion and a snake's tail. Variegated plants with stripes or splashes of colourless mutant tissue (which appear white or cream by reflected light) are also examples commonly met with. Sometimes the mutant tissue forms a complete layer on the outside of a plant or plant organ, in the same way that a glove covers a hand. The russet-skinned potato 'Golden Wonder' is of this origin. If shoots can be induced to form from the inner tissue and are grown on, the original 'Langworthy' variety develops. The variegated form of mother-in-law's tongue (*Sansevieria trifasciata* 'Laurentii') is of similar origin and if propagated by leaf cuttings (where shoots arise from the inner tissue) the resultant plantlets are of the original non-variegated species. Chimaeras can arise artificially on grafted plants. The best known example is *Laburnocytisus adamii* where the tissues of the laburnum stock and purple broom scion have become joined together, the resulting tree bearing shoots and flowers of both plants side by side.

Chromosome All living creatures, including plants are made up of numerous microscopic units or cells. An essential part of the contents of each cell are the chromosomes, minute rod-shaped bodies which are made up of bead-like structures known as genes. The genes are the basic units of inheritance, passing on from one generation to the next all the basic characteristics such as flower shape and colour, leaf shape, degree and type of hairiness, etc. Each species of plant and animal has a set number of chromosomes to each cell. Growth takes place by each cell dividing in two. When this takes place the chromosomes divide also. Chromosomes in the cells of leafy shoots (body cells) all split in two, a complete set migrating into each new cell. In the sex cells, however, which will eventually develop into seeds, the chromosomes do not split but divide into two equally numbered groups. For example in the body cells of sweet violet there are 20 chromosomes, while in the sex cells there are 10. Sex cells in plants are known as ovules (female) and pollen grains (male). So, when the pollen grain unites with the ovule the two sets of 10 chromosomes come together forming the usual complement of 20 and uniting characters from each parent. The basic number of chromosomes in each body cell is known as the diploid (two sets) number, those in the sex cells as the haploid (half set) number. Sometimes a plant has double the diploid number and is then known as a tetraploid, having four sets instead of the normal two. This state can be induced by drugs such as colchicine, or radiation by X-rays and radioactive substances. Tetraploid flowers and vegetables are often larger and more sturdy and may crop more heavily.

Cloche A temporary structure of glass sheets and wire clips, or plastic sheeting supported on cane or wire hoops, for covering rows of vegetable or flower crops to hasten their maturity. The modern cloche evolved from the bell-glass (q.v.).

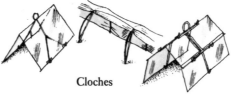

Cloches

Clone A term to cover all the plants raised by vegetative means from a single individual. It is particularly used for named varieties of garden flowers, vegetables and fruits. For example, all bushes of the rose 'Peace', provided they are raised by budding, grafting or cuttings, are members of the same clone; the same is true of all plants of 'Royal Sovereign' strawberry if raised from runners, or 'Mount Hood' daffodil if raised from a splitting of the original bulb.

Composite A plant belonging to the daisy family, botanically known as *Compositae*. This family, the largest among the flowering plants, contains over 900 genera and almost 14,000 species. It is typified by having numerous tiny tubular flowers, known as florets, clustered together on a disk-shaped flattened stem tip known as a receptacle. There are two kinds of florets, those with six tiny petals arranged around the top (the disk florets) and those with the petals fused together and drawn out into a strap-shaped organ like a single petal (the ray florets). The two forms are often present in one head, as in the common lawn daisy which has closely packed yellow disk florets surrounded by a ring of white, strap-shaped ray florets. In the dandelion all the florets are strap-shaped and in the cornflower the outer disk florets are larger and much more elongated than those in the centre.

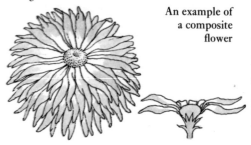

An example of a composite flower

Compost A term with two different meanings.
1. A brown crumbly peat-like substance resulting from the decay or breakdown of plant and or, animal remains. This is most efficiently achieved by building an enclosure or bin of gapped boards or chicken wire in which is placed vegetable remains from the kitchen, grass mowings, pea and bean haulms and other trimmings from the vegetable plot, manure etc. Diseased material should not be used. The bacteria that break down the plant and animal remains require abundant nitrogen and to get a quick and efficient breakdown a nitrogenous fertilizer must be applied; sulphate of ammonia or Nitro-chalk are suitable and should be spread over the surface of the heap at 3–4 oz. per square yard as soon as a layer of 6–9 in. has built up. The stack or heap should not rise above 5 ft. or exceed this measurement in width, so that air can penetrate easily. If the weather is dry the heap should be kept moist by watering.

2. Compost also refers to the rooting medium used for growing plants in pots or other containers. Traditionally, this medium was a mixture of loam, peat and coarse sand, sometimes with the addition of well-decayed manure. The components of a compost of this sort can be varied in quantity to suit the needs of the plant. A standardized compost which is still much used is that formulated by the John Innes Institute and consists of 7 parts of loam, 3 parts of peat and 2 parts of sand, plus a 2–2–1 mixture of hoof and horn, superphosphate and powdered chalk at 5 lb. per cubic yard. Nowadays, more simple mixtures of peat and sand or peat alone, plus nutrient fertilizers, are used, especially for short-term pot plants.

Cone The woody fruiting spike of a coniferous tree (pine, larch, fir, cedar and cypress) composed of a central axis bearing overlapping woody scales which shelter the seeds. Cones of cypress have angular umbrella-shaped scales which touch but do not overlap. Some cypress cones are barely as big as a pea, while the cone of Coulter's pine is larger than a pineapple and weighs up to 5 lb. Not all coniferous trees bear cones; yew and the maiden-hair tree (ginkgo) have fleshy fruits. Some plants that are not related to the conifers have cone-like structures, notably cycads and the primitive spore bearing horse-tails (equisetum).

Cone

Conifer Any tree or shrub which bears cones. (See Cone above).

Cordate (See Leaf Shapes).

Cordon A fruit tree or bush, usually apple, pear or gooseberry trained to a single stem with very small side branches. Sometimes, particularly with gooseberry, two or three stems are grown up from the same root; double or triple cordons. Apples and pears grown as cordons are particularly suitable for the small garden as they take up very little room and several varieties may be grown in the space normally required for one traditional orchard tree.

Corm, Cormlet, Cormel A bulb-like organ which consists of a short, greatly thickened stem clothed with papery or fibrous scale leaves; crocus, gladiolus and acidanthera are familiar examples. Tiny corms that form around the base of a larger corm or on the stem of such plants as *Watsonia bulbillifera* are known as cormlets or cormels.

Cotyledon The name given to the first leaf or leaves that are present in the seed and emerge on germination. These seed leaves, as they are also known, must not be confused with the first true leaves that occur first above the ground in such plants as garden peas and runner beans. In these plants, the cotyledons remain below ground as food reserves. Cotyledons are frequently a different shape from the true leaves that follow; those of cabbage, for example, are inverted heart-shaped, quite distinct from the adult cabbage, while the broad, wavy, kidney-shaped cotyledons of the common beech tree are nothing like the adult ovate leaves. One can frequently identify a plant species from the shape of its cotyledons and this knowledge can be especially useful in distinguishing weeds from the sown crop at an early age. The flowering plants can be divided into two groups on the number of cotyledons present in the seed, Monocotyledons with one seed leaf and Dicotyledons with two. Monocotyledons are mainly grassy-leaved plants and include the true grasses, rushes, orchids, and most bulbous plants. Dicotyledons usually have broader leaves and include most trees and shrubs and such familiar plants as daisy, buttercup, borage, delphinium and antirrhinum.

Crown, Crown Bud The term crown is usually applied to that part of a border perennial plant at soil level, or just below, where young growth emerges each spring. The best examples are those herbaceous perennials such as peony and golden rod which die back to the crown each autumn and form resting buds just beneath the soil. Crown is also applied to the whole rootstock, with resting buds attached, of such plants as lily-of-the-valley and rhubarb when they are lifted for forcing, or for sale. Crown is also an alternative name for the cup, trumpet or corona of such flowers as daffodils and narcissi. Crown bud is a term used by chrysanthemum growers for a particular kind of flower bud. Depending on the variety, chrysanthemum plants are stopped (q.v.) once or twice to promote branching and to secure flower buds that will open at a particular time. Flower buds that appear after a first stopping are known as first crown buds and those appearing after a second stopping the second crown buds. A further distinguishing feature of these buds is that they are surrounded by shoot buds which will grow into leafy stems and subsequently produce further flower buds unless removed while young. Alternatively, if the crown bud is removed these lateral shoots will produce a later crop of blooms.

Cultivar A term derived from an abbreviation of cultivated variety. A cultivar (also further abbreviated to cv.) is a variant or mutant form of a species or hybrid, sufficiently distinct to merit a separate name, and maintained in cultivation. It may arise as the result of the plant breeder's skill or as a chance seedling or mutation. It is not necessary for the chance seedling or mutation to have arisen in the garden. For example, colour variants and double-flowered mutants often arise in the wild but soon die out because they are sterile. Propagated vegetatively, however, and maintained in cultivation by this means they are then best considered as cultivated varieties, or cultivars. Cultivars, because they are not part of a naturally breeding wild population should not be given names of Latin form as are true botanical varieties, forms or subspecies. The *International Code of Nomenclature for Cultivated Plants* recommends that all cvs be given fancy names, only those names of Latin form given prior to January 1959 being still valid. An example of an old name of Latin form that is legitimate and is retained is *Cornus alba* 'Elegantissima'. Note that the name is in Roman lettering, starts with an initial capital letter and is enclosed in single quotation marks. This is to distinguish it clearly from a true botanical variety which is always written with a lower case initial letter and set in italics thus: *Rosa banksiae normalis* (the original wild, creamy white single-flowered Banksian rose). All fancy names must also be enclosed in single quotes and have a capital initial, for example Rose 'Peace', *Erica carnea* 'Springwood Pink'.

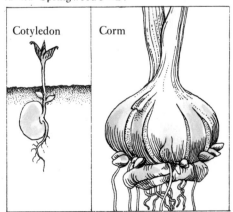

Cotyledon | Corm

Cutting The name for a particular method of vegetative propagation, whereby a piece of stem or leaf is severed from the parent plant and induced to form roots of its own. In its simplest form, a cutting consists of a length of stem, usually severed beneath a node (q.v.), and placed in a suitable rooting medium. Stem cuttings of this type can be divided into three sorts; hardwood, semi-hardwood and soft. Hardwood cuttings are used for trees and shrubs, mature ripened stems about 1 ft. long being inserted into the open ground in late autumn; mock orange (*Philadelphus*), poplar and black-currant are good examples. Semi-hardwood cuttings are taken from mid to late summer and consist of side shoots that are just becoming woody at the base. Such cuttings are usually placed in a propagating frame in sand or peat and sand medium; examples are provided by ceanothus, pyracantha and heathers. Soft wood cuttings are made from soft, sappy shoot tips and placed in a propagating case, often with bottom heat (q.v.): examples are geranium (zonal pelargonium), busy Lizzie (*Impatiens*) and cherry pie (*Heliotropium*). Modifications of the stem cuttings are bud cuttings, either with or without the leaf attached. In the grape vine, the ripened stem of the previous season's growth is cut into one bud sections, each about 1 in. long. These have a thin slice removed from the stem away from the bud and are buried shallowly so that the bud only projects above the rooting medium. Leaf bud cuttings may be made of such woody evergreens as camellia. In this case, the bud, with leaf attached is removed from the stem by slicing through just behind the bud taking a shield-shaped piece of wood with it. These cuttings are inserted in the rooting medium by just burying the bud and shield at an oblique angle. Several plants can be propagated by either whole or sections of individual leaves. Most plants that have somewhat or very fleshy leaves, such as begonia, saintpaulia, peperomia, sedum, crassula, can be treated in this way. Saintpaulia is usually propagated by whole leaves with about 2 in. of leaf stalk attached, half of which is inserted in the rooting medium. Peperomia and begonia may be treated in the same way or the leaf blade may be cut into wedges or squares. Such succulent plants as *Sedum stahlii* need only to be placed on the surface of the soil and will soon form roots and new growth.

Damping Off An expression used to cover the effects of several fungi that attack seedlings. These fungi are encouraged by overcrowding and over moist conditions and produce a stem rot near ground level resulting in the toppling and subsequent death of the seedling. Several fungicides are available to cure this condition.

Damping Down The wetting of greenhouse paths and staging to produce extra humidity. This operation is usually carried out during the warmest part of the year and apart from raising the humidity also slightly cools the greenhouse atmosphere. It is particularly beneficial to plants that come from warm countries that enjoy plenty of atmospheric moisture.

Deciduous Referring to plants that lose all of their leaves at the end of each growing season. The best examples are among trees and shrubs such as elm, lime, chestnut, apple and pear.

The Gardener's Glossary

Dibber, Dibble A blunt, pointed tool used for transplanting seedlings and small plants. Depending on the size of the seedlings to be dealt with, a dibber may be about the size of a pencil up to that of a spade handle. An old spade or fork handle top does, in fact, make a good large dibber for transplanting young cabbage plants, etc. Iron points can be fitted, but a blunt point is best as there is less risk of an air pocket forming under the seedling roots. Dibble is an alternative term, but is usually used as a verb, i.e. to dibble out seedlings.

Digitate (See Leaf Shapes.)

Disbudding Referring to the thinning of excess flower buds or shoots. This is done to produce large quality blooms by removing all but the strongest bud or buds in a cluster. Growers of exhibition blooms of such flowers as dahlias, carnations and chrysanthemums need to carry out a rigorous programme of disbudding.

Disk The swollen or inflated stem tip of members of the daisy family, upon which are borne the small flowers or florets. See Composite.

Division A method of propagating clump-forming perennial plants by pulling or breaking them apart into smaller pieces, each with one or more rooted shoots. Dense or woody herbaceous perennials such as Michaelmas daisies, golden rod, phlox and pyrethrum are best levered apart by inserting two forks back to back, tines vertical, into the centre of the clump and pulling the handles together. Greenhouse perennials such as streptocarpus and saintpaulia should be treated more gently, the individual tufts or rosettes being severed with a sharp knife.

Dot Plant An expression used for individual plants of character dotted in among lower bedding plants to lend height and contrast. A common example would be the use of heliotrope grown on a stem or leg, planted among petunias, tagetes, geraniums or other spreading flowering or foliage bedding plants.

Double Flower Referring to flowers with more than the normal number of petals. These extra petals are usually modified stamens and known as petaloids (q.v.). Good examples are carnation, many varieties of peony, ranunculus (buttercup), camellia and hybrid tea roses.

A double-flowered camellia and peony

Drawn Used of plants that are thin and pale, with extra long internodes (q.v.) as a result of being overcrowded or grown where there is insufficient light. Badly drawn plants, particularly those of vegetables take a long time to recover and are often always weak. For this reason attention must be paid to the siting of such plants, making sure that they are given plenty of space and away from shaded areas.

Drill The narrow depression or furrow made with a pointed stick or the corner of a hoe for the purposes of sowing seeds. Alternatively it can be used as a marker for setting out plants in rows. Drill depths for seed sowing must suit the seed size; the smaller the seed the shallower the drill. After sowing, displaced soil is gently raked on top and firmed with the back of a rake or hoe.

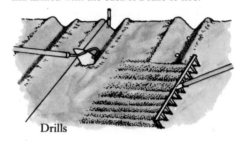
Drills

Drupe Fleshy, one-seeded fruits, the seed protected by a 'stone' (q.v.), are botanically known as drupes. Cherries and plums are examples, as also are the separate sections of the fruits of blackberries, loganberries and raspberries.

Earthing-up The act of drawing soil up around the base of a plant, usually to blanch the base, as in celery, or to prevent light getting to a crop such as potatoes. Sometimes it is necessary to earth up such plants as tall winter cauliflower or sprouts to stabilize them against strong winds.

Elliptic (See Leaf Shapes.)

Epiphytic A term applied to a plant which grows upon another, using it merely as a support and drawing no nourishment from its host as do parasites. In temperate and tropical rain forests many species of orchids and bromeliads grow on tree branches, drawing their sustenance from the air, rainfall and the detritus resulting from decaying leaves and mosses.

Eye As a horticultural term, eye usually refers to single dormant buds such as are found on a potato tuber or on the crown of a cluster of dahlia tubers. It also refers to buds on woody plants such as grape vines, particularly when the stems are cut into single bud cuttings for propagation purposes. Eye can also refer to the centre of a flower when it is of a contrasting colour to the rest of the blooms; single-flowered border pinks provide good examples. The flowers of primroses and other *Primula* species are sometimes spoken of as pin-eyed or thrum-eyed. This refers to whether the stigma or stamen cluster are visible in the centre of the flower; the stigma looking like a pin head and the stamen cluster a thrum or tassel.

Falcate (See Leaf Shapes.)

Falls Referring to the three outer petals of an iris flower which curve outwards and, in some species, hang vertically.

Family A unit of plant classification. Plants are classified and named primarily on the basis of floral similarity. Individual plants are species (q.v.) (or a form or variety of a species) and are the basic units of classification. Species with flowers of the same basic structure are grouped together into assemblages called genera, and genera with affinities in common are grouped together into larger units known as families. Thus all the genera with daisy-like flowers, for example *Bellis*, *Chrysanthemum*, *Dahlia*, *Aster*, *Tagetes*, etc., are grouped in the family *Compositae*.

Fasciation A term applied to freak plant growth that takes the form of several stems fused together side by side. This produces a ribbon or strap-shaped stem, often ribbed and bearing many more leaves than usual. Many border plants

may produce stems of this kind, notably lupin, delphinium, lilium and pyrethrum. Shrubs also may bear fasciated stems, *Forsythia intermedia* 'Spectabilis' being particularly prone. Several cacti and other succulents produce this multiple growth and are known as cristate, such plants being sought after by collectors. The exact cause of fasciation is not known, but it is thought that damage to the minute growing point of the shoot, perhaps by insects such as the capsid bugs, may be the initial cause.

Fastigiate Referring to the habit, mainly of certain trees and shrubs, that have a narrow head of erect growing branches. Many fastigiate trees are mutant forms of normal broad-headed species, for example Lombardy poplar is a form of the broad-headed black poplar (*Populus nigra*) and the Japanese cherry 'Amanogawa' is a similar form of the spreading *Prunus serrulata*.

Feathered A maiden tree (q.v.) before the young side shoots or 'feathers' have been removed from the main stem. Sometimes feathered is used to describe those varieties of tulip and carnation etc., which have flowers with contrasting splashes or streaks of another colour. The more usual term for this condition is broken or flaked.

Earthing up celery

Fertilization The coming together and union of the male cell (pollen grain) with the female cell or ovule, resulting in the formation of a seed which, under the right conditions, will grow into a new plant. Fertilization takes place after the pollen has arrived on the stigma (see Pollination). At this point the pollen grain germinates and sends down a tube into the ovary and finally into an ovule where the pollen nucleus fuses with the ovule nucleus.

Filament The stalk which unites the anther to the base of the flower. (See Stamen.)

Forcing The bringing on of vegetables, fruits and flowers ahead of their normal season, by applying artificial heat and sometimes light. Bulbs, flowering shrubs and such vegetables as rhubarb, chicory and seakale all respond to gentle heat, provided the plants have had a short period of rest under cool conditions beforehand.

Form Derived from the purely botanical term *forma*, this means a naturally occurring variant of a species which breeds true from seeds. The variation is usually a small one such as the presence of hairs on the calyx or leaf veins or a change in colour shade. In a more general way, form is used for any plant which is different from its parent and is even applied to strains (q.v.) of vegetables and flowers raised by the breeder.

Frame A low structure of brick, wood or concrete, ideally with a sloping roof, which can be covered with glass or plastic transparent sheeting. Some modern frames are like miniature greenhouses and are glazed down to ground level. Frames have various purposes; to raise plants from seeds or cuttings, to produce early crops of salad vegetables and carrots, etc., to harden off (q.v.) young flower and vegetable plants raised in a heated greenhouse and to over-winter plants which are too tender to stand the winter outside. Artificial heating will be required during the winter to keep the frost out for the more tender plants.

Fungus (plural fungi) A primitive form of plant life which lacks the green colouring matter chlorophyll found in most higher plants. Chlorophyll enables plants to utilize the sun's energy and to produce essential food substances such as sugars. Lacking this ability, fungi have to obtain their food ready manufactured and do so by becoming parasites or saprophytes. A parasite obtains nourishment from living plants and a saprophyte from the remains of dead ones. A fungus plant consists of branching whitish threads often forming a labyrinthine tangle. Fungal threads may also be shades of brown and in some species combine to form stem or root-like structures known as rhizomorphs, e.g. the boot-lace fungus, also called honey fungus from the colour of its fruiting bodies. The fruits or fruiting bodies of fungi are of all shapes and sizes, but the most familiar ones are the mushrooms, toadstools and bracket fungi which are commonly seen on rotting and living trees, on manure and compost heaps, in grass, etc. These fruiting bodies produce spores, minute structures of one or a few cells that reproduce the species by growing into new fungus plants.

Gall Malformed plant tissue caused by a variety of parasitic organisms, notably insect, mite, eelworm, fungus or bacterium. Galls vary greatly in shape and size, each different sort having a characterisitic form; thus the oak marble gall is a woody sphere $\frac{1}{8}$ to $\frac{3}{4}$ in. across, while the artichoke gall of the yew tree resembles a tiny artichoke at the tips of the shoots. Whatever its shape the substance of each gall is entirely derived from the host plant. The gall causer merely provides the stimulus which results in the curiously localized malformed growth known as a gall. Familiar galls of the garden or countryside include oak apple, a soft green or whitish and reddish somewhat knobbly structure, not unlike a small slightly withered apple. On wild rose may be seen the red, mossy, robin's pincushion gall and on willow leaves the reddish swellings of the bean gall sawfly. All these are caused by insect parasites. A tiny mite is the cause of the swollen big bud gall on blackcurrant, while the swollen red distorted leaves on peach–known as peach leaf curl–is due to a fungus. Bacteria cause the similarly distorted leaves on deciduous rhododendrons (azalea gall) and the soft or woody, usually subterranean, lumpy growths known as crown gall which may occur on trees, shrubs and such herbaceous plants as chrysanthemum and dahlia.

Gene (see Chromosome).

Genus A unit of plant classification. Plants are classified mainly on a basis of floral similarity, i.e. same number of sepals, petals, stamens and ovaries of similar form, Individual plants are species (or a form or variety of a species) and are the basic units of classification. Species with flowers of the same basic structure are placed together in an assemblage known as a genus (plural genera). Thus, the bulbous buttercup, the field buttercup, the creeping buttercup, the lesser celandine, water crowfoot, spearwort and corn crowfoot, all with buttercup-shaped flowers, are placed in the genus *Ranunculus*.

Germination The initial stage of growth of a seed. When a seed is placed in a moist position with adequate air and warmth it absorbs water, often noticeably increasing in size, and, after a predetermined period has elapsed (varying from species to species) the seed coat splits and the first root emerges. At a later stage, the seed coat completely ruptures and the seed leaf or seed leaves (see Cotyledon entry) emerge and grow

up into the light. In some plants the cotyledons are fleshy and remain below ground, the first leaves to appear being true leaves.

Glabrous A botanical term meaning without hairs and used to describe plants or plant organs which are hairless.

Glaucous A botanical term meaning blue-white or blue-grey. It is usually used of leaves that have a bluish patina or 'bloom' like that on a plum.

Grafting In the usual sense, this refers to the union of two plants, often closely related but distinct, one providing the root, the other the bud or stem that will eventually grow into a new plant. In a wider sense, this can include natural grafting, but here, two stems or branches, often on the same plant or from separate plants of the same species growing close together, eventually unite. Grafting in the nursery or garden has a twofold purpose; to propagate a particular species or variety and, in fruit trees, to produce a plant of known vigour and performance by using a special clonally reproduced rootstock. Many methods are used to unite the rootstock with the shoot or scion as it is known. Budding (q.v.) is the most commonly used in nurseries, followed by whip and tongue. This latter method involves the top of the stock and the bottom of the scion being sliced off obliquely so that they fit together. Making a small nick in the cut surfaces at a sharp angle forms two small tongues that fit in to each other when stock and union are pushed together. Another common method is rind grafting where the trunk (if a small tree) or the main branches, are cut off cleanly and the scion shoots are inserted between the wood and bark after a long slit has been made. This method is used when one wishes to change the variety of an existing, probably inferior, fruiting tree. Cacti are among the most easy of plants to graft as it is necessary only to press the two cut surfaces together and secure them either with a spine, wooden toothpick or an elastic band.

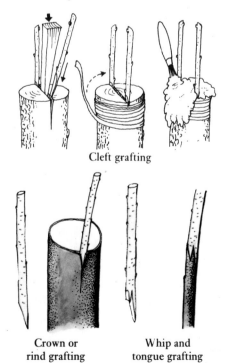

Cleft grafting

Crown or rind grafting   Whip and tongue grafting

Hardy A relative term, depending on the climate of the area where one lives. It means that any given plant will grow outside the whole year round without any artificial protection, and, in particular, will not suffer damage from frosts.

Hastate (See Leaf Shapes.)

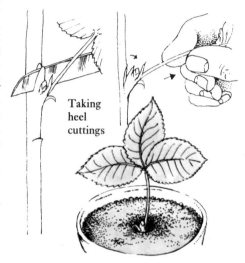

The Gardener's Glossary

Heel Applied to the preparation of a certain type of cutting used for propagation. Semi-hard and hard-wood cuttings (see Cutting) often root more efficiently if a sliver of the parent stem is retained. This is achieved by gently pulling the cutting shoot away from its parent stem (thick cuttings should be sliced off to avoid bruising). The resulting cutting should have a shield-shaped piece of old wood at the base, which, ideally should be trimmed around with a sharp knife to remove the tail of bark and ragged edges.

Taking heel cuttings

Heeling in An expression used to describe the temporary planting of trees, shrubs and other hardy plants that, for one reason or another, cannot be placed in their permanent position. The procedure is to draw out a shallow trench, usually at an angle to the surface of the soil, lay in the plants thickly and cover with the removed soil, or from the next trench if several rows are made. The soil should be lightly firmed and watered if dry.

Herbaceous Any plant which dies down to ground level after each season's growth is completed. In a botanical sense, this includes annuals as well, but in the garden it is usually restricted to hardy border perennials.

Hormone A growth-regulating substance which occurs naturally in plant (and animal) tissue. Such substances are responsible for rate of growth, the bending of plant organs in response to light and gravity, formation of roots, flowers, fruits, etc. Synthetic hormones are now available for garden use and will aid the rooting of cuttings, produce fruits without seeds and prevent premature drop. They can also be used as weed killers, by upsetting the growth rate balance of the plant.

Hose-in-Hose Referring to the abnormal formation of certain flowers, notably primroses, which appear to be two flowers, one sitting within another. There are two types; one, as in the primrose and polyanthus is a kind of doubling (q.v.) with two sets of petals sitting separately one inside the other. The other type is seen in rhododendron and Canterbury bell where the calyx becomes enlarged and coloured the same as the petals or corolla.

The Gardener's Glossary

Hotbed (see Bottom heat).

Humus From a purely gardening point of view, this is the brown, sweet-smelling crumbly substance that results from the efficient break-down of plant and animal remains after composting (see Compost). Pure humus results at a somewhat later stage and is a dark brown colloidal substance, i.e. a jelly-like material, which coats the soil particles. It holds water round soil particles in a sponge-like way without the soil becoming water-logged and is an important medium for soil bacteria. The healthy rhythm of the soil demands that there be a continual flow of humus through the soil. This is achieved by the bacteria breaking down plant and animal remains, which in turn releases essential plant foods, and use the humus itself to feed upon. It is, therefore, a cyclic process which is quickly slowed down if insufficient humus is applied, especially to vegetable crops which are being continually removed and not allowed to die *in situ*.

Hybrid A plant produced by crossing two species, either in the same genus (q.v.) or from different genera. From a horticultural point of view, it is also used to denote crosses between forms and varieties within the same species. Hybrids combine the characters of both parents in varying degrees (see Chromosome). The first generation offspring of hybrid origin may all blend the two sets of parental characters equally, or there may be a range of character expression, some plants resembling one parent, some another, with yet others forming a transition between the two. Sometimes also the characters of one parent are dominant and the first generation progeny all resemble one parent. When hybrids are crossed among themselves or are self pollinated the characters combine and recombine in a complex way, giving rise to a very variable progeny. In this way the plant breeder is able to select plants for particular purposes. However, not all hybrids are fertile, particularly those that are made between the less closely related parents. In such cases, there may be an unequal number of chromosomes as when a diploid and tetraploid are crossed. Sterile hybrids of this origin may sometimes be rendered fertile by artificially doubling the number of chromosomes by the use of such drugs as colchicine or atomic radiation or X-rays. The crossing of two pure breeding strains (see Strain) of a particular species or variety often results in plants which are more vigorous than either parent and are very uniform in appearance. This is known as hybrid vigour and varieties of this origin are known as F_1 hybrids. Many kinds of vegetable and flower seed are of this origin, as a glance at any seedsman's catalogue will show.

Incurved Applied to a particular group of chrysanthemums, the flowers of which have petals (florets) that curve over and into the centre of the blossom.

Inflorescence A term used to describe that part of a plant which bears the flowers. It may be a single flower as in tulip or a large conical cluster as in lilac. Inflorescences are classified by the way they branch and the flowers are borne. The main types, each followed by a familiar example are: spike–lavender; raceme–delphinium; panicle–pampas-grass; umbel–hogweed; capitulum–daisy; corymb–candytuft; cyme (scorpioid) borage, (dichasial) snow-in-summer.

Internode Leaves are borne at points on a stem called a node (q.v.). The internode is the section of bare stem between nodes.

Knot (see Parterre).

Lanceolate (see Leaf Shapes).

Lateral A side-shoot growing out from a leading stem of a tree or shrub. The term is mainly applied to fruit trees as a means of explaining what and how to prune. Broadly speaking, the laterals are the fruit producers, while the leading shoots extend the branch system.

Layering A method of propagation, whereby an aerial shoot is induced to form roots while still attached to the parent plant. This may be achieved by various methods. In the easiest way a shoot is selected that can be bent down to ground level without breaking. The tip is bent in a U-shape and buried in the soil, the U being secured by a peg. Plants usually produce roots more readily if the buried part of the stem is nicked or sliced part the way through, the cut being kept open either by some sand or a tiny stone, or by bending the stem sharply away from the cut. Carnations and many trees and shrubs respond to this method. Hormone (q.v.) rooting compounds may be applied to the cut surface of those species known to be difficult to root. Where it is inconvenient to peg a shoot down to ground level, the layering may be done *in situ* by using plastic sheeting or sleeving secured around the shoot to be rooted and packed with a suitable rooting medium – usually a mixture of sphagnum moss, peat, sand and loam. The mixture must be just moist only and the sheeting or sleeving firmly sealed with adhesive tape; this is known as air-layering. Dense-growing plants such as heaths and heathers may have the centre mounded with peat and sand and when the stems have rooted the whole plant may be separated into small plants ready for permanent sites.

Leaf shapes 1. Acuminate. 2. Cordate. 3. Digitate. 4. Elliptic. 5. Falcate. 6. Hastate. 7. Lanceolate. 8. Linear. 9. Lyrate. 10. Palmate. 11. Pandurate. 12. Peltate. 13. Pinnate. 14. Oblong. 15. Obovate. 16. Orbicular. 17. Ovate. 18. Reniform. 19. Sagittate. 20. Trifoliate.

Legume, Leguminous Any plant which is a member of the great pea family or *Leguminosae*. Legume is the name for a particular kind of seed pod of elongated shape, often laterally flattened, with a single row of seeds. Examples are pea, bean, gorse, broom, laburnum, false acacia, etc. Many legumes rupture suddenly when ripe, the two valves that form it twisting suddenly and projecting the seeds often several feet or more away. Not all species of leguminous plants have the bean-shaped pod; clover, for example has a single-seeded pod which does not explode and the medicks have spirally twisted pods, sometimes with hairs or spines, which are distributed on the coats of animals.

Linear (see Leaf Shapes).

Lyrate (see Leaf Shapes).

Maiden A nursery term for a young tree during the first growing season after budding or grafting and before formative pruning has been carried out. A maiden tree is usually a single stem, but vigorous varieties of fruit or ornamental cherries or crab apples may have a number of laterals and are then spoken of as feathered maidens. (See Feathered).

Monocarpic A botanical term which means once-fruiting and refers to plants which grow to maturity, flower, seed and then die. In the strict sense this refers to annuals and biennials also, but from a horticultural point of view it is used to describe plants which take several years to reach flowering size. *Agave americana*, the so-called century plant is one of the more spectacular examples. It does not take 100 years to reach maturity, but can take anything from 15 to 50 years before it flowers and seeds. Most houseleeks are monocarpic as are several bromeliads and the giant lily, *Cardiocrinum giganteum*. All these plants however usually leave behind a few tiny offsets and it might be argued that they are not truly monocarpic.

Moraine (see Scree).

Mosaic (see Virus).

Mulch A layer or top-dressing of bulky organic matter such as compost, decayed manure, peat, grass mowings, etc. They serve several purposes, to provide a source of plant food, to conserve moisture and keep roots cool and to smother weeds and prevent others growing from seeds. Mulches should not be applied unless the underlying soil is thoroughly moist, and ideally only after the winter cold has left the soil, because the mulch acts as an insulating barrier. Nowadays, black polythene sheeting and aluminium foil are used as mulching materials and though they do not feed the plants, they perform all the other functions.

Mutation An aberrant plant, or part of a plant, that exhibits characters different from the species or variety to which it belongs. Sometimes the mutation may be hardly discernible, then again it may be dramatic, as when a flower changes colour or leaves show white or cream variegation. Such mutations are also called chimaeras (q.v.). Mutations are a result of changes in the genes within the cells of the growing points. Such changes take place as a result of shock. Artificially they can be induced by drugs such as colchicine and the radiation from radioactive substances and X-rays. Certain hormone weedkillers may also be responsible. In nature, mutations are usually the result of the cosmic radiation which continually bombards the Earth. Mutations of this origin provide the variability by which natural selection evolves new forms, species and even genera.

Mycelium (see Fungus).

Nicking and Notching A method used to bring dormant buds into growth, or *vice-versa*, during the formative training period of a young fruit or ornamental tree. Not all buds formed in any one year will break into growth the following season. Many remain dormant and never grow unless those above are damaged by frost, gale or pests. When a nurseryman is training a tree to a particular form he may need a branch where one has not grown naturally. If dormant buds are present, they may be stimulated into growth by removing a small sliver, wedge or crescent of bark, down to the wood, just above a suitably placed bud. This concentrates the sap flow in the vicinity of the bud and usually promotes its growth. This should be done in April or at least just before general bud burst. To render dormant a bud that may be needed later, perhaps as a further lateral growth or a fruiting spur, the nick should be made below the bud in early spring before the buds in general start to swell. Making a cut above a bud is usually called notching and below a bud nicking, but both terms are used indiscriminately for either operation.

Node The point on a stem where the leaves arise. Most plants have only one leaf from a node, others such as privet and lilac have two or more. In the axils of the leaves buds and subsequently branches arise. A node is often known as a joint.

Obovate (see Leaf Shapes).

Opposite Used mainly of leaves that arise two at a node, one opposite the other; privet and lilac provide good examples.

Oval (see Leaf Shapes).

Ovary That part of a flower where the ovules are borne. Some ovaries are within the flower as in buttercup and poppy, others just beneath as in apple and quince. Ovules become seeds when the egg cells they contain are fertilized by the pollen. (see Pollination).

Ovate (see Leaf Shapes).

Palmate (see Leaf Shapes).

Pandurate (see Leaf Shapes).

Papilionaceous Plants bearing pea-shaped flowers, which belong to the *Papilionoideae* section of the *Leguminosae* family. (See also *Leguminous*).

Parterre A French term which began to be used in Britain in the seventeenth century. It refers to a garden area on a level site which is laid out to flower beds in flowing or geometrical patterns edged with low clipped plants such as box. Such beds, especially when of intricate pattern, were known as knots and a garden area composed of them a knot garden. The beds were usually filled with low-growing bedding plants, though in earlier times they may have been surfaced with coloured gravels or sands or turfed over.

Peltate (see Leaf Shapes).

Perennial In a gardening sense, a herbaceous plant (q.v.) which lives at least two years and by implication indefinitely, flowering and seeding year after year. Monocarpic plants are also perennial but flower and seed but once.

Petal, Petaloid Part of a flower. The vital organs of a flower, the ovaries and stamens (q.v.) are in most plants surrounded by two rings of specially modified leaves, the sepals and petals. Both are protective in the bud stage, but when the flower opens, the petals, which are often brightly coloured, become a device for attracting pollinating insects. Petals may be leaf-like and separate as in poppy and buttercup or united into a cup or tube as in gentian, rhododendron and morning glory (*Ipomoea*). Botanically, the ring of petals, whether separate or fused, is known as the corolla. Petaloid refers to the extra petals seen

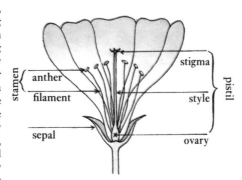

Parterre

in a double flower (q.v.). They are derived from stamens, the anther aborting and the filament becoming expanded into a petal-like organ.

pH A numerical scale used to express the alkalinity and acidity of a liquid, based upon the gradual neutralization of an acid by the addition of an alkali (lime). Chemically, the neutral point is a balance between the hydrogen ions (acid) and hydroxyl ions (alkali). The process has been numerically graded, with 7 as the neutral point. In horticulture this has been applied to the assessing of soil acidity and alkalinity, each number in the scale being given a colour rating also. A soil to be tested is mixed with distilled water and a special indicator (often alcohol of potassium thiocyanate), plus a quantity of barium sulphate to settle the soil rapidly after shaking. The whole is vigorously shaken and allowed to stand. Soon a zone of clear coloured liquid is visible and may be compared with a special chart. Green is neutral, grading down to red for acid and up to blue for alkaline. This is the basis of soil indicator sets that can be purchased from horticultural sundriesmen and chemists.

It is important to know if one's soil is acid or alkaline as certain plants will not grow satisfactorily in one or the other. For example, many of the best flowering shrubs, rhododendron, pieris, kalmia, gaultheria, pernettya, etc., will not tolerate an alkaline soil. Conversely, most of the brassica crops (cabbage, sprouts, cauliflower), do best where lime is present.

Pinch To remove the tip of a shoot with the nails of thumb and forefinger thus encouraging the formation of lateral growths and a more bushy habit.

Pinnate (see Leaf Shapes).

Piping A particular kind of cutting (q.v.) used for propagating pinks and carnations. The tips of a non-flowering shoot of these plants is pulled straight out and without further preparation inserted into the rooting medium.

The Gardener's Glossary

Pistil A term sometimes used for the female organ of a flower. It comprises the ovary, style and stigma (q.v.).

Plunge A bed of ashes, coarse sand, peat, or well-drained soil used for keeping pot-grown plants so that they do not dry out so readily and are not toppled by wind. The pot is either buried flush with the rim or, for young shrubs in a soil plunge, buried an inch or so deep. Bulbs in pots or bowls being prepared for blooming indoors are also plunged several inches deep until a good root system is formed.

Pollard Derived from the word poll, meaning to cut short, this term is used of trees that have all their branches removed back to the trunk at regular intervals. It is done to willows or osiers to produce the young pliant shoots for basket making called withes. In the garden, certain trees that have coloured bark on young shoots, especially *Salix alba* 'Chermesina' ('Britzensis'), are cut back annually to maintain a colourful winter display.

Pollen, Pollination Pollen grains are the male sex cells of a plant and are borne in anthers (q.v.) within the flower. Although very tiny, pollen grains are very variable in shape and size and often exhibit exquisitely sculptured surfaces when viewed under a microscope. Some grains are adapted to be carried by the wind and have small air sacs to make them buoyant, some have a rough surface to enable them to adhere to the furry bodies of insects, yet others are borne in sticky chains which enable them to stick readily to the insect visitors. Pollination is effected when the pollen grains reach and adhere to the stigma (q.v.). Once there the grain germinates and sends out a tube-like growth to the ovary. (see Fertilization).

Pompon Refers to the shape of a double flower, in particular a type of dahlia with a small rounded flower head. Pompon is a French word meaning a top-knot or tuft.

Pot A container for growing plants. Formerly pots were always made of a porous baked clay, but nowadays various kinds of plastic materials are also used. Traditionally pots are inverted, truncated cones in shape, sometimes with an expanded rim for safer stacking. Depth and width ratios vary greatly and those which are wider than they are deep are known as pans. All pots have drainage holes in the bottom to allow surplus water to get away rapidly. There is now a wide range of fancy pots, some square in outline, others straight tubular. Others are united at their rims into units and are useful for propagating purposes. Pots for growing epiphytic orchids are specially made with large holes round the sides for extra ventilation. Pots are classified in two ways; by the inside top diameter measurement and cast size. Cast size can only be applied to the clay pots, a cast being a lump of clay, from which one to many pots can be made, grading 1 to 72 and above. For example if one pot only is made from the cast this is number 1, if 16 are made these are no. 16s, if 60 they are known as 60s. The pots of each cast size have a more or less constant inside diameter, a no. 1 being 18 in. across, a 16 being 8½ in. across and a 60 varying from 3–3½ in.

Pricking Out or Off This is an expression used to describe the operation of transplanting small seedlings from the pot, pan or box in which they were sown, to a larger receptacle or nursery bed. The seedlings are gently eased out with a pointed stick or label so as not to damage the roots and placed singly in holes made with a dibber (q.v.). The seedlings are firmed by pushing in the side of the hole with the point and side of the dibber. Seedlings should be pricked off as soon after the cotyledons (q.v.) have expanded as possible and while the root system is still small or unbranched, as it is very easy to damage such frail young roots and so severely check the growth of the seedling.

Prickle A particular kind of spine which arises as an outgrowth from the surface tissues of a stem. The so-called thorns of a rose are, in fact, prickles. (see also Spine).

Propagation A general term for all methods of increasing or reproducing plants. (see Budding, Cutting, Division, Germination, Grafting, Layering.

Pruning The controlled cutting back of a plant, usually a tree or shrub, with a particular end in view. Pruning is carried out for one of the following reasons: to keep a plant within bounds; to remove dead or diseased growth; to control the fruiting capacity of a fruit tree; and to train a young tree, shrub or other plant to a particular form. Pruning of any kind tends to promote further, often more vigorous, growth; the harder a shoot is cut back, the more vigorous the response. This vigour can be harnessed in various ways. For example hybrid tea roses when cut hard back will produce robust stems and large flowers of high quality. Shrubs and trees which rely upon brightly coloured stems for their main attraction, for example *Cornus alba* 'Sibirica' and *Salix alba* 'Chermesina' ('Britzensis'), can have this feature heightened by cutting back hard annually to promote extra long vigorous shoots. Clean cuts which heal rapidly and thus lessen disease risks should always be aimed at. Always use a sharp knife or secateurs and special pruning saws for the larger stems and branches. Large wounds should be covered with bitumastic paint to prevent fungal infection.

Puddling An ancient planting practice seldom used nowadays. It involves the dipping of a plant's roots into a slurry of soil and water prior to planting. This is said to help the plant to root and grow away quicker and to protect against drought. Some of the older gardeners also believed that it was a protection against root fly of cabbages and related crops. There is, however, no modern evidence to substantiate any of these claims.

Pyramid A name given to a particular trained form of fruit tree, usually pear and sometimes apple. The resulting trees grow up to 20 ft. and more tall and are now seldom seen and unobtainable commercially. Nowadays, the dwarf pyramid has taken its place and is used mainly for apples. It is a small tree on a dwarfing rootstock and is very suitable for the suburban garden and for intensive orchard practice. The tree is trained from a maiden (q.v.) by shortening the leader and laterals from a half to two thirds each year with summer pruning from the second or third year onwards. Pruning laterals to an outward pointing bud creates shortish side branches which are almost horizontal. By the third year a roughly pyramidal outline results.

Ray Usually referring to a ray floret of a daisy flower. (see Composite).

Recurved, Reflexed Mainly used to describe a particular kind of chrysanthemum flower head with the florets bent outwards and curving back towards the stem. In a general way these terms can be applied to any plant organ which curves over and downwards.

Reniform (see Leaf Shapes).

Reversion This term is used in several senses in the garden, the most common one being when a variegated plant gradually turns green again because the original green shoots are stronger than the variegated ones. Grafted plants sometimes sucker from the stock and as these growths are often more vigorous than the scion variety they swamp it out unless what is happening is observed early on. This also is spoken of as reverting. Herbaceous plants such as lupins are also said to revert when different coloured flowering spikes appear. What has usually happened is that a seedling has grown up in the centre of the choice variety which then dwindles rapidly and dies out. Reversion is also a term applied to the virus which attacks blackcurrants. This virus reduces the cropping capacity of the bush and produces smaller leaves with fewer lobes, making them appear more like the wild ancestor of the currant.

Rhizome A botanical term for a particular kind of underground stem which spreads the plant through the soil and acts as a storage organ during the dormant summer or autumn/winter period. Bearded irises have thick fleshy rhizomes which are only partly buried in the soil, while our native wild anemone has an equally fleshy but much thinner one well underground. The latter are dormant from late summer until early winter. Not all rhizomes are fleshy, however; the underground stems of couch grass and Yorkshire fog grass are thin, tough and wiry.

An iris rhizome

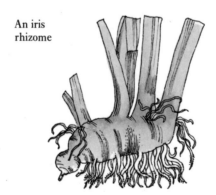

Ridging A method of cultivating the soil so as to expose as large a surface area as possible to the ameliorating actions of frost. Heavy sticky soils containing much clay are treated in this way so that they can be broken down to a good tilth in the spring. The ground to be so treated is marked out into strips about 30 in. wide (or three spades width). As one digs, the centre spadeful is taken out first and the ones to the left and right piled on to either side thus creating a ridge.

Rootstock A term with two meanings in the nursery and garden world. One means a crown (q.v.) with roots attached, the other refers to the stock (q.v.) plant used in budding and grafting which provides the root system of the new plant after grafting.

Ridging

Rosette A ring-like tuft of leaves, usually overlapping, which arise very close together on a short section of stem and spread out horizontally over the soil or at an oblique angle to it. Houseleeks, echeverias, and the first year plants of foxglove and Canterbury bell are good examples. The term is derived from a rose and formerly referred to sculptured or moulded ornaments of rose-like form.

Rotation This refers to the planning of a vegetable garden so that no crop occupies the same patch two years in succession. This helps to minimize the build up of pests and diseases, also some crops do best on freshly manured ground, others are best following such a crop. For example, leafy crops such as cabbages and cauliflower and salad lettuce may be planted after manuring, to be followed by all root crops. A proper rotation should be drawn up for the vegetable garden by dividing it into three equal sections. Each year the crops grown in one section are moved to the next. In this way no crop is grown in the same spot more frequently than every third year.

Runner A slender, fast-growing stem which grows over the surface of the soil rooting and producing plantlets at the nodes (q.v.). This natural method of reproduction is frequently taken advantage of by gardeners and is the sole means of propagating strawberry varieties. The sweet violet and mother-of-thousands (*Saxifraga stolonifera*) are other good examples.

Sagittate (see Leaf Shapes).

Scion A term used in grafting (q.v.), the scion, or graft, being a piece of the plant variety to be propagated, usually a short length of stem, or a single bud as in budding (q.v.).

Scree, Moraine A scree is the usually fan-shaped mass of rock debris that accumulates at the foot of steep mountain slopes as a result of weathering and gravity. A moraine is a similar accretion of rock debris which forms along the margins of and terminates a glacier. Certain plants are characteristic of these rock formations, some growing nowhere else. Generally they are low-growing and often of rosette or cushion-like form. Some are very garden worthy but difficult to grow unless a growing medium like that in their native homeland can be provided. To this end, scree beds are sometimes made by mixing together 8–10 parts of coarse stone chippings (granite or limestone according to the requirements of the species of plants grown), with one part each of loam, peat and sand. This mixture is placed about 18 in. deep, preferably on a sloping site, though a level site may be used if the ground is very free draining. The edges of a bed so formed are best supported by natural boulders, but bricks, concrete blocks or old railway sleepers may be used as substitutes. An extension of this idea is the raised bed for growing rock and alpine plants in general. These are, table-like structures of almost any shape or size, edged with dry-walling about 2–2½ ft. tall and filled with a mixture which contains rather more peat and loam.

Seed Leaf (see Cotyledon).

Selection (see Strain).

Semi-Double Referring to double flowers (q.v.) which have only a few extra petals or petaloids, the centre remaining open with at least some stamens and pistils (q.v.) remaining functional.

Sepal The outer ring of modified leaves which form the flower (see Calyx).

Set As used in horticulture a term with two distinct meanings.

1. Small potatoes, onion bulbs and shallots used for starting off a crop instead of true seeds are spoken of as sets. Up to the end of the last century this term also referred to cuttings, suckers and young plants, and to this day it is usual among nurserymen to talk about setting out young plants when they mean planting out.

2. Set is often used to describe the formation of young fruits just after the flowers fade and forms the basis of the expression 'a good set', meaning that many young fruits are forming.

Shrub A plant with woody stems that increase in length and girth year after year. Such plants are branched at, or close to, ground level and usually do not have a single main stem, or if they do it is very short in relation to the growth above. When a shrub is very large, i.e. above 12 ft. tall, it may then equally be considered as a small tree, regardless of whether it has a main trunk or not.

Single (see Double flower).

Side-Shoot (see Lateral).

Singling (see Thinning).

Snag The stump of a branch, or smaller stem, resulting from bad pruning practice. Such stumps are a source of infection by the fungal diseases silver leaf, coral spot and others. The removal of snags is known as snagging, a term also used for the operation of removing that part of a young budded tree stock above where the bud was inserted and which for the first year is used as a support for the scion shoot.

Snag

Snagging

Soil Block A temporary alternative to the use of pots for short term crops. Moistened potting compost is compressed into blocks, that can be round, square or hexagonal in cross-section, by the use of a specially constructed mould, which also leaves a depression at one end. Into this depression one or two seeds are sown and covered with a little compost in the usual way. The strongest seedling only is retained after germination. This is a particularly good method for raising such plants as tomato, cucumber, melon, zinnia, etc., as they do not suffer a pricking off (q.v.) check. As soon as roots appear on the surface of the block the seedlings should be planted out into permanent positions. Soil blocks should not be handled more than necessary and it is usual to place them in trays after manufacture. Watering must be done carefully with a rose nozzle on can or hose. Peat blocks are used in a similar way. These are purchased ready made.

Spadix A fleshy flower spike, usually unbranched, which bears tiny stemless flowers. This kind of inflorescence is characteristic of the palm and arum families (see also Spathe).

Spathe A modified leaf or bract associated with an inflorescence, usually in a protective way. For example, the papery sheath close to and below a daffodil flower or cluster of 'Paper White' narcissi is technically a spathe. The best examples of spathes are found in the arum family, where they may act as an aid in pollination by trapping tiny insects, as in our native lords and ladies or cuckoo pint, or in the anthurium (also known as 'tail flower' or 'flamingo flower').

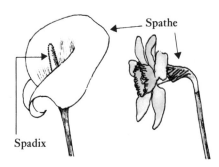

Spathe

Spadix

Species A unit of classification for all living things, members of which are so closely allied as to appear identical to the uncritical eye. In plants, the primary classifactory organs are the flowers and fruits (seed pods). A series of individual plants which have flowers and fruits of identical form are placed in the same species. There may be small differences in size and colour and such variants are known as varieties or cultivars (q.v.). Groups of species are placed in larger units known as genera (singular, genus (q.v.)).

Spike Botanically, an elongated inflorescence, usually unbranched, in which the individual flowers are stalkless, e.g. lavender and mullein. To the gardener, spike is used for any slender, spire-like flower cluster, including such familiar plants as delphiniums, antirrhinums, stocks and hyacinths. In all these, however, the individual flowers have a stalk and the cluster of blooms is botanically a raceme (q.v.).

Spine These are the hard sharp points that appear on the stems or leaves of certain plants and which apparently give protection against grazing animals. The term often, but wrongly, includes prickles (q.v.) and thorns which have different origins. Botanically a spine is a modified leaf – as in gorse, or part of a leaf – as in holly. A thorn is a modified stem which terminates in a point and often bears leaves at its base; hawthorn and firethorn (*Pyracantha*) provide well-known examples. The spines of cacti and those which tip the leaf-like stems of butcher's broom (*Ruscus*) are also technically thorns.

Spit 1. An expression meaning a spade's depth of soil. Thus, one speaks of digging one spit deep, meaning that the soil is dug and turned over to one spade's (or fork's) depth. In the past, spit meant the actual thrust of the spade during digging and the amount of soil that could be lifted with this tool.

2. Prefaced by the word cuckoo, spit also means the spittle-like froth that is made by and protects the soft-bodied young frog-hopper, an injurious sap-sucking insect.

Spore The equivalent of a seed among such primitive plants as fungi, mosses, horsetails, club mosses, and ferns. Spores are microscopic single-cell structures, usually with a thickened or strengthened coat. Unlike true seeds, they often give rise to a plant body that is different from the familiar mature plant. For example, mosses start off as a mass of green threads known as protonema, upon which, eventually the moss plant is borne. Fern spores give rise to small flattened leafy bodies known as prothalli upon which male and female organs are borne. Only when these have fused and fertilization has taken place does the familar fern plant begin to grow. Spores from toadstools and mushrooms and other fungal fruiting bodies produce, usually whitish, threads (see Mycelium and Fungus) which may grow for several years before producing the well-known toadstool.

Sport The more spectacular and often sudden plant changes, such as flower colour and the appearance of white or cream variegations on leaves, are popularly known as sports. The technical term, however, is mutation (q.v.).

Spur There are two definitions of this term.

1. Many flowers, for example columbine, delphinium, violet and nasturtium (*Tropaeolum*) have the petals or sepals drawn out into a hollow projection in which insect-attracting nectar is stored or secreted. These are floral or nectary spurs.

2. Fruiting spurs are the small, often gnarled stems or branchlets of a fruit tree (apple, pear, plum, cherry) which bear the flowers and subsequently the fruits.

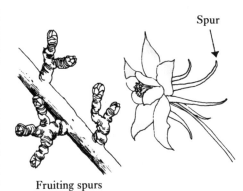

Spur

Fruiting spurs

Stamen The male reproductive organ of a flowering plant, borne within the flower. It is composed of a stalk or filament and an anther. The latter body is usually ovoid in shape and divided into two pollen-bearing cavities known as pollen sacs (see Pollen). Stamen number is usually constant in the flowers of any given species and can vary enormously. For example in Indian shot (*Canna*) each flower has one petaloid stamen only, which bears a half anther, while in all the poppies there are many dozens to each blossom.

Standard A term with two widely differing meanings.

1. Botanically it is the erect, often largest, petal of a pea-flowered plant, or of an iris.

2. Horticulturally, standard is used for a tree or shrub grown on a single unbranched stem or leg. Many weeping trees are grown in this way to display better the pendulous growth habit.

The Gardener's Glossary

Sterile The inability of any plant to produce viable seeds. Certain mutant plants which produce completely double flowers, e.g. the snowball bush (*Viburnum opulus* 'Sterile'), double stocks and the wallflower known as 'Harpur Crewe' are good examples. Some plants, such as the 'hortensia' hydrangeas, have a mixture of sterile and fertile flowers, the sterile ones being much larger and more highly coloured and acting as petals to the small fertile ones which are wholly or partially hidden. Self sterility or incompatibility is found in members of the potato family and among certain fruit trees, notably sweet cherries. In these, special sterility genes prevent the pollen grains from germinating properly down the style of the male flower. To obtain fruit, another cultivar or clone must be planted nearby so that bees can transfer pollen from one tree to the other.

Sterilization Horticulturally this is the act of partially sterilizing soil to kill harmful bacteria, fungi and weed seeds. This can be effected in several ways, the usual and most efficient being by heat. Steaming is frequently used in nurseries and special apparatus has been designed to heat the large quantities of soil needed. The amateur gardener can deal with small amounts of soil in a domestic steamer, provided a temperature of not less than 180°F (82°C) or more than 200°F (93°C) can be maintained for 10 minutes. There are various improvizations for home use, and if a steamer is not available a saucepan can be used and the soil placed in a bag of coarse cloth resting on a grid just above the boiling water. There are also special electric sterilizers in which damp soil is placed between electrodes, the resistance of the soil causing it to heat up and thus sterilizing it. It is most important not to overheat the soil. This will kill all the life present, including the beneficial bacteria, and if hot enough, all humus will be destroyed as well. Soil may also be partially sterilized by chemical means. Such substances as formaldehyde and cresylic acid are watered on to the soil and the fumes trapped by covering the surface with tarpaulins, sacking or plastic sheeting. The disadvantage of these substances is that several weeks must elapse before it is safe to replant or sow seeds.

Stigma The receptive part of a pistil (q.v.) where pollen is caught or held and can then germinate down into the ovary. Stigmas vary greatly in shape and size. Usually they are attached to the ovary by a stalk known as the style (q.v.) but sometimes they sit right on top of the ovary as in the common poppy. Wind pollinated flowers have feathery or hairy stigmas, e.g. those of grasses and trees such as hazel and walnut, to catch the wind-borne pollen grains. Insect-pollinated flowers have sticky stigmas to capture the grains adhering to the bodies of insect visitors; rhododendron is a good example.

Stock A name given to that part of a grafted plant which provides the root system. For example, the stock used for budding roses is usually the wild rose or briar, that for culinary and dessert apples various named clonal selections of crab apple (see Grafting).

Stone The hard seeds of plum, cherry, apricot, peach and nectarine are referred to as stones because of their densely woody almost stone-like texture. For this reason trees that bear fruits of this kind are sometimes spoken of as 'stone fruits'. Stoning is an expression referring to that period in the development of a stone fruit when the hard woody covering of the seed is being formed. It is particularly applied to grapes, though the seeds of grapes are not stones in the strict sense. Botanically, the stone fruits are drupes (see Drupe), fleshy fruits with a single, centrally placed seed arising from a single ovule.

Stool A term with somewhat variable meaning, but basically a plant which produces many shoots from at, or below, ground level. It is often applied to aspects of propagation. For example, a chrysanthemum plant which has finished flowering and has been cut down ready for the young basal shoots to emerge to be be used as cuttings, is spoken of as a stool. Stooling is a method of propagating several trees and shrubs, particularly apple clones to be used as stocks for grafting. The plant to be propagated is cut down close to ground level at planting time. When young shoots have reached about 9–12 in. tall they are earthed up at the base and will subsequently produce roots. At the end of the growing season these rooted shoots are removed and the cycle is repeated, year after year. Stooling is also sometimes used in the same sense as pollarding, particularly when a tree or shrub is grown like a herbaceous plant and cut down to ground level each year to provide a display of extra large decorative leaves, e.g. tree-of-heaven (ailanthus) or paulownia, or coloured stems as with *Cornus alba* 'Sibirica'.

Stopping Basically this is the same as pinching, i.e. to remove the growing tip of a shoot to promote branching. Stopping is particularly important with such plants as chrysanthemums, as it can largely determine the timing and number of flower buds (see Break). Stopping for a different purpose is carried out on crops such as melons, cucumbers and grapes. Grapes are very vigorous and all laterals are pinched out at two leaves beyond the fruit cluster and any subsequent growth is removed back to one leaf. This reduces the vigour and helps to fill out and ripen the fruits. In melons and cucumbers most female flowers are borne on the lateral and sub-lateral shoots, so continuous stopping is aimed at, to produce more of these growths. At the same time, when a fruit has formed, the stem beyond is pinched in the same way as for the grape. Stopping, as for pinching, is carried out with the nails of the thumb and forefinger, or a sharp knife may be used if the shoot is a thick or fleshy one.

Stopping

Stove This is a now largely obsolete term, except in some botanical gardens. A stovehouse is a greenhouse artificially heated to 70–75°F (21–24°C), or above, for the growing of tropical plants. The term is directly derived from the mode of heating. Some of the earliest greenhouses were, in fact, heated by coal or wood burning stoves placed inside them.

Strain A term used particularly by plant breeders or gardeners who produce a fine selection of an already existing cultivar (q.v.), variety, or even species. A strain usually refers to plants raised from seeds, such as vegetables and annual flowers, and is produced by careful selection of the best plants only for use as seed parents. However, strain can be applied to certain vegetatively propagated plants that either habitually mutate or carry virus diseases. If a non-mutating or disease-free specimen can be produced this can become an 'improved strain'. Although it has common usage among gardeners, 'strain' is not accepted as a valid term by the *International Code of Nomenclature for Cultivated Plants*, which recommends that a new cultivar name be given to any plant that differs recognizably from its seed parents, or vegetative progenitor.

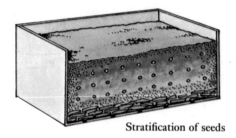

Stratification of seeds

Stratification The seeds of many plants, particularly those of trees and shrubs, with woody or fleshy fruits have a period of dormancy. Various factors are responsible; it may be the tough nature of the seed coat or that the fleshy fruit needs to be removed. It may also be a chemical inhibitor in the seed coat that needs soaking. Quite often a simple period of chilling is required. All these factors may be removed by a pre-sowing practice known as stratifying or stratification. Simply, this is performed by placing layers of the fruits alternately with layers of sand, peat and sand or sandy compost in pots or pans and placing the containers in a sheltered spot outside. (The seeds and peat and sand can also be uniformly mixed together.) Fleshy fruits such as berries should ideally be bruised first to facilitate rotting and the pots should be kept watered during any dry spell. Fruits and seeds should be stratified as soon as they are ripe and looked at from time to time from the following March onwards. As soon as the first sign of germination is observed, proper sowing must be carried out. Generally speaking, this method is only advantageous when large quantities of a particular species have to be dealt with. Small quantities are best sown in the usual way and placed outside in a plunge bed (q.v.) for the winter. This saves the double operation of stratifying and sowing. A thin layer of gravel placed on the surface of the compost prevents the soil from becoming panned down by winter rain.

Strike A cutting (q.v.) beginning to root is said to 'strike', or 'take', and when a batch of cuttings all root well one can say there is a 'good strike' or a 'good take'. Similarly, 'striking' or 'taking' a cutting is to place it under the right set of conditions to induce the cutting to produce roots.

Style The stalk which unites the stigma to the ovary. (See Pistil and Stigma.)

Sub-shrub In the botanical sense this is a semi-shrub, that is a perennial plant with a woody base, bearing branches annually that either partially or wholly die back at the end of the growing season. The tree paeony is a good example. Some normally shrubby plants which are not fully hardy in this country may behave as sub-shrubs. Fuchsia is the best example. Horticulturally, the term also covers any small low-growing shrubs such as rock rose (*Helianthemum*), thyme, *Gaultheria. Erica carnea* and crowberry (*Empetrum nigrum*).

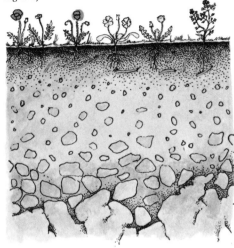

Sub-soil Soils which overlie the parent rock from which they were derived usually have a layered or graded appearance. At the surface, the soil is often darker and less stony and contains a percentage of humus. This is the zone where worms and soil insects live and the main feeding roots of plants are found. Below this is the sub-soil which is lacking in humus and gets progressively more stony until the rock-bed is reached. The only roots which penetrate this zone are primarily for anchorage. In a more general and less accurate way, the soil below the usual digging depth of one spade's length is often spoken of as sub-soil.

Succulent A plant adapted to a life under arid condition by producing water storage tissue in leaves or stems. Such plants have markedly swollen stems or leaves and sometimes roots, which are very fleshy and juicy when cut or squeezed. Most of the true cacti (members of the *Cactaceae* family) are good examples of stem succulents. Houseleeks, stonecrops and such plants as *Echeveria, Crassula* and *Lithops* provide good leaf succulents. The curious climbing succulent, elephant's foot (*Dioscorea elephantipes*), has a fleshy tuber with a hard, woody, corrugated rind, that sits in the soil surface with the top exposed.

Sucker This is a young shoot which develops at, or near, the base of a plant, or direct from its roots. Plum, lilac and elm often produce sucker growths from the roots and raspberries are propagated from root suckers. Suckers can be a nuisance on grafted plants as they arise from the stock (q.v.) and if not observed in time and removed, may eventually swamp the scion (q.v.).

Systematic Referring to the classification of plants (and all living things) by the similarity of their flowers and fruits. (see Family, Genus, Species, Variety).

Systemic This is descriptive of the way in which certain modern insecticides and fungicides work. The active killing substance is dissolved in water and either applied as a drench to the roots of the plant or sprayed on in the usual way. By this means the insecticide gets into the vascular system of the plant (the sap stream) so that any insect sucking or feeding on the leaves imbibes the poison. It is particularly effective against sucking insects such as aphids and capsid bugs.

Take (see Strike).

Tap root In a botanical sense this often applies to the first downward-growing root that emerges from the seed. In a gardening sense it applies to any delving root which is primarily of an anchoring nature, though it may also tap the lower water levels. Many trees and larger shrubs have tap roots, also some herbaceous plants, especially those which normally live in dry areas such as sand dunes. In some plants the original tap root becomes a storage organ; carrot, parsnip and beetroot are good examples.

Tender This term is applied to any plant that cannot be grown out of doors the whole year round because of low temperatures during the winter. The term is relative to the part of the country where one lives. The western and southern coastal areas in Great Britain experience milder winters than the rest of the country and thus certain plants that thrive there may be tender elsewhere. Sometimes a plant is winter hardy but the young growths are killed by spring frosts. If such frosts occur regularly then the plant is really too tender to be grown there. Many tender plants can be grown outside with a minimum of protection; siting against a sheltered south wall, covering with straw or sacking or polythene sheeting, or if a herbaceous or bulbous plant, mounding the site with ashes or coarse sand, are protective methods.

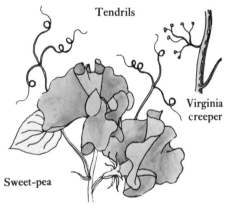

Tendrils

Virginia creeper

Sweet-pea

Tendril This is a modified leaf stem or other plant organ that assists or enables plants to climb. Tendrils often take the form of hair–or bristle-like appendages which are sensitive to contact and quickly wind round the nearest support. Garden peas, sweet-peas, and passion flowers are good examples. In some climbers the tendrils have sucker tips e.g. Virginia creeper; in others the tips are clawed or hooked (cat's-claw creeper *Bignonia unguis-cati*). Although not strictly tendrils, the leaf stalks of nasturtium (*Tropaeolum*) and most kind of clematis behave in the same way.

Terminal This is a self-descriptive term meaning the topmost shoot or flower bud on a stem or branch.

Tetraploid A term referring to plants of which the cells contain double the normal number of chromosomes. This may occur naturally or be induced by drugs such as colchicine. Sometimes tetraploids are more robust, more hardy or more freely fruiting than the original diploid. (see also Chromosome).

Thinning This term usually concerns the reduction of seedlings in a row to give those remaining more room to grow. This kind of thinning may be done by hand or with a hoe and is also known as singling. Fruit trees often produce more fruits than they can mature to optimum size, or extra large or fine fruits may be required, when thinning must be resorted to. Thinning is also applied to overgrown trees and bushes, and sometimes over-productive fruit trees need to have their fruit spurs thinned during winter.

Thorn (see Spine).

Tine The individual prong or tooth of a fork or rake. It may be flat or round in cross section. It may be hollow in the tool used for aerating lawns.

Tip-bearer A strictly fruit-growing term referring to certain cultivars of apple, notably 'Worcester Pearmain' and 'Lady Sudeley', that produce many fruiting buds on the tips of the young shoots. Lateral fruiting spurs are also produced in the normal way but are fewer. Tip bearers are, therefore, not suitable for restricted trained trees such as cordons, espaliers and pyramids, where young growths are regularly pinched or pruned.

Top-dressing The application of fertilizers or manures to the surface of the soil and allowing them to act *in situ* rather than working them into the surface. Top-dressing also applies to the practice of renewing the top layer of soil on permanent pot or container-grown plants when repotting is not necessary or is inconvenient. The replacement soil should be richer than ordinary potting compost, containing added fertilizers for feeding purposes.

Top-soil The upper, fertile, humus-rich layer of soil in which most of the feeding roots of plants are found. (see Sub-soil).

Topiary The practice of training and clipping trees and shrubs into the shapes of animals or inanimate objects such as balls and pyramids, etc. It is an ancient art, known to have been practised by the Romans. Many evergreen woody plants have and can be used, but yew and box are favourites. Training should begin while the plants are young and the more complex shapes will need special wire frames to start them off.

Topping (see Stopping).

Trenching A method of deep cultivation suitable only for the deepest soils. The plot to be trenched should be divided up into two halves longitudinally, then at the top end of one half mark off and take out a trench 2 ft. wide and a full spade's depth. The soil removed should be placed at the same end of the adjacent strip, ready to fill at the end of the operation. The bottom of the trench should now be forked over to a full fork's depth. Next mark off another 2 ft. wide trench and place the soil in the first trench on top of the forked sub-soil, repeating the operation until the end of the first half plot is reached. Now turn round and work up the second half, placing the first trench of excavated soil in the last trench of the first half. Completion of the second half will leave a trench ready to be filled by the original excavation. It is important to make sure that the trenches are all of the same size so that there will not be too much or too little soil to fill in the terminal trench. Manure or compost may be worked into the soil during this operation. In the past it was placed in the second spit, but it is known to be much more beneficial and acts more quickly if it is worked into the top spit.

The Gardener's Glossary

Triploid Normal plant cells contain two sets of chromosomes and are known as diploids. Sometimes individual plants arise with twice this diploid number (see Tetraploid) either spontaneously or by the aid of drugs such as colchicine. When plants of a diploid and tetraploid nature are crossed together a triploid can result, with three sets of chromosomes. Triploids are often sterile or partially so because the odd number of chromosomes cannot pair off satisfactorily. Triploids are often more robust than diploids and if reasonably fertile can produce larger flowers and fruits. The apples 'Bramley's Seedling' and the new 'Mutsu' are triploid and set good crops if other apple cultivars are flowering nearby to supply good pollen.

Tuber A swollen storage organ derived from a modified stem or root, usually but not invariably, underground. The potato is the most familiar example of a stem tuber. Its stem origin is clearly observable as the eyes are lateral buds. Dahlias and Persian ranunculus are good examples of root tubers. They do not bear buds, these being found only on the short length of stem that unites the individual tubers. Some of the yams (in particular *Dioscorea bulbifera*) and the succulent *Ceropegia woodii*, both bear aerial tubers, those of the former sometimes achieving several pounds in weight.

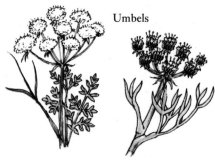

Umbels

Umbel A particular kind of inflorescence or flower head in which all the individual flower stalks arise from the same point at the summit of a stem like the ribs of an umbrella. This kind of flower cluster is typical of members of the *Umbelliferae* family. Quite often the main ribs of the umbel terminate in further smaller umbels and such an inflorescence is described as a compound umbel. Parsley, carrot, parsnip and giant hogweed are familiar examples.

Variegated As generally accepted this refers to foliage which bears white or cream markings due to lack of the essential green pigment chlorophyll. Sometimes the markings are arranged in a regular way to form a pattern, sometimes they are an irregular series of spots or blotches. The latter are often caused by a virus which inhibits the formation of chlorophyll, but the more regular types may be due to a mutation (q.v.). The grey or silvery markings seen on such plants as rex begonias and aluminium plant (*Pilea cadieri*) are not of this origin, but are caused by the presence of an air space under the leaf skin or epidermis, not by lack of chlorophyll.

Variety In the true botanical sense, a variety is a naturally occuring variant of a species which breeds true from seeds and is found as a self-perpetuating population in the wild. For example,

the small-flowered catch-fly, *Silene gallica*, an annual weed of arable farmland and some gardens, typically is white or pale pink in Britain. In the Channel Islands and on the Continent one finds the variety *S.g.*var. *quinquevulnera*, a much more decorative plant with the petals blotched crimson. Sometimes it occurs as a mixture with the typical species, sometimes by itself. Variety is also used in a general sense among gardeners, to mean any plant which differs from its parent, whether of mutant origin or purposefully raised by breeders.

Vegetative This term is used in relation to propagation practices and refers to any plant not raised from seed. All plants raised from cuttings, layers, division or grafting are said to have been propagated vegetatively.

Virus A general name for many kinds of disease-causing organisms, the individual particles of which are much smaller than the smallest bacteria. They live in the sap streams or cells of plants and cause a variety of disease symptoms by upsetting the chlorophyll production and general metabolism of the plant. The more usual symptoms are a paler streaking, mottling or stippling of the foliage, often accompanied by distortion or severe crippling. In the worst cases plants get progressively weaker and die out. Some viruses do not produce visible symptoms as mentioned above. For example many fruit trees, especially apples, are virus infected but although it may reduce cropping, does not do so dramatically and so remains unsuspected. The potato 'King Edward' is another example of a plant which crops satisfactorily with a virus infection. By special laboratory techniques, involving heat treatment, this potato has been freed of the virus. It then produces a much heavier crop but is so late maturing that few growers are interested in it. Some viruses have no recognizable weakening effect on plants even though they produce prominent white spots or blotches known as variegation (q.v.). Infected plants such as spotted laurel (*Aucuba japonica* 'Variegata') are, in fact, sought after for garden decoration. The tulips with curiously streaked and feathered patterns to the petals and sometimes known as 'broken tulips', are also caused by a virus. Viruses are frequently spread by sap-sucking insects and occasionally by birds which eat leaves, buds or young fruits. In the garden they can easily be transmitted on pruning tools or even the fingers. It seems that only rarely does a virus find its own way into another host plant and this is via the roots. Because viruses permeate the innermost parts of a plant they are virtually impossible to eradicate by traditional methods. As already mentioned, special techniques can be used to free a plant variety from virus. This involves heat treatment and the culturing of the minute growing point of a shoot under specially sterile conditions on an agar culture medium. In the garden all virus infected plants should be removed as soon as detected and burned.

Weeping Usually a tree or shrub in which the branchlets hang vertically instead of growing upwards in the normal manner. In such trees as the true weeping willow (*Salix babylonica*), the weeping spruce (*Picea breweriana*) and *Forsythia suspensa*, this weeping habit is natural. Quite often, however, weeping trees arise as mutants (q.v.). Sometimes they do not readily form trunks of their own and are grafted on to stems of the normal erect growing species. Examples are weeping ash and elm. In other cases it is necessary to train the leading growth up a cane or other support until it thickens out and becomes self-supporting. The weeping wellingtonia, *Sequoiadendron giganteum* 'Pendulum', is an example.

Whorl A wheel-shaped arrangement of leaves or flowers on the stem. Instead of the usual one or a pair of leaves at a node (q.v.) three to many arise together radiating outwards like the spokes of a wheel. The Canadian pondweed (*Elodea canadensis*) and the umbrella pine (*Sciadopitys verticillata*) are good examples. Many flowers are borne in whorls, notably such candelabra primulas as *P. japonica* and *P. malacoides*.

Wing, Winged Leaf stalks, stems and some seed pods are spoken of as winged when they bear thin keeled outgrowths or wings. The stems of sweet pea and the shrub *Euonymus alatus*; the leaf stalks of common and blue comfrey; and the pods of asparagus pea (*Tetragonolobus purpureus*) all bear winged outgrowths. Wing or wings is also used to describe the two side or lateral petals in the typical pea flower.

Witch's Broom Several kinds of trees, notably birch and elm often produce dense clusters of small twiggy stems that look like a bird's nest or broom from a distance, and are commonly known as witch's brooms. Sometimes they are of mutant origin, but quite often they develop in reaction to attacks of fungi or mites. Witch's brooms arising as mutations may be propagated by cuttings and remain dwarf and compact growing. Many dwarf conifers are of this origin.

Xerophyte A botanical term used for plants which are adapted to living in countries or areas that are dry for long periods. Various modes of growth have developed either to conserve moisture or to cut down water loss from the surface of the plants. The basic modifications are less pores in the leaf surface and imbedding in deep pits, rolled leaves (as in many grasses), a waxy coating, and reduction of shoots to leafless spines. In broom and gorse, the leaves are very short lived and sparsely borne, their functions being taken over by green stems. In heather, the leaves are reduced to scale-like proportions to cut down water loss, and several conifers also have reduced leaves. In other plants water-holding tissue is formed, producing the swollen leaves or stems characteristic of succulents (q.v.).

Zygomorphic A term referring to flowers of irregular formation, usually with petals of different shapes and sizes. Orchids provide good examples, as well as such common plants as antirrhinum, schizanthus and all the pea-like blossoms. Generally, such flowers are borne at right angles to the main erect-growing flowering stem and have a distinct top and bottom. Most orchids have an erect standard petal at the top, a lip or labellum at the bottom, and lateral or wing petals on either side. Such a flower can only be divided into mirror halves by cutting in a vertical plane down through the standard and lip petals. This is the test of a true zygomorphic flower. The more usual regular flower such as a buttercup or a bellflower can be cut in any plane through the centre and identical halves will result.

Antirrhinum, an example of a zygomorphic flower

Index

Acknowledgements
The publishers are grateful to the following photographers for providing photographs:
P R Chapman, R J Corbin, Ernest Crowson, Valerie Finnis, Brian Furner, Iris Hardwick, Peter Hunt, A J Huxley, G E Hyde, D J Kesby, Ray Procter, Elsa Megson, Kenneth Scowen, Donald Smith, Harry Smith and Dennis Woodland.